SOUTHEAST ASIA

A MODERN HISTORY

For Charmian O'Connor

Nicholas Tarling

SOUTHEAST ASIA

A MODERN HISTORY

OXFORD

UNIVERSITY PRESS

OXFORD
UNIVERSITY PRESS

253 Normanby Road, South Melbourne, Victoria, Australia 3205
Oxford University Press is a department of the University of Oxford.
It furthers the University's objective of excellence in research, scholarship,
and education by publishing worldwide in

Oxford New York

Athens Auckland Bangkok Bogotá Buenos Aires Calcutta
Cape Town Chennai Dar es Salaam Delhi Florence Hong Kong Istanbul
Karachi Kuala Lumpur Madrid Melbourne Mexico City Mumbai Nairobi Paris
Port Moresby São Paulo Shanghai Singapore Taipei Tokyo Toronto Warsaw

with associated companies in Berlin Ibadan

OXFORD is a registered trade mark of Oxford University Press
in the UK and certain other countries

National Library of Australia
Cataloguing-in-Publication data:

Tarling, Nicholas.
  Southeast Asia: a modern history.

  Bibliography.
  Includes index.
  ISBN 0 19 558397 3 (PB)
  ISBN 0 19 558441 4 (HB)

  1. Asia, Southeastern—History.
  2. Asia, Southeastern—Politics and government.
  I. Title

959

Edited by Janet Mackenzie
Cover design by Modern Art Production Group
Cover photograph supplied by PhotoDisc
Typeset by Desktop Concepts Pty Ltd. Melbourne
Printed through Bookpac Production Services, Singapore

Contents

Maps

Preface

This book is a history of modern Southeast Asia. It is the second one the author has attempted, and perhaps he should know better than to try. Over thirty years or so the task has become in one sense easier, indeed, but in other senses more difficult. Much more has been written. But that not only increases the indebtedness of the author, which gratitude can hardly encompass, but also the challenge to do justice to the work on which he draws. Much more has happened. Yet it is no longer sufficient to regard the gaining of independence from colonial rule as the focus or climax to a book. On the other hand, Southeast Asia has become more of a reality as a region, and there is less need to question the writing of a regional history.

Much has happened also to the discipline of history in thirty years, if not to the capacity of the author to take account of it. The perennial problems of historiography remain: the marriage, divorce, or de facto relationship between narrative and analysis; the distinguishing of similarity and difference; the shifting relationship of present and past; objectivity and subjectivity. To them have been added, though not necessarily as problems, not only new practices in historical research but also new or renewed challenges to the bases of the discipline itself. Historiography has its own history, and its current state must also influence a historian's approach.

Every writer of a general history is still a specialist, and certainly has to be selective. The present writer is no exception. He has also been influenced by a late-twentieth-century perception of a world of nation-states, of which the states of Southeast Asia form part. Every writer of a general history also faces in an extreme form the problems all historians face in providing both a chronological sequence and a discussion of topics.

Though in some sense thematically organised, Part One of the present work provides the reader with some kind of narrative sequence. That may help in tackling Parts Two and Three, where the topical emphasis is much firmer, though the reader will be made conscious of chronological phasing. In format Part Four is more like Part One, but will be better understood in the light of both the narrative and the topical treatments that have preceded it. In other words the parts and the chapters within them can be read on their own, but may also have a cumulative effect. Within these frameworks the experiences of particular states and peoples are related and juxtaposed.

In adopting this structure the author was affected by his wish to see Southeast Asia as unique but also as part of a wider human experience. That prompted, too, his rather risky attempt at the outset of each section to reflect more generally about the topic to come under discussion. It is a means not only of rationalising and comparing the experiences of Southeast Asian states, peoples, and regimes. It also represents some attempt to link those experiences with those of states, peoples, and regimes in other parts of the world. A reader may find such passages over-ambitious or too simplistic. But they may at least begin to serve two purposes: helping to understand Southeast Asian history; but also helping to see it as part of world history.

Part Five of the book offers comments on the historiography of Southeast Asia. Again this is introduced by some consideration of the issues in modern historiography and their relationship to the writing of Southeast Asian history. In this the author has drawn on the major theoretical contributions historians of Southeast Asia have made, as elsewhere on the practical: they have indeed been too little recognised in recent writings on historiography.

In a work of this nature, the topics are selective, and so, too, is their coverage. The author hopes in part to remedy this, and also to indicate a measure of his indebtedness, by his bibliography.

The author gratefully acknowledges the academic hospitality of the New Zealand Asia Institute of the University of Auckland; the University of Hull; and Universiti Brunei Darussalam; and the supportive criticism of Dr Brook Barrington.

Abbreviations

AFP	Armed Forces of the Philippines
AFPFL	Anti-Fascist People's Freedom League, Burma
AFTA	Asian Free Trade Area
ARVN	Army of the Republic of Vietnam
ASA	Association of South-east Asia
ASEAN	Association of South-East Asian Nations
BIA	Burma Independence Army
BNA	Burma National Army
BO	Boedi Oetomo
BSPP	Burma Socialist Programme Party
CBCP	Catholic Bishops' Conference of the Philippines
CCP	Chinese Communist Party
CIA	Central Intelligence Agency (United States)
CLC	Communities Liaison Committee
CPP	Communist Party of the Philippines
CPT	Communist Party of Thailand
DAP	Democratic Action Party, Malaysia
DK	Democratic Kampuchea
DRVN	Democratic Republic of Vietnam
GAPI	Gabungan Politiek Indonesia (Indonesian Political Union)
GCBA	General Council of Burmese Associations
GEACPS	Greater East Asia Co-Prosperity Sphere
ICP	Indo-China Communist Party
IMF	International Monetary Fund
IMP	Independence of Malaya Party
INA	Indian National Army
InterFET	International Force for East Timor
ISDV	Indische Sociaal-Democratische Vereniging (Indies Social-Democratic Association)
JAS	*Journal of Asian Studies*, Ann Arbor
JMBRAS	*Journal of the Malayan/Malaysian Branch of the Royal Asiatic Society*, Kuala Lumpur
JSEAS	*Journal of South-East Asian Studies*, Singapore
JSEAH	*Journal of South-East Asian History*, Singapore
JSS	*Journal of the Siam Society*, Bangkok
KBL	Kilusang Bagong Lipunan (New Society Movement)

KMM	Kesatuan Melayu Muda (Union of Young Malays)
KNIL	Koninklijk Nederlands Indisch Leger (Royal Netherlands Indies Army)
KOSTRAD	Komando Strategis Angkatan Darat (Army Strategic Reserve Command)
MAS	*Modern Asian Studies*, Cambridge, UK
MCA	Malay Chinese Association
MCP	Malayan Communist Party
MCS	Malayan Civil Service
MIAI	Madjlisul Islamil a'laa Indonesia (Greater Islamic Council of Indonesia)
MIC	Malayan Indian Congress
MIM	Muslim Independence Movement
MNLF	Moro National Liberation Front
MPAJA	Malayan People's Anti-Japanese Army
MPR	Madjelis Permusjawaratan Rakyat (People's Deliberative Congress)
NEP	New Economic Policy
NIC	newly industrialised country
NLD	National League for Democracy
NLHS	Neo Lao Hak Sat (Lao Patriotic Front)
NOC	National Operations Council
NPA	New People's Army
NU	Nahdlatul Ulama
NUF	National Unity Front
OPM	Organisasi Papua Merdeka (Free Papua Movement)
OPSUS	Operasi Khusus (Special Operations)
PAP	People's Action Party, Singapore
PAS	Partai Islam se Tanah Malaya (Pan-Malayan Islamic Party)
PBF	Patriotic Burmese Forces
PC	Philippines Constabulary
PDI	Partai Demokrasi Indonesia (Indonesian Democratic Party)
PI	Perhempunan Indonesia
PKI	Partai Kommunis Indonesia (Indonesian Communist Party)
PKK	Pak Kommunis Kampuchea
PNG	Papua New Guinea
PNI	Perserikatan (Partai) Nasional Indonesia (Indonesian National Association (Party))
PPP	Partai Persatuan Pembangunan (United Development Party)
PRB	Partai Rakyat Brunei
PRC	People's Republic of China
PRRI	Pemerintah Revolusioner Republik Indonesia (Revolutionary Government of the Republic of Indonesia)

PSII	Partai Sarekat Islam Indonesia
PUP	Princeton University Press
PUSA	Persatuan Ulama Seluruh Aceh (All-Aceh Ulama Association)
PVO	People's Volunteer Organisation
RAM	Reform the Armed Forces Movement
RPKAD	Resimen Pasukan Komando Angkatan Darat (Army Commando Regiment)
RTC	Round Table Conference
RV	Republic of Vietnam
SEAC	South-East Asia Command
SEATO	South-East Asia Treaty Organisation
SI	Sarekat Islam
SLORC	State Law and Order Restoration Council
SNAP	Sarawak National Party
SUPP	Sarawak United People's Party
TNI	Tentara Nasional Indonesia (Indonesian National Army)
UCP	University of California Press
UDT	Uniao Democratica Timorense (Timorese Democratic Union)
UMNO	United Malays National Organisation
UNIDO	United Democratic Opposition
UP	University of the Philippines
USAFFE	United States Armed Forces in the Far East
VOC	Verenigde Oostindische Compagnie (United East India Company)
VNQDD	Viet Nam Quoc Dan Dang
ZOPFAN	Zone of Peace, Freedom, and Neutrality

Part One

Peoples and States

The modern world is a world of nation-states, among which the states of the Southeast Asian region are numbered. The notion that the world is one, however, dates back only to the so-called voyages of discovery, while 'globalisation' is an emerging force, affecting nations, states, and regions.

The nation-state is a modern development. Still more recent is the logic that identifies nation and state to the extent that every 'nation' may lay claim to a state, no other kind of state can exist but a nation-state, and the relations of states are 'international'.

Other kinds of state existed in the past. The first part of this book discusses the kinds of state that have existed in Southeast Asia: the 'premodern' states and empires; the commercial empires of the Portuguese and the Dutch; the colonial states and protectorates; the Japanese empire; and the independent nation-states of the post-colonial period. It also discusses their relations with one another.

States are shaped by, but also shape, the identity or identities of those who form part of them. That is one reason for making their history the backbone of the opening part of the book. It also establishes a framework and a chronology for approaching the topics covered in Parts Two and Three of the book.

Those are concerned with the relationships that states and peoples have established with their environment, and with the societies and systems of government that they have created or sustained. The politics of the Southeast Asian states are covered in the fourth part of the book.

Southeast Asia, to about the middle of the thirteenth century CE

1.1 Peoples and Identities

Southeast Asia is marked by what is often called 'ethnic' diversity. The differences among its peoples are not simply the result of a series of migrations. They are better seen as the results of a continuing process, in which states have played a substantial role.

Often peoples do not have a single sense of 'identity'. One of the most common in Southeast Asia is formed by the relationship of patron and client. It may be that the paucity of Southeast Asia's population throughout most of its history contributed to the creation of a pattern that has continued into modern times.

Southeast Asia is marked by ethnic diversity. That results in part from its geographical location: peoples have penetrated it by land from the northern direction, by sea from all directions. It also results from the challenges Southeast Asia itself presents to human settlement. The ethnic diversity of the area does not result simply from successive migrations to the area. The obstacles that jungle, mountain, and swamp present to human settlement have assisted over time in adding to the diversities among the peoples of Southeast Asia by cutting them off from one another and promoting their distinctiveness in different parts of the region. Ethnic diversity is to be attributed both to migration and to *in situ* differentiation. The processes of acculturation in Southeast Asia have continued for centuries and still continue, promoted by governments and by other institutions, promoted by pressures from within the region and from outside it. Their effect has rarely been so complete as to eliminate existing diversities entirely. Sometimes they have increased them, adding to or sharpening the divisions.

Among these ambivalent processes is that of state-building. States of one kind or another have bound together, though also divided, the peoples of Southeast Asia in their endeavours to come to terms with their environment and to draw a living from it. In some cases those states have pursued cultural integration. In others it has been thought unnecessary. In others, again, it has been opposed, though it may still have taken place. In others, yet again, the process has provoked a counter-action, an assertion of distinctiveness. Other processes, such as the expansion of trade and the advance of religious conversion, have also operated, again not without ambivalence.

But it is the three-way relationship of peoples, states, and resources that provides the chosen theme of this history, and other processes are discussed largely in that context, to which indeed they are often highly relevant.

Clearly states in Southeast Asia have varied over time, not only in size, but in nature. It is less clear, but also true, that the identities of peoples have also changed. Indeed, even in speaking of ethnic diversity among its peoples, we are applying, in one form or another, a modern kind of categorisation that those peoples would not for the most part have recognised. Identity shifts, not merely in the eyes of the beholder. An individual or a group may, moreover, have more than one kind of identity, though one kind may predominate.

The states of Southeast Asia have taken many forms, those creating them adopting a range of devices, structures, and ideologies: patron–client relationships, bureaucracy, and democracy are among them. The relations among them have also taken different forms: 'mandala', empire, colony, nation-state. New forms have not always replaced old, but rather retained or reutilised them. Identities have been established in relation to these forms. People may be seen, and see themselves, primarily as clients of a patron or subjects of a ruler or citizens of a state. Their relationships with other groups may involve their elimination or their assimilation, a halfway tributary status, its mutation into a 'minority' over against a 'majority'.

Such identities do not preclude the formation of other identities: identities can compete and coexist. But the state is likely to shape them, since it may reinforce them, or, by its actions, turn people towards them in protest. A sense of religious identity may, for example, be an asset to a state, but it may also be a challenge. The state may encourage people to find other identities and internalise identities that have been thrust upon them. Colonial and modern census-takers have been obsessed with ethnicity. 'There is no doubt', a North Borneo census report remarked in 1931, 'that a good deal of confusion and doubt exists not only in the minds of the enumerators but of the natives themselves as to which [tribal] subdivision they really belong in'.[1] The same emphasis was applied to the past. Nineteenth- and twentieth-century historians saw, for example, Aniruddha's conquest of Thaton in 1057 as a Burman conquest of the Mon people, instead of an attempt to secure control of the coast justified in religious terms and in terms of the ideology of kingship.[2] Modern Indonesia accepts the existence of *suku*, so that people may be Acehnese or Sundanese or Javanese, as well as being Indonesian. Its government has not sought 'to eradicate diversity', as Greg Acciardi says, 'but to emasculate it'.[3] Ethnicity, as Robert Taylor puts it, has been 'reified and politicized'.[4]

Other categorisations are offered, sometimes as if they were 'primordial'. The anthropologist Clifford Geertz's categorisation of *aliran* in Indonesia—ways of life, such as *santri*, pious, *abangan*, folk, *priyayi*, aristocratic—indeed entrenched them more firmly in Indonesians' perception of themselves,[5] as did the politics of the 1950s that he observed. But while these examples are modern, and often emphasise the 'ethnic', the process is not entirely new, if now more self-conscious. Under

Spanish rule, the inhabitants of the lowland Philippines came to identify themselves with regions—Kabikolan, the land where Bikol was spoken; Katagalogan, the land where Tagalog was spoken, the land of the Tagalogs—and only later, and in addition, with the Philippines, as 'Filipinos'. In Borneo, a 'non-Malay' tribesman might become 'Malay', chiefly by becoming a Muslim. In nineteenth-century Bangka there was a category—non-Muslim indigenes—called 'Orang Lom', those who were 'not yet' Muslim.[6] Being 'Vietnamese' or 'Khmer' usually involved seeing the hill peoples as 'savage', not, or not yet, acculturated.

The process takes place indeed among a number of peoples, states, religions, and cultures. What one group does is related to what others do. The sense of being Vietnamese is constructed in the context of antagonism to the Chinese and also to the Chams. The sense of being Malay and Muslim and also a subject of the Sultan of Pattani is boosted by opposition to the advancing Thai state. The major challenge of the last two centuries was the creation of colonial regimes and of independent states in the 'modern' image. A sense of 'national' identity was built partly by appropriating Western ideology and techniques, but also by opposing Western domination. The modern governments seek to identify people and state ever more closely. Immigrants from other states are seen only as guest workers, often without any rights to speak of, and without the prospects of assimilation that, to a varying degree, were available in the pre-colonial and colonial phases.

To write of the peoples of Southeast Asia risks reifying the relatively recent and the present, and tempts us to over-simplify the historical past. We should have that in mind when we consider the attempts to reconstruct the peopling of the region in prehistoric times. They draw on archaeological and linguistic evidence and on what biology and anthropology may offer.

Most of the contemporary inhabitants of the archipelagic part of Southeast Asia— the area now covered by Indonesia, Malaysia, and the Philippines—are considered to be of the Southern 'Mongoloid' type. Others are in the 'Australoid' grouping, such as the Andamanese, the Negritos of the Philippines and those formerly called Semang in peninsular Malaysia, or, in more easterly parts of the archipelago, in the 'Melanesian' grouping. Most of the Negritos were indeed absorbed into the Mongoloid population. In eastern Indonesia the Southern Mongoloid settlement extends over the western boundary of Melanesia. The Southern Mongoloid peoples in general speak languages of the Austro-Asiatic family, such as Mon-Khmer, Vietnamese, Aslian, and Nicobarese, or the Austronesian, those spoken in modern Malaysia, Indonesia, and the Philippines. The latter abut on the realms of the Papuan complex, and the former on the Tibeto-Burman branch of the Sino-Burman family, including Chin, Naga, Kachin, and Karen, and on the domain of the Thai-Lao-Shan languages.

Diversity among the peoples of the archipelago, and among the Southern Mongoloid peoples themselves, has in the past often been attributed to successive waves of migration, a series of southerly movements of 'progressively more Mongoloid peoples'.[7] Bellwood's view is that the Negritos and their hunting and gathering lifestyle 'must be considered as autochthonous to the Indo-Malaysian Archipelago, whereas the agricultural lifestyle of the Austronesian speakers is to a great (but not total) extent the result of an original expansion from more northerly latitudes'. The present variations among them he attributes not to 'mixing between clearly differentiated and successive races and cultures', but to 'the slow expansion and adaptation of a relatively unified ethnolinguistic population, combined with inter-group contact and the successive influences of external civilisations'.[8] The Austronesian founder groups, he believes, indeed came from the north, starting perhaps around 3000–2500 BCE, but through Taiwan and the Philippines, and so to the west and south. 'The old idea … that the Austronesians migrated from the Asian mainland through the Malay Peninsula or Vietnam, is absolutely wrong.'[9]

Aside from the Southern Mongoloid Cham peoples in what we call central and southern Vietnam, the mainland peoples do appear to have originated from the north. The Tibeto-Burmans, it has been suggested, had been descending the Irrawaddy valley probably since the later centuries BCE, but penetrated the lowlands of the dry zone shortly before the eleventh century CE. There they came into contact with the Mons. The related Khmer peoples were pressed by the advancing Thais. The Shan-Thai-Lao peoples had been moving down the Salween and Menam valleys in the early centuries CE. The Burmans presented an obstacle that limited the Shans mainly to the plateau country, but the Mon-Khmer peoples of the Menam basin offered less effective resistance to the Thais. Such an account, however, may again overplay the extent to which differentiation resulted from waves of migration, rather than *in situ* change over a longer period, including the creation of states. That may be even clearer in the case of the Vietnamese. They originate with a kingdom which in the second century BCE spanned what is now the China–Vietnam border, subsequently for a time incorporated in China. Breaking away, the Vietnamese began to expand southwards, conflicting with and absorbing the Chams, and then contending also with the Khmers.

The geographical environment offered peoples two major kinds of opportunity for state-building. One encompassed the fertile soils and climatic conditions that permitted the intensive cultivation of rice by natural or technical irrigation. The other was presented by positional advantage in relation to the trade of the region, and in particular to its commercial connexions with other parts of the world. The first set of opportunities was available chiefly on the mainland, in the great river valleys of the Irrawaddy, the Menam Chao Praya, and the Red River. In the archipelago it was available, more exceptionally, in Java. In that part of the region, by contrast, lay the main positional opportunities, particularly once traders began to use the route through the Straits of Melaka.

Southeast Asia's contacts with the outside world were amplified by the expansion of trade that occurred in the early centuries of the Common Era. To some extent this had a European origin: Rome unified the shores of the Mediterranean and inaugurated through the Middle East and India a demand for Southeast Asian products, gold, spices, scented woods, and resins. Furthermore, nomadic disturbances in the pre-Christian era had closed the routes through Bactria to Siberian gold, and Indian merchants thus looked to Southeast Asia. Chinese records also suggest a Chinese commercial interest in the maritime route, fluctuating with China's own access to overland routes, 'but the actual evidence for any Chinese presence in South-East Asia outside Vietnam before the Song dynasty (960–1279) is really very slight'.[10]

Initially international trade took advantage of land portage across the narrow part of the peninsula around Kra, and between the first and fifth centuries CE small indigenous states developed in southern Indo-China and in the northern Malay peninsula. One of them the Chinese called Funan. French archaeologists have investigated its port at Oc-eo in southern Vietnam, where Roman and Indian imported items date from the second century CE. It established its supremacy in the isthmian region in the third century. Among the other states there was Lankasuka, in the area of modern Pattani. Its fortunes revived with Funan's decline in the late fifth century.

That decline may have related to the opening of the Straits, encouraged by the Chin dynasty when it lost access to the caravan route in the late fourth century, for the maritime route then became more important than the portage. Funan was finally conquered by its Khmer neighbour, Chen-la. The change may also have helped the Chams, whose states, founded perhaps in the late second century CE, were initially centred somewhat south of modern Hué, colonising the fertile pockets in the mountains of present-day central Vietnam at the expense of more primitive tribes. The change certainly opened up the opportunity to create a trading state or states at the southern end of the Straits, on the tip of the peninsula, on the islands beyond, or in southeastern Sumatra, though for a while at least it was still important to control the isthmus.

The decline of Funan led in the seventh century to the first of several attempts to create a commercial empire in this region. Based at Palembang in southern Sumatra, Sri Vijaya centralised the trade of a number of petty river-mouth statelets or levied exactions upon it, and created a fragile political structure dependent on command of the sea. But its main advantage was positional, and, lacking the agricultural resources that would sustain a substantial population, that it had to maximise.

The states of the archipelago were less enduring than those that were being built up on the mainland by the Burmans, Thais, and Vietnamese. Even so the Southern Mongoloid peoples continued to dominate the Indo-Malaysian archipelago. There were occasional raids from the outside, like those of the Chola of southern India who attacked Sri Vijaya in the eleventh century, or the Mongol intervention in the Javanese kingdom of Singosari. Generally, however, the Southern Mongoloid peoples were not displaced. Rather they continued at once to assimilate and to diversify. The traces of earlier inhabitants diminished, but the current inhabitants became more differentiated.

On the mainland, however, they had more difficulty in surviving. The Thais moved down the peninsula, challenging the Malays in the north. More seriously still, the Vietnamese advanced relentlessly at the expense of the Chams. No more peoples from further north challenged the Burmans, Thais, and Vietnamese, however, and in that sense the mainland, like the archipelago, had come to enjoy a kind of stability. That did not, any more than in the archipelago, mean the end of conflict. The main theme of mainland history indeed came to be the struggles among the major peoples now established there. In the case of the Burmans and the Thais, it was often a matter of war and invasion, in some measure designed to determine the fate of the lands occupied by the Mons and the peninsular Malays. In the case of the Thais and the Vietnamese, it was a struggle to determine the fate of the intervening state of the Khmers.

A new series of incursions starting in the early sixteenth century had more effect on the archipelago than on the mainland. On the mainland the Portuguese were suppliers of arms and mercenaries in the war between the Burmans and the Thais that reached a new level of intensity. Neither they nor their successors, the Dutch, had more than a marginal effect, though they left behind the first Eurasian communities, useful, if controversial, in subsequent encounters, and the Thai and Vietnamese states welcomed Chinese traders and settlers.

In the archipelago, too, small Eurasian communities emerged. Neither the Portuguese nor the Dutch created states that colonised or assimilated on any substantial scale, though their intervention provoked a strong political and religious reaction. The Dutch venture did, however, expand the opportunities for Chinese traders and artisans in the archipelago, and Chinese communities of a more or less permanent nature appeared in their towns and in the hinterland.

The same was true in the Philippines. There, too, European settlement was limited in extent. Europeanisation was, however, more intense than elsewhere in archipelagic Southeast Asia, and it was as a result of it, and in reaction to it, that lowland and hill peoples became more distinct, and that lowland people, identified by the Spaniards as indios, came to speak a selection of languages that identified them regionally.

The peopling of Southeast Asia continued alongside the process of state formation, influencing it and influenced by it. Assimilating the Chinese proceeded in a more differentiated way, for example: their experience in the Thai state of Ayudhya or even in the Spanish state of the Philippines contrasted with that in other parts of the archipelago, now increasingly Muslim. The colonial phase—a phase, too, of economic transformation—expanded immigration to Southeast Asia, not only from China, but also from India.

Southeast Asia had been relatively uninhabited. Though there were many peoples in the region, there were not many people. For most of its history it has, unlike neighbouring India and China, been sparsely populated. The policy of the northern Thai kingdoms was to acquire population: 'take vegetables and put them in the basket, take slaves and put them in the *muang* [lordship]'.[11] 'The first essential in these States', the British Resident in Negri Sembilan wrote in 1899, 'is Population, the second Population and the third Population.'[12] In 1830 there were perhaps about 30 million people in Southeast Asia as a whole, in 1900 perhaps 80 million. In 1991 the total was 415 million. It was not surprising that the area continued to attract migrants, particularly from India and China, during the economic expansion after about 1830. Even today, the boom economies do not draw their 'guest workers' merely from their regional neighbours. Now, however, it is hard to recapture a Southeast Asia that is short of people.

Yet that paucity may be connected with a feature of its societies that persists, despite the demographic transformation, and lies alongside, reinforcing or weakening, the state structures that have been erected. What was important was people. Only with people could resources be turned to account, surpluses created, states built and defended. Compulsion was necessary, but clearly had its limits. That may help to explain the mutuality of the relationships that developed, between master and slave, between superior and inferior, between patron and client, and that continued.

In such a context it may be suggested that 'Southeast Asians' have been simply—though in a complex way—sustaining an additional identity. They might be at once Indonesians, Muslims, Acehnese, followers of Daud Beureu'eh; at once Filipinos, Christians, Ilokanos, clients of Marcos; at once Saw Karens, Christians, opponents of the Burman state and the SLORC regime.

Notes

1 q. M. Clark Roff, *The Politics of Belonging*, KL: OUP, 1974, p. 207.
2 Michael Aung-Thwin, *Myth and History in the Historiography of Early Burma*, Athens: Ohio U; Singapore: ISEAS, 1998, p. 146.
3 q. G. Wijeyewardene, *Ethnic Groups across National Boundaries in Mainland Southeast Asia*, Singapore: ISEAS, 1990. p. 3.
4 'Disaster or Release … ', MAS, 29, 1 (February 1995), p. 59.
5 cf. R. B. Cruickshank, 'Abangan, Santri, and Prijaji: A Critique', JSEAS, 3, 1 (March 1972), pp. 39–43.
6 Mary F. Somers Heidhues, *Bangka and Mentok Pepper*, Singapore: ISEAS, 1992, p. 95.
7 C. A. Fisher, *South-east Asia: A Social, Economic and Political Geography*, London: Methuen, 1964, p. 67.
8 P. Bellwood, *Prehistory of the Indo-Malaysian Archipelago*, Sydney: Academic P, 1985, p. 130.
9 ibid., p. 124.
10 ibid., p. 137.
11 q. Wijeyewardene, p. 49.
12 q. J. M. Gullick, *Malaya*, NY: Praeger, 1963, p. 31n.

Kingdoms and Super-Kingdoms

The kingdoms created in mainland Southeast Asia before the fifteenth century included those of the Khmers, above all Angkor; of the Vietnamese, centred on the Red River; of the Thais, the greatest of which was Ayudhya; and of the Burmans, with a capital at Pagan in central Burma. The kingdoms in the archipelago were based either in the Straits of Melaka, like Sri Vijaya, or in Java. The greatest of the latter was Majapahit.

Monarchy is the predominant form of rule in European history, but it assumed very different forms over the centuries. Kingdoms, too, changed their shape and their frontiers and their relationships with one another. In some countries they became the basis of nation-states, though at the outset there was little, if any, sense of nationality. Nations that constituted themselves in the nineteenth century called in monarchs, often from the princely houses of Germany, originally the substructure of the Holy Roman Empire. In writing about early kingdoms, it is too easy to picture them in the bureaucratic and national forms they may later have assumed. Writing about later ones, it may be too easy to assume an identification between people and monarch that elsewhere was the result of a long process. Monarchy and kingdom had to come to terms. The same might apply to an alternative form of state, the republic. Borrowed from the city-state, that had to be domesticated in Europe, as later in Asia. The historian who writes about Europe has to be ready to shift perspective and accept that sources might have their own perspective.

Writing about Southeast Asian monarchies makes similar requirements, but involves an additional burden, since for much of their earlier history the sources are limited. Our knowledge partly comes from inscriptions often hard to interpret. Nor is the interpretation of written material from Chinese sources straightforward. Official scribes, like the Emperor, were indeed interested in the actual situation among the barbarians to the south. But, as Hermann Kulke has put it, 'they "translated" the information not only into their own language but also into their own officialese. Its idiom was deeply pervaded by the Chinese conception of their own centralized State.'[1]

Kulke suggests three phases or levels in state formation: the local, the regional, and the 'imperial'. 'Very generally speaking, the first step always had to be the successful establishment and consolidation of a solid local power within a limited territory.[2] This he characterises as 'chieftaincy'. Next might come the conquest of one or more neighbouring nuclear areas, incorporated not by administrative unification, but by the establishment of more or less regular tributary patterns. These were the somewhat precarious 'early kingdoms' of Southeast Asia. From the early ninth century a small number of what Kulke calls 'imperial' kingdoms, or perhaps one might say super-kingdoms, emerged, which unified two or even several core areas of former early kingdoms.[3] But they, too, were fragile, challenged by their attempts to secure sufficient resources, in material but above all in manpower, to ensure the continued retention of their acquisitions. The characteristic form is often described, as by Kulke, in terms borrowed from Europe, tributary and vassal. Oliver Wolters adopts a Sanskrit term used in Indian manuals of government, 'mandala', or 'circles of kings'. 'Mandalas would expand and contract in concertina-like fashion. Each one contained several tributary rulers, some of whom would repudiate their vassal status when the opportunity arose and try to build up their own networks of vassals.'[4]

Khmer states

Funan was 'less likely a dominant empire than the largest and most aggressive of a number of principalities', Ian Mabbett writes.[5] Of these there were, he adds, 'quite a few ... , called into being by the Indian trade and possessed of Indian court culture'. He includes the states of the Cham peoples to the east and to the west, 'a string of coastal city-states extending round the Gulf of Siam and down the Malay Peninsula'.[6] Into this pattern the Khmers, who lived on the fringes of the forest or in clearings within it, were drawn.

Khmer kingdoms appear in the seventh and eighth centuries, known to us from inscriptions and from the Chinese records. The latter speak of a state called Chenla, but historians differ over its nature: a single state or just one among contending principalities? Out of this Angkor, a Khmer empire or super-kingdom, was built up, 'a constellation of communities sustained by stretches of water',[7] though the process is unclear. 'Unification was an irregular and fitful process, not a once-for-all achievement; but in the end it came to be embodied in the Khmer state that survives today.'[8] Those who look back on it see Jayavarman II (r. 790–c.835) as starting the pan-Khmer regime. The site of his final capital, Roluos (Hariharalaya), is about eight miles southeast of Siemreap.

Yasovarman I (r. c.889–c.911) chose a capital site that enabled him to place a real hill, Phnom Bakheng, at its centre, a symbol of the kingdom's position in the world. Round it lay the city of Yasodharapura. A successor, Rajendravarman (r. 944–c.968), sought to give the kingdom a bureaucratic structure, and another, Suryavarman, engraved the loyalty of his officials in stone. From the eleventh century onwards, Angkor was a major empire. Suryavarman II (r. 1113–c.1145–50) was the builder of Angkor Wat, 'the most spectacular of all the monuments that remain to attest the empire's glory'[9].

The Khmers expanded westward, contending with the Mons who had founded the kingdom of Dvaravati, centred at the present city of Nakorn Pathom, and with the Thais of the Menam valley. To the east they also contended with Champa, now thought to have been a 'polyethnic' country, including uplanders, Jarai and Rhade, Mnong and Stieng, as well as Chams. In 1177 Champa was able to defeat Angkor, but its success was only temporary. The prince who redeemed the Khmers was Jayavarman VII (r. 1181–1218). '[T]he imperial unity that the second Jayavarman had so proudly celebrated, ardently pursued by subsequent kings yet never irrevocably mastered, required a mighty effort if it was to be seized once more.'[10] Of this Jayavarman was capable. The Chams were defeated and the empire extended into present-day Laos. Temple foundations were dedicated to his mother, the Ta Prohm, and to his father, the Preah Khan. His capital city was Angkor Thom, and within it was the central shrine, the Bayon.

That reign, however, represented the peak of Angkor's glory. In 1369 the capital was temporarily abandoned, and in the fifteenth century the Khmer rulers moved to the Phnom Penh vicinity. Several reasons have been suggested for these changes. One is the pressure of the Thai kingdoms. Another, developed by Bernard Groslier, emphasises ecological factors: its agricultural system proved unsustainable. Mabbett also draws attention to the changes in China and to their impact on Southeast Asia. Under the Sung dynasty the bulk of its population came to be concentrated in the south, and it gave a new impulse to the trade to the south. That strengthened coastal centres on the Southeast Asian mainland, such as Ayudhya, and in that sense the Khmer shift to the Mekong may have been a positive move and not a mere retreat. But it had, as Mabbett adds, now reverted from its 'imperial' standing to 'that of a regional kingdom engaged in a struggle for survival with its neighbours'.[11]

The Vietnamese state

The Chams had also been contending with the Vietnamese to the north. Conquered by the Han in the first century CE, the Red River area became the site of a relatively stable polity, built up by Chinese frontier administrators and leading local clans, sensitive to dynastic interests but ready also to take advantage of dynastic weakness. 'Giao Province has gone its own way', a Ch'i dynasty official lamented in the late fifth century. 'It is located at the edge of the horizon and is joined to the Southern Barbarians beyond. It produces valuable merchandise; incomparably strange and curious things are gathered from the mountains and the sea. The people trust in their remoteness and the dangers of the road; they often rise in rebellion.'[12]

As part of its frontier reorganisation, the succeeding T'ang dynasty set up the Protectorate of An-nam, Pacified South, in 679. In its later years the T'ang was able to drive back a ninth-century invasion from the kingdom of Nanchao in Yunnan. That, as Keith Taylor puts it, 'affirmed Vietnam's long-standing ties to Chinese civilization'.[13] Yet the T'ang were now too weak to dominate Vietnam, and the regime that emerged from the post-invasion reconstruction was 'the first of a number of transitional regimes that finally led to the establishment of an independent Vietnamese monarchy'.[14] At the battle of Bach-dang River in 938, the Vietnamese led by Ngo Quyen, the son of a provincial magistrate, defeated an assault by Southern Han forces, and the following year he took the title of king. A period of anarchy followed his death in 944. Out of this Dinh Bo Linh fashioned a new kingdom, which he called Dai Co Viet. At the same time, though he called himself emperor, he managed to come to terms with the new Sung dynasty. His successor, Le Hoan, repelled the Sung's attempt to benefit from his assassination, and the Vietnamese gained a century free of northern pressure, in which they could lay the foundations for continued independence. This was the work of the Ly dynasty, which based itself at Thanh-long (Hanoi), and of the Buddhist monks it employed. In 1076 it was able to defeat a second Sung invasion.

Fending off the Chinese to the north, the Vietnamese expanded to the south. Ly Phat-ma led a successful expedition against Champa in 1044, and his son, posthumously known as Ly Thanh-tong (r. 1054–72), repeated the attack in 1069. In the late thirteenth century the Tran dynasty succeeded in defeating the armies of the Mongol (Yuan) dynasty, which approached from the north, and also from Champa. The Viet–Cham conflict weakened Champa in its contest with Cambodia. But the collapse of the Tran in the late fourteenth century enabled the Chams, under a redoubtable leader known to the Vietnamese as Che Bong Nga, to ravage Dai Viet, and even to occupy Thang-long for six months in 1383. Ho Quy Ly, the chief minister, proclaimed himself ruler in 1400, only to provoke the intervention of the new Ming Dynasty. Posing as restorers of the Tran, the Ming endeavoured in the event to restore the province of Giao. That endeavour was abandoned in the 1420s.

Vietnamese resistance had gathered behind a wealthy landowner from Thanh-hoa, Le Loi. 'Finally it became possible to overcome violence with righteousness, to displace tyrannical force with humanity … Our territory from now on shall enjoy peace. … An unprecedented task has been accomplished. The Four Seas shall be quiet forever. An era of renovation shall be announced at every place.'[15] So read Le Loi's proclamation of 1428, composed by his scholar adviser Nguyen Trai. He began a new dynasty. The rule of his grandson, Le Thanh-tong (1460–97), was famous. Keeping the Ming at arm's length, he dealt Champa a decisive blow, capturing its capital, Vijaya, in 1471, and annexing everything north of what is now the border of the province of Binh-dinh. With that, however, Dai Viet came into closer contact—and into more intense conflict—with the Khmers, who were at odds also with the Thais.

The Thai and Lao states

The Shan-Thai-Lao peoples had been moving down the Salween and Menam valleys under constant Chinese pressure in the early centuries CE. Early in the twelfth century tiny Thai states appeared in the upper Menam valley, and Shan states appeared in this region and in Burma and Assam in the thirteenth century. The weakening of Khmer power helps to explain the expansion of these peoples. The principal movement was, however, caused by the Mongols' destruction of the kingdom of Nanchao in 1253. A last great dispersal ensued and Thai military ruling classes took control in new regions in the Irrawaddy and Menam valleys. By the end of the thirteenth century, the mainland was no longer dominated by superkingdoms: its political landscape, as David Wyatt puts it, was 'fractured into numerous much smaller states, relatively more equal in their political and military power'.[16] In the 1290s Chiengmai became the capital of the Lan Na kingdom, its ruler, Mangrai, fending off the Mongols, who settled for the presentation of tribute. To the south Ramkhamhaeng built up the kingdom of Sukhotai after his accession in 1279, but it fell away after his death in 1298. The way was open for the creation of a new southern Thai state. Its centre was at Ayudhya on an island in the Menam, where the king was crowned in 1350, its influence based on 'an uneasy alliance between Tai manpower … , Khmer prestige and statecraft from Lopburi and the eastern provinces, and Chinese (and other Asian) commercial power concentrated at the center in the port-capital'.[17] To the north lay the Lao states, welded into the kingdom of Lan Xang by Fa Ngoum in 1353, as well as Chiengmai. Characteristically Ayudhya struggled with Cambodia, and looked south, gaining some form of control over much of the peninsula. Its great king Borommatrailokanat (Trailok) (r. 1448–88) strengthened its institutions.

The Burmans and the Mons

The Tibeto-Burmans had been descending the Irrawaddy valley probably since the later centuries BCE. Till the early ninth century the Pyu people, perhaps an 'advance guard',[18] occupied the central as well as the southern zone, but in 832 and 835 they raided by Nanchao, and they lost their last city in central Burma. That probably gave the Burmans their opportunity to create a kingdom of their own. A city, started on a Pyu site in 849, was to become Pagan. Its 'great unifier' was Aniruddha, who established Burman hegemony over the Mon kingdom of Thaton.[19] The super-kingdom, like Angkor, was held together only with difficulty, and external stress was coupled with internal disruption. In 1271 the Mongols vainly endeavoured to assert Pagan's tributary status. The Mons rebelled in 1273, but the Burmans had to focus on the north, where the Mongols invaded in 1283, and again in 1288. The notion that a subsequent period of anarchy gave the Shans their opportunity, and that they founded the kingdom of Ava in 1364, has recently been exploded by Michael Aung-Thwin. Ava was a Burman kingdom, 'Pagan writ small', deflecting the Drang nach Osten of the Shans.[20] The kingdom was not, however, able to secure the submission of the Mon kingdom of Pegu, which had established its independence after the collapse of Pagan.

Moreover, Arakan, which had hitherto been a field of conflict between Mons and Burmans, was able also to establish its independence after 1430, and a new capital was set up at Mrohaung.

Sri Vijaya

Pointing to the collapse of the Cham state, and also that of the archipelagic state of Sri Vijaya, Kulke again draws his distinction between early kingdoms and what he calls imperial kingdoms. Did they disappear from the political map of Southeast Asia because they failed to transform their structure?[21] Sri Vijaya—Georges Coedès' placing of which in Palembang has been confirmed by recent archaeological work[22]—was certainly a different kind of state from Angkor, a different kind, perhaps it might usefully be said, of imperial kingdom, as the very dearth of monumental remains suggests. With the decline of Funan, and the increasing use of the Straits, Sri Vijaya made itself from the late eighth century what proved to be the first of a number of commercial states or empires in the peninsula and the archipelago. Those sought to centralise the trade of a number of petty river-mouth statelets, and establish an entrepot for traffic with the wider world. Their political structure remained somewhat fragile, requiring command of the sea, naval battles and blockades, and it was not backed by the major resources of land and people that supported mainland imperial or super-kingdoms like Pagan or Angkor. For a while it remained important to control isthmus as well as Straits, and that was an important objective for the Sailendra dynasty that ruled Sri Vijaya. 'The Sailendra thalassocracy was made up of a confederation of trading ports on the fringe of the primeval forest', and land routes were unimportant save on the isthmus.[23] Among the areas over which Sri Vijaya established the sort of supremacy that a maritime empire could expect to maintain were Kedah and the isthmus, the islands south of the Straits, east and north Sumatra, and possibly the Nicobars.

An entrepot is always difficult to sustain, even apart from the weaknesses of a state that may be built upon it. On the one hand, it is exposed to rivals, who may plunder it, even if they cannot displace it; and Sri Vijaya was attacked both by the Javanese in the tenth century, and in the eleventh by a power from outside the region, the Cola dynasty of Tamil Nadu. An entrepot is, on the other hand, also exposed to economic dissolution, in particular through the development of alternative connexions between its dependencies and the outside world. 'The recalcitrance of the vassals was the major threat to this empire.'[24] The growth of Chinese shipping in Southeast Asia, particularly under the Sung, enabled other ports to operate independently of Sri Vijaya, and its supremacy unravelled. In the thirteenth and fourteenth centuries, other overlords spread into the area, the Thais from the north, and the Javanese from the east, where a new 'imperial' kingdom had been established, Majapahit.

Javanese states

State-building in Java, unlike that in the peninsula and Sumatra, could draw not only on commercial but also on agricultural resources. Javanese coastal towns were well placed for linking the trade to the eastward with the world trade that began to flow through the Straits of Melaka, and were at times at odds with Sri Vijaya. But the fertile soils and growing population, particularly of central and eastern Java, also suggested the possibility of creating 'early kingdoms' like those on the mainland, and even 'imperial' or super-kingdoms. In the eighth century a Saivite king established himself at Mataram in south central Java, which became the basis of a Sailendra dynasty, Mahayana Buddhist rulers who built the Borobudur, a huge terraced monument in the Kedu plain. A subsequent Saivite king responded with the temple complex at Prambanan.

In the mid-tenth century the royal centre moved further east: the kingdom of Airlangga (r. 1016–49) was based on the delta of the Brantas and Solo rivers. So, too, were its successors, Kadiri and Singosari, though the latter, under its most famous king, Kertanagara (r. 1268–92), sought to assert control over Sri Vijaya as well as over Madura and Bali. His successors were to create Majapahit. That was an 'imperial' or super-kingdom in the sense that its rulers were able to unite all of eastern Java. Taking up Kertanagara's ambitions, it became 'imperial' in another sense. The concept was of an archipelago-wide empire, *nusantara*, ruled by the Javanese. Under a great minister, Gajah Mada, and a great king, Hayam Wuruk, something of this was realised, and celebrated in Prapanca's epic poem, the *Nagarakrtagama*, written in 1365.[25] The extent of the empire has been disputed. But in any case it was for the most part a loose hegemony that rapidly disintegrated with the passing of the men who had created it.

Melaka

The decline of Majapahit, coupled with a renewal of Chinese commercial and political activity in Southeast Asia under the Ming, created the opportunity for another attempt at commercial 'empire' in the Straits. That originated with a Malay prince who first appears as a vassal of Majapahit at Palembang, and then at Temasek, which he renamed Singapore, and finally, after he was expelled by the Thais, at Melaka in 1400–01. There he competed with Ayudhya, using his contacts with the Ming to help fend off the Thais. The state he founded established its supremacy over parts of the peninsula and coastal Sumatra, and thus guaranteed its dominance of the Straits. It also established contacts with the north Javanese ports, restive under Majapahit's dominance, and thus indirectly with Maluku and the further parts of the archipelago. It utilised its position and its politics to make itself the leading entrepot for the international trade of the area. In a sense it was a new Sri Vijaya. One major difference was its adoption of Islam in 1436, after it had ceased to be a base for the Ming voyages.[26] Its expansion was now associated with Islam. That, as well as its entrepotal control of Southeast Asia's trade, made it a prime target for the Europeans at the beginning of the sixteenth century.

Conclusion

The Europeans did not secure commercial monopoly nor, till the nineteenth century, political control. On the mainland their impact in the next three centuries was to be quite limited, and in the archipelago and the peninsula their activities, though more persistent, stopped short of giving 'empire' the meaning they gave it in the nineteenth and twentieth centuries. Southeast Asians continued an active and substantially autonomous commercial and political life. Their response to change was conditioned by the experience of the previous period. The impact of the Europeans led to innovation, modification, and reinforcement.

The states of this period had consolidated the concept of monarchy in general, not only among the rulers but also among those they ruled. In part as a result, they determined that the mainland would be predominantly Buddhist and the archipelago Muslim. They had also left behind the recollections, recorded or inscribed in memory, of legendary heroes, like the 'great unifier' Aniruddha or Ramkhamhaeng or Gajah Mada. They left behind, too, accounts of states, like Pagan, that seemed at least in retrospect to be ideal, and monuments of states, like Angkor, that were to seem in retrospect almost incomprehensibly grand. In related ways, the period had seen the creation and consolidation of the traditional cultures that identified the main peoples of the region, Burman, Thai, Khmer, Vietnamese, Javanese, and Malayo-Muslim.

Notes

1 in David Marr and A. C. Milner, *Southeast Asia in the 9th to 14th Centuries*, Singapore: ISEAS, and Canberra: RSPacS, ANU, 1986, p. 2.

2 p. 5.

3 p. 8.

4 *History, Culture and Region in Southeast Asian Perspectives*, Singapore: ISEAS, 1982, pp. 16–17.

5 Ian Mabbett and David Chandler, *The Khmers*, Oxford: Blackwell, 1996, p. 73.

6 p. 74.

7 ibid., p. 93.

8 ibid., p. 92.

9 ibid., p. 103.

10 ibid., p. 205.

11 p. 217.

12 q. Keith Weller Taylor, *The Birth of Vietnam*, UCP, 1983, p. 123.

13 p. 249.

14 p. 249.

15 q. Truong Buu Lam, *Patterns of Vietnamese Response to Foreign Intervention*, Yale UP, 1967, p. 61.

16 David K. Wyatt, *Thailand: A Short History*, Yale UP, 1984, p. 39.

17 ibid., p. 67.

18 D. G. E. Hall, *A History of South-East Asia*, London: Macmillan, 1964, p. 10.
19 M. Aung-Thwin, *Pagan*, U Hawaii P, 1985, pp. 17, 20–2.
20 *Myth and History in the Historiography of Early Burma*, Athens: Ohio U; Singapore: ISEAS, 1998, p. 142.
21 Marr and Milner, p. 8.
22 Pierre-Yves Manguin, 'Palembang and Sriwijaya ... ', JMBRAS, 66, 1 (1993), p. 29.
23 P. Wheatley, *The Golden Khersonese*, KL: U Malaya P, 1961, p. 298.
24 O. W. Wolters, *Early Indonesian Commerce*, Cornell UP, 1967, p. 249.
25 newly translated by S. Robson, Leiden: KITLV P, 1995.
26 O. W. Wolters, *The Fall of Srivijaya in Malay History*, KL: OUP, 1970, pp. 160, 162.

1.3 Empires

In the sixteenth century the Europeans established direct contact with Southeast Asia. The Portuguese captured Melaka and secured a share of the trade of the archipelago. Less than a century later, the Dutch East India Company (VOC) followed them to the region, but its application of force was more persistent and more methodical. Only in parts of the archipelago did the VOC establish political control, but in the eighteenth century it came to dominate Java.

By contrast the Spaniards had established control over much of what they called the Philippines in the late sixteenth century. Like the Portuguese and the Dutch, they met Muslim opposition. Indeed the 'Moros' continued to raid their possessions in Luzon and the Visayas.

The chief states of the mainland—Ava, Ayudhya, and Dai Viet—were much less affected by the European incursions than those of the archipelago. Their history was more concerned with their own internal problems and their struggles one with another.

'Imperial' states had existed within Southeast Asia, whether or not Kulke's definition is adopted or modified. He would include the kingdoms that extended beyond an initial core area, like Vietnam, the ruler of which indeed imitated and countered China with an imperial title, but not a state like Sri Vijaya, which had but a limited core area throughout its history. It has seemed permissible, however, to see his 'imperial' kingdoms as super-kingdoms, and to use the word 'empire', somewhat riskily, for the loose commercially oriented hegemony established by Sri Vijaya or the *nusantara* of the Javanese monarchs.

Southeast Asia is more typically seen in terms of empires whose centre was outside the region. Its neighbours, India and China, were powerful, but even when united did not exert their power in this way. The Europeans did. Particularly at first, however, the structure of their empires in Southeast Asia resembled those of the commercial empires they tended to displace. Unlike those empires, however, they were part of larger empires not based in the region. They were to give way to a different kind of empire, territorial and colonial. In some ways, however, that too was to resemble the empires or super-kingdoms it largely replaced: it both challenged them and utilised them. British Burma was in some sense the successor of Pagan, French Indo-China of the Vietnamese empire, and Netherlands India of Majapahit.

India and China

Economic contacts with India had been substantial, but political interventions from India were few. Its impact was felt rather through the domestication of India's religions and cultures, largely on the initiative of Southeast Asian rulers, who over time became, as Wolters puts it, 'capable of forming independent judgments on the practical advantages of strengthening their institutions of government by means of certain Indian kingship doctrines, a process of borrowing which in time meant that courtly society in Indonesia felt that it was part of, and on equal terms with, the Indian, or "civilised" world'.[1] Economic links with China were also substantial. Its culture was less susceptible of domestication, and its political example less relevant. Vietnam was an exception that proved the rule. Once incorporated in China, the core of the kingdom secured its independence in part as a result of that experience, and at times even claimed equality with China within a Confucian world. Yet it could also be characterised as a Southeast Asian kingdom, its Confucian borrowings fitful and inappropriate.

Sporadically China made its power felt in the region, sometimes with catastrophic effect, but its control, even in Vietnam after the tenth century, never lasted long. One period of vigorous activity was connected with the creation of the Mongol empire, and under the Yuan dynasty there were attacks on Pagan and Dai Viet, and also expeditions against Singosari and Champa. In the early fifteenth century, a time when southward trade was again expanding, the new Ming dynasty not only tried to re-establish control over the Vietnamese kingdom: it also was responsible for a remarkable series of voyages, mostly led by the eunuch admiral Zheng He (Chengho). Between 1405 and 1433, in some seven voyages, he visited Champa, Java, Sumatra, India, and Sri Lanka, and even Arabia and East Africa, and called at Melaka several times. The object was to re-establish a tributary pattern of trade.

Both the spasmodic assertions of control and the maintenance of tributary patterns of trade were designed to mark the influence of China in Southeast Asia, to sustain order, and to check the over-mighty. A tribute mission was, for a Southeast Asian state, a means of avoiding something worse—pre-empting a more forceful deployment of China's power—but it also had a more positive aspect. 'The emperors thought that they were manipulating their vassals by techniques of indirect control; the vassals were manipulating the China trade ... to amass wealth as a means of asserting their authority'.[2] 'Vassalage' might also directly assist one kingdom to maintain itself over against another. Promising to accept Kublai Khan's overlordship secured the founder of Majapahit the help of Mongol troops. A fourteenth-century king of Burma, Mingyi Swasawke, was recognised as 'Governor of Burma', and the two powers cooperated to some extent against the Shans. Sukhotai sent missions to

Beijing in the Mongol period, and the Thais had the support of China as a splinter movement in the Khmer empire. Generally the Chinese sought fragmentation, as well as submissiveness. Ayudhya expanded when the Mongols were in decline, but it sought to cultivate good relations with the Ming. So did the ruler of Melaka, though the ruler of Brunei was the first southern ruler to journey personally to Nanjing.

The Portuguese and the states of the archipelago

It was Melaka that the Portuguese defeated in 1511. The commander, Affonso de Albuquerque, gave his soldiers two reasons for the attack:

> the first is the great service which we shall perform to Our Lord in casting the Moors out of this country. ... And the other reason is the service we shall render to the King D. Manuel in taking this city, because it is the source of all the spiceries and drugs which the Moors carry every year hence to the Straits [of Bab-el-Mandeb]. ... Cairo and Mekka will be entirely ruined, and Venice will receive no spiceries unless her merchants go and buy them in Portugal.[3]

The Iberian voyages of 'discovery' were described by a sixteenth-century Spanish historian as 'the greatest event in the history of the world, apart from the incarnation and death of Him who created it'.[4] Together with other European adventurers—Italian, Dutch, English, French, Russian, Danish, Swedish—the Portuguese and Spaniards 'made humanity conscious, however dimly, of its essential unity'.[5] Commercial links had long existed across Asia and between Asia and Europe across the Middle East, and in the fifteenth century Asia and Europe were caught up in a new phase of economic expansion, in part the result of recovering from the Black Death, the great plagues of the fourteenth century, in part the result of the Chinese initiatives. But though the Ming voyages were connected with those developments, it was the Europeans whose 'discoveries' encompassed the whole world. If the novelty of their achievement perhaps prompted an exaggeration of their initial impact, at least in Asia, it was still a decisive event in world history.

While estimating the impact of the voyages is difficult, it is also difficult to explain their origins, though Albuquerque's order-of-the-day offers some hints. 'Only the hope of great profit and the courage of reckless adventure could induce men to undertake voyages on which the prospect of safe return was at best fifty-fifty.'[6] An inspiring goal was all the more important inasmuch as the Europeans had few other advantages in their favour. The expansion of this period cannot be explained by capitalism or industrialisation. Portugal and Spain, the countries most involved in the sixteenth century, were not even the most economically advanced of the European states, and the former was a small country with a population of only a million in 1500. Nor were the ventures the necessary result of advances in technology or geographical knowledge. The Portuguese had the compass—probably in fact derived from the Chinese through Arab and Mediterranean sailors—and the astrolabe and quadrant in simple forms, but navigation at sea remained somewhat haphazard. Geographical information was lacking. The Portuguese patiently explored the west coast of Africa, only then leaping from the Cape to the coast of India. Columbus would not have 'discovered' America had he thought it was there. His goal was the fabled China.

The hope of great wealth was certainly a stimulus, and it stimulated the state as well as the individual. The Renaissance offered first the Italian city-states, and then the larger states elsewhere in Europe, new ways of cultural expression, new means of exerting political power. In every case, European expansion was backed by the state, by the Portuguese government that employed Genoese to outwit Venetians, by the Spanish government that patronised the Genoese Columbus, by the Russian government that chartered Novgorod merchants, and by the English and the Dutch who chartered East India Companies. But if the venture was 'European' in scope, it also depended on the divisions among Europeans. 'Whoever is lord of Malacca has his hand on the throat of Venice.'[7] The expansiveness of Europe was partly explained by its breakup into states, which sought security or domination *vis-à-vis* each other. This rivalry drove them to seek wealth overseas, and their ventures there were marked by that rivalry, though also by attempts to accommodate it, the initial attempt dating back to 1494, when by the treaty of Tordesillas Portugal and Spain sought to divide the world. Intra-European rivalry was to extended into the subsequent period of imperialism, which was indeed partly driven by it.

The Spaniards found great wealth in Mexico and Peru, though they went on to Asia, and established themselves in islands they named after the future Philip II. For the Portuguese, though they 'discovered' Brazil, Asia was the main source of wealth. Their strategy, as Albuquerque indicates, was to secure a share of the burgeoning trade within Asia, by violence if need be, and to re-route the trade in spices that Europe found so necessary in order to make meat palatable at a time when the winter shortage of cattle-fodder meant that cattle had to be slaughtered, but refrigeration did not exist. To this end they established 'factories' or trading agencies and, where necessary, fortified them. The Dutch, displacing them in the early seventeenth century, followed their example, both in pursuing an Asia-wide trade, and in selectively seeking control of products that were in demand. The English, then a lesser commercial power, found it difficult to compete.

Albuquerque pointed to another motive, striking a blow at Islam. It was true that the 'land route', of which Venice was the terminus, was in large part in the hands of Muslims, in particular the Mamluk kingdom of Egypt, and that their control of the trade in Asia had increased, particularly with the rise of Melaka. The Portuguese could thus depict their venture as dictated not only by the need to acquire wealth and serve the king, but also to save souls, in effect an extension of the long struggle against Islam on the Iberian peninsula itself. That remained a motive with the Catholic powers, stimulated indeed by the Counter-Reformation of the sixteenth century and the creation of the militant Jesuit order. The real Portuguese attempts at conversion belong to the later sixteenth century. Their intolerant nature did nothing to restore declining Portuguese authority. The Dutch and the English were to be far more cautious. Their predecessors had provoked an Islamic reaction, which they wished to avoid.

The Portuguese, indeed, never achieved the dominance of which Albuquerque spoke. The capture of Melaka struck down the major Muslim entrepot. Now the Portuguese sought to build their own commercial empire in the archipelago, differing from earlier empires in its more formal connexion with other parts of Asia, let alone Europe, but using methods probably differing rather less. 'The years were filled with piracy and naval warfare by the Portuguese, defense against assaults, and attacks on trading ships, war fleets, and fortresses, guerilla warfare with a strong element of vendetta to it.'[8] One novelty, it seems, was the fortification of their 'factories', otherwise similar to the *fondachi,* the residential quarters of Italian merchants in Muslim ports in the Mediterranean. Their violence was also accompanied by a superiority in the use of weapons and gunpowder. Those were not unfamiliar to Southeast Asian states, and, as Leonard Andaya writes, they 'invested time and effort to develop their own arms and gunpowder. Ultimately, however, the new weapons were used to reinforce traditional ways of fighting rather than to transform the tactics of warfare.'[9] Even so the Portuguese did not destroy the opposition. Instead they both diffused it and inflamed it. The destruction of Melaka prompted a dispersion of Malay power and the creation of a number of new Malayo-Muslim states. None of them, however, had the ability to create an 'imperial' kingdom along the lines of Sri Vijaya or its Muslim successor.

Melaka had been fostering the independence that the coastal trading cities of east and central Java were attempting to secure from Majapahit. That super-kingdom appears finally to have disintegrated between 1513 and 1528 in face of a coalition of Muslim states, Madura, Tuban, Surabaya, and Demak, and the sultanate of Demak became the most powerful state in Java. It controlled the northern rice-growing plains from Jepara to Gresik, exporting rice to Melaka and trading to Maluku. The Portuguese gained a foothold in west Java by agreement with the petty Hindu state of Pajajaran at Sunda Kelapa. By 1527 the neighbouring ruler of Bantam, forcibly acquired in the name of the sultan of Demak as an outpost against the Portuguese, had taken over, renaming it Jayakarta (Jakarta). Bantam was to become in 1568 an independent sultanate, extending over all west Java and to Lampung and southwest Sumatra, its swidden lands becoming a great source of pepper.

The independence of the sultanate was achieved as a result of a struggle in east and central Java which, however, ultimately created a new super-kingdom in the later sixteenth century. The collapse of Majapahit had left the interior of Java a political chaos, but a new dynasty arose, based on Mataram, which was at the very heart of central Java. It had been a small district under the ruler of Pajang, itself part of Demak. In 1582 an official of that ruler, Senapati, an adventurer of low origin, was able to usurp the government of Pajang, and in 1586 he shifted its seat of government to Mataram. The new sultanate attempted to control the coastal towns, which were perhaps weakened by their struggle with the Portuguese. At Senapati's death in 1601 it was still, however, an inland state. Its chances of becoming an 'empire' that shared Majapahit's dual character—both Javanese and archipelagic—were to be prevented by the Dutch.

Partly as a corollary of the competition of the Javanese, the Portuguese were not as strong in Maluku as is sometimes thought. The Javanese towns still had an influence not only in western Borneo, source of diamonds, and in Timor, Aru, Ceram, and Kai, but in the spice islands themselves. Their colony at Hitu on Ambon—a key to the clove trade—was early a centre of resistance to the Portuguese. The latter never occupied Banda, the source of the other fine spice, nutmeg, and they met Javanese as well as Spanish and local opposition in Tidore and Ternate, centres of commercial kingdoms in Maluku. Ternate at first welcomed the Portuguese while Tidore welcomed the Spaniards, but struggles in the 1560s forced the former to move to Tidore. In succeeding years the ruler of Ternate claimed parts of Sulawesi, the Sula islands, Sumbawa, and Buton, while Tidore claimed supremacy over neighbouring southern Halmahera and northwest New Guinea (Irian Barat). The Portuguese, however, established themselves more firmly at Ambon, and benefited from the struggle between the Javanese towns and Mataram.

The Javanese towns also competed with the Portuguese in the western parts of the archipelago, attacking Melaka itself on a number of occasions—in 1513, 1535, 1551, and 1574—but failing to capture it. In this area, however, other Malayo-Muslim states had emerged, rivals to the Portuguese, but also to the Javanese. Some Melaka traders had fled to Aceh in northern Sumatra, and in the first half of the sixteenth century Aceh extended its control over the pepper-producing ports of Pedir and Pasai and over part of Menangkabau, and in pursuit of pepper it stretched down the west coast as Bantam stretched up it. The Portuguese were driven south from Pasai, and had to obtain their pepper from central east Sumatran ports like Inderagiri, Kampar, and Jambi. Aceh attacked Melaka itself several times—in 1537, 1539, 1547, 1568, 1573, 1575—and it endeavoured to establish control over states on the peninsula, like Kedah and Perak, sources of tin.

Aceh did not face only the Portuguese. The rulers of Melaka created a new state, despite the repeated attacks of the Portuguese, its centre based at the southern end of the straits in Johore and the Riau-Lingga islands. The rivalry that developed between Aceh and Johore, particularly over Deli and eastern Sumatra, helped the Portuguese to survive. In 1539 Johore, with Perak and Siak, defeated the north Sumatrans. In 1564, on the other hand, Aceh sacked Johore. When the Acehnese followed up by an attack on Melaka, Johore came to its aid. In 1582 the Portuguese helped Johore beat off another Acehnese attack. Then Melaka and Johore fell out, to the advantage of Aceh.

Other traders fleeing Portuguese Melaka settled in Pattani on the peninsula, in Makasar, in Brunei, Sulu, and Mindanao, contributing to the development of

Malayo-Muslim sultanates in those regions. Many of them became significant states, some, like Aceh and Pattani, centres of Islamic learning, one, Brunei, extending its commercial range and influence well beyond the peninsula and the archipelago. The successor-state of Johore retained much of the mana, if not all the power, which it had inherited from Melaka, and which the Portuguese could not inherit. Johore, Aceh, Sulu, and Brunei were still politically active in the late nineteenth century. Yet, while the Portuguese had prompted an assertion of Malayo-Muslim political power, it was and remained diffused. Portuguese Melaka did not play the role of pre-Portuguese Melaka. None of the Malayo-Muslim states were to emulate Sri Vijaya either. The establishment of Dutch power made that even less likely, just as it impeded the creation of a new Majapahit.

The Dutch company and the states of the archipelago

The Dutch empire, like the Portuguese, was Asia-wide, and linked politically with Europe. It was also more methodised, and it proved longer-lasting. While the Dutch East India Company, or VOC, created no general commercial monopoly in the archipelago, and established no overall political supremacy, it curbed not only its European but also its local rivals. It did not eliminate all of them. But it prevented their empire-building and it tried to channel the international trade of the archipelago and the peninsula. The VOC, it might be said, built a new kind of Sri Vijaya. Though its power in Java increased, it was not until the nineteenth century that the Dutch built a new kind of Majapahit.

The VOC's approach was novel in another way: its emphasis on contractual relationships. In a sense the Dutch were thus extending to the archipelago a system of international relations that was being developed in Europe, but they were denying its implications. At this stage Europeans were disposed to see Southeast Asian states as equal partners, sovereign states with which equal treaties might be made. The Dutch treaties with Indonesian princes, though made on the ostensible basis of equality, tended, however, to diminish it by undermining their relations with third parties. That the English, then a minor power, vainly questioned in their discussions with the Dutch in 1613 and 1615.[10] For their part it seems that Malay rulers saw treaties in terms of the tributary patterns that traditionally regulated relations among Southeast Asian states: treaties were temporary in duration, reflecting the current state of power relationships, and the partners' obligations personal and mutual in nature. In Europe, indeed, treaties were not necessarily perpetual: they were understood to be only a part of a pragmatic system of diplomatic relations among states. In Southeast Asia the Dutch were able to develop a more lopsided view of emerging European practice. In due course the 'international law' the Europeans followed outside Europe was to diverge yet further from the practice within Europe.

In Europe the Dutch had greatly benefited from the commercial expansion precipitated by the Portuguese and Spanish voyages, and by the end of the sixteenth century, when the Portuguese and Spanish crowns were temporarily united, had determined themselves to enter world trade. Their initial ventures into Asia were marked by the decentralisation of the new Republic of the United Provinces that had been set up to consolidate independence from Spain. Amsterdam fleets were able to trade at Bantam, despite Portuguese opposition, to establish a 'factory' at Lonthor in the Banda islands, and, though unable to subdue the Portuguese fort at Ambon, briefly to establish a Dutch one, and make some contracts for the delivery of spices. The Middelburg fleet of 1601 established a factory at Aceh and one at Pattani, and in 1603 a factory was established in Johore.

The Dutch state wanted a more organised approach, since it wished to wage war in Asia against the Iberian powers without expense to the government. The States-General created a united company, the VOC, in 1602, and gave it exclusive rights beyond the Cape of Good Hope. Within three years thirty-eight ships had been sent to the East. In 1609 a governor-general was appointed, and in 1610 the Directors, the Heeren 17, ordered the acquisition of a central rendezvous at Johore, Bantam, or Jakarta. The choice fell on the last, for the ruler was only 'a nobleman ruling over a small coastal town without much trade and a small hinterland which could yield only a limited amount of pepper',[11] yet the position, midway between the two points traditionally the focus of power in the archipelago-peninsula region, was superb. There Governor-General J. P. Coen created the new city of Batavia.

It was soon threatened by Mataram. The great Sultan Agung had been conquering the north Javanese towns and Madura. As 'Susuhunan' he claimed overlordship over the whole of Java. In 1629 he laid siege to Batavia with a vast force, defeated because it could not be supplied by food overland, and the Dutch had command of the sea. After this the energy of Mataram was concentrated against local powers to the eastward. Its influence spread to western Borneo: in 1622 it conquered Sukadana and forced Bandjermasin to submit. Though the Balambangan region of eastern Java was conquered in 1639, Bali yet contrived to maintain its independence. Its rulers sought to preserve its Hindu culture in the face of the advance of Islam from Mataram in the west and also from Makasar in the east. The VOC 'paralyzed' them both, as H. Schulte Nordholt puts it,[12] and the rulers legitimated themselves by claiming to be the successors of Majapahit.

In Maluku the VOC faced not only the opposition of the Portuguese and the Spaniards but also of the English. England, too, was at odds with Spain, anxious to ensure its independence and boost its wealth by ventures in the world at large. The position of the Netherlands, moreover, gave England an enduring interest in its independence from a major European power, since it was from that part of the continent that it was itself most vulnerable to attack. England and the Dutch state were also, however, commercial rivals, and indeed their relations were long to be marked by this duality. The Dutch obstructed the first expedition sent out by the East India Company that had been chartered in 1600. With smaller resources, and dominated by the need to sell home manufactures, the English Company was less able than the VOC to secure a share in intra-Asian trade. In Coen's period there was outright conflict. He conquered Banda, wiping out the inhabitants, and parcelling out the spice lands for cultivation by slave labour. 'Things are carried on in such a criminal and murderous way', wrote an ex-officer of the VOC, 'that the blood of the poor people cries to heaven for vengeance'.[13] The erosion of the English position was completed by the massacre at Ambon in 1623. The Company now concentrated on pepper rather than fine spices, using a factory at Bantam, though also 'smuggling' other spices via Makasar.

In the Straits Melaka yet remained in Portuguese hands, and this was also a period of great prosperity for Aceh. In 1607 Iskandar Shah seized the throne, and he expanded Aceh's control over the pepper- and tin-producing areas of the Straits, over the coastal regions of Sumatra, and over the peninsular states of Pahang, Kedah, and Perak. The Acehnese fleet of 1629 was, however, defeated by the united forces of Melaka, Johore, and Pattani, and this setback began a period of decline, which the Dutch capture of Melaka was to accelerate.

That finally took place—with aid from Johore—in 1641. 'With reinforcements', Governor-General van Diemen told the Heeren 17, 'we shall be able to drive the Portuguese out of India within a short time. The English and Danes must then dry up and the Company will have full control of the rich trade.'[14] The Dutch now began a more rigorous policy. In part this was the result of the economic recession that took hold from the 1630s. That had major effects in Europe, in particularly advantaging France over Spain, so that the latter part of the century witnessed the glory of Louis XIV's reign and also renewed French activity overseas, commercial and missionary. It was also an age of mercantilism, in which England, among other states, took measures designed to weaken the Dutch control over the colonial and carrying trades. The reaction of the VOC was to intensify its attempt to secure spice monopolies, to drive down prices by political means, and to constrain, if not eliminate, Asian as well as European competitors.

The capture of Melaka affected both and enabled the Dutch to pursue command over the tin and pepper trades. 'When the Dutch first came here', the ruler of Jambi had complained, 'they said my place would be rich, but now they are trying to shut out the Chinese who give the most trade'.[15] The Dutch wanted to direct the junk trade to Batavia, and by the mid-century efforts to divert the junks from the Bangka straits had been successful. Sultan Agung proclaimed himself the protector of Palembang, but the VOC defeated his fleet in 1641. In 1642 it made a contract with Palembang securing exclusive rights to its pepper, and after a dispute in 1658 it sent a punitive expedition, designed not only to enforce the contract but to provide a lesson 'to surrounding Moor princes'.[16] Relations later in the century were good, despite the restrictions the Dutch put on Palembang's trade both to the east and the north: if the ruler of Palembang no longer feared the Susuhunan, he was for a time apprehensive of Bantam, while the *orang laut* of Johore and Jambi sought slaves in Palembang waters. At the same time, he and his subjects were able to engage in 'smuggling' pepper, and the Dutch managed to secure only about half the harvest.

The VOC's pursuit of a pepper monopoly affected Aceh. So did its interest in tin. In 1642 the Dutch made an agreement with Kedah for the delivery of half of its production, and the following year Ujong Salang (Phuket) promised all it produced. Kedah had to be blockaded, but was never completely coerced. Perak remained under Acehnese suzerainty, but in 1650 the Dutch extorted from the queen of Aceh a treaty whereby they were to share the tin trade equally with her to 'the exclusion of all other nations, Europeans as well as Indians'.[17] In 1651, however, the Dutch factory was attacked and plundered, and a sequence of punitive expeditions to Perak and deputations to Aceh ensued. What made Perak come to terms, however, was its fear of the Thais, who were now, under Narai, reasserting their claims over the northern Malay states, and against whom the enfeebled Aceh could offer no help. In 1670 the VOC established a post on Pangkor. But though the ruler of Perak sought good relations with the VOC, he could not, by contrast to the Palembang ruler, overcome his subjects' opposition to the Dutch, their blockades, their low prices.

After it had assisted the Dutch to turn the Portuguese out of Melaka, Johore was given a number of commercial privileges by the Dutch that made the pass system that they used in order to limit the trade in 'contraband' goods less burdensome. For a while, on the other hand, Johore needed Dutch protection against Mataram and against Aceh, and the two thus came to a kind of working relationship. Johore regained Siak and Rokan, but a long if sporadic war with Jambi was to ensue in the latter half of the century. In 1673 Jambi destroyed the Johore capital. In this case the Dutch could not assist, since Jambi was also an ally. But the Johore kingdom quickly revived and took vengeance on Jambi in 1679.

Dutch attempts to capture the pepper trade of the west coast of Sumatra promoted the decay of Aceh. The pepper, like that of the east coast ports, came down from the interior regions of Menangkabau, where pepper gardens had been developed from the sixteenth century. The Dutch displaced Acehnese supremacy on the west coast, and under the Painan contract of 1663 a number of rulers in the Padang region granted the VOC 'an absolute monopoly over the pepper trade'.[18] It was to southwest Sumatra that the English were to retreat when the Dutch secured control of Bantam.

That, too, was done in an attempt to control the pepper trade. An independent sultanate, it was visited by Chinese, Indians, English, French, and by ships of the Danish East India Company, reorganised in 1670. The Dutch were aided by a succession dispute, one party to which their troops assisted. As a result the victor made a treaty with them in 1684, surrendering his claim to Cirebon, paying the VOC's war costs, granting it an exclusive right of trade, and agreeing to expel all non-Dutch Europeans. The fortress of Speelwijk was constructed nearby.

The advance of Dutch power in the western parts of the archipelago deeply affected Mataram. Sultan Agung had sought to prolong the resistance of Melaka, and had sent an embassy to the Portuguese at Goa in India in 1633. After the fall of Melaka his successor, Amangkurat I, sought to maintain an influence in southeastern Sumatra, but the VOC contested it. The Dutch also sought to constrain the

Javanese trade to the eastward. In 1646 the VOC made a peace treaty with the Susuhunan, but they now quarrelled over northern Java. Batavia depended on it for rice and timber. Amangkurat I needed its resources more than ever as his larger empire fell away. His violent rule—'the harsh time of broken nails'[19]—provoked rebellion, however, and the VOC, though recognising that intervention meant 'certain costs and uncertain profits',[20] decided to support the authority of Mataram in the hope of restoring peace and stability. A comprehensive treaty was concluded in 1677, in which the Susuhunan promised to meet the VOC's costs, to grant the Company the right to trade throughout his dominions, to deliver rice, and to prohibit trade with Makassarese who did not have a VOC pass. A further treaty was made with Amangkurat II in 1678: the northern seaports were ceded to the VOC until his debts were repaid; it was given a monopoly over the import of textiles and opium; the boundaries of Batavia were extended; and Semarang was made over to the Company. '[T]he Dutch have gradually extended their hegemony over various places to the point where many of the coastal areas are now in their possession', the representative of a Chinese junk reported at Nagasaki.[21]

The VOC had, however, thus begun its first major war in the interior of Java, unaware that it was the 'the beginning of fifty years and more of discord, battle and chaos',[22] recently so brilliantly elucidated by Merle Ricklefs. Amangkurat II was crowned with the so-called crown of Majapahit, while VOC soldiers fired salutes. But his realm was no Majapahit. And the defeated prince Trunajaya's admonition tellingly pointed out: 'Your Highness' ancestors never before had anything to do with Christians for they wished to settle their own affairs, for they [the Dutch] are like grafts which are attached to a tree and finally wither the trunk. ... '[23] Humiliated by his dependency, and by the loss of Cirebon, the king indeed supported the Balinese adventurer Surapati in his massacre of a VOC mission to his capital, Kartasura, in 1686. Trade languished. 'May the good God make things turn out otherwise', the governor-general and Council prayed in 1703.[24] Shortly, indeed, the VOC was able to turn its recent acquisitions to account: coffee was successfully introduced in west Java, and Java coffee became quite popular in Europe. 'The VOC had now become a territorial power with vital economic interests to protect on the island of Java.'[25] Melaka seemed more of a 'strategic outpost',[26] and a peaceful relationship with Johore more important. 'By 1700, Batavia had come to rely on the strength of Johore as a safeguard to the peaceful traffic of the Straits',[27] even if its authorities at Melaka found their commercial interests sacrificed.

Obtaining a monopoly of fine spices, then grown only in a very limited area, was easier than obtaining a monopoly of pepper. The VOC had gone a long way towards securing control at the source in the early part of the seventeenth century. What it did in the latter part was mainly designed to prevent 'smuggling' by Europeans and Asians. Makasar was a base for that. God, said Sultan Hasanuddin, 'has created the world so that all men can enjoy the use thereof. Or do you believe that God has reserved for your trade alone those islands which lie so far distant from your own country?'[28] From the late sixteenth century Portuguese, Chinese, and English merchants visited Makasar, especially after the establishment of Javanese and, later, Dutch influence at Bandjermasin, and Mataram's oppression of the coastal towns tended to drive the Javanese traders to it too. The ruler, as the Dutch governor-general commented, was 'attempting to expand his dominion more and more, so that, in time, in order for it not to become too big it will need to be stopped, either by dexterity or open violence'[29]. In 1660, following what David Bassett termed a 'seventeenth century version of Pearl Harbour'—the VOC attacking all the Portuguese ships at Makasar without warning[30]—Hasanuddin agreed to prohibit all sailings to Maluku and expel the Portuguese. He failed to carry out the undertaking, however. In 1667 he was finally defeated by a Dutch force under Speelman, aided by Buginese allies from Bone led by Arung Palakka, whose remarkable career Leonard Andaya has traced so absorbingly.[31]

Alongside Dominican missionaries, the Portuguese were in the Lesser Sundas, a source of sandalwood and slaves, from the mid-sixteenth century. They had come to Timor in 1516, when it was on the trade routes of the Javanese. The Portuguese refocused on the area after the Tokugawa turned them out of Japan in 1638. They remained at Larantuka on Flores. On Timor they lost Kupang to the Dutch in 1653, but constructed Lifau, at Oecusse, to replace it, effectively dividing the island. In the eighteenth century, the governors were to have difficulty in controlling the feuding 'black Portuguese', and in 1769 moved their base from Lifau to Dili.

The Spaniards had evacuated Tidore in 1663, concerned at the threat to the Philippines from 'Koxinga' (Zheng Chenggong), the Ming loyalist in Formosa. Speelman forced its ruler to follow neighbouring Ternate in accepting Dutch overlordship. 'What Aceh had practised on the pepper coast, what the Portuguese applied in the Moluccas, what the rulers of Ternate and Tidore were accustomed to carry on against each other—*hongi* expeditions were now elevated by the Dutch Company to a system'. These fleets of large prau or cora-cora 'served first of all to punish the wicked violators of the monopoly contracts for selling spices to the foreign traders and by intimidation to make trade impossible for competitors, in the second place to maintain the spice prices by limiting production (destroying plantings)'.[32] That meant increasing poverty and revolt in the islands. It also meant that for the VOC 'the gross profit from the spices became overwhelming, often more than 1000 per cent'.[33] In the last decades of the seventeenth century the Company could fix the price of clove and nutmeg in Europe and Asia. Too high a price might, however, stimulate competition.

The long-sought monopoly of fine spices became less relevant in the eighteenth century. The provision of winter cattle fodder and culinary changes reduced their significance for the Europeans, who, on the other hand, developed new demands, for Indian textiles and for China tea. To these the British proved better able to adapt than the Dutch. Indeed British traders increasingly penetrated the archipelago itself, supplying arms and opium, seeking jungle and marine produce for the China market. The position of the Dutch in the peninsula and archipelago was also undermined by Bugis adventurers, dispersed by the intervention in Sulawesi and by the establishment of Arung Palakka's overlordship. Their numbers and their mobility indeed meant that few states could repel them, though some tried to use them.

Increasingly the Dutch focused on Java. The wars had by no means come to an end: they had in fact become more costly and also more destructive. The VOC backed a usurper, who became Pakubuwana I, against Amangkurat III, and he turned to Surapati. The latter was killed in 1706, and in 1708 Amangkurat was exiled to Sri Lanka. Yet the new Susuhunan's dependence on the Dutch was to heighten political opposition to him, and his successor, Amangkurat IV, was described by the authorities in Batavia as 'an emperor who was deserted by all his people and had acquired virtually the whole of the Javanese world as his enemy'.[34] Another war of succession burdened the kingdom with ever greater debts and obligations. The dynasty had been preserved, but at great cost. Nor was Java more stable, though Batavia was free of threat. The peasants, as Ricklefs says, 'had fought and died, grown their crops in order to turn them over to the Company or to their lord, suffered famine and disease and doubtless sought to escape to places quieter, richer, healthier than wherever they were'.[35] Vast tracts of East Java were devastated and depopulated.

The relations between Company and Susuhunan were uneasy, even perhaps contradictory. The former wanted stability, money, and products. The rulers it supported wanted to establish and exploit their realms, and were unwilling to allow their subordinate lords autonomy or to see the kingdom's wealth drained off to foreigners. Their reliance upon the VOC they tended to resent. Their opponents saw it as shameful and a threat to Islam.

The uneasy relationship broke down again in the 1740s. The sugar industry had expanded in the *ommelanden*, 'a kind of Wild West *avant la lettre*'.[36] A reduction in prices led to mill closures and to unemployment and banditry among the Chinese workers. Repression and the threat of deportation produced revolt in October 1740, and the Chinese within Batavia paid the price in a three-day massacre. The Susuhunan, Pakubuwana II, mistakenly involved himself and his forces, and in 1743 he was made to sign a new contract, involving the cession of Pasuruan, Madura, Surabaya, Rembang, and Jepara, and in 1746 Governor-General van Imhoff secured the cession of all the coastal regencies for a yearly sum.

Yet further military action followed in 1749–57. Mangkubumi, his brother, opposed the Susuhunan, and when his successor received the crown from the Dutch as Pakubuwana III, most of the Mataram chiefs joined Mangkubumi. For a time the Dutch were hard pressed, but the outcome was the partition of Mataram. In 1755 Mangkubumi, who had taken the name Hamengkubuwana, accepted Pakubuwana III as ruler of the eastern part of the kingdom, centred at Surakarta, while he received the western half, with a capital at Yogyakarta. Another rebel, who became Pangeran Adipati Mangkunegara, was bought off with a princely domain in 1757.

The VOC had dropped the policy of the 1670s of seeking stability and trade through a malleable monarch. It now ruled the northern coast directly, while accepting the division of Mataram. Though the VOC was weaker as a whole, it was now the master of Java, save for the remnants of Surapati's followers in the east.

East of Java the VOC continued to dominate the spice islands. In a further bid to protect the approaches to Maluku, it made a new agreement with Bandjermasin in 1756. West of Java their position, and that of the Malay rulers, was complicated by the Bugis incursions. Johore allowed them to settle on the periphery, in Linggi and Selangor, but, when they fell out, could not expel them. Johore was also threatened by Menangkabaus from Sumatra led by Raja Kechil, who claimed to be the son of Sultan Mahmoud, assassinated by his Bendahara in 1699. He conquered Johore in 1718, and established himself as ruler at Riau, and had Sultan Abdul Jalil murdered. In turn the Bugis took the part of Abdul Jalil's son, Raja Sulaiman, and installed him as sultan. A Bugis leader became Yamtuan Muda. That in a sense provided legitimation for the Bugis. But the sultan belonged to the usurping Bendahara dynasty, and himself depended on their strength, rather than the mana of the dynasty that it had replaced.

The VOC sought to make capital out of the rivalry between Malay sultan and Bugis Yamtuan—it saw the former as the *speelpop* (puppet) of the latter[37]—and in 1755 it helped Sulaiman against Siak, where Raja Kechil had set up as ruler. It hoped this would pacify the area, but it triggered a Bugis revolt. The VOC then offered the sultan assistance in return for tin from Selangor, Kelang, and Linggi, but those were in Bugis hands. Sultan and Company attacked Linggi in 1756, but the Bugis retaliated against Melaka. Abandoning interventionism once more, the VOC made peace with the Bugis in 1758, securing Linggi and Rembau, and in 1760 they returned to Riau. Its trade flourished: 'an object of anxious uneasyness to the Dutch and of great mercantile convenience to the English'.[38]

In the fourth Anglo-Dutch war, the Dutch, allied with France, dropped their caution, and the VOC attacked Riau in 1784. The result was a fiasco, but van Braam's fleet, sent out by the Republic itself, and on a scale never before seen in the archipelago, drove the Bugis from Riau. The sultan himself then revolted against the dominance the Dutch thus secured. He encouraged 'smuggling' and called in the Ilanun (Maranao) pirates, while the Temenggong, one of his ministers, took to privateering. Completely disrupting the commercial interchange between the Bugis and the British Asia-based 'country traders', the Dutch action also 'impelled the British to occupy Penang two years later'.[39] Its founder, Francis Light, also alluded to French action in Cochin-China.[40]

The relations between Johore and the VOC had always been subject to tension. The sultan did not control the tin the Company sought, and his kingdom was the centre of the free trade to which the VOC was opposed. With other states in the region it had come to an accommodation. In Palembang it had no monopoly. Instead it acted as 'protector', and secured a delivery of tin—recently discovered on Bangka—at a privileged price as a kind of tribute. The relationship might be compared more with the tributary patterns of Southeast Asian tradition than with the contractual relationships the Dutch had introduced.

A similar relationship developed with Perak: the VOC traded the political support it could offer as 'the greatest and most stable political power in the region'[41] for the tin the sultan controlled. Van Imhoff wanted Melaka to revive its trade, while

Sultan Muzafar wanted a buttress against the Bugis in Selangor and the rival they backed, Raja Iskandar. The VOC fort on Pangkor was rebuilt, and a treaty concluded in 1746, 'seen by the Malays not as a passing flirtation with a minor princeling, but as a grand alliance with the most important European power in the area'.[42] To this treaty Perak remained loyal in the coming struggles. On becoming sultan Iskandar followed his predecessor's policy, and it led to 'an unprecedented period of prosperity and peace', celebrated in the *Misa Melayu*.[43]

The VOC's deployment of force and diplomacy old- and new-style had been assisted by the divisions among and within the mainly Malayo-Muslim states they faced. Those had indeed tempted its officials at times to intervene incautiously or over-ambitiously. That led to the long and devastating wars in Java. Out of them, however, the VOC emerged as the predominant power on that island. Increasingly, too, it began to see Java as the centre of its empire. In the seventeenth century it had sought to control the trade of the peninsula and archipelago and to establish monopolies over selected products. In the eighteenth century it deployed its power to exact tribute from the protection it might afford. A number of the major states accepted that relationship, in part because of their internal instability, but also because of the new threats of instability from the Bugis and the Thais. The Dutch themselves could not be dislodged, save by a European power. Becoming the leading maritime state, and increasingly interested in the trade of the archipelago, the British were yet restrained by their relationship with the Dutch in Europe. The Dutch resort to violence in Johore and the Straits was an over-reaction to the penetration of the British country traders, backed by article 6 in the Anglo-Dutch peace treaty of 1784. Penang was beyond the limits of the Dutch empire.

The Spaniards and the Philippines

The first major British venture in island Southeast Asia in the new phase was the capture of Manila in 1762. The Spaniards' venture in Southeast Asia had meanwhile been shaped by their relationships with the Portuguese and the Dutch, and above all with the Muslim sultanates to the south of what was called the Philippines. It began, of course, as part of their attempt to reach the riches of the East by travelling west, and they linked Southeast Asia in yet another way with the outside world, across the Pacific from their conquests in Mexico and Peru. The objective of the voyage begun in 1519 by Magellan—a Portuguese who had fought with Albuquerque against Melaka, and subsequently joined the Portuguese expedition to Maluku—was the spice islands. He reached Samar and Cebu, then an entrepot for trade with China. Its ruler, Humabon, welcomed him, and sought to enlist his support against his rival Lapu-lapu on Mactan. Lapu-lapu refused to recognise the Spanish-supported ruler, and the ensuing battle led to Magellan's death.[44] The remaining ships went on to Palawan, Brunei, and Tidore, and the *Victoria* completed the circumnavigation of the globe. This and subsequent expeditions met Portuguese opposition in Maluku, but a new expedition sent to the 'western islands' in 1542 named them after the

Infante. As King Philip II, that prince ordered a new expedition to the Philippines, which left New Spain in 1564. It made a settlement in Cebu, but partly as a result of Portuguese prodding, its commander, Legazpi, shifted to Panay in 1569, and then to Manila in 1570. Over the succeeding decades, with aid from Mexico, the Spaniards established a territorial control in Luzon and the Visayas, where they met little organised resistance.

There indeed no Malayo-Muslim sultanates had been established. But Manila had been an outpost of Brunei, and the capture of the settlement after a clash with its Raja Suleiman began a long conflict with opponents to the south whom the Spaniards called 'Moros'. The Sultan of Brunei, Governor Francisco de Sande reported, claimed that 'the whole archipelago would very willingly render obeisance and pay tribute to him if we were not here. The Moros of Borneo preach the doctrine of Mahoma, converting all the Moros of the islands.'[45] In 1578 he sent an expedition to demand that the sultan stop spreading Islam and exacting tribute, and admit Christian missionaries. The response was a refusal, and the Spaniards captured the city, but soon withdrew, driven out by disease or resistance or, perhaps, both. A second expedition, of a more peaceful nature, made no progress, but after the defeat of a conspiracy of the Brunei elite in Manila the relationship settled down.

The Spaniards, however, continued to face opposition from the other Moro sultanates, in particular Sulu, which made itself independent of Brunei in the seventeenth century, and indeed laid claim to part of northern Borneo. The 1578 expedition had exacted a capitulation from Sulu, and a Spanish expedition was sent against Mindanao in 1596. But the Moros reacted by frequent raids upon the Spanish coastal settlements to the north. The first major attacks were on Cebu, Negros, and Panay in 1590–91. In 1616 Sulu Moros plundered as far as Camarines and Cavite. A Spanish attack on Sulu in 1630 was followed by a retaliatory raid on Leyte and Samar in 1634. The Spaniards constructed a base at Zamboanga and from there attacked Sultan Kudrat of Mindanao and also the Sulus in the 1630s. In the 1640s the Spaniards withdrew, making treaties with both sultanates, and in 1663 they left Zamboanga.

The Spaniards were indeed facing pressure from the Dutch as well as from the Moros. The VOC wished to dislodge them from Maluku and to secure Manila as a means of access to the China trade. One of the Rotterdam fleets of 1598 had plundered vessels in Manila Bay in 1600, but been driven off. The VOC followed the example, and in 1614 Iloilo, the supply base for Maluku, was sacked. In 1616–17 van Spilbergen appeared before Manila. The Dutch were drubbed, but kept up a blockade until the mid-1620s. 'We must do our utmost to destroy the trade between China and Manila, for, as soon as this is done, we firmly believe that … the Spaniards [will] leave the Moluccas, and even Manila of their own accord.'[46] The Dutch did not take Manila, but their activities limited Spanish activities to the south, and in the 1640s they intensified their pressure in this region as elsewhere, prompting the Spanish compromise with Sulu and Mindanao, though it was yet another threat that prompted Spain to leave Maluku.

It was perhaps a sign of the change in the VOC's position in the eighteenth century that the Spaniards were able to recover some ground *vis-à-vis* the Moros. In 1718–19 Zamboanga was rebuilt, and several sharp encounters with the Sulus followed. Sultan A'zim-ud-din sought an understanding with the Spaniards, however, and in 1737 the two parties made a treaty, promising mutual aid in the event of an attack other than one from a European power. H. de la Costa suggests that the sultan wanted to strengthen his government 'against the turbulent and unruly aristocracy of Sulu', and that the treaty gave him 'time'.[47] The notion is perhaps strengthened by recalling the relationships Palembang and Perak developed with the Dutch. But, if he looked for Spanish help, it came at a high price. The Dutch abstained from missionary activity, but in 1747 the Spanish government sought permission to preach the Christian religion in Sulu, at the same time offering an alliance against European powers as well as Asian. The sultan's agreement increased the opposition to him, and he was displaced by his younger brother. He appealed to Spain and even accepted baptism. An expedition was sent to restore him, but the Spaniards decided that they could not trust him. He was imprisoned, and the Spain–Sulu war was renewed'.

Raiding increased. In 1753, for example, the Moros attacked the provincial capital of Mindoro, and took one-third of the inhabitants prisoner. The following year they attacked all the coastal towns of Mindoro, a particular target because of its strategic location. By 1755 they were entrenched in Marinduque. Their presence hindered resistance to the British, and after the British left they were stronger than ever. In 1788, after repeated raids, only three towns in Mindoro were still standing. 'Iranun raiding in the period before 1790 often involved wanton destruction of Filipino lands and communities', James Warren writes, 'suggesting that marauding was then viewed as an extension of *jihad,* with political not simply economic motives'. After 1800, he suggests, 'slaves were the prime object'.[48]

Spain's ambitions had extended more widely, contributing, for example, to the distrust of the Christians in Tokugawa Japan. Their intervention in mainland Southeast Asia was, however, confined to attempts on the part of adventurers backed by Governor Luis Dasmarinas to help the Cambodians against the Thais in 1596–99. In general, indeed, the Europeans played a far more limited role on the mainland than they did in island Southeast Asia, even at the height of the economic boom. The dynamic of inter-state politics was not greatly affected by them, and it followed established patterns. Merchants, missionaries, and mercenaries, the Europeans did not establish empires, nor even lay the foundations for them.

Burma under the Taung-ngu dynasties

The kingdom of Ava had been able to maintain some semblance of authority in the fifteenth century only when China was pressing on the Shans who threatened it. In 1527 they finally sacked the capital, and the remaining rulers up to 1555 were all Shan chiefs. Then it was incorporated in a new super-kingdom created by the rulers of Taung-ngu, who had also incorporated the Mon kingdom of Pegu.

Among the forces with which Tabin-shwei-hti attacked Martaban in 1541 were Mon levies and also a contingent of Portuguese mercenaries, and his victory against Ava was won with the help of Portuguese gunners. Though he was crowned in Pagan, his capital was in Pegu. Indeed the expanding commerce of the sixteenth century focused his attention, and he attacked Ayudhya in 1548, thus beginning a long struggle between the Burmans and the Thais for the old Mon lands and the northern peninsula.

His kingdom collapsed when he was murdered in 1550, but his successor, Bayin-naung, renewed his ambitions. In 1551, with Burman, Mon, and Portuguese forces, he recaptured Pegu, and in 1555 he took Ava. His attack on Chiengmai, or Lan Na, was but a step towards his chief object, the conquest of Ayudhya, and the vast expedition of 1563–64 forced its king ruler to submit. A second expedition in 1568–69 installed a vassal king. A first attempt to take Vientiane, the capital of the neighbouring Lao state of Lan Xang, failed, but in 1574 it was captured, and the king sent into exile. Facing revolt in the north, his successor, Nan-da-bayin, also tried to deal with Ayudhya's attempts to regain its independence. In 1587 he besieged Ayudhya, but the invasion ended in a disaster that might have been even worse but for a Cambodian invasion of the Siamese state. By 1593, however, Nan-da-bayin had failed in five full-scale invasions, and the Thai king, Naresuen, turned the tables. Dealing first with Cambodia, he turned on southern Burma, acquiring Tavoy and Tenasserim and then, with the help of Mon rebels, Moulmein. In 1595 he threatened Pegu, and Nan-da-bayin's kingdom collapsed.

The dynasty was restored by the Nyaungyan prince, who now once more based the kingdom in the dry zone of central Burma. He first dealt with the Shans. His son and successor, Anauk-hpet-lun, turned south, taking Prome in 1608 and Syriam in 1613, invading Tenasserim, but stopping short of Mergui. He re-established control over Chiengmai, but accepted the independence of Ayudhya, and the new king, Thalun, pursued a peaceful policy. In 1658, however, Yung-li, the last of the Ming emperors, fled by the old Burma road from Yunnan to Bhamo, and upper Burma was ravaged by Ming supporters. The challenge the Burmans thus faced in the north precipitated a Mon revolt in the south, a flight of Mons into Siam, an ineffectual invasion of Siam, and Ayudhya's capture of Chiengmai. But a revolt in Chiengmai, and the establishment of Manchu control over Yunnan, helped Burma to recover, though it had to surrender Yung-li.

The Restored Taung-ngu dynasty lost control over the outer zones of its domains in the early eighteenth century. 'Day by day and month by month, the great tributary states that made up the empire—the crowned saw-bwas and [Tai] myo-zas— broke away and deserted the king. Each withdrew and fortified himself within his own principality.'[49] That opened up a threat from the Manipuris to the north, galvanised by Hinduisation, and their incursions encouraged the Mons to revolt in 1740. Aided by their use of European ordnance, they captured Ava in 1752, though neither neighbouring Arakan nor Ayudhya afforded them support.

The disaster revitalised the dry zone, and the Burmans reasserted themselves under a great warrior, Alaung-hpaya, founder of what turned out to be the last Burman dynasty, named after Kon-baung, the traditional name for the country round his village. In 1754 he took possession of Ava. In 1755 he entered Dagon, opposite Syriam, renaming it Yan-gon (Rangoon) (The Enemy is Consumed). Syriam was taken in 1756, and Pegu sacked in 1757. He went on to attack Ayudhya, and his successor, Hsin-hypu-shin, sacked it in 1767. You can visit the extensive ruins that remain.

Raiding into Manipur, the Konbaung dynasty was also to establish control over Arakan. That the Taung-ngu dynasty had attempted. Tabin-shwei-hti had led a vain expedition against Mrohaung, and Bayin-naung had been about to attack it when he died in 1581. The Arakanese took advantage of Nan-da-bayin's difficulties and seized Syriam in 1599, placing it under the control of one of their Portuguese mercenaries, Philip de Brito. His power was to be destroyed by the Restored Taung-ngu dynasty, and he was impaled by Anauk-hpet-lun. The ambitions of the 'feringhi' had been a source of concern to the king of Arakan himself. But the real threat to both parties came from the rise of Moghul power in India. Moghul control of Bengal was followed by the annexation of Chittagong in 1666, and a weakened Arakan was exposed to the Burman revival of the eighteenth century.

In these events Portuguese mercenaries played some part and European weapons were used. There was, however, no opportunity for European empire-building. Even the commercial opportunites were limited. Welcomed as a balance against the feringhi, and later against the Moghuls, the VOC was able to establish a factory in Arakan for a number of years. In Thalun's reign it established a factory at Syriam, the first in Burma, and, when order was re-established in the north, it sought to establish one at Bhamo. But the Ava government forbade the project, and the VOC closed its Burma factories in 1679. That led the English Company to display an interest in Burma.

Its other motive derived from its growing contest with the French in India, and, more immediately, from their involvement in Ayudhya in the late seventeenth century. Both powers saw the significance of southern Burma, not only in respect of the supply of teak and thus of naval construction and repair, but also, and increasingly, in respect of its strategic position in regard to the Bay of Bengal. They were thus tempted to take advantage of the Mon revolt. Rumours of Dupleix's plans to aid the Mons prompted the English Company to seize Negrais in 1753. That, however, led to conflict with the victorious Alaung-hpaya, and the withdrawal upon which the Company had decided was not completed without a massacre in 1759.

Ayudhya

The kingdom of Ayudhya, like other coastal kingdoms, had generally been strengthened by the commercial expansion of the fifteenth and sixteenth centuries, as well as, more specifically, by the use of European weapons and the employment of Portuguese mercenaries. Its position as an international trading centre had made it a target for the Burmans, but helped it to recover from their invasions, and so did the statecraft of king Naresuen and his successors. Foreign traders were welcome, European, Chinese, Japanese—'the confluence of Japanese increased considerably', Jeremias van Vliet reported, as did 'their natural pride and impudence'[50]—and they were used by the monarchs to conduct their trade. The VOC—itself interested in Ayudhya's intra-Asian trade—was especially important, first as a counter to the Portuguese, and later, under Prasat Tong, for its political support, for example in dealing with the recalcitrant Malay vassal state of Pattani.

His successor, Narai, opened relations with the French, with whom he had made contact through missionaries of the Société des Missions Etrangères, and the connexion was encouraged by a Greek adventurer, Phaulkon, who hoped that king and people might be converted to Christianity. The arrival of an imposing French mission in 1687, with six warships, 500 troops, and Jesuit missionaries, was followed by Phaulkon's overthrow in 'the revolution of 1688'. The Portuguese were apprehensive of wider consequences,

> for when it is rumoured throughout these realms that the Europeans (for very few can distinguish between the French and Portuguese), under the cloak of propagating the faith, would have raised a revolt in the Kingdom of Siam, they will drive out all the missionaries and Europeans, and close all the ports to them, as was done in Japan, fearing that we will do as the French did in Siam.[51]

The French troops had to leave, and Narai's successor made a new treaty with the Dutch. The conspirators, Wyatt suggests, 'may have felt more comfortable in a world in which commerce and international relations were conducted on a simpler, smaller scale',[52] and in a more traditional way. Ayudhya no longer employed European administrators and courtiers, though 'Moors' and Chinese still made it cosmopolitan.

Laos and Cambodia

After the Burman interventions of the 1570s and 1580s, Lan Xang had fallen apart, and it was only restored by the great king Surinyavongsa (r. 1637–94). The first European to visit Vientiane, van Wuysthoff was sent up from the Dutch factory in Cambodia in 1641 to attempt to open up trade with the 'land of gumlac and benzoin',[53] but nothing came of his mission, partly owing to the impassability of the Mekong. The death of the king was followed by a succession dispute. Just as those in Mataram opened the way to Dutch intervention, that dispute led to the intervention of the neighbouring Vietnamese. The subsequent break-up of the kingdom into three states—Luang Prabang, Vientiane, and Champassak—indeed led to the intervention of the Thais as well, and later to that of the Burmans under Alaung-hpaya. The Lao kingdoms 'were easy prey to hostile or ambitious neighbors, and the longer their disunity prevailed, the more difficult their reunification became'.[54]

Also uncomfortably placed among the three major mainland kingdoms, Cambodia, too, was a prey both to its own weakness and to the aggression of its neighbours. Its king had sought to take advantage of Ayudhya's weakness in the 1580s, and then sought assistance against the avenging Thais, even appealing to the Spanish governor of the Philippines, and securing dubious help from the Spanish adventurers. Though the capital, Lovek, fell in 1594, the early seventeenth century proved to be a period of prosperity for Cambodia. For the first time since Funan, it became, as David Chandler puts it, 'a maritime kingdom',[55] and in the 1640s the king married a Malay and converted to Islam. He was overthrown in the 1650s by rival princes. They were assisted by the Vietnamese, who subsequently choked off the international trade of Cambodia. Increasingly, too, the Mekong delta was made part of the Vietnamese state, though it was still known to many Khmers even in the twentieth century as Kampuchea Krom (lower Cambodia).

Dai Viet

The Southeast Asian kingdoms found it difficult to retain central control and to avoid the debilitating localisation of power. That was true of Dai Viet as it was of Mataram and of Pagan and its successors. The early sixteenth century was a period of bloody chaos. Out of this the emperor Mac Dang Dung emerged in 1527. Though a descendant of the Le sought the intervention of the Chinese, he bought them off in 1540. But the Le, with their generals Nguyen Kim and then his son-in-law Trinh Kiem, recovered the provinces of Thanh-hoa and Nghe-an in the early 1540s, and the following decades saw struggles that culminated in the defeat of the Mac in the early 1590s by Kiem's younger son, Trinh Tung. The restored Le emperors were, however, now powerless; and under their nominal sovereignty the Trinh dominated the north, and the Nguyen built their power on newly acquired lands to the south. Supported by the Chinese, the Mac remained for three generations in the province of Cao-bang. That perhaps encouraged the Trinh to retain the Le: a usurpation might have provoked a further intervention. But a unity that depended on division was but a semblance.

From the 1620s, indeed, civil war developed between the Trinh and the Nguyen, and it lasted till the 1670s. In that period both parties welcomed European merchants, particularly as a source of arms and munitions: Portuguese brass cannon, made in Macao, were the best, and the Portuguese also built a gun-casting foundry for the Nguyen at Hué, apparently in 1614. Both parties also offered a much more tempered welcome to European missionaries. Not surprisingly the Nguyen, outside the traditional heartland of Vietnam, were probably the more alive to the need to tap external resources.

Stalemate between the two regimes followed civil war, and a kind of boundary was established along the Song Gianh, once the division between the Viet and Cham lands. Though possessed of the heartland, the Trinh had been restrained by continued opposition from the Mac and apprehensions of Chinese intervention. After the truce, the Trinh were able to end the power of the Mac in 1677, and to secure peace with the Manchu dynasty, having perhaps persuaded it that the Mac were remnants of the Ming order.[56] The latent threat of Manchu intervention, however, restrained the Trinh, who had fought the Nguyen during the weakness of the Ming. The Nguyen had survived partly because they tapped the resources of the south, not only through their traffic with foreigners, but through colonisation. 'By following the Cham example', as Li Tana puts it, 'seventeenth-century Cochinchina found the resources and vitality to undergo a great period of expansion in population, wealth and land, despite having to fight a war with the north which lasted fifty years'.[57] The Nguyen continued along these lines.

The division of Vietnam did not make it less of a threat to its neighbours: rather the reverse. The Trinh moved against a divided Laos, and the Nguyen against a weakened Cambodia. Champa's independence was terminated in the 1690s, and the Vietnamese moved on to colonise the Mekong delta, in part with Vietnamese captives and refugees, and also with Chinese settlers.

Despite its economic expansion, the Nguyen regime was politically fragile. Nor did it secure from the Manchus the recognition of a separate political status for Cochin-China. The eighth lord, however, assumed the title *vuong* (prince or king) in 1744. He also welcomed a French East India Company mission under Pierre Poivre in 1748–50. Pursuing its rivalry with the British in India and China, France looked to Cochin-China as well as to Pegu. Poivre failed to secure permission for a factory at Tourane, but a modest one was established after 1753, and the ban on Christian missions modified.

The Nguyen regime, and indeed that of the Trinh, was to be overthrown by the Tay-son rebellion that began in the 1770s. But, as the Canadian scholar Alexander Woodside suggests, the political failure of the southern regime did not mean that it was unimportant. The Nguyen 'were the Vietnamese gatekeepers of a relatively thinly populated Southeast Asian seaboard society at a time when Southeast Asia had to face great demographic and commercial expansion',[58] and they ensured its future was Vietnamese. Though their realm was in many ways distinctive, they did not achieve the creation of a separate Cochin-China polity, 'which would have begun to give eastern Indochina the Latin American quality of a common civilization with multiple states'.[59]

Conclusion

Commercial expansion had attracted Europeans to the mainland as well as to the archipelago in the sixteenth and seventeenth centuries. In the former, however, they played a far smaller role than in the latter, both commercially and politically, and it was in its impact on the traditional dynamics of the region that commercial expansion had its main political significance. It added, for example, to the tension between the Burmans and the Mons, it contributed to the resilience of Ayudhya, and it sustained and shaped the Nguyen regime. Weapons and mercenary personnel were involved in these struggles, but the influence of European adventurers was never lasting. Nor were missionary endeavours successful, except in the creation of small but enduring Christian communities in Vietnam. The outset of the next phase saw renewed conflict between Burma and Siam, the overthrow of Ayudhya, the Tay-son revolt in Vietnam. Out of all this, however, the chief mainland states emerged with yet greater cohesion, for a time, at least, able to deal both with the renewed expansion of Chinese economic enterprise and with the growth of British trade and power.

Archipelagic Southeast Asia presents a different picture. There the Europeans had had a greater impact, both because their commercial objectives were more urgent and more specific and because their opponents were weaker and more exposed to seapower. Their incursions, however, tended to diffuse political power and entrench Islam. No traditional 'empire' could emerge, and super-kingdoms found it difficult to survive. Yet Aceh and Sulu, like the mainland states, were, for a time at least, able to respond to the changes of the closing years of the eighteenth century. The mainland states, Lieberman has suggested,[60] should, however, be compared not so much with them as with the emerging colonial polities. The Dutch, though slow to build an empire of their own, had consolidated their hold on Java. The Spaniards, though challenged by the Moros, undertook a reform programme after the British attack, seeking, too, to orient the trade of the Philippines away from the trans-Pacific galleons and opening Manila to foreign trade in Asiatic goods. The British were to follow a different line again. In 1819 they founded a new entrepot, more attractive than Penang to traders of the archipelago, made free of customs by subsidies from India, and becoming a focus for Chinese activity. 'Singapore's commercial system rested mainly on an interrelation of European capital and Chinese enterprise.'[61]

Notes

1 *Early Indonesian Commerce*, p. 64.
2 Wolters, *Fall*, p. 37.
3 *Commentaries*, London: Hakluyt Society, 1875–84, III, pp. 116–18.
4 q. J. H. Elliott, *The Old World and the New*, CUP, 1970, p. 10.
5 C. R. Boxer, *Four Centuries of Portuguese Expansion*, Johannesburg: Witwatersrand UP, 1965, p. 1.
6 C. P. Fitzgerald, *The Chinese View of their Place in the World*, London: OUP, 1964, p. 50.
7 Tome Pires, *Suma Oriental*, trans. A. Cortesao, London: Hakluyt Society, 1944, XC, second series, p. 287.
8 J. C. van Leur, *Indonesian Trade and Society*, The Hague and Bandung: van Hoeve, 1955, p. 164.
9 *CHSEA*, I, p. 395.
10 A. F. Rubin, *The International Personality of the Malay Peninsula*, KL: Penerbit Universiti Malaya, 1974, p. 44.
11 Van Leur, pp. 181–2.

12 *Bali: Colonial Conceptions and Political Change, 1700–1940*, Rotterdam: Erasmus U, 1986, p. 13.
13 q. B. H. M. Vlekke, *Nusantara*, The Hague: van Hoeve, 1965, p. 141.
14 q. B. Andaya in Kernial Singh Sandhu and Paul Wheatley, eds, *Melaka*, KL: OUP, 1983, I, p. 194.
15 q. B. W Andaya, *To Live as Brothers*, U Hawaii P, 1993, p. 55.
16 q. ibid., p. 68.
17 q. B. W. Andaya, *Perak, the Abode of Grace*, KL: OUP, 1979, p. 45.
18 Hall, p. 527.
19 q. Soemarsaid Moertono, *State and Statecraft in Old Java*, SEAP, Cornell U, 1963, p. 44.
20 q. M. C. Ricklefs, *War, Culture and Economy in Java, 1677–1726*, St Leonards: Allen and Unwin, 1993, p. 33.
21 q. Yoneo Ishii, ed., *The Junk Trade from Southeast Asia*, Canberra: ANU; Singapore: ISEAS, 1998, p. 204.
22 Ricklefs, p. 42.
23 q. ibid., p. 56.
24 q. ibid., p. 125.
25 L. Y. Andaya, *The Kingdom of Johor, 1641–1728*, KL: OUP, 1975, p. 197.
26 Dianne Lewis, *Jan Compagnie in the Straits of Malacca*, Athens: Ohio U, 1995, p. 28.
27 ibid., p. 40.
28 q. C. R. Boxer, *Francisco Vieira de Figueiredo*, The Hague: Nijhoff, 1967, p. 26.
29 q. B. Schrieke, *Indonesian Sociological Studies*, The Hague, Bandung: van Hoeve, 1955, I, p. 74.
30 'English Trade in Celebes, 1613–67', JMBRAS, 31, 1 (May 1958), p. 29.
31 *The Heritage of Arung Palakka*, The Hague: Nijhoff, 1981.
32 Schrieke, I, p. 73.
33 K. Glamann, *Dutch–Asiatic Trade, 1620–1740*, Copenhagen: Danish Science P; The Hague: Nijhoff, 1958, p. 93.
34 q. Ricklefs, p. 187.
35 ibid., p. 221.
36 L. Blussé, 'Batavia, 1619–1740 … ', JSEAS, 12, 1 (March 1981), p. 172.
37 B. W. Andaya, *Perak*, p. 57.
38 q. R. Vos, *Gentle Janus, Merchant Prince*, Leiden: KITLV P, 1993, p. 121.
39 D. K. Bassett, 'British "Country" Trade and Local Trade Networks … ', MAS, 23, 4 (October 1989), p. 643.
40 B. E. Kennedy, 'Anglo-French Rivalry in Southeast Asia, 1763–93 … ', JSEAS, 4, 2 (September 1973), p. 206.
41 Vos, p. 57.
42 B. W. Andaya, *Perak*, p. 93.
43 ibid., p. 148.
44 K. R. Hall, 'The Opening of the Malay World to European Trade in the Sixteenth Century', JMBRAS, 58, 2 (1985), p. 93.
45 q. G. Saunders, *A History of Brunei*, KL: OUP, 1994, p. 54.
46 q. W. L. Schurz, *The Manila Galleon*, NY: Dutton, 1939, p. 35.
47 *Asia and the Philippines*, Manila: Solidaridad, 1967, pp. 82–3.
48 *The Sulu Zone*, Singapore UP, 1981, p. 171n.
49 Konbaungset chronicle, q. V. Lieberman, *Burmese Administrative Cycles*, Princeton UP, 1984, p. 207.
50 'Description of the Kingdom of Siam', JSS, 7, 1 (1910), p. 47.
51 *Records of the Relations between Siam and Foreign Countries*, Bangkok: Vajiranana Library, 1921, V, p. 59.
52 David K. Wyatt, *Thailand: A Short History*, Yale UP, 1984, pp. 117–18.
53 q. Hall, p. 415.
54 Wyatt, p. 123.
55 *A History of Cambodia*, St Leonards: Allen and Unwin, 1993, p. 88.
56 K. W. Taylor, 'The Literati Revival in Seventeenth-Century Vietnam', JSEAS, 18, 1 (March 1987), p. 3.
57 'An Alternative Vietnam' … ', JSEAS, 29, 1 (March 1998), p. 118.

58 A. Woodside, 'Central Vietnam's Trading World ... ', in K. W. Taylor and John K. Whitmore, eds, *Essays into Vietnamese Pasts*, Cornell SEAP, 1995, p. 170.

59 p. 170.

60 'An Age of Commerce ... ', JAS, 54, 3 (August 1995), pp. 804–5.

61 M. Turnbull, *A History of Singapore*, KL: OUP, p. 40.

1.4

Colonies and Dependencies

Between the late eighteenth century and the early twentieth almost all Southeast Asia was divided into colonies or protectorates held by the Western powers, and new boundaries were drawn with the object of avoiding conflict among them. Stage by stage the Dutch rounded out the realm they called Netherlands India. The British established themselves in northern Borneo, but the Philippines was held by Spain until it was challenged by the revolutionaries in the 1890s, and then taken over by the United States. The British also established themselves on the Malay peninsula, but avoided too great a challenge to the Thais. Their kingdom indeed survived, partly as a buffer between the empire the French created in what they called Indo-China, and the province of India into which the British made Burma.

Trade had long linked Southeast Asia with other parts of the world. Along with commercial links, other connexions had been established: cultural and religious, sometimes political. The early European empires had not inaugurated the commercial expansion that had involved Southeast Asia in the fifteenth century, but, after the initial disruption their violence caused, they added to it, in particular by throwing into world trade the precious metals of the Americas, by establishing in the various continents products that had once been peculiar to but one of them, and by opening up new routes, in particular a trans-Pacific connexion that was entirely novel. The political connexion they established with their European homelands was also novel, however tenuous and indirect it might be.

In the nineteenth century the nature of world trade, and of the commercial relations of Southeast Asia with other parts of the world, was again to be transformed. The origins of the change were on this occasion more clearly in the West. Indeed the initiative lay with one state, Britain, which became the first industrial society. But it is easy to antedate the economic transformation that industrialisation effected: it was not always a rapid process, and it was often, like the earlier changes, a complex one. It is also easy to over-simplify its relationship to the political changes which Southeast Asia underwent in this period. The establishment of colonial states was not simply the result of the advance of capitalism or the demands of industrialisation. The process was a long one, and began before industrialisation transformed the economic connexions between Southeast Asia and the West. When it did, the relationship developed more clearly and more fully at the micro-level than at the macro-level. In the case, for example, of the Dutch, J. Th. Lindblad suggests that there was 'an incessant interplay between the interests of private capital and political or administrative measures at the local level'.[1]

Britain's position as the first industrial society was to give it an enormous advantage *vis-à-vis* other states, even if it was likely not to be a permanent one, since they would catch up as industrialisation spread. But its temporary primacy was enhanced by other advantages that it had secured even before industrialising, or when only in the early stages of that process. One set of advantages related to Europe, one to India.

In respect of Europe, it had by 1815 attained an unprecedented degree of security. It had, of course, certain inbuilt advantages, such as its island position, but they had never been entirely sufficient. Command of the sea was again facilitated by its island position, and its relationship to the Channel, but it was not automatic, and it had to be struggled for. To complement and reinforce these advantages it was important that the Continent of Europe should not be dominated by any one major power that by cumulating the armies and navies of the Continent would be able to eliminate Britain's natural and acquired advantages. The defeat of the France of the Revolution and Napoleon vastly enhanced Britain's security by 1815. To maintain the 'balance of power' on the Continent and to prevent one-power dominance became a prime aim.

In Asia Britain had gained a unique position even before industrialisation gave it one. It had acquired an empire in India without precedent among European powers. That, too, had in a sense been precipitated by the struggle with France. The rivalry among European states had helped to prompt the projection of European power beyond Europe in the sixteenth and seventeenth centuries, and the same was true in the eighteenth. It was the attempt of the French to counter British commercial success that prompted their struggle in India, but the outcome was the subordination of many of the Indian states to British control or their elimination. That extraordinary venture enhanced the resources available to the British, human as well as physical, but it also preoccupied them. Their unique empire gave them unique problems. The command of the sea offered security in Europe, and indeed, while only European powers could build modern navies, it offered security for their possessions overseas. But for India it was not enough. The empire there was a continental empire, not a maritime one, and its security requirements were different.

Indeed Britain came in some sense to have two foreign policies. One was predicated on its political security in Europe and for most of its overseas possessions. There it could pursue safely, and indeed with advantage, the kind of foreign policy that its increasing economic strength indicated was appropriate. Its aims should of course include a prime concern with the security of Britain and its possessions. But beyond that it should attempt, not to add to those possessions, but to guarantee commercial access to other parts of the world by keeping the major routes free of threats, and by seeking overseas conditions of political stability under which its trade and investment might prosper. Such a policy was compatible with the concept of the 'balance of power'. Indeed that might be more easily upheld if minor European states were supported by their possession of colonial empires, likely in such hands to be no threat in themselves. Major European states, indeed, could well have similar outlets that might make them more satisfied with the European status quo, recognising but attenuating the sense of rivalry that had so long driven the European system and its connexion with the rest of the world. The perception of the world that was supported by the advance of the first industrialised society was not indeed entirely compatible with that. It envisaged a world of stable states trading freely with each other. But it was recognised that this could not be achieved in the short term.

The foreign policy suggested by the security needs of India was different. A continental state is concerned to limit the threat on its frontiers, and it is likely to seek a measure of subservience among its neighbours, as a guarantee against any threat. In this British India was no exception. Indeed it was, perhaps, particularly sensitive to challenges on the frontier, because they might stimulate, or be combined with, challenges within the boundaries. Given that British India was sustained with a minimum level of armed force, much of it Indian in origin, the risk was ever present. It conduced to a foreign policy that did not always coincide with the policies that Britain's own priorities suggested, those of a power that put trade with other nations first, rather than subordination. In Southeast Asia the 'Indian' approach particularly affected neighbouring Burma.

The British recognised the exceptional nature of their Indian empire. At home, as the empire, governed till the mutiny of 1857 through the East India Company, expanded, the government took steps to assert its control, in particular through the establishment of the Board of Control under the India Act of 1784. Less obvious, but even more significant, was the desire to avoid the extension of an empire of this kind, especially outside the sub-continent. That affected Britain's policy towards the rest of mainland Southeast Asia and towards China.

There was another implication. Earlier European empires in Asia, the Portuguese and the Spaniards more than the Dutch, had challenged Islam, though in so doing tending to provoke its expansion. The acquisition of an empire in India was to make Britain, the leading power in predominantly Christian Europe, the leading Muslim state in the world in the sense that it ruled over more Muslims than any other state. That helped to shape its policy towards other states and in its own dependencies. Even more clearly than the Dutch, perhaps, it saw the danger in provocation.

The widespread creation of colonies in what some have termed an age of imperialism has been the subject of much controversy among historians and others. The study of the Southeast Asian case, perhaps too often neglected, suggests that an explanation may be found in a shift in the relative power of states as between European and non-European, brought about in part by industrialisation, but also by the increased efficiency and military effectiveness forced on European states by intra-European conflict. The previous period had left many Asian states in no position to develop a positive response, and the impact of economic change in the new period often undermined the capacity of others. Companies and concessionaires added to traditional factionalism. Up-to-date and objective advice on dealing with a changing world was hard to find, let alone use.

The establishment of colonies and protectorates was, however, a prolonged process. Before about 1870 it was slowed by Britain's primacy: its own interests did not require their creation, and it looked to Asian countries to transform themselves. It is the subsequent decades that may more truly be described as 'imperialist'. From about 1870 Britain ceased to be the only industrial society, and the vast potential of Germany and the United States began to be turned to account. The rivalry among the European powers was sharpened, and indeed it extended to powers outside Europe. The challenge to Britain's primacy also challenged the arrangements that it had earlier favoured, and they were challenged, too, by the inability of existing states to cope with increasingly rapid economic and social change. The result was the establishment of colonial authority throughout almost all of Southeast Asia by a series of moves in which Britain's role was often reactive or defensive.

Industrialisation was the major factor in the redistribution of power that took place. But again it shaped, without entirely determining, the policies that the Western powers pursued. A need for 'markets', for example, might be part of the rhetoric of 'imperialists', but trade and investment also crossed the frontiers, even of alleged rivals. States that were industrialising only relatively slowly, if at all, did not refrain from creating, or attempting to create, colonial empires. What was at issue was the possession and application of power at a time of change in its relative distribution, and a variety of motives were involved and arguments employed. To a remarkable degree Britain's policy retained the character it had taken on in earlier decades: it did not, unlike all the other major powers, turn to protectionism; and it did not abandon the devolutionary approach it had adopted towards the colonies of settlement.

All the Western powers, though to differing degrees, were affected in this phase by changes within as well as changes among them. States became more democratic and their peoples more literate, and the concept of public opinion took on a wider meaning. That affected Western approaches to the colonial world. Whatever the motives for acquisition or retention, they had to be presented in a different way: 'for the general public in the Netherlands, Ethical perspectives were the easiest to understand', Locher-Scholten writes. 'Gradually involved in the political process through the extension of the vote between 1870 and 1918, the voting public was not acquainted with the intricacies of colonial policies and reacted emotionally on moral grounds.'[2] Colonial discourse now emphasised the 'white man's burden' rather than his profit. The involvement of the public did not, however, necessarily make it easier to abandon territories that might now be seen as 'national' possessions rather than Company factories or royal appurtenances.

Southeast Asia was also affected by changes in the concept of the state that had been taking place in Europe. Rivalries within Europe had been a factor in the creation of inter-state borders. Enlightenment map-making made it possible to represent territorial divisions yet more clearly, while the French Revolution identified state and citizen yet more closely. The colonial venture transferred such concepts to Southeast Asia, particularly after 1870, when both economic expansion and political rivalry intensified. Colonial governments seldom saw their subjects as citizens, though they often took up the cause of residents or protégés, European or not. They certainly affirmed a concept of territorial border in a region hitherto dominated by often overlapping and temporary tributary relationships. Those they displaced, both by using and by rejecting them.

Because of its power Britain's policy was for the greater part of the century bound to be decisive, and the policy of other states would tend to be shaped in reaction to it. It did not use its power with any determination to unify the Southeast Asian region, nor indeed in any uniform way. The changes brought by the West, though they had common features, thus had a variety of inflections.

In the nineteenth century, during which the colonial regimes were set up, Britain's interests in Southeast Asia were indeed limited, even extraneous: it was only in the early twentieth century, when its primacy had been challenged, that Malaya came to be of major economic importance, and Singapore of major strategic importance. In the late eighteenth century, by contrast, Britain's policy in Southeast Asia had been largely determined by its interests elsewhere, in Europe, in India, in China. It wanted to ensure the security of its growing dominion in India, by keeping European powers at a distance and ensuring that neighbouring states offered no challenge. It wanted to guarantee the security of the route to China, in particular through the Straits of Melaka. And it wanted a balance of power in Europe, where France was still a threat.

The export of tea through Canton, the only open port in China, had become the Company's major commercial enterprise, and it retained a monopoly of the British trade in tea till 1834. Its ships needed safe passage, and the same was true of the 'free' trade after 1834, when the British sought to take wider advantage of the trading opportunities China seemed to offer. The industrial revolution encouraged the notion that there was a vast market for British manufactures that only needed to be 'opened up'. The British secured Hong Kong in 1842, and forced the Manchu dynasty, in a series of 'unequal' treaties, to open other ports and to accept extraterritorial jurisdiction, though the trade never realised all their hopes.

Meanwhile, however, the China market was more receptive to the import of opium, a source of revenue for the Company in India, and to the import of marine and jungle produce and tin from their traditional sources in Southeast Asia. Supplying the means to pay for tea, then a product of China rather than of India or Sri Lanka, the trade of the archipelago gave the British a limited interest in its commerce. But their other main concern in Southeast Asia was with the European powers. The long-established Dutch and Spanish empires were not displaced: they were not a threat in themselves and were in some sense an insulation against a threat from others, while alienating them might reduce Britain's security in Europe. Even France, a major power and a historic rival, was in due course to be accepted as effectively the ruler of Vietnam.

Britain's interests in Southeast Asia were limited, and it used its power in a limited way. It was still necessary for other states, European and Southeast Asian, to take account of those interests: their survival might depend on their success in so doing. For some of the Southeast Asian states the task was more difficult than others, not only because of their different history and their different geographical position, but also because of the different attitude of the British. Their position was also complicated by the presence of other European powers. That might appear to offer the opportunity of playing off one against another. More often, however, the Europeans, rather than engage in open conflict, tended to come to terms among themselves at the expense, explicitly or implicitly, of Southeast Asian states, and the borders established between their respective territories tended to reflect the need to avoid conflict among the Europeans rather than the realities of Southeast Asian history or geopolitics. Avoiding conflict with the British required the other Europeans even so to pay a price. In particular they had to offer the British commercial opportunity as the price of political survival. This, too, the Thais recognised, though the Vietnamese did not. The position of Burma, by contrast, was determined more by its relationship with India than with Britain itself, and the policy Britain pursued was impelled more by its 'continental' than its 'commercial' priorities.

The Dutch empire

The Dutch empire in the Indonesian-Malaysian area in the latter part of the eighteenth century still retained many of the characteristics it had acquired in the preceding phase. It was linked with Dutch factories elsewhere in Asia, administered by the VOC, and even in Java its territorial control was limited. But during the nineteenth century the Dutch were able to establish their power throughout the archipelago, largely because the British did not challenge them, nor allow others to do so. The agreement between the two powers both helped to exclude other European states, and reduced the chances that Indonesian states could sustain their independence. Indeed it permitted the Dutch in some areas to defer the establishment of their actual control, allowing the Indonesian rulers meantime to enjoy a practical independence that could not, however, endure.

In the late eighteenth century the Dutch position still rested largely upon treaties and contracts with Indonesian and Malayan rulers, more concerned with questions of commerce than government, with deliveries of produce than surrenders of sovereignty. The exclusion of European rivals remained critical both for the VOC and for the Indonesian-Malayan states. Despite their commercial interests in the area, the British were cautious over presenting a direct challenge. Their long-standing possession of Benkulen in west Sumatra was on the periphery of Dutch power, and so was the newly acquired Penang. Article 6 of the Anglo-Dutch treaty of 1784 was not a contradiction of the Dutch right to exclude their trade from states with which they had established contractual relationships.

The first of a number of attempts at a formal Anglo-Dutch deal followed the Anglo-Prussian intervention in the Dutch Republic of 1787. The British proposed to guarantee the Dutch monopoly of fine spices and not to trade or settle east of Sumatra. In return the Dutch would transfer the naval base at Trincomalee in Sri Lanka, a protection for the Bay of Bengal, and also the island of Riau, where the country traders had been active. Even a friendly Dutch government could not accept that. In the European wars that followed, French influence was established in the Netherlands, and the British took over many of the Dutch possessions overseas, including Melaka and Maluku in 1795–96, the Cape and Sri Lanka, and in 1811 Java itself, with the Dutch Asian capital, Batavia.

The defeat of the French, and the establishment of an independent Dutch kingdom, including the Belgian provinces of the Habsburgs, was the signal for another attempt at a deal in Southeast Asia. In fact, while the British retained the Cape and Sri Lanka, the convention of 1814 provided for the return of all the Dutch possessions in the archipelago and on the peninsula. The British did not even try to secure Riau as they had pre-war.

On their return, however, the Dutch began to renew their treaties and contracts with the Indonesian-Malayan states, and this aroused protests, not only from the merchants at Penang, and also those established in Java during the British interregnum, but also from Stamford Raffles, who had governed Java, and was from 1818 back in the archipelago at Benkulen. He argued that the Dutch would not only interfere with British trade: they would also undermine the security of the route to China. His own view was that the British themselves should create an empire in the archipelago, though the connexion with the Malay peoples would be on 'a very different footing from that with the people of India. … it is by the reciprocal advantage of commerce, and commerce alone, that we may best promote our own interests and their advancement'.[3] Even that had no support in London. But his strategic argument persuaded the governor-general in India to give him instructions that he used to acquire Singapore from some of the dispersed princes of Johore, while the India Board and the Foreign Office in London decided on a new attempt at a deal with the Dutch.

The result was the treaty of 17 March 1824. The fundamental British objective was set out by the Foreign Secretary, Lord Castlereagh. The Dutch, he believed, should hold Java and other old possessions in full sovereignty, but preferably dropping their claim to 'exclusive trade'. The other islands should certainly be opened to commercial competition, but 'without the establishment of any preponderating military or political authority in those seas to counterbalance that which the Dutch now and long have exercised'. He felt that 'a good understanding is to both states more important to their general interests than any question of local policy'.[4] The limited British interests in the area were to be pursued without establishing a rival colony in the archipelago.

The treaty, finally signed after prolonged negotiations, endeavoured to effect this in two ways. First, while the spice monopoly in Maluku would continue, the Dutch undertook to limit the protection they gave their trade in ports in their possession, and to abandon it and any attempt at exclusion in ports over the trade of which they had made or would make treaties with local rulers. Second, there was a delimitation. The British transferred Benkulen, and the Dutch transferred Melaka, along with their factories in India, and also withdrew their opposition to the settlement on Singapore. They agreed not to make treaties with states on the peninsula, and the British made the same undertaking with respect to Sumatra.

In these ways the British sought to provide for the security of the route to China and for commercial opportunity in the archipelago: they would possess Penang, Melaka, and Singapore, the 'Straits Settlements'; and the Dutch would be precluded from intervening on that side of the Straits. The Dutch sacrificed remnants of their Asia-wide empire and their position on the peninsula, which they had increasingly seen as an outlying defence for a Java-focused empire; and they accepted limits on their ability to protect their trade even in areas where they were sovereign. They did, however, avoid the challenge Raffles had advocated, and there was to be no rival British empire in the Indies. The deal with the British indeed brought another advantage, no less real for being unspoken. No other power was likely to challenge the Dutch either.

The British and the Dutch had certainly had other European powers in mind. 'The situation in which we and the Dutch stand to each other is part only of our difficulties', George Canning had written; 'that in which we both stand to the rest of the world as exclusive Lords of the East, is one more reason for terminating our relative difficulties as soon as we can'.[5] Neither wanted another power in the area. The British were careful to avoid a close enquiry into the 'title deeds' of the Dutch, lest others followed suit, while the Dutch realised that the high price that they were even so paying the British was also an investment in deterring others. The two parties phrased the treaty to avoid too open a challenge to Western powers, but in effect they were claiming to be 'exclusive Lords of the East'. Their claim was to be in large measure respected. The Dutch, a minor power, owed much of their security *vis-à-vis* major powers to the unwritten support of the British.

The deal of 1824, of course, also affected the Indonesian and Malay states, the rulers of which were not consulted. The division between the peninsula and archipelago that the treaty involved, though not in so many words, was unprecedented. It did not necessarily mean, as is sometimes assumed, that the British would establish control of the peninsula or even the Dutch of Sumatra. But it did mean that the rulers all the same lost some of their independence. In particular, of course, those on the 'Dutch' side of the 'line' could not hope to involve the major power of the day in determining their fate. Only over Aceh, with the deposed sultan of which Raffles had made a treaty in 1819, had the British expressed a reservation.

For a time, however, many Indonesian rulers would not have realised that their position had deteriorated. Deeply embroiled in the Java war of 1825–30, and then in the Belgian breakaway struggle after the revolution of 1830, the Dutch largely avoided expansion in the outer islands, following a policy of abstention or *onthouding*. They were, however, drawn into West Sumatra by local initiative. Back in Padang after the occupation, the Dutch committed themselves to helping the Menangkabau *penghulu* or chiefs against the Padris, Wahhabi-style religious reformers, though a settlement was made while the Java war was on. On its conclusion the governor-general, van den Bosch, favoured a more active policy in the outer islands, but still a limited one. In Sumatra it would be sufficient to occupy ports, river-mouths, selected interior market towns. But in West Sumatra he agreed that order must be re-established, and from 1837 the war with the Padris was prosecuted with vigour.

The east coast states, to which Menangkabau trade had been flowing, were also brought to acknowledge Dutch sovereignty, Jambi in 1833–34, Inderagiri in 1838, then Panei and Bila, and the sultan of Siak sought Dutch protection. Merchants in the Straits Settlements protested. Rather surprisingly, the British Foreign Office took their part. The 1830s was a time of recession. But the major reason, it seems, was the belief that the Dutch had not fulfilled their treaty pledges in their treatment of British trade in Java. By 1838 the official view had already shifted from that of 1824: 'an extension of Dutch Influence, or Territorial possession, would in all probability be attended with consequences injurious to British interest, and should be looked upon with jealousy by the Government of this country'.[6] The reaction of J. C. Baud, van den Bosch's successor, was twofold. He withdrew from the East Coast *pro tem*, without abandoning Dutch claims. But, concerned lest European adventurers in the areas that the Dutch had hitherto felt that they could safely neglect might now receive official support, he ordered an archival survey of Dutch treaties and contracts—the 'title deeds'—and sent out special commissioners to fill the gaps revealed.

In general, however, they did no more than paper over the cracks: occupation rarely followed. Only in Bali, which had developed a rice trade with Singapore in the 1830s and 1840s, was there a major deployment of force, something the Dutch were generally anxious to avoid. There the Dutch commissioner, Huuskus Koopman, had secured treaties only by promising aid against the Mataram kingdom in Lombok. The help was not forthcoming, and the treaties were not ratified. Three Dutch expeditions were sent to Bali. In 1848 the raja of Buleleng-Karangasem was able to defeat the Netherlands Indies army, and the 1849 expedition was larger than the British expedition that took Hong Kong. Clearly, however, the Anglo-Dutch dispute did not assist the Indonesian rulers in maintaining their independence, those of East Sumatra temporarily apart. Apprehension lest the British abandon the treaty drove the Dutch to strengthen their position and reduce that of the rulers.

The British did not abandon the treaty. Moreover the prosperity of the 1850s removed any domestic pressure on the British government, while after 1848 the Dutch began slowly to liberalise. When the Dutch renewed their policy of extension on the east coast of Sumatra in the late 1850s and 1860s, the Foreign Office did not support the renewed protests of the Straits merchants. Instead it used them to secure a new settlement with the Dutch, the treaty of 1871, under which all the British objections to Dutch rule in Sumatra were withdrawn in return for the promise of a commercial open door. The concern about other powers was another argument for it. As Lord Wodehouse had written in 1860, when Under-Secretary at the Foreign Office:

> It seems to me in many respects very advantageous that the Dutch should possess this Archipelago. If it were not in the hands of the Dutch, it would fall under the sway of some other maritime power, presumably the French, unless we took it ourselves. The French might, if they possessed such an eastern empire, be really dangerous to India and Australia, but the Dutch are and must remain too weak to cause us any alarm.[7]

With the treaty of 1871, the British abandoned the reservation they had made in 1824 in respect of Aceh. That had been a factor in the Dutch failure to extend their system over the sultanate in the subsequent decades. Instead they had resorted to piecemeal extension over the west and east coasts, which had in a number of cases challenged Acehnese claims and antagonised the sultanate. Now they were concerned lest other powers would find an opportunity to intervene, provided by the resentment of the sultanate and the publication of the new treaty. 'An end must come to the equivocal policy of Atjeh towards the Netherlands government. That state remains our weak point so far as Sumatra is concerned. As long as it does not recognise our sovereignty foreign intervention will continue to threaten us like the sword of Damocles.'[8] The Dutch attempted a coup. Its failure led them into a thirty-year war. In it 2000 Netherlands Indies troops were killed, 10 000 died of disease, and 25 000 forced labourers died from disease or exhaustion. The Acehnese lost some 60 000–70 000.[9] Their resistance was stiffened by Islam, and the war ended only with a deal with the territorial chiefs, the *uleebalang*. Even then guerrilla opposition continued: 10 000 more Acehnese were to die.[10]

In any attempt to generalise about Dutch policy, Aceh might, indeed, be seen as the exception to prove the rule. Most colonial powers were sparing in the use of force and anxious to maximise its effect when it was used. That was perhaps especially true of the Dutch, now a small power, anxious to use its resources efficiently. Their answer was to apply their power in the context of a system of treaties and contracts derived from their earlier empire in the archipelago. Aceh had not been part of that system, and the use of force was risky. Caution over provoking Islam was another continuing feature of Dutch policy, again set aside in this case.

The relationship with other Western powers was also part of the equation. The understanding with the British, shaken as it sometimes was, helped to avoid the intervention of others. The changes among the Western powers after about 1870 might, however, revive the political threat, even though the abandoning of differential duties in 1873 firmly opened the commercial door: 'a liberal trade policy in our possessions will constitute an essential contribution to the defence of our territory against a foreign enemy', the States General had been told.[11] The question now was not whether the British would abide by the treaty of 1824. Could their influence help to ensure that others would?

The internationalisation of the colonial endeavour, particularly with the emergence of a unified Germany, put that in question. After the Berlin West Africa conference of 1884–85 it seemed clear that actual occupation would be necessary to ensure that other powers respected a colonial possession: mere paper claims would not be enough. The Dutch were apprehensive lest the principle were applied in the Indies. Sent to Lombok the year after the conference, J. A. Liefrinck urged an end to the policy of 'benevolent indifference'.[12] Its Balinese raja refused to make a supplementary treaty. The Council of the Indies urged forceful action, 'so that it will not appear as if the war in Aceh has broken our power elsewhere in the Netherlands Indies since this could be fatal to us'.[13] The governor-general was anxious to avoid precipitating another conflict, but his successor authorised an expedition. It succeeded only with difficulty, the climax being a fanatical attack upon the Dutch forces, a *puputan*. Hundreds fell before the bullets.

The Dutch then introduced 'protection' into Bali itself, but the impulse to annexation was spurred by the adoption of 'Ethical Policy'. Queen Wilhelmina spoke in 1901 of the Netherlands' 'ethical obligation and moral responsibility' to the Indies.[14] 'We … shall, wherever there is injustice … not be able to remain inactive in the protection of the weak and oppressed', wrote Governor-General Rooseboom. 'To be sure,' the Colonial Minister commented, 'but to take this ethical direction as a guiding principle is to come into conflict everywhere; hence self-restraint is needed'.[15] Bali's turn came in 1906–08. Three dynasties compromised, three collapsed, one, Badung, with another *puputan*. 'People who had initially fled before our fire, returned as it were ashamed of their vacillation and sought death.'[16]

Only indirectly the result of the industrial revolution, the renewed rivalry of the powers pressed the Dutch to affirm and intensify their control over the Indies, prompted, too, by the Ethical Policy. For most of the century their privileged relationship with Britain, and its primacy, had facilitated a policy of abstention and limited intervention. That was now modified. The direct impact of the industrial revolution—its demand for food and raw materials, its transformation of economic relationships—might affect Dutch policy in areas where hitherto their intervention had been limited. There were, however, two processes at work, and they did not necessarily coincide. The incorporation of new areas in the Indies did not simply result from the demands of a capitalistic imperialism. Nor, of course, were those without effect in areas of the Indies long under Dutch control.

Either process would affect the position of the Indonesian rulers. For much of the century they might have enjoyed *de facto* independence, unaware of the deterioration of their international standing. Now that independence was lost, and any attempt to restore it by asserting their *de jure* independence could only make their position worse. Revised treaties, including the 'short contracts' developed from 1898, prepared the way for a modern administration that might open the way for the 'development' that the industrial revolution could bring, and that Ethical Policy mandated. In some cases, the impact was more immediate, intensified, for example, by the discovery of oil.

The Dutch had begun to speak of a 'Netherlands India' that stretched 'from Sabang to Merauke'. Though the Dutch position was often still 'contractual' in form, and many areas were in that context 'self-governing', it was a colonial realm quite different from the earlier commercial empire, and different also from the fragmentary realm to which the Dutch had returned after 1816. What had made this transformation possible? In part it resulted from the lack of challenge from other powers, and from the support of the British. It also resulted from the skill of the Dutch in building on their earlier relationships with Indonesian states and in the selective use of force. But that in turn in part depended on the divisions among the Indonesians, which the Dutch turned to account. Now, somewhat paradoxically, they were creating a new political entity. Their policies, and the impact of the industrial revolution, were also creating the conditions for the rise of a group of Indonesians who aspired to control that entity themselves and saw it as the basis of a nation-state. Not surprisingly, their struggle put a premium on unity.

Brunei and Sarawak

Like Aceh, the sultanate of Brunei had not become part of the Dutch system. At the time of the treaty of 1824, however, the British had probably seen the whole of Borneo as within the Dutch sphere. The change in their attitude partly arose from dissatisfaction with the Dutch treatment of their commerce, which made them think that further Dutch expansion was disadvantageous. That was not, however, sufficient to account for British intervention in Brunei. Nor was an increased interest in the north coast of Borneo, as a result of the expansion of British trade with China that followed the end of the Company's monopoly in 1833; nor even the fact that the area was a possible source of coal for the steam vessels, naval and commercial, increasingly penetrating Asian waters. The intervention would not have taken place without the initiative of an individual adventurer, James Brooke.

A former officer in the Company's Madras army, Brooke sought to create a new career for himself in the Indies. He conceived the ambitious aim of undoing the policy of 1824 and reviving Raffles' concept of a British empire in the archipelago. The Dutch had 'gradually and effectually destroyed all rightful authority'.[17] The

British should intervene where their influence was weak or non-existent, and reform and revive the indigenous monarchies. Brunei came to his attention only when he reached Singapore in his yacht, the *Royalist*, in 1839, but it became a field of activity and also, he hoped, an example. Initially he planned to restore order in Sarawak, then an outlying province of Brunei, assisting the Raja Muda Hassim. He was then attracted by the opportunity to govern the province and secured the title of raja. He still, however, saw this as part of a scheme to restore and modernise Brunei. By setting an example in Sarawak, and by backing Hassim at the capital, he would start a process that he hoped would secure the backing of the British government, and indeed lead it to modify its policy towards other states in the archipelago.

He made some progress. The British government was committed to suppressing piracy—indeed that had been reaffirmed in the treaty of 1824—and Brooke encouraged vessels of the Royal Navy and of the Company's marine to go to Borneo to do so. He also emphasised the importance of Borneo coal, an argument his supporters used in Britain in a campaign to secure government support, and in 1844 he was appointed Agent with the Sultan of Brunei. Intervention there on behalf of Hassim and his faction prompted a coup against them in 1846, and that led to further intervention, and indeed a naval demonstration. Labuan, an island standing off Brunei already offered to the British, was formally made a colony, and in 1847 a treaty was made with the sultan. By this he undertook to cooperate against piracy, granted the British a measure of extra-territorial jurisdiction, and undertook not to make cessions to other powers without the approval of the British government. The British had not acquired a colony on Borneo itself, nor offered Brunei protection, but they had made a breach in the understanding of 1824, though they rejected the protests of the Dutch, who were concerned not only about the Brooke venture itself, but also about the example it might set. At the same time Brunei's position had changed: still independent, it had, however, lost some of its room for manoeuvre.

Though the British government had not done everything Brooke wanted in respect of Brunei, it appointed him Commissioner and Consul-General to the Sultan and Independent Chiefs of Borneo, a position, as the instructions given him in 1848 put it, designed 'to afford to British commerce that support and protection … peculiarly required in the Indian seas in consequence of the prevalence of piracy … and by reason of the encroachments of the Netherlands authorities in the Indian Archipelago'.[18] The British government did not, however, wish to go so far as Raffles or Brooke: its policy was designed to secure better treatment from the Dutch rather than to set up a rival empire. At home, too, a campaign now developed against the raja, particularly after a major conflict with Iban pirates at Beting Marau in 1849. Were they really pirates or were they rather enemies of the Brooke raj? Should Brooke be in a position to call on naval forces? Were his various roles incompatible? When a new British administration appointed a commission of inquiry in 1853, the expansive policy of the 1840s, such as it was, was dropped.

Labuan was, however, retained, and the 1847 treaty continued. Nor did Britain dislodge Brooke from Sarawak: public opinion would not have accepted that.

Frustrated in respect of his earlier policy for Brunei, he increasingly argued that Sarawak was an independent state, and sought to extend its rule by acquiring the cession of further rivers from the sultanate. He coopted local support from the Malayo-Muslim elite and from his erstwhile Iban opponents, but, like the Dutch, he was ultimately dependent on the British government. That was, of course, committed to defending the lives and property of British subjects, but it did not accept that one of them could be an independent ruler. Raja James threatened to look to other European powers for protection, to the Dutch themselves, to Leopold, the future creator of the Belgian Congo, to Napoleon III, who had begun to create the colony of Cochin-China on the opposite shores of the South China Sea. These moves were disputed by Brooke's supporters, and particularly by his would-be heirs. But they helped—with the support of friends in high places—to produce a measure of recognition for the raj: a British consul was appointed in Kuching in 1863.

The second Raja of Sarawak, Charles, less anxious than his uncle about the security of the raj, was also more determined to expand it and Brunei was, moreover, becoming more difficult to hold together. But the British government was concerned about the continued extension of a raj whose relations with Britain were so anomalous, and invoked the treaty of 1847 against Sarawak's take-over of the Baram in 1868. The treaty of 1847, though prescribing a much clearer relationship, was, however, itself becoming more difficult to uphold. In 1865 some American adventurers had secured concessions of rivers to the north and even settled briefly at Kimanis, and in the changing conditions of the 1870s a more serious infringement of the treaty seemed possible. New concessions to Overbeck and Dent led to the founding of the British North Borneo Company, and the British government gave it a charter in 1881. That did not make North Borneo British territory. But, as the Foreign Office saw, it excluded other powers without directly confronting them, and provided for law and order without incurring direct responsibility.

Sultan Abdul Mumin had perhaps hoped that other concessionaires could be played off against Sarawak. If so, his diplomacy had apparently failed. The Company acquired additional rivers, while the British government gave the raja the go-ahead. In 1888 the British government concluded agreements with all three Borneo states, granting them protection while respecting their independence. But that was designed to provide further against the interference of other powers, not to preclude the final break-up of Brunei.

The break-up did not in the event occur. Resentful of the chartering of the Company, Raja Charles pressed ahead, hoping ultimately to take over the remnant of the sultanate himself. In 1890 he occupied the Limbang. But Sultan Hashim refused to accept the cession money he offered. Indeed the raja's coup helped the sultan to consolidate the opposition in Brunei to the further dispersal of its territories, and in that sense his diplomacy paid off. His determination would not, however, have been sufficient on its own. The British also changed their policy.

The Colonial Office in London had seen the creation of the Company alongside the raj as adding anomaly to anomaly, and from the 1870s had begun to think that a more regular assertion of British responsibility was required in Borneo. At first officials thought it might be done by supporting Sarawak. Then in the 1890s the creation on the peninsula of the Federated Malay States seemed to offer another possibility: the creation of a similar structure in northern Borneo. 'I look in future', Charles Lucas wrote in 1896, 'to an administration of North Borneo & Sarawak on much the same principles as the native states of the Malay peninsula, with a resident General at Labuan and residents on the mainland, the whole under the High Commissioner at Singapore'.[19] The appointment of a British resident at the sultan's court, discussed but rejected in the 1880s, now became a possibility: it would be a step towards implementing this plan. A persuasive report from M. S. H. McArthur, an official of the Federated Malay States sent to Brunei in 1904, won over doubters in the Foreign and Colonial Offices. Sultan Hashim accepted a Resident as a way of preserving his dynasty and the last remnants of its empire.

'British Borneo', to a greater extent than Netherlands India, remained, however, a collection of fragments, the future of which in a world of nations was unclear. That is explained in part by the extent of British power in the nineteenth century and by the contingent and prudential decisions the British made about exerting it. In the interwar period, their position was weaker, and cautioned them against taking the political initiative, though they did arrange to appoint a 'British Representative' to the raj in 1941. But the outcome was not simply the result of the decisions of the British government. British adventurers also played a part. So, too, did the Sultans of Brunei, who managed to preserve a small portion of their original empire, but one which, it turned out, brought them enormous wealth, in turn enabling them to create or recreate a Malay monarchy.

Besides protesting against the activities of the Brookes and the Company, the Dutch had sought to affirm their authority elsewhere in Borneo. Once the protectorates were set up, however, they agreed to a border settlement in 1891. That in general followed the line of the watersheds, and so, if unprecedented, was not entirely unrealistic. The establishment of North Borneo also brought about another delimitation which, like that between the peninsula and Sumatra, was unrealistic as well as unprecedented. For Sulu, another old Malay sultanate that Spain claimed as part of the Philippines, had a long-standing connexion with northern Borneo, particularly with the east coast, and the Company had sought a lease from the Sultan of Sulu as well as from the Sultan of Brunei.

Sulu

Britain's policy towards the Philippines in some ways resembled its policy towards the Dutch East Indies, but it was not encoded in treaties. Like the Netherlands, Spain was no longer a threat by the late eighteenth century, but it was important that it should not come under the control or influence of Britain's major rival, France. So long as it did not do so, it could retain possessions like the Philippines. Britain had in any case no wish to take them over. It preferred to see them in the hands of a minor power, such as Spain had now become, particularly if it granted British commerce adequate opportunities.

In the case of the Dutch East Indies, these objectives were set out in policy documents and in treaties. In the case of the Philippines, they have rather to be inferred from actions. It was during the Seven Years War, for example, in the course of which Spain allied to France, that the British captured Manila in 1762, but they restored it in 1764 after the war ended. The demonstration of British power, but also the limitations on its use, were evident, and the Spaniards acted accordingly. If they were to retain the Philippines, they must not antagonise the British. Though no treaty prescribed the way in which they should treat British trade, they increasingly opened their colony to foreign enterprise, and the British were the main participants. In deciding on this policy, the implicit political bargain was a major factor, though it was also true that, until the latter decades of the century, Spain, undergoing no industrial revolution, had little to invest in its colony.

Manila was opened to foreign trade—formally in 1834, in fact well before that—and Sual and Iloilo followed in 1855. At the same time Spain attempted to assert its authority over the islands. Exerting control in the mountains of Luzon was delayed by the French wars, but the tobacco monopoly—and Igorot sabotage of it—prompted punitive raids in the cordillera in the 1830s, and by the 1860s Spain had established politico-military commanderies on the western slopes. The introduction of steamers helped to protect the coasts from the marauders of the south: the last major raid on Sorsogon and Kabikolan was in 1860. The attempts of the Spaniards effectively to incorporate the south itself, and so to round out what they called the Philippines, were more contested and more controverted.

Spain intervened in Mindanao in 1860, exploiting dynastic rivalry, and up-country broke the power of Datu Utu of Buayen. But though Governor-General Claveria attacked Balanguingi in 1848, and his successor Norzagaray established a garrison of Balabac in 1858, Sulu and the southernmost islands were not brought under effective control. The major reason was the vigour of their resistance, a centuries-old Islamic-inspired struggle. But the conflict also had an international dimension. The British were reluctant to accept that Sulu was part of the Philippines, and only dropped their objections in 1885.

The position of Sulu in some ways resembled that of Aceh. The Dutch had not been able to inveigle that sultanate into their system of contractual relationships, and, fearful of foreign intervention, had finally resorted to the application of force outside that context. The result had been a long struggle, inflamed by and inflaming Islam. By contrast to the Dutch, the Spaniards had not generally based their authority in the Philippines on contractual relationships, but rather on resettlement and conversion. Spain had made treaties with Sulu, but neither side had much confidence in the other. Spain resorted to sheer displays of force, particularly when it seemed that other powers might intervene, but it was never able to establish effective occupation.

The Moro areas had attracted the British at the outset of the period as a possible base for expanding their trade in the region without alienating the Dutch. Before the conquest of Manila, Alexander Dalrymple, an emissary of the Madras government of the Company, had secured from the reigning sultan of Sulu the cession of the island of Balambangan, which he occupied early in 1763. In Manila the exiled sultan, baptised Fernando, offered part of the territory first to the Spaniards, and then, when they conquered the capital, to the British. Dalrymple was apprehensive that, on their return, the Spaniards would use these dealings to undermine his acquisition of Balambangan, and the additional cession of northern Borneo that he had subsequently secured. He arranged that Fernando should return to Sulu, renouncing all the treaties he had made in his absence, and confirming the cessions to the British. Sulu, he hoped, would be an independent state, standing between the Spanish and British possessions. A Sulu governor should be appointed to administer northern Borneo, the purpose of the acquisition of which being the exclusion of the Dutch.

Dalrymple argued the case for Balambangan: it would expand British trade in 'Oriental Polynesia'. It became linked, too, with a scheme to open up trade with Vietnam. But, restored to the Philippines, the Spaniards protested at the infringement of the frontiers they claimed for their colony, and the British government resolved not to approve nor to support the venture. It did not, however, countermand it either, and the East India Company sent an expedition to occupy Balambangan. The settlement did not last long. Established in 1773, it was destroyed by a Sulu attack in 1775. The Sulus were no doubt jealous of so near a neighbour. It was also true that the British had occupied Balambangan without continuing the supportive relationship with the sultanate that Dalrymple had envisaged.

Brooke included Marudu in northern Borneo in the prospectus for his voyage. He came to focus on Brunei and Sarawak, but he also interested himself in Sulu. Like Dalrymple, he sought to maintain its independence, and in 1849 he made a treaty with it along the lines of the treaty he had made with Brunei in 1847. Again Spain protested. 'The question is to sleep', wrote the British Foreign Secretary.[20] The British government did not ratify the treaty, though they did not formally recognise Spanish sovereignty either.

Brooke's intervention prompted a further Spanish expedition to Sulu, and another treaty was made, though again no occupation followed. The spread of Islamic revivalism and the threat of intervention by other powers prompted still more violent Spanish action against Sulu in the 1870s, cutting off its trade and sinking its ships, and in 1876 an expedition secured a foothold on the island itself. The German government had protested against Spanish proceedings, and Britain, interested in ensuring that newly unified Germany did not itself turn to territorial acquisition, joined in securing the protocol of 1877, by which Spain agreed to refrain from any interference with British or German vessels, and to levy no duties on trade except where its authority was definitely established. But though theoretically this deal still kept open Sulu's traffic with the outside world, including the arms trade the

Spaniards so much resented, it could, of course, only prompt them to make further efforts to establish their authority. In 1878, indeed, Sultan Jamal-ul-A'zam was compelled to sign a new treaty.

It was just at this point that Dent and Overbeck secured from the sultan the lease of the Sulu territories in northern Borneo that was designed to supplement the leases they had secured from Brunei. Jamal-ul-A'zam's motives were obvious: it would interpose another obstacle to the Spanish advance. The British government indeed rejected Spanish protests, and insisted that it had not recognised Spanish sovereignty. But that was now a negotiating device. Its aim was to settle the differences with Spain by agreeing on a partition. The British would recognise Spanish sovereignty over the Sulu archipelago, but Spain would renounce the sultan's claims over North Borneo. That was the basis of a new Anglo-Spanish-German protocol concluded in 1885.

Once more the Europeans had come to an arrangement, to which the Malayo-Muslim rulers were not a party, in order to avoid conflict among themselves. Once more, too, their arrangement created a frontier that was without historical precedent or geographical reality: it went through the realm of Sulu. Politically North Borneo remained linked to it only insofar as the Company was bound to pay the sultan an annual sum for its perpetual lease. Otherwise the territories were separated politically, despite long-standing commercial and cultural links.

Spain had secured a border for the Philippines, but a rather porous one. The problem that presented was soon, however, to be faced by its successor, the United States, and then by the independent Republic of our own time. In the remaining years of their regime, the Spaniards sought still to strengthen their position in Sulu. But their garrison lived in fear, as Ada Pryer reported on her visit. 'At night, at frequent intervals, was heard the sharp cry of Alerte passing from one water tower to another along the city wall.'[21] When the United States displaced Spain, moreover, it made a separate treaty with Sultan Jamal-ul-Kiram. That was in the event but a temporary move. When it had dealt with opposition in Luzon and the Visayas, the United States determined to bring the Moro lands under control. That was not done without a great deal of violence. But this time colonial authority was firmly established, and the sultan deprived of all but his religious authority.

The United States acquisition of the Philippines

The American intervention in the Philippines had made a Spanish fear real. Ever since the British capture of Manila, which had stimulated the rebellion of Diego Silang in Ilocos, the Spaniards had been apprehensive lest foreign threat should coincide with internal opposition. In 1896 a revolt began in the Tagalog provinces, and then the war with the United States, begun in the Caribbean, spread to East Asia. The outcome was never in doubt, though the New York Times declared that Admiral Dewey's victory at Manila rivalled 'the glories of Trafalgar'.[22] Under the treaty of

Paris of 10 December 1898, Spain withdrew from the Philippines, while the United States made it a payment of $20 million. The United States had earlier purchased Louisiana and Alaska, but Thomas B. Reed, an anti-annexationist, branded the transaction as the purchase of ten million people 'at two dollars a head, unpicked'.[23] The Americans had indeed not conquered the islands, and now they had to deal with the Filipino revolutionaries, who sought, not the 'benevolent assimilation' that President McKinley offered, but independence for the republic they had proclaimed on 12 June. The struggle was a long one, since some of them, like the Acehnese, resorted to guerrilla struggle.

Not all the revolutionaries believed in persisting with the struggle. They were conscious of internal weakness in at least two respects. One was, as it were, horizontal: the rebellion was initiated in the Manila region; and they had to make it a Filipino revolution, not merely a Tagalog revolt. Another aspect was vertical: the elite was afraid that political revolution might unleash social revolution. At the height of the Republic's success, it attracted elite support as a guarantee of order. The elite was ready to turn to the Americans when its future came into question, thus accelerating its collapse.

Independence ill-prepared for would end in dominance by a foreign power, the great polymath José Rizal had prophesied.[24] There was indeed an interplay between the revolution and the outside powers, counterpart to the long-standing apprehensions of the Spaniards. The revolutionaries were conscious of their international weakness. 'Whenever a people have risen against another people that ruled them, a colony against a metropolis', Ferdinand Blumentritt had warned Rizal, 'the revolution has never succeeded on its own strength.'[25] Unlike the earlier Spanish American revolutionaries, the Filipinos were not likely to receive great power support, even if they set up an orderly government, which they saw as necessary on this ground, too. Unlike later anti-colonial revolutionaries, they had no fellow revolutionaries in Asia either. Concerns about the outside world linked up, however, with knowledge of internal weakness. If order could not be ensured—thus making foreign opposition more likely—the elite might be all the more ready to accept a modification or postponement of the claims to nationhood as the means of avoiding internal subversion—thus making the acceptance of foreign rule more certain.

The policies of the outside powers varied. American opinion was deeply divided by this imperial adventure, and questioned whether this was the way the industrialising United States should expand its role in East Asia. Annexationists and anti-annexationists conflicted, and indecision, only dissolved by McKinley's re-election in 1900, prolonged the uncertainty of some of the Filipino elite. Now, too, the United States acted with even greater vigour. 'Everyone was to be made to want peace and want it badly.'[26] The British would have preferred the status quo. Not that they were unequivocally for Spain. Hong Kong was a source of arms for rebels and a venue for exiles. Like other revolutionaries Galicano Apacible acknowledged the 'English spirit of equity'.[27] Continued Spanish rule was in any case out of the question. The British did not consider that the Filipinos could set up a viable regime, even though they had been proponents of the independence of the Latin American republics earlier in the century. Their relative power diminished, they did not wish to intervene themselves. Of the choices that remained, control by the United States was preferable to control by Germany. The United States now in fact became a colonial power. Its presence tended to support the the colonial structure Southeast Asia had assumed, and it also stood in the way of the Japanese, who had taken over Formosa/Taiwan after winning their war with China in 1894–95.

Some of the revolutionaries had looked to Japan, and some of the more radical Japanese were interested in the Philippines. Before the rising José A. Ramos and Doroteo Cortes had vainly contacted Oi Kentaro, and the revolutionary Katipunan organisation delivered an appeal to the captain of a Japanese training ship, *Kongo*. Some Europeans, even in 1896, thought Japan would aid the Filipinos as the United States had the Cubans. The Tokyo government was, however, cautious. After acquiring Formosa, it had made an agreement with Spain, setting out spheres of interest. When the revolution began, it feared to provoke the intervention of others, and did not want the renegotiation of its own 'unequal' treaties interrupted. Okuma Shigenobu, the foreign minister, indicated that the extension of American sovereignty or protection was acceptable. If, however, the United States did not wish to undertake that, Japan was ready to join the United States, singly or with another power, 'to form, subject to proper conditions, suitable government for the territory in question under the … protection of the guaranteeing powers'.[28]

'One really cannot wish victory on either of them', wrote the Dutch prime minister in the Spanish–American war.[29] Spain's failure was an argument for the Ethical Policy. '[T]here is no better way of ensuring that we keep the East Indies than a policy of righteousness and honesty', as its advocate, C. Th. van Deventer, put it.[30] In the event, while US occupation held off the Japanese, its experiments in colonial rule were to disturb the Dutch.

West New Guinea and Timor

The Germans secured the Carolines by a money payment, though Bulow suggested that it would stimulate the people and the navy to follow the Kaiser 'further along the path which leads to world power, greatness and eternal glory'.[31] Itself gaining little, Germany had helped to bring other powers together at the expense of the Asian states. German activity helped to define another Southeast Asian frontier. The Dutch claimed part of the coast of West New Guinea/West Irian, on the ground that it was claimed by a vassal, the Sultan of Tidore. Apprehensive of British moves in northern Australia in the 1820s, they had taken possession up to 141 degrees east, and occupied a settlement at Triton Bay between 1828 and 1836. Bismarck's demonstration of interest in New Guinea prompted the hoisting of the British flag at Port Moresby in 1884. A settlement between the British and the Germans followed in

1885. Ten years later the Dutch reached a boundary agreement with the British along the 141-degree line, and in 1910 the Germans also accepted what that decided. In 1902 the Dutch had established their post at Merauke.

German 'world power' ambitions brought the future of Portugal's African colonies into question. In Southeast Asia the Portuguese and the Dutch had made a deal in 1859. The former abandoned their claims to Solor and Larantuka, while the Dutch paid over f200 000, and made over the coffee region of Maubara west of Dili. In the 1890s, as bankruptcy threatened Portugal, it seemed that it might sell its colonies, including East Timor. The Dutch sought explicit recognition of preferential treatment if it did, given that, as the Dutch ambassador in Lisbon put it, 'all the governments are like hungry ravens, with their eyes fixed on everything that Portugal will or might have to cede'.[32] A declaration, made mutual to please Portugal, was signed on 1 July 1893. There were further boundary revisions in 1904 and 1914. The Portuguese preserved the enclave of Oecusse.

The Straits Settlements and the Malay peninsula

The activities of the Germans in North Borneo and Sulu in the early 1870s may have added to the suspicion that they might intervene on the Malay peninsula. From that the Dutch had been excluded under the treaty of 1824. But though the British did not establish their control on the peninsular side of the 'line', the treaty reduced the effective independence of the Malay rulers, as it did those of Indonesia. The presence of the British in the Straits Settlements also tended to fend off the intervention of other Western states, though they were to become more nervous about it after 1870.

For the Malay rulers it was, however, not all loss. The Thai state had a long-standing interest in the peninsula, and, after the Burmans had overrun the northern Malay states, the new dynasty at Bangkok sought to reduce them again to the status of Thai tributaries. Kedah, as Francis Light put it, had 'kept peace with both. Paying homage sometimes to one and sometimes to the other and often to both'.[33] That was no longer possible. Kedah and Trengganu paid tribute to Bangkok, and when Pattani declined to do so, it was crushed. The withdrawal of the Dutch under the treaty of 1824 removed an obstacle to Thai expansion, and it was not at first clear whether or to what degree the presence of the British in the Straits Settlements would prove a sufficient substitute.

Indeed, though the Sultan of Kedah had ceded Penang in 1786 in the expectation of assistance from the East India Company, no such assistance had been offered, nor was it offered when the Company, seeking to add to the security of the harbour, procured the further cession of Province Wellesley in 1800. The Company wanted to avoid any conflict with Siam, not only because of its general desire to limit extension outside the sub-continent, but also because Siam paid tribute to China, and the Company had no wish to see its profitable monopoly of the tea trade at Canton disturbed. In 1816, however, the Thais instructed the sultan, as their vassal, to procure the submission of Perak, and in 1821 they invaded Kedah themselves. Could the British still stand by?

British merchants in Penang thought not. During the French wars, the competition of the Dutch had been eliminated, and commercial ties with the peninsula had been expanded, particularly with Perak, a source of tin. Some officials in Penang argued that they had the same kind of obligations as the presidencies in India. 'We have become a preponderating Power on this side of India and we ought ... to protect the weaker power against the usurpations of the stronger, to mediate between them all on every occasion when our interference can be effectual, and even at times to exhibit a tone of superiority to check the extravagant pretensions of the different states.'[34] The Supreme Government in India did not accept this approach, even after the conclusion of the Anglo-Dutch treaty of 1824.

The war between the Company and Burma, which broke out soon after the conclusion of that treaty, brought about negotiations with Burma's long-time enemy, Siam, and at one point the British contemplated offering the Thais some of southern Burma in return for their disavowing or moderating their claims in the Malay peninsula. In the event, however, Henry Burney, the negotiator at Bangkok, arrived empty-handed, and he was not able to secure what the Penang government hoped for. The Burney treaty of 1826 in fact established a kind of Anglo-Thai-Malay tripartite relationship. It differed from state to state, but in all cases it reduced the international status of the rulers. Apart from Pattani, however, it prevented the complete absorption of the states within Siam.

Pattani was not brought into the discussions. Nor was the Sultan of Kedah restored: indeed the British government undertook not to permit him 'to attack, disturb, or injure in any manner the territory of Kedah', and to arrange for him to live outside Penang, Wellesley, Perak, and Selangor. Siam, however, undertook not to obstruct commerce in Kelantan and Trengganu, and not to attack Selangor or Perak. Perak itself could send tribute to Siam if it so decided. Disappointed with most of this, Governor Fullerton sent a mission to Perak to ensure that the sultan decided in the right way. The emissary also secured the cession of the island of Pangkor, and was subsequently sent on an expedition to Kurau. There his task was to attack a chief who was allegedly connected with the pirates from Johore, but who was also a supporter of the Thais.

In Calcutta, however, these actions were disapproved, and the governor-general, Lord Amherst, insisted that good relations with Siam had priority over Britain's interests on the peninsula. The policy of non-intervention adopted by the superior authorities did not, however, preclude all intervention by the local authorities: it meant that their intervention had to take a different form. They had to operate by influencing the rulers. In so doing they established a practice that profoundly affected the relationship Britain established with the peninsula when it abandoned non-intervention.

The practice had to differ from state to state. In Kelantan and Trengganu, Burney had avoided recognising Thai supremacy, and the Straits authorities tried to prevent its establishment. The rumour of a Thai attack in 1832, for example, led S. G. Bonham at Singapore to have HMS *Magicienne* sent up to look for pirates: 'the Siamese ... would at once conceive that the visit had been caused by them and would by no means call on us for further interference'.[35]

Over Kedah, however, Thai suzerainty had been recognised, and a different course had to be followed. At first sight, indeed, it seems different in purpose as well as in execution, but closer analysis suggests another conclusion. Though the government was obliged under the Burney treaty to keep the sultan away from Kedah, it was in fact unable legally to do so. As a result of his intrigues, the Siamese regime in Kedah was overthrown by expeditions led by his relatives in 1831 and again in 1838. Against the advice of the Supreme Government, the Penang authorities cooperated rather ostentatiously with the Thais, and sought to emphasise the piratical connexions of the expeditions so as to ensure naval cooperation. Their rationale, it seems, was that, given that Thai claims had been endorsed, merely temporising was impossible: it would alienate their Thai neighbours without winning over the Malays. Arguably the policy worked. The attacks helped to persuade the Thais to change their policy, while the attitude the British had adopted made it easier to accept their mediation. The outcome was the restoration of the sultan as a Thai vassal in 1842. The tripartite sharing of power was restored, though in a way peculiar to Kedah. Orderly government characterised the subsequent period: the sultan and chiefs wanted to avoid British complaints that might lead to Siamese intervention.

Thai claims did not extend to the south of the peninsula. There the British and the ruler of Johore developed a relationship that was unique, but influenced the relationship between them and other rulers. Raffles had secured Singapore from the Temenggong of the Johore sultanate, in whose appanage it lay, and from a claimant sultan, Hussein, who was the rival of the sultan whom the Dutch recognised, based in Riau-Lingga. The Temenggong's successor, Ibrahim, was quick to see advantage in dissociating himself from the piratical activities of the Johore chiefs and their followers, and of associating himself with the British, in whose settlement he in fact lived. The anti-piracy operations undertaken in 1836 by HMS *Andromache* and the Company's steamer *Diana* only strengthened his conviction. Association with the British enhanced Ibrahim's authority, while it also helped to expand their informal influence. Furthermore, Ibrahim persuaded his neighbour, the Bendahara of Pahang, another former officer of the old Johore empire, also to work against piracy and the slave trade.

In the 1850s the close connexion of the Straits government and the Temenggong began, however, to have a destabilising effect. Other rulers became jealous of him and of his power, and even looked to the sultan in Lingga as a counterbalance. Hussein's son, Ali, was more or less bought off by a treaty of 1855, but a civil war in Pahang was more serious. Johore intervened on one side, and Sultan Omar of Trengganu on the other. He was not opposed to the British: rather he resented their rather exclusive relationship with the Temenggong. Governor Blundell attempted to build relationships with all the rulers. His successor, Orfeur Cavenagh, reverted to a pro-Johore policy, apparently convinced that Omar would be too fearful of the Thais to continue his opposition. He was mistaken, and late in 1862 he ordered a punitive bombardment of Trengganu.

That did not prevent the success of the Temenggong's opponents in Pahang, which in effect restored the equilibrium of the east coast. But it did affect the position of states over which the Thais had claims. The Thai government protested against the bombardment, and the British government disapproved of Cavenagh's proceedings. His successor, Ord, the first Colonial Office appointee, was thus inclined to recognise Thai claims even over Trengganu, and also to attribute the stability of the state to them rather than to Omar. But though the British attitude changed, the sultan was not dislodged, and the tripartite system continued.

Ord was contrasting the orderliness of the northern states with the disorder in Selangor, and even more in Perak. In those states there were no strong rulers through whom the British might work and so make up for their own limited capacity to intervene. Yet the development of tin-mining, the immigration of Chinese, and disputes among the Malay elite, presented problems far greater than those in Johore or Trengganu. Neither Cavenagh nor Ord could, however, secure a reversal of the official non-intervention policy. That came only with the instructions issued to the next governor, Sir Andrew Clarke, in 1873.

The reason for the change has been the subject of substantial controversy. Were the British more concerned with protecting the growing trade in tin? Or were they concerned to avoid the intervention of other powers who might argue that they were restoring order in troubled native states? The latter explanation appears the more persuasive, even though there is no evidence that another state was planning to intervene. The security of the route through the Straits was an essential objective of the British, as the treaty of 1824 had shown. The changing relationships among the European powers, and their changing relationship with the rest of the world, suggested the need to take precautions. 'We are the paramount power on the Peninsula up to the limit of the States, tributary to Siam', the Colonial Secretary, Lord Kimberley, formerly Lord Wodehouse, told the prime minister, Gladstone, 'and looking to the vicinity of India and our whole position in the East I apprehend that it would be a serious matter if any other European Power were to obtain a footing on the Peninsula'.[36]

While it could be argued that it was now necessary to do something more to fend off other powers than merely rely on the treaty of 1824 and the existence of the Straits Settlements, it could also be argued that it was not necessary to do very much. That probably helped with the change of policy. Most of the states did not require intervention. Where it took place—in Perak, in Selangor, and in neighbouring Negri Sembilan—it did not appear to require the direct exertion of British control, still less annexation. Clarke went further than his instructions suggested. But what he did was to make treaties with the rulers under which they would be bound to seek and follow the advice of British Residents appointed to their courts on all matters 'other than those touching Malay religion and custom'. That was an idea that Lieut.-Governor George Campbell had put up in 1872. 'In India, in many a native-ruled state, it is marvellous what work a single well-selected British officer has effected.'[37]

Applying the concept to Malay states had been suggested before. The reason it was expected to work, however, was surely the experience gained in the previous decades of alleged non-intervention, in particular with the ruler of Johore. What was needed, it was concluded, was not a take-over, but better means of giving advice and carrying it out. The judgment seemed mistaken, for the first British Resident in Perak, J. W. W. Birch, was assassinated, though arguably that was because Clarke's successor, Jervois, had, as Peter Burns puts it, 'left the Malays in no doubt that Britain intended to take direct control of the country'.[38] In any case the punitive expedition that followed—more troops were sent than needed, displaying the power that backed the system in India—helped to preserve the myth of government by advice. Now that advice was sure to be taken. 'The Colonial Office still would not acknowledge facts, but at least it was ready to be party to a fiction.'[39] The British never acquired sovereignty in Malaya.

The system was extended to Pahang. In 1887 Sultan Ahmad—'almost in tears'[40]—accepted an agent and in 1888 he accepted a Resident. The states in which there were by now Residents were, under new treaties, pulled together into the Federated Malay States in 1895–96. In approving the draft treaty, the Colonial Secretary, Joseph Chamberlain, insisted that 'no pains should be spared to safeguard the position and the dignity of the Native Rulers, ... and to give them the assurance that such changes as shall be made are solely intended to promote strength by combination, uniformity of policy and harmony of purpose'.[41] 'The Sultan of Perak signed and sealed the Treaty at once', reported Frank Swettenham. 'The Sultan of Pahang returned it to me in four hours, the Sultan of Selangor affixed his seal in an hour.' Told of his swift success, Andrew Clarke 'rolled with laughter' and said, 'Yes, but you know what a Native's consent amounts to, when he is told that the Government wants a thing consented to'.[42] Under the treaty, indeed, the rulers seemed to lose even more of their power to rule, and other Malay rulers became wary of joining the federation. Moreover, they preferred, if they had to receive British officers, that they should be termed Advisers. 'British Malaya' was variegated.

The Colonial Office had become critical of Johore. It did not, however, back the British concessionaires and speculators. Rather it saw them as obstructions to the introduction of good government which would have to be undertaken. A kind of exemplar of the Resident system, Johore paradoxically held out till 1914, when a General Adviser was installed. The time had come for Trengganu and Kelantan after the Thais transferred their rights over the northern Malay states in 1909. The tripartite sharing of power thus became bipartite. Over that transaction the rulers were indeed not consulted, and the Sultan of Trengganu said that 'he could not understand how Siam could transfer what it had never possessed'.[43] Siam behaved in a sense like a colonial power. But had those states been more fully incorporated in the Thai state in the preceding decades, the transaction might have been more difficult for it to agree to and to carry out, and indeed the Malay states might not even have existed. That they had not been so incorporated owed something to the leadership their rulers had given, but something also to the British, and in particular to the authorities in the Straits Settlements, who had worked to ensure the preservation of the Malay monarchies south of Pattani. In this way a new border was created in 1909.

The Bangkok kingdom

The 1909 deal was prompted by the Thais' determination to retain the independence of their kingdom in a region now almost entirely dominated by colonial powers. It was necessary not only to come to terms with them, but to behave like them, if that objective was still to be attained. In the period of British primacy the course they needed to follow was more obvious, though their major neighbours failed to follow it. It was to yield to the British, but not totally, and keep others in play, but not dangerously.

The phase of revolution and reconstitution through which the three major mainland kingdoms passed in the latter half of the eighteenth century—affected both by economic opportunity and political rivalry—helped to determine their response to the changes of the nineteenth century. There was a possibility that Britain could deal with them as with the Philippines and Netherlands India. The Lao states and Cambodia, on the other hand, were unable to benefit from economic expansion and became indeed a prey to their neighbours. Western powers shaped their policies accordingly.

The destruction of Ayudhya in 1767 destroyed the central authority of the Thai kings. Taksin, a former governor, rebuilt the capital down-river at Thonburi, well-placed, not only for control, but for commerce. Part Chinese, he also re-established Thai links with China, the Manchus proving responsive because of their difficulties with Burma. Asserting control over the core of the old kingdom, he also renewed control of the peninsular states and over Chiengmai, and he brought the major Lao states, Luang Prabang and Vientiane, under control. His kingdom was inherited by Rama I, founder of the Chakri dynasty, who moved the capital across the river to Bangkok. Again he reasserted control on the peninsula, partly for fear of Burma. It was that which brought about contacts with the British.

Their settlement in Penang, their contacts with the Malay states, and their conflict with Burma gave the British an interest in Siam, but they had no wish to add it to their empire. Siam's tributary relationship with China gave them an additional reason for avoiding conflict, though they realised that their conquests in India meant that the Thais could not but be suspicious of their intentions. Sent to Bangkok after the founding of Singapore, John Crawfurd recommended against installing a British envoy there: it would only be a source of irritation. The Supreme Government indeed hesitated about sending Burney:

all extension of our territorial possessions and political relations on the side of the Indo-Chinese nations is, with reference to the peculiar character of those states, to their decided jealousy of our power and ambition, and to their proximity to China, earnestly to be deprecated and declined as far as the course of events and the force of circumstances will permit. … Even the negotiation of treaties and positive engagements with the Siamese Government … may be regarded as open to serious objection lest any future violation of their conditions should impose upon us the necessity of resenting such breaches of contract.[44]

But Burney was sent, and Rama III accepted the treaty of 1826, which not only covered the Malay states, but also provided for British trade at Bangkok, though it did not establish any British official there.

The attempts of the Penang government to remedy what it saw as the deficiencies in the treaty, in particular by its exploits in Perak, prompted the Supreme Government in Calcutta to reassert the priorities in British policy in the new context it created:

Our only national object of policy hereafter in relation to the Siamese should be to endeavour to allay their jealousy of our ultimate views … and to derive from our connection with them every attainable degree of commercial advantage, by practising in our intercourse with them the utmost forbearance, temper and moderation both in language and action, and … by faithfully observing the conditions of the treaty which fixes our future relations.[45]

That policy discouraged intervention on the peninsula. It also made the Indian government unwilling to take up complaints from British merchants about their treatment at Bangkok. Nor did the Company's attitude change when the British relationship with China changed, and it no longer seemed necessary to take account of Siam's vassal status. British policy towards China was now, however, in the hands of the Foreign Office. Advised by Charles Gutzlaff, an ex-missionary, its officials argued that, since China had been made to change its attitude towards foreign trade, its erstwhile feudatories could readily be persuaded to follow its example, open their ports, and accept extraterritorial jurisdiction. The idea of a new mission to Bangkok was also taken up in Singapore, and in 1848 the Chamber of Commerce made a direct approach to the Foreign Secretary, Lord Palmerston, following it up the following year with the proposal that Sir James Brooke, who had just made his treaty with Sulu, should be the emissary. The India Board was doubtful. But the Board of Trade declared that 'the manufacturing districts in the North of England' were in favour of 'an attempt to extend our commercial relations with Siam and Cochin China',[46] and Palmerston resolved to give Brooke this additional task.

He was instructed to visit Bangkok if he thought that he 'might be able to make some arrangements that would effect an improvement in the British Commercial Relations with that Country'. The commercial stipulations he could include should be comparable with those in treaties made with 'other imperfectly civilized States', such as China and Turkey. The instructions did not cover the political issues that so much concerned the Indian authorities. But Brooke was 'to be very careful not to get involved in any dispute or hostile proceedings which would render our position in Siam or Cochin-China worse than it now is, or which might compel Her Majesty's Government to have recourse to forcible measures in order to obtain redress'.[47]

At first Brooke seems to have planned a policy of 'conciliation', undermining rather than overthrowing Thai prejudices: 'as we have delayed for thirty years doing anything, ... in the course of this policy we may wait till the demise of the king brings about a new order of things. Above all, it would be well to prepare for the change, and to place *our own* king on the throne', Mongkut, 'a highly accomplished gentleman, for a semi-barbarian'.[48] The approach he advocated towards the states in the archipelago seems to have been in his mind. But when Rama III rejected a new treaty, he entirely abandoned it. An 'expedient' policy did not preserve peace: it led to 'embarrassment', 'the sacrifice of a favourable prestige', and war. 'An adherence to this principle has raised our Indian Empire, and established the reign of Opinion which maintains it; and the departure from this principle has caused the present deplorable condition of our relations with Siam.' Britain should demand 'a more equitable Treaty in accordance with the observance of civilized nations'. If Siam refused, a British force should destroy the defences on the Menam, 'which would place us in possession of the capital and by restoring us to our proper position of command, retrieve the past and ensure peace for the future, with all its advantages of a growing and most important commerce'.[49]

Opinion in Singapore was divided. Some were in support of this approach, arguing that, if it damaged trade in the short term, it would bring long-term benefits that Singapore would share. Others offered a different opinion. Negotiations should be resumed when the Thai government changed. 'A warlike demonstration' might 'convulse the whole Kingdom, put a stop for years to all trade, and perhaps render the establishment of British power in the Country indispensable'.[50] It was this line, not Brooke's, that the British government followed.

The accession of Mongkut led it to send a new mission. The controversy over Borneo, which was to reach its climax with the commission of inquiry, meant that Brooke was not sent back to Bangkok, as was initially intended. The new mission was carried through by Sir John Bowring, the Superintendent of Trade at Hong Kong, in 1855. The old system of measurement duties and monopolies, which had caused much of the earlier friction, was replaced by a system of import and export duties, and the rice trade, hitherto closed, was opened. A British consul was to be appointed, and British subjects placed under extra-territorial jurisdiction.

These were indeed the kind of stipulations Britain made with 'imperfectly civilised' states like China. By them it hoped to secure commercial advantage without incurring territorial responsibility. Siam accepted what had been forced on China. It was, however, also making a bargain that could be compared with the deals, explicit or implicit, that the Dutch and the Spaniards made with Britain in respect of their Southeast Asian empires: political independence at the price of commercial opportunity. A deal with Britain, the leading power, also helped to limit the scope for others. The Kalahom minister indeed said he was glad Bowring was 'the pioneer of the new relations to be opened between them and the West, as they could then count upon such arrangements being concluded as would both be satisfactory to Siam, and sufficient to meet the demands that might hereafter be made by other of the Western Powers'.[51] The treaty gave Britain an additional stake in the independence of Siam.

The following year Harry Parkes concluded a supplementary treaty. He also brought with him a letter from Queen Victoria. That, he said, touched King Mongkut's heart 'and flattered his ambition'.[52] Correspondence between monarch and monarch was a further sign that, albeit at some cost, Siam had strengthened its position in the emerging world of states. It also extracted itself from the old world of states. Further tribute to China was evaded. The last was paid in 1852. In 1862 the Chinese reminded the Thais that tribute was overdue. The head of the Chinese merchants was asked to reply and he pointed to the rebels and bandits in southern China. Further evasion followed another reminder in 1863: it was agreed to say that the vessels used had rotted away.[53]

At first the new arrangements strengthened Siam's position in Malaya. The topic had come up in 1855, but Bowring had no instructions to deal with it, and the new treaties left that part of the Burney arrangements untouched. The presence of a British consul in Bangkok was, however, to contribute to a change in practice. It became more difficult for the British authorities in the Straits to deal directly with the tributary states. It also provided a direct avenue of protest against Cavenagh's bombardment of Trengganu in 1862.

The establishment of a French colony in Cochin-China, moreover, made Siam no longer a marcher territory for the British, but a buffer state. French penetration of Laos in the 1880s led the Straits authorities to question Thai claims over the northern Malay states, lest France acquire Siam and the claims as well. But there was also the risk that, if in fact Siam preserved its independence, it would be alienated, and also that France might be encouraged in its course by British example.

It was indeed possible that Siam might have to pay a further price if it was to retain its independence. According to Prince Prisdang, it sought to claim as much as it could, both in Indo-China and Malaya, with the idea that some day it might, 'like Medea', save the country, or part of it, by throwing dependencies at its pursuers.[54] The Siamese forward movement in Laos—undertaken while Vietnam was weak—provoked the French, however, and they took up Vietnamese claims. The French saw the annexation of eastern Laos as necessary for the security of Indo-China, and the fact that Vietnamese opponents found sanctuary there underlined it. They also saw it as an initiative in the expected showdown with the British over the future of Siam itself.[55]

A naval demonstration at Bangkok in July 1893 was designed to secure Siam's compliance with French claims. The reaction of the British disappointed the Thais.

While attempting to restrain France in Cambodia—the absorption of Battambang and Siemreap (Angkor) 'would be not only a monstrous invasion of the integrity of Siam, but would equally destroy her independence', France was told[56]—they urged the Thais to accept French demands so as to avoid their being stepped up. In the event the Mekong became the frontier in Laos, though Siam retained for the time being its claims over western Cambodia, and Delcassé did not secure Siemreap and Battambang, as he hoped.

In 1896 Britain and France reached an agreement under which each power undertook not to advance in the Menam valley without the other's consent. That did not explicitly provide against their further acquisition of Thai territory. King Chulalongkorn had appointed a number of Western advisers, having seen, as J. G. D. Campbell put it, 'that if Siam is to preserve her independence … she must put her house in order, or keep up an appearance of doing so'.[57] The General Adviser, the Belgian Rolin-Jaequemyns, thought that the 1896 treaty improved Siam's position, inasmuch as it took away from the French, at least while they were at peace with the British, 'the fearsome weapon of an attack on the Menam (be it understood that I leave aside the wicked hypothesis of an agreement between these two countries re this attack)'.[58] Of that, of course, there was some suspicion, for example on the part of the Japanese: the arrangement was 'of the same nature as the compact between two highwaymen not to molest a certain richly-laden coach'.[59] At the time, however, the two powers had expressed their solicitude for the security and stability of Siam, and Lord Salisbury wrote to the British ambassador in Paris a despatch for publication, denying that the agreement threw doubts on the Thais' rights to 'the remainder of their kingdom'.[60]

There was also the question of yet other powers, in particular Germany. Salisbury had sought to deal with the risk to the peninsula by the secret treaty of 1897, in which the king of Siam agreed not to cede any rights south of Muong Bang Tapan, nor to allow any special privileges, while the British undertook to support him in resisting any third-party attempts to acquire dominion or influence there. The Thai government had, partly for security reasons, begun to implement a policy of closer integration, but it proved counter-productive, and the opposition aroused in Pattani made the British apprehensive of foreign intervention, against which the secret agreement might be ineffectual. At the same time, the British still did not wish to alienate the Thais, which could in turn be counter-productive. Swettenham was told to reject the appeal of Sultan Abdul Kadir of Pattani, and the new agreement of 1902 did not cover that state. Under it Siam was required to appoint advisers of British nationality to the rulers of Kelantan and Trengganu.

The French had already hinted at a wish to establish 'spheres of influence' outside the Menam valley. Now they felt justified in advancing their influence in eastern Siam. More influential was the Anglo-French rapprochement in face of the growth of German power in Europe. The agreement of 1904 recognised that outside the Menam valley the French had a sphere to the east and the British to the south. Even before that agreement was finalised, the Thais, recognising that Britain would not help, had yielded to French demands, and both Cambodia and Luang Prabang had been extended. In 1907 the French finally secured Siemreap and Battambang. Agreement between the Europeans served the Thais no better than rivalry.

The Thais had thus had to supplement the bargain they had made, by which commercial opportunity was offered in return for political independence. The two were, however, still connected. The secret treaty of 1897 had imposed inconvenient restrictions on concessions. In the treaties of 1907 and 1909, the European powers reduced their extra-territorial rights. The kingdom's survival required a measure of consolidation: it would be leaner but keener. It was fortunate for the Thais, as Prisdang had seen, that they had entered this dangerous phase when their empire was at its greatest extent. They could concede territory now that it was necessary to do so, and yet remain, in Mongkut's phrase, 'within our house and home'.[61]

Nguyen Vietnam

The rivalry of the French in the eighteenth century had helped to set the British on the path towards creating a territorial empire in India. Their success prompted the French to look elsewhere, in particular to Dai Viet. Their impact at this time was, however, limited. A century later, the position was very different: in 1859 they began to establish a colony in Cochin-China. In the meantime, unlike Siam, and indeed Netherlands India and the Philippines, Vietnam had not come to terms with the British, nor had it thus given them a stake in maintaining its independence. They did not oppose the French venture, though they took some precautions. Vietnam had escaped the threat that European rivalry often brought to Asia, but it succumbed to European agreement.

Vietnam was in some sense condemned by success in a more traditional objective: the creation of a unified state. The Nguyen regime had been overthrown by the movement led by the Tay-son brothers. Beginning very much among the upland peoples and the remnant of the Chams, in reaction to Nguyen attempts to control the Mekong delta, it had become something far wider, partly because, seeing an opportunity, the Trinh ruler had marched south in 1774–75. In 1786 the brothers invaded the north in the name of the Le and destroyed the Trinh regime. Le Chieu-tong appealed to the Chinese, who crossed the border in 1788, but that only precipitated the triumph of one of the Tay-son brothers who called himself emperor Quang-trung. Though this was a period of commercial growth, stability did not follow, and he was challenged by the Nguyen pretender. In 1792 the latter marched north, in 1801 took the Tay-son capital Hué, and in 1802 secured Hanoi. The reunited country was formally called Vietnam and Nguyen Anh became the emperor Gia-long. Yet the unity thus regained was fragile, and the Nguyen, coming from the south, were always uncertain of the allegiance of the Vietnamese as a whole. That uncertainty turned to negativism in its dealings with foreign powers.

French ministers, particularly Choiseul, had seen Dai Viet as a possible source of 'compensation' for the success of the British in India and China. Vergennes was apprehensive lest they intervened first. 'If they decide on that place before us, we will be excluded for ever and we will have lost an important foothold on that part of Asia which would make us masters by intercepting in time of war the English trade with China, by protecting our own in the whole of India, and by keeping the English in a continual state of anxiety.'[62] The involvement of France in the war of American independence, and the British conquest of their possessions in India, brought this plan to nothing. The British themselves sent a mission to Dai Viet, headed by Charles Chapman, partly in the hope, earlier expressed by Dalrymple, of expanding their trade with China. But the chaotic conditions created by the Tay-son rebellion did not encourage them to go further.

That rebellion seemed, however, to offer the French another opportunity to take up their venture when they returned to India after the war. Nguyen Anh reluctantly sought their aid in his struggle with the Tay-son through the head of French missionary activities in Vietnam, Pigneau de Behaine. He and Nguyen Anh's son, Canh, went first to Pondicherry and then to Paris, where he argued that 'the political balance in India is so inclined towards the English nation … that we must consider it a most difficult task to bring it back to equality. Perhaps of all the methods one could use an establishment in Cochin-China would be the surest and most effective'.[63] Louis XVI's minister, Montmorin, accepted the idea after the founding of Penang and the Anglo-Prussian intervention in the Dutch Republic, and he and Pigneau, as the Nguyen representative, signed a treaty in 1787, in which France offered military aid in return for the eventual cession of Callao island off Da-nang harbour and the cession of Pulau Condore. Carrying out the French commitment was, however, left to the discretion of the authorities at Pondicherry. They were more cautious, and Pigneau had to recruit volunteers. 'What in fact materialised was a private venture organised by Pigneau.'[64] Their help probably contributed little to Nguyen Anh's ultimate success, and the treaty of 1787 was not implemented.

The limited role of the French was not the main reason why, once he had reunified Vietnam, Gia-long sought to cut down European influence still further. Nor was it his fear that a connexion with the French might provoke the intervention of their British rivals, of whose conquests in India he was aware. His main concern was to strengthen Vietnamese unity, which foreign influence might subvert. His successor, Minh-mang, invoking the Confucian heritage, went further, and under him the last remaining Frenchman left the emperor's service. Isolation, feasible in the short term, was not, however, a credible policy in the long term, particularly when it came to be combined with suppression of the Christian missions, of which the French had long seen themselves as patrons. Minh-mang, the Bishop of Veren wrote in 1822, 'is the greatest partisan of Confucius and of all the literati. He threatens to chase us all out of the kingdom'.[65]

The British had been concerned lest Nguyen Anh's success should lead to an expansion of French influence, and the governor-general had sent two missions under John Roberts to Vietnam in 1803–04. The ruler 'strongly evinced a determination to avoid all intercourse with the English'.[66] They were reassured by the defeat of the French, and the negative response of Gia-long to the attempt of the restored Bourbon monarchy in 1817–18 to revive the treaty of 1787. Now, too, given their command over the supply of Indian opium, the British were no longer interested in Vietnam as a means of amplifying their imports into Canton. Following the establishment of Singapore, however, the Company sent Crawfurd to the Nguyen capital, Hué, as well as to Bangkok. Unlike Roberts, he was not even received by the Emperor, on the ground that he was the emissary only of a governor-general. Minh-mang also refused to accept the governor-general's presents. Crawfurd then declined to accept the return gifts, and the Vietnamese withdrew their reply to the letter he had brought.

Crawfurd saw no need to assume 'a higher tone'. The Vietnamese were 'far removed from the sphere of our Indian politics'.[67] No threat in themselves, they harboured no foreign influence either. 'Of all European nations the Cochin Chinese entertain great jealousy, nor is it in the least degree probable as long as the country remains as it now is, united and free from insurrection or internal dissention, that they will permit any European party to establish an influence of the least importance to their councils.'[68] The commercial opportunities that Vietnam offered Crawfurd thought had been exaggerated. An American visitor referred to the shuffling, chicanery, and rapacity of the merchants at Saigon, and 'the rapacious, faithless, despotic, and anti-commercial character of the government'.[69]

The response of the Nguyen monarchs to British approaches was very different from the response of the Chakri monarchs, and they developed no relationship with the leading European power. That was the more dangerous because they proceeded to worsen their relationships with other powers, particularly the French. The Le Van Khoi rebellion in the south in 1833 intensified suspicion of the Christians, and in the following years a number were put to death, including seven missionaries. That did not, however, stop missionary activity: it held out the prospect of martyrdom. Missionaries, too, had previously called for political intervention, and might again do so.

Minh-mang's policy, and the similar policy of his successor, Thieu-tri, was the more dangerous because of the change in the relationship between China and the Western powers after the Anglo-China war of 1840–42. Vietnam saw itself as a tributary of China, and, if that had been a restraining factor in European policy, it no longer operated. Even more important, the opening of China led to an expansion of Western naval forces in the China seas, including the French, but others as well. The French prime minister, Guizot, insisted that France could not be absent from so great a part of the world, when other European nations had settlements there. France had little commerce for its navy to protect, however. It responded to the appeal of missionaries in Vietnam. In 1845 USS *Constitution* had set a precedent for violent action. In 1847 the French ship *La Gloire* acted with still greater violence. Several junks were destroyed at Danang, and perhaps 1300 Vietnamese killed.

The change in the Anglo-Chinese relationship also, however, prompted a different approach to Vietnam, a renewal of the British attempts to open it up commercially. Gutzlaff argued that Thieu-tri would respond positively to a new approach. Vietnam, he suggested, had benefited from China's defeat: trade with China had expanded, and politically it had become less oppressive. So far royal monopolies had limited the opportunities of European vessels in Vietnam, though Vietnamese vessels had gone to Singapore. The earlier resort to French advice and assistance suggested that the Vietnamese were not averse to 'foreign intercourse', and it should be possible to persuade them of the advantage of 'a free intercourse and moderate duties'. This misreading of Vietnamese policy made Gutzlaff optimistic about a mission led by 'an accredited Envoy from Her Majesty'.[70] The Foreign Office in London authorised Sir John Davis to carry it out.

Based on misunderstanding, the mission was, not surprisingly, a complete failure, its chances, slim as they were, having been further reduced by the 'unfortunate collisions' with the French and the Americans, which 'increased to a high degree of animosity the unfavourable prejudices ... previously conceived against foreigners'.[71] Though he had a commission from the Queen, Davis was not permitted to proceed to Hué, let alone secure an audience with the emperor.

While the Nguyen failed to come to terms with the British, they fell out with the French. Napoleon III had been considering missionary proposals for intervention in Vietnam, and the execution of a Spanish bishop provided the occasion. France, the Brenier committee argued, could not expand in Europe: 'it would be unacceptable if ... she were forced to restrict her capabilities for action to these narrow confines while other maritime nations try to strengthen their power and resources in regions which Providence seems to have held in reserve to receive the superabundant expansionary capacities of Europe while inspiring true civilization with the legitimate aim of trying to penetrate them'.[72] French domination would be a 'deliverance' for the people.[73] In August 1858 a joint Franco-Spanish expedition seized Danang, but it could not attack Hué overland or by sea. Against the protests of the missionaries—whose interests lay mostly in Tonkin, where they looked for a pro-Le rising—the French admiral moved on Saigon early in 1859. The French began to create a colony they called Cochin-China.

Their rejection of Britain's approaches meant that the Nguyen could not enlist its support. Nor by this time could they draw on a feeling of rivalry. The old jealousies of Pigneau's time had died out, the Hong Kong *Register* declared: a commercial settlement at Da-nang might benefit 'the whole of commercial Europe', not France alone, if it helped to spread 'western civilisation and a more liberal policy in this quarter of the globe'.[74] There was no opposition in the Straits Settlements. 'Even news of the French seizure of Pulau Condore, still nominally a British possession, took second place in the *Straits Times* in December 1861 to a leader on amateur theatricals.'[75] The

Foreign Office in London told its ambassador in Paris to ascertain the 'ulterior object' of the French: to protect Christians or Catholics? to open commerce? to occupy territory permanently? He was, however, 'not to convey the impression that the French operations are viewed with jealousy or suspicion'.[76] The last option was clearly in mind, but the Foreign Office took no further steps.

A French colony in Vietnam could be tolerated, the British believed, so long as it remained within limits and did not trench upon Laos. Encouraged by the strain in Anglo-Thai relations caused by the Trengganu bombardment, Admiral La Grandière felt free to move at the expense of the Siamese claims over Cambodia. A treaty signed at Udong in 1863 brought that kingdom French protection. The British still felt that, so long as French proceedings did not interfere with Siam, they could be viewed without anxiety.

Initially the French colony covered the eastern provinces of Cochin-China. Saigon was effectively occupied only by February 1861. Then the French spread out over the surrounding provinces, Gia-dinh, Bien-hoa, and Dinh-tuong, and, pressed, too, by Ta Van Phung's anti-dynastic rebellion in the north, the imperial government ceded them in a treaty of June 1862. Taking Cambodia under protection was followed in 1867 by Admiral La Grandière's annexation of the three western provinces, meeting little opposition from the dynasty, more from partisans. The Tu-duc emperor believed 'that strengthening rather than attenuating Confucian preeminence was the appropriate response to the challenge of the West'.[77] Hoping to regain the lost provinces, he followed a course of appeasement, even during the Franco-Prussian war of 1870–71, when a Catholic mandarin, Nguyen Truong To, suggested an offensive against the French: they 'would treat our people like fish on the chopping block'.[78] The policy was a complete failure.

In the 1870s the French authorities in Cochin-China became disposed to move north, especially as they conceived that the Red River might provide the access to China that they had found that the Mekong did not provide. At first the Paris government restrained them—the adventurer Francis Garnier's death at Hanoi in 1873 was an embarrassment—and then it removed its curb. In 1882–83 the French secured control over lower Tonkin, and defying the intervention of the Chinese, whose help the dynasty had invoked, they proceeded to establish a protectorate over the rest of the empire, contested by partisans inspired by the Ham-nghi's emperor's final flight from Hué. Only at the last did the Nguyen seek to invoke the kind of loyalty that had once helped Vietnamese leaders to oppose Chinese invaders. Turning out the European invaders was to take more than that. In 1887 the French created the Union Indochinoise under a governor-general. The future of Laos and of Siam itself came into question.

Cambodia and Laos

Unlike its bigger neighbours, Cambodia had not consolidated itself in the late eighteenth century, and it was the more open to their intervention because of its own factionalism. 'Please let me be subjected to the merit and power of both great king-doms', the king pleaded, 'so that my people can live in peace and happiness'.[79] Cambodia looked to British protection, and then to French. Under French protection, King Norodom lost much of his power, and he played an equivocal role in the revolt of 1885. The French, however, retained the monarchy, and regained the provinces the Thais had kept in the 1860s. The 1907 treaty meant the regaining of Angkor—'my Alsace-Lorraine', as King Sisowath called it[80]—though there was some guerrilla oppo-sition to the take-over. Cambodia was thus reconstituted by imperialist intervention.

The division of Laos after the collapse of Lan Xang had left it, too, exposed to its more effective neighbours. The Burmese capacity to intervene depended on pos-sessing Chiengmai, which they finally lost in 1798. The Thais had invaded Vientiane in 1778, marking their success by taking the Emerald Buddha to Bangkok, and their general, who became Rama I, used his opportunity to intervene in the Lao states. Anu, the king installed at Vientiane, rebelled in 1826, following a rumour that the British were set to attack Bangkok. That prompted a harsh Thai military interven-tion: Vientiane was torched in 1827.[81] 'If the goals of the current armed invasion are only to satisfy their hatred, to pillage goods, and to seize young girls and bring them to Siam', Hoang Kim Hoan, a high Vietnamese official, wrote, 'then we have nothing to say about it. But if they occupy the kingdom of the Ten Thousand Elephants, our buffer zone would disappear.'[82] Minh-mang was cautious, and Anu met an appalling fate at Thai hands.

Under the mandala system, the Lao states had offered tribute to Vietnam as well as Siam. Taking over Vietnam, France determined to back its claims, though they were flimsy, and the Lao had seen them as a means of reducing the influence of Siam and maximising their own independence. The Thais were forced to surrender all their claims east of the Mekong, but the French did not go further. Thus, though they reconstituted Cambodia, they did not seek to reconstitute Lan Xang. They pressed no claim to Isan, left under Siam. Nor did they treat what they secured in a unified way: Luang Prabang was protected territory, the rest directly administered. For the French Laos was a protection for and a hinterland to Vietnam. 'The effect … was perma-nently to divide the Lao territories and to relegate French Laos to the status of a remote colonial backwater, landlocked, underpopulated and underdeveloped.'[83] Imperial intervention saved Laos from extinction, but permanently reduced it to a minor power, in which ethnic Lao were no more than 50 per cent of the population. Extending it further, however, would have met British opposition as well as Thai.

Kon-baung Burma

Laos was important to the British because their interests in Malaya and Burma prompted them, once the French established themselves in Vietnam, to see Siam as a buffer state. Over Burma they had long been especially sensitive, for, to a greater extent than the other states of Southeast Asia, it fell, to use Crawfurd's phrase, 'within the pale of our Indian diplomacy'. Indeed, British policy towards Burma was influenced less by the commercial concerns of an industrial power than by the security concerns of a territorial power, less by those of the United Kingdom than those of the Indian Empire. Those security concerns covered, of course, the possibility of a direct threat, but they went beyond that. A territorial empire needs to insulate itself from such a possibility by ensuring that its immediate neighbours offer no challenge. In this the British empire in India was not exceptional. In another sense, however, it was, and that was underlined by the Mutiny of 1857. It depended, as James Brooke had put it, on the reign of 'opinion', on 'prestige'. That could be undermined by a threat from the outside, still more by a defeat. Neighbouring states were expected to show a degree of submission as the price of their continued independence. States elsewhere in Southeast Asia, colonial or otherwise, could secure their independence by offering commercial opportunity. Burma's case was different.

If British requirements were exceptional, the Burmese monarchy was in no position to offer an exceptional response. The building-up of the Company's territorial dominion in India coincided with the expansion of the assertive new monarchy of Alaung-hpaya and his successors. Like Vietnam and Siam, Burma had been revolutionised and reconstituted, and it renewed earlier objectives in a new context. Its success did not make it easy to respond to the British in the way they wanted, though it was incomplete. Pressed by the Burmans, the Shan saw-bwas had appealed to China, and its intervention led the Burmans to withdraw from Ayudhya after sacking it. That allowed Taksin to rebuild the Thai kingdom, and Bodaw-hpaya vainly attacked again in 1785–86. But, partly in order to contend with Siam, Burma deported population from Manipur, which raids kept in subjection, and after 1784–85 it held Arakan in subjection, too. That gave it a common frontier with the British Company in Bengal. The questions that raised also raised the larger questions: what relationship could be established between empire and monarchy, British and Burmese, given their different history and perspective?

The contact between Company and dynasty had begun badly with the massacre at Negrais. Alaung-hpaya had also destroyed the French settlement at Syriam, but the French continued to see Burma as a means of threatening the British in India. In the War of American Independence they used naval bases at Rangoon and Mergui, but after it, they abandoned their more ambitious plans. At the same time, however, Bodaw-hpaya's conquest of Arakan brought a new risk of conflict between his kingdom and the Company. Many refugees fled across the frontier, and in 1794 there was a major rebellion, after which the Burmese army crossed the Naaf in pursuit of its opponents. To improve relations, to ascertain that the French had not renewed their interest with the opening of the European war, and to investigate the commercial prospects, the governor-general sent a diplomatic mission to the Burmese capital, headed by Michael Symes. He was told that the king could not treat equally with a viceroy. He concluded that, proud and victorious, the Burmese had 'an extravagant opinion of their own power'. Any aggression must be repelled, but a 'reasonable allowance' should be made for their 'mistaken principles'. Britain should work for a good understanding, but not a close connexion: 'it is to our interest to maintain their independence and to guard it from foreign encroachment'.[84]

More refugees were settled at Cox's Bazaar in 1799. While the Company would not decline to receive them, it was not able to prevent their using British territory as a base for attacking their conquerors. William Francklin advised Governor-General Wellesley that the proper course was to conclude with Burma the kind of 'subsidiary alliance' the Company made with Indian states. Symes was sent on a second mission in 1802. But it was, not surprisingly, completely vain. His only consolation was that French influence was also rejected. A further mission, led by John Canning in 1803, got no further than Rangoon. 'It seems', he reported, that Bodaw-hpaya 'will treat with no power on earth as an equal, but he graciously receives under his protection China, Ceylon, Assam, and the British Empire in India. He will grant a boon but will not make a treaty.'[85]

The renewal of Arakanese opposition both added to the Burman king's distrust of the British and diminished his estimate of their strength. After 1817 he intervened in Assam, and a new series of border incidents followed. Moreover, fleeing the Burmans, Manipuris moved into British-protected Cachar, and news came that the Burmans were planning to attack Chittagong. It was at this point, early in 1824, that Governor-General Amherst determined on war: 'no permanent security from the aggression of the Burmese … can be safely calculated on, until that people shall have been made to feel the consequences of their provoking the British government to depart from the pacific tone of policy it has hitherto pursued'.[86] The aim was 'to produce such an impression of the power and resources of the British empire in India as will deter the Court of Ava from any attempt again to disturb the friendly relations which may be re-established by the result of the present contest'.[87]

The British emphasis was on the demonstration of their power. Acquiring territory was not the initial aim. It became necessary only because the demonstration of that power proved unconvincing. It had to be demonstrated in a different way, one that would in the event make it more difficult to develop in the future the kind of relationship the rulers of British India sought. Without new peace terms, as the Court of Directors said, 'success would not have been manifest … and the powers of India might have been tempted to believe that the British government had at last encountered an enemy whom it had failed to humble'.[88]

The war-plan had been a good one: to attack from the south and compel the Burmese to divert their attention from the north. Rangoon was taken in May 1824. But the Burmese did not surrender, the Mons did not rise, and the lack of transport prevented further advance before the monsoon set in. A total of 11 000 men died in Rangoon, including 5000 Europeans. In 1825 the British took Prome, and early in 1826 the fighting approached Pagan. The peace negotiations that had been intermittently conducted during the struggle were now concluded at Yandabo, three days from Ava. Under it King Bagyidaw ceded Arakan, Assam, and Tenasserim, promised to abstain from interference in Manipur and Cachar, and undertook to pay an indemnity of one crore of rupees. A British Resident was to be sent to Ava, and a Burmese envoy to Calcutta, and another treaty was to settle commercial relations.

The annexation of Burmese territories was a poor substitute for the confession of submissiveness that the British had aimed to obtain. Indeed it produced resentment, and a wish to undo the treaty, rather than to build upon it. The first Resident, John Crawfurd, secured a commercial treaty late in 1826, but the monarchy saw it as no more than a licence to trade. Crawfurd indeed recommended against making the position of Resident permanent: he would be 'an object of perpetual jealousy to a Government indescribably ignorant and suspicious'.[89] A Burmese embassy to Calcutta sought to reopen the treaty of Yandabo, and there were raids across the now much-extended common frontier. Their continuance led the governor-general to reconsider the acceptance of Crawfurd's advice, and Henry Burney was appointed Resident late in 1829.

Successful at Bangkok, Burney was at first successful at Ava. Compromising on protocol by removing his shoes, he was able to make direct contact with the king. On his advice, too, the governor-general agreed to a settlement of the disputed boundary of Manipur in Burma's favour, though he would not back down, as the Burmese wished, on the indemnity. The real problem, at least with Bagyidaw, remained the one to which Crawfurd had referred. 'More than any other man in his empire', Burney wrote, 'he feels and broods over the disasters of the late war; and of all this nation that war has left the least impression of our superiority upon his mind'.[90]

The attitude of the next king, Tharrawaddy, who seized power in 1837, was no more positive: he sought to reject the treaty of Yandabo without actually breaking it. He told Burney 'that the English had not conquered him or made the treaty with him, and that he was determined to have nothing to say to it'. If he sought its modification, Burney replied, he should send an embassy to Bengal. The king replied that, if he sent an embassy, it should be to the king, not to a mere governor-general. 'I am determined to place the relations between the two countries on precisely the same footing as they were previous to the reign of the late King who committed a blunder in going to war with you.'[91] Burney left the capital for Rangoon. He thought it necessary to place British relations with Burma 'on a more solid and secure footing'. If Tharrawaddy would not distinctly acknowledge the subsistence of the treaty and the authority of the governor-general, the British should 'intimidate' him by 'an extensive military demonstration' before he grew too strong or was able to 'take advantage of any occupation which some other power may give our armies in Hindustan'.[92]

The recommendation was not followed, and the Calcutta government appointed a successor to Burney. Resenting the treatment he received, he left the capital in 1839, and his assistant was withdrawn from Rangoon in 1840. No 'military demonstration' ensued. Lord Auckland was indeed concentrating on 'some other power', Afghanistan. A war with Burma, he had argued, might secure Pegu, and it might in time pay for 'the expense of its acquisition and maintenance', but he had 'no ambition to try this experiment'. He considered it 'a settled maxim of Indian policy that a war with Ava is to be avoided if possibly it may be avoided without dishonour or the sacrificing of undoubted and essential rights, and in support of such maxim I need scarcely dwell upon the degree to which the strength and resources of the state are likely to be elsewhere employed'.[93]

Appointing a Resident was, as Crawfurd had suggested, always a doubtful policy, since the kind of treatment he received might not be the kind of treatment the British authorities in India could accept. The absence of any representative at the Burmese court, however, removed a means of settling other disputes that arose along the common frontier or as a result of the opening of Rangoon to foreign trade. Receiving a Resident was not made easy, however. He was indeed the envoy of a governor-general, and his appointment followed a war which had not achieved its real purpose. The British government in India was not anxious for another war, of which further territorial acquisition was the likely outcome. But there was little prospect that the succeeding years would be used in a way that might reduce the risk of it. A stand-off was not a solution.

The origins of the second Anglo-Burman war are easily misinterpreted: the acquisition of Pegu seems to result from a minor dispute involving some not very reputable British traders. In Britain, indeed, Lord Dalhousie was the target of Richard Cobden's pamphlet, 'How wars are got up in India'. But an explanation of the conflict has to take account of the larger issues involved in the relationship of the British with Burma, in particular those that related in their view to the security of their dominion in India. The decision to take up the complaints of the British traders may have represented, as Pollak argues, an attempt of the Calcutta authorities to assert themselves while the governor-general was up-country,[94] and Commodore Lambert, sent with the demand for redress, certainly proved more 'combustible' than expected. Even so, it was essential that the Burmese demonstrate their compliance: as Dalhousie put it, 'we can't afford to be shown to the door anywhere in the East'.[95] The somewhat paradoxical answer he found to his dilemma was to face the Burmese government with a still more stringent demand—for an indemnity of ten lakhs of rupees—the acceptance of which would put Burma in its proper place without the need for a war. When Dalhousie's ultimatum expired, and the expedition he had prepared stood off Rangoon, a steamer was sent ahead with a flag of truce to ascertain whether the king had responded: a threat, but also a last attempt at peace. '[A] blow struck promptly and severely' might convince the Burmese of the superiority of British military power, 'recall to their memories' the unhappy result of the previous war, and 'deter them from entering on the hazards of another encounter'. If it succeeded, 'a vast political advantage would be gained by the restoration of the friendly relations between the states'. If it did not secure immediate submission, the defeat of the Burmese army and the retention of Rangoon would convince Burma of its inferiority and aid in an 'extended' war.[96]

He prosecuted the war much more effectively than Amherst had conducted the first, but no sign came from the court. How then was the acceptance of British

superiority to be demonstrated? Only, as Amherst had found in rather different circumstances, by taking territory: Pegu itself. That was 'the only adequate measure for
the punishment of the Burmese, for the reimbursement of expenses, and for ensuring peace by crippling Burman power'.[97] It was, however, enough. The Secret
Committee of the Company wanted the acquisition accepted by the Burmese in a
treaty. Dalhousie did not think that a treaty, even if it was worth having, could readily be secured. It would, he believed, require the conquest of the Burmese capital
itself. That the Burmans would not welcome, though the Mons might. 'The British
have stripped them of all their conquests one after another. … And if we shall still
proceed, and … shall invade their own soil, drive out their sovereign, and impose
dominion upon them; on what conceivable ground can it be supposed that they will
view us with favour, and hail our supremacy?' The annexation of Pegu, by contrast,
would give the British security 'by depriving the Burmese of much of their means for
carrying on the war, and by arming us with commanding advantages calculated to
deter them from attempting it'.[98]

The new king, Mindon, was, as Arthur Phayre put it, 'afraid to incur the odium of
signing away the lower provinces of his kingdom'.[99] But he saw the value of peace, and
he made a real attempt to improve relations with the British. Even though his initial
hope that he would persuade them to leave Pegu was disappointed, the complimen-
tary mission he sent to Calcutta in 1854 was received with great state, and the governor-general sent a mission to his capital in response the following year. The fact that
British representation at the court was at this time informal rather than an official
also assisted the restoration of relations: Thomas Spears, a Scottish merchant, was an
intermediary acceptable to both parties. The Burmans made no attempt to take
advantage of the British during the Crimean War or the Indian Mutiny: indeed the
king gave a thousand pounds to the Mutiny relief fund. In 1862, Phayre, now Chief
Commissioner of British Burma, was able to negotiate a commercial treaty, permitting British traders to operate all along the Irrawaddy, the main objective being to
open up backdoor access to the trade of China. A Resident was appointed, and in
1867 a further treaty was negotiated by Phayre's successor, Fytche, including the abolition of monopolies. But by this time relations had begun to deteriorate.

Mindon's attempts at 'defensive westernisation'[100] were not in themselves a threat
to the British. His attempts to emulate Siam in another way were more risky. In 1854
he had turned aside the proposal to appoint a Sardinian consul, lest it might 'provide the thin end of the wedge the British were looking for'.[101] But he sent a mission
to the United States in 1857, and early in the 1870s he expanded Burma's contacts
with other powers. A number of approaches were made to Russia, and the oriental-
ist P. I. Pachino, who visited Burma, claimed that Mindon was deeply interested in
Peter the Great.[102] A mission headed by the Kinwun Mingyi U Gaung went to Italy
and France, as well as to Britain. In London it secured no government contacts, but
in Paris it was able to conclude a commercial treaty in 1873. This, however, the
French, apprehensive of British protests, did not ratify. For Mindon wanted to go

further, seeking an alliance and a supply of firearms. The latter he needed to sustain the monarchy's position in the mountain territories, but the Calcutta government had resiled from an annexe to the Fytche treaty more or less guaranteeing their availability while the countries maintained friendly relations. Anglo-Burman relations were also damaged in Mindon's later years by the 'shoe question'. Like Burney, other British envoys had all compromised on court protocol, so that they did not appear in the royal presence with shoes on. In 1875, however, Sir Douglas Forsyth protested, and the governor-general ruled out the compromise. The result was that British envoys lost their direct contact with the king. 'As the old King was his own Minister of Foreign Affairs', wrote the Resident Horace Browne in 1879, 'and no negotiations were ever concluded except at personal interviews with him, this sudden change put an absolute stop to all important business'.[103]

The accession of the new king, Thibaw, had been accompanied by a massacre of members of the royal family, but the government in London did not accept that this was an argument for intervention. In October 1879 the Residency was withdrawn after the murder of the Resident in Afghanistan. The overthrow of a traditionalist faction at the court led, however, to an attempt to put Anglo-Burman relations on a new footing, and a Burman mission left for Calcutta and Simla. The Secretary of State, Lord Ripon, responding to its statesmanlike suggestion, agreed that the Indian government should make a commercial treaty with Burma, while there should also be a friendship treaty between Queen Victoria and King Thibaw. Burma would thus gain the direct connexion with the government in London that had evaded Mindon, while the arrangements would also reflect the dual origin and nature of British interests. But the Burmese, hoping for more because of Britain's current embarrassment in Egypt, let the opportunity slip.

More dangerous still, the Burmese government sent a new mission to Europe, led by the Myotat Atwinwun. It made a commercial treaty with Germany, which did not arouse British suspicions. Its activities in France did, particularly because the French were at this time establishing themselves in northern Vietnam. The French now ratified the 1873 treaty, though without the disputed articles. Ferry indeed sought to reassure the British, telling Lord Lyons, the British ambassador, about the negotiations for a supplementary treaty: it had, he said, no political or military articles. But he had given the Burmese ambassador a note, promising to supply arms and military equipment from Tonkin when peace and order had been established there.[104]

In the capital, Mandalay, Italian and French concession-seekers were interested in mines and forests, and the activities of the French consul, who arrived in May 1885, alarmed his Italian counterpart. Agent for a British firm, the Bombay Burmah Trading Corporation, he feared that its timber concessions would be transferred to the French, and he made use of the Ferry letter, of which he had secured a copy. French commercial and political dominance at Mandalay could not be allowed, the British government decided. The Burmese government rejected the British proposal for arbitrating its dispute with the timber company, and that was made the occasion for the ultimatum with which it was presented on 22 October, requiring Burma to put its foreign relations under British control. The ultimatum was rejected. Troops crossed into Burma on 14 November, and Mandalay was occupied on 28 November.

The reasons for the third Burma war have been the subject of controversy. D. P. Singhal argued in *The Annexation of Upper Burma*[105] that the main motives for Britain's policy were economic. In fact the government was not responding primarily to the needs of the merchants at Rangoon or even the BBTC, but rather to what it saw as security imperatives. Only briefly, in the early years of Mindon's reign, had Burma fitted into what the British saw as its proper role. But there had never been any chance that the British could accept at the Burmese capital the kind of foreign influence against which they had sought to guard for more than a century. 'It is French intrigue which has forced us to go to Burmah', Lord Randolph Churchill told the House of Commons on 18 November; 'but for that element we might have treated Theebaw with severe neglect. … If … you finally and fully add Burmah to your dominions before any European rights have had time even to be sown, much less grow up, you undoubtedly prevent forever the assertion of such rights, or attempts to prepare the way for such assertion.'[106]

Above all because of its proximity to India, the British treated Burma in a way that differed from their practice elsewhere in Southeast Asia. Furthermore, they now proceeded not only to exile Thibaw, but to abolish the monarchy. The ultimatum had not envisaged that, and Lord Dufferin, the governor-general, at first opposed annexation. But no 'protected prince', he was advised, could maintain his throne without Indian troops, and the Indian government would be burdened with responsibilities without having control. 'Upper Burma' was incorporated into the Indian empire on 26 February 1886. That the Chinese did not like, but they made only a mild protest at the destruction of a former vassal, and in a convention of July 1886 it was agreed that Burma would send a mission every ten years on a basis of equality.

Pacification was, on the other hand, to prove a major task. The British neglected the possibility that their taking direct control would magnify rather than reduce the opposition they were already facing from guerrilla groups. They were more than mere dacoits. They were led by real or pretended princes, and by hereditary *thugyi*, with monks behind the scenes, attesting to a concern that Buddhism was under threat. '[I]t had been supposed', as Commissioner Crosthwaite put it, 'that our coming was welcome to the people and that "the prospects of the substitution of a strong and orderly government for the incompetent and cruel tyranny of their former ruler" was by the people generally regarded with pleasure. But by July [1886], it had become evident that a considerable minority of the population, to say the least, did not want us.'[107] By the early 1890s the British had 35 000 troops in upper Burma. There was some disorder in lower Burma, too.

The British also extended their authority over the 'minorities', initially 'visiting' the hill chiefs with a substantial force, 'essentially an indigenous tactic',[108] putting down resistance, and securing allegiance. The Shan chiefs had been challenging Mandalay, but, unlike the Saw-bwa of Yawnghwe, not all turned to the British. British military expeditions would, as Chief Commissioner Bernard put it, allow the British to 'con-firm all *de facto* rulers and overawe intending breakers of the peace'.[109] The states kept their autonomy, a resident adviser being attached to each saw-bwa. When the Shan states were federated in 1922, a federal council of saw-bwas was set up.

French motives in Burma may be clarified, Patrick Tuck has suggested, by a later statement by François Deloncle, a participant in the Franco-Burmese negotiations. Ferry, he said, had asked him to negotiate the new agreement

> in such a way that the British might become aware of our desire to develop an interest in independent Upper Burma, where they were so jealous of their own influence, and that, thenceforth, they might be prepared to make exchanges which would allow us, if need be, against the withdrawal of our interest in Burma, to obtain concessions in Siam. This would at least enable us to keep the British on tenterhooks in the Malay Peninsula. What Jules Ferry wanted was to conclude an agreement with Burma which would give him the tiller in Siam.[110]

In a sense, therefore, the French had risked the independence of Burma for a possi-ble gain on the other side of the mainland. There, indeed, the British were to resist their incursion into Siam with some effect.

Though the 1896 agreement established a ' buffer state', French Laos and British Burma had a common frontier on the upper Mekong. The British had extended their control over the Shan states that had paid tribute to the Burmese monarchy, but abandoned those beyond the river, 'trotting out Burmese claims whenever it suited them, or ignoring such claims whenever necessary', as Chao Tzang Yawnghwe puts it, though never, he regrets, dropping Shan vassalage to Burma.[111] The Chin tribes accepted British authority in 1895. A boundary with India was readily agreed. One with China was less easily secured. In 1900 it agreed to a line between Myitkyina in the Kachin territory and the Salween river, and the Namwan tract was leased to Britain to facilitate communication between Bhamo and the Shan states. Over the rest of the frontier the Chinese acquiesced rather than agreed.

The Andaman and Nicobar islands

The security of the Bay of Bengal that interested the British Company in Negrais, in Trincomalee, and in Penang, interested it also in the Andaman islands. Lieut. Archibald Blair was sent to survey them in 1788, the object being

> the acquisition of an Harbour where fleets in time of war can refit by any means, on leaving the coast of Coromandel upon the approach of the stormy monsoon, or to which any part or the whole may retire in the Event of a disastrous conflict with an Enemy and so obtain a Central position in the Bay, whence the ship may return to the Scene of Action, as soon as possible.[112]

The settlement, made in 1789, was also designed to shelter the shipwrecked, and to check Malay pirates, to whose slave-raiding Blair ascribed the Andamanese hostility to strangers. Placed at the present Port Blair, then called Cornwallis, it was moved to what proved to be a more unhealthy site, and abandoned in 1796. Sir A. Campbell's expedition against Burma made rendezvous there, however, in 1824.

In 1856 the commissioner in Arakan suggested the establishment on the Andamans of a Burmese penal settlement. Lord Canning, the governor-general, was opposed: 'we must consider our means and the … liabilities which we may bring upon ourselves'. His colleague, J. P. Grant, asked for 'some visible sign of actual dominion. … I take it for granted that no foreign power should be allowed to estab-lish herself in the Andamans or Nicobars. Whatever was the case before, the conquest of Pegu has made the Bay of Bengal a British Sea.'[113] He also argued the case for a con-vict station. The outbreak of the Indian Mutiny was the clinching argument. 'Port Blair' was reoccupied. Clashes with the Andamanese ensued, including the so-called 'battle of Aberdeen' on 14 April 1859. A more conciliatory policy followed, but proved even more destructive of those who were won over: they were devastated by 'the gifts of civilization (tobacco, alcohol, venereal and other diseases)'.[114]

The French used Nancowry in the Nicobars in the wars of American independ-ence and the Revolution. The Danish East India Company, based at Tranquebar, had attempted to settle on the islands after 1756, and maintained a small guard there between 1793 and 1807. Postwar a Danish settlement was established on Kamorta in 1831. It was withdrawn in 1838, though Danish claims were not abandoned. Two French missionaries, sent from Siam, were present when Denmark resumed posses-sion in 1845, but it again abandoned its effort in 1848. The subsequent renewal of allegedly Malay-led attacks on visiting ships, often described as piracy, but partly at least due to provocation, prompted the British to establish a settlement at Nancowry in 1869. Maintained till 1888, it was resumed after World War I.

Conclusion

An extended discussion of this phase is justified both by the changes that it brought and by their long-term implications. Almost all of Southeast Asia became more or less formally divided into colonial states, more or less effectively under the control of metropolitan powers in the West, and even Siam, which retained its independ-ence, was dramatically changed. The nature of the state in Southeast Asia, and the relationship between Southeast Asia and the rest of the world, were transformed.

In a major sense, the changes were brought about by the projection of European power into the region on an entirely new scale. That began even before Europe began to industrialise, in particular with the conquest of India. Nor was it ever prompted merely by economic motives: the search for security, the handling of rivalry, the need to respond to a domestic political constituency, all played their part. But it was true that, as industrialisation gained momentum and spread from Britain to other countries, the search for markets and resources took on new dimensions, and its intensification added to the complexity of the problems that non-European states had to face, and the range of Europeans with whom they had to deal.

The shift in power relationships was accompanied by a shift in attitude. In the phase of commercial empires, Asian states might be dealt with ruthlessly, but also without condescension. In the early nineteenth century, men like Raffles began to think, somewhat romantically, of the past glories of states which they might help to restore. By the late nineteenth century, the attitude had altered again, as, for example, the changing attitudes of the Brookes to Brunei suggested. There were 'dying kingdoms', as there were 'dying peoples'. The discovery or rediscovery of ancient monuments now seemed the testimony to an irrecoverable, even inexplicable, past. A shift in the Western concept of international law also took place. 'Natural law' theorists gave way to 'positive law' theorists. The former tended to see non-European political groups as 'states' like European states. The latter, basing their views on consent, tended to exclude them from equality. 'The conversion of Asian States, which before the nineteenth century had been members of the universal family of nations, into candidates for admission to this family or for recognition by the leading powers was brought about by doctrinal changes, particularly by the abandonment of the natural law doctrine and adherence to positivism of the European brand.'[115]

The discussion should not, however, imply that the outcome, in Southeast Asia or elsewhere, was simply the result of the application of Western power, and entirely in accordance with Western policy. The study is properly one of the interrelationship between the Europeans and the Southeast Asian states and peoples. In some cases that interrelationship was complicated by the relationships among the Europeans. Rivalry was a long-standing feature of their activities overseas, and in the nineteenth century it was still influential, though modified by the temporary primacy of the British. They supported minor European powers over against major ones, but also tended to conciliate and accommodate major powers when they offered no clear threat.

Those relations affected the position of the Asian states. Playing off one European power against a rival had always been a high-risk strategy, and it remained so. The better strategy in this period was to conciliate the major power, whose interest, moreover, was generally not in territorial expansion but in commercial opportunity. But the deals it had made, explicitly with the Dutch and implicitly with the Spaniards, in effect precluded the development of political connexions between it and the Malayo-Muslim rulers of the archipelago. For much of the century they maintained a *de facto* independence. It could not, however, be actively exerted.

On the mainland, it was more difficult for the Burmans to maintain their independence than their neighbours, for there the normal requirements of British policy were overlaid by the exceptional security requirements of the Indian empire. At the same time, it is clear that the Burman monarchy was more inflexible than the Thai. So, too, was the Vietnamese, though for different reasons. The Thais were able to come to terms with the British, but the Vietnamese, apprehensive of a threat to their hard-won unity, neglected the opportunities they were offered. They lost their independence to a France that had not yet undergone an industrial revolution but was ruled by regimes that all sought the glory of territorial empire and was represented by adventurers and adventurous naval commanders.

In a retrospective account, such as this, it is easy to assume that contemporaries then knew what seems evident to us. What was at issue, it may be suggested, was whether the Southeast Asian states would in the new circumstances remain autonomous actors among the other states of the world or not. Only Siam effectively achieved it. The other states of the world were in, or were entering, an international framework that had developed in Europe since the collapse of the Holy Roman Empire: one in which states were equal in sovereignty, but not in power, and in which continued independence might therefore depend on modifying in practice what was claimed in theory, one in which, too, written commitments played a role in affirming political relationships, though not rendering them permanent. Southeast Asia's approach had differed. States, it was recognised, were unequal in power, and were in competition. But the inter-state pattern was set in the form of a collection of mandala, which reflected inequality and competition through shifting and overlapping tributary relationships.

Survival depended in part on skilful diplomacy, and that depended in part on good information. Information, moreover, has to be processed. In the nineteenth century Asian rulers had often to change their 'personal constructs of the world if their states were to survive'.[116] Southeast Asian rulers were often at a loss. In the 1840s 'the Rajas of Buleleng, Karangasem and Klungkung, as well as the Raja of Lombok, regarded the Dutch as a potential ally in the struggle that really mattered: the struggle among themselves'. None realised that the Dutch were 'a threat of a different order'.[117] What Southeast Asian states knew about European states was far less than what European states knew about each other. Their sources of information were not only limited: they were also prejudiced. And even when it was available information might be misinterpreted.

The ruler of Johore preferred on the basis of past experience to renew its old working relationship with the Dutch after the French wars, rather than to offer the British the port they sought: the Malays, as Dianne Lewis has put it, 'had been misled by the vagaries of a policy whose foundations they had no means of knowing'.[118] The result was the acquisition of Singapore and the effective break-up of their empire. In 1865 King Mongkut commented to King Norodom of Cambodia on the catastrophe their neighbours faced in Cochin-China: 'it so happened that the Vietnamese were stubborn and determined to hold on to their old policy. They did not know the real strength of the maritime powers and there was nobody to tell them of the real might and custom of these distant lands.'[119] Which was the cat and which the rat? Pengiran Mahkota of Brunei asked James Brooke, when they discussed the British and the Dutch.[120] The answer in this case was clear. But on what sources could Thibaw rely?—he had never moved more than five miles from Mandalay—or Sultan

Hashim of Brunei?—an illiterate among self-serving consuls and courtiers, who had probably never ventured beyond Labuan, he was *katak di-bawah tempurong,* a frog under a coconut shell.[121]

Lack of information made it difficult to take the decisions that would maximise the chance of independence. Information was also manipulated by court factions or obscured by court protocol. At Thibaw's court the Taingda advocated war, and the Kinwun was against it. The queen turned the balance against the Kinwun: 'Bring him … a petticoat and a fan'.[122] Two factions offered Tu-duc advice in the 1860s: the advocates of war, *chu chien,* Confucian hardliners; and the advocates of peace, *chu hoa,* who pointed out that, though the West had humbled China, it had not deprived it of territory.[123] Among the partisans there was an 'almost total lack' of intelligence about the enemy: they could not know how 'politically precarious' the venture was in Paris.[124]

For their part, the European powers preferred to get their way with a minimum of force. That may be true of all regimes. It was perhaps particularly true in this case. The British used their great power sparingly, and the Dutch and the Spaniards wished to avoid displaying their weakness. The preference was for demonstrating power in a convincing manner, so that it would not need to be continuously deployed. In many cases that worked, but not always. In some cases, too, a regime might surrender or be displaced, but a guerrilla war continue. That was true in Aceh, in Burma, in Vietnam.

In some cases, too, the colonial powers would seek to utilise the remnants of the regimes that they brought under control. To varying degrees old forms and old structures persisted, embedded in the new context of colonial power, or inspiring elements of continued resistance. The establishment of the colonial regimes in Southeast Asia was a striking change, but the extent of their hold on Southeast Asia was still in question. Their establishment and their maintenance depended on the application of force in the context of local collaboration. Their weakness was to be conclusively demonstrated by the incursion of another outside power. But even before the Japanese invasion, the colonial powers, it may be suggested, had demonstrated their transitional character. Their territories were not modern states; they were modernising. Their future in a world of states was in question.

In one sense they were modern, but even in that sense incompletely. They had borders of a definiteness that often earlier states had not. What had traditionally concerned rulers was the people not the place. The sense of geographical or locational entity was less strong. 'Thus a British surveyor trying to demarcate the boundaries of a Malay state in 1875 could elicit no more exact information from the local potentate concerning the limits of his territory than that if you wash your head before starting, it will not be dry before you reach the place.'[125] European states had developed quite a different view. States had definite borders, within which the population was composed of subjects or citizens. It was this concept of the frontier that the colonial powers brought with them to Southeast Asia, and accordingly they drew lines on their map of the region. One object was to avoid dispute among themselves.

The lines they drew might be quite arbitrary so far as long-standing economic and political realities were concerned, as the treaty of 1824 or the protocol of 1885, for example, clearly indicated.

It was in that sense that the frontiers differed from those in Europe, though they were ostensibly similar. There, by contrast, they had developed over a long period, during which states had both consolidated their control and fought out or resolved disputes with each other. Within the frontiers the state had increasingly asserted control over the population, in its final form identifying state and nation. No national ideology identified the colonial state with its rulers, nor could it. Whether an alternative could be found was doubtful. Yet the process of modernisation was set in train, and merely colonial bonds could not suffice once the state became more active and expected more of those it ruled.

The Japanese invasion underlined the weakness of the colonial states, but their interregnum did not remedy it. Instead it contributed to the creation of a Southeast Asia of independent states. Their rulers were inspired by the nationalist ideologies they had derived from Europe and used against the Europeans. But the frontiers of the states they sought to rule inherited the frontiers of the colonial period, created for quite a different purpose. The ensuing tension is one of the long-term results of the phase of colonial state-building.

Wang Gungwu called the colonial regimes 'transitional states', since they were never colonies in the true sense, and apart from the 'semi-colonial' regime in Siam, 'never gained legitimacy in the eyes of the vast majority of their subjects'.[126] They were transitional in another way. Though rarely by intention, the economic and political changes they undertook or mediated were transforming the 'subjects' they claimed. The outcome, we recognise, was the creation of what are seen as nation-states, whose relationships are regulated by a developing pattern of international law and practice. There might, perhaps, have been another 'transitional' phase that took account of the weakness internal and external of the post-'colonial' state. Partially invented, indeed, that was foreclosed in part by its conceptual difficulty: it was also discredited by the interregnum and the postwar struggles in Southeast Asia, and by the triumph of the nation-state concept in general.

Notes

1 'Economic Aspects of the Dutch Expansion in Indonesia, 1870–1914', MAS, 23, 1 (1989), p. 23.
2 'Dutch Expansion in the Indonesian Archipelago … ', JSEAS, 25, 1 (March 1994), p. 106.
3 q. H. E. Egerton, *Sir Stamford Raffles*, London: Unwin, 1900, p. 229.
4 Castlereagh to Clancarty, 13 August 1819, private. F.O. 37/107, Public Record Office, London.
5 Note on Courtenay's memorandum of 15 January 1824, Dutch Records 1/2/32, India Office Library, London.
6 Strangways to Barrow, 9 January 1838. F.O. 37/ 213.
7 Memorandum, 18 August 1860. F.O. 12/28.
8 Loudon to Van de Putte, 25 February 1873, q. A. Reid, *The Contest for North Sumatra*, KL: OUP, 1969, p. 95.

9   H. L. Wesseling, 'Colonial Wars and Armed Peace, 1870–1914 … ', *Itinerario*, 5, 2 (1981), pp. 60–1.

10 A. Reid, *The Blood of the People*, KL: OUP, 1979, p. 7.

11 q. G. J. A. Raven and N. A. M. Rodger, eds, *Navies and Armies*, Edinburgh: Donald, 1990, p. 59.

12 A. van der Kraan, *Lombok: Conquest, Colonization and Underdevelopment*, Singapore: Heinemann, 1980, p. 32.

13 q. ibid., p. 34.

14 H. Sutherland, *The Making of a Bureaucratic Elite*, Singapore: Heinemann, 1979, p. 45.

15 q. H. S. Nordholt, *The Spell of Power* … , Leiden: KITLV P, 1996, pp. 210–11.

16 q. H. S. Nordholt, *Bali: Colonial Conceptions and Political Change, 1700–1840*, Rotterdam: CASP, 1986, p. 5.

17 q. N. Tarling, *The Burthen, the Risk and the Glory*, KL: OUP, 1982, p. 80.

18 Palmerston to Brooke, 23 February 1848. F.O. 12/6.

19 Minute, 18 June 1896. C.O. 144/70 [10680].

20 q. N. Tarling, *Sulu and Sabah*, OUP: KL, 1978, p. 88.

21 N. Tarling, ed., *Mrs Pryer in Sabah*, Auckland: Centre for Asian Studies, 1989, pp. 102–3.

22 q. R. Sullivan, *Exemplar of Americanism*, Ann Arbor: U Mich, 1991, p. 31.

23 q. U. Mahajani, *Philippine Nationalism*, St Lucia: UQP, 1971, p. 120n.

24 John N. Schumacher, *The Propaganda Movement*, Manila: Solidaridad, 1973, p. 197.

25 q. L. M. Guerrero, *The First Filipino*, Manila: National Heroes Commission, 1963, pp. 311–12.

26 q. Luis Camara Dery, *From Ibalon to Sorsogon*, Quezon City: New Day, 1991, p. 184.

27 q. R. C. Ileto and R. Sullivan, *Discovering Australasia*, Townsville: JCU, 1993, p. 36.

28 q. P. Oblas in Chaivat Khamchoo and E. B. Reynolds, eds, *Thai–Japanese Relations in Historical Perpective*, Bangkok: Innomedia, 1988, p. 53.

29 q. M. Kuitenbrouwer, *The Netherlands and the Rise of Modern Imperialism*, Oxford: Berg, 1991, p. 239.

30 ibid., p. 258. See also H. T. Colenbrander and J. E. Stokvis, *Leven en Arbeid van Mr C. Th. van Deventer*, Amsterdam: van Kampen, 1916, II, pp. 42–3.

31 q. Paul Kennedy, *The Rise of the Anglo-German Antagonism*, London: Allen and Unwin, 1980, p. 236.

32 q. Kuitenbrouwer, p. 255.

33 q. R. Bonney, *Kedah, 1771–1821*, KL: OUP, 1771, p. 26.

34 Minute by Clubley, 16 September 1823, G/34/9, India Office Library.

35 q. N. Tarling, *British Policy in the Malay Peninsula and Archipelago, 1824–1871*, KL: OUP, 1969, p. 43.

36 q. W. D. McIntyre, *The Imperial Frontier in the Tropics*, London: Macmillan, 1967, p. 205.

37 q. ibid., pp. 198–9.

38 *The Journals of J. W. W. Birch*, KL: OUP, 1976, p. 30.

39 E. Sadka, *The Protected Malay States*, KL: UMP, 1968, p. 102.

40 q. A. Gopinath, *Pahang, 1880–1933*, KL, 1991, p. 87.

41 q. J. S. Sidhu, *Administration in the Federated Malay States, 1896–1920*, KL: OUP, 1980, p. 39.

42 q. P. Loh Fook Seng, *The Malay States, 1877–1895*, Singapore, KL: OUP, 1969, p. 99.

43 q. J. M. Gullick, *Rulers and Residents*, Singapore: OUP, 1992, p. 151.

44 GG in Co. to Gov. in Co., 19 November 1824. G/34/99.

45 GG in Co. to Gov. in Co., 23 July 1827. G/34/142.

46 Board to FO, 22 November 1849. F.O. 17/163.

47 Palmerston to Brooke, 18 December 1849. F.O. 69/12.

48 Brooke to Stewart, 17 June 1850. J. C. Templer, ed., *The Private Letters of Sir James Brooke*, London: Bentley, 1853, II, p. 304.

49 Brooke to Palmerston, 5 October 1850. F.O. 69/1.

50 Memorial by Boustead et al., 1850. *Singapore Free Press*, 17 January 1851.

51 q. N. Tarling, *Imperial Britain in Southeast Asia*, KL: OUP, 1975, p. 180.

52 q. ibid., p. 219.

53 Chadin Flood, trans. , *The Dynastic Chronicles Bangkok Era Fourth Reign*, Tokyo: Centre for East Asian Cultural Studies, 1965–7, II, pp. 283–5, 302–4.

54 E. Thio, 'Britain's Search for Security in North Malaya, 1886–97', JSEAH, 10, 2 (September 1969), p. 285.

55 M. Stuart-Fox, 'The French in Laos, 1887–1945', MAS, 29, 1 (February 1995), p. 115.

56 q. Thio, p. 292.
57 *Siam in the Twentieth Century*, London: Arnold, 1902, p. 171.
58 q. Walter Tips, *Gustave Rolin-Jaequemyns and the Making of Modern Siam*, Bangkok: White Lotus, 1996, p. 114.
59 Inagaki to Okuma, 10 September 1897, q. Oblas, p. 54.
60 q. J. Chandran, *The Contest for Siam, 1889–1902*, KL: Penerbit UKM, 1977, p. 222.
61 q. A. L. Moffat, *Mongkut, the King of Siam*, Cornell UP, 1961, p. 124.
62 q. A. Lamb, *The Mandarin Road to Old Hué*, London: Chatto, 1970, p. 64.
63 q. A. Lamb, 'British Missions to Cochin China: 1778–1822', JMBRAS, 34, 3 & 4 (1961), p. 84.
64 Lamb, *Hué*, p. 144.
65 q. ibid., p. 233.
66 q. ibid., p. 221.
67 *Journal of an Embassy ... to the Courts of Siam and Cochin China*, London, 1830, I, p. 473.
68 Lamb, JMBRAS, p. 196.
69 John White, *A Voyage to Cochin China*, OUP: KL, reprint, 1972, pp. 246–7.
70 Memorandum, 12 July 1845. F.O. 17/100.
71 Note in Parkes to Hammond, 3 August 1855. F.O. 12/236.
72 q. P. Tuck, *French Catholic Missionaries and the Politics of Imperialism in Vietnam, 1857–1914*, Liverpool UP, 1987, p. 51.
73 p. 49.
74 31 August 1858.
75 M. Turnbull, *The Straits Settlements*, London: Athlone, 1972, p. 240.
76 Malmesbury to Cowley, 21 November 1858. F.O. 27/1240.
77 Mark W. McLeod, 'Nguyen Truong To ... ', JSEAS, 25, 2 (September 1994), p. 319.
78 q. ibid., p. 327.
79 q. Thongchai Winichakul, *Siam Mapped*, U Hawaii P, 1994, p. 85.
80 q. John Tully, *Cambodia under the Tricolour*, Monash U, 1996, p. 10.
81 Tej Bunnag, *The Provincial Administration of Siam*, KL: OUP, 1977, pp. 32–3.
82 q. Mayoury Ngaosyvathn and Pheuiphanh Ngaosyvathn, *Paths to Conflagration*, Cornell U, SEAP, 1998, p. 229.
83 M. Stuart-Fox, *Buddhist Kingdom, Marxist State*, Bangkok: White Lotus, 1996, p. 24.
84 M. Symes, *An Account of an Embassy to the Kingdom of Ava*, London, 1800, pp. 463–4.
85 q. D. G. E. Hall, *Europe and Burma*, London: OUP, 1945, p. 96.
86 q. G. J. Ramachandra, 'The Outbreak of the First Anglo-Burmese War', JMBRAS, 51, 2 (1978), p. 82.
87 Instructions to Campbell, 26 March 1824, q. G. P. Ramachandra, 'Anglo-Burmese Relations, 1795–1826', PhD thesis, University of Hull, 1977, p. 391.
88 q. Ramachandra, thesis, p. 433.
89 *Journal of an Embassy ... to the Court of Ava*, London, 1834, II, Appendix, p. 26.
90 q. N. Tarling, ed., *The Journal of Henry Burney*, Auckland: The University of Auckland New Zealand Asia Institute, 1995, p. 27.
91 q. W. S. Desai, *The History of the British Residency in Burma*, Rangoon: University of Rangoon P, 1939, pp. 295–6.
92 q. ibid., p. 309.
93 q. ibid., p. 392.
94 O. B. Pollak, *Empires in Collision*, Westport: Greenwood, 1979, p. 68.
95 q. D. G. E. Hall, ed., *The Dalhousie–Phayre Correspondence*, London: OUP, 1932, p. xix.
96 q. Aparna Mukherjee, *British Colonial Policy in Burma*, Delhi: Abhinau, 1988, p. 121.
97 q. Hall, p. xxv.
98 Minute, 3 November 1852. *Papers Relating to Hostilities with Burma, presented by Command*, London, 1852, pp. 82–4.
99 q. Pollak, p. 110.
100 ibid., pp. 113–14.
101 ibid., p. 155.
102 R. Quested, 'Russian Interest in Southeast Asia ... ', JSEAS, 1, 2 (September 1970), p. 55.

103 q. Mukherjee, p. 326.

104 C. L. Keeton, *King Thebaw and the Ecological Rape of Burma*, Delhi: Manohar, 1974, app. D, pp. 370–1.

105 Singapore: Eastern Universities P, 1960.

106 q. Keeton, p. 243.

107 q. M. Aung-thwin, 'The British "Pacification" of Burma … ', JSEAS, 16, 2 (September 1985), p. 250.

108 ibid., p. 252.

109 q. Ni Ni Myint, *Burma's Struggle against British Imperialism*, Rangoon: Universities P, 1983, p. 114.

110 q. P. Tuck, *The French Wolf and the Siamese Lamb*, Bangkok: White Lotus, 1995, p. 72.

111 *The Shan of Burma*, Singapore: ISEAS, 1987, p. 78.

112 q. L. P. Mathur, *History of the Andaman and Nicobar Islands, 1756–1966*, Delhi: Sterling, 1968, p. 45.

113 q. Tarling, *Imperial Britain*, pp. 250, 251.

114 *Census of India, 1951*, vol. xvii, Delhi: Manager of Publications, 1955, Introduction, p. ix.

115 C. H. Alexandrowicz, *An Introduction to the History of the Law of Nations in the East Indies*, Oxford: Clarendon P, 1967, p. 235.

116 D. Gillard, 'British and Russian Relations with Asian Governments in the Nineteenth Century', in Hedley Bull and A. Watson, eds, *The Expansion of International Society*, Oxford: Clarendon P, 1984, p. 97.

117 A. van der Kraan, *Bali at War*, Monash U, 1995, pp. 185–6.

118 in B. Barrington, ed., *Empires, Imperialism and Southeast Asia*, Clayton: Monash Asia Institute, 1997, p. 32.

119 q. N. Snidvongs, 'The Development of Siamese Relations with Britain and France in the Reign of Maha Mongkut', PhD thesis, University of London, 1961, p. 209.

120 N. Tarling, *The Burthen, the Risk and the Glory*, KL: OUP, 1982, p. 30.

121 A. V. M. Horton, 'British Administration in Brunei', MAS, 20, 2 (April 1986), p. 357.

122 q. Keeton, p. 257.

123 Mark W. McLeod, 'The Treaty of Sai-gon … ', PhD thesis, UCLA, 1988, pp. 120–3.

124 D. Marr, *Vietnamese Anticolonialism*, UCP, 1971, p. 33.

125 q. C. A Fisher in W. G. East and O. H. K. Spate, eds, *The Changing Map of Asia*, London: Methuen, 1950, p. 197.

126 in A. Reid, ed., *Sojourners and Settlers*, St Leonards: Allen and Unwin, 1996 p. 8.

Puppets and Partners

Though the Japanese had long had an interest in Southeast Asia, they had not planned to invade it. Their occupation policies were therefore improvisatory. Between the world wars the weakness of the Western powers had, however, been apparent. The regimes of the Americans, British, and Dutch were quickly overthrown. They planned to return at the end of the war, but took too little account of the changes that the occupation, by accident and design, had brought about.

The concept of a world of states the Europeans perceived at the outset of their endeavours in Asia was never entirely abandoned and, even at the height of the colonial period, it could be argued that imperialism was but a necessary step towards it. When the natives of India 'in some future age [were] sufficiently enlightened to frame a regular government for themselves, and to conduct and preserve it', it would 'probably be best for both countries', Sir Thomas Munro had written, 'that the British control over India should be gradually withdrawn'.[1] 'Security and order, are the bases of government, and from these, in the progress of time, must be evolved an enlightenment and civilization suited to the people', Sir James Brooke had written of Sarawak in 1856. ' ... A *hundred years* of precept and practice may establish just principles and just notions in the native mind, and 500 years hence, Sarawak may become a great country.'[2] The issues became clearer as the changes of the nineteenth century took effect. The kind of criteria and timetable implicit in such concepts came under discussion. What were the requirements of a state? Who should judge them? The discussion could not avoid being a political contest, with colonial powers more likely than their nationalist opponents to set tough criteria and vague timetables. 'I am always being asked in connection with ... [our] policy of autonomy: when?' said the conservative Dutch Governor-General B. C. de Jonge (1931–36). 'Now I believe that since we have worked in the Indies for some 300 years, another 300 will have to be added before they may perhaps be ready for some kind of autonomy.'[3]

Such a contest undermined the chances of developing an intermediate kind of state in which collaboration might continue but on a different basis. That was in any case a difficult concept, as the best example, the 'self-governing' colonies of the

British Empire that became Dominions and then members of the (British) Commonwealth of Nations, tends to show. Yet it is not surprising to find the first Southeast Asian nationalists, the Filipinos, concerned over their internal and external weakness, looking for something like it. Early in 1899 even the revolutionary Apolinario Mabini was prepared to accept 'protection'—though he preferred 'aid'— if the United States would accept Philippine independence.[4] Jacob Schurman thought that, if negotiations could be started, Emilio Aguinaldo would seek 'a Canadian-style autonomy'.[5] Pedro A. Paterno attempted many compromises, one of which was 'protection', while Pedro Roxas thought Filipinos could manage with an autonomy like that of Australia.[6] A new colonial regime was, however, established.

Opposing the West in the Pacific War, the Japanese sponsored the 'independence' of the Philippines, as well as of Burma, and later Vietnam and Indonesia. In some sense, as Akira Iriye has argued,[7] they were echoing the rhetoric of their opponents. Independence was, it is true, to be qualified by acceptance of the new form of relationship the Greater East Asia Co-Prosperity Sphere was intended to represent. That, too, however, had a parallel in the 'partnership' concept the British were developing.

The Japanese invasions of 1941–42 dramatically destroyed the colonial governments set up in the nineteenth century. How far were they even so a turning-point in the history of Southeast Asia? The answer cannot be attempted without considering not only the nature of their regime, but what followed its destruction: it turned out to be an interregnum, but not one that was followed by the restoration of the colonial governments. The answer must also, of course, take into account the strength of the colonial governments before the Japanese invasion. They already faced challenges from within their territories, partly as a result of their own inevitable, if incomplete, commitment to modernisation. But their establishment had been closely connected with factors that had affected the relationship of Southeast Asia with the rest of the world, in particular the growth of Western power and the evolution of Britain's relationships with other Western states. Indeed the regimes, unable to base themselves on a loyal citizenry, were to an unusual degree reliant upon outside strength. Changes in other parts of the world affected that relationship, and in turn the prospects for colonial Southeast Asia.

World War I

Their primacy challenged, the British did not resort to a protectionist policy, at least before the Great Depression of the 1930s. Politically they sought to accommodate the ambitions of other powers, while putting a priority on the defence of what they saw as essential interests. That pattern had begun to emerge in the late nineteenth century, though the shift from permitting the expansion of other powers to coming to terms with it had been somewhat masked by precautionary steps and imperialist rhetoric. More apparent, perhaps, was the impact of prioritisation on this process. It was easier to accommodate some powers than others, not only because of their approach, but because their ambitions affected Britain's interests less seriously. Though the history of Britain's relations with the United States had been quite stormy, and its relations with Germany rather good, Germany came to present a threat to Britain's main interest, its security in Europe, for nearly a century sustained by the absence of a continental threat. That even tended to override the long-standing British concern over Russia, a major participant in European politics, but also, throughout the nineteenth century, an expanding power in Asia. In 1902, Britain had even made an alliance with Japan, the first of the Asian states to industrialise, in order to check Russia. But within five years it made not only an agreement with France, but also one with Russia, France's ally, in the hope of checking Germany by restoring the 'balance of power' in Europe. Neither this, nor the maintenance of Britain's naval supremacy, sufficed, however, to prevent Germany's resort to war in 1914.

The European war, far more engulfing and prolonged a conflict than many had expected, became a world war. Above all, the United States entered the conflict in 1917, thus signaling more clearly than ever before that the distribution of power in the world was, thanks to the spread of industrialisation, no longer to be decided only in Europe. Partly in order to compete with the Bolsheviks, who seized power in war-torn Russia later in the year, the United States also sought to change the character of the inter-state diplomacy that Europe had built up, on which there was a tendency to blame the war. President Wilson's Fourteen Points endorsed the concepts of self-determination and nationality with Europe in mind, but they were susceptible of wider application. Indeed they could be associated with the development of different attitudes towards colonialism, not only in the United States or among the Russian Communists, but in the metropolitan states themselves, and indeed in the colonies. 'The decisions of Versailles', as the Indonesian leader Hatta put it, 'could only bring about new sentiments of nationalism'.[8] In India, a source of troops in the war, the British declared in 1917 that their aim was to develop, in the phrase of Edwin Montagu, the Secretary of State, 'responsible government'.

The new government in Russia initially hoped to ignite revolution in Europe. When that failed, its leader, Lenin, put forward the thesis that capitalism might be overthrown by attacking imperialism. Communism should support the peasant movement, giving it a revolutionary character, and organising soviets wherever possible. The Communist International (Comintern) was also 'to create a temporary cooperation, even an alliance, with the revolutionary movement of the colonies and the backward countries; it must not, however, amalgamate with it but must maintain absolutely the independent character of the proletarian movement—albeit only in embryo form'.[9] That boosted the nationalist movement in China, which had established a republic in 1911, and also the anti-colonial movements in Netherlands India and Vietnam. But the formulas were full of internal contradictions and open to different interpretations.

They were also very general compared with the specific circumstances of each country. The struggle was global—working-class against capitalism—but it was also

possible to think of each Asian country in terms of a national struggle, the communist party thus fighting feudalism and capitalism and winning independence.[10] But
then the relationship with proletarian movements in the metropolitan countries
was unclear. Would they be in support or opposed? Particularly after the break
between the Chinese nationalists in the Kuomintang and the Chinese Communist
Party in 1927, Lenin's successor, Stalin, neglected the national liberation issue, and
with the rise of Fascism in Europe, put his emphasis on a Popular Front, endorsed
in the Seventh Congress. Comintern weakness left scope for confusion, but also for
Asian Marxist initiatives, such as the national liberation strategies of Mao Zedong
and the Vietnamese. On the other hand the colonial powers' concern was increased
by their sense that it was an international movement. They tended to cooperate
against it, though never very completely.

The Japanese

The world war had also changed the position of Japan. There the defeat of China in
the 1840s had brought about the change of policy the British had sought in vain in
Vietnam, and the seclusion associated with the Tokugawa regime had been abandoned. The wider opening prescribed by the treaties of 1858 led to a civil war and to
the destruction of the Tokugawa, but its successors, ruling in the name of the Meiji
emperor, pursued a policy designed to maintain the independence of Japan by attaining 'equality' with the nations of the West. It modernised and industrialised. What
foreign policy should it follow? Industrialisation, combined with a lack of natural
resources, suggested an emphasis on overseas trade. An image of over-population
argued for emigration or for colonial settlement. There were security considerations,
too. If China could not defend itself against the West, the West would dominate East
Asia, and Japan's own position would be under threat. Japan must either support
China in a 'pan-Asian' opposition to the West, or itself step in, if need be at China's
expense, to pre-empt the West. The ruling oligarchy favoured the latter approach,
though the idealism of the former was never quite abandoned. Pending progress with
Japan's self-strengthening, however, it tended to pursue a moderate policy. Like other
powers, Japan took account, too, first of Britain's primacy, and then of its relative
decline. Before World War I it established its control in Taiwan, and, triumphing over
Russia in the war of 1904–05, in Korea and in southern Manchuria. In the war it
secured the German leasehold in Shantung and faced the Chinese government with
the twenty-one demands of 1915.

After the war the Japanese took account of the rise of American power and the
new approach to international relations. Japanese governments for most of the 1920s
combined a more democratic approach at home with international cooperation
abroad. They concluded the Washington agreements in 1921–22, and they pursued
the policy of 'China friendship' associated with Shidehara. The emphasis was on
commercial rather than imperial expansion. Even before the Depression, however,

the Japanese began to change their approach, particularly in response to an impatient Chinese nationalism. The Depression after 1929 only made 'China friendship' yet more difficult to pursue, and the Manchurian 'incident' followed in 1931. A 'puppet state' was created, Manchukuo. The Konoe government of 1937 adopted a yet bolder approach, unleashing the 'undeclared war' with China. By the end of 1938 he was defining Japan's objective as the establishment of a 'New Order' in East Asia, and by 1940 it had become, with rather more of a pan-Asian overtone, the creation of a 'Greater East Asia Co-Prosperity Sphere'. In that, Southeast Asia was to be included.

Southeast Asia had been in Japanese minds before this, of course, both in terms of pan-Asian idealism, and in terms of imperialism. The end of seclusion recalled the seventeenth-century contacts that predated Tokugawa dominance. The acquisition of Taiwan had brought Japan to the confines of Southeast Asia, and some radicals had wanted to intervene to help the Filipinos against the Spaniards. Japan's success against Russia in 1904–05 stirred nascent nationalist feeling in Burma and Netherlands India. Nervous about the Anglo-Japanese alliance, the Dutch extended most-favoured-nation treatment to the Japanese in a conciliatory gesture of 1912. In the war the Japanese proffered not altogether welcome assistance to the British authorities in Singapore when the Indian troops there mutinied in 1915. 'What', Tsukuda asked his Tokyo readers in 1916, 'is the significance to be attached to the fact that the flag of the Rising Sun was set up in the centre of Singapore?'[11] The Dutch, neutral in the war, were again nervous. After it, they were reassured by the undertakings of the Washington powers, and by the moderation in Japanese policy of which they were in part a testimony. The Japanese, on the other hand, benefited by the lack of commercial competition in the war, and then by the rationalisation they undertook after the 1920–23 recession.

The Japanese, a British official commented, were interested in the trade of the Indies and its oil. They had

> no definite political ambitions in this region. But they are obsessed by the idea that their country is one day destined to be mistress of the Pacific and of its islands. They regard Holland as a very weak Power, and her colonial empire as doomed to disruption. Japan must have a say in the disposal of this rich empire. So she is steadily increasing her knowledge of the country, her vested interests therein, and the numbers of her merchants and colonists,

and keeping an eye on the native movement.[12] The Manchuria incident renewed Dutch apprehension, in particular about the security of the oil-bearing parts of Sumatra and Borneo. Might the Japanese not make a sudden descent upon them? Once they were there, it might not be possible to get them out. The Dutch nevertheless risked the crisis import ordinance of 1933, largely, of course, directed at Japanese competition.

It was only in the middle of the decade, however, that Southeast Asia began to feature in Japanese policy-making at cabinet level, in particular as a result of the interest of the Imperial Japanese Navy. It was at once nervous about access to the resources of the region, and apprehensive about trying to guarantee it. Japan's oil mostly came from the Americas and had to cross the American-dominated Pacific. A more secure source, nearer at hand, would make Japan better able to pursue its policies in Asia without the risk of American interposition. Securing such a source, however, might not be feasible if the Americans stepped in, and taking on the Americans was not something the Navy could readily contemplate. The Fundamental Principles of 1936 thus endorsed 'footsteps' in the south, including the promotion of semi-governmental economic enterprises.

In China the Japanese achieved major successes but no final triumph. The frustrations they faced made them look towards Southeast Asia, and they tried to restrict supplies that reached the Chinese overland through Burma and Vietnam. The opening of the war in Europe in September 1939, and in particular the dramatic surrender of France in June 1940 in face of the German onslaught, led Japan to step up its pressure. The British closed the Burma Road, and the Japanese were able to move troops into northern Vietnam by agreement with the Vichy regime. Konoe, in power again, was again optimistic, and again indulged in a dramatic foreign policy, the conclusion of the tripartite pact with Germany and Italy in September.

Again, however, Konoe was too sanguine. For the United States had come to attach a greater importance to Southeast Asia than it had attached to China. In order to prolong the resistance that, in spite of the fall of France, Britain was offering the Germans in Europe, and thus limit the German threat to the Atlantic, the Americans wanted to keep open British access to the resources of Southeast Asia and the manpower of India and Australasia. Just at the time, therefore, that the Japanese were attaching increased importance to securing the resources of Southeast Asia, the Americans were becoming more determined to prevent it. Crucially, there was also a time factor. The United States had also reacted to the fall of France by determining to build a two-ocean navy. In the coming years that would mean that Japan would lose the superiority it currently enjoyed in East Asian waters. If it could not achieve its objectives soon, it might not be able to do so at all.

It was for this reason that, when Konoe's diplomacy failed, his successor, Tojo, resorted to force, and in December 1941 the Japanese attacked both British Malaya and the American base at Pearl Harbor. His opponents were surprised. 'We're all astounded over Japan. We never thought she would attack us and America at once. She must have gone mad', wrote Oliver Harvey.[13] It was, perhaps, desperation more than madness. The Japanese had no certainty of victory, particularly in the longer term: their industrial capacity was 10 per cent of that of the United States. Military action, they believed, would put them in a better position to negotiate a satisfactory settlement. The aim, as Admiral Tomioka Sadatoshi put it, was a limited war, the objective of which was 'to attain an overwhelming supremacy over the enemy in its initial stages and create a strategic equilibrium against the Allies; then to seek a favourable opportunity to enter into negotiations with our enemies for a compromise peace'.[14] Their initial military success was far more complete than their success in China, yet their future strategy was unclear. Would they, as in China, simply go on expanding? As there, a deal evaded them.

Throughout its short existence Japanese rule in Southeast Asia indeed retained a provisional quality, though its improvisations had a background in Japanese policy and practice both at home and in the puppet territories. Nevertheless, though historians reach different judgments over its impact, in one sense it was decisive. Colonial Southeast Asia had been destroyed, and it was never restored, neither politically nor economically. In a sense, the Japanese achieved their objective, though not through any negotiated settlement.

The improvisatory character of their rule related to a lack of preparation. Though they had been collecting information and building up their interests, they did not seriously envisage the use of force till mid-1940. Indeed their very success in those tasks suggested that there would be no need to do so. The weakness of the colonial powers and the growth of nationalist movements were in their favour, and they had been able to secure a share in the trade of the region. The guidelines of March 1941 concentrated on the immediate objectives of the occupying forces, and the emphasis was on acquiring resources, using existing organs of government. These principles were made over to the Planning Board, set up only on 26 November.

The European war changed the timing of the Japanese advance in Southeast Asia, and thus its nature. The German triumphs in Europe in 1940 opened up an opportunity with an element of precaution: Southeast Asia was more open to pressure, but Germany itself might be a rival, too. One purpose of the tripartite pact was to avert that. The German attack on the Soviet Union in June 1941 expanded the opportunity, but increased the risk, this time of US intervention. The world was being divided up anew, it seemed. Japan had to use force to stake its claim to that 'fair share' it had long sought while its relative strength was sufficient to affect the outcome.

Interwar Southeast Asia

Between the wars the colonial framework of the nineteenth century had clearly been under pressure. The American acquisition of the Philippines in 1898 had been a barrier to Japan's advance beyond Taiwan, and had in a measure boosted the colonial regimes in Southeast Asia by recruiting to their ranks, at a time when Britain's primacy was declining, the major power of the new century. But, even though it rejected Filipino compromises, its attitude to empire was always ambivalent, and it rationalised it by holding out the prospect of independence. The Filipino leadership, wanting that, also wanted a guarantee: the expansion of Japan was in their minds. In 1916 the Jones Act set independence as the aim, though without fixing the date. The pressure of the Filipino elite, but still more the impact of the Depression, which prompted American and Cuban producers of sugar to oppose the tariff preferences accorded their Filipino rivals, led to the setting of the date. Under the Tydings–McDuffie Act, a Commonwealth of the Philippines was set up, given a substantial degree of independence other than in foreign affairs, and promised complete independence ten years later. Its President, Manuel Quezon, aware of Manchuria, was nervous about American ambivalence over the defence of the Philippines: 'in the haphazard tesselation of American Far Eastern policy there was no clear design for the Philippines'.[15] The United States, he had told Roy Howard in 1933, should either fortify the Philippines and build a navy, or 'leave bag and baggage': he wanted an 'alliance, or ... partnership in commerce and defense'.[16] Quezon even looked to joining the British Commonwealth.

Quite unable to respond to that, the British wanted the United States to indicate a clear commitment to the Philippines, which they were of course anxious should not fall into Japanese hands. The British also recognised both the importance to them of the security of Netherlands India and the impossibility of their guaranteeing to support it. In 1936, for example, the Chiefs of Staff in London declared 'that the integrity of the Dutch East Indies is vital to our security in the Far East, and the occupation of the Dutch Islands near Singapore by a hostile Power would be a most serious event'. But they did not 'recommend that a guarantee of military support under all circumstances should be offered to the Dutch'.[17] Indeed, the defence chiefs were to remain opposed to a guarantee until the United States indicated that it was committed, and that was not until 1 December 1941, shortly before the Japanese attack on Pearl Harbor and Malaya.

Within Netherlands India the Dutch had affirmed their position, but they had been internally challenged. Faced by revivifying Islam, Snouck Hurgronje's answer had been 'association': 'the creation of a Netherlands nation consisting of two parts widely separated geographically but spiritually closely united'.[18] But the Ethical Policy, economic changes, and the impact of communism, conduced to a partial politicisation of Indonesian life, and to that the Dutch reacted ambivalently. A moderate nationalism might be acceptable, but not a movement that sought early independence. Against a statement by President Taft of 1911 that the Americans 'were likely to retain the Philippines for a considerable time', an unnamed hand in the Dutch Foreign Ministry wrote: 'Hoera!'[19]

Though they did not take part in World War I, the Dutch moved to set up the Volksraad (People's Council). In November 1918, seizing the opportunity provided by the threat of revolution in the Netherlands to by-pass his conservative superiors, the liberal Governor-General van Limburg Stirum declared that he envisaged a transfer of power to the Volksraad. 'The new course which the latest world events have prescribed for the Netherlands will also determine the direction of our affairs here. With us, however, it is not so much a matter of changing course as of increasing speed. The government and the Volksraad are faced with a period of new relationships and changes of competence.'[20] In the following years, however, the Dutch turned against this policy, while unrest in the Indies increased. Governor-General de Graeff was unable to find a middle way, to create 'trust' as he put it.[21] The Depression encouraged the more reactionary policies of de Jonge, and even cooperating nationalists received no concessions.

Singapore had acquired a new importance for the British—'undoubtedly the naval key to the Far East', Admiral Jellicoe had declared[22]—but the decision to build a naval base there was not a sign of strength. During World War I, it had become clear that relative naval power was no longer merely a matter among Europeans, and it was necessary for a state with worldwide interests to be able to deploy effective naval strength worldwide. Britain, however, could not readily afford to build a two-ocean navy. Its strategy was to have two bases for a one-ocean navy, so that it could be deployed to meet crises in different parts of the world. Singapore would be 'made into a place where the British Fleet can concentrate for the defence of the Empire'.[23] Security in Europe naturally was first priority, and the main fleet could not be sent to the East if there were a major crisis there. Admiral Richmond was to refer to the 'illusion that a Two-Hemisphere Empire' could 'be defended by a One-Hemisphere Navy'.[24] It was, however, assumed that Japan would not act unless there was a crisis in Europe.

Britain was indeed overcommitted. That may also have contributed to the paralysis of its colonial policy in Malaya. There, unlike the Dutch in the Indies or the Americans in the Philippines, they did not face a nationalist movement. They had, however, come to realise that their nineteenth-century arrangements were under pressure. Malay rulers, such as Sultan Idris of Perak, were restive at the dominance of the bureaucracy in the Federated Malay States structure, while the sultans in the northern states were unwilling to join it. That made it difficult to conceive of a more unified British Malaya without a persuasive degree of decentralisation. At the same time, however, the British had also to consider the role of the Chinese and the Indians, the so-called immigrant communities brought in to develop Malaya's rubber and tin, who were in fact becoming increasingly domesticated. Any advance towards a more democratic structure, such as was occurring in other parts of the empire, would enable them to swamp the Malays, and perhaps undermine the long-term basis of Britain's interests in a territory where they were now, thanks to the ability of rubber to earn dollars, vastly more important than when intervention was first formalised. It was not easy to settle on a policy, let alone carry it out. There was, however, no immediate crisis. The communities were not at odds, and neither jointly nor singly did they challenge the British. It was easier to do nothing much. An attempt at a bold new policy might fail, and both increase and demonstrate Britain's weakness.

Nor did the rationalisation of British Borneo make much progress. Lucas's grand plan had not been carried out. The British government had hesitated to tackle embittered old Raja Charles, and his successor, Vyner, proved evasive. An advocate of decentralisation on the peninsula, Sir Cecil Clementi advocated federation in Borneo. The Company was willing to sell, but, affected by the Depression, the government was not ready to buy. The raja's brother persuasively argued that appointing a British resident to advise a British raja would damage rather than strengthen: the raja's position would be 'anomalous'.[25]

In Burma, by contrast, constitutional change had already been set in motion in the early 1920s, as a result both of Indian example and Burman pressure. In such a case, there was no alternative for the British but to press on with that course. Under the 1935 Act Burma was separated from India, and from 1937 parliamentary Burma had a widely though not completely responsible government, though the non-Burman areas remained for the most part directly under the governor. The British had not explicitly declared that their goal for Burma was Dominion status, but increasingly they had to treat it like a Dominion.

The position in Indo-China was quite different. The French, like the Dutch, had been concerned about the Japanese successes at the opening of the century. Reassured by a mutual acknowledgment of interests and possessions in a treaty of 1907, the French again became apprehensive in World War I. Nevertheless they had to withdraw French troops to fight in Europe. The government also recruited 'volunteers', though without the *quid pro quo* of a declaration like Montagu's. Heavy-handedly suppressing the Yen-bay mutiny and the Nghe-an-Ha-tinh peasant revolts in the early 1930s, the French yet failed to offer any real alternative to nationalists who might have preferred to avoid communist leadership. The weakness of their international position, in Europe and Asia alike, was evident. Indeed their common border with China underlined it. 'The fact that Indochina is practically lacking all the means of maritime defence and has only an inadequate aviation can lead to an aggression or even a blockade of our coasts.'[26] In 1938 France reached an informal deal with the Japanese—a ban on the transit of munitions in return for the status quo in Hainan—but they did not adhere to the bargain.

The weakness of the Western powers, evident to Japan, was evident also to the Thais. They had declared war on Germany in World War I and 1200 volunteer soldiers went to France. The object was to secure a place at the peace conference and to assert their equality with other states, and during the 1920s and 1930s the Thais renegotiated the unequal treaties. Sent to Bangkok as British envoy after the coup of 1932 ended the absolute monarchy, Sir Josiah Crosby was expected to reassure its promoters of Britain's wish for friendly relations with the new regime. But he admitted that Japan had attained a 'predominant position' in Asia, and Siam was bound to take it into account as 'one of the pivotal points around which her foreign policy must turn'.[27] In 1933 it abstained from the League of Nations censure of Japan in respect of Manchuria. Later some of its leaders, especially the military clique led by Pibun, began to consider the possibility of regaining the territories earlier lost to France and Britain when those powers were stronger. They were stimulated by the Anschluss.

But for the European war, the Japanese goals in Southeast Asia might have been secured without violence, even the violence as a prelude to some kind of negotiated settlement that was, it seems, their aim. The impact of the European war made it impossible. When they did resort to violence, the weakness of their opponents, how-ever, maximised its effect, and, like Hitler, they increased it still further by a ruthless *Blitzkrieg*, the resort, it may be, of states whose governments know that they must apply what strength they have in a way that causes terror and panic. In a sense, how-ever, the Japanese, too, were unprepared, not simply for the stunning speed and magnitude of their initial victory, but for the administration of the territories that they had so precipitately acquired. Nor, indeed, did they even have a strategy for the future if a settlement was still not forthcoming. If there was any chance of bringing the United States to terms, it was in the early months of 1942, but the collaboration between Germany and Japan that it would have required was not forthcoming. The defeat of the Imperial Navy at Midway in mid-1942 meant that the Japanese could only expect a counter-attack. Their disastrous Imphal offensive of 1944 was but an attempt at forestalling. It was in these circumstances that they created the Co-Prosperity Sphere.

The Pacific war

The invasion of Southeast Asia was an entire novelty. It was, as Tony Stockwell puts it, 'a stroke more compelling than the fall of Melaka to the Portuguese in 1511'.[28] Before the Portuguese, the Chinese had sent expeditions to Java or to Vietnam. After them, the Dutch had used force sparingly, if tellingly, often drawing it from one part of the archipelago to apply it in another. Disposing of far greater power, the British in the nineteenth century had abstained from seeing the region as a field of military or territorial dominance. Now, for the first time, an outside power brought all Southeast Asia under its effective military control. But it was not sustained by a coherent policy, and while its violence maximised the initial effect, it soon became counterproductive.

The war began on 7–8 December 1941. The US fleet was crippled at Pearl Harbor, and half the US air force in the Far East was destroyed at Clark airbase in the Philippines. The two ships that Britain sent to Singapore, the *Repulse* and the *Prince of Wales*, were, in the absence of air support, sunk off Pahang on 10 December. While the Japanese had thus quickly achieved superiority at sea and in the air, their ground troops, which had landed in northern Malaya and the Philippines, also advanced rapidly. Early in January 1942, they captured Manila and Cavite, though the fort at Corregidor held out till May. The British evacuated Penang on 17 December, and on 11 January the capital of the Federated Malay States, Kuala Lumpur, fell. Miri had been taken on 15 December, Kuching on Christmas Day, Labuan on 1 January, Jesselton on 9 January. Sandakan fell on 19 January. By the end of the month, Singapore was besieged, and it surrendered on 15 February, 'the worst disaster and largest capitulation in British history', as Churchill, the prime minister, put it.[29]

The Dutch had recognised that their security depended on the British. Now the battle of the Java sea laid Netherlands India open to the Japanese. The capital,

Batavia, fell on 6 March, and the commander-in-chief, General Hein Ter Poorten, surrendered on 9 March. The Japanese had bombed Medan at the end of December and then the other major Sumatran ports. Troops landing in southern Sumatra in February were quickly successful, and Palembang fell before Singapore. The Dutch retreated north, finally surrendering on 28 March in Aceh, 'which itself', as an Indonesian nationalist put it, 'had been the very last area of Indonesia to be colonized by the Dutch'.[30] Within another month or so the Japanese had virtually completed their conquest of Southeast Asia. Rangoon had been bombed on 23 December, and the Indians began to flee: some 400 000 were to trek out by land, 'the real end of the Indians in Burma'.[31] The British evacuated Rangoon the day after Batavia fell, and the advance of the Japanese, with some Burman allies, took them to Mandalay by 2 May.

A diplomatic deal over Timor had been rumoured in March 1939. The advancing Japanese would guarantee Macao, while Portugal would join their Anti-Comintern Pact with Germany, recognise Manchukuo, and grant an airbase on Timor. Nothing came of that, but over Timor the Portuguese had to 'walk warily', as one of them put it,[32] because Macao was exposed. A Japanese raid, the governor thought, would be attempted only if there were a general attack on the British and the Dutch. When that threatened in 1941 the Portuguese were unwilling to accept cooperation with the Allies in advance. The result was an occupation by the Australians, and then an invasion by the Japanese late in February 1942. The Australians fought a guerrilla war till early 1943.

In French Indo-China the 1940 deal had offered Japan's recognition of French sovereignty in return for a privileged position in northern Vietnam, including the right to introduce troops, ostensibly to pursue the conflict with China. The Vichy foreign minister believed that his government had to accept: 'if we refuse Japan, she will attack Indo-China which is incapable of being defended. Indo-China will be 100 per cent lost. If we negotiate with Japan; if we avoid the worst, that is to say the total loss of the colony, we preserve the chances that the future may perhaps bring us.'[33] The deal was carried through, though not without incidents provoked by the Japanese military in Kwangsi. Japan's decision to continue the southward advance, despite its German ally's invasion of Russia, was followed by the move on southern Indo-China late in July 1941. The Vichy government reacted in the same spirit as before. A compromise, though humiliating, was better than a total loss. But it brought the Japanese significantly nearer Malaya and Singapore.

Vichy had hoped that the 1940 agreement would also restrain the Thais and that the Japanese would uphold the integrity of Indo-China against their aspiration to regain the 'lost provinces'. In fact Pibun had in October undertaken to permit Japanese troops to cross Thai territory in order to attack Malaya and Singapore in return for Japan's support for Thai irredentism. After conferring with the army and navy, Foreign Minister Matsuoka decided to offer 'mediation' in the dispute, in which Japan would take Thailand's side in return for its adhesion to the New Order.

Mediation was reluctantly accepted by the French in January 1941. Agreement was reached only on 11 March, and the treaty signed only on 9 May. Under it much of northwestern Cambodia went back to Thailand. Neither France nor Thailand were to make pacts with third countries that could be considered hostile to Japan. In December 1941 Pibun kept his bargain. There was minimal resistance to the passage of Japanese troops. On 21 December Thailand and Japan solemnly concluded a treaty of alliance before the Emerald Buddha, a secret protocol to which covered the restoration of some of the 'lost provinces'. On 25 January Thailand declared war on the United Kingdom and the United States.

These moves testified to the prowess of Japan's diplomats, but they compromised the idealism of the Greater East Asia Co-Prosperity Sphere. Though dedicated to the exclusion of the white man from Asia—and German firms were to be offered no special status under Japanese rule, nor even compensation for their losses—the Japanese had come to terms with Vichy, and French authority was sustained in Indo-China. The promises made to Thailand—to be redeemed in July 1943, when Tojo visited Bangkok—were presented as gestures against the colonial powers: 'Britain with warcraft and guns robbed Thailand of these territories', it was inaccurately proclaimed.[34] But more Malays were thus placed under the Thai rule that those in Pattani so resented, while Ba Maw told Tojo of the 'unhappiness' of the Burmese and the Shans. It was clear, too, that Japan would not protect Laos even as much as France had.

In any case, the emphasis in the Sphere was realistic rather than idealistic. The priorities were the maintenance of peace and security, the acquisition of important raw materials, and local self-sustenance. The larger political gestures were made only when it became clear that Japan was on the defensive and could not mount another offensive. In 1943 Burma and the Philippines, politically the most 'advanced' of the pre-war colonial territories, were granted independence within the Sphere. Ba Maw's regime had to offer complete military collaboration. Laurel's was not at first required to declare war: he argued that the pro-American movement was so strong that doing so would threaten stability. Prime Minister Tojo spoke of 'political participation' in Indonesia in mid-1943, but no promise of independence was held out till his successor's declaration of 7 September 1944. Even then Koiso avoided using the word 'Indonesia', and, in true colonial style, avoided naming the date. Only on 17 August 1945, after the Japanese surrender, were the Indonesians in a position to declare independence. In Malaya there was no promise of independence, and four states had been made over to Thailand. In July 1945 the Japanese decided to appeal to the Malay radicals by promoting inclusion in 'Indonesia Raya'.

The French were dislodged only on 9 March 1945. When the Japanese lost control of the South China Sea, the forces in Indo-China had to plan for self-sustenance, and when the allies reopened the Burma Road, they had to deploy troops in the north. Their position was worsened by the failure of the Imphal offensive, and with the return of de Gaulle to Paris, the loyalty of Decoux, the governor-general, became even less reliable. On 17 January the Army and Navy agreed on Operation Meigo, the takeover. The Indo-Chinese states were offered independence, however, partly to avoid worsening relations with the Soviet Union, with which the Japanese were not yet at war, and which might, they hoped, provide the way to a negotiated peace. But Cochin-China was kept apart from the rest of Vietnam till 8 August.

Japan had been concerned about the loyalty of Thailand since November 1943, when Pibun had not attended the Greater East Asia conference in Tokyo: would it change sides, becoming the Italy of the Orient? The Japanese did not, however, seize power there. Thailand would resist, and that would divert troops needed elsewhere, by contrast, as ambassador Yamamoto suggested, to Indo-China, where Japan had only to deal with 'a few thousand Frenchmen who didn't have the cooperation of 26 million colonials'.[35]

'Our policies for the people we shall free', the popular magazine *Kaizo* had declared, 'will require great sagacity and great boldness'.[36] Instead, as Grant Goodman puts it, the Japanese 'out-colonialed' the colonials.[37] The *sook ching* in Singapore is notorious: Yamashita's aim was to establish security for an under-strength army and to avoid the type of guerrilla warfare faced in China. But he unleashed terror and massacre. The regime was not merely harsh and insensitive but exploitative, too. As Leon Salim put it, 'freed from the mouth of the tiger', Indonesia 'was in the jaws of the lion'.[38] Forced labour did not come only from prisoners-of-war Asia-style, but from Java and Malaya as well: about 75 000 Malays and Indians were sent to Thailand; the death rate was over 30 per cent.

'Lack of understanding and sympathy disappointed the indigenous peoples and even engendered their anti-Japanese sentiments, after the initial enthusiastic reactions with which they greeted Japanese troops as the arrival of a holy army', wrote Fujiwara Iwaichi, a leading intelligence officer. The *kosaku* (intelligence operations), 'impatient for success', aroused 'false hopes'.[39] Yet that trend still did not deprive Japan's conquest of its effect, and the regimes it set up to counter the return of the colonial powers were of longer-term significance as well. 'If the Japanese can make their forced withdrawal seem to be a further invasion of Asia by imperial white powers, they can leave behind them the foundation for another effort sometime in the future', George Kerr commented, discussing a possible Japanese peace offer at the time of the Cairo conference.[40] More subtle than the army-dominated Ministry of Greater East Asia, the Foreign Ministry argued that 'the ideological foundation developed during the war of liberation in Greater East Asia by the Empire, is regardless of the course of the war, an eventuality which even the enemy must follow and accept'.[41]

Wartime plans

The French had indeed realised that, once interrupted, colonial rule would be difficult, even impossible, to restore. During the war, however, the colonial powers prepared to return, developing not only military plans for what they in turn called the 'liberation' of their territories, but also plans for revising the colonial relationship.

In some ways, as Akira Iriye has argued, the ideology of the Allies and their Japanese opponents became remarkably similar. The Allied leaders believed that the old colonial system could not simply be restored, nor even that it should be. Yet, while they could apply the word 'puppet' only to the creations of the Japanese, they also believed that their former dependencies should for the time being become something less than fully independent. That was the case, indeed, even with the Philippines.

They were not, however, the only parties involved. 'The Europeanised "Far East" has gone', the British consul-general at Batavia wrote as early as March 1942, 'and the organisation of European activities there in the future will have to be rebuilt on entirely different foundations from those prevailing before 1939'.[42] Quite how different it was difficult to realise. The interregnum unleashed a variety of movements, nationalist and otherwise, both as a result of Japanese policies, and of the unintended outcomes that their policies, like those of earlier colonial powers, tended to produce. About them, the Allies were not often well-informed, nor did they always share the information they had. For their part, the Allies sought the support of the inhabitants in ways that they had avoided pre-war, and encouraged guerrilla movements the agenda of which were broader than their own.

World War II added further international dimensions to the relationship between colonial powers and their territories. Even before World War I, a kind of 'world opinion' had begun to emerge, on colonial as on other questions, and it was affected by Wilsonian idealism and by the Bolshevik revolution. It did not merely affect metropolitan opinion about the colonies: it affected opinion within the colonies. In general colonies were becoming less isolated, their elites better informed about developments in other parts of the world, and the movements they organised securing a better chance of international support. In World War II the colonial powers had to reckon with a need to justify their return.

Though the attitudes of each government and the conditions in each territory varied, it was generally recognised that all the Allied powers would have to take more account of nationalism than pre-war. Yet, though there was from August 1943 a South-East Asia Command—one of the first occasions on which this description of the region was used—its task lay in the military rather than in the political field, despite the connexion of the two and the zest with which the Supreme Commander, Lord Mountbatten, played politics. The Allies did not therefore coordinate their approach to nationalism. The British indeed developed a clear appreciation of the need for more regional coordination, but, though they were still the main European power involved, they were in no position to enforce it. The French and the Dutch had different views, and so had the Americans, the most powerful of all. The endorsement of self-determination in the Atlantic Charter of 1941, drawn up with Europe in mind, arguably applied in Asia as well. Certainly Roosevelt thought so. By contrast, Margery Perham declared the British empire 'a self-liquidating concern, dissolving itself by an orderly process into a commonwealth of peoples united by a common ideal of partnership in freedom'.[43] And Roosevelt and the French were poles apart.

Though it was neither well-informed nor coordinated, there was, however, a great deal of planning. In that, colonial 'liberation' contrasted with the original colonial ventures of the Europeans, as well, of course, with those of the Japanese. There was, after all, plenty of time. In the event, however, the war ended more suddenly than had been expected, since the Japanese capitulated after the unleashing of atomic weapons on Hiroshima and Nagasaki in August 1945. The war ended, too, in a way the planners had not expected, and in some ways they were more hampered by what they had prepared than helped.

In the interwar period planning had indeed become more fashionable, a response both to the Depression and, no doubt, to the example set by the Soviet Union. The war itself spread a military practice. But the magnitude of the disaster in Southeast Asia pointed the same way. It seemed a judgment on the caution and adhockery of the preceding years. Planning, too, should go beyond restructuring governmental or administrative systems. It should engage in economic and social reconstruction. 'The Malayan disaster has shocked us into sudden attention to the structure of our colonial empire', wrote Perham in March 1942.[44] The war, she argued, had shown the weakness of 'plural societies' like Malaya. 'But there is a level of education and of potential common interests upon which we are held back only by our prejudices from cooperation and friendship. Yet, without these, imperial rule cannot change into the working partnership which the coming age demands.' The concept of 'partnership' replaced that of colonial trusteeship.

Even so, the plans of the Allies were often unrealistic. For the British to see their loss of Malaya as 'a God-sent chance to clear up all the country's troubles', as Roland Braddell put it,[45] was a new kind of hubris. Was Britain going to be in any position to make Burma, in Bevin's phrase, 'an Empire gem'?[46]

British planning for the future of Burma began as early as 1942. More politically advanced than Malaya, Burma had a 'government-in-exile', based in Simla, and the governor, Sir R. Dorman-Smith, with British and Burmese officials, had little to do but plan. They developed the view that further constitutional advance should be deferred and that during a period of direct gubernatorial rule Burma would be 'reconstructed' with substantial aid from the British, designed not only to undo the effects of wartime destruction, but to build a better Burma. Constitutional progress would resume after a fixed period of time, and Burma would then be in a position to advance to Dominion status.

The planning for Burma continued on this basis for much of the war, but its lack of realism had soon become evident. On the one hand, the prime minister, Winston Churchill, son of the Secretary of State under whom Upper Burma had been conquered in 1885, saw it as giving Burma away as soon as it was regained. The funding on which the concept depended was in any case unlikely to be available, given Britain's virtual bankruptcy by 1943, even supposing that Burma could usefully apply the large sums proposed. Above all, however, the programme was politically unrealistic. Whatever benefits Britain might be able to bring, restoring direct rule, even for a fixed period, was unlikely to be acceptable in Burma or indeed, perhaps, in the United States, on which Britain's dependence had increased.

The policy the British pursued in Burma made the programme, finally set out in the White Paper of 17 May 1945, still more unrealistic. Burma had been fought over again. The reconquest/liberation began in 1944 when Slim's Fourteenth Army first withstood the Imphal offensives and then began to turn them back. The British had been working with minority groups, but Force 136 contacted Aung San's nationalists. They offered their cooperation, which was accepted, and the Burma Defence Army of the puppet state changed sides on 27 March. That speeded up the destruction of Japanese power, and Rangoon was occupied on 3 May. But it implied a political commitment, and Mountbatten indeed argued for the policy on political grounds. Britain would be working with the leaders of the future in the Anti-Fascist People's Freedom League, founded in August 1944, and that would guarantee that Burma, when it gained its independence, would remain in the Commonwealth. Dorman-Smith did not share that view. Nor did the officials, nor, at least at first, the Labour ministers who succeeded Churchill late in July.

No government-in-exile existed for Malaya, and planning was developed in the Colonial and War Offices in London. There, again, however, it was believed rather curiously that the destruction of British power provided an opportunity to do a better job, to end 'botching', as Edward Gent of the Colonial Office called it.[47] If in Burma the planning was designed to remedy the drawbacks in the working of the pre-war constitution, in Malaya it sought to provide the basis for constitutional advance. A bold attempt must be made to build a nation out of a plural society, and a united state out a plethora of governments. In May 1944 the British Cabinet, concluding that 'efficiency and democratic progress alike demanded a change in the pre-war constitutional and administrative system',[48] approved a plan to create a Malayan Union, to include all the states and all the settlements except Singapore. The special position of the sultans would be reduced, while the Chinese would be given the opportunity to obtain Malayan citizenship, thus also fending off the risk of intervention on the part of China, one of the Allies, with which a new treaty had been made.

Those in London who argued that this was a drastic change in policy were told that it was rather a new attempt to fulfil Britain's obligations as in effect a trustee. But it took little account of the arguments it might meet in Malaya. There indeed the British in advance of the intended reconquest/liberation were making contact through Force 136 with a Chinese-dominated guerrilla movement, but they were less informed about the changes in Malay attitudes that the occupation had brought about. Nor, of course, was the basic assumption proved correct that implementing the plan would follow a reconquest/liberation: the war ended before the British had even begun the task that they had completed in Burma.

The reorganisation of Malaya was not designed only to provide for its constitutional advance, and through that a long-term association with Britain. It was also designed to strengthen its security in the postwar world. The British planners also covered the Borneo territories. None of them, they thought, could survive on their own, but it was at least premature to include them in a wider union. Instead it was proposed that the British government should secure greater authority in Sarawak, and take over from the Company, as proposed in the 1930s. The Borneo territories would not themselves be federated, but their administrations would cooperate more closely. Coordination among all the territories was to be enhanced by the appointment of a governor-general, though, unlike other governor-generals, he would have no territory of his own to govern.

Convinced of the importance of regaining Indonesia—it in fact added 5 per cent to Dutch domestic product 1840–70 and 8 per cent 1921–38[49]—the Dutch had begun to prepare the way for their return with an eye to the Americans. In December 1942 Queen Wilhelmina had spoken of 'a commonwealth in which the Netherlands, Indonesia, Surinam and Curacao will participate' in 'a combination of independence and collaboration':[50] 'a poorly designed and unrealistic proposal … better characterized as an improvised concession to the language of the times rather than a map of the road to independence'.[51] It was indeed not at all clear that the Dutch had reckoned with a real change in their policy towards the Indonesians, though that was necessary, too. They were not well-informed about what was happening in their colony, but even with better information, they might not have been ready to alter their approach. In any case they were to be taken by surprise by the intensity of the opposition they faced, and were to react to it very negatively. There was no guerrilla movement in their favour, nor any reconquest/liberation in which, had they had any forces available, they might have taken part. Instead they were confronted by nationalists, and affronted by them, in their eyes a small bunch of jumped-up collaborators. If the British had to adapt their plans, that at least meant that they kept political objectives in mind. Unable simply to return as colonial rulers, the Dutch had to improvise, and they found it difficult.

The re-establishment of the French in Indo-China again depended in part on the support of the Allies. During the war Roosevelt had more than once declared his opposition to their return: 'for every dollar they have put in', as Chiang Kai-shek had told him, 'they have taken out ten, and … the situation is a good deal like the Philippines were in 1898'.[52] His death, the attitude of the British, and the establishment of the Free French government diminished the international obstacles. French ability to come to terms with nationalism was another question. The French Committee of National Liberation had offered 'a new political status within the French community'.[53] The Brazzaville conference early in 1944 stood, however, against self-government, but envisaged some kind of federal structure for the French empire. Its principal architect, Henri Laurentie, accepted the need to accommodate nationalism, for repression could no longer be backed up by the myth of colonial invincibility. The difficulty of doing so was indicated even before the policy had been finalised, when the Japanese coup in March 1945 took the French by surprise. A Declaration on Indo-China was rushed out on 24 March, but it offered far less than the nationalists sought: an Indo-Chinese federation as part of a French Union; and Vietnam in that federation still divided into three parts. And the French, recently dislodged with a minimum of heroism, were not returning in the course of a major struggle of reconquest/liberation.

Like Burma, and also North Borneo, where the Australians landed in June 1945, the Philippines was, by contrast, fought over once more, one result being destruction on a vast scale, in Manila itself, for example. Unlike Burma, of course, the Philippines was being regained by the major power, the United States. That had no need to shape its policy to suit the convenience of its Allies. It was, however, anxious to mark its victory by reasserting its pre-war policy, and sticking, despite all that had occurred in the interim, to the plan by which the Philippines became independent after ten years of 'Commonwealth' government. That, moreover, would afford an example to other colonial powers. It was also a response to the fact that, while some Filipinos had collaborated with the Japanese and accepted 'independence' from them in 1943, others had participated in the guerrilla struggle against the Japanese. That was a further reason for the Americans to fulfil their promise, hedged about though the fulfilment turned out to be.

The Thais, who had not lost their independence in the colonial phase, retained it in the Japanese phase that followed. When the war turned against the Japanese, the Thais sought to improve their relations with the Allies without prompting the Japanese to take over. They succeeded brilliantly. Pibun was driven from power in July 1944. Khuang Aphaiwong led a new government, in which civilian elements in the coup group predominated, while Pridi, the leader of the underground movement in Thailand, became sole regent for the young king, then in Switzerland, and expanded contacts with the Allies. Those contacts were subtly differentiated. The European powers, they believed, would be especially resentful of their wartime conduct, and the British at least in a position to make their resentment felt. The Americans, however, had never recognised the Thai declaration of war in January 1942, and the Thai ambassador in Washington, Seni Pramoj, led the Free Thai movement in the United States. The Thais made the most of this relationship, playing on American opposition to European 'imperialism', and exaggerating the threat to Thailand of the policies that Britain was preparing. Those, it was argued, had an element of the punitive. Not only did the British expect the return of the territories the Japanese had given to the Thais. Anxious to avoid famine in the territories to which the colonial powers were returning, they also looked for a free delivery of Thai rice, one of the pre-war staples of Southeast Asia. With less justification the Thais were apprehensive lest the British sought strategic control over Kra as a defence for Malaya. That had, however, received some consideration in London. Bringing Pattani into Malaya received very little.

Conclusion

In the Japanese phase Southeast Asia had come, for the first time, under the control of one power. The effect was lessened by the improvisatory nature of the policies that power adopted. The territories, already under different regimes, were taken over by different means and at different times. But in any case the Greater East Asia Co-Prosperity Sphere had a variety of inflections, ranging all the way from the harshly assimilative policies of Japanese colonialism in Korea and Taiwan to the puppetry of Manchukuo and the Wang Ching-wei regime, also incorporating practices borrowed from the metropolis itself; and those inflexions partly varied with the authority concerned, army or navy, partly with the variety of agencies involved, and, as with all empires, partly with the individuals on the spot. The forces the Japanese had were thinly spread, and soon engaged in defensive operations. That produced more improvisations, more diverse initiatives. Even what was common to the whole enterprise, the humiliating elimination of the colonial regimes, was also differential. The French were left in occupation till March 1945.

Allied victory again brought change to the whole region. But this time it was not all encompassed in one military endeavour: the bombs brought Japan's surrender before the wars of reconquest/liberation had been completed. Nor were the Allies agreed among themselves. The leading power, the United States, was not prepared to oppose the return of its European allies to their colonies in Southeast Asia, but it was not anxious to support them. Nor did the Europeans entirely agree. The British wanted the French and the Dutch to return to Southeast Asia, but wished them to pursue more liberal colonial policies than they had pre-war. Their own plans were based on what they believed was a new kind of relationship which would enable Europeans still to play a major role in Southeast Asia. But those plans would have a better chance of success if their European allies followed a similar approach. What had been a colonial region which European powers had divided among themselves, but otherwise made few attempts to view as a whole, must now be viewed more positively. Too close a collaboration would arouse the suspicion of the Americans and increase rather than diminish local opposition. But a common approach was desirable.

That was going to be difficult to achieve. For one thing, the colonial powers were under different domestic pressures. For another, they faced very different situations in their several Southeast Asian territories. And the former reacted on their chances of pursuing a flexible approach to the latter. They, too, improvised, in the case of the French and the Dutch without that sense of an overall political aim which the Japanese, too, had lacked, but which the British at least possessed. There was, however, a common outcome. The idea that there was some halfway house between colonial status and national independence did not survive. Paradoxically the Co-Prosperity Sphere had helped to evoke a sense of nationalism that made an alternative impossible.

The British no longer possessed as surely as before the military force they had drawn from India. Japan had sought to turn their instrument against them, initially by fomenting disloyalty, and then by creating the volunteer Indian National Army. After the British collapse, many joined, though officers tended to be constrained by their oath, but the cautious approach the Japanese army adopted was alienating, and the INA collapsed after the arrest of its leader Mohan Singh in December 1942. It was revived during 1943, when Subhas Chandra Bose returned from Germany, and formed a Provisional Government of Free India. It was permitted to join the Imphal offensive, which was a disaster. The INA had some effect, however. During the war Indians had numbered 700 000 of the one million Allied troops in Southeast Asia, and they were still essential to the British. But the reaction to the trials of INA personnel that began in November 1945 made the British apprehensive of their continued loyalty and cautious about they way they used them.

S. C. Bose was allowed to call himself head of state. 'What then is the state of his head?' K. P. P. Menon wondered.[54] In November 1943 the Japanese announced that the Provisional Government of Free India would take over the Andaman and Nicobar islands, which they had captured in March 1942. Bose said it was 'symbolic', as the islands had been used for political prisoners. In fact deportation had diminished interwar, and the government had looked towards the creation of a self-supporting community, the origins of which lay in the ticket-of-leave system begun in the 1860s. For the indigenous islanders the Japanese occupation was another disaster. Food was short because of the Allied blockade. The Japanese commander's policy was ruthlessly to 'eliminate the old and infirm', leaving only those who could work for the invaders.[55]

Notes

1 q. G. Bennett, ed., *The Concept of Empire*, London: Black, 1962, p. 70.
2 Brooke to Jolly, 22 November 1856. MSS Pac. s 90, vol. 1, Rhodes House Library, Oxford.
3 q. H. Benda, 'The Pattern of Administrative Reforms in the Closing Years of Dutch Rule in Indonesia', JRAS, 25, 4 (August 1966), p. 591n.
4 C. A. Majul, *Apolinario Mabini*, Manila: National Heroes Commission, 1964, pp. 123–4.
5 q. R. Paredes, 'The Partido Federal, 1900–1907, Political Collaboration in Colonial Manila', PhD thesis, Michigan U, 1989, p. 194.
6 Ileto and Sullivan, p. 40.
7 *Power and Culture*, Harvard UP, 1981.
8 q. Mavis Rose, *Indonesia Free*, Cornell UP, p. 19.
9 q. R. McVey, *The Rise of Indonesian Communism*, Cornell UP, p. 59.
10 cf. R. B. Smith, 'The Foundation of the Indochinese Communist Party, 1929–30', MAS, 32, 4 (September 1998), p. 77.
11 Notes in W.O. to F.O., 21 January 1918. F.O. 371/3235[13287].
12 q. N. Tarling, *Britain, Southeast Asia and the Onset of the Pacific War*, CUP, 1996, p. 22.
13 *The War Diaries*, London: Collins, 1978, p. 71.
14 q. Ikeda Kyoshi in Ian Nish, ed., *Anglo-Japanese Alienation*, CUP, 1982, p. 144.
15 T. Friend, *Between Two Empires*, Yale UP, 1965, p. 195.
16 q. G. Goodman, 'Consistency is the Hobgoblin ... ', JSEAS, 14, 1 (March 1983), p. 90.
17 COS 1245B. CAB 4/24, Public Record Office, London.
18 q. C. L. M. Penders, ed., *Indonesia: Selected Documents*, St Lucia: UQP, 1977, p. 159.
19 q. N. A. Bootsma, *Buren in de koloniale tijd*, Dordrecht: Foris, 1986, p. 23.
20 q. B. Dahm, *History of Indonesia in the Twentieth Century*, London: Pall Mall, 1971, p. 49.
21 q. J. Ingleson, *Road to Exile*, Singapore: Heinemann, 1979, p. 40.
22 q. W. D. McIntyre, *The Rise and Fall of the Singapore Naval Base*, London: Macmillan, 1980, p. 22.
23 Balfour, q. W. D. McIntyre, 'The Strategic Significance of Singapore ... ', JSEAH, 10, 1 (March 1969), p. 73.

24 q. ibid., p. 94.
25 q. N. Tarling, 'Sir Cecil Clementi and the Federation of British Borneo', JMBRAS, 44, 2 (1971), p. 14.
26 q. J. F. Laffey, 'French Far Eastern Policy in the 1930s', MAS, 23, 1 (1989), p. 133.
27 q. Tarling, *Pacific War*, p. 50.
28 *CHSEA*, II, p. 329.
29 q. Turnbull, *Singapore*, p. 193.
30 Leon Salim, ed. A. Kahin, *Prisoners at Kota Cane*, Cornell UP, 1986, p. 97.
31 H. Tinker, 'A Forgotten Long March … ', JSEAS, 6, 1 (March 1975), p. 4.
32 q. Tarling, *Pacific War*, p. 276.
33 P. Baudouin, *The Private Diaries*, London: Eyre and Spottiswoode, 1948, pp. 198–9.
34 q. Thamsook Numnonda, *Thailand and the Japanese Presence, 1941–45*, Singapore: ISEAS, 1977, p. 48.
35 q. Reynolds in Khamchoo and Reynolds, p. 183.
36 q. Usui in Nish, *Alienation*, p. 96.
37 *Japanese Cultural Policies in Southeast Asia during World War 2*, Basingstoke: Macmillan, 1991, p. 4.
38 Salim, p. 112.
39 Fujiwara Iwaichi, *F. Kikan*, Hong Kong: Heinemann, 1983, pp. 226, 227.
40 q. Iriye, p. 166.
41 q. H. Benda et al., *Japanese Military Administration in Indonesia*, Yale UP, 1965, p. 242.
42 q. N. Tarling, *Britain, Southeast Asia and the Onset of the Cold War*, CUP, 1998, p. 3.
43 q. John W. Cell, *Hailey*, CUP, 1992, p. 269.
44 q. W. R. Louis, *Imperialism at Bay*, Oxford: Clarendon P, 1977, p. 136.
45 q. A. Stockwell, 'Colonial Planning during World War II: the Case of Malaya', JICH, 2, 3 (1974), p. 335.
46 q. N. Tarling, *The Fourth Anglo-Burmese War*, Gaya: Centre for South East Asian Studies, 1987, p. 42.
47 q. A. J. Stockwell, *British Policy and Malayan Politics*, KL: MBRAS, 1979, p. 37.
48 q. Stockwell, JICH, p. 341.
49 A. Maddison, 'Dutch Income in and from Indonesia', MAS, 23, 4 (October 1989), p. 646.
50 q. Yong Mun Cheong, *H. J. van Mook and Indonesian Independence*, The Hague: Nijhoff, 1982, p. 202.
51 H. L. Wesseling, 'Post-Imperial Holland', JContempH, 15 (1980), p. 127.
52 q. E. J. Hammer, *The Struggle for Indochina*, Stanford UP, 1954, p. 44n.
53 ibid., p. 43.
54 q. H. Toye, 'The First Indian National Army', JSEAS, 15, 2 (September 1984), p. 380.
55 Census, p. x.

Nation-States

In the aftermath of World War II, independent nation-states emerged in Southeast Asia, often not without struggle, and then sought to consolidate their position. In Burma the struggle was less overt than in Indonesia. In Malaya the British had to jettison their plan for a Union, though they persisted with making Sarawak and North Borneo (Sabah) into colonies. Malaya became independent in 1957. The Malaysia scheme of 1961, designed to include the three Borneo territories and Singapore in a wider federation, was challenged by Indonesia's policy of 'confrontation', as well as the Philippines claim to Sabah. Till then the United States had generally been supportive of Indonesia. In Vietnam, on the other hand, it supported the French against the communist-led nationalist movement. After the Geneva agreements of 1954, it supported the non-communist government in the south, and in Thailand it supported the military-led regimes.

The independent states of Southeast Asia emerged into what was becoming a world of nation-states, and they were to benefit from that process and to contribute to it. Though they had all come under Japanese control in the previous phase, they did not secure their independence simultaneously or in similar circumstances. They did, however, have one common feature: they inherited the borders established, though for other purposes, in the colonial phase. The arbitrariness of the Japanese towards those frontiers had not undermined them: rather the reverse. The creation of the United Nations and the Cold War struggles tended to preserve them.

In the Japanese phase, as indeed in the colonial phase, international factors had a major impact on Southeast Asia. The same was still the case during the struggles for independence and indeed subsequently. To adopt the Indonesian terms, independence was won, not simply by 'struggle' but by 'diplomacy'. Some independence movements were more fortunate than others. Not merely was it important to recognise the international factors that might work in their favour: the attitude of other powers, particularly the super-powers; but also the emergence of other independent states. It was also a question of timing. And that was something the nationalist leaders could not alone determine.

Nor indeed could the colonial powers. Yet international factors were also crucial to them. They were, too, in any case engaged in a venture in which they needed more than ever to control the process of change over time. Returning to their colonial possessions seemed, to borrow Dorman-Smith's phrase, to be 'setting back the clock',[1] and in fact their initial plans, such as they were, proved largely irrelevant. In the hope of controlling the process of change they adapted their plans, though seldom sufficiently. They also sought to combine those political initiatives with a judicious use of force, their object being, as in the previous phase, to establish a framework of collaboration within which the application of minimal force could achieve maximum effect. Indeed, the concepts involved in their attempt to return after the war still resembled those upon which their earlier colonies had been built: they involved not merely the application of force, in which they were now indeed quite deficient, but the winning-over of collaborators. For this, they soon recognised, they needed time. They were tempted to use force to secure a 'breathing space'. But it had now become difficult to use in the old way, even if it was available. It could no longer be an exemplary demonstration of power, since defeat had lost the Europeans their prestige. Nor could it readily be placed in the context of collaboration, which nationalism was doing so much to dislodge. Indeed it could be counter-productive. The British were better than the French and the Dutch in setting their use of force in a political framework. But their flexibility did not mean that they were everywhere entirely successful in restoring their control.

The international context

In the war, as before it, Europe was the priority of the major powers, and that continued to be the case at the end of the war. Other parts of the world, including Southeast Asia, tended to be seen in that perspective. The United States and the Soviet Union, whose prophesied rise as the super-powers of the world the war had finally brought about, were clearly potential rivals in Europe, even before the so-called Cold War in which they were subsequently engaged had begun. For a while at least, the United Kingdom conceived that there was an opportunity for a 'third force' in Europe. Of this, it saw itself as the leader, a victorious power, possessor still of an empire, in a position to give leadership on the continent. That required the development of good relations with the Western European states, in particular with France, with which indeed the treaty of Dunkirk was signed in March 1947, but also with lesser states, including the Netherlands. The policy was always an over-ambitious one, and as the Russians became more threatening, the British turned increasingly to the United States, though hoping still to be the main link between it and Western Europe. The United States announced the Marshall Aid programme in June 1947. The Russians did not participate, but set up the Cominform in September. The 'Zhdanov line', stressing that the world was divided into two camps, one social imperialist and anti-democratic, the other democratic and anti-imperialist, was reaffirmed at the Calcutta Youth Conference in February 1948. That year the growing Cold War was intensified by the seizure of power in Czechoslovakia and by the Berlin blockade. It was in the context of the Cold War that the United States viewed the victory of the Chinese communists and the setting-up of the People's Republic in October 1949, and the outbreak of the Korean War in June 1950 was seen in the same light.

Those events indeed shifted the perspectives on Southeast Asia that the outside powers adopted. Initially the super-powers gave it limited attention. Britain endeavoured to take a lead among the returning powers, both by utilising the influence that its role in Mountbatten's South-East Asia Command gave it, and by setting an example. It argued that the Europeans could re-establish themselves in the short term and sustain their interests in the longer term only by coming to terms with the nationalist movements that the war had stimulated. That Britain sought to do itself, adjusting its ambitious postwar plans to meet the unanticipated circumstances under which the war had ended. But the British believed that setting an example was not sufficient, and that the other European powers must be persuaded to move along the same lines. Britain recognised that, as a result of the war and the interregnum, nationalism was active throughout Southeast Asia, and that the region was becoming more quickly than had been anticipated part of the world of states. The imperial approach to Southeast Asia was outdated. A new regional approach should succeed it: indeed it was a counterpart to the recognition by the independence movements that the success of one could help another. There was another reason for the policy the British adopted. They needed the friendship of the Dutch and the French in Europe. Their programmes in Europe and Southeast Asia would come together better if those powers adopted the same kind of strategy in their part of the region as the British. But example and persuasion might not suffice, and, as in colonial times, the British were generally unwilling to risk their European policies for the sake of their Southeast Asian interests. In general they put more pressure on the Dutch than on the French. Partly as a result, the Indonesians secured international recognition of their independence in 1949. The Vietnamese were far from it.

By that time Southeast Asia was being seen in Cold War terms. In the immediate postwar period the Soviet Union had given the struggles that developed there relatively little attention, and indeed, in the hope that it would secure a triumph in Europe in 1946–47, it had avoided taking up the colonial cause, only shifting with its disappointment, as the creation of the Cominform and the enunciation of the Zhdanov 'struggle line' suggested. The colonial powers had, however, sought to emphasise the role international communism was allegedly playing in support of the resistance they faced in the hope of eliciting US interest. From 1948–49, US aid was more forthcoming. The Korean War led the Americans to implement a policy of containment, believing that it would not have occurred 'but for an equivocal American statement regarding South Korea's expendability'.[2] It involved a peace treaty with Japan, the ANZUS pact, and support for the Kuomintang on Taiwan. In the eyes of the British, the policy put excessive emphasis on military alliances and security com-mitments. They sought to moderate it, and to stress other values, partly in order to avoid a full-scale war with China, partly in order to accommodate the views of the leaders of India, which had secured its independence within the Commonwealth in 1947, and partly, and in particular by that means, to maintain a role in the making of Western policy towards Southeast Asia. The French, by contrast, secured American support for the military struggle in Indo-China into which they had entered late in 1946, but which they had been unable to bring to a satisfactory conclusion.

A stalemate between the two super-powers became apparent in 1952–53 and, with the 19th Congress, Stalin's death, and the Korean armistice, Soviet policy began to shift towards one of peaceful coexistence and economic competition. China's adoption of this policy produced a detente in its relations with India, and Zhou Enlai and Nehru endorsed the five principles of coexistence in 1954. Nehru accepted that India needed peace, and that its influence in world affairs was 'very strictly lim-ited'.[3] His principles of coexistence created an 'atmosphere' in which force became a little more difficult to use. For China, of course, India's opposition to imperialism in Southeast Asia was an advantage. The principles were included in the preamble to the Sino-Indian agreement on Tibet in 1954, and reiterated at the conference Indonesia convened at Bandung in 1955, where Zhou demonstrated 'sweet reason-ableness'.[4] China had also accepted the Geneva agreements on Indo-China, which it could see, too, as a step towards the exclusion of Western influence from neigh-bouring mainland Southeast Asia.

That, however, was not acceptable to the United States, which formed the South-East Asia Treaty Organization (SEATO), and took steps to deny success to commu-nism in Southeast Asia. That could not be done by applying the doctrine of 'massive retaliation' the new Eisenhower administration had announced, and the United States had finally to introduce troops into Vietnam as it had unprecedentedly, but under UN auspices, in Korea. The struggle became a focus of the split between the Soviet Union and the PRC, allies since 1950. China could not compete as an eco-nomic power: the Great Leap Forward failed, and after 1957, and still more after 1959, it came to see its ally as a rival, too soft to the imperialists, while the Soviet Union withdrew its technicians and more or less suspended its aid. The British were appre-hensive lest the Chinese should be prompted to join in the Vietnamese conflict as they had in the Korean. The India card could not be played. To the Soviet Union's regret China had also challenged India on the Tibetan frontier in 1959, and defeated it in an outright clash in 1962. But, though the United States bombed north Vietnam as well as introducing troops in the south, it stopped short of action likely to produce overt Chinese counter-action. The PRC had detonated its bomb in September 1964.

The decision to withdraw US troops from Vietnam was facilitated by the contin-uance of the Sino-Soviet rift. It led to another deal, this time between China and the United States. Under the Guam doctrine of 1969, the United States stressed more than ever that Asian countries would have to defend themselves, albeit with aid and advice and a shield against nuclear attack. At the same time the United States encouraged Japan to play a strong economic role in Southeast Asia. It had encouraged Japan to look to that region in the early 1950s, when it could not look to the markets and resources of China, and believed it could contribute to its 'stabilisation' and the 'economic integration' of 'the free nations of Asia'.[5] It was thus prominent in forming the Aid-Indonesia International Consortium in 1966 and played a leading part in the Asian Development Bank. The United States had contributed to the 'miracle' of Japan's economic success, and in Southeast Asia Japan was helped by information acquired in the war, by links with Chinese commercial networks, and by paying reparations. Japan's international trade indeed gave it a strategic interest in Southeast Asia as well: 90 per cent of its oil—now from the Middle East—came through the Straits. By contrast the British were, after confrontation, withdrawing east of Suez.

In Malaya the British had identified the opposition they faced in the 'Emergency' from mid-1948 as communist, though they were never entirely sure that it was supported from outside. Their answer was, however, characteristically not merely military but also political. Indeed they quickly saw that their time-scale must change, and Malaya must advance to independence much more quickly than they had anticipated. It became an independent state in 1957. That also seemed to offer a way for providing for the independence of Britain's remaining dependencies in the region. In the 1950s no one thought that small states could survive: the world was too dangerous; development seemed to require a strong domestic economic base. Those were reasons why Britain resorted to creating a series of federal structures as a means to decolonisation. Of these Malaysia was one. The connexion, represented so far by the war-time concept of a governor-general and by the subsequent appointment of a commissioner-general, was in 1963 consolidated into a form of federation, only the protected sultanate of Brunei standing out.

At that point Vietnam was the site of intensifying conflict. Two rival regimes competed, as the Trinh and the Nguyen had in the seventeenth century. In some sense, it was again a civil war, seen now in terms of a single nation-state. In another sense, it was an international war of quite a different order. The United States identified the cause of the regime in the south as the cause of the 'free world' in its Cold War with communism, while the regime in the north looked both to the Soviet Union and the PRC. Only in 1975 did the United States finally withdraw. With that, the region became almost entirely part of the world of states. But that made it possible, and perhaps necessary, for those states to conceive of themselves more as part of a region.

In their attempts to influence the way the Dutch and the French handled the nationalist movements they faced on their return, the British pointed to the example of their dealings with India and Burma. In neither case, it was true, had things gone according to plan. But at least the British could point up the need to develop a plan in the first place, and then to be flexible in attempting to implement it. In Burma, they accepted independence more quickly and completely than they had contemplated. The new government was, however, challenged from the start, and the British ceased to be confident in pointing to Burma as an example. The steps they took to support the new government enabled them to enlist the cooperation of newly independent India, however, and they could at least offer the spectacle of Commonwealth collaboration. The new state was also put at risk by a covert American attempt to open a second front in the Korean War by financing Kuomintang troops who penetrated the Shan states. Not surprisingly Burma was to affirm a policy of neutralism, to make a border settlement with the PRC, ceding the Namwan tract, and to conclude a treaty in 1960 binding each party not to enter a military alliance against the other. The Kuomintang intervention also boosted insurgency (and opium-growing) and thus helped to overthrow civilian rule.

On one point at least the British had surely been right. What was emerging, as they recognised, was a region of nation-states. They shaped their policy accordingly and wanted others to do so, too. That did not always happen. Yet the Cold War struggles led that way as well. The super-powers competed for the allegiance of nation-states. The principles of coexistence affirmed the endorsement of their borders, and they were rarely openly challenged. Now and then the British were concerned about the implications for small states. Could they survive? That was one question. Could they be denied? That was another. Was the 'Commonwealth club' to be 'the R.A.C. or Boodles'?[6]

Aung San

Mountbatten, among others, blamed the returning governor, Dorman-Smith, for the failure of Britain's policy in Burma. Had he collaborated with Aung San and the Anti-Fascist People's Freedom League, the argument ran, he might have been more successful in restoring an economy devastated by two series of battles, and ensured that Burma would have agreed, like India, to remain in the Commonwealth. In turn, the minority peoples might have felt less defenceless against the Burman majority, and Burma would not have faced the instability that it was Britain's purpose to avoid. The latter part of this argument has some credibility, but the former not.

Aung San and the AFPFL had certainly been strengthened, both politically and militarily, by the collaboration they had offered the British during the reconquest/liberation. The governor was, however, in no position to accept their dominance even if he had been so disposed. Though allied since 1941 with the Soviet Union, the United Kingdom saw itself as having fought for democracy against totalitarianism. One-party rule was not at this time acceptable in Burma or elsewhere. 'We do not want to see, in Burma or in any other country, the rapid seizing of power by any particular group of people.'[7] Sir Stafford Cripps had so made the point in the House of Commons in June, and when his party formed the government, it reiterated that view. The Secretary of State agreed that Dorman-Smith could not accept the terms Aung San set for joining his Executive Council in October. The British government, not merely its governor, wanted a plural system of politics.

That was, it seemed in retrospect, a decisive moment, T. L. Hughes believed: 'Failure to persuade AFPFL to join the governor's Executive Council on mutually acceptable terms was probably the seed which ultimately led to the severance of ties with Britain'.[8] For without the cooperation of the AFPFL, the governor could not carry out the programme envisaged by the White Paper of 17 May. He sought to revive politics by bringing back pre-war politicians, even the pre-war premier Saw, whom the British had detained during the war on the ground that he had offered his services to the Japanese, but that only added to his embarrassment. One of them accused Aung San of a wartime crime, but the British could not risk bringing him to trial. The prime minister, Clement Attlee, decided that the governor had lost his grip, though it would be fairer to say that he had failed to work an unworkable policy. He was replaced. Aung San concluded that he was winning what he hesitated to call the fourth Anglo-Burmese war, since the Burmans had lost the first three.[9]

Though the British rarely saw the use of force as a substitute for policy, it was also true that they felt particularly hampered in Burma's case. They had seen their rule in Burma from the very start in an Indian perspective, and they continued to do so. Deploying additional troops in Burma, so as to increase the governor's leverage, was virtually ruled out, since, given the demobilisation of British troops, they would have to come from India, and employing Indian troops against a nationalist movement would make it even more difficult to come to terms with the politicians in India, even perhaps risk the security of the raj in a transition period. The INA trials and the fact that Indians had already been used in Indo-China and Indonesia in order, as the British hoped, to secure a satisfactory settlement there, only made it more difficult to use them in Burma, and Mountbatten perhaps took some pleasure in pointing it out to Dorman-Smith in January 1946. When the governor contemplated arresting Aung San, he was stopped, not by his own indecisiveness, but because the British government were concerned lest it affect the Cabinet's mission to India. On the other hand, AFPFL 'still retained its potent military arm'.[10] Of the Patriotic Bumese Forces, 5700 were in the regular army, and the rest in the 'People's Volunteer Organisation'.

Dorman-Smith was replaced by Mountbatten's nominee, Hubert Rance, in mid-1946. Aung San was not prepared 'to start all over again' as he had put it,[11] and the new governor was confronted on his arrival by nation-wide strikes that demonstrated AFPFL strength. The British government now conceded an AFPFL majority on the Executive Council, the more readily because of Aung San's break with communist elements, and agreed to talks in London in January 1947 that might result in independence after elections had been held. Aung San had apparently won the 'war'. But the British hoped that, with these concessions, the Burmese would at least remain in the Commonwealth, even though at that time membership still involved accepting the sovereign of Great Britain as the head of state, and a republican regime, to which the AFPFL had, like the Indian Congress, committed itself, was impossible. The fourth Anglo-Burmese war might thus end with honour, even with a kind of victory.

Any hope of this—and it was always slim, if not negligible, though Aung San had declared that Burma's aim was to be 'another Egypt'[12]—was ruined by his assassination on 19 July 1947. A session of the Executive Council that morning was sprayed with Sten gun bullets, apparently at the behest of the disappointed Saw. Aung San's successor, Nu, could not take the risk of advocating that Burma should stay in the Commonwealth, particularly given the suspicion that Britons were involved in the assassination. Burma became independent outside the Commonwealth on 4 January 1948. The British accepted that to press the regime to stay in, as India, and also Pakistan, had in the event done, might only reduce the prospects for stability.

In their extensive planning for postwar Burma, the British had also taken account of what had come to be seen as the 'minority' peoples. Some were to remain apart from parliamentary Burma for the time being, as they had been under the 1935 constitution—the Shans and Kachins, for example. In early 1947 time was suddenly up, and the British could do little more than ease their conscience over the terms on which these peoples entered the Union of Burma and trust in Aung San. The Karens were an even greater problem, since in the lowlands they were intermixed with Burmans. Their concept of a 'Karenistan' was never viable, but it is not clear that the British fully realised the seriousness of their opposition to the new structure. Leaving the Commonwealth, furthermore, was in some sense the last straw. While Britain could not in any case have intervened, the minorities felt all the more abandoned and desperate at the prospect of 'majority' Burman rule. Membership of the Commonwealth and stability were not after all alternatives.

Indonesian independence

To the Dutch in Indonesia the British offered the example of India and Burma: Admiral Helfrich countered by comparing Sukarno and Hatta with S. C. Bose, a 'much less comfortable parallel'.[13] The British also brought pressure to bear. That was possible because at the end of the war the Dutch had neither land nor sea forces available, and they were therefore dependent on SEAC and the British who dominated it. The task of the SEAC forces was to disarm the Japanese and to rescue the prisoners-of-war and civilian internees. But the British believed that they had to go beyond that. Even to achieve those tasks, they were committed to a measure of intervention. Aware of the contribution that the Dutch had made in the European war, and seeking their future collaboration, they concluded that they were obliged to give them a measure of assistance. The relationship was not entirely unlike that at the end of the French wars 130 years earlier, though placed in the new context of nationalism. The British wanted the Dutch to return, but the Dutch thought their approach ungenerous. The support they offered was insufficient. Indeed the British had to reckon with the fact that they were for the most part using Indian troops. Moreover, they had recognised that the Europeans' position in Southeast Asia in future would depend on reaching an accommodation with the nationalists in each country. Attached to the offer of help, therefore, was a price: a reasonable deal with the nationalists.

What, however, was a reasonable deal? The European powers depended on finding collaborators on whom they could rely: they had never been able to rely solely on compulsion and certainly could not do so now, despite Helfrich's view that 'when dealing with native rabble, the most effective way is to hit immediately and hit hard'.[14] But the Dutch, shocked by the strength of the nationalist movement, found it difficult to deal with its leaders, and they found it particularly difficult to deal with those who, like Sukarno, had 'collaborated' with the Japanese, since, after their experience of Nazi rule, 'collaboration' was a dirty word. Impressed by the determined opposition they met in the battle of Surabaya in November, the British found their attitude quite unrealistic, but had difficulty in bringing about the negotiations between the two parties that they believed offered the only possibility of a solution in the short or the long term. They adopted the risky policy of offering the Dutch further support on condition that they negotiated. But the negotiations were pursued in such a way that it was easy to conclude that the Dutch were simply playing for time and getting Britain to prevent the Indonesian Republic's attaining complete control before they had built up their forces.

That, perhaps, was not entirely fair, for the Dutch also had elections to face in May 1946, and the politicians did not want to enter them facing the accusation that they had abandoned the colony on which it seemed the revival of the kingdom might depend. Indeed the Dutch political system did not offer the government the flexibility that Labour, with its huge 1945 majority, enjoyed in Britain. A multi-party approach conduced to caution, to the politics of formula rather than statesmanship. Lieut.-Governor-General van Mook believed that he had found, in the French accord with the Vietnamese of 6 March, a way of approaching the Indonesians. But the negotiations that followed at Hoge Veluwe got nowhere.

Developing in the new context the concept put forward in the Queen's speech of 1942, the Dutch also developed earlier federalist ideas. They now planned a federal Indonesian state, which should be a partner with the Netherlands in the Kingdom of the Netherlands. Of this federation, the Republic which the nationalists had proclaimed would be a part, along with other states set up in other parts of Indonesia. Immediate reoccupation was impossible, but such a structure, the Dutch hoped, could be set up stage by stage. In this way, indeed, they hoped, as in the colonial phase, to mix force and diplomacy. A military build-up would be more useful if it contributed to a diplomatic approach, rather than substituted for it. In parts of the outer islands, particularly in East Indonesia, where the Japanese navy had not encouraged nationalism and the Australians had taken over promptly, their task was relatively easy. The Republic was far stronger in Java, and most of Sumatra identified with its cause. The use of force was at once more necessary and more problematical. The Dutch hoped to find collaborators, whom they could, if necessary, back by the limited application of force. But, amid the nationalist fervour of postwar Java, their concept of a collaborator was too limited, and the application of force only likely therefore to weaken rather than strengthen those who might work with them.

That was underlined by the tension among the Republicans themselves, which in a sense turned on a different perception of the same strategy. Some advocated 'struggle', others 'diplomacy'. The former sought to prevent compromise with the Dutch, the latter tried to use the former to gain leverage and secure a satisfactory compromise with the Dutch. They had, they recognised, an advantage the Indonesians had not possessed in their contentions with the Dutch in the colonial phase. Then the Anglo-Dutch agreement isolated them from the outside world, and no state took up their cause. Now the position differed in both respects. That 'internationalisation' was indeed another condition with which the Dutch failed fully to come to terms.

Determined to withdraw their troops by the end of November 1946, the British brought about negotiations between the Dutch and the Republic, which led to the Linggadjati agreement in November. In the subsequent months, despite further British diplomatic intervention, negotiations over implementing the agreement became deadlocked. Those among the Dutch who favoured the use of military force—either as a substitute for a diplomacy that had failed, or as a back-up to a diplomacy they thought might then succeed—had their way in July 1947. 'It is not wishful thinking', van Mook had declared, 'that with military action, I hope to create the conditions for a sound implementation of Linggadjati on the basis of cooperation from inside out'.[15] The build-up had put the Netherlands under great economic pressure, and this seemed the way both to secure control over the most valuable areas and to secure the Republic's compliance. It did neither, but it strengthened international opposition.

The fortnight-long 'police action', begun on 20 July, certainly produced territorial gains for the Dutch, but, while two-thirds of Java and one-third of Sumatra were occupied, guerrilla warfare continued. At the same time, Australia and India brought the matter before the United Nations. 'The spirit of new Asia will not tolerate such things', Nehru declared.[16] To avoid worse alternatives, the United States secured the establishment of a Good Offices Committee, including members from Australia, Belgium, and the United States itself. 'Good offices' alone did not suffice to bring the antagonists together, but a further agreement was finally signed early in 1948 on board the USS *Renville*.

The conflict was not resolved, however: in a sense it was repeated. The Dutch pressed ahead with creating in the areas they controlled states that would form part of the federal structure. The Republic, unable to accept what it saw as unilateral actions, continued guerrilla activities. The Dutch had difficulty in meeting them with military force, though as before they also hoped that deploying it would at once elicit the cooperation of those they saw as 'moderates', strengthen their leverage in negotiations, and put them in a better position to resort to direct military action should that prove necessary. Over that the Dutch coalition hesitated, apprehensive of renewed international intervention. The Republic indeed continued to seek support from outside, and its government's success in putting down the ill-prepared communist-oriented revolt at Madiun in September 1948 won it a new degree of support from the United States, which during the year had become increasingly concerned over the threat of international communism. 'At a time of irresistible communist advance in China', the suppression of the revolt 'seemed to suggest that the Sukarno–Hatta government could be an anti-communist bulwark in Southeast Asia'.[17]

Despite US pressure, the right-wing elements in the Dutch coalition now had their way, and a second 'police action' ensued just before Christmas 1948. It enjoyed a measure of military success, but it was a complete political disaster. The Republican leaders were taken prisoner, and strategic sites were occupied, but guerrilla warfare continued, throwing power to the military, and still more to local units. The Dutch Resident in West Sumatra thought the situation 'strongly reminiscent of the Netherlands under German occupation'.[18] That affected the loyalty of the federalists, and so did the international reaction, far more intense than on the occasion of the first 'police action'. By attacking the moderate Sukarno–Hatta government, 'which is the only Government in the Far East to have crushed an all-out communist offensive', said the American Acting Secretary of State, 'the Dutch may have destroyed the last bridge between the West and the Indonesian nationalists, and have given the communists everywhere a weapon of an unanswerable mass appeal'.[19] Despite its European priorities, the United States threatened the Netherlands with a reduction in Marshall Aid and a deferral of military equipment assistance. The Dutch had no alternative but to return to the negotiations, now on a more unfavourable basis than ever. Enough had been lost already, business interests believed.

At The Hague Round Table Conference of 1949, the Dutch had thus to concede the independence of the Republic of the United States of Indonesia, without indeed either firmly establishing the proposed Netherlands–Indonesia Union or securing useful guarantees of their interests. What they did obtain again proved damaging rather than helpful. Anxious to ensure the support of the States General for an outcome that conservatives saw as a catastrophe, the cabinet wanted to be able to say that the flag still flew in Asia. That was a major factor in a dispute over the inclusion of West New Guinea in the new Republic, which claimed to inherit the frontiers of the colonial state. In 1949 the matter was deferred, but further discussions did not resolve it.

The dispute intensified throughout the 1950s, becoming the focus of the nationalistic trend in Indonesian domestic politics pursued by Sukarno and those Herb Feith has described as 'solidarity-makers'. The Dutch sacrificed their business interests to their policy conceptions. 'Even a child could have seen the serious risks involved.'[20] In 1957 Dutch properties were expropriated and Dutch citizens left. The Indonesian government also sought to internationalise its case, mobilising support from the increasing number of independent Afro-Asian countries, one object of the Bandung conference, and bringing it before the UN General Assembly, though in what was then a much smaller body, without gaining the two-thirds majority it needed. The government was in effect repeating the strategy that had helped to win independence, mixing force and diplomacy, as the colonial power itself once had. 'Military plans are to be geared to the diplomatic battle', Sukarno told Suharto.[21] It finally worked.

The United States had been associated with the winning of independence, but it had become increasingly concerned over the revival of the Indonesian Communist Party (PKI) in the early 1950s, and in particular over its association with Sukarno and the solidarity-makers. Secretary of State Dulles told Ambassador Cumming that preserving unity could be a danger: in China it had led to communist domination. Rather than a communist-leaning unity, he would prefer a breakup of Indonesia, 'furnishing a fulcrum which the United States could work later to help them eliminate Communism in one place or another, and then in the end, if they so wish arrive back again at a united Indonesia'.[22] The idea reappeared after the provincial elections of 1957. Dulles favoured the idea of supporting non- and anti-communist elements in Java, and for that purpose, and to provide 'a fall back should Java be lost', of supporting the dissident army leaders in the outer islands.[23] Some support was given to those who set up a rival government at Bukittinggi in February 1958. The rebels were, however, disappointing, the army unexpectedly effective. The policy was dropped after an American pilot was shot down and a more traditional view reasserted itself. The Indonesian government and the armed forces had, moreover, been turning for aid and arms to the Soviet Union, and the United States believed it had to compete.

The outcome was that it intervened over West New Guinea in support of the Indonesian claim. In October 1961 the Dutch had offered to transfer it to the United Nations in 'a last vain effort to avoid the necessity of turning the territory over to Indonesia'.[24] Now the United States promoted a settlement in 1961—turning West New Guinea over to the United Nations only briefly, and paying lip-service to 'the self-determination trick'[25] that the Dutch played—that virtually ensured the Indonesian take-over that in fact ensued after a so-called 'act of free choice' in 1969. In the meantime, despite the Americans' hope that the Indonesian government would now concentrate on economic and social development, the regime had gone on to 'confront' Malaysia.

Union and Federation

The British had returned to Malaya with a plan designed, like that for Burma, to remedy what they saw as defects in its social and political structure, and so enhance its security and put it on the path to self-government within the empire. The plan was bold—to create a Malayan Union of the disparate territories on the peninsula and to offer citizenship to the non-Malay communities—but the circumstances under which they attempted to implement it were not those that had been anticipated. There was no campaign of 'liberation', in which the British would have demonstrated their military strength; in which, too, the Malayan Chinese, strongly represented in the Malayan Communist Party with which Force 136 was in contact, would have played a substantial role. Instead there was an uneasy interregnum between the surrender and the reoccupation, marked by racial clashes, which continued even after the British returned.

Sir Harold MacMichael succeeded in concluding with the rulers the new treaties that were necessary to lay the basis for the Union by enhancing Britain's jurisdiction, rather as Jervois had planned in 1875. But, though they did not explicitly deprive the rulers of sovereignty, the Japanese occupation and the events of the interregnum had made the Malays more politically conscious, and the United Malays National Organisation, formed in March 1946 and led by Dato Onn, son of the first *mentri besar* of Johore, protested against the treaties, and persuaded the rulers to boycott the installation of Sir Edward Gent as first Governor of the Union on 1 April. He promptly advised a change in policy. The object, he now argued, must be to win over the Malays, lest they be radicalised by the example of the Indonesians, or even attracted to their cause. L. D. Gammans was amazed to find 'Malay women, who in my day took no part in public affairs at all, making speeches. The Malays have undoubtedly become politically conscious overnight.'[26] Prolonged discussions with the Malay leaders, but not with the leaders of the other 'communities', led to a revised proposal. The Union would be replaced by a Federation. Still, like the Union, excluding Singapore, the Federation would provide the political unity the British had sought. But the proposal not only restored the states structure that the Union had more or less eliminated; it also curtailed the access to citizenship it had offered to the non-Malay communities.

The leaders of those communities had not offered the Union much support, but they strongly opposed the new Federation. Their alienation offered the communists an opportunity. Despite, or perhaps in part because of, its relatively strong position at the end of the war, the Malay Communist Party had not presented the British with a direct political challenge. Now, possibly encouraged by the signals given at the Calcutta conference, and ever more clearly realising that their hopes of securing power by peaceful means were being frustrated, the communists turned to violence. A spate of terrorist acts prompted the British to declare an 'Emergency' in June 1948 and even to ban the Communist Party, though concerned lest that should harm the prospects of political development in Malaya and tarnish the political reputation of the British.

The uprising could be presented as a communist rather than a nationalist movement, and it received little sympathy or support outside Malaya. Its suppression, however, required a costly military effort, and even that was successful only because the British, unlike their neighbours, put their use of violence in a viable political context. The British encouraged moderate Chinese leaders, who set up the Malayan Chinese Association, and the Commissioner-General, Malcolm MacDonald, took a special interest in the Communities Liaison Committee. General Harold Briggs never lost sight of the political objectives, as Frank Furedi puts it.[27]

As early as 1950, the Defence Secretary in London was clear that it might be necessary to concede independence to Malaya 'prematurely', in order to contain nationalism.[28] Indeed what had at first been conceived as an attempt to regulate events in Malaya, and to gain time for orderly political advance, became a step in a race to independence. Twenty-five years were really needed, MacDonald said in June 1950, but 'we must be mentally prepared' to 'accept a quickening of the pace' because 'if we were to resist the pace of change we should lose the support of Asian leaders'.[29] That Malays and Chinese could work together politically, at least at the elite level, was demonstrated at the Kuala Lumpur elections of 1952, and still more persuasively by the elections to the Legislative Council in 1955. Independence followed on 31 August 1957. The Malay Communist Party had never got to the guerrilla phase, and had fallen back on terrorism. With independence 'the last support was knocked away from the MCP's pretensions to be the party of national liberation'.[30] The Emergency ended in 1960. A total of 2473 civilians were killed, 1865 members of the security forces, 6711 communists. The cost to the British and Malayan governments was 180 million pounds.

Singapore and Borneo

Singapore had not been included in the Malayan Union, nor in the Federation. For that there were a number of reasons. One was strategic. For the foreseeable future, Britain would have to retain forces in the area, though also encouraging its Commonwealth partners, Australia and New Zealand, to contribute to the defence of what R. G. Menzies had called the 'Near North'. Either way, a base was needed. The inclusion of Singapore in Malaya might make the control of that base problematic. Certainly it would put Britain's attempts at social and political engineering at risk, for Malays would be even more concerned for their future if the predominantly Chinese city were part of the new state: unification would be 'assisted by the non-inclusion of Singapore at any rate at the first stage', as Gent had put it.[31] Yet the British, conceiving that small states could not survive, believed that 'merger' would have to come, and that the question was again one of timing. The view was shared by the People's Action Party that won the Singapore elections of 1959. Only 'merger' would offer Singapore an adequate market for the socialist economy it wished to develop.

In the course of the struggles with the British in Singapore in the 1950s, it seemed that the political trend was continually to the left. The new rulers of Malaya began to contemplate the idea that the trend could be contained by the 'merger' they were at first unready to accept, and that was seized upon by the PAP leadership. Including the Singapore Chinese in the federation could, moreover, be balanced by also including the three Borneo territories.

There the plans the British had made during the war had in fact been carried out after it, and Sarawak and North Borneo had become colonies in July 1946. In the case of North Borneo, greatly in need of assistance after extensive destruction during the war, the British had been able to deal with the Company, and in 1949 the arbitrator awarded it 1.4 million pounds to liquidate the share capital. There had been no opposition in the territory itself. The Philippines, gaining their independence at the same time, considered raising a claim based on the 1878 lease from the Sultan of Sulu, but, anxious to avoid antagonising the British, decided against it.

Britain faced more difficulty in implementing its policy in Sarawak. There was opposition within the Brooke family. While the old raja, Vyner, believed that it was impossible to continue the old raj in the new circumstances, his nephew and would-be successor, Anthony Brooke, thought differently: he did not believe that Raja Vyner had the right, particularly after granting a constitution in 1941, to dispose of the raj. Nor was the way the assent of the Malay chiefs was secured creditable. The British government was compelled to review the process, but it did not, as in Malaya, abandon its policy. 'Cession' was finally carried in the Council Negri by nineteen to sixteen, but a majority of the non-Europeans voted against it. The first Colonial Office governor was faced with a Malay-led anti-cession movement, couched in pro-Brooke terms, which he treated with some severity. The struggle culminated in the assassination of his successor, Duncan Stewart, at Sibu in December 1949. After that it collapsed, but the divisions among the Malays the movement had caused continued.

The next step, in some sense a recurrence to the policy of Lucas or Clementi, was to bring the Borneo territories into some kind of closer relationship with one another. Thought premature in 1943, the plans were now, however, put off by the anti-cession movement in Sarawak. Nor was Sultan Ahmad Tajudin of Brunei helpful: 'Sarawak', he said, 'was not a *Kebun Getah* [rubber estate] to be sold off by the Rajah'.[32] He also resented the 1948 decision to make the Governor of Sarawak also High Commissioner for Brunei, though the only sign of public opposition to that, the Colonial Office was told, came from 'isolated members of now dormant youth association, notably school teachers who have tried to suggest this announcement of *fait accompli* is undemocratic'.[33] Even Sarawak and North Borneo, though both colonies, became, as time went by, more different rather than less. The unexpectedly rapid approach of Malaya's independence again raised the question of the future of Borneo. The idea of federation aroused little enthusiasm in Sarawak's Council Negri, and in Brunei, as the high commissioner put it, 'the quality are dead against it'.[34] The emergence of Azahari's more radical Partai Rakyat Brunei, and its advocacy of a unitary state of Kalimantan Utara, renewed Britain's caution over federation. Yet it seemed clear that the territories, like Singapore, would not be able to survive as independent states, and that the rise of the SUPP foretold left-wing Chinese dominance in Sarawak.

The prospect of including the Borneo states in a Malaysian federation, along with Singapore, thus attracted the British. That was what the Malayan prime minister, Tunku Abdul Rahman, envisaged. Some think, he said, 'that they should wait until the three territories have formed a federation of their own. ... But ... how long will this take? Years, I am afraid. Knowing the British for what they are, the longer the better—what you can do tomorrow, why bother to do today?'[35] At the same time, it was clear that the local leaders would require some persuasion. On this task the British and Malayan governments embarked in 1961–62. Their success with the Sarawak and Sabah leaders was considerable: 'by the end of 1961 the zealousness of the Borneo leaders to preserve their emerging national identities had toned down to mere uncertainty about getting on the band-wagon'.[36] A five-state consultative committee produced a memorandum supporting the concept, and a commission of inquiry headed by Lord Cobbold, set up by Britain in respect of its colonies of Sarawak and North Borneo, found that one-third of the people were strongly in favour, another third wanted safeguards, and the rest wanted independence first or wanted Britain to stay. In August 1962 Britain announced its agreement to form Malaysia and set the date at 31 August 1963. An intergovernmental committee, representing Britain, Malaya, North Borneo, and Sarawak, and chaired by Lord Lansdowne, worked out the conditions.

For Brunei, state-by-state inclusion in Malaysia was no better than inclusion in a Borneo bloc. Arguably Sultan Omar Ali Saifuddin III was never keen on either, nor on the democratisation that the British felt they had to advocate, despite the emergence of the PRB, and their interest in Brunei's oil. The sultan may have had some sympathy with the PRB, but it certainly gave him some leverage both against the Borneo federation proposal and against democratisation. Faced with direct incorporation in Malaysia, he evaded that as well. The British became protectors of a sultanate in which democracy retreated.

Denied the results of electoral success, and recognising that the creation of Malaysia would frustrate Kalimantan Utara, the PRB had led a revolt in December 1962. That internationalised the issue. It was, of course, always unlikely that so major a step as creating a new state in Southeast Asia out of the former British and British-protected states could have been simply seen as a *fait accompli* by its neighbours. Their own position was sure to be changed by it: would it, for example, add to or diminish their security? In addition to such basic questions, however, they possessed special interests in the area under consideration.

For the Philippines that was represented by the Sabah claim, which it had decided not to raise when North Borneo had been turned into a colony. Now, however, it would become part of a nation-state, and the chances of making good the claim, in a world of nation-states, would be virtually nil: if it was to be pursued at all, it had to be pursued now. The new President, Macapagal, had, moreover, identified himself with it and made it a political cause. It was, too, a step that might indicate that the Philippines could still pursue an independent foreign policy, though its independence was qualified. 'The published text of the new American–Philippine Treaty makes reservations as regards bases which detract considerably from the grant of full and sovereign independence', Lord Killearn had commented in 1946. Rehabilitation had been tied to economic concessions to US citizens, and those had required an amendment to the constitution. Being the first to gain independence, the Philippines had not had the advantage of precedent or example or pressure from others, even though still closely tied to the United States.

The British tried, perhaps too off-handedly, to dismiss the Sabah claim. A dispute 'might even lead to territorial claims being put forward by other South-East Asian countries. … Such developments would impair the stability of South-East Asia and the capacity of the peoples concerned for resolute united resistance to Communist encroachment and subversion.'[37] The claim, Taylor suggests, did not have only a pecuniary objective. It would give the Republic 'a voice in the future of the Malay area' and, if Malaysia did not eventuate, could be used to prevent an Indonesian takeover.[38] Macapagal spoke of a greater Malayan Confederation—Malaya, the Philippines, Singapore, and the three Borneo territories—as an 'Asian project', better than that of the colonialists.[39]

Nor were the British prepared to countenance the claims of the Indonesians. Unlike those of the Philippines, those were not, at least openly, territorial: they had claimed West New Guinea on the ground that it had been part of the colonial state, and the argument did not apply in northern Borneo. They could, however, argue a concern over security. Foreign occupation of West New Guinea left them with a weak frontier. The creation of a Malaysian state would change the status of the territories on their Borneo border. If they did not themselves seek to acquire them, the Indonesians had a legitimate interest in that change. Again the British tended to act in a way that seemed to recall the age of the colonial states rather than to be in keeping with the world of nation-states.

That said, however, it must also be admitted that it was not easy to find a means to involve Indonesia in the process without running the risk of its complete derailment. Lord Selkirk, however, visited Jakarta in August 1961, and discussed Malaysia with Foreign Minister Subandrio. At first, it seemed that Indonesia would not oppose, but that attitude shifted with the outbreak of the revolt in Brunei in December 1962. Indeed, the 'confrontation', or *konfrontasi*, of Malaysia now became, in succession to the campaign for West Irian, the new focus of Sukarno's search for domestic political consensus. Once more, too, he adopted the mixture of force and diplomacy with which Indonesia had secured its earlier successes. But this time it failed.

On the diplomatic front, it seems that, not surprisingly, the British left the initiative to Tunku Abdul Rahman, the Malayan prime minister. His approach to Brunei was so brusque as to be counter-productive, but towards the Philippines and Indonesia he was more accommodating. Indeed, during 1963, the three leaders agreed to set up an association, called Maphilindo, within which their differences might be resolved. Echoing ideas of the revolutionaries of the 1890s, the concept, larger than Macapagal had at first envisaged, appealed to the Filipinos, while to please Indonesia the leaders agreed to describe the foreign bases in the area as 'temporary'. Following Sukarno's protest against the conclusion of the UK–Malaya agreement on the formation of Malaysia, the leaders also agreed to ask the UN Secretary-General to determine whether the wishes of the people of Sarawak and

North Borneo had been accurately assessed. The report was positive. But the Malaysian leaders had gone ahead before that was announced. Sukarno declined to recognise Malaysia and stepped up his use of force. The British embassy in Jakarta was sacked and British estates taken over. The Sarawak frontier, already crossed, was infiltrated by regular troops, ostensibly 'volunteers'. In September 1964 paratroopers landed in Johore. The use of force was, however, ineffective, since it was not set in a compatible diplomatic context.

Certainly the British reacted strongly. If Malaysia had been a step in decolonisation, it was clearly going to require the application of force on a greater scale than they had anticipated. They remained, however, somewhat apprehensive lest the United States would once more, as in the West Irian case, resolve to conciliate Indonesian nationalism as a means of retaining Indonesian allegiance in the Cold War. Initially, indeed, ambassador Howard Jones was 'outraged' by Britain's 'cavalier and provocative tactics'.[40] The United States, said Robert Komer of the White House staff in July 1964, was 'jollying Sukarno along'. 'Rather a neutralist Sukarno than a Communist running the country. So it will make sense for us to lean over backwards (without sacrificing Malaysia), so long as there's even a reasonable chance that we can keep the lid from blowing up.'[41] But the militarisation of the conflict compelled Britain to withdraw troops from Germany, and US alarm contributed to the overruling of Jones's accommodationist policy. Even he lost sympathy with Indonesia when it began probes into Sarawak and landings on the peninsula. 'To Hell with your aid!' Sukarno had shouted.[42] He went too far. His use of force made Malaysia seem a victim, while internationally he began to seek support from the People's Republic. Supporting Malaysia was very costly for the British, and probably speeded their virtual withdrawal from Southeast Asia in the following years. But Sukarno's regime, and the leftward trend in Indonesian politics, were fatally undermined.

Malaysia survived, but it did not long remain intact. Within less than two years of its foundation, Singapore was excluded. It had, after all, threatened the intercommunity compromises on which Malaya had been based. Lee Kuan Yew wept. In the meantime, however, Singapore's involvement in the formation of Malaysia had facilitated the destruction of the left-wing on the island, while the chances of its sustaining its independence, though still widely doubted, had been enhanced by the prospects of economic expansion that both US investment and the revival of Japan were bringing about.

Vietnam before and after Geneva

The policies pursued by the leaders of Singapore, and indeed by those of Malaya and of Indonesia, were much influenced by the shifting relationships among the superpowers. The Soviet Union had turned to policies that the PRC saw as 'revisionist', envisaging the communist struggle with the capitalist world as one that was now to be fought out more in economic than political competition. The struggle in

Vietnam was a focus of their differences. There the United States, after supporting the French, had itself intervened, and committed itself to preventing a communist triumph. Their intervention the Americans saw partly as a demonstration to the world at large that they would defend the 'Free World'. It was also seen as a means of ensuring that the rest of Southeast Asia would not 'fall', like a heap of dominoes. Indo-China was regarded, as in 1941, as a key to the south, the 'loss' of which would endanger Thailand and Burma and make Singapore, the Malay peninsula, and Indonesia more vulnerable.

The French had argued that, once dislodged, it would be difficult, if not impossible, for them to return. The Japanese, pressed by the Allies, finally overthrew them. 'If it had not been for the victory of the Allies,' the communist leader Pham Van Dong was to comment, 'no one knows how long our independence struggle would have had to last'.[43] Assisted by the Chiang Kai-shek regime over the border, Ho Chi Minh had been organising the Viet Minh in northern Vietnam since 1941, and a guerrilla force had been built up under the guidance of Vo Nguyen Giap. The March coup expanded their opportunities, and after the Japanese surrender they secured Hanoi. Initially, however, French prospects seemed unexpectedly bright. SEAC forces, under General Douglas Gracey, offered the French far more support in Cochin-China than the Dutch were to secure in Java, and the Viet Minh's Committee of the South had no chance of retaining control.

At the same time, however, the French seemed inclined to adopt a conciliatory policy towards the north, where Ho Chi Minh had proclaimed independence in September. In mid-1945 he had sought from President Truman the same treatment as the Philippines: tutelage, then independence;[44] and his declaration of independence was designed to appeal to the United States. The northern area, however, came under the military control, not of SEAC, but of the Kuomintang Chinese. Their departure, secured by abandoning French extra-territoriality in China, was associated with the conclusion of an accord between Ho Chi Minh and Jean Sainteny on 6 March 1946, under which, in the spirit of Brazzaville, France agreed to recognise Vietnam as a free state, having its own government, parliament, army, and finances, belonging to the Indo-Chinese federation and the French Union, while Vietnam declared itself ready to receive French troops. As Laurentie noted, 'opinion in Asia is generally hostile to the colonial powers. Britain's difficulties in India, and those of the Dutch in Indonesia are ample proof of this. It is therefore remarkable that our country should by amicable means have arrived at a definition of common ground with Annamite nationalism.'[45]

Ho Chi Minh had hoped to launch an insurrection, Bolshevik-style, at the end of World War II: it would be *thoi co*, the opportune moment that comes once in a thousand years.[46] If so, the accord was, as Vo Nguyen Giap put it, a 'Vietnamese Brest-Litovsk'.[47] 'I am not happy about it', Ho told Sainteny. ' … But I understand that you cannot have everything in a day.'[48]

The fact that the accord inspired van Mook was not, perhaps, a happy augury, however. It was based on a formula, and about its elaboration there were bound to be differences.

Over these the two parties negotiated during 1946, but they reached no real agreement. At the same time, the establishment of the authority of the French in the south encouraged the idea of military action in the north, which might assist in setting up a more amenable regime. The high commissioner, Admiral d'Argenlieu, tended to see the accord as simply a device to get the Chinese out, and while his mentor, de Gaulle, had resigned in January, he continued to offer advice, and it was not of a conciliatory nature. Perhaps the most important factor of all was the weak and distracted nature of the government in Paris. Policy was in effect determined on the spot. When the authorities in Indo-China took matters into their own hands and bombarded Haiphong at the end of November 1946, the government in Paris was in no position to intervene.

And yet that episode—blamed on the Viet Minh: another Pearl Harbor, said Marius Moutet, the Minister of Overseas France[49]—started a war which the French were in the event unable to bring to a victorious conclusion. What had begun as a means of reframing the context of negotiations was in fact the first step in a long conflict. Like the Dutch, the French miscalculated: the effect of the use of force in a nationalist context differed from its effect in a colonialist context. Unlike the British, they were unable to adjust their diplomacy. No doubt the accord could never have led to the kind of Francophone empire Brazzaville contemplated. The French could perhaps, however, have achieved, as Martin Shipway suggests,[50] some face-saving solution of the type the British secured. That would have needed a stronger metropolitan control over policy-making, and a real, rather than merely formulaic, measure of agreement within the metropolitan governments.

The position had indeed differed in another sense. Thanks in part to pre-war French policy, the Vietnamese nationalist movement was led by communists like Ho Chi Minh. At first that had not seemed a major obstacle to the *politique des accords*, particularly as the French Communist Party adhered to Popular Front line, while Ho Chi Minh, his Leninist line failing, sought compromise. But when that too evaded him, he had to yield to men like Truong Chinh, who argued for a people's war, Mao-style. The French attitude to communism also began to change, and the Saigon authorities sought to justify their action by the need to avoid a communist triumph. At first the British Foreign Office was sceptical, but the development of the Cold War, and in particular the events of 1948, encouraged the Western powers to emphasise Ho Chi Minh's communist rather than his nationalist orientation.

At the same time, it became increasingly evident that the French had no chance of military victory. Belatedly they searched for alternative political options. D'Argenlieu had initially attempted to set up a separate regime for Cochin-China, but that experiment failed. The other option that emerged was to accept the unity of

Vietnam, and to make the abdicated emperor Bao Dai its head. Such a regime was never likely to win nationalist support away from the Viet Minh, but the French government further reduced its chances by its reluctance, despite the advice of its allies, to grant the regime a convincing degree of autonomy. Only in face of the triumph of the Chinese communists did the United States and the United Kingdom recognise the Bao Dai regime early in 1950.

In Indonesia the United States had endorsed nationalism as a means of combating communism. In Vietnam that was more difficult. In fact, while urging them to take steps to make the Bao Dai regime more credible, the United States had to aid the French. It did not want them to leave, lest it then had to step in itself. 'We are the last French colonialists in Indochina', an American diplomat declared late in 1953.[51] The outbreak of the Korean conflict, and the Chinese participation in it, only seemed to make it more necessary to avoid a communist triumph in Vietnam. The Chinese offered aid and—something impossible in Malaya—sanctuary. But the armistice in Korea, signed in July 1953, was associated with a French decision late in June to seek peace in Vietnam rather than victory. 'The armistice is a sign that when the Communist world is certain that it cannot achieve a military victory without risking a general conflagration, it accepts at least a pause, at least a truce', said prime minister Laniel.[52] But it was a way out for France, too. Its forces had lost 92 000 men, mostly Africans, Indochinese, and Legionnaires, but also over 20 000 Frenchmen, 40 per cent of them officers and NCOs.

The French favoured a five-power conference on Indo-China, including the United States, the United Kingdom, the Soviet Union, France, and the PRC, and that became an agreed Western objective late in February 1954. It was important that France should be in the best possible military position before the negotiations got under way. Its seizure of Dien Bien Phu in November, designed to stop Viet Minh penetration of Laos, had, however, been followed by a siege, the outcome of which would thus be politically as well as militarily decisive. Equally the prospect of a conference encouraged the Viet Minh to press for victory. Anxious to avoid a communist triumph, the United States ruled out massive retaliation, nor would it send in troops, as it had, under the UN flag, in Korea. The administration found, however, that Congress leaders were prepared to accept air strikes only if the United States were acting as part of a coalition. 'The most influential men on the Hill would not condone unilateral intervention in behalf of a colonialist cause.'[53] The British indeed declared that they were 'ready to take part, with the other powers principally concerned, in an examination of the possibility of establishing a collective defence'.[54] But the Foreign Secretary, Eden, denied that this meant, as Secretary of State Dulles thought, that Britain was committed to any military action before or in substitution for the conference. He believed that this was not the moment to challenge China, but that agreement could be reached. Armed intervention to save Dien Bien Phu, he told the House of Commons, 'might well have led to a general war in Asia'.[55]

After the fall of the Laniel government, the new French premier, Pierre Mendès-France, declaring that he would resign unless a satisfactory solution were secured by 20 July, met Zhou Enlai in Berne: essential to the Chinese, he was told, were an armistice in Vietnam, Laos, and Cambodia, and elections in Vietnam. These would, of course, make it possible to secure unification, despite a temporary partition. The partition line Mendès-France thought too far to the south. On 20 July, he and Pham Van Dong agreed on the 17th parallel, somewhat north of the old divide between the Trinh and the Nguyen regimes, and set July 1956 as the date for elections, the latter being the price the Viet Minh exacted for the former. Partition—or as Ho called it, 'readjustment of zones'—was 'a temporary affair leading to reunification'.[56] The 'whole hoggers' among his colleagues could hardly criticise China, and so had to accept the compromise.

Two regimes had coexisted in Vietnam before the Nguyen restoration, though there had been a phase of civil war between them, followed by stalemate, and they had, to a greater or lesser degree, acknowledged the nominal sovereignty of the Le. The experience perhaps made any attempt to repeat it less rather than more likely. Above all, of course, the concept of unity was now seen in national terms. Geneva envisaged national elections. The competitors would be not two parties, but two potential national regimes.

The United States took note of the agreements and undertook not to upset them by threat or force. 'It is not what we would have liked to have', President Eisenhower observed. 'But ... if I have no better plan I am not going to criticise what they have done.'[57] It was impossible for the United States openly to reject the agreements, but it could not accept them either, since that would result in a communist triumph. It had failed to keep the French fighting long enough for American training and equipment to create a Vietnamese army to replace them. But it was now determined that no more of Indo-China should be lost to the 'Free World', and proceeded to train and equip armies and to give Laos, Cambodia, and South Vietnam the backing of the South-East Asia Treaty Organisation, a policy incompatible, as James Cable puts it, with the essence of the Geneva agreements,[58] but not inconsistent with a notion that Dulles, relying on Korean precedent, had earlier advanced, of holding a bridgehead long enough to train an anti-communist army.

Late in June the Americans and the British had resumed discussion of the collective defence arrangements that Eden had refused to proceed with in April. In September the Manila treaty created SEATO, the price paid by the United Kingdom for US acquiescence at Geneva. A 'zoo of paper tigers', as Cable calls it, it did not deter enemies nor reassure friends, but it was 'a figleaf for the nakedness of American policy that was occasionally useful in Washington'.[59] Thailand was a member, but not the other mainland states. But under article 4, it was possible for the parties to 'designate' a 'state or territory' in which armed aggression would endanger one of the parties, upon which the parties would 'act to meet the common danger', subject to the invitation or consent of the government concerned, and subject, so far as the United

States was concerned, to its being communist aggression. About other actions short of aggression, the parties agreed to consult. The French had insisted on 'designation', arguing that 'alliance' would infringe at least the spirit of Geneva.[60]

The Bao Dai regime had not accepted the Geneva agreements, its foreign minister protesting against partition. Increasingly, its prime minister, Ngo Dinh Diem, had been, with American encouragement, acting as if the state really were independent. Never at ease with Bao Dai, Diem set up a republic after a rigged referendum, and held elections for a constituent assembly. The elections contemplated by Geneva were not held. The co-chairmen of the conference did not reconvene it. The Soviet Union did not press the point, while for the British the prime concern was their relationship with the United States, and they had no wish to see that strained again, as it had been in 1954. Furthermore, at that time the prospects for the southern regime did not seem unhopeful, while the Democratic Republic in the north ran into trouble with the agrarian reforms of 1956–57.

After 1959 fighting expanded in Vietnam and spread to its neighbours. At a symposium that year, David Hotham argued that it was a national conflict, not a Cold War one: the object should be reunification on the best terms possible while the United States was still in a position of strength.[61] Perceiving the conflict still in Cold War terms, however, the United States was determined to avoid defeat. 'China is so large, looms so high beyond the frontiers, that if South Vietnam went', said President Kennedy, 'it would not only give them an improved geographic position for a guerrilla assault on Malaya but would also give the impression that the wave of the future in Southeast Asia was China and the Communists'.[62] The Vietnamese communists sought victory, though they were prepared for a transitional government in the south. Their stance had some attraction there, for Diem himself in 1963, for the 'neutralists' supported by the Buddhists, but none for the United States. Kennedy increased the number of American advisers in South Vietnam, while accepting that Ngo Dinh Diem, whose leadership now seemed inadequate, should be displaced, and he was assassinated in November 1963, shortly before the President himself.

'You have to go all out', ex-President Eisenhower told the new President, Lyndon Johnson, because 'we are not going to be run out of a free country that we helped to establish'.[63] Johnson stepped up the American commitment, backed by Congress with the Gulf of Tonkin resolution of August 1964. The north was bombed in an attempt to sustain the south, where the United States supported post-Diem military-led governments, to coerce the DRVN, and to stem the flow of supplies along the Ho Chi Minh trail to the guerrillas in the south. 'Most of the non-communist nations of Asia cannot, by themselves and alone, resist the growing might and the grasping ambition of Asian communism', Johnson declared. ' ... If we are driven from the field in Vietnam, then no nation can ever again have the same confidence in American promise, or American protection.'[64] The United States stopped short of a level of intervention that might have provoked the intervention of China, and it stopped short of using nuclear weapons. Those fundamental restraints, however, perhaps conduced to greater violence and ruthlessness in the ground warfare. So, perhaps, did the time factor. How long would the US people support a land war in a cause, avoiding defeat, that seemed far from heroic?

Resistance continued, and bombing tended to evoke patriotic determination and international condemnation. Never clearly placed in a political context, so that it was clear what Hanoi would have to do in return for cessation, it was never intense enough to drive the DRVN to seek settlement short of its full goals, for all that 4 million combat sorties were flown, 8 million tons of bombs dropped, and 8500 aircraft lost.[65]

In the north two kinds of approach persisted, the long-term radicalism associated with Truong Chinh, envisaging protracted war, and the 'Bolshevik' line, now associated with Le Duan, seeking a 'general uprising' in the south. The latter faction leant towards the Soviet Union, which, wanting to stalemate the United States, encouraged a more conventional war. The People's Republic, unable to respond to the US escalation because of its military incapacity and its fear lest hostilities spread, offered what help it could in order to avoid driving the DRVN entirely into the Russian camp. It was, too, a rear base, capable of dissuading US invasion, and providing a route for Soviet aid.

The Tet offensive of 1968 is generally seen as the turning-point in the struggle. It was not the turning-point that the Vietnamese had sought: they had hoped that the offensive would precipitate the 'general uprising', and it did not do so, though there was a bloody battle in Hué. To that extent US policy had been successful. But its demands upon the United States were too great. The US government had never elicited sufficient consensus for a major struggle, and the growth of the protest movement forced Johnson to announce that he would not seek a second term in office. His successor, Richard Nixon, determined to extract the United States from the war, without admitting total defeat. One route that he and his Secretary of State, Henry Kissinger, pursued was through Beijing. Profiting from the intensifying of the Sino-Soviet split after the fall of Lin Biao, they now recognised the PRC regime, and the President visited China in 1972. In Vietnam they proceeded more intensively with the build-up of the South Vietnamese army and they bombed Cambodia.

Tet had given Truong Chinh an argument for concentrating on reconstruction in the north, but Le Duan stuck to the offensive strategy, while moderates, led by Pham Van Dong, advocated negotiation. Le Duc Tho, a mediator between the groups, became the negotiator, biding his time for success on the battlefield, and determined not to be sold out, Geneva-style, by his patrons. The Kissinger–Nixon visits to Beijing were worrying, but Soviet aid increased, and confirmed the position of the south-firsters over Truong Chinh. In 1972 the DRVN decided to accept a ceasefire, dropping its insistence on a coalition government in the south. In January 1973, after the Christmas bombing of 'Linebacker II', they signed the Paris Peace Accords, and the United States insisted that President Nguyen Van Thieu should sign too. The DRVN leadership believed that, using Soviet doctrine and weapons, they could gain on the ground what they appeared to lose at the negotiating table, and the military success they enjoyed at the expense of Thieu's army proved them right. In April 1975 they captured Saigon. Between 1965 and 1973 the United States spent $109.5 billion and suffered 349 588 casualties (about 50 000 were killed). The 'enemy and innocent' suffered two million casualties: more than a million died.[66]

Sihanouk

The Cambodian communists had already taken Phnom Penh when Saigon fell to the communists. That was to boost their pride, and to contribute to the hubris of the Khmer Rouge regime. Another factor in it, overlaying even the ideology its leaders brought from France, was a determination that Cambodia should survive. Its main historical enemy had been Vietnam. It was not surprising that the relations between the two communist movements were full of tension, nor even perhaps that the two victorious regimes were to go to war in 1978. The fact that, during their long war, first with France and then with the United States, the Vietnamese determined their policy towards Cambodia largely in accordance with their own strategic needs, did nothing to ameliorate those relations. Engelbert and Goscha have persuasively argued that, because of the geographical shape it had assumed, Vietnam was intensely vulnerable. Securing its western flank became the dominant objective of its leaders.[67] It was a concept that those who made 'French Indo-China' in the 1880s and 1890s would have understood.

The pre-war Comintern had, like the colonial power it opposed, focused on 'Indo-China', but in 1945 Ho Chi Minh had proclaimed a Republic of Vietnam. Possibly that was in deference to the Free Thai, who supported the Lao. Possibly, too, the Viet Minh feared to alienate the Thais and the Chinese by establishing a Vietnam-dominated Indo-China, more of a threat than a French one. The future of Laos and Cambodia was nevertheless important to them: the future of the Vietnamese revolution itself might indeed depend on it. It was necessary to ensure that they were amenable, whether that was done by establishing or supporting local communist parties or by other means.

They had less success in building a communist network in Cambodia than in Laos. Their attempts were impeded by inter-ethnic conflict as well as by the return of the French. It was only in western Cambodia that the Vietnamese communists made progress, in the provinces made over to Thailand by the Japanese and not returned to the French by the reluctant Thais till late 1946. The coup in Siam in November 1947 lost the high-level support afforded the revolutionaries by the post-war Free Thai governments led by Pridi and his associates. Late in 1948 Pibun, who had resumed power, clamped down on Vietnamese activities in Thailand. The victory of the Chinese communists opened up a vast new rear base for the Viet Minh, but it now had none in the south.

In the closing years of the French war, the Vietnamese sponsored a provisional Khmer People's Revolutionary Party. More dramatically, their military forces thrust into northeastern Cambodia from lower Laos, so as to secure their flank and disrupt the French north–south supply lines. 'If the Rhine was the first line of defense for Britain, the Mekong River was Viet Nam's first line of defense', the fifth central executive conference of the ICP concluded in August 1948.[68]

Cambodia's independence had 'fallen out of the sky' when the Japanese overthrew the French.[69] King Sihanouk proclaimed independence on 12 March 1945, and a pre-war nationalist, Son Ngoc Thanh, brought back by the Japanese, became foreign minister in May. On 15 August, the day of the Japanese surrender, he became prime minister, and in September he held a kind of referendum, to determine whether Cambodians wanted 'to be as free as they were under Jayavarman, with the temples of Angkor Wat'.[70] That favoured an end to French protection, and he appealed to Pridi and to the Viet Minh. But General Gracey needed Cambodian rice, and the loyalty of the Cambodians in Cochin-China was in doubt. French, British, and Indian troops took over Phnom Penh, and arrested Son Ngoc Thanh. Sihanouk reluctantly welcomed the French protectors back—they promised to regain the lost territories—and a new agreement was signed. Some of the opponents of the French fled to Thailand or the western provinces, forming the Khmer Issarak, but many surrendered when the provinces were regained, and became the 'Democrats'.

'[R]ecognizing that his position was imperiled by the strength of popular nationalist sentiment', Sihanouk 'moved to master it and make himself the spokesman of it.'[71] In 1953 he visited the United States, where Dulles told him: 'Your difference with France will only serve the cause of our common enemy.'[72] Returning, he set up first in Bangkok, and then in Siemreap. He was able to secure a full transfer of power from the reluctant French and returned to Phnom Penh in triumph on 8 November.

Geneva dealt the Cambodian resistance a harsh blow. It now had to work within a political system increasingly dominated by Sihanouk, who as king had led the 'crusade for independence', and, ceasing to be king, now founded a political movement, the Sangkum, that left little room for political alternatives. Nor did the DRVN help the resistance, counselling them to stay with a political line, though it was impossible to pursue one. The DRVN came to rely on Sihanouk's neutrality as a buffer on their southern flank. Neutrality, however, Sihanouk saw in terms that reflected the history of Cambodia as well as the developing Cold War struggle. No longer protected by France, Cambodia faced its traditional enemies, the Thais and the Vietnamese. There was a boundary dispute with the former. There were long-standing disputes with South Vietnam, involving, for example, complaints about the treatment of the Khmer Krom and counter-charges about the treatment of Vietnamese in Cambodia. A separate commercial outlet at Sihanoukville was completed in 1959. Thailand was a member of SEATO and South Vietnam supported by the United States. 'Our neighbours bugling their indefectible adhesion to the American bloc ... take turns at causing serious trouble for us', Sihanouk complained.[73]

If the communists won in neighbouring Laos, Sihanouk said he would have to 'entreat China to make North Vietnam confine itself to South Vietnam'.[74] He hoped for a neutral Laos. The failure to achieve that, and pessimism about South Vietnam, led him, for fear of a unified Vietnam, to look to China. It was to play the role of France. In August 1963 he broke off relations with South Vietnam, and in May 1965, when US troops began to land there, he broke off relations with Washington.

The escalation of the Vietnam War threatened growing involvement. From 1966 Sihanouk allowed the supply of arms through Sihanoukville. In such circumstances the Vietnamese could not countenance armed revolution in Cambodia, though the communist leader Saloth Sar (Pol Pot) sought it. But early in 1968 Sihanouk's balancing act—the successor to neutrality—needed adjustment, and he seems to have allowed US forces 'hot pursuit' across his border. Whether or not with Sihanouk's consent, or merely with his acceptance, the following year the United States began 'secretly' to bomb the Vietnamese sanctuaries in Cambodia, as part of Nixon's strategy for delaying a communist victory in Vietnam and withdrawing American troops safely. The Vietnamese feared a land attack on the sanctuaries, and their fears came true when Sihanouk was overthrown by Lon Nol in March 1970. In April US and RV troops entered Cambodia.

Now the Khmer and the Vietnamese communists could collaborate, the former no longer thwarted by the latter's alliance with the ruler of Cambodia. Even so, 'serious cracks' appeared in the alliance. Saloth Sar feared that his movement would be swamped by the Vietnamese, and distrusted the Khmer communists of the 1950s who now returned to Cambodia. The differences expanded when in mid-1972 the Vietnamese resolved to negotiate a cease-fire, and in January signed the Paris accords. Saloth Sar was determined not to negotiate. Massive US bombing did not affect that decision, though it helped to bring about the collapse of rural society and to drive Cambodians into the cities. Neither Vietnam nor China had abandoned hope of a peaceful solution, and the Khmer communists were apprehensive that they would play the 'Sihanouk card'. Possibly, however, the Chinese were offering them some support, as a means of checking Vietnamese expansionism. As they planned their final assault on the south, too, the Vietnamese saw that continued action in Cambodia would tie down Lon Nol's forces and buffer key bases in eastern Cambodia so that the Ho Chi Minh trail could function.

The Khmer Rouge were able to mount three 'storming attacks' in 1973. Their attack on Phnom Penh from May onwards prompted a new outburst of US bombing, but that was stopped by Congress in July, and Nixon, already embroiled in Watergate, lost the 'keystone of [his] strategy'.[75] More attacks followed in 1974, and on 17 April 1975 the Khmer Rouge troops appeared in the capital. They ordered its occupants, citizens, and refugees, young and old, sick and healthy, to leave. For Cambodia 1975 was also year zero.

Laos and neutralism

In Laos the Vichy regime tightened its links with the Lao elite in face of the Thais and Japanese, and in August 1941 agreed that Luang Prabang should extend its authority over Xieng Khouang, Vientiane, and Nam Ta. When the Japanese dislodged the French, the king was reluctant to proclaim independence, and did so in April only when they sent troops to Luang Prabang. Prince Petsarath formed a government. Some, like Katay Don Sasorith, thought collaboration the only possible policy in face of the Vietnamese threat, while others looked to the Free Thai movement. They formed the Lao Issarak. When the Japanese surrendered, Petsarath reaffirmed independence, and declared Laos a unitary state, including Champassak (whose prince Boun Oum was serving with the Free French), though not, of course, Isan, once part of Lan Xang. Not dislodged by the occupying forces—Chinese, not French— Petsarath was at odds with the king, and, backed by the Issarak, deposed him. He was joined by the forces of his half-brother Suphanuvong, who believed that Laos had to look to the Viet Minh. The French returned when the Chinese left, and attacked Suphanuvong's stronghold at Thakhaek: many Laos and Vietnamese fled to Thailand. But, securing the return of the trans-Mekong provinces, France was able to finalise unification under the king of Luang Prabang, and take steps towards an independent Laos. The Lao Issarak government-in-exile dissolved itself in October 1948. Most of the Lao elite looked once more to France.

France now regarded Laos not, as before, as the hinterland of Vietnam, but as an independent state, and that was a reason for making their, albeit vain, stand at Dien Bien Phu. At Geneva the Lao communists enjoyed more success than the Cambodian. Laos agreed not to join a military alliance, nor to request foreign military aid except for defence. But two provinces, Samneua and Phongsali, were set aside for the regrouping of the communist Pathet Lao forces pending reintegration. The Pathet Lao was in any case reluctant: their idea of integration was infiltration. But it was the involvement of other powers that did most to defeat the reintegration that, under Prince Suvanna Puma, the Royal Lao government attempted.

His policy had two aspects, to elicit the cooperation of outside powers, and to create a coalition government. He thus went to Beijing and Hanoi in 1956 to secure Bandung-style cooperation, and he also attempted to set up a National Union government. But that, Dulles saw, could not be counted upon to request help under article 4 of the SEATO agreement, and it was opposed by the US ambassador: 'I struggled for sixteen months to prevent a coalition'.[76] A second attempt followed in November 1957, but when the communist Neo Lao Hak Sat (Lao Patriotic Front), did well in the supplementary elections of May 1958, the United States held up aid, and Suvanna Puma resigned. The anti-communist Phuy Sananikon took over, renouncing Geneva. Viet Minh troops then entered southern Laos, and the Viet Minh assisted a remilitarised Pathet Lao to regain control of Sam Neua. In December the army, led by Phumi Nosavan, a cousin of the Thai strongman, Sarit, seized power, supported by the CIA, and the rigged elections of 1960 eliminated the NLHS.

'[T]he US was attempting to push the conservative nationalists into a role that they were unable, and a significant number were unwilling, to sustain.'[77] In August 1960 Konglae, a parachute battalion commander, son of a Kha, seized power in

Vientiane. He was anxious to restore neutralism, and Suvanna Puma set up a government. After attacking Vientiane in December, Phumi Nosavan and Boun Oum replaced it by a rightist government, which was endorsed by the United States. The Soviet Union, concerned to demonstrate to the DRVN that, despite China's criticism, it was still radical, flew in arms and Vietnamese personnel to bolster Konglae and the Pathet Lao. Beset by the Cuba crisis, the Kennedy administration supported Britain's efforts to work out a compromise with its Geneva co-chairman the Soviet Union. 'Thank God the Bay of Pigs happened when it did', Kennedy said later. 'Otherwise we would be in Laos by now—that would be a hundred times worse.'[78] An international conference began in May 1961. Bolstering the anxious Thai helped: US marines were flown into Thailand in 1962, as well as small contingents from the United Kingdom, Australia, and New Zealand. So, on the other hand, did the military defeat of the Lao conservatives. The factions agreed to accept a coalition in June, and the Thais reluctantly signed a declaration on the neutrality of Laos in July.

Laos declared its intention not to seek protection from any outside government or from SEATO. The United States tried to provide for genuine neutrality, for example by giving neutral neighbours a role, but in vain.[79] There was in fact no effective support for Suvanna Puma's renewed attempts at setting up a neutral regime. Neutrality became a mere shell. The Viet Minh needed to control the Ho Chi Minh trail and to keep the Plain of Jars out of enemy hands. The United States acknowledged Suvanna Puma, but secretly bombed the trail, and set up a mercenary army. A third coalition, set up in 1974, consisted of equal numbers from the left and right: the only neutralist was Suvanna Puma. It collapsed with the demoralisation of the right after April 1975. At the end of that year, the monarchy was abolished, and the Lao People's Democratic Republic was proclaimed.

Pridi, Pibun, and Sarit

The struggles in neighbouring Indo-China were of deep interest to the Thais. They were long-standing rivals of the Vietnamese and they had long-standing relationships with and claims over the intermediary states of Laos and Cambodia. At the same time they had long recognised, more effectively than any other Southeast Asian leadership, the significance of outside powers. They had made concessions to the French in the heyday of colonialism, particularly when the British failed to support them. The weakness of the West and the power of the Japanese persuaded them to go to war with France in 1940–41, and in the Pacific war itself they accepted the transfer of territories in Burma and Malaya that the British had controlled. Listening to Tojo, Pibun 'displayed a joyful countenance. But it was not to the point of a broad smile.'[80] The Thais were quick to notice and to act on the defeats of the Japanese, and sought, in particular by developing their relations with the United States, to put themselves right with the Allies as victory approached. In that they largely succeeded, though the French territories had to be returned, and their peace treaty with Britain burdened them with a requirement to deliver rice for the relief of other parts of Southeast Asia that was much resented.

That did not help the postwar governments, since it exposed them to nationalist criticism, as well as encouraging smuggling and corruption. But it should not be supposed that the civilian governments led by Pridi and his associates were deaf to the nationalist cause. They saw it, however, in a rather different way. Though the colonial powers were returning, they were greatly weakened. Siam should recognise that change by building relationships with the Indo-Chinese independence movements. In the post-transfer discussions with the French on border adjustments, Pridi sought to claim the territories lost since 1893. His idea, it seems, was that he would reconstitute Lan Xang, and offer Lao nationalists their independence.[81] France and Siam would jointly sponsor a South-East Asian Union. But the idea was a failure, and he failed to secure even an adequate frontier.

Pridi's difficulties, and the attempt to connect him with the death of the young king, prepared the way for the coup of 1947, and in turn that led to the return of Pibun in 1948. The Thai governments closely identified themselves with the United States as the Cold War intensified. Pibun recognised the Bao Dai regime early in 1950 and Thailand was one of the first countries to respond to the UN call for assistance in Korea. Bangkok housed the SEATO headquarters. Under Sarit, Thailand backed the right-wing in Laos, and in March 1962, as he sought compromise there, Kennedy pledged US support for Thailand's independence and integrity. In due course Thailand became a base for US aerial warfare and intelligence operations in Laos, Cambodia, and Vietnam. By 1968 there were 46 000 American servicemen in Thailand. The shifts in US policy in the early 1970s undermined the dictators who succeeded Sarit, and they fell in 1973. The communist triumphs of 1975 in neighbouring countries helped to prompt a right-wing reaction in Thailand in 1976.

East Timor

By this time most of Southeast Asia had become, as Thailand had always been, free of direct Western rule. Only Brunei remained under British protection, though it had secured the substance of self-government. The Andaman and Nicobar islands, though geographically and in other ways clearly part of Southeast Asia, remained part of India's inheritance from the British, and part, too, of its security system in the Indian Ocean. The Portuguese had belatedly returned to East Timor in April 1946, the idea of annexation or co-rule that the Australians had entertained being rejected. The Portuguese revolution of 1974 was followed by a call for independence. The Indonesians intervened, though East Timor had not been part of Netherlands India, and in face of substantial opposition within the territory and outside, proceeded to incorporate it in their republic.

Conclusion

The incorporation of East Timor was, indeed, an exception to the rule that the new nation-states of Southeast Asia inherited the borders of their colonial predecessors. States in Europe emerged in competition with one another and regulating their borders was often part of a long process. The colonial frontiers had emerged from a process of competition, but it was among states outside the region, which in general sought to avoid conflict in the region. As a result they tended to have a more arbitrary character. The frontiers might cut across long-established ties or encompass peoples who had enjoyed very few previous ties at all. It was only now, and not in the course of a long process, that these territories came to be governed as nation-states. Thailand was the only one which had so far been able to experiment with that.

There was, however, no real chance that the borders could be adjusted. The ways by which independence had been secured did not make that likely. If it had been secured without an armed struggle, as in the case of Malaya/Malaysia, the rulers were certainly no more likely to accept adjustment or disintegration than those in states where armed struggle took place, Singapore's extrusion being an exception to the rule. In the latter, of course, the struggle itself had often created a sense of unity which, as in Indonesia, the rulers were unwilling to forgo. In the case of Cambodia, the determination to regain independence was so intense that it wanted to regain territory lost even before the colonial period, but of that there was no chance. Frontiers were unlikely to be changed by war.

Nor were the borders likely, as in the colonial phase, to be changed by diplomacy. For one thing, the world in this phase was dominated by two super-powers, the United States and the Soviet Union. Any change among other states, or indeed within them, was a subject of their jealous interest. It was not a world without any conflict, but it was one without major conflict: the tension of the Cold War between the super-powers increased but it limited the conflict among others. The borders of states rarely changed, though battles might be fought across them or within them. Moreover, the borders were now those of states in a world of states, enforcing a sense of common interest in preserving them, enhanced by the existence of international organisations. They were also nation-states in a world of nation-states. Their citizens could not be bargained away like the subjects of a ruler.

They did, however, have a reciprocal loyalty to the state. The governments, though inheriting the frontiers of colonial states, had now to see them as nation-states, commanding the allegiance of their citizens in ways that the colonial powers had not contemplated. Governments, too, were now expected to do more, while the global forces that played upon them and upon those they ruled were more intense than ever. If the struggle for independence stretched over a thirty-year period, the building of nations would take even longer. The tensions would not necessarily be less, but they would be different, and the level of formal violence involved in dealing with them would generally be of a different order.

Ethnicity became a political issue. Strengthened by the colonial regimes, the concept was also strengthened by their successors. Nation-states sought an ethnic basis for the loyalty of their citizens. That put a new stress on the sense of identity among Southeast Asian peoples. The responses varied from assimilation to separatism. The inheritance of colonial divide-and-rule did not make it easier to experiment with federalism or with devolution. And it was possible that the 'globalisation' of the future would strengthen, rather than weaken, the nation-state.

Notes

1 q. Tarling, *Burmese War*, p. 7.
2 C. A. Fisher, 'The Vietnamese Problem in its Geographical Context', *Geographical Journal*, 131, 4 (December 1965), p. 508.
3 q. Ton That Thien, *India and South East Asia, 1947–1960*, Geneva: Droz, 1963, p. 54.
4 q. N. Tarling, '"Ah-Ah": Britain and the Bandung Conference of 1955', JSEAS, 23, 1 (March 1992), p. 105.
5 q. Sueo Sudo, *The Fukuda Doctrine and ASEAN*, Singapore: ISEAS, 1992, p. 28.
6 Macmillan, q. W. D. McIntyre, 'The Admission of Small States to the Commonwealth', JICH, 24, 2 (May 1996), p. 269.
7 in House of Commons debate, 1 June 1948, Hansard, vol. 411, cols 495–550.
8 Eur. E 362/5, p. 47, India Office Library.
9 J. Silverstein, *The Political Legacy of Aung San*, Cornell UP, 1972, p. 17.
10 U Ba Than, *The Roots of the Revolution*, Rangoon: The Guardian, 1962, p. 61.
11 q. Tarling, *Burmese War*, p. 225.
12 q. Silverstein, p. 79.
13 P. Dennis, *Troubled Days of Peace*, Manchester UP, 1987, p. 113n.
14 q. Yong Mun Cheong, p. 62.
15 q. ibid., p. 127.
16 q. G. Kahin, *Nationalism and Revolution in Indonesia*, Cornell UP, 1952, p. 215.
17 A. Reid, *The Indonesian National Revolution*, Hawthorn: Longman, 1974, p. 146.
18 q. A. Kahin, ed., *Regional Dynamics of the Indonesian Revolution*, Hawaii UP, 1985, p. 165.
19 q. Oey Hong Lee, *War and Diplomacy in Indonesia, 1945–50*, Townsville: JCU, 1981, p. 209.
20 H. Baudet in D. C. Coleman and P. Matthias, eds, *Enterprise and History*, CUP, 1984, p. 269.
21 q. Dahm, p. 209.
22 q. A. and G. Kahin, *Subversion as Foreign Policy*, NY: New P, 1995, p. 75.
23 ibid., p. 126.
24 Vandenbosch, 'Indonesia, the Netherlands and the New Guinea Issue', JSEAS, 7, 1 (March 1976), p. 115.
25 q. Dahm, p. 208.
26 q. L. Manderson, *Women, Politics, and Change*, KL: OUP, 1980, p. 43.
27 in R. Holland, ed., *Emergencies and Disorder in the European Empires after 1945*, London: Cass, 1994, p. 96.
28 q. ibid., p. 96.
29 q. ibid., p. 104.
30 A. Short in Wang Gungwu, ed., *Malaysia: A Survey*, London: Pall Mall, 1964, p. 159.
31 q. A. Lau, *The Malayan Union Controversy*, Singapore: OUP, 1991, p. 58.
32 q. B. A Hussainmiya, *Sultan Omar Ali Saifuddin III and Britain*, KL: OUP, 1995, p. 52.
33 q. A. V. M. Horton, 'A Note on Post-War Constitutional Change in Brunei, 1944–1948', JMBRAS, 63, 1 (1990), P. 50.
34 q. Greg Poulgrain, *The Genesis of Konfrontasi*, Bathurst: Crawford, 1998, p. 148.
35 q. J. M. Gullick, *Malaysia and its Neighbours*, London: Routledge, 1967, p. 41.

36 J. P. Ongkili, *Borneo's Response to Malaysia, 1961–1963*, Singapore: Moore, 1967, p. 43.
37 q. *Philippine Claim to North Borneo*, Manila, 1968, I, p. 151.
38 G. Taylor, *The Philippines and the United States*, NY: Praeger, 1964, p. 267.
39 *The Philippines Looks East*, Quezon City: Mac, 1966, pp. 28–30.
40 Kahins, p. 221.
41 q. P. Sodhy, 'Malaysian–American Relations during Indonesia's Confrontation', JSEAS, 19, 1 (March 1988), p. 124.
42 q. J. A. C. Mackie, *Konfrontasi*, KL: OUP, 1974, p. 223.
43 q. S. Tonnesson, *The Vietnamese Revolution of 1945*, Oslo: IPRI; London: Sage, 1991, p. 415.
44 J. Siracusa, 'The United States, Viet-Nam, and the Cold War', JSEAS, 5, 1 (March 1974), p. 94.
45 q. M. Shipway in R. Holland, ed., *Emergencies and Disorder*, p. 5.
46 Thai Quang Trung, *Collective Leadership and Factionalism*, Singapore: ISEAS, 1985, p. 17.
47 q. John T. McAlister, *Vietnam: The Origins of Revolution*, London: Lane, 1969, p. 287.
48 q. Ellen J. Hammer, *The Struggle for Indochina*, Stanford UP, 1954, p. 153.
49 ibid., p. 198.
50 ibid., p. 14.
51 q. ibid., p. 319.
52 q. ibid., p. 312.
53 M. Gurtov, *The First Vietnam Crisis*, New York: Columbia UP, 1967, pp. 95–6.
54 q. James Cable, *The Geneva Conference of 1954 on Indochina*, Macmillan, 1986, p. 57.
55 q. G. McT. Kahin and John W. Lewis, *The United States and Vietnam*, Delta, 1967, p. 39.
56 q. C. Thayer, *War by Other Means*, Sydney: Allen and Unwin, 1989, p. 9.
57 q. Cable, p. 115.
58 p. 139.
59 p. 139.
60 V. Bator, *Vietnam: A Diplomatic Tragedy*, London: Faber, 1967, p. 152.
61 Richard W. Lindholm, ed., *Viet-Nam: The First Five Years*, Michigan State UP, 1959, pp. 348ff, 361–2.
62 q. Chester A. Bain, *Vietnam: The Roots of Conflict*, Englewood Cliffs: Prentice-Hall, 1967, p. 30.
63 q. David L. Anderson, *Trapped by Success*, New York: Columbia UP, 1991, p. 205.
64 Statement, 28 July 1965. *Times*, 29 July.
65 Earl Telford in Phil Melling and Jon Roper, eds, *America, France and Vietnam …* , Aldershot: Avebury, 1991, pp. 112–14.
66 Siracusa, p. 82.
67 T. Englebert and C. E. Goscha, *Falling out of Touch*, Clayton: Monash Asia Institute, 1995, p. 14.
68 q. Takashi Shiraishi and Motto Furuta, *Indochina in the 1940s and 1950s*, Cornell UP, 1992, p. 147.
69 q. D. Chandler, 'The Kingdom of Kampuchea … ', JSEAS, 17, 1 (March 1986), p. 92.
70 q. ibid., p. 89.
71 Hammer, p. 296.
72 q. Roger M. Smith, *Cambodia's Foreign Policy*, Cornell UP, 1965, p. 46.
73 q. ibid., p. 129.
74 q. ibid., p. 120.
75 G. Porter, *A Peace Denied*, Indiana UP, 1975, p. 205.
76 q. Arthur J. Dommen, *Conflict in Laos*, London: Pall Mall, 1964, p. 85n.
77 C. J. Christie, 'Marxism and the History of the Nationalist Movements in Laos', JSEAS, 10, 1 (March 1979), p. 151.
78 q. U. Mahajani, 'President Kennedy and United States Policy in Laos, 1961–3', JSEAS, 2, 2 (September 1971), p. 92.
79 G. Modelski, *International Conference on the Settlement of the Laotian Question*, Canberra: ANU, 1962, p. 28.
80 q. E. Bruce Reynolds, *Thailand and Japan's Southern Advance*, NY: St Martin's, 1994, p. 158.
81 Kobkua Suwannathat-Pian, 'The Wartime Leadership Reconsidered … ', JSEAS, 27, 1 (March 1996), p. 172.

1.7 | Regionalism

The independent states of Southeast Asia sought to limit differences among themselves and the intervention of other powers by developing regional cooperation. The Vietnamese invasion of Cambodia was both a challenge to this process and a catalyst of it.

Southeast Asian states had, throughout their history, developed in a larger context. In their earliest phase the most important relationships were with India and China. Though they were not entirely displaced in the next phase, the relationships with Europe became more direct, and came increasingly to incorporate not merely the commercial, but the political and cultural. The struggle for independence was itself deeply affected by the relationships to the rest of the world, the European conflict, the Japanese attack with which it was connected, the victory of the Allies, the beginning of the Cold War between the super-powers. Gaining independence was not simply a matter of 'struggle' against the return of the colonial powers, but of 'diplomacy' that would exploit the international situation. The independent states found themselves in a world of states, in which the relations among states were an essential focus, and as 'nation-states' they had to conduct 'inter-national' relations. That required knowledge of the system as it had been built up by the Europeans and Americans over a century and more, and information as to the changing ways in which it was now being further developed and utilised.

The prime aim in the foreign policy of the modern nation-state must be to maintain its territorial integrity and its security. In that it is not unlike earlier states, but the objectives are the more significant because of the sense that a national community is involved. Partly as a result, it has also come to be accepted that a state—the authoritarian as well as the democratic, perhaps even more—has to seek the prosperity of its citizens, and that its diplomacy cannot therefore be solely concerned with political issues. But the nation-state system—like the colonial system and the puppet system and indeed others that preceded it—mixed rhetoric and reality. In it states are equal in sovereignty, but not in power. A state had to be 'recognised' by others, and that came normally to be associated with the right to a seat in the General Assembly of the United Nations. But in fact independence was bound to be a matter of degree. To enjoy as much of it as was possible, a state had to recognise the limits of the possible. To be independent, a state had to recognise that others were more independent. Only an acceptance that power was differentially distributed made the concept of theoretical equality viable.

A state may thus have a third series of aims. In part to ensure its security, its sovereignty, and its integrity, but also in part because of the dynamics of the system, a state must expect and be expected to exert an influence in its region and in the world at large commensurate with its size, its power, and its wealth, and also with the skill with which they are deployed. The acceptance of that, both on the part of the stronger, but also on the part of the weaker, lies at the heart of the system. It could not work if the theory of equality were not tempered by the acceptance of inequality, nor if the reverse did not also apply. That consideration must inform the diplomacy of the system if it is to encompass moderation, consideration, mutual antagonism but also forbearance, the successful reconciliation of divergent interests. Nor are states merely divided between the weaker and the stronger. Some are even stronger than others, even 'super-powers'. Some are nearer than others. A weaker state may find a connexion with a stronger state that is more remote some kind of insurance of its independence with respect to a state less strong but closer at hand. Caution is always needed, of course, but especially if your neighbour is of super-power capability.

Not all of this, of course, is peculiar to the nation-state system. Indeed it cannot practically ignore, but only formally push into the background, the kinds of relationship upon which the earlier mandala system had been based. Its novelty is found partly in its worldwide range, and in the nature of the states it involves. It is also affected by the novel ways in which power may now be deployed, not only in terms of direct offence, but in terms, too, of propaganda, subversion, and guerrilla warfare. It is possible to conduct warfare of one kind or another while yet maintaining apparent adherence to the basic principles of the system. Intelligence has become even more important. Without it a state can neither pursue its policies nor deflect those of others. Not entirely paradoxically, states have found it difficult to control or make accountable services that so often must deal in secret, while those services have been tempted to lose a sense of reality, let alone morality.

Understanding the foreign policy of states in a world of states requires some additions to this simple model. The model emphasises interests rather than ideologies, perhaps unduly. For again, authoritarian states no less than democratic states, and perhaps more, may be tempted to apply in foreign affairs the approach they adopt at home. Pursuing an ideology may support the pursuit of an interest; it may complicate it; it may even damage it. It is also likely to change the perception of a state's policy on the part of other states. Even if a state does not avowedly include an ideological formulation in its foreign policy, it may approach foreign policy in preconditioned ways, affected, say, by the education or experience of its policy-making elite, or, perhaps, by public opinion. The role of the latter has long been a source of controversy. To what does the phrase refer? How far is it the creation of the elite, even a fiction it invents? Certainly, once evoked, it may prove a dubious advantage for the diplomat, as likely to reduce as to expand the room for manoeuvre in negotiation. The discrediting of secret diplomacy in World War I led to a demand for more openness. But that was not very practical. More common is an appearance of openness in which diplomats are indirectly engaging in negotiation, while also responding to a constituency at home.

In established states, public opinion seems for the most part extraordinarily diffident on foreign policy issues. They may be more significant for newer states, particularly for those engaged in a process of nation-building. Invoking a national cause may help to unify the nation, but there may be a cost in foreign policy. Will it drive foreign policy objectives beyond their rational limits? Will it prejudice rather than sustain security, prosperity, an influence in the world commensurate with the possession of power?

In their search for independence, Southeast Asian statesmen had already shown a striking awareness of the factors at work in the world they were seeking to enter, and that had helped the cause. The experience they had gained helped to guide them afterwards. In particular they came to see the advantage of a regional approach. That itself changed its nature in the closing decades of the century. But it was a striking sequel to the struggle to set up independent states, though not necessarily in contradiction with it. Southeast Asian statesmen increasingly saw Southeast Asia as a region, as foreign statesmen, Chinese, Japanese, British, Russian, and American, had long tended to do, and they encouraged public opinion to do the same. But that was because they saw it as the best means of pursuing their national objectives amid the international changes that were taking place.

Those changes were in part political in nature, but by no means merely so. The most important for Southeast Asian countries, if not the most important of all, was the changing relationship among the two super-powers and the People's Republic of China. Nixon had played the China card in the early 1970s. His successors increased the pressure on the Soviet Union, and in the late 1980s it buckled under the strain of maintaining the status it had so long sought. At the same time, post-Mao China began to approach its economic development in a way quite different from Mao's, becoming at once an exciting opportunity for the capitalist world, and a new kind of influence on its neighbours, if not a potential threat to their security. The nature of Japan's policy came into question: how was it to preserve its security without itself alarming its neighbours? So, too, did the policy of India. China had sharply defeated it in 1962. The break-up of Pakistan in 1971 had reduced the outside threats, but the Sino-American rapprochement and China's modernisation were of increasing concern, particularly with the collapse of India's long-standing ally, the Soviet Union. With Britain's withdrawal from east of Suez—announced in 1967, speeded by *konfrontasi*—the European states ceased to play more than a residual political or strategic role. Their economic role remained considerable, and it was advanced nationally and through the European Community.

These major political changes were indeed accompanied by a new 'globalisation' in economic life, clearing the path for 'free trade' capitalism and for international competition in an ever more comprehensive way. As a result of that process the 'developing' countries might find their economic advance was only temporary, their initial advantage, in cheap labour or raw material, quickly lost, and their future niche difficult to capture. Culturally they might be overwhelmed by an all-embracing consumerism, which could defuse ideological differences, but also raise expectations. Socially and politically they might face the tensions associated with rapid change, including, perhaps, a more fundamentalist approach to religious experience and a new level of ethnic assertion and inter-ethnic tension.

These changes established the international and transnational circumstances in which the Southeast Asian nation-states had to develop their foreign policy after 1975. Politically China looked for a Southeast Asia in which the governments were friendly or at least not hostile: its smaller neighbours should not be allied to an enemy and ideally they should be within its sphere of influence. In a sense this was a new version of a traditional policy, one designed to ensure submissiveness in its neighbours rather than control over them, but it now had international overtones. It was particularly concerned, as traditionally, with the aspirations of Vietnam, and with its connexions with the Soviet Union.

Southeast Asia, as I. I. Kovalenko put it in 1980, was 'of vast importance from the angle of military strategy. Located here are the main centres of supply and it is through the sea-lanes that Japan ships in most of the raw materials it needs. In the final analysis, Japan's snag-free economic activity depends on the situation in this part of the world.'[1] In fact, for Japan Southeast Asia was, as it once had been for Britain, more important strategically than it was commercially. Japan's economic interests in Southeast Asia were substantial, but its stability was essential above all because its oil now came not from Southeast Asia or the United States but from the Middle East, and its tankers as well as its freighters passed through the Straits.

The interest of Japan in Southeast Asia also helped to define the interest of the United States. It had, of course, been deemed essential to seek the stability of Southeast Asia in order to deny it to the Soviet Union, and promote 'development' as an antidote to communism. For those purposes the United States had rightly or wrongly conducted a prolonged war in Indo-China, justified by some, not of course by the measure of success in Indo-China itself, but by its 'buying time' for anti-communist movements and governments elsewhere in Southeast Asia, now expected to be better able to stand on their own feet. 'The American presence for example in South Vietnam has certainly bought time for the democratic forces in Indonesia', wrote M. Lubis in 1971. 'The non-communist forces in Indonesia, in or outside the army, would have lost heart and confidence in themselves had the American forces left before 1965.'[2] But the policy of the United States was also affected by its relationship with Japan, and that motive became predominant in the 1980s and 1990s.

The association was reaffirmed in 1969. The United States, Oran R. Young observed in 1968, 'is currently beginning to show an interest in supporting the continued development of Japan ... to provide a balancing force that is likely to become increasingly important as a function of the emergence of China as an important actor in the Asian subsystem.'[3] Late in 1969, in a speech described as part of a Japan-US policy statement, prime minister Sato Eisaku announced a 'new Pacific age', in which 'a new order will be created by Japan and the United States'.[4] But sponsoring Japan in Southeast Asia was something of a two-edged weapon, as the United States had realised in the 1950s, since the memories of the war were still alive. It had been focused on economic development. But in that it was almost too successful, and now Japan seemed but a trading animal, and a greedy one. Visiting Southeast Asia in 1974, premier Tanaka found more anti-Japanese feeling than he expected. That, the oil crisis, and the end of the Vietnam War, led to the Fukuda doctrine of 1977. That encouraged industrialisation in Southeast Asia. But it also staked a claim to the economic opportunities that Southeast Asia offered now that the regimes in the region both promised stability and sought it. Those opportunities had become more necessary to Japan. The dearth of factory sites, labour shortages, high costs, an outcry against pollution, were leading private Japanese industry to move lower-level operations to other countries. In Southeast Asia it entered renewed partnerships with local Chinese capital.

Not surprisingly there was no wish to see Japan take a military role in addition. Japan, said its ambassador to Malaysia in 1983, rejected that, though it was concerned over the security of the Straits as well as investment. 'It makes things easier for Japan for the United States to be present in Southeast Asia, whether in regard to the problem of [Japan's economic] over-presence, or the problem of the defense of the sea-lanes.'[5] The US forces that remained in Southeast Asia—even after the bases in the Philippines were abandoned in 1990—were there to defend US interests in eastern Asia, and, as Robert O. Tilman suggested in 1987, 'only secondarily to protect American direct interests in East Asia's southeastern appendage'.[6]

There were continuities in India's policy, too, stretching back to the imperial period. One was concerned with the Burma frontier. Northeast India became especially difficult to defend after partition, and India's policy was to maintain good relations with Burma, even when the regime there acted against the Indian community. India had also inherited the Andaman and Nicobar islands. Allegedly Sukarno had offered to help Pakistan in its 1965 war with India by seizing them.[7] Certainly they acted as a gateway to the Indian Ocean. India decided against building a naval base on Great Nicobar, as rumoured in 1986, preferring the advantage of greater mobility. Either way, its policy was, as in the case of Burma and the rest of Southeast Asia, affected by its concern over the growth of China's power.

China and Vietnam

In the previous phase the Southeast Asian states had often sought to turn the interest of outside powers to account in the pursuit of their foreign policy objectives. Where those objectives encompassed the winning of independence, as with Vietnam, or could be presented as a continued anti-colonial struggle, as with Sukarno's Indonesia, that was especially evident. In its campaign for West New Guinea, Indonesia looked to the Soviet Union and to the United States, and in *konfrontasi* it turned increasingly, but counter-productively, to the PRC. In their contest with the United States, the Vietnamese leaders looked both to the PRC and the Soviet Union, however complex the changing trends in Sino-Soviet relations made their task. But their triumph in 1975 made that impossible to continue.

China's distrust of its southern neighbour became evident: it sought in vain to fit Vietnam into a satisfactorily compliant relationship. It gave the newly unified state only limited aid, and the Vietnamese emissary, Le Duan, went on to Moscow, where in October 1975 he secured four times as much. China aided the Khmer Rouge government in Cambodia—which was deeply inspired by Pol Pot's anti-Vietnamese nationalism and increasingly raiding Vietnamese territory in a new kind of 'storming attack'—as a means of constraining the Socialist Republic of Vietnam, and when it took steps against the Chinese community, it cut off aid. Moscow airlifted arms to Vietnam, and in November 1978 concluded a treaty of friendship and cooperation that offered it sufficient international reinsurance for it to risk going to war with the already internationally discredited Khmer Rouge regime. That it did on Christmas Day 1978. Phnom Penh fell on 7 January, and the Soviet leaders congratulated the leader of the new regime, Heng Samrin. The following month PRC troops invaded Vietnam, but the 'lesson' their incursion gave the Vietnamese was less effective than the one given India back in 1962. Furthermore the Soviet Union sent ships into Vietnamese waters, and Cam-ranh became a base for the blue-water navy it had been building up. It also became the chief source of aid to the People's Republic of Kampuchea.

These events seem to form a turning-point in the development of regionalism in Southeast Asia. The Japanese had seen it as part of Greater East Asia. The Allies had set up a South-East Asia Command. Postwar the British had appointed a commissioner-general for Southeast Asia. The Americans had set up the South-East Asia Treaty Organisation. Now the regional concept was, as it were, regionalised. Regionalism did not, of course, mean that the Southeast Asian states had ceased to pursue the objectives of a national foreign policy. Rather it offered, like the access to other powers, a means of pursuing a national foreign policy. But it also showed that in certain respects the interests of the states were held in common, and furthermore that they were prepared to work in such a way that those common interests might expand. The events of 1978–79 suggested both that Southeast Asia was once more open to intervention by outside powers and that there was an opportunity, if not a necessity, for a regional diplomacy that would limit that in the future.

Indonesian foreign policy

In realising this Indonesia seems again to have shown an ability to recognise changes in the international scene and to turn them to account. Without them, indeed, the resolution of the Cambodian crisis would not have come about. But it was also a testimony to Indonesia's role as the most populous and powerful state in the region, and to its recognition that such a role had to be exercised in a way that would be acceptable to other states in the region and give them also an opportunity to pursue their foreign policy objectives.

That recognition itself took time to emerge, and it took time for the other states themselves to recognise that it had taken place, since Indonesia's policy had not always shown them much consideration. At the same time, even during such crises as *konfrontasi*, the principles on which a wider regional understanding could be based were also taking shape and taking hold. They remained part of the foreign policy debate in the region throughout the tortuous negotiations on Kampuchea in the 1980s, forming a kind of framework within which differences could be resolved or mitigated and elements of commonality brought out.

These ideas owed some of their currency to one of Indonesia's earlier ventures, the Bandung conference of 1955, and it was not surprising that the Suharto regime chose to celebrate the thirtieth anniversary of one of the main initiatives of the regime it had displaced. That conference was partly designed to rally support among the newly independent nations for the claim to West Irian, but it had a larger purpose and a larger significance. It demonstrated the resourcefulness of Indonesia's diplomacy and its capacity to play a role in the region and beyond. But, even more important, it was an opportunity to generalise the principles on which nations might live alongside each other without overt involvement in the Cold War. Those principles had been set down by Nehru and Zhou Enlai in 1954, but the fact that China and India were later to fall out did not destroy their validity. Non-interference and respect for sovereignty and territorial integrity were essential to the relationships among the new states. Indeed they were essential to the working of the world of states in general, and had their origin in ideas articulated by men like Wilson and Hull and were implicit or explicit in the founding documents of the League of Nations and the United Nations, even though the current super-powers might criticise what was seen as 'non-alignment' or 'neutrality'. What was indeed at issue, as so often in foreign policy, was the extent to which the principles were applied in practice. Quite often the principles were best served, not by insisting on their total implementation, but by acknowledging exceptions to them. They might still retain some force, and still influence behaviour.

In the course of the *konfrontasi* crisis, Malaya, Indonesia, and the Philippines had sought to accommodate their interests in the Maphilindo agreement. Though what it sought to set up was described as a confederation, it in fact tried to stress the need for regional consultation on foreign policy and looked towards the elimination of foreign bases in the area. It was still-born and Malaysia went ahead as planned. In this case, Indonesia had sought to use a sense of regionalism too blatantly in its own interest for it to be acceptable to its neighbours. Attempting to secure a proper recognition of the degree of influence Indonesia should have as the major regional state, its statesmen had in fact provoked apprehension rather than acceptance.

It went on to provoke alarm, and also the mobilisation of British power in Southeast Asia once more. Sukarno's supplanters were to change his approach.

Soon after Malaya had secured independence in 1957, the Tunku had mooted regional cooperation against communist subversion, and he and President Carlos Garcia had in January 1959 agreed to a Southeast Asian Friendship and Economic Treaty. Interested in economic collaboration, Thailand's foreign minister, Thanat Khoman, sought to include the other countries of the region, apart from the DRVN, but in vain. Instead Malaya, Thailand, and the Philippines set up a loose Association of Southeast Asia in July 1961. Not surprisingly, Sukarno's Indonesia would have no part in an association among three members of the Western bloc, two of them members of SEATO, and one connected with Britain under the Anglo-Malayan Defence treaty. The Philippines claim to Sabah, reawakened by the Malaysia proposal, meant that the association made no progress in the following years, though Thailand helped to restore the ties between Malaysia and the Philippines that the Sabah claim had broken.

Bangkok was the site of the normalisation talks between Indonesia and Malaya in May 1966. Even before the Gestapu coup of 1965, the Indonesian army, especially KOSTRAD (the strategic reserve), had become doubtful about *konfrontasi*: it was enhancing the power of the PKI, while the army's campaign against Malaysia was a fiasco. Malaysia, on the other hand, might be a barrier against the advance of communism from the north, while the extrusion of Singapore reduced the perception of it as Chinese-dominated. The head of KOSTRAD, Suharto, sought contacts with Malaysia through Operasi Khusus, and that groundwork helped to end *konfrontasi* soon after Suharto assumed power in March 1966. To erase the memory of *konfrontasi*, the New Order demonstrated a new enthusiasm for regional cooperation. That would, moreover, also enhance Indonesia's security, and give it a new leadership role, welcome to nationalists at home, but acceptable in the region, too. Furthermore, other countries were coming to share Indonesia's view that the presence of foreign military powers in the region was unacceptable, a view that was reinforced by the announcement of Britain's withdrawal, and by the recognition that the United States would not win in Vietnam, even if it would not altogether lose. It was important, as General Panggabean was to put it, that the power vacuum should be filled regionally, not by outside forces.[8]

ASEAN

The idea of a new regional organisation emerged at the normalisation talks, when Adam Malik proposed that it should replace ASA and Maphilindo. A SESKOAD (staff college) paper of July advocated a Confederation of Southeast Asia. ASEAN was set up by the Bangkok declaration of 8 August 1967. It affirmed that Southeast Asian countries had primary responsibility for security, and also affirmed non-interference. Indonesia had long seen foreign bases as a threat, and the United States had indeed aided the 1958 rebels. The US bases still in the Philippines were covered in the declaration by a compromise formula: such bases were not to be used to threaten or subvert countries in the region. ASEAN was not a military alliance. That might have made it more difficult for its members to cooperate. But it did facilitate military cooperation, and there were to be bilateral military exercises.

Early in 1968 Tun Ismail of Malaysia articulated the idea that Southeast Asia should be neutralised, and after the United States had announced the Guam doctrine in November 1969, he again indicated that his country favoured neutralisation, guaranteed by the United States, China, and the Soviet Union. At the third ASEAN ministerial meeting in December 1969, Malik had responded to both the British and American announcements by advocating a more autonomous regional order. In September 1971 he outlined three possibilities: aligning with a foreign power; getting foreign powers to declare Southeast Asia a neutral zone; and developing an indigenous form of stability; and it was the last that he favoured. Following Kissinger's visit to Beijing, a special meeting of the ASEAN foreign ministers produced the Kuala Lumpur declaration of 27 November 1971, endorsing the concept of a Zone of Peace, Freedom, and Neutrality (ZOPFAN), 'free from any form or manner of interference by outside powers'.[9]

In February 1976, less than a year after the triumphant capture of Saigon, the ASEAN leaders met at the Bali summit. That endorsed ZOPFAN as an objective, and adopted a Declaration of ASEAN Concord that put a new emphasis on political cooperation among members. A Treaty of Amity and Cooperation set out criteria for the conduct of relations among members that stressed the avoidance of threat and the resolution of conflict by peaceful means. In a new context members endorsed familiar principles, mutual respect for independence, sovereignty, equality, territorial integrity, national identity, and non-interference. The treaty aimed to promote cooperation for economic development, peace, and stability.

Overall agreement covered a range of differences among members. Clearly the development of ASEAN reflected the view of the region formulated by its largest member, Indonesia, and the organisation was in a sense a recognition of the leadership it could expect to give its neighbours. At the same time, it proceeded cautiously and avoided formality, so as to enhance their acceptance of that leadership. Malaysia, for example, had preferred the outside guarantee that Indonesia opposed. Singapore, the smallest member at the time, believed that stability was best achieved by a balance among the outside powers, and was certainly opposed to the complete withdrawal of the United States from Southeast Asia.

The differences among the members were also reflected in their attitude to Vietnam. In the war, their policies had differed. Thailand and the Philippines sent military forces, and allowed the Americans to use bases. Indonesia recognised Hanoi, but feared the spread of communism. All were apprehensive about the implications of the success of the Vietnamese communists, for the reunified Vietnam had a large army and received aid from the Soviet Union, and there was a possibility, it seemed at first, that it would be rehabilitated by the United States and Japan, on the model of Germany and Japan itself after World War II, even though they had been defeated and Vietnam had not. But a communist Indo-China was a reality that had to be accepted, and the Bali agreements were designed to suggest ways in which, on the basis of the Bandung principles, it might be accommodated. ZOPFAN was vague, as Weatherbee said, thus permitting 'a fragile value consensus. It does ideally provide ASEAN a normative context for the integration of Vietnam into a peaceful Southeast Asia.'[10]

Again members might differ. Indonesia was particularly opposed to the emergence of two blocs in Southeast Asia, while smaller states were concerned lest Vietnam and Indonesia, the two largest, should collude. The differences increased with the crisis of 1978–79. Yet ASEAN unity was not destroyed, and the principles it had endorsed played a role in the prolonged attempt to reach a settlement.

The Cambodian settlement

Early in 1979 the ASEAN foreign ministers had deplored Vietnam's invasion of Cambodia as an inroad upon its independence, sovereignty, and territorial integrity, and demanded the withdrawal of its forces, confirming Cambodia's right to self-determination. Not surprisingly, they stood together on these points, and perhaps not surprisingly, even given the nature of the Pol Pot regime, they enjoyed success at the United Nations in denying the Cambodian seat to the Heng Samrin regime. The European Community supported ASEAN, and the British representative describes how it became the custom 'to leave the Assembly Chamber at speed to avoid the outstretched handshakes of the Pol Pot delegation'.[11] At a UN-sponsored conference on Cambodia in July 1981, ASEAN legitimated its programme in the international community: ceasefire; withdrawal of foreign forces; and free elections under UN supervision. To give added respectability to the cause, it supported non-Khmer Rouge opponents of the new regime, including Son Sann's National Liberation Front, and Sihanouk's National United Front for an Independent, Neutral, Peaceful, and Cooperative Cambodia, and it hammered together the Coalition Government of Democratic Kampuchea in June 1982, designed to keep the Khmer Rouge forces in the field, but at a political distance. That, of course, ASEAN had to persuade China to accept, a task carried out by Prem of Thailand and Lee Kuan Yew of Singapore. Arms were supplied, Malaysia and Singapore aiding the non-communist elements through Thailand, where the refugee camps offered sanctuaries and bases.

ASEAN demonstrated its unity as well as its determination, but its members still differed, particularly over the role of China. Its invasion of Vietnam had enhanced the suspicions of Malaysia and Indonesia. Indonesia and also Singapore were concerned, too, over the close relations between the PRC and Thailand, which was apprehensive over Vietnam's de facto control over neighbouring Cambodia. Indonesia played a leading role in seeking a conclusion, for it believed a prolonged conflict would only tie the Chinese and the Thais more closely together, while it saw Vietnam not as a threat but as a buffer against China. 'Some countries say that Vietnam is a threat to Southeast Asia', said Suharto's trouble-shooter, Murdani, on visiting Hanoi in February 1984, ' but the Indonesian army and people do not believe it'.[12]

Indonesia played a leading role in the tortuous negotiations that led to the Cambodian settlement of 1991. The main decisions were indeed still taken outside the region. For Vietnam's venture Soviet backing had been essential, and Soviet aid helped to keep it going. India initially supported Vietnam, since it saw a strong Vietnam as a guarantee against Chinese dominance over Southeast Asia. But the convergence of ASEAN and China in opposition to Vietnam and its Soviet backer led to a change in India's policy in 1987–88: it should try to narrow the differences between ASEAN and Vietnam, lest they promoted China's dominance. The essential change was, however, in Soviet policy. Under Gorbachov it sought to normalise relations with China in order to relieve the pressure the United States was exerting, and to open the way to sharing in the development of the Asia-Pacific, the climax of the diplomacy being a meeting in Beijing in May 1989. For that to succeed it was important to remove the Vietnam–Cambodia irritant in the relationship. Vietnam had already announced troop withdrawals, and perhaps Gorbachov took more credit than he deserved. But while Vietnam's reformist leaders had domestic motives, they were also aware of the shift in PRC–Soviet Union relations. An international conference on Cambodia, chaired by the French and Indonesian foreign ministers, produced the Paris agreement of October 1991.

The expansion of ASEAN

The following year Vietnam and Laos acceded to the Treaty of Amity and Cooperation and were given observer status in ASEAN. It was at last possible at least in one sense to realise the objectives ASEAN had set itself in the 1970s. During the 1980s, indeed, the parties had in a sense signalled to each other through the ZOPFAN principles. The communiqué of the Indo-China foreign ministers of 28 January 1984, for example, had suggested, among the options, a solution that involved the withdrawal of all foreign armed forces, an end to external intervention, and the establishment of 'a zone of peace, friendship and cooperation'.[13] Direct intervention had now ceased. ASEAN could resume its search for regional security, at once fending off the intervention of outside powers, and avoiding or resolving intra-regional disputes that might invite it. The year 1984 itself saw the mooting of the Southeast Asian Nuclear-Weapon-Free Zone, finally signed on 15 December 1995.

The Bangkok declaration of 1967 had not covered political cooperation. Economic collaboration was intended to be the association's main focus. To that there were two aspects, collaboration among the members within the region, and collaboration among them in dealing with countries, organisations, and agencies outside the region. With the former, progress was slow. The economies of the members were more competitive than complementary, and the less industrialised feared unequal competition with the more industrialised: 'economic nationalism collided with economic efficiency'.[14] In 1992, however, ASEAN committed itself progressively to liberalise intra-regional trade through AFTA (ASEAN Free Trade Area) by 2003. A number of 'growth triangles' were set up, designed to promote cross-frontier economic advance.

Even so ASEAN was more effective in dealing with the outside world. It was a bargaining tool with the Dialogue Partners it established among the developed countries. It could make a stronger stand than any single country could in face of a contracting world market for commodities and increasing protectionism directed against manufactures from newly industrialised countries. ASEAN solidarity could be used to get better terms of trade, and the regional stability it offered could attract investment.

Over the balance between the two aspects of ASEAN's economic activities its members again differed. For Indonesia, for example, extra-regional cooperation was far more important than intra-regional. What it wanted was to obtain extra funds from donor countries and agencies, and ASEAN improved its bargaining position and helped in international forums like the General Agreement on Tariffs and Trade (GATT) and the North–South dialogue. Singapore, by contrast, was interested in the Indonesian market for its goods.

Other areas of collaboration were not precisely defined in the ASEAN documents, but nevertheless significant. Limiting the political intervention of outside powers, ASEAN also prescribed respect on the part of each member for the frontiers of the others. Through regionalism each country was pursuing its foreign policy objectives, and regionalism guaranteed their integrity and sovereignty. A military exercise with the Philippines in Panay in 1977 was partly designed to show that Indonesia would not endorse separatism, even though it would not endorse the suppression of the Moros. Indonesia was thus confirming that other members would not support separatist movements in Aceh or West Irian. The other members indeed accepted its incorporation of East Timor, only Singapore, concerned that a big country could annex a small with impunity, registering a modest form of disapproval, while Brunei, joining ASEAN in 1984, saw it as a guarantee of what it called 'full independence' against its larger neighbours. ASEAN stands against intervention by outside powers, but also for the consolidation of the existing states. That involves mutual respect.

Indeed, it may involve mutual support. Increasingly the regimes joined in rejecting Western intervention of an ostensibly different kind, that in favour of human rights, for example, or the environment. The economic crisis that began in 1997 offered a new challenge. Had ASEAN a role in resolving it? And if it had not, would it lose the initiative? If there were political fall-out, could it handle that? The position of China, though it took no advantage of the economic crisis, might yet help to keep ASEAN together. It seems to have been a factor in the decision to admit Burma, despite the widespread distaste for its regime. The object, of course, is not confrontation, but dialogue.

The PRC had laid claim to the Spratly islands, which were of strategic and potentially of economic importance, and had occupied seven islets after a clash with Vietnam in March 1988. Some islets were also claimed by other ASEAN states, including Malaysia and the Philippines. In 1995 the PRC was found to have built permanent structures on Mischief Reef, claimed by the latter. On the eve of the meeting that year of the ASEAN Regional Forum—started in 1993 to provide for consultation on security in the post-Cold War era—it offered to recognise international law, including the 1982 convention on the law of the sea, as the basis for a negotiated settlement.[15] No such settlement followed. The dispute between the PRC and the Philippines intensified.

Economic, demographic, and technological developments in the postwar world had promoted a new interest in the resources of the sea, and the nation-states into which the world was divided made new 'frontier' claims. Three UN conferences on the law of the sea sought to regulate them by agreeing on principles, rather as the colonial powers had sought in the 1880s to agree on principles for the partition of Africa. Before World War II, the sea had in general been seen as open to all, though the right of coastal states or colonies to a territorial jurisdiction extending three nautical miles offshore had come to be widely accepted. Postwar more intensive fishing methods, the dumping of waste, and above all the extraction of oil and minerals gave the sea a new economic importance. States began to extend the limits of their territorial waters, and to claim exclusive economic zones extending up to 200 nautical miles offshore, or even to the limit of a 'continental shelf' if it went further. These concepts were largely recognised in the third conference (1973–82). States had already been putting them into operation.

In Southeast Asia—much of which was, of course, deeply penetrated by the sea— the new approach produced many overlapping claims. In addition both the Philippines in 1955 and Indonesia in 1957—with a kind of echo of the VOC—had claimed to be archipelagic states, rendering their seas 'internal'. Agreements were, however, reached between Malaysia and Indonesia in 1969 and 1981, and among Indonesia, Malaysia, and Thailand in 1971. The Vietnam wars made the other claims more difficult to settle.

The Spratly question, too, was not merely an economic one. The issue—like the recognition by the United States, Japan, and the major states that Indonesia's archipelagic claim put it in a position to close the passages between the Indian and Pacific Oceans—was a reminder, moreover, that outside powers retained a political interest in Southeast Asia.

So, too, was the crisis over East Timor in 1999, with which ASEAN failed to deal. Following the collapse of the New Order regime in Indonesia, Suharto's successor allowed a referendum on its incorporation, and it went in favour of independence. The violence that ensued led to intervention under UN auspices. The Americans were notably cautious, the neighbouring Australians much less so. But, if ASEAN took no initiative, the Thais were second-in-command of InterFET. That, as

The Nation (24 September) suggested, was a means of reducing 'tension and hostility' between the Indonesians and the multinational forces, and it was also 'a face-saving measure for Indonesia'.

Notes

1   q. R. A. Longmire, *Soviet Relations with South-East Asia*, London and NY: Kegan Paul, 1989, p. 149.

2   q. Dewi Fortuna Anwar, *Indonesia in ASEAN*, Singapore: ISEAS; NY: St Martin's, 1994, p. 38.

3   q. B. K. Gordon, *Towards Disengagement in Asia*, Englewood Cliffs: Prentice-Hall, 1969, p. 63n.

4   *New York Times*, 22 November 1969.

5   q. Khamchoo and Reynolds, p. 254.

6   *Southeast Asia and the Enemy Beyond*, Boulder and London: Westview, 1987, p. 127.

7   Mohammed Ayoob, *India and Southeast Asia*, London and NY: Routledge, 1990, pp. 13–14.

8   Anwar, p. 129.

9   ibid., p. 178.

10 Donald E. Weatherbee, ed., *Southeast Asia Divided*, Boulder and London: Westview, 1985, p. 8.

11 A. Parsons, *From Cold War to Hot Peace*, Penguin, 1995, p. 161.

12 q. Weatherbee, p. 20.

13 ibid., p. 124.

14 Anwar, p. 78.

15 Muhammad Kamlin, 'ASEAN in the 1990s: The Beginning of a New Era in Southeast Asian Regionalism', in *Purih Kumpulan Esei Mengenai Negara Brunei Darussalam*, Bandar Seri Begawan: UBD, 1996, p. 335.

Part Two

Environment and Economies

The first part of this book dealt with the peoples of Southeast Asia and the states under which they lived. The second part deals with the relations of the peoples and states of Southeast Asia with their environment and with their economic activities.

It is divided by topic, though there is also a chronological approach. The topics cover the changing position of Southeast Asia, and of parts of Southeast Asia, in international trade; domestic production and production for export; communications and industry; villages and cities.

Southeast Asia, fourteenth and fifteenth centuries CE

Regional and International Trade

From early in the first millennium CE Southeast Asia had commercial connexions with India and China and, indirectly, with Europe. The European voyages of 'discovery' established a direct connexion with Europe and a connexion with the Americas. Most of the trade, however, remained, as before, trade within Asia. In the nineteenth century the pattern changed. Increasingly Southeast Asia supplied food and raw materials to the industrialising world, taking manufactured goods in return.

Trade expanded its reach as societies grew in size and states were consolidated: exchange and markets at the village and town level were supplemented by commerce at the regional and super-regional level. It became intra- and inter-continental: traffic within Asia was supplemented by traffic between Asia and Europe. Opinions differ as to the nature of the trade. 'The objects of oriental trade are splendid and trifling.' Van Leur borrowed Gibbon's phrase to characterise intra-Asian trade before the arrival of the Europeans.[1] He under-emphasised its volume and its significance, but clearly conditions did not favour bulk transport over long distances until the nineteenth and twentieth centuries. Most of the latter phase was also marked by unprecedented economic growth, above all the result of the industrial revolution, briefly interrupted by the Depression of the 1930s.

States varied in the extent to which they were able to call or rely upon the creation of agricultural surpluses. For those in Southeast Asia, commerce, whether regional or international, was a desirable supplement, and for some it was essential. It provided a means by which rulers could secure and reward a political following in a region where population was scarce, and itself the most desirable of commodities. The early modern phase of economic expansion, dating from the fifteenth century and termed by Anthony Reid 'the age of commerce', showed the close interest of Southeast Asian rulers in economic development, and their recognition of its significance in building the state.

The economic expansion of the nineteenth century and the early decades of the twentieth largely escaped the control of the Southeast Asian states, for most of the region was divided among European empires. Empire was not acquired simply to further the interests of Western industrial capitalism. The two processes interacted more at the micro than at the macro level. Once established, however, the colonial regimes were clearly not going to take the political steps that independent states could take to advance their position in an industrialising world, or even themselves to industrialise. The regimes, though modernising, were modernising only in a limited sense. Not only were they cautious over political advance: they were cautious over economic advance. In that sense the regimes came to stand in the way of economic internationalisation.

The dissolution of the colonial regimes, however, produced a kind of competition between the aspirations of their nationalist successors and the objectives of international capitalism, and it continues. Some of the older economic structures—which had depended on the use of political power at the micro level—gave way in the 1950s. Attempts to industrialise—to leap forward—largely failed. Even in the 1970s and 1980s it was clear that industrialisation in Southeast Asia was limited by the international interests that dominated 'globalisation'. In the 'international division of labour', its role was to provide cheap labour and raw materials, and technology transfer was restricted.

What emerged, it might be said, was a new version of an older Southeast Asian experience. As in the earlier 'age of commerce', governments took what they could get, and their use of wealth, even though population was no longer in short supply, was heavily influenced by the clientelistic practices of the past. The future of their states was uncertain, while the environment was plundered. '[I]t does seem apparent that Southeast Asia's periods of prosperity have been built upon an unstable, and often unsustainable, exploitation that has been succeeded by conflict and collapse', Al McCoy wrote on reviewing its history in 1997. 'There is little indication that the region's current prosperity rests on firmer foundations.'[2] Yet more recent events tended to support his doubts.

International trade up to the fifteenth century

International trade in Asia expanded some two thousand years ago with the establishment of the Roman empire at one extreme and of the Han empire at the other and the growth of commerce in India. Southeast Asia was not only a route for that trade, but took part in it. Indeed participation in the intra-Asian trade remained the major pattern in its commerce until the nineteenth century, when it was overlaid by a range of contacts with other parts of the world. But over the centuries the contact-points between regional and international trade changed; the trade expanded in size and in range of products, one function of its internationalisation indeed being the transfer of animals, trees, and seeds from one part of the world to another; and the relative role of Southeast Asian peoples and peoples from other regions varied. Three phases may be discerned.

The initial points of contact were in the northern Malay peninsula and at Oc-eo in the Mekong delta. Some raw materials were brought to Funan across the eastern

sea, while west Asian goods, hitherto taken to China overland, were taken to different parts of the mainland. Another, more indirect, link between Southeast Asia and
international trade, mainly with India, was located in the area of the Sunda Strait,
called Ko-ying in the Chinese transcription, again, it seems, distributing west Asian
goods, and collecting Southeast Asian goods.

From the fifth century, the international trade route no longer crossed the peninsula, but went round its tip, giving the Straits of Melaka an enduring importance. It
thus made direct contact with the Sunda region. Over the next two centuries the
trade of the archipelago, Java, western Borneo, and the islands further to the east,
involved Indonesians and came to focus on the region controlled by the empire of
Sri Vijaya. International trade, boosted by the unification of China under the T'ang
dynasty, included the goods of India and China, but it now incorporated products
from Sumatra itself, resin, benzoin, and camphor, and from further eastward, cloves,
nutmegs, dragon's blood (a resin), and other forest products.

In the tenth and early eleventh centuries the trade route shifted and Sri Vijaya's
control diminished. The Khmer empire at Angkor and the Burman state of Pagan
were 'beginning to involve themselves in international trade'.[3] Indian and Chinese
traders were attempting to go more directly to the source of supply of Southeast
Asian goods, such as spices. East Java was beginning to develop its own trade, and
though Sri Vijaya sought to establish itself with both the Chola power of South India
and the new Sung dynasty in China, it could not maintain its old entrepotal position.
The Cola attack of 1025 shattered its hegemony. North and west Sumatra began to
trade direct with foreign traders, and they began to trade direct to east Java. East Java
indeed became the means of trading indirectly with the islands to the east, the source
of spices. In the Sung period writings of Chau Ju-kua, Java is thus identified with
spices, increasingly popular in Europe from the twelfth century, and in China, too.[4]
Trade increasingly involved bulkier products, no longer simply drugs and jungle and
marine produce, but also cotton goods from India and porcelain from China.

This set the pattern of the regional and international trade of the thirteenth,
fourteenth, and fifteenth centuries. With its control of the spice trade, Java, as
Whitmore puts it, ' … must be seen as the dominant commercial power during this
time and … this dominance influenced much that was going on around it.' The new
Mongol dynasty moved directly on Java in 1292—no accident—but Java continued
to exert its power over southern Sumatra in the fourteenth century, 'resisting even
the intrusion of the newly founded Ming dynasty in China'.[5] Its power in the outer
islands was, however, relatively loose, its focus being on the trade to the east, and
ports like Pasai in northern Sumatra were thus free to handle their local trade, in
pepper in its case, and even to market 'Javanese' spices to international traders from
the west. It was in this context that Melaka emerged in the first half of the fifteenth
century, first as part of the Ming tributary system, and then fitting into the pattern
of international trade by linking up with the Javanese merchants and their trade to
the further islands. Pasai was left with the pepper trade, though Sumatran rivals
emerged even for that, Pedir and later Aceh.

In the Irrawaddy delta Pegu also took part in the commerce of northern Sumatra and the Straits as well as of the Bay of Bengal. In the mid-fifteenth century it developed a strong trading relationship with Melaka as its status as a regional and international trading centre grew. Oriented towards China, the new centre at Ayudhya, by contrast, tended to see Melaka as 'an intruder into its sphere', as Whitmore puts it.[6]

The Sung had turned to Southeast Asia when its overland routes to the west were closed. They were closed again after the fall of the Mongol dynasty, and that led the Ming to interest themselves in the maritime region.[7] The Ming dynasty manifested its interest by sustaining the Zheng He voyages, renewing the tributary patterns within which it expected trade to take place. Once barbarian envoys were supplying it with tropical commodities, the court enforced prohibitions on private trade. Then in the 1430s it stopped sending its own fleets. A network of private trade nevertheless emerged, despite the authorities,[8] until in 1567 the emperor partially lifted the prohibitions and allowed trade under licence. The network had two main routes, the 'Western Ocean' to Java and the spice islands, and the 'Eastern Ocean', to Luzon and the spice islands. The Europeans were to link up with this network.

The Ming ventures helped to expand the trade of Southeast Asia in the fifteenth century, though they did not change its nature. Expansion was also, more indirectly, prompted by the changes at the extreme end of the framework, in Europe, where the economy revived after the devastation of the Black Death in the previous century. These changes together inaugurated 'the age of commerce' in Southeast Asia, which may be treated here as a second phase in the development of its international trade. They precede the incursions of the Europeans themselves, whose violence in fact led initially to a temporary interruption of the expansion of trade. Subsequently, however, the Europeans added novel elements to the traditional trading pattern, though again without displacing it, and, partly as a result, they helped to make the sixteenth and seventeenth centuries part of 'the age of commerce' as well.

'The age of commerce'

In one sense the pioneers in this venture, the Portuguese, offered nothing new. Others before them had entered the pattern of trade within Asia with the aim of securing more direct access to the products involved. The novelty, of course, lay in the fact that this time the initiative came from so far away as Europe. Hitherto it had been an extreme point in the pattern, and it had been linked with it through Venice and its post-Crusade connexions with Mamluk Egypt. The Iberians' ventures, particularly that of the Portuguese, are best conceived in terms of their perception of an intra-Asian and inter-continental trade, into which they might insert themselves at the expense of the middlemen, including Venice. It was no accident that the Genoese, rivals of the Venetians, played a part in the Iberian enterprises.

The initial focus of the Portuguese was on the western side of the Indian Ocean, where their success dated from the defeat of the Egyptians at Diu in 1509. They acquired Hormuz and Goa and tried to control the pepper of Malabar. In 1518, searching for cinnamon, they established themselves at Colombo, and, seeking a share in the Indian textile trade, they set up on the Coromandel coast as well. After the middle of the century, they extended their activities to the eastern extreme of the framework, occupying Macao in 1557, and securing a welcome as arms suppliers in the Japanese civil war. Their capture of Melaka in 1511, and the expedition sent thence direct to Maluku, source of clove and nutmeg, not only struck at what had become the major link between the regional and the international trade of Southeast Asia, but also broke the hold of the Javanese on the trade to the eastern parts of the archipelago.

The capture of Melaka did not lead to Portuguese dominance. Rather it removed the focus of trade from the Straits region, and dispersed it among other centres. Those included the new state of Aceh in north Sumatra, which dealt direct with international traders, and responded to the increased demand for pepper by expanding along both the northern and eastern coasts. The Melaka rulers, setting themselves up in Johore, competed with Aceh in Sumatra, but came to focus more on the eastern trade.

Indeed the Portuguese did not secure a monopoly of the trade in fine spices. Maluku became instead the focus of competition among several groups, including the Javanese towns, despite their growing conflict with the new state of Mataram, and also the Spaniards. To the north Spain conflicted with the sultanates of Brunei and Sulu, which were developing another link with China and the eastern archipelago.

The existing Asian networks acquired another new link, with Mexico. The original goal of the Spanish voyages had been to acquire wealth in Asia, and their unanticipated acquisitions in the Americas did not entirely distract them. Legazpi was sent to the Philippines to discover the return route to New Spain, 'bringing or sending spices and other valuable articles of those regions'.[9] But while the Spaniards, competing with Brunei and Sulu, continued to show an interest in Maluku, Manila became their commercial focus. 'This trade is so great and profitable and easy to control that the Spaniards do not apply themselves to, or engage in, any other industry', Antonio de Morga was to write in 1609. ' … They do not engage in the many other industries to which they could turn with great profit, if the China trade should fail them.'[10]

The trade was in a sense peripheral to Southeast Asia, since it chiefly consisted of the exchange of Chinese products for precious metals from Mexico. The Portuguese sought to fund their acquisition of the goods Europe sought from Asia by engaging in intra-Asian trade. The Spaniards based it on American silver, brought across the Pacific in the famous Manila galleons. But the supply of precious metals promoted economic expansion in East Asia. 'Still more dramatic than the flow of American silver was the sudden expansion of production and export from the Japanese silver mines, following improvements in technology in the mid-sixteenth century.'[11]

The Spanish enterprise, however, also contributed more indirectly to the expansion of Southeast Asia's trade. Making the world one by including the Americas created a rudimentary world economy. The Spanish monarchy became an instrument for spending the wealth it had adventitiously acquired. Though the Portuguese incursion had interrupted the expansion of Asian commerce, the Spaniards were to contribute to its further expansion by creating the boom conditions in the West of the later sixteenth and early seventeenth centuries.

The Dutch, the main carriers of trade within Europe, benefited from Spain's prodigal expenditure of the wealth it acquired from the Americas. Even after they revolted against Philip II and created the Republic of the United Provinces, Spain remained largely dependent on their commercial services. Well-informed about the Asian trade by Dutchmen who had been in the service of the short-handed Portuguese, such as van Linschoten, and by the persecuted Portuguese Jews, they conceived that they, too, might break into the intra-Asian trading framework. They took their decisive moves when the king of Spain, having become king of Portugal also in 1580, tried to close Lisbon to the Dutch rebels. A number of fleets were sent into Asian waters in the 1590s and the VOC was founded in 1602.

Like the Portuguese the Dutch traded almost throughout maritime Asia, and their activities in Southeast Asia were part of a larger enterprise. For example, they realised the importance of the trade in Indian textiles, and in 1605 planted commercial 'factories' at Masulipatam and Petapoli on the Coromandel coast. They also established themselves at Cambay in Gujerat, the other great textile area, and later Surat became an important source of textiles from northern India. In Ceylon, despite the opposition of the Portuguese, they obtained a share in the cinnamon trade. In East Asia, they were less successful than on the sub-continent. They failed to drive the Portuguese from Macao in 1622. They gained a footing in the Pescadores, but had to leave under threat of attack by the Chinese governor of Amoy. The VOC moved to Taiwan in 1624, but it never gained a footing on the mainland. By contrast it obtained a factory at Hirado in 1609, and it was to be able to continue trading in Japan even when others were excluded under the policy of seclusion adopted by the Tokugawa in the 1630s, and the Japanese were themselves prohibited from overseas trading.

In Southeast Asia itself the early fleets had traded at Aceh, at Bantam, and at Pattani, and they had also penetrated into Maluku in search of fine spices. The VOC's new city of Batavia was by 1660 to become the trade centre of the Malay world, the 'New Melaka', as the old ruler of Cirebon put it.[12] That was not, however, the result merely of positional advantage: it required the application of force, designed to eliminate rivals, focus and control regional and international trade, and secure the most important products on privileged if not monopolistic terms. The directors indeed insisted that the VOC's trade must be 'based on the common right of all peoples, consisting in freedom of commerce, the which being granted in neutral places by free nations where We find laws and do not have to bring them, We may not appropriate the aforesaid trade according to our own ideas and constrain such nations thereto by force.'[13] The practice differed from the precept. 'It is *mare liberum* in the British seas', as Sir George Downing said, 'but *mare clausum* on the coast of Africa and in the East Indies'.[14] Whatever rights they claimed for themselves in Europe, the Dutch in Southeast Asia sought control, and after 1640 their application of force had become more determined.

The VOC's attempts to enhance its control of Asian trade after 1640 were not confined to Southeast Asia. On the Coromandel coast it had taken Negapatnam, and a treaty of 1644, following its regaining independence from Spain, gave Portugal only a respite in Ceylon. By 1663 it had lost all its possessions there, and all but Goa and Diu in India. In East Asia Governor-General van Diemen drove the Spaniards from Taiwan in 1642, but Zheng Chenggong (Koxinga) in turn forced the Dutch to abandon their factory in 1661.

The policies of the Dutch, in Asia in general and in Southeast Asia in particular, were influenced by the downturn in the world economy, brought about in part by the decrease in the flow of precious metals from Spanish America. They were also reacting against the mercantilist policies this trend encouraged in the other European states, directed against the Dutch hold on the carrying and colonial trades. In these conditions the VOC used its political power to strengthen its commercial control and to eliminate competition. Both the recession, and the Dutch reaction to it, contributed to what Reid has seen as the mid-seventeenth century crisis in Southeast Asia.[15] It is with this period that he was thus disposed to terminate the 'age of commerce', and which is taken here as completing a second phase in the development of the international trade of Southeast Asia. The volume of trade diminished, and what continued was often in different hands, those of the Chinese and, at least in the archipelago, of the VOC. The role of Javanese traders 'became redundant and they disappeared from the scene'.[16]

The Portuguese had been active in the mainland states as mercenaries and adventurers rather than traders. Their destruction of Melaka, however, enabled Pegu and Ayudhya to expand their direct foreign contacts, and Cambodia established a port on the Mekong linked to the population on the northern fringe of the South China Sea. Before seclusion Japanese traders, unable to operate in China, were active in the ports of the eastern mainland, seeking raw silk in particular. After seclusion, Japan obtained its foreign goods from the former competitors of the Japanese traders, the Dutch and the Chinese, who were both permitted to trade under regulation at Nagasaki.[17]

The Dutch had made contact with Ayudhya, and also established a factory at what had become the vassal state of Pattani, and for a time the English followed their example. In 1634, after its political intervention, the VOC was permitted to build a small settlement on the river-bank at Ayudhya, but its position was by no means so strong as in the south. In 1649 the Company's agent, Jeremias van Vliet, threatened to call in a Dutch fleet when the court failed to satisfy some of the claims he had made. As a result the Dutch factory was seized and its employees arrested. The VOC staged a naval demonstration in 1654, and a decade later secured a treaty granting it a monopoly of the trade in hides, which went to Japan, and a virtual monopoly of the trade between Ayudhya and China.

The VOC also reached out to Arakan and Burma, but there again its penetration was even more limited, given the Moghul threat to the former and the disintegration and discouragement of the latter. The struggles between Burma and Ayudhya and the internecine strife in Dai Viet contributed to the security and prosperity of Laos in the early seventeenth century, but the VOC's venture there was also unsuccessful.

In Vietnam itself the Nguyen regime was particularly alive to the benefits of foreign trade, and its port, Fai-fo (Hoi-an) became 'the Vietnamese powerhouse of a South China Sea trading economy'.[18] Among its traders, indeed, the Europeans were only one element: before seclusion the Japanese were prominent, as in Ayudhya, and after it the Chinese took their place. The Portuguese had no factories in the area, but had gone to Tonkin to buy silk for the Japanese market, and traded to Fai-fo. The Nguyen invited the Dutch to trade, but their establishment of a factory at Pho-hien in Tonkin led to quarrels with the Nguyen, and the factory in the south was abandoned in 1641, reopened in 1651, and finally closed in 1654. The end of the civil war reduced the scope for European traders: after the truce both regimes became less tolerant of them. The Dutch stayed on in Tonkin, despite a further cut in Japan's trade, but finally left in 1700. The English Company had established a factory in Tonkin in 1672, its eyes also on the Japan trade, but it was never a success, and was abandoned in 1697. For a while (1702–05), however, a rival English company occupied Pulau Condore, its venture terminating when the Makassarese garrison massacred the Europeans. There were now no European factories in Vietnam. But Cochin-China still wanted foreign trade, and the restrictions on the Japanese and the distaste for the Europeans provided an opportunity for the Chinese, to whom the Nguyen were more open than the Trinh in the northern heartland could ever be.

The Dutch sought to drive the Spaniards not only from Maluku but from Manila itself. That they hoped would provide them with additional access to the China trade. But though they succeeded in Maluku, they did not succeed in the north. The war limited Spain's attempts to control the Moros and imposed great burdens on the population that they did control. But here again, as on the mainland, the VOC's success was limited.

In most of maritime Southeast Asia, by contrast, it greatly increased its commercial control in the later seventeenth century, above all by wielding its political and military power. The combination of its endeavours, and those of the sultanate of Mataram, played a major part in destroying the long-standing trade of the Javanese; their entrepot at Batavia displaced the Straits as the focus of international trade; and many of the states in the area were compelled to deliver products on a privileged or even monopolistic basis. Those elements whose role they thus curbed in the recession of the latter half of the seventeenth century would find it difficult to take advantage of the expansion that followed in the eighteenth. Nor indeed was the VOC well placed to take advantage of the new opportunities of the eighteenth century.

From the 1690s to the early nineteenth century

A revival in foreign trade began around 1690. It was associated with the expanding activities of the English, and with the new European demand for textiles—the

'Indian craze'—and for China tea. It owed something to the activities in the Bay of
Bengal of the Armenian, Indian, and other Muslim merchants excluded from the
archipelago. In the South China Sea it also owed a great deal to the Chinese merchants, particularly after the Manchu dynasty raised the ban on overseas trade it had
imposed until it had finally defeated the Ming in 1683, and their empire entered a
phase of unexampled prosperity. Trade was still predominantly intra-Asian, but to
an important extent had come to focus on different areas and different products.

Attuned to the previous phase of recession and monopoly, the VOC was not able
to adapt, even though it had certain advantages it might have turned to good account
in the changed circumstances it now faced. At the end of the century, for example,
Indian textiles occupied a dominant position among the Asian goods received in the
Dutch Republic. The Coromandel textile trade had suffered from local civil wars, and
the VOC had taken the initiative in developing trade in Bengal. It was, however, soon
left behind by English commercial competition there, and in the first third of the
eighteenth century the English definitely took the lead. The same was true in China.
'The VOC itself recognised in the 1690s that it was more efficient to trade with China
through Chinese shipping on Batavia than to send Dutch ships to China where they
always encountered distrust and obstruction from local officials.'[19] 'As a whole the
Dutch Company during these years lost ground in the European race for China tea.
The English competing company had … become the greatest importer.'[20] The
English familiarised themselves with the Chinese market, 'and thus had a flying start
into the eighteenth century, the Age of Calicoes and Tea and Opium'.[21] The East India
Company secured a permanent base at Canton in 1762.

Their interest in tea gave the English a new interest in Southeast Asia. China was
not yet a market for European manufactures, and if the trade in tea were not to be
funded simply by the import of specie, it required an expansion of the trade from
other parts of Asia. Increasingly Indian opium was to fill the gap, but the age-old
trade in tin and jungle and marine products from the archipelago continued to be
important. This trade the British Company left to the 'country traders', those based
in Asia, while itself retaining the direct trade to India and from China. The country
traders, buoyed by the demand for tea, and increasingly able to distribute opium and
arms as well, stimulated what the Dutch saw as 'smuggling'. They traded at ports
outside Dutch control, made contact with the Bugis, who had reacted against the
conquest of Makasar by adventuring elsewhere in the archipelago, and infringed the
contracts the Dutch made with Malay and Indonesian rulers.

The VOC reacted in several ways. It sought to retain its monopoly of the fine
spices of Maluku, even though they were now less important to the Europeans. It
sought still to secure deliveries of other products, if not by enforcing treaties, then
by offering protection. The VOC, too, turned a blind eye to some of the 'smuggling',
if it were secure enough in its own share of the trade. It did, however, seek to curb
an excess of 'smuggling', as in Riau. A fourth approach was, as the British Company
put it, 'an extraordinary Claim to an exclusive Right … as if the Seas themselves were

theirs and the bare Navigation through them was an Invasion of their Property'.[22] It was this that the treaty of 1784 was designed to deny.

In one way the VOC was innovative. From the 1640s the Dutch had tried to supply the European market with sugar from estates around Batavia. In the new century, while the English ministered to the European demands for tea and textiles, the Dutch began to satisfy another new craving, for coffee. For that they turned to account their growing territorial power in Java. The great breakthrough of Java coffee on the European market came in the 1720s. That broke with the traditional pattern of intra-Asian trade, and separated Java even further from it. But it was still not a reciprocal trade with Europe. In fact coffee quickly came to be secured by 'forced deliveries', for the most part secured through the 'Regents' and other Javanese officials, in some sense renewing a traditional pattern, and taking it into the nineteenth century.

The impact of the industrial revolution

Typically, however, that century, inaugurating a fourth phase in the history of the international trade of Southeast Asia, was marked by the emergence of a new pattern of trade, both within the region, and in respect of its relationship with the rest of the world. That was mainly the result of the industrial revolution in the West. That put those countries in a better position than ever before to compete with the traditional industry of Asia, though China still remained a challenge rather than a fulfilled opportunity. In general the trend was for Europe, and later the United States and Japan, to become exporters of manufactured goods, and for countries like those in Southeast Asia to become suppliers of food and raw materials, sometimes concentrating on just one or two commodities. How and when that took place and in what form was determined by a number of factors, including of course the distribution of the relevant resources and the availability of capital and labour.

It also depended on the regime in each territory. The colonial regimes were not simply the instruments of capital, but they were influenced by its interests. They were set up with a range of motives and they had different perspectives on economic change, just as their state-building, another source of change, had elements of difference as well as similarity. Some regimes were more interventionist than others, some more protectionist: some anticipated the new connexion with international trade, some delayed it, some promoted or facilitated it, some rather stood aside. In the previous phases the interrelationships between Europe and Asia were worked out at the micro-level as well as, or even more than, at the macro-level. The same was still true.

In any case it is easy to antedate the development of the economic relationships that the industrial revolution brought about. The old intra-Asian pattern was slow to recede, let alone disappear. The 1870s may mark a turning-point. In Europe and in the United States, industrialisation both spread and intensified. Unification, and then protection, boosted it in Germany. The end of the civil war boosted it in the United States, and it, too, adopted protection in 1891. Russia moved more slowly, and French and Italian industrialisation did not really get under way till the new century, by which time the Europeans had an Asian imitator, Japan. Britain lost the advantage of being first, though gaining opportunities for investment and in the modernisation of other economies overseas.

If the world was transforming itself, it was also brought closer together. Much of the early impulse to industrialisation, and of the government involvement in it, was infrastructural in nature. Communications were dramatically improved, not only within countries, above all with railway-building, but among them. The most striking development in that respect was the opening of the Suez Canal in 1869. Other ties developed about the same time. The electric telegraph reached Singapore in 1871 and linked Southeast Asia to Europe, China, and Australia during these years.

Trade within Asia did not, of course, disappear, but it changed its character. Previously it had focused on the export of Indian textiles and of Indian drugs to other parts of Asia, on the importation into China of tin and jungle and marine products, on the export of manufactures from China. Such activities were not at once displaced, but they were put into the background. The new emphasis on an export–import relationship with the rest of the world was accompanied by an intra-regional differentiation. While, for example, tin and later rubber were exported from Malaya, rice was taken to Malaya and also to Indonesia from the Burma delta. Siam became a major exporter after the treaty of 1855, and so did French Indo-China after the expansion of the ricelands of the colony of Cochin-China.

Even before 1870, a mixed pattern had been emerging. The merchants in early Penang and even in early Singapore were still concerned with the 'country trade', with textiles, opium, and goods for China. Those established in Java after the British conquest of 1811 still retained close ties with India, but they were also distributing British textiles. The disputes over the Anglo-Dutch treaty of 1824 related to duties charged upon goods from Europe as well as those upon goods from other parts of Asia.

The same overlaying of patterns is apparent in the Philippines, too. The opening of Manila facilitated the export of rice to China. Then new opportunities opened up for sugar, particularly after the collapse of the West Indian industry that followed the abolition of slavery. Grown in Luzon and the Visayas, it was taken to Europe and Australia, while hemp, produced in the Bikol region, was exported to the United States. The Philippines, like tin-focused Malaya, then became an importer of rice.

The intervention of governments helped to create the mixed pattern of trade. Some sought to establish new economic relationships with Europe well before the 1870s tended to transform the trading pattern more generally. In the Philippines the efforts of the Spanish government proved somewhat ineffectual. After the British capture of Manila in 1762, and its subsequent return, the Spaniards had sought to develop the islands for fear of losing them again. In particular they tried to link them more effectively with the rest of the world, instead of merely with Mexico, by opening up the route round the Cape of Good Hope. Under the impulse of 'enlightened despotism' at home, they also established the Royal Philippine Company, and an

Economic Society, designed to develop new resources in the Philippines. But their endeavours enjoyed limited success. The loss of Mexico and the other major possessions in America in the early nineteenth century meant that the Philippines had to seek other means of ensuring its survival. The only way was to facilitate foreign trade. That had the advantage of appeasing the British, though it ran the risk of subverting Spanish authority in other ways.

The Dutch, by contrast, intervened in the economy of Java with determination and effect. In the French wars they had lost the bases from which the VOC had conducted its trade elsewhere in Asia. The economy of the new Dutch kingdom was not in a position to industrialise or to invest. What it did, from 1830, was to take up and develop the compulsory delivery of products to which the VOC had turned in the eighteenth century. Though commodities were thus secured for the European market, it was done by methods that were outdated by the 1870s, and indeed before; but the village remained a source of cheap labour after 1870. Java was treated as an appendage of the Dutch economy, and with the surpluses it created Dutch infrastructure was built and industry made to flourish.

Singapore was part of the old pattern and part of the new. Its initial success in many ways showed that it belonged to the old, though 'Kota Baru', as it was long known to indigenous traders,[23] provided new routes and new products. It was but the latest in the series of entrepots for intra-Asian and Southeast Asian trade that had triumphed at the tip of the Straits, and a concept of the history of Temasek seemed to be in Raffles' mind. Singapore had, however, the special advantage of 'free trade', partly as a result of support from British India. For the Dutch, it was another Riau, thrust into the heart of their empire and absorbing its trade. It distributed Indian textiles and opium; it welcomed traders from China, from the archipelago, from Vietnam, from Siam; and it also distributed British manufactures. 'Since Singapore has become a settlement chintzes from Europe have been used as bathing clouts, broadcloths as trousers, Bugis satins and the batek silks of Java as hats. People carry silk umbrellas in their hands and wear leather sandals, and talk fluently in English, Bengali and Tamil. If an Englishman addresses them in Malay they reply in English.'[24]

Singapore faced the problems other entrepots face. One was the setting-up of rivals. Its superb situation, and the almost total freedom from taxation, meant that they had little chance. Riau was a total failure in the nineteenth century. A more serious prospect was the erosion of Singapore's entrepotal position, as with the expansion of trade, it became more feasible for other ports in Southeast Asia to renew or develop a direct contact with the outside world, rather than an indirect: Bangkok, Saigon, even Makasar. In the event, despite continued apprehension, Singapore kept ahead. It benefited from the development of neighbouring Malaya, but it retained a hold on the trade of other parts of Southeast Asia, particularly of Indonesia, partly by providing additional services. Some believed, for example, that Makasar, made a free port in 1847, 'would rise, like another phoenix, literally from her ashes'.[25] In fact it stimulated Singapore's trade with Sulawesi, though reducing the Bugis role.

By the early twentieth century the industrial revolution had moved into a new phase, often requiring higher levels of technical know-how and capitalisation, and it exerted new demands on the outside world. One feature was the emergence of the automobile industry. There was a demand for oil, and also for rubber. That could be grown on plantations, but also by smallholders. Different parts of Southeast Asia again tended to respond in different ways. Rubber tended to be a plantation crop in Cochin-China, a smallholder crop in Netherlands India, a plantation crop and a smallholder crop in Malaya. Oil was exploited in Burma, in eastern Borneo, in southern Sumatra, and later in Sarawak and Brunei.

The worldwide Depression after 1929 brought to an end the long period of expansion that the industrial revolution had promoted. During that period there had been phases of recession and boom, sometimes prompted by economic factors, sometimes by political factors, such as World War I. To those the Southeast Asian economies had responded, particularly as they had become more closely linked with the international commodity markets. The Great Depression had much more profound effects. Java's sugar industry was dealt a crippling blow. The Dutch government tried to stem the flow of cheap Japanese imports by abandoning its free trade policies. The British supported planter production of rubber more effectively than smallholder. Yet in some ways, despite all the hardships it involved, the Depression prepared the way for the future. Java's sugar industry was already becoming non-competitive on world markets. Smallholder production could revive. Japanese competition was a portent.

Some historians have indeed been tempted to make the Depression the watershed in modern Southeast Asian history, rather than choosing the Japanese invasion. That seems an exaggeration, but some changes are too easily ignored. The approach of World War II produced a boom that affected some of the raw materials that Southeast Asia produced, such as rubber. Then the war itself prompted a complete disruption of the patterns of Southeast Asia's international trade. The return of the colonial powers was accompanied by attempts to restore the pre-war patterns. They were, however, no more than partially successful, in the economic field as in the political. The way was in fact prepared for a wider participation in a new phase of economic expansion, promoted by the free trade policies of the United States, the recovery of Japan, the development of multinational corporations, and the emergence of international funding and aid agencies.

The late twentieth century might thus be characterised as a new 'age of commerce' in Southeast Asia. Once again Southeast Asian rulers enthusiastically took up the opportunities that their geographic exposure to the outside world offered them. Historians could compare the changes that each period saw. They could also wonder whether the new age would create more permanent rewards for the endeavours of the Southeast Asian peoples than the old one. Would their prosperity last? Would their economies take off? How widely would the benefits be shared? Would absolutism persist? Would diversity be reduced? Would the environment be irretrievably damaged? The 1997–98 crisis encouraged gloomy responses to such questions. Yet it could teach useful lessons.

Notes

1 *Indonesian Trade and Society*, p. 85.
2 Review of *CHSEA* in *Journal of the Economic and Social History of the Orient*, 40, 1 (1997), p. 116.
3 John K. Whitmore in Karl L. Hutterer, ed., *Economic Change and Social Interaction in Southeast Asia*, Ann Arbor: U Mich, 1977, p. 143.
4 K. R. Hall, 'Trade and Statecraft in the Western Archipelago at the Dawn of the European Age', JMBRAS, 54, 1 (1981), pp. 22, 23.
5 p. 145.
6 p. 146.
7 K. R. Hall, 'The Opening of the Malay World … ', JMBRAS, 58, 2 (1985), p. 85.
8 L. Blussé, 'No Boats to China … ', MAS, 30, 1 (February 1996), p. 57.
9 q. E. J. McCarthy, *Spanish Beginnings in the Philippines*, Washington, 1943, pp. 27–8.
10 q. Schurz, p. 39.
11 A. Reid, 'An "Age of Commerce" in South East Asian History', MAS, 24, 1 (February 1990), p. 20.
12 q. C. R. Boxer, *The Dutch Seaborne Empire*, London: Hutchinson, 1965, p. 189.
13 q. Van Leur, p. 243.
14 q. Boxer, p. 92. *Mare liberum*, free sea; *mare clausum*, closed sea.
15 *Southeast Asia in the Age of Commerce*, Yale UP, 1993, II, pp. 297–8.
16 S. Arasaratnam, *Pre-Modern Commerce and Society in Southern Asia*, KL: UM, 1972, p. 17.
17 Yoneo Ishii, ed., *The Junk Trade from Southeast Asia*, Singapore: ISEAS; Canberra: ANU, 1998, pp. 1–2.
18 A. Woodside in K. W. Taylor and John K. Whitmore, eds, *Essays into Vietnamese Pasts*, Cornell UP, 1995, p. 182.
19 Ishii, p. 195.
20 K. Glamann, *Dutch–Asiatic Trade, 1620–1740*, Copenhagen: Danish Science P; The Hague: Nijhoff, 1958, p. 243.
21 Blussé, MAS, p. 76.
22 q. Vos, p. 159.
23 A. van der Kraan, 'Bali and Lombok in the World Economy', RIMA, 27, 1 &2 (1993), p. 95.
24 Abdullah bin Abdul Kadir, *The Hikayat*, trans. A. H. Hill, KL: OUP, 1970, p. 162.
25 q. Wong Lin Ken, 'The Trade of Singapore, 1819–69', JMBRAS, 33, 4 (December 1960), p. 103.

Subsistence and Exports

During the four phases in which the international trade of Southeast Asia developed—before the fifteenth century, the 'age of commerce', the period from the 1690s to the early nineteenth century, and the period since the industrial revolution—the region, predominantly based on a rice economy, produced a range of export goods. They came from different areas and their production had differential effects, social and political.

International trade is clearly still in a process of development, and the world of nation-states is still coming to terms with 'globalisation'. That implies not only a further, if contested, extension of the principle of the division of labour. It implies major economic and social adjustments. Peoples and governments seek to position themselves to take advantage of those changes or avoid their disadvantages. Much depends on their resources, human as well as physical, and their ability to mobilise them in the most effective way. Issues such as human rights and the environment, though not new, gain a new importance. The world focuses on the debate at the outset of the twenty-first century. It can also, however, be seen in a historical context. The experience of the Southeast Asian region can be taken as an example, though, like any example, it has its special features.

The growing involvement of Southeast Asia in international trade over the centuries depended, of course, on the participation of its peoples and on their relationship with those who came to the region or sought its products. The peoples and those who led them had to achieve a balance between their domestic needs and their foreign involvement, and that changed over time. Both in turn depended on the resources that Southeast Asia possessed, and also on the availability of technologies capable of exploiting them. Those technologies could open up resources, but could also deplete them.

Characteristic of the volcanic mountain structure of the region are its mineral riches. The Indo-Malayan mountains contain not only lead, silver, zinc, and antimony, but the greater part of the world's tin and tungsten, more easily worked further south, in Malaya, Bangka, and Biliton, because heavier rains have washed it down in alluvial mud. There are scattered deposits of iron in eastern Malaya, in the Philippines also, and in the Riau-Johore area there is bauxite. Gold lured early Indian traders to Malaya; and gold was a welcome resource for the Philippines in the Depression of the 1930s. The area has little good coal, but considerable mineral oil and gas, in Upper Burma, in Sumatra, and in Borneo, in both Kalimantan and Brunei. Exploiting such deposits has depended on demand, domestic and foreign, but also on technological capacity. Continuing to do so also depends on the extent of their depletion.

The sea-girt nature of the region has not only contributed to its exposure to international trade: it has also provided it with rich marine resources. Fish, dried or fermented, were an important source of food, drawn also from lakes and swamps. The sea provided delicacies that were in demand in China as well as in the archipelago itself, such as trepang and shark-fin. Pearls from the Sulu seas were included in the regalia of Malay monarchs and adorned society beauties in Victorian London.

Jungle produce also became part of the traditional trade to China. For some of the peoples of Southeast Asia itself the jungle was also an almost complete source of subsistence, and for others again it was an important supplement. But, for those who sought a living by sedentary cultivation, its density and diversity could be misleading. Only some of the soils of Southeast Asia are fertile. Generally they are poor sterile red laterites, created by the leaching action of heavy rainfall which, with low organic content, has washed the silica away and left clays. The process is, of course, less noticeable in drier areas, where indeed evaporation may draw up plant nutrients into the soil, for instance in east Java and central Burma. Elsewhere elaborate vegetation—there are in the archipelago alone some 45 000 species of flowering plants—is no indication of fertility. The vegetation is the result of a delicate balance, and it lives off its decaying self rather than from the soil. Excessive destruction of the vegetation leads to erosion and further impoverishment. The fact that Borneo supported 'a luxuriant tropical rain forest is no indication of the value of its soil', Karl Pelzer wrote, 'since these forests depend on decayed plant material for nourishment'.[1]

Fertile soils in part result from volcanic outpourings. Not all of those enhance fertility. In Sumatra the ejecta are largely acidic in character rather than basic. The reverse is true in Java and Bali where the volcanoes produce basic ejecta and fertilise the soils, and peasants press riskily close to the summits. The other source of particularly fertile soils in Southeast Asia is the alluvial deposits created by the great rivers, the Irrawaddy, the Chao Praya, the Mekong, the Red River, the Solo. High rainfall means considerable erosion, especially where, as in central Burma, it is preceded by a period of drought. The rivers thus carry considerable deposits, borne far afield in time of flood. The Irrawaddy delta, though eroded by the sea, expands some three miles each century; the deltas of the Mekong and the Solo more rapidly still. The shallow seas of the Sunda shelf and the mangroves help to retain the silt. In the

Philippines both sources of fertile soils are present: the soil is renewed by streams in the Cagayan valley, by ash on Negros.

Rice

The practice of shifting cultivation or swidden agriculture, under which clearings in the jungle, made by slash-and-burn methods, are used and then abandoned for substantial periods, was adapted to the poorer soils of Southeast Asia. An agriculture that inserts itself in the self-renewing process of the jungle, it has to be delicately managed, lest it lead to erosion. Assumed, perhaps questionably, to be the earliest form of settled agriculture, it persists, examples including the *ladang* cultivation in many parts of the outer islands of Indonesia, the system of *ray* in Vietnam, of *taungya* in Burma, of *caingin* in the Philippines. Yet governments dislike it. Pre-colonial Javanese kingdoms were inimical to shifting cultivation and shifting cultivators, while the forest offered 'sanctuary to those wishing to escape or remain outside the effective control of the state'.[2] Colonial rulers also opposed shifting cultivation, like the British in Malaya: 'their main concern', as Lim Teck Ghee tells us, being 'that only one crop was taken off the land which then reverted to valueless secondary forest and could not be recultivated until it had remained fallow for several years'.[3] Post-colonial political and business leaders echo their pre-colonial and colonial predecessors, concerned, like them, to establish their authority, and seeing swidden as 'backward'. They are concerned, too, that it requires a large area of land, which, with the substitution of artificial fertiliser for the nutrients created by the traditional burn-off, might be used more productively, and concerned also at times simply to displace the shifting cultivators who obstructed the clearing of the jungle for other more immediately profitable purposes. For the cultivators, the staple is, as it always has been, millet, or dry rice, though other crops are also grown.

Sawah, or wet-rice cultivation, became common, it is thought, in the early centuries of the common era, although, as K. R. Hall points out, surviving records can substantiate 'only that wet-rice agriculture in permanent fields was practised in eastern Java and the Kyaukse area of Burma by the eighth century'.[4] This system was far more productive, even making it possible to harvest two crops a year, and it was able to sustain a more substantial peasant population, and to create a surplus for consumption by others. It could be sustained only in rich alluvial plains, or where irrigation brought in dissolved volcanic matter, or where fertiliser was added, traditionally by the water buffalo used for the ploughing that made the land suitable for seed or transplanted seedlings. Its development required a long-term commitment on the part of the cultivators, and they were likely to occupy the same land for generations. The surplus they produced made it possible to sustain states, but early state elites had to come to terms with the sawah producers, offering them protection and rewards and invoking suitable deities.

The subsequent centuries were not, of course, unmarked by change, but it took the form of extension and replication. Only in the nineteenth century did rice become a major item in international trade, and this changed the pattern in several ways. Traditional rulers, seeing the production of rice as a fundamental basis for the power and prosperity of their realm and apprehensive of the risks of scarcity, had prohibited its export. The Spanish government in Manila, so often comparable to a traditional government, also prohibited export by foreigners, if not by others, when the price rose so high that it might provoke discontent. Now those barriers were broken down by the establishment of British rule in Burma and of French rule in Cochin-China, by the Bowring treaty with Siam, by the liberalisation pressed on the Spaniards by the loss of their American possessions and the diplomacy of the British.

That led to a vast expansion of wet-rice cultivation in the Chao Praya basin and the deltas of the Irrawaddy and the Mekong, and for a time the Philippines became a rice exporter. Rice exports from Siam rose 25-fold between 1850 and 1900: they constituted 60–70 per cent of exports. In 1830, 66 000 acres of Lower Burma were under rice; in 1860, 1 333 000; in 1890, 4 398 000; in 1920, 8 588 000; and in 1940, 9 932 000.

> The soil did not really laugh with a crop when it was tickled with a hoe; it was equally likely to give an ugly leer. … And the loans that were necessary initially to provide food and clothes were to be obtained only at a distance at high rates of interest, which in a year of fever could not be paid but must go to swell the debt which, as it grew, first nibbled at the *morale* of the pioneer and finally swallowed him up completely.[5]

Cultivating the delta fields was exacting, but the rising price of rice urged it on. In Cochin-China the French auctioned off land to pay for the canals they constructed, and rice was grown to the advantage of a new landed elite. A rich landlord class emerged: out of 6530 landowners with over 125 acres in all Indo-China in 1930, 6300 were in southern Vietnam. '[W]e have given vast territories to individuals who doubtless have been of service to us', wrote Paul Bernard in 1945, 'but who were only our creatures and did not deserve such rich presents'.[6]

Initially the main markets were in Europe, though Philippines rice went to China, and Burma rice to India. Increasingly, however, exports went to other parts of Southeast Asia, where the population was turning to other export-oriented activities, such as tin-mining and rubber-planting in Malaya, or sugar cultivation in the Philippines, and where rice cultivation was relatively more costly. Java exported its best rice to Europe, while importing cheaper rice for home consumption from other parts of Southeast Asia.

These patterns were disrupted by the Pacific War. In some parts of Southeast Asia, in Java and northern Vietnam, there was famine before the war ended. In Java growing foodstuffs had the highest priority, but it was undermined by the random conscription of *romusha,* the Japanese version of forced labour, and by bad management. That discouraged the production of rice and inhibited its movement from surplus to deficit areas. Hunger spread: in 1944 in all residencies except Jakarta and Priangan the death rate exceeded the birth rate. Returning to Southeast Asia, the British were particularly anxious to restore the supply of rice from Siam and Burma: the return of the colonial powers must not be associated with renewed famine. The experience encouraged the independent states to think in terms of self-sufficiency. Those who fought the Cold War also emphasised the need to avoid hunger and unrest.

The term 'Green Revolution' was apparently invented by William S. Gaud, an official of the US Agency for International Aid: the 'new technology' would avoid 'Red' revolution.[7] The Japanese had made attempts to introduce Northeast Asian strains of rice and seed fertiliser techniques. After the war Ford, Rockefeller, and the Philippines government established the International Rice Research Institute at Los Baños, with the aim of developing strains that would yield more abundantly in tropical Asia. At the same time as Clifford Geertz was writing gloomily of Java, the institute was working on North Asian hybrids, the first of which was released as IR 8 in 1966. It needed a great deal of fertiliser, and its resistance to disease was weak, but other strains followed. The 'miracle rice' was soon being grown extensively in the Philippines, and it was taken up in Indonesia in the 1970s. The yields, Anne Booth notes, were highest on small holdings.[8]

Market and other forces

These changes in the rice economies of Southeast Asia were associated with other changes, in particular their increased involvement in production for overseas markets. Such production had, of course, a much longer history, and in it several phases may be discerned. Before about 1400, as Reid has pointed out, most Southeast Asian exports were of jungle and marine produce, 'that exotic inventory of medicines, delicacies, perfumes and aromatic woods described in Chinese manuals of the T'ang and the Sung'. After 1400 in response to the expansion of international trade the situation changed. Forest produce was gathered on an increased scale. There was also, however, a qualitative difference. 'Whole communities devoted themselves to cultivating pepper, clove, cotton, sugar and benzoin, and became dependent on the international market for their livelihood.'[9] The third phase begins as the end of 'the age of commerce' ends. But from late in the seventeenth century parts of Southeast Asia responded to China's prosperity, while the Dutch in the new century began to experiment in Java with the forced cultivation of coffee for the European market. In the fourth phase, set off by the industrial revolution, export economies developed on a large scale, and involved a range of products, often sent to remote markets.

The VOC had adopted a new development of an old practice in the eighteenth century, the forced delivery of produce, and it was continued in the nineteenth. And it is, of course, necessary to consider, with regard to all the phases through which Southeast Asia's involvement in production for export has passed, the inducements or pressures under which hunters, gatherers, and cultivators created and parted with their surplus, and the means by which, and the intermediaries through which, it reached the market. In particular an attempt has to be made to distinguish what we would see as the political and the commercial factors involved.

In modern capitalist society, it is easy to point to the distinction, but also to the relationship, and public discussion focuses on the extent to which governments should 'intervene' to promote, restrain or regulate the working of 'market forces'. In some other twentieth-century societies governments have sought to direct and control the economy, rather than rely on capitalist enterprise or market forces to create wealth and produce a surplus. In pre-modern societies, such as those of Southeast Asia up to the end of the age of commerce, the position is different again. There governing elites, and those connected with them, took an interest in both promoting the creation of a trading surplus and benefited from it either by direct participation or by taxing and licensing. The activities of the VOC in Southeast Asia in the following phase may be seen in that context. By enforcing contracts and offering protection it used its political power to secure goods and to lower their cost. The 'cultivation system' of its successors involved 'intervention'.

Nor did the subsequent colonial phase bring a sudden transition to a capitalist model. The 'modern' sugar planters of late colonial Java, for example, relied on the maintenance of the village (*desa*), not only as a pillar of peace and order, but as a source of cheap labour. In colonial Indo-China the European employer did not have to pay what we call social security.[10] The extended family and the village still looked after the child, the old, the helpless. 'Those who organised trade maintained the worker on the level of the traditional economy, but sold the product of that work on the level of the city economy', as Paul Mus put it.[11] It was a kind of capitalist system that in that respect its post-colonial successors had some reason to emulate: if government should not intervene, the family became all the more important. At the same time they were tempted to behave like earlier elites, participating, taxing, licensing.

Agricultural exports

The earliest phase in Southeast Asia involved the collection of marine and jungle produce, and its transmission to markets largely outside Southeast Asia, above all China. The practices that involved continued to mark this trade, insofar as it persisted through later phases. They tend to be described in terms of 'exchange', with hunters and gatherers from the upland interior producing forest products in return for goods from the lowland, in particular salt, as well as goods from the outside world. In turn, indeed, the lowlanders would 'exchange' the local goods for goods brought by traders from or in touch with the outside world. These 'exchanges', however, involved political, even ritual, as well as commercial transactions. Leaders who possessed both commercial and political power were involved at the points of intersection in this system, controlling the supply of salt, taxing the passage of goods, creating but profiting from a market at the river-mouth.

It is in such a context that the 'age of commerce' should next be considered. In this phase there was an export-led boom in cotton, sugarcane, benzoin, and pepper, which had probably been introduced in Pasai and Pedir before the fourteenth century by Muslim traders from Malabar. How were those products secured and by what means? 'Some growers undoubtedly became very wealthy', Reid writes, 'but the principal beneficiaries were the rulers of the port-cities which marketed these goods, the traders, and the intermediaries who financed the new frontiers of cash-cropping'. The key figure, he points out, was the entrepreneur who could mobilise labour and advance money to growers who would be bound to deliver produce, and in some cases were more or less slaves. 'In all cases a large share of the profit would go to this intermediary financier and broker, who might in time become the chief of a small river-system; a percentage would also go as tribute to the ruler of the city-state where the international market was located.'[12]

The end of the 'age of commerce', it seems, added to the element of political compulsion in the extraction of trade goods. The VOC adopted the practice, but did not originate it. 'Such a system, requiring every adult male or nuclear family to cultivate a stipulated number of pepper vines, was enforced by the rulers of Banten during the second half of the seventeenth century',[13] using the indigenous administrative hierarchy to enforce compliance and to collect the produce. The VOC followed the model when it introduced the cultivation of coffee into Java and determined to make it competitive with other sources of supply. In 1723 coffee was made an article of monopoly. Around 1760 the planting of a given number of trees was made obligatory, the Regents organising production in conformity with the requests of the commissary for native affairs appointed by the governor-general, and being aided by 'coffee sergeants'.[14]

The leaders of eighteenth-century Mataram needed cash. They were, as Luc Nagtegal has put it, political entrepreneurs.[15] Rice could not be converted into political power, but wealth could win supporters, buy rarities to distribute as gifts, guns to protect or terrify. Though the VOC was now very much a presence in Java, it seems doubtful that such an attitude was entirely novel, but the Susuhunan (sultan) himself had to pay for a Dutch garrison and was short of money, and gifts and bribes were welcome. What was new was that some *bupati* (regents) sought wealth by growing coffee and indigo for the VOC. 'Because there was no fundamental difference between public and private funds, we cannot speak of political corruption', Nagtegal adds. But political entrepreneurship had long been part of the state, and the *bupati* were expected to be loyal supporters, not an impersonal and functional bureaucracy.[16]

In the British interregnum on Java, Raffles made some attempt to limit the role of the Regents. Government was to become more dependent on taxation than on production. Like his trusted Dutch adviser, H. W. Muntinghe, he believed that this would awaken the spirit of enterprise among the peasants. 'Let the Javanese be deprived of every prerogative, of a right of property, and of every prospect of ameliorating his situation, and he naturally will be what he now is, an indolent, poor and wretched creature. But grant him a right of property, and open to him a view of mending his situation, and naturally he will display the principles and faculties innate to every human being.'[17] The peasants paid dues in money, but even more in kind, and also owed labour service. 'The oppression, abuses, and hardships to which this system must give rise are evident and striking. While there exists no defined or limited extent of these feudal services and it is impossible to define precisely the demands of the public service, it must naturally be expected that persons in authority will avail themselves of the convenience thus placed within their reach.'[18] Raffles was expressing ideas associated with the fourth phase in the development of Southeast Asia's exports. So great a change as he contemplated could hardly be carried through by an interim administration, under pressure, furthermore, not to run at a loss, and not very well-informed.

On their return to the Indies after the French wars, the Dutch found themselves no more able to pursue the new system. '[The] King himself, and his leading minister, seem to mean well', Raffles wrote in 1817, '[but] they have too great a hankering after profit, and *immediate* profit, for any liberal system to thrive under them'.[19] The system failed to deliver export revenues at the level the Dutch needed, particularly after the outbreak of the Java war in 1825 and the onset of the Belgian secession crisis from 1830. 'I shall not assert that it is impossible to raise the industry and prosperity of the Javanese people', the Dutch Resident of Pekalongan wrote in 1828, 'but rather that under the present circumstances, in which the mass of people are still oppressed by the secret vexations of thousands of minor chiefs, this will always remain exceedingly difficult'.[20] The Dutch turned back to the old system in a new form, the 'culture' or 'cultivation system' advocated by van den Bosch. This was a new attempt to employ political power to ensure the availability of export surpluses at a profitable rate—to mobilise the unused labour power of the peasantry 'to cultivate products fit for the European market, at prices which can stand the competition from other countries', as he put it[21]—not dislodging the Javanese elite from the process but again involving them in it. Compulsion lay behind the use of the traditional mechanism. As to cultivation by the inhabitants, '*must* is the ultimatum', said Inspector L. Vitalis in 1835.[22]

In that sense it was systematic. In practice it varied widely, and the judgments made about it at the time and since have, partly for that reason, varied widely also. Van den Bosch was himself opposed to systems. It was 'dangerous to lay down prescriptions or regulations that are too explicit. ... It is better to leave a great latitude to the Residents and to follow their point of view.'[23] There was, however, a general concept, defined by Cees Fasseur as 'that form of agricultural-industrial exploitation of Java in which the government uses its authority and influence to force the peasantry to grow tropical export products in return for payments that were unilaterally fixed and low; these products subsequently were sold for the benefit of the treasury'.[24] What is missing from that succinct definition is the role of the native elite. That was essential, and a great deal of discretion went with it. They benefited not only from 'culture percentages', but also, particularly at the level of the village headman, through their role in the assessment of the government's land-rent, against which, in some cases, the payments were set off, and in the apportionment of corvée and cultivation services.

The government initially concentrated on crops that were likely to produce the most immediate returns: indigo, already grown for domestic consumption; sugar, increasingly planted in irrigated fields in a one-in-three-year cycle with rice; and above all coffee, grown in cooler foothill and upland country, in plantations, as a forest crop, or in small gardens. Other crops were introduced, and some proved of long-term significance, such as tea. But more immediately coffee, sugar, and indigo were responsible for bringing about a vast increase in revenue, not only from the sale of produce but also from direct taxes and tax-farms, and, as the Dutch claimed, of peace and prosperity, although the people of Cirebon were not themselves allowed to drink coffee, and those in the Kunungan regency had to hand in their kettles.[25]

The famines of the late 1840s questioned Dutch optimism, and started a debate about the system that has in a sense never ceased. It had been based on the idea of capitalising what appeared to be unused or underused labour in Java. Its success depended, as Elson puts it, 'upon the tricky task of keeping a balance between the material and labour requirements for the production of sufficient domestic sustenance and those for the Cultivation System'.[26] The famines indicated that the balance had not been kept. He argues convincingly that a weak colonial government had created a system which it could not control. In particular the Javanese elite could turn its power to account, and European officials were in no position to restrain them or prevent the abuses that resulted. An uneasy coalition of interested players flourished briefly, but led, as it was bound to lead, to corruption and maladministration.[27]

In the 1850s, the state, stronger and aware of the abuses, began to curb them, and that, as Elson suggests, virtually ended the system. Though not the first, the most famous of the critics was an ex-official, Eduard Douwes Dekker; he was the creator, under the *nom-de-guerre* Multatuli, of a marvellous novel, *Max Havelaar,* published in 1860, which—as another critic, W. R. van Hoevell, put it—'sent a shudder through the land'.[28] There were other arguments, too, which a stronger Dutch middle-class could endorse and put forward in the States-General, a body that after the Dutch monarchy felt the tremors of 1848 was able to play a larger role in colonial policy. If the government relinquished the role of 'planter and merchant', D. C. Steyn Parvé argued, and limited itself to the role of 'sovereign', the Javanese would seek their own advantage in 'free labour', and become more productive.[29] This was the time, too, that the United States was challenging slavery as a means of production and Tsarist Russia serfdom.

There was some evidence, indeed, that the Javanese could behave like the 'economic men' of the capitalist world. Crop payments, though kept low, offered disposable incomes in the form of cash. In Kedu, even in the 1830s, 'as soon as they have any money over from the yield of their produce, the natives … spend it on purchasing plough animals and tools, and on ornaments for themselves, their women and their children'.[30] Indigenous commerce expanded, as increased purchasing power satisfied old needs and generated new. 'The colonial rulers were content to employ the old system', as Elson puts it, 'but they were aiming to replace it with a new one in which peasants were economically dependent upon the resources not of village chief, district chief or Regent, but of the Dutch-managed colonial export economy'.[31]

The changes that were made in the 1850s and 1860s stopped short, however, of implementing the 'free labour' concept, as indeed did the changes made in Russia, if not the United States. Even the legislation of the 1870s produced, as it were, a halfway house. It provided for the abandonment of the cultivation system in respect of sugar, and permitted private concerns to lease 'waste lands' on a regular long-term contractual basis, and to lease village lands on a short-term basis, while guaranteeing the non-alienation of land by the peasants. Private entrepreneurs became free, often despite themselves, since they preferred a government contract. For labour, it was a different matter.

Like the Tsars the government sustained the village as a pillar of peace and order and avoided the alienation of village land. But that also sustained the village as a source of cheap labour, and the sugar entrepreneurs negotiated with the village chiefs not only for the use of sawah land but also for labour, as they had under the previous system. The new 'liberal' system reduced the role of the Regents and the higher levels of the native hierarchy, but not that of the village headmen. Nor were the 'plantations' even now operating in an entirely 'free' market. 'The village, which aggregated and managed this cheap labour supply, had to retain its traditional ties and bonds in order to fulfil this function which was not eliminated by transforming forced labour into wage labour, for the low level of the wages depended on a continued symbiosis between private-export and village economy'.[32]

Indeed it became a question whether the interventionist policies the Dutch followed were 'transitional' or whether they were inhibiting 'transition'. By the 1890s van Deventer was concerned over 'diminishing welfare' in Java, and, in language that reflected a new sense of responsibility among colonial powers, he called for the Dutch to redeem their 'debt of honour':

> a situation must be prepared in which the greater share of the riches deriving from the soil of the Indies no longer falls to the foreign *entrepreneur* working with foreign capital, but in which also, and above all, the person native to the country can demand his share in those riches. To that end the level of his knowledge and abilities must be raised considerably; to that end he must be reinforced economically and fortified to self-reliance; to that end the resource bestowed upon him by nature, his excellent and sacred land, must be developed to its highest productivity; to that end he must be reformed morally; to that end a great number of unsavoury abuses must be abolished.[33]

The Ethical Policy of the early twentieth century accordingly included a programme of irrigation, education, transmigration, and rural credit. The response disappointed the Ethici, devotees of the Ethical Policy. But there was, of course, something of a paradox in their concept that what was needed was not less government intervention, but more, though oriented in a different way. What villagers were now expected to do seemed incomprehensible and alienating. Government became more intrusive, but welfare could not be created by *perintah halus* (gentle pressure). 'And as for "uplift"—the Natives don't want to be "uplifted". The more I did my best to "uplift" them, the more trying they thought me.'[34] The redemption of the debt of honour benefited others as much, if not more.

Attempts to analyse the problem contributed to the theory of 'dualism' that J. H. Boeke advanced in a number of forms. 'The mass product of the new Western industries was thrown upon the Eastern market', he declared in 1930, 'sweeping away Native handicrafts, Native trade, and the Native system of distribution'. Capitalism offered only new products, not 'new sources of labour. ... It forced a population with a rapid natural increase to revert to small-scale farming, and ... stunted its differentiation.'[35] The basic reason, however, was 'that there was no force for vigorous development operative in the cultures of such Eastern peoples'.[36] No doubt, so far as Java at least was concerned, that was to over-emphasise 'cultural' factors, and to downplay the 'political' factors that had continued to operate. 'The financial success of the Western economy was a function of the structural immobilization of the peasant economy.'[37] Ethicism could only protect peasants from the more naked abuses of the sugar industry. Boeke hoped for a small Westernised elite.

Outside Java, as he recognised, the position was rather different. In Menado, coffee cultivation had been started in 1822, and incorporated the *walak* chiefs.[38] In 1847, after the Padri war, the government made it compulsory for every able-bodied male in the Menangkabau highlands to raise coffee and deliver it at a low fixed price, though it strained the supra-village elite, already weakened in the war.[39] There was, however, no cultivation system outside Java, only some 'arrangements that resembled it'.[40] Government intervention in the economy, even where government was effectively established, was much less, and the 'opening up' of the Outer Islands, to which the Ethici also committed themselves, benefited not only European planters and miners but also peasants and indigenous entrepreneurs. Some of the Menangkabau— disposed by the practice of *merantau* (travelling) to seek wealth and advancement in non-traditional ways—founded trading firms that became significant in the Indonesia of the 1950s.[41]

On the east coast of Sumatra, indeed, a plantation industry had already been established, growing tobacco for the European market, marginalising local *ladang* cultivators, and employing Chinese and later Javanese labour held there by the 'penal sanction'. But that system was untypical. The concept—taken up by Nienhuys, but originating with an Arab businessman, Sayid Abdullah ibn Umar Balsagih[42]— could be implemented only because it involved 'a rare quality product with a monopoly position in the world market', the Sumatra wrapper leaf.[43] There were strict regulations against native planting, officially because of the risk of disease,[44] but smallholders did get into rubber in the early twentieth century, not because of the government, but because of the interest of Muslim and Chinese traders from Singapore. The swidden lands of the outer islands were indeed suitable for products that could be grown by smallholders, traditional crops such as coffee and pepper, products for which there was now a new demand, like copra, as well as new products, like rubber, grown also in southeast Kalimantan.[45] The opportunities were taken up by a class of individualistic smallholders and petty capitalists, the kind of elite, perhaps, that Boeke hoped would transform Java. In 1894 native export agriculture was valued at 17 million guilders, 7 million from Java and 10 million from the Outer Islands. In 1925–27 the annual average was 438 million, 83 million from Java and 350 million from the Outer Islands.

Java was thus exceptional. The situation elsewhere in Southeast Asia in the nineteenth- and early-twentieth-century phase was again varied, and comparisons can be made with both Java and the Outer Islands. Under Governor Affonso de Castro, Portugal, for example, began a kind of cultivation system in Timor in the 1860s, using the *liurai*.[46] It may still be that Java is unique, not so much because of the impact of cultural factors, as Boeke implied, but because of the emphatic role colonial government had assumed in a society already highly and hierarchically structured. If the peasants could behave like economic men, it had not been made easier for them to do so.

In Malaya rubber, suited to the relatively poor soils of much of Southeast Asia, became a plantation crop in the early twentieth century, but also, as in Sumatra, a smallholder crop. Technical innovations—Goodyear's vulcanisation of 1839 and Dunlop's invention of the pneumatic tyre in 1888—had increased the potential of natural rubber, and the development of the automobile industry from the turn of the century vastly increased the demand, particularly from the United States. Seedlings of *Hevea brasiliensis* were brought from Kew and transplanted in the Singapore Botanical Gardens, and its director from 1888, H. N. Ridley, begged planters, currently concentrating on coffee after disease had destroyed the industry in Ceylon, to make a trial. His persistence paid off, and, while Brazil dominated the coffee market, rubber took over in Malaya, aided by loans from merchant houses in Singapore and from the government itself.[47] 'By 1919 Malayan net export exceeded the net exports of the rest of the world put together.'[48]

In sparsely populated Malaya, much of the labour the plantations needed came from Indian and Chinese immigrants. Malays took some part, for example in timber-felling. More controversially, peasants were also prepared to sell their land, a process which undermined the Federated Malay States government's wish to retain a stable 'Malay yeoman-peasantry', and led it to pass the Malay Reservations Enactment of 1913.[49] But early on, peasant smallholders became decisively involved in rubber production. To that the British Residents were generally unsympathetic. It would compete with the plantations, and it would cut into rice production. But by 1912 it was 'on its way to becoming the dominant peasant economic activity'.[50]

In fact the main effect of the Enactment was to set aside large areas of undeveloped and unalienated land for future development.

Malaya became a dollar-earner for the British empire, but it also became strikingly dependent on a single crop. The disadvantage of that was shown in the postwar slump of the early 1920s. The government adopted the planters' answer, the Stevenson restriction scheme of 1922, 'introduced for the purpose of saving the extremely valuable position in the plantation rubber industry built up by British enterprise in the East', as the Colonial Secretary put it.[51] The scheme indeed favoured planters, European and Chinese, rather than smallholders, though an increase in price helped both. It also, however, encouraged planting in Netherlands India, which did not take part, and it prompted the United States to look to other sources.

In addition the Stevenson plan encouraged planting in French Indo-China, which again did not take part. There plantation rubber had spread rapidly from the 'grey lands' round Saigon to the 'red lands' of northern Cochin-China, southwest Annam, and northeast Cambodia, where it used Vietnamese labour. French investment in Indo-China was, however, relatively limited: before World War I, indeed, 25 per cent of French private investment was in Russia, its political ally, and only 10 per cent in the colonies as a whole. Nor did the government invest except in infrastructure, where it also made extensive use of forced labour, though it offered loans and subsidies in the 1920s. It largely confined itself to trade protection, particularly after the Méline tariff of 1892 ended the liberal regime inherited from the second empire. French trading and currency principles were thus imposed on traditional farming and cultivation methods, as Martin J. Murray says, without significantly modifying them.[52]

Capitalist agricultural enterprise indeed depended on that. The villages were reserves of cheap labour, and the profitability of capitalism was related to the maintenance of the traditional sector, as in Java. Plantation workers were 'temporary proletarians', 'partial peasants'.[53] The village offered a reserve for upturns in the market, and a dumping-ground for downturns. It also meant that workers had to accept lower wages, the villages offering the competition that immigration from populous lands offered in Malaya.

In the Philippines, the government made no attempt to introduce a cultivation system. The German traveller Feodor Jagor argued that van den Bosch was copying the model provided by the tobacco monopoly in the Philippines. That, however, was primarily a means of taxation on the part of a government desperately insecure after the British conquest of 1762. Begun by Governor Basco in 1781, it had by 1786 extended over all Luzon, though initially prohibiting cultivation in one of the best areas, Cagayan. 'The problem for the Spaniards was not how to mobilize native labor to grow tobacco, but how to limit the number of people already engaged in this occupation.' Opposition to it was greatest, not where it was grown, but where it was sold.[54] The monopoly could not meet a demand from Spain when it was imposed after 1839. 'Farmers were resentful, consumers dissatisfied, even the government disenchanted.'[55] It was finally abolished in the early 1880s.

Though the government—based on principles that differed from those of the Dutch—otherwise kept out of trade, the *alcaldes* (governors) enjoyed a trading privilege, the *indulto de comercio,* till 1844. They used it, for example, when rice exports to China began in the 1830s, working with foreign merchants in Manila. Thus John Shillaber, acting for Jardines in Canton, could report in 1834: 'We have made arrangement with a respectable Gentn. in conjunction with the Alcalde of the Province of Pangasinan to purchase Rice for our a/c exclusively and as the Alcaldes have power over the natives to induce them to bring so much of the Rice to them as they wish to buy, we think our purchases in that quarter will be satisfactory.'[56] The agents, he added, had 'a host of sub-agents, natives, belonging to all the rice villages around the Province'.[57]

With the removal of the *alcaldes* from the equation, foreign trade was increasingly organised on capitalist lines, involving foreign merchants, given increased access by the opening of ports outside Manila, and the enterprise of Chinese, mestizo, or 'native' agents and contractors. Sugar replaced rice as the main export, and the demand for it led to the transformation of Panay and Negros. In that foreign merchants such as Nicholas Loney played a major role, and so did Chinese mestizos. He wrote in 1861

> that many new estates had been opened, particularly at Negros, by parties, both mestizo and European, who have been attracted by the promising future of the sugar planting interest. The liberal distribution of funds to some extent in aid of both old and new plantations, and the opportune supply of iron mills and sugar-boiling Pans on credit, against the yield of the different estates, with the additional security of mortgages, has naturally also had a beneficial influence. ...

The European planters were mostly Spaniards. Many Iloilo mestizos were also involved. They had moved out of the textile trade in part as a result of Chinese competition. But they were themselves, as Loney put it, 'a remarkable commercial, industrial and speculative race, increasing yearly in social and political importance'.[58]

Indeed the mestizos were founding the fortunes of the powerful sugar barons of the Visayas. In response to the new opportunities the opening of Iloilo provided, they drew on the loans and equipment men like Loney offered. They also utilised the traditional practice of share-cropping, thus integrating the new enterprise with an older labour system, but without the direct intervention of government. Sugar was to benefit under subsequent US rule from privileged access to the large American market, although its privilege was also to become an argument in the United States, under the impact of the Depression, for speeding independence, for America to 'free itself from the Philippines'.[59]

Americans took a more direct role in the development of the export trade in abaca (hemp), grown on the slopes of the Bikol-speaking provinces of Camarines, Albay, and Sorsogon. The supply of abaca had been one reason for the establishment of the Spanish shipbuilding in the area: it became part of the tribute the people owed the government, while supplying hardwood was a burdensome corvée or *repartimiento*.[60] In the late eighteenth century, as it began to seek new sources of revenue and worked to suppress the Moro attacks which particularly affected those provinces, the government toyed with a silkworm scheme. But the explosive growth of abaca that came to dominate Kabikolan in the nineteenth century was, as Norman Owen puts it, 'a small facet of a global phenomenon—the expansion of a capitalist world-system'.[61] Initially supplying the growing shipping industry, the fibre was later used for other purposes, such the 'binder twine' used in the mechanical grain-binders developed from the late 1870s. American houses in Manila were prominent in the trade for much of the century, making advances to middlemen and producers, and so, like other merchant houses, becoming 'commodity speculators as well as commission agents'.[62]

From its origins to World War II, Owen calculates, the Bikol abaca industry produced nearly 60 million pikuls of fibre, worth about one billion pesos at Manila prices. It brought prosperity to an elite and, particularly in the late nineteenth century, better wages for the labourer. That prosperity collapsed even before the Great Depression. Exposed already to the market fluctuations of a single crop—which the colonial governments did nothing to mitigate—the Bikolanos were now, as Owen says, 'left as poor as they had been a century and a half before. Worse, they were no longer self-sufficient, but commercially dependent on a capitalist world-system which no longer had any great use for them.'[63]

It was to that system that Southeast Asia had to a greater or lesser extent accommodated itself. The Great Depression did not only hit the Bikolanos: it struck at the commodity export trade elsewhere as well. In Malaya the fall in the price of rubber led to unemployment, the repatriation of immigrant labour, a drastic fall in revenue, and a decline in imports. Again a restriction scheme was introduced, this time joined by the Netherlands. By the time it came into operation in 1934, however, prices were reviving, and the scheme seemed, deliberately or not, to be designed to protect European plantations against smallholder competition. The onset of war in Europe produced a boom, as a result of US stockpiling. In the Depression the market for Javanese sugar collapsed, too, and the impact of the Depression was all the greater in Netherlands India because the Dutch stuck to the gold standard.

The Japanese war still further disrupted the pattern that had been established in the colonial phase, and that integrated export and subsistence crops, no longer simply within territories or states, but within the region as a whole. The export market was almost completely destroyed, and for many of the products of Southeast Asia Japan and its satellites had little need. Its attempts to create a Co-Prosperity Sphere, which involved attempts to establish new export crops, like cotton and jute, could have little success in the short term, and shipping within the Sphere was increasingly disrupted.

Supplying rice to postwar Southeast Asia was a British priority, not only for the sake of security. It was essential for restoring the pre-war regional pattern, by which some areas concentrated on export crops, and others helped to feed them. 'We can only … reiterate that the solution of many, if not most of Malaya's industrial troubles depends on the availability for consumption of more and cheaper rice', wrote S. S. Awbery and F. W. Dalley in a report on trade unionism.[64] The British, for whom it was a much-needed dollar-earner, proved markedly successful in rehabilitating the Malayan rubber industry and, despite the threat the Emergency presented, the 1950s saw major replanting. Though the world war had encouraged the United States to develop synthetic rubber, the Korean War led it to stockpile natural rubber. Independent Malaya became 'the most important rubber producer in the world'.[65]

Java sugar, by contrast, did not revive. The main reason, it seems, was not the impact of the Depression, nor even of the occupation. Its success had always depended either on the 'gentle pressure' of the Dutch bureaucracy or on the commitment of the *lurah* (village headman) as both agent of the government and of the sugar-mills. Now the industry no longer had those political advantages. Republican bureaucrats had no incentive for making Dutch plantations work, and the *lurah* had his mind on elections and the influence of the political parties.[66] Even so, an element of compulsion remained, though no attempt could be made to export sugar.

Jungle and forests

In the centuries before the capitalist phase, the forests of Southeast Asia had featured in economic life in several ways: hunter-gatherers had lived in them and from them; swidden cultivators had drawn subsistence from the temporary clearings made by slash-and-burn methods; collectors had secured produce for the cities and courts and gutta percha and ratan for overseas trade; and farmers and others had seen them as a source of fuel and food supplement. Houses, tools, artefacts, and boats were made of wood. In the age of commerce the demands of shipbuilders increased the demand for timber in particular areas, at Sorsogon, for example. Their interest in timber for shipbuilding encouraged both the French and British to make contacts with Lower Burma in the eighteenth century.

There was a nineteenth-century interest in jungle products. Charles Brooke granted monopoly rights in *cutch* (wood oil) and *jelutong* (wild rubber) to Western companies.[67] In the capitalist phase, especially in recent times, it was the timber itself that became an export product. That, and the drive to extend plantation agriculture into areas that might be artificially fertilised, has now led to a great reduction in the size of Southeast Asia's forests. 'Southeast Asia's rainforests, the most bountiful in the world, are disappearing', Margaret Scott wrote in 1989. 'Unless the destruction is stopped, by the year 2010 most will have gone or been seriously damaged.'[68] The fires that swept the Outer Islands and blanketed large parts of Indonesia, Malaysia, and Brunei in palls of smoke in the 1980s and 1990s were effect rather than cause. They were sometimes unconvincingly blamed on slash-and-burn cultivators, whom governments continued to see as wasteful. Their role in deforestation is at once less significant and more complex.

The growth of the market economy, the expansion or transmigration of population, and the constraints imposed by government, tend to lead to the undermining of the swidden system through its over-use: the soils become exhausted as the cultivation cycles become shorter. Logging at least temporarily may give the cultivators new opportunities: it makes slash-and-burn easier. Ultimately it is a competitor, rendering more of the forest unavailable, even leading to its displacement by plantations. Fires may be caused by the swidden cultivators, though their experience with the use of fire is age-old, unlike that of the logging companies. But the risk is greatly enhanced by the methods of logging that have been used, particularly when tractors and bulldozers are employed and not, as in Thailand, elephants, and inflammable debris is left behind. Governments have responded more by rhetoric than regulation, and most of their rules have been ignored in practice. Some of them have in any case been misconceived: concessions have been granted on too short or uncertain a basis to allow the operation of cutting cycles, for example. Selective logging, often advocated, damages the forest canopy, without necessarily helping growth. Reafforestation often involves exotics, designed to supply the processing industry, like the eucalypt, which makes excessive demands on water, provides poor shade, and drops toxic leaf litter. Conservation is rare. The Taman Negara (national park) in peninsular Malaysia was established by the British in 1939.

The British had made some attempt to develop a forest policy when they moved into Burma. The commissioner in Tenasserim, A. D. Maingy, opened the forests to private enterprise in 1829, and Moulmein became a timber and shipbuilding centre. Short-term leases, however, meant a 'cut and run' strategy, and regulations against it were not enforced.[69]

Pegu was the focus of attempts at a more systematic management of forest resources. 'I deem it the duty of the Government of India to safeguard the forest resource of Pegu and not to permit them to be devastated like the forests of other provinces', Governor-General Dalhousie declared in 1855. He appointed Dietrich Brandis the first Superintendent of Forests in the newly acquired province, and his first Forest Order laid the basis for forest administration in India. He insisted on planned cultivation, despite the traders' claim that the forests were inexhaustible.[70] He also developed the idea of actually using the shifting cultivators to plant trees. U San Dun, a Burmese forester, was the first to carry out what was called as a result the *taung-ya* system of forestry.[71] It would, of course, undermine the Karen lifestyle, and it was not adopted without pressure from the colonial state. The breakthrough came in 1869, when a deal between forest officials and a Karen village set a precedent: the counter-offer was exemption from capitation tax, payment per acre, and land for Karen use. The *taung-ya* plantations were designed to complement a network of reserved forests, and the system was not extended to Upper Burma. But such forms of 'social forestry' have been widely used in Southeast Asia since the 1950s.

Western interest in Siam's teak began in the 1860s, but the major expansion began in the 1880s, initially prompted by over-felling in Burma, and the strict regulations there after the British takeover of the remainder of that kingdom in 1886.[72] The creation of the Forestry Department in 1896 was designed both to strengthen the Bangkok government's control in the north, and to avoid exhaustion of the forests. Siamese officials were sent to train at Dehra Dun in India. The new system, and the exhaustion of the more accessible stands, tended to put the business into the hands of larger firms, and drive out the Burmese and Shan foresters.

After 1932 the Forestry Department's jurisdiction expanded, and in 1947 it organised the Forestry Industry Organisation and in 1951 the Thai Plywood Company. Only in the 1960s did it set aside areas for conservation, but the national development plans of the period put their emphasis elsewhere, and reforestation was delegated to the Plywood Company. In the late 1970s sawmills produced 6.5 million cubic metres as against a legal annual production of 2.5 million.[73] In 1985 the 'great give-away' leased degraded forests at a low rate for tree plantation. Reforestation reached 90 000 hectares in 1988, but in the period 1961–85, 12.5 million hectares had been destroyed.[74]

There were other reasons beside the expansion of commercial logging for the great reduction in Thai forests. Agriculture was still critical in developing Thailand for maintaining self-sufficiency in food, and for stabilising the balance of trade. The pressure of population led to extension at the expense of forest land, those without the means to improve their land resorting to squatting in the designated reserves. In the poor northeast tenants and squatters, encouraged to grow cassava for EEC livestock by the army during counter-insurgency campaigns in the 1960s and 1970s, were in turn displaced by agribusiness enterprises. Those planted eucalypt, designed to supply domestic pulp and rayon needs, as well as pulp and wood chip for the Japanese and Korean markets. Swidden cultivators were driven into marginal areas, where their practices were ecologically more damaging, particularly if they resorted to monoculture, like cropping opium.

The results were dramatised in Thailand by the flash flooding that culminated in the landslides in deforested Nakorn Sri Thammarat in November 1988, which killed over 350 people. The government enacted a ban on logging. That led to illegal logging in Thailand, but it also transferred deforestation back to neighbouring Burma, where the military government was desperate for cash; to Laos, a field for Thai investment; and to Cambodia, where rival groups needed to buy weapons.

The drama of Indonesian deforestation was found not in floods but in the great fires of 1988, 1994, and 1997. In both the colonial and post-colonial phases, the government ostensibly followed the German principles of 'scientific forestry'. One problem was that, apart from those in Java, the forests differed from those in Burma, and the application of the principles had to vary between the monsoonal teak stands of the mainland and the more complex dipterocarp forests of the islands. Clear-felling was tried in the 1930s, with the object of producing even-aged stands of the most valuable timber, but once upland forests had to be used, select felling was preferred.[75]

Independent Indonesia prescribed that 25 per cent of the medium-sized trees had to be retained. But, even if concessionaires had stuck to the rules, that would not have attained the objective, sustainability over 35-year cycles. Enforcing the rules was in any case a problem. That the colonial government had attempted, for example by the Timber Ordinance of 1934. It had found the operation of Japanese firms in southeast Kalimantan particularly scandalous.[76] Suharto's New Order government was at best ambiguous. Timber concessions might, after all, be a reward for loyalty. Exhausting its concessions Weyerhauser of the United States went into partnership with International Timber Corporation of Indonesia, which had rights to 386 000 hectares of primary hill forest in Kalimantan: the major shareholders were seventy-three generals.[77]

The New Order government set 1985 as the target date for stopping the export of raw logs. It wanted more value added and pushed both domestic companies and foreign investors that way. That meant that plywood firms took over control of the timber industry. In 1986 Indonesia became the leading exporter of tropical plywood, and for a while it became its leading export after oil. The government levied a fee for a reforestation fund. But it committed itself to creating industrial forest, with fast-growing eucalypts, much of the product only useful for pulping, and the demands of the mills set up in fact led to the cutting down of natural forest, as well as to the planting of village land.

The transmigration programme, again begun by the colonial government but vastly expanded by the New Order, also led to the destruction of primary tropical rain forest, and to the exhaustion of the soil. It was phased down in the fifth Five-Year Plan. In 1987, the World Bank had decided to allocate new loans only for the rehabilitation and consolidation, and not for the expansion of the sites.[78] That year annual forest losses were 100 000 hectares in the Philippines, 23 000 in Malaysia, 325 000 in Thailand, and 550 000 in Indonesia.

Another episode in the drama was set in Malaysian Sarawak, where, in 1987, the government arrested hundreds of Penan tribesmen attempting to block logging. The Malaysian prime minister, Dr Mahathir, blamed the Penan for destroying the forest by shifting cultivation, but they are not shifting cultivators. In October it was made a criminal offence to barricade timber roads. Timber exports were all-important to the elites in Sabah and Sarawak, and timber was currently Malaysia's third-largest export. After the intercommunal crisis of 1969, the Sarawak coalition government had used the New Economic Policy to create rich Muslim businessmen, pushing Foochow *towkays* to collaborate with Melanau leaders: timber concessions were part of the strategy, and high party and government officials were prominent in the timber companies. Longhouses often found out what was happening only when the bulldozers moved in. In twenty-two years 30 per cent of Sarawak's forests were logged. Little replanting was done—concessions could be granted and revoked by the Chief Minister—and as a state assemblyman put it: 'nobody gives a damn about regulations'.[79] The political vulnerability of concessions meant that Sarawak logging was 'characterized by a grab-and-run philosophy'.[80]

In Sabah, as the North Borneo Company had recognised, the primary forests of the east coast were, in the absence of exploitable mineral deposits, 'the strategic natural resource'.[81] In Malaysian Sabah, as in Sarawak, timber concessions were 'handed out … as a means of strengthening political allegiances or as rewards for favours',[82] and disputing factions traded allegations. Since 1970, after all, timber has formed about one-third of Sabah's gross domestic product.

In neighbouring Philippines most virgin forests had gone by the mid-1980s. In parts of Mindanao they were transformed into denuded mountains: there were fires and a long drought in 1982. Regulations were not enforced. 'What would you do as a forestry officer manning an isolated road block if a dozen armed men pushed the barrels of their rifles down your nose and politely requested you let their log laden trucks through?'[83]

The Malaysian prime minister was outspoken in defending his country's policies in face of mounting overseas criticism: it had as a sovereign state a right to control its development; and criticism came from countries that wanted to secure a market for temperate timber. The internationalisation of trade indeed internationalised other issues. In the nineteenth century it had been connected, for example, with the campaign against slavery, and the British had discriminated against slave-grown sugars and the trade of those states that produced them. In the 1990s the focus was on 'human rights' as well as on sustainability. But, like the earlier campaigns, those involved political as well as economic and ideological issues. They were also placed in a world of nation-states, and were, therefore, diplomatic issues, too. Whatever steps EEC states took, for example, their effect would be diminished if Japan did not follow them. That was particularly clear in the case of timber. It bought 89 million cubic metres of logs, worth M$12.3 billion, from Sarawak alone between 1982 and 1989.

Minerals

By this time oil and gas were also major exports from the Malay world, suppliers in particular to energy-deficient Japan above all. Minerals had, of course, long formed an element in the export trade of Southeast Asia. Tin, for example, was not only used locally as a component of bronze in the manufacture of musical gongs and weapons. It was also exported to China, where it was used in alloys for mirrors, teapots, candlesticks and vases, and beaten into leaves and burnt in sacrificial offerings. For that, alluvial tin was particularly suited, coming from the Malay peninsula, and from the eighteenth century particularly from Bangka.[84] The availability of alluvial tin was, however, insufficient to meet the needs of the wider international market of the nineteenth century. They resulted from the development of the trade in food surpluses and from technological improvements in the tin-plate industry. The expansion of canning demanded new supplies of tin, and, even before the development of rubber, it made the west coast states of the Malay peninsula major producers for an international market, in turn, indeed, helping to locate rubber planting there as well. Between 1874, when the British 'intervened', and 1895, when they created the

Federated Malay States, the proportion Malayan tin bore of the world's production rose from 10 to 55 per cent.

If plants are transported, minerals have to be found, and then effectively exploited. The steam pump permitted the reopening of mines which the earlier chain pump could not fully exploit and the opening of new mines where there was inadequate hydraulic power. Initially, however, Western technology was not of prime importance. Prospecting, which became more important with the development of deep open-cast mining, was often done by traditional methods. The *lanchut kechil* was a kind of washbox of great advantage to fossickers, and it led to a rush for land in Kinta after 1888.

Western enterprise entered the industry, indeed, only when hydraulic mining techniques came into play, involving higher capitalisation and less labour, and able to exploit relatively less stanniferous ground. There were, however, two main problems, disposing of the tailings without damaging valuable agricultural land, and diverting water to work the monitors. The answer was to be found in bucket-dredging, which became more popular in the new century, and gave the more highly capitalised European firms a decisive advantage. 'By 1920, Chinese control was definitely on the decline',[85] the destruction of the secret societies and the abolition of the tax farms having struck additional blows. The Depression brought tin control schemes that restricted production, but did not have a 'Stevenson effect'.[86] Tin production peaked in Perak, the state chiefly concerned, with the outbreak of the war in Europe in 1939. By then fifty-eight dredges contributed 51 per cent of total output, and about 70 per cent of the total output of the Federated Malay States came from European-owned mines.[87] The Japanese were unable to restore Malayan production: over the whole occupation, the total produced in Perak was only slightly more than in the year 1940. The postwar rehabilitation loans tended to favour the European enterprises, and many small mines did not reopen. An 'even higher stage of mechanization' was reached.[88]

High capital requirements also tended to place the exploitation of Southeast Asia's energy resources in Western hands. Low wages, however, helped to make the anthracite produced in French Indo-China competitive in international markets, even in Canada.[89] In the interwar period Indo-China was the chief coal exporter in East Asia, though not the chief producer. In the archipelago coal production was generally less successful, and the British attempt to work the coal in Labuan and Brunei failed. The Dutch were rather more successful in southeast Kalimantan.

Borneo, both northwest and southeast, proved, however, to be a major source of mineral oil, which the internal combustion engine made an essential fuel. First Sarawak, and then from the late 1920s Brunei yielded oil, and after the Pacific War the latter developed not only its oil reserves, making it in the 1950s the largest oil producer in the Commonwealth, but also substantial offshore gas reserves, too. In the southwest Shell had begun drilling in the Mahakam delta in the 1890s, and the results had been fabulous. In the new century it joined its rival Royal Dutch, and in 1907 the joint Bataafsche Petroleum Mij took over all the installations in southeast Kalimantan. In the years before World War I it produced 14 000 barrels a day, 53 per cent of Indonesia's total. The other centre in Indonesia was in the Palembang region of south Sumatra. The more recent production of natural gas, however, is mainly drawn from Aceh. Oil production had also been transformed in Burma in the early years of the present century: it produced 50 000 barrels in 1886, when the Burmah Oil Company was formed, and 6 366 000 barrels in 1914. A major refinery was built at Syriam.

Migrants

The development of Southeast Asia's exports over the centuries often, though by no means always, involved peoples from outside Southeast Asia, in particular Indians and above all Chinese. For that, there were no doubt several reasons, general and specific, related to their homeland and related to Southeast Asia itself. Generally, it may be suggested, migrants are alive to opportunities, which may be created by the opening-up of new routes or the development of new products or the change in systems of government. At the same time, they may retain links with their homeland and with other migrant communities, which can be useful at the entrepreneurial level, or they may be so conditioned in their homeland or rendered so dependent in the process of migration that their labour can be readily exploited.

Indian merchants came to the archipelago not indeed as the imperialists that some Indian historians felt bound to conjure up—'swarms of daring adventurers … anticipating the enterprise of the Drakes and Frobishers, or more properly of the Pilgrim Fathers', as Mukherjee put it[90]—but not merely as the pedlars that van Leur depicted either: some at least were important figures. In the colonial phase, Indians found other opportunities, too. There were Tamil labourers on the Malayan rubber plantations, Sikh and Pathan policemen and watchmen, Jaffna Tamils from Ceylon in government service, law, and medicine, Chettiar moneylenders from Madras in the Irrawaddy delta and port-labourers in Rangoon, artisans and policemen and professionals in many of the cities, particularly of the areas dominated by the British, with whose administrative and commercial practices they had the advantage of familiarity. '[I]n Burma the people were in no position to compete with the influx of Indians who flooded in to exploit the resources of the country and to take up posts for which no trained Burmans were available.'[91]

Even more significant, except in Burma, were the Chinese. Their role as traders predated the early modern and colonial phases, but in those phases they secured many opportunities. There were push-factors: the wish to escape the dominance of the Qing dynasty; the prospect of sharing in the commercial expansion brought to Southeast Asia by China's prosperity under that dynasty in the eighteenth century; and the economic and demographic pressures of the nineteenth century. There were also pull-factors: the need of local rulers for efficient and compliant merchants and tax-collectors; the need of the Europeans for a range of workers, agents, and inter-mediaries; and the need of the European and the independent states for labour to take advantage of the expansive conditions of the nineteenth century. Colonies of Chinese labourers appeared in Siam in the late Ayudhya period, sugar and pepper planters; in Palembang-Bangka, tin-miners; in Brunei, pepper planters; on the west coast of Borneo, gold-miners. In the colonial phase, the Chinese were tin-miners, agents, shopkeepers, and entrepreneurs.

The Chinese clearly did not appear as middlemen as a result of the colonial order. Their relationship with it was more complicated. Non-colonial rulers had balanced them off against over-mighty subjects,[92] contrasting their peaceful behaviour with that of the Europeans.[93] Their opportunity in seventeenth-century Java was pro-vided in part by Mataram's attacks on the coastal towns. Nguyen Vietnam encour-aged their settlement. 'Siam's regeneration [after 1767] was aided by the China trade, Chinese capital and labour.'[94] Encouraged by the Temenggong after his break with the pirates, Chinese played a major role in developing Johore.[95]

On the other hand, the Chinese might be too much of a good thing for the Europeans. Not only was there a massacre at Batavia in 1740: the Spaniards also reg-ulated the Chinese by a mixture of slaughter—as in 1609, 1639, and 1662—and con-straint: only Christian converts were allowed outside the Parian, the Chinese quarter in Manila. In 1765 the post-invasion government expelled the Chinese on the ground that they had helped the English. Thus, in the Philippines, by contrast to the mainland states, the Chinese did not benefit from the expansion of the late eigh-teenth century, though the mestizos did. In the nineteenth century many of the restraints on the Chinese were removed. 'The Chinese dealers have the [import] trade entirely in their own hands', wrote the British vice-consul at Cebu in 1878. ' … European competitors would have no chance with these Chinese distributors of goods, who have one or more shops in all the principal villages on the coast and in the outlying districts.'[96] In Netherlands India many of the restrictions on the Chinese were eliminated under the Ethical Policy, and the *totok* (immigrant) com-munity expanded, bringing with it contacts with regional commercial networks.

The ambivalent relationship between rulers and Chinese had not been confined to the colonies. For Rama VI of Siam the Chinese were 'the Jews of the East'.[97] In the post-colonial world it continued. The departure of the Europeans indeed opened up a new set of economic opportunities for the Chinese. Their know-how and their regional networks were all the more important to the nation-states. Yet that did not mean that they were not resented. Sukarno's Indonesia followed the Philippines in banning foreign participation in the retail trade. That was, of course, directed at the Chinese, and in Indonesia, *totok* or *peranakan* (Indonesia-born), citizen or non-citizen, they tended to be butts in times of crisis. The New Order's approach was selective. It patronised individuals and established 'Ali Baba' relationships, though it destroyed Chinese chambers of commerce and other organisations. But, as Jamie

Mackie put it, 'it would be naive to assume that because some (or even many) high officials have such relationships with a few very wealthy Chinese they would feel a strong commitment to restraining anti-Chinese sentiments in general'.[98] The riots of May 1998 suggested the truth in that observation.

Notes

1   in R. McVey, ed., *Indonesia*, Yale UP, 1963, p. 5.
2   G. Bankoff, *Changing Perceptions of the Environment: State and Society in Maritime Southeast Asia*, Murdoch U: Asia Research Centre, 1993, p. 7.
3   *Peasants and their Agricultural Economy in Colonial Malaya, 1874–1941*, KL: OUP, 1977, p. 48.
4   *CHSEA*, I, p. 188.
5   Report by S. G. Grantham, 1920, q. Cheng Siok-hwa, *The Rice Industry of Burma, 1852–1940*, KL and Singapore: U Malaya P, 1968, p. 7n.
6   q. J. Buttinger, *Vietnam: A Dragon Embattled*, London: Pall Mall, 1967, p. 39.
7   B. H. Farmer, 'Perspectives on the "Green Revolution" in South Asia', MAS, 20, 1 (February 1986), p. 176.
8   *Agricultural Development in Indonesia*, Sydney: Allen and Unwin, 1988, p. 165.
9   *CHSEA*, I, p. 468.
10 Martin J. Murray, *The Development of Capitalism in Colonial Indo-China*, UCP, 1980, p. 214.
11 q. McAlister, p. 77.
12 *CHSEA*, I, p. 470.
13 J. Kathirithamby-Wells, *CHSEA*, I, p. 597.
14 Vlekke, p. 198.
15 in G. J. Schutte, ed., *State and Trade in the Indonesian Archipelago*, Leiden: KITLV P, 1994, pp. 77–97.
16 p. 96.
17 Minute by Muntinghe, 27 May 1812, q. J. Bastin, *The Native Policies of Sir Stamford Raffles in Java and Sumatra*, Oxford: Clarendon P, 1957, pp. 22–3.
18 q. ibid., p. 23.
19 q. ibid., p. 66.
20 q. R. E. Elson, *Village Java under the Cultivation System*, Sydney: Allen and Unwin, 1994, p. 40.
21 q. ibid., p. 43.
22 q. R. E. Elson, *Javanese Peasants and the Colonial Sugar Industry*, Singapore: OUP, 1984, p. 33.
23 q. ibid., p. 33.
24 C. Fasseur, *The Politics of Colonial Exploitation*, trans. R. E. Elson and Ary Kraal, Cornell UP, 1992, p. 27.
25 Frans v. Baardewijk in Schutte, pp. 165–6.
26 *Village*, p. 108.
27 R. E. Elson, 'From "States" to State', in J. Th. Lindblad, ed., *Historical Foundations of a National Economy in Indonesia*, Amsterdam: North-Holland, 1996, p. 129.
28 q. Fasseur, p. 226.
29 ibid., p. 105.
30 q. Elson, *Village*, p. 199.
31 p. 200.
32 R. Van Niel, 'The Legacy of the Cultivation System for Subsequent Economic Development', in Anne Booth et al., *Indonesian Economic History in the Dutch Colonial Era*, Yale UP, 1990, p. 85.
33 q. *Indonesian Economics*, The Hague: Van Hoeve, 1961, p. 260.
34 Resident G. L. Gonggrijp, q. ibid., p. 31.
35 ibid., p. 172.
36 p. 172.
37 Elson, *Sugar*, p. 182.
38 David E. F. Henley, *Nationalism and Regionalism … Minahasa …* , Leiden: KITLV P, 1996, pp. 38–9.

39 Kenneth R. Young, 'The Cultivation System in West Sumatra … ', in Booth et al., pp. 98, 101.

40 Fasseur, p. 27.

41 R. Robison, *Indonesia: The Rise of Capital*, North Sydney: Allen and Unwin, 1986, p. 22.

42 D. Lombard, *Le Carrefour Javanais*, Paris: Ecole des Hautes Etudes, 1990, II, p. 93.

43 Van Gelderen in B. Schrieke, ed., *The Effect of Western Influence on Native Civilisations in the Malay Archipelago*, Batavia, 1929, p. 92.

44 K. Pelzer, *Planter and Peasant*, The Hague: Nijhoff, 1978, p. 50.

45 J. Thomas Lindblad, *Between Dutch and Dayak*, Dordrecht: Foris, 1988, pp. 59, 61.

46 C.-J. Telkamp in Francien van Anrooij et al., *Between People and Statistics*, The Hague: Nijhoff, 1979, p. 78.

47 Chai Hon-chan, *The Development of British Malaya, 1896–1909*, KL: OUP, 1964, p. 161.

48 Lim Chong-yah, *Economic Development of Modern Malaya*, KL: OUP, 1967, p. 75.

49 Lim Teck Ghee, *Peasants and their Agricultural Economy in Colonial Malaya, 1874–1941*, KL: OUP, 1977, pp. 111, 74.

50 ibid., p. 79.

51 q. ibid., p. 143.

52 p. 195.

53 p. 216.

54 Ed. C. de Jesus, *The Tobacco Monopoly in the Philippines*, Quezon City: Ateneo UP, 1980, pp. 105–6.

55 p. 188.

56 q. N. Tarling, 'Some Aspects of British Trade in the Philippines in the Nineteenth Century', *Journal of History* (Manila), 11, 3 & 4 (1963), p. 295.

57 p. 296.

58 Consular report, 10 July 1861. F.O. 72/1017, Public Record Office, London.

59 q. Norman G. Owen, *Prosperity without Progress*, UCP, 1984, p. 161.

60 Luis Camara Dery, *From Ibalon to Sorsogon*, QC: New Day, 1991, pp. 106–7, 56–7.

61 Owen, p. 43.

62 p. 64.

63 p. 246.

64 q. D. M. Nonini, *British Colonial Rule and the Resistance of the Malay Peasantry, 1900–1957*, Yale UP, 1992, p. 111.

65 Lim Chong-yah, p. 91.

66 Alec Gordon, 'The Collapse of Java's Colonial Sugar System … ', in van Anrooij et al., pp. 256, 258–9.

67 A. Kaur, *Economic Change in East Malaysia*, Basingstoke: Macmillan, 1998, pp. 57–8.

68 FEER, 12 January 1989, p. 34.

69 Raymond L. Bryant, 'Shifting the Cultivator … ', MAS, 28, 2 (May 1994), p. 228.

70 Herbert Hesmer, 'Dietrich Brandis and Forestry in Burma', in anon., ed., *Southeast Asia and the Germans*, Tubingen-Basle: Erdman, 1977, pp. 184–5, 198.

71 Bryant, p. 231n.

72 Ian Brown, *The Elite and the Economy in Siam*, Singapore: OUP, 1988, pp. 110–11.

73 Philip Hurst, *Rainforest Politics*, London: Zed, 1990, pp. 228–9.

74 Bryan Hunsaker, 'The Political Economy of Thai Deforestation', in Hunsaker et al., *Loggers, Monks, Students and Entrepreneurs*, DeKalb: N Illinois U, 1996, pp. 14–15.

75 L. Potter, 'Forestry in Contemporary Indonesia', in Lindblad, *Historical Foundations*, p. 374.

76 Lindblad, *Between Dayak and Dutch*, pp. 103–4.

77 Hurst, p. 34.

78 Maria Seda, 'Global Environmental Concerns and Priorities …', in Seda, ed., *Environmental Management in ASEAN*, Singapore: ISEAS, 1993, p. 19.

79 q. Hurst, p. 106.

80 Amarjit Kaur, 'A History of Forestry in Sarawak', MAS, 32, 1 (1998), p. 141.

81 D. W. John, 'The Timber Industry and Forest Administration in Sabah under Chartered Company Rule', JSEAS, 5, 1 (March 1974), p. 80.

82 Hurst, p. 103.

83 q. ibid., p. 189.

84 Wong Lin Ken, *The Malayan Tin Industry to 1914*, Tucson: U Arizona P, 1965, p. 13.
85 ibid., p. 217.
86 Lim Chong-yah, p. 59.
87 Francis Loh Kok Wah, *Beyond the Tin Mines*, Singapore: OUP, 1988, p. 37.
88 ibid., p. 69.
89 Murray, p. 330.
90 q. Van Leur, pp. 343–4.
91 q. J. S. Furnivall, *Colonial Policy and Practice*, CUP, 1948, p. 116.
92 Hall, JMBRAS, 58, 2, pp. 96–7.
93 A. Reid, 'The Unthreatening Alternative … ', RIMA, 27, 1 & 2 (1993), p. 14.
94 Hong Lysa, *Thailand in the Nineteenth Century*, Singapore: ISEAS, 1984, p. 48.
95 C. Trocki, *Prince of Pirates*, Singapore UP, 1979, p. 205.
96 q. M. Cullinane in McCoy and de Jesus, p. 274.
97 q. Wyatt, p. 229.
98 *The Chinese in Indonesia*, U Hawaii P, 1976, p. 134.

Transport and Industry

Southeast Asia shared in the revolution in transport and communications that coin-cided with the colonial and post-colonial phases. The colonial powers concerned them-selves with infrastructure, but not with industrialisation. The nation-states attempted industrialisation, first directed at import substitution, and then oriented to exports.

It is only in recent times that mankind has been able to travel and communicate by air as well as by land and by water. For much of history, indeed, communication by land has been slow and difficult, and, while air transport was a twentieth-century revolution, it is perhaps easy to forget that it was only in the nineteenth century that the railway revolutionised land transport. That revolution was, of course, followed by the revolution created by the invention of the automobile and the lorry and the creation of road and motorway networks. Transport by sea and river, by canal, aque-duct, and portage, has been more important throughout history, and it is only rela-tively recent generations that have had to decide, on the basis of political and economic arguments, in what ways the various systems may best be combined, whether by planning, by competition, or by regulation.

Political as well as economic factors have always been present, for the control of the main means of communication helped, of course, to support the building and maintenance of states. Their size and their durability depended not only on the trade that might pass along river and road, but on the capacity to mobilise and to apply force. The most famous example in European history is that of the Roman empire, seeking to extend a Mediterranean empire by a road system laid down with such determination that it located settlements and towns and is still visible today

The political significance of the more recent revolutions in transport were recog-nised as well as the economic. Railways were built to carry passengers and goods, but they were also political statements, and they were often the means of realising them. 'War by timetable' seemed to offer the Germans the prospect of victory in 1914. In the United States and Canada the railways conquered the west, and the Russian empire perhaps dissipated too large a proportion of its resources on the building of the Trans-Siberian railway. In post-Mutiny India the British had built the railways with strategic and political purposes in mind, though they came to serve other purposes and still do.

The Southeast Asian terrain gave communication by sea and river the greatest importance. The obstacles presented to other forms of transport—by jungle, mountain, and above all by swamp—were formidable. On the other hand, water made so much of Southeast Asia accessible that it was remarkably open to the outside world throughout its history. Nineteenth-century 'explorers' and entrepreneurs hoped to exploit neglected opportunities in the water transport systems of Southeast Asia rather than to replace them, putting emphasis, for example, on access by the upper Irrawaddy to the trade of the Chinese interior or, more disappointingly, on access along the much less navigable Mekong. Even in recent times the convenience of water transport has accentuated the difficulty of land transport. The traveller in northwestern Borneo may still prefer to go by sea or by air than by gruelling bus, and the little railway in Sabah moved from construction to curiosity without the intervening prosperity once enjoyed by the railways of the West. Generally, it might be said, the innovations in transport came initially to supplement or complement the commercial facilities long provided by water transport rather than to replace them.

In the pre-colonial phases of Southeast Asian history political power depended on the control of river systems or on the control of their links with the sea or on both. That naturally continued to be the case in the colonial phase. But while the newer forms of communication had at first a supportive role in the commercial world, their novel political possibilities were not neglected. As in the West, the motives for railway-building were mixed, designed both further to 'open up' Southeast Asia to external trade, but also, not always consistently, to increase political control or affirm political integrity.

Railways

In the Philippines, as Frederick L. Wernstedt and J. E. Spencer point out, 'railroads have never played the important role they have in so many countries. ... the archipelagic nature of the land areas restricts the length of the railroads and seriously hinders their effective integration'.[1] Work began in Luzon in 1887 with British capital, a minor part of the great overseas investments in infrastructure that the British undertook in the later nineteenth century, and the assets were transferred to the government, which the United States was 'filipinizing', in 1917. The line was built above all for the transport of export produce, and the same was true of the railroad operating in Panay from 1907. Not completed till 1938, this limited system was not well-placed to withstand the competition of mechanised road transport.

Sarawak's railway was opened in 1915. It extended only ten miles, and lasted only sixteen years. The railways the Company built in North Borneo were more extensive and lasted longer. The section from Weston to Beaufort was opened in 1898; that from Beaufort to Jesselton (Kota Kinabalu) in 1902; that from Beaufort to Tenom in

1905, and to Melalap in 1907. The railway encouraged rubber-growing, much of it by smallholders, and focused development more on the west coast than the east, the Company's previous focus. It was 'a major casualty of the War'.[2]

On the Malay peninsula the development of rail transport was associated with the expansion of tin-mining in the west coast states after the 'intervention' of 1874, and it helped to locate the subsequent development of rubber on the peninsula. Initially, as Amarjit Kaur has related, river transport had been supplemented by bridle-paths and cart-tracks, but 'a more efficient system' was needed. 'With revenues from tin, the first railways were constructed connecting the inland mining centres with the ports', tin extraction providing both motive and means.[3] The first railway in Perak, from Port Weld to Taiping, opened in 1885, and the first in Selangor, from Kelang to Kuala Lumpur, in 1886.

For some at least, there was a political motive as well. Linking the railways in the states would help 'to consolidate the union'[4] created by the formation of the Federated Malay States in 1895. Like the Colonial Secretary, Joseph Chamberlain, the first Resident-General, Frank Swettenham, shared the idea, not only that railways would draw the Malay states together, but that they would help to draw the empire as a whole together. Their more ambitious view overcame the doubts of Governor Mitchell. But, as Amarjit Kaur puts it, 'railways were not conceived in terms of stimulating well-rounded economic development in the country as a whole'. The major towns on the west coast and the Straits Settlements were connected with one another and with the areas producing raw materials, but there were fewer links with or on the east coast. Freight rates favoured the long haul of primary products and the movement of imported manufactures to the interior, and favoured larger clients, too.

The modern road system began as a supplement to the rail system on the west coast, though it was more important than that in Pahang and the east coast states, and it was generally extended during the Depression as a means of providing employment. As elsewhere the railway began to face competition, and as elsewhere, now as well as then, governments were faced with the problem of providing, by competition or otherwise, the most effective transport system.

Though the road system so greatly helped the Japanese invaders, they sought to use rail, as had the British, for exporting the raw materials they needed from Malaya, in their case, chiefly iron and bauxite. Rail also had a role in the integration of their empire, particularly because of their weakness at sea. Locomotives and wagons were taken to Burma and Indo-China, and part of the permanent way of the interior line was removed to build the infamous death railway between Burma and Thailand.

The Thai railway down to the south had become a means of supplying rice to the peninsula. Yet the main purpose of the construction of the Thai system was political. 'Politically the railway will always play a leading role as it ties the outlying provinces more firmly to the government', wrote Luis Weiler, one of the German engineers involved.[5] Building it was one of several steps taken under Chulalongkorn to strengthen his kingdom in face of the colonial powers in the 1880s and 1890s.

Apart from a short line between Paknam and Bangkok, opened in 1893, the first rail-way to be built was the Korat line, 'a fact', as Charles Fisher put it, 'which should be viewed against the background of the French advance into Laos in 1893'.[6] The next priority was to strengthen control over the north, though the line did not reach Chiengmai till 1921. A southeastern line was begun in 1908, the year after the French secured Battambang and Siemreap. Part of the Siamese deal with the British in 1909 involved a loan for the completion of the railway into the southern provinces, and it linked with the Malayan system in 1917. In those ways rail extended and reinforced the control the river system had already given the superbly positioned Bangkok.

In neighbouring Indo-China the crucial administration of Governor-General Doumer also belonged to the end of the nineteenth century. He sought to give the union real meaning, not only by administrative and political reforms, but also by a programme of rail construction, financed partly by taxation, partly by loan. One great project was the Transindochinois. The difficulties of the coastal route meant, however, that Saigon and Hanoi were not linked till 1936, while Cambodia and Laos remained without rail connexions to the Vietnamese lands. Doumer's other great project had priority. That was the Yunnan railway, designed to 'open up' southwest China. The 290-mile line, with 172 tunnels and 107 bridges, was built at monu-mental expense of life as well as treasure: 30 per cent of the 80 000 coolies involved died, and 40 of the 300 European personnel[7]—an earlier death railway, it might be said. Reaching Kunming in 1910, it returned, however, a better revenue than other railways in Indo-China, since it did not face competition from road transport.

The river-system of Burma provided a greater level of accessibility than those of the other mainland states, even Siam. The Burman monarchies focused their system on the dry zone, but the British focused on their ocean-oriented capital Rangoon. Burma's 4000 miles of commercially navigable waterways remained 'the most funda-mental component in the country's transport network',[8] the Irrawaddy itself naviga-ble for 874 miles year-round, and a further 105 miles for seven months of the year. The British-owned Irrawaddy Flotilla Company, together with the Arracan Flotilla Company, also British-owned, carried over 8 million passengers a year in the 1930s, and 1.3 million tons of cargo. Competing also with 'country' boats, the railways car-ried nearly 19 million passengers and 4 million tons of cargo.[9] They had been built by the British with Indian capital, and the debt was to remain unpaid until a deal was made between Burma and India in 1954.[10] The first line, opened in 1877, ran from Rangoon to Prome, but after that, to avoid duplicating the main river route, it followed the Sittang valley. By 1889 it had reached Mandalay, and by 1899 an extension ran from Sagaing to Myitkyina. 'Even more spectacular' was the line from Mandalay to Lashio, completed in 1903.[11] The gap between Mandalay and Sagaing ceased to exist with the completion of the Ava bridge in 1934. The effectiveness of water transport and the construction of railways delayed the building of a road network—the rivers, as J. S. Furnivall puts it, were a hindrance and a substitute[12]—and, aside from the trunk road that often paralleled the railway, it was largely designed to feed rather than compete.

The Burma transport system served the delta and the dry zone, and it served the remoter areas, mainly in the Shan states, that produced tin, lead, and zinc, and also tungsten. It did not, as Fisher puts it, weld Burma together into 'a coherent whole'.[13] He even suggests that the rivalry of rail and river was 'merely one aspect of a division which ran through national life',[14] and contrasts old capitals and river villages with 'upstart railway towns', especially between Mandalay and the delta, often with substantial Indian populations, and above all Mandalay itself and Rangoon. The lack of links between the core of Burma and the 'fringe' was also striking. That presented a contrast with neighbouring Siam, and tended to deepen rather than diminish their political divergence. Unlike the French and the Thais, the British did not use the rail system to integrate their territory.

Overall the transport systems on the Southeast Asian mainland in the colonial phase share another striking feature, also with political implications. Whatever the relevant weight of economic and political factors in the building of the railways in each country, the systems that were built did little to link the countries. The connections at the Siamese–Malay borders were exceptional. While the geographical obstacles were often, of course, very great, it was also true that there were no economic or political pressures to overcome them. Rail was built either to facilitate exports or to promote political integration or both. Only the Japanese had the motivation to build a Siam–Burma railway. Burma was never linked with neighbouring India, even when they were both under British rule. The dreams of railway projectors were undermined by the convenience of water transport, put off by expense, and then destroyed by the advent of motorised transport.

Netherlands India was highly accessible by sea and river, and railways played a supplementary role in economic life. The first section was built in 1867 in Java, and Java remained the main focus of the railway network, designed, of course, to improve the links between the interior and the main ports, Batavia, Semarang, and Surabaya, but also linking the principal towns. In Sumatra the system was much more fragmentary, three separate 3-foot 6-inch systems being unconnected, and that in Aceh using a different gauge. There were 47 kilometres in south Sulawesi. But in the other islands there was no rail system, and in the 1930s the Dutch resolved to concentrate on roads. By 1940 a north–south road linked Aceh and Oosthaven (Palembang).

What neither road nor rail could do in Netherlands India was to draw the archipelago together into a political whole by enhancing its communications links. One means of effecting that was to modernise traditional links. For most of the nineteenth century the Outer Islands remained part of the older maritime system of island Southeast Asia, and were oriented towards its current entrepot, Singapore. The Dutch government supported the KPM (Royal Packet Company) with a view to reorienting trade away from Singapore, and by 1915 it had eliminated all Singapore-based shipping east of Bandjermasin, though in the west it still had to use the British port.[15]

The nineteenth and twentieth centuries offered other communications technologies that could be used for both political and economic purposes. One was the

telegraph. Linking Southeast Asia with the outside world in the 1870s, it also operated within each territory, and, unlike rail, among territories. Singapore and Batavia
were connected by wire in November 1870, and Penang and Singapore in December.
Early the following year the British Indian Extension Company opened the line
between the Straits and Europe. The connexion with Hong Kong followed in 1871,
and telegraph construction began in Siam in 1875. The telegraph was important to
administrators, both for day-to-day activity, where it tended to reduce local initiative and enhance conformity, and in respect of emergencies. It was also important
economically, especially for the export sector. 'Mining, mercantile, and planting
interests were enabled to maintain speedy and efficient contacts with the ports and
world market conditions.'[16] While telegraphic communication relied on wire, it
tended to follow in the wake of other kinds of communication, and to reflect the relative importance placed on economic and political factors in their development. In
Malaya, for example, 'states with inadequate road and rail communications had correspondingly inadequate social communications, and lagged behind the more
developed states'.[17] Its integrative function might be limited. Wireless communication, begun in Malaya in the 1930s, changed that.

The development of air transport again did not simply replicate or reinforce
existing patterns. In some cases it did. Partly as a result of their geographical position, and partly as a result of determined efforts to take advantage of it, Bangkok and
Singapore quickly became the leading international airports: Singapore was on the
main route Europe–Australasia, and the secondary route East Asia–Australasia, but
somewhat off the Europe–East Asia route, which passed via Bangkok. Links within
Southeast Asia echoed older entrepot patterns. Within the region, too, air offered a
means of communication that could overcome obstacles hitherto intractable. The
Dutch, for example, were 'quick to appreciate the possibilities which air communications afforded for closer integration of their scattered and largely undeveloped
territories'.[18] The KNILM was set up in 1928, subsidised, like the KPM, by the government, and by 1938 its regular flights covered 150 000 miles a month, connecting
Medan, Tarakan, Makasar, and Den Pasar with Batavia and Surabaya. The Siamese
government again was 'quick to appreciate that the aeroplane might afford the most
effective means of linking up the outlying parts of the country'.[19]

The colonial phase coincided with revolutionary developments in transport and
communications. Those were turned to account by the governments of the region,
colonial or not, each exploiting, though in varying proportions, their political and
economic potential. Their preoccupation was in any case with infrastructure. They
were not concerned to establish in Southeast Asia the revolutionary developments
in industry that the nineteenth century also brought: rather the reverse, indeed. It
was to require a change in government, as well as a redefinition of the 'Asia-Pacific'
role in the world economy, for Southeast Asia to realise the potential to industrialise
that had been increased by the growth of population and the extension of infrastructure. Even then it was not clear that it could be sustained once the initial

comparative advantages had been exploited. Nor was it clear what role governments could, should, or would, continue to play.

Industry

The industrial revolution held out the prospect of a reciprocal trade, in which the counterpart of the export of agricultural and mineral products from Southeast Asia would be the importation of the manufactures of Europe. In developing infrastructure, merchants and administrators thought along these lines, and their policies were designed to promote such a pattern, sometimes favouring it by protectionist measures directed against local, Asian, or other European rivals. As Lieut.-Governor of Java during the British interregnum, Raffles wrote:

> The population of Java may be estimated at about five millions, and the lower classes of people, unlike those of Hindustan, are accustomed to wear clothing. … It may at the same time be observed that no political objection exists [as in India] against restraining or superseding, to such an extent as may be deemed profitable, the cotton manufacture of this colony, because the persons employed therein do not form a specific class of the people, and the population is so inadequate to the extent and capability of the land that it would be advantageous to attach their time and attention as exclusively as possible to agricultural pursuits.[20]

Under the more interventionist cultivation system that the Dutch introduced, that tended to happen. Peasants bought goods from outside their locality. In Pasuruan, for example, monetisation and the requirements of sugar cultivation destroyed the cotton and weaving industry.[21]

The importation of textiles was, of course, nothing new in the archipelago, for the trade in Indian piece-goods was centuries-old. What Raffles sought to do was to compete with that trade, as well as with the Javanese textile trade, with which it was integrated. The textile trade became three-cornered and, with the return of the Dutch, four-cornered. In 1830, for example, the Batavia government put an extra duty on the import of beeswax, in order to discourage the manufacture of batik handkerchiefs and sarongs, in the dyeing of which it was used. That would also discourage the importation of British white shirtings and cambric muslins from which batik was by then largely made.[22] The Anglo-Dutch dispute over the commercial clauses of the 1824 treaty largely turned on the discriminating duties imposed on British imports into Java. Despite the duties, one British merchant wrote, 'our manufactures have hitherto been able in some degree to compete with those of the Netherlands, but the consequent enhancement of price has had the effect of perpetuating several native manufactures in the remoter parts of those countries, and of narrowing the consumption of European manufactures throughout them all'.[23] The commercial rivalry of the European states, like their political rivalry, could help, as well as hinder, the survival of independent Asian activities. Even after the Dutch abandoned differential duties in 1872, Javanese manufactures survived, only to face a further measure of competition when Chinese traders, helped by the assimilationist element in Ethical Policy, penetrated the interior in the early years of the new century. The Depression changed the nature of the contest again. Dutch textiles could not compete with cheap Japanese imports. But behind the barrier of the Crisis Import Ordinance that the Dutch put up in 1933, Javanese textile manufacturing boomed.

The colonial government had not had the macro-economic policy weapons that would have directly promoted the industrialisation of Java. A number of the conditions were right: a far greater population than in Raffles' day, providing a domestic market and a labour-force; a village system that avoided the need to cost in a safety net. Van Deventer's cures for 'diminishing welfare' were irrigation, education, transmigration, better rural credit. Abraham Kuyper, prime minister in 1901, argued by contrast that the proper policy was 'to advance the people of the Indies from the agricultural to the industrial state',[24] and Idenburg, the colonial minister, envisaged indigenous industry based on indigenous capital. Plantation interests, however, were opposed: it would raise the cost of labour. Industrialists and workers in the Netherlands were also opposed: they wanted to retain the market. Only the fear of Japanese competition in the Depression encouraged the setting-up of factories making tyres, textiles, bikes, paints, beer, soap, and margarine. Other policies of the Depression were clearly those of a colonial regime. The Dutch used discriminatory quotas against imports, rather than tariffs. They stuck to the gold standard. Debt default was precluded.[25]

In the Depression the French retained the protectionism introduced in Indo-China in 1892. Colonies were to produce raw materials and import manufactures. Import substitution industries would have been possible by the end of World War I. But while there was no prohibition against them, there was also no assistance for them: there were no subsidies, and small-scale entrepreneurs were excluded from metropolitan trade associations. 'Better that Indo-China and her twenty million inhabitants should perish, than a single French sock-factory!' *La Tribune Indochinoise* summed up the 1928 tariff.[26] The banker Paul Bernard argued that France should create an internal demand for goods, currently limited by the poverty of the population. But even the Popular Front government did not favour that: Moutet preferred peasants and artisans to unruly workers.[27] Even so some ancillary activities emerged, processing to reduce the bulk of raw materials, and small-scale production for the local market. In an isolated Indo-China Vichy officials were tempted to change policy, but Pétainism again preferred peasants and artisans. The *dirigisme* that attracted the French postwar had no chance in a disturbed Indo-China.

Exporting sugar, tobacco, and hemp, the nineteenth-century Philippines imported manufactures mainly from Britain. The protective tariff of 1891 helped Spain, raising its share of imports from 4–8 per cent to 24 per cent.[28] The United States opened up its markets for sugar, and saw the Philippines as a market for manufactures. Gaining self-government and fearing the loss of privileged access for primary products on independence, the Philippines embarked in the later 1930s on 'a substantial programme of import-substitution, in which a government company, the National Development Company, took a leading role'.[29] In Malaya/Singapore in the 1930s manufacturing was on a 'very small scale'.[30]

It was indeed at this point that the macro-level tie between imperialism and industrialisation came to predominate. The establishment of colonial regimes was not closely tied to the penetration of Western capitalism, though the two became linked at the micro-level. Once established, however, the regimes tended to prevent Southeast Asia's following the trajectory of Europe. '[T]he natural dynamic of colonialism … lowered mortality [but] perpetuated high fertility. Colonial policy did not favor the industrialization, urbanization, and advancing education that were associated historically with declining fertility among Western peoples. … In so far as the partial diffusion of the Western economy and society influenced the fertility of the East it tended toward increase rather than decrease.'[31]

The Thai divergence

The divergent role of Siam illustrates the significant role of government, and also its limitations. In the nineteenth century, though it was not a colony, its economy was subject to the then current version of the international division of labour. '[W]hen rice became a general product of commerce, people more and more applied themselves to cultivation alone and in consequence gradually commenced to neglect other such occupations, as did not prove to be as profitable or easy as rice growing.'[32] Weaving, spinning, smelting, iron manufacture, pottery, and papermaking gave way to rice- and timber-milling, shipbuilding, and the manufacture of construction materials. Industrialisation was not attractive: the domestic market was small; and the treaties limited tariff protection.[33] Cement was an exception to prove the rule: the Siamese Cement Company, formed in 1913, enjoyed a *de facto* protection provided by the high freight charges on imports.[34]

Siam was, however, an exception more generally, as the Cement Company again suggests. It was an initiative of Chaophraya Yomarat, the Minister for the Capital, a government leader. The capital for the enterprise could not be raised in official or commercial circles in Bangkok, so three-quarters of it was drawn from the king's privy purse. What prevented the government going further, it seems, was not, as some have argued, the 'feudal' values of its leaders, but 'the openness of Siam to the powerful and diverse influences of the world economy', as Ian Brown puts it.[35] The Thais, unlike the Japanese, could not protect their industries. They also pursued cautious financial policies, behaving like the colonial powers for fear of losing their independence to them. The subsequent 'radical' criticism of their policies at this time is justified only perhaps to the extent that their apparent success discouraged a rethinking. The elite accepted the orthodoxy of the late nineteenth and early twentieth centuries:

the economies of the non-Western world would prosper by producing agricultural and mineral commodities in which they had a comparative advantage.

That view was challenged by the Depression, and Siam's reaction to it differed from that of the colonial governments. Already in the 1920s revision of the unequal treaties had assisted a number of small industries: ice, biscuits, toothpaste, canned fruit, matches, paper, textiles, fertiliser. The new government of the Promoters went much further. Though Pridi, its leading civilian, was accused of 'communism' by his political opponents, he probably owed more to List than Marx, and like those of the dominant military leader, Pibun, his policies were nationalist. The treaties were again renegotiated, and increasingly the state invested in a range of enterprises industrial and otherwise. The role of Western capital, never so great as in the colonial territories, was reduced. As elsewhere, however, imports from Japan expanded, overtaking those from Britain in 1933–34.

About the role of the Chinese in those changes there has been controversy among the historians of Thailand. It is a topic worth exploring for its own sake, but also for its possible contribution to the study of industrialisation in more recent times, not merely in Thailand. The 'feudal' (*sakdina*) values that 'radical' historians have attributed to the elite led it, it has been argued, to avoid utilising or encouraging the entrepreneurial skills of the Chinese, and prevented their emerging as an innovative bourgeoisie. Against that, Brown renews his argument: what limited the elite was Siam's international position, economic and political. The elite was, he adds, anxious to encourage a diversification of Chinese merchant capital, but it could only be done within those constraints.[36]

The 1932 coup, Chai-Anan suggests, was supported by a largely Chinese bourgeoisie,[37] and for a while the new regime gave it a new political influence. Then, he suggests, the Thai official elite took steps to diminish that influence, compelling the Chinese to revert to older patron–client approaches or to secret societies. The Chinese economic role nevertheless persisted. One example is provided by the Thai Rice Company, founded at the end of 1938 in order to break the Chinese hold on the trade, especially in view of the anti-Japanese boycotts that followed the opening of the undeclared war in 1937. It was a successful venture. But the managing director was a hastily naturalised Chinese, Ma Bulakul, and many of the mills the company rented or purchased were his. It had strong political backing, too. In the new Thailand Chinese business leaders tended to survive, though other Chinese were discriminated against. Many adopted Thai names and became Thai citizens, and worked with Thai political figures who could secure permits, licences, and contracts. 'The lines separating bureaucrats, politicians, and capitalists became at best indistinct.'[38]

These Thai examples suggest two conclusions. One is that in the colonial phase Chinese enterprise was limited by the overall constraints of the dominant Western political and economic system. If that seems to be true in Siam, it is even clearer in the non-independent territories. There, as in Siam, some very wealthy Chinese emerged. As in Siam, again, some of the wealthiest were tax-farmers, and it has been persuasively argued that their tax-farming was not only a convenience for rather thinly spread governments, but also a necessary support for the other enterprises, such as mining, in which the farmers were also engaged. For example, Hugh Low, the second British Resident in Perak, established three-year revenue farms to help open up Kinta. 'The Perak River has hitherto been much neglected, but by interesting the Penang Opium Farmers in its prosperity I am inclined to hope that they will assist in the introduction of labourers and capital which, while increasing their income from opium, will increase that of the Government from the export of tin.'[39] Industry, however, did not attract their enterprise. Nor did it after the first decade of the new century, when governments modernised their taxation practices, partly under the impact of campaigns against the consumption of opium, and tax-farmers' capital was freed for other purposes. Siam abolished the opium farm in 1908–09, the gambling and lottery farms in 1916–17. 'The Chinese turn increasingly to private enterprise', as the king put it, 'of which rice milling is an example'.[40]

The second conclusion is linked to the first. In taking up the opportunity to industrialise, elite elements will work together, as they had in the Siamese system of tax-farms, even if the ideology of the regime suggests otherwise. What counts is the existence of that opportunity. The Depression opened it up, a little in the case of the colonial territories, but rather more in the case of Thailand.

ISI and EOI

The Japanese occupation sought to displace the old colonial pattern by a new one. On the defeat of the Japanese the returning colonial powers sought to rehabilitate the old pattern. Their success was patchy, but the civilian regime in Siam was itself anxious to restore the export of primary products and to appease Western investors, for instance by relinquishing the controversial state oil monopoly. By the late 1940s, however, a different pattern was emerging. The 1947 coup brought Pibun back. The Philippines had become independent in 1946, and now Burma and Indonesia joined it. Though they still had to work within the limits of a Western-dominated world economic system, governments in Southeast Asia could adopt policies no longer determined by colonial interests.

It was not surprising that, like that of the Thai Promoters, the new governments expected to play a large role in the economy. Interventionism, as it is now perceived, was indeed then as fashionable in the world at large as it is now unfashionable: five-year plans were not confined to Marxist states. Post-colonial governments, moreover, were under pressure to undo the impact of colonialism, and to respond to the high expectations that event had aroused among the people they now ruled. The new states had, as Elson puts it, 'a sense of aggrieved paternalism',[41] and adopted an intrusive and proprietorial role. It was not surprising either—whether or not it was wise—that governments tended to put a priority on industrialisation. That seemed the way to modernity.

In the Philippines, indeed, industrialisation was promoted less as a result of a plan than an accident, but it enjoyed government protection. Once the postwar windfall dollar receipts—from the US army, from veterans' payments, from rehabilitation—were exhausted, the new republic entered a balance-of-payments crisis, and, since the peso was pegged to the dollar as part of the deal with the United States, it could not devalue. The position was worsened by the election expenditures of 1949, and the government sought President Truman's approval for the imposition of exchange and import controls. Anxious to avoid the collapse of the republic, he agreed. 'The immediate aim of the controls', as Doronila tells us, 'was to halt the sharp decline of the exchange reserves, but they were gradually intensified in the 1950s and increasingly developed as an instrument for industrialization via import substitution.'[42] 'Stimulated by an effective barrier against foreign products and by preferential access to foreign exchange ... an entire spectrum of new or expanded local industries came into existence. The traditional trading-in-finished goods orientation of the non-agricultural sector soon changed into packaging, assembly, and light manufacture.'[43] Import-substitution industrialisation (ISI) had its limits, however, and it had its opponents, including the sugar-planters. The 'Filipino First' campaigns of the late 1950s and early 1960s were a defensive reaction. But the end of the controls was followed by direct protection.

In Thailand ISI began, Ruth McVey writes, as an ad hoc attempt to save the remnants of Pibun's state capitalism of the late 1930s and 1940s.[44] But the effects of the end of the Korean War boom were worsened by the droughts and poor harvests of the mid-1950s, and the collapse of the National Economic Development Corporation established in 1954 suggested the failure of the state intervention policy. The way was open for the 'developmentalism' of the Sarit 'strong-man' regime.

In Indonesia 'development' was caught up in the argument between technocrats of a neo-classical bent and those concerned to promote 'national' economic leadership. The Benteng programme was designed to establish Indonesian dominance in imports, as against Chinese. In fact it produced 'a group of licence brokers and political fixers',[45] and individuals associated with politicos and bureaucrats onsold the licences to the Chinese. In 1957–65 the programme was displaced by 'nationalist' policies that enhanced the role of the state, including army take-overs. After 1965, and especially after 1973, bureaucratic capitalism was to become the path to capital accumulation, and to a massive industrialisation, transcending ISI.

'Owing largely to its former character as a peripheral region of the Indian Empire', Burma was one of the least industrialised countries in Southeast Asia, and 'the desire for rapid industrialization ... was particularly intense'.[46] Embarking on a Two Year Plan in 1948, the government called in an American firm of consultants, KTA. The primary aim was to reduce dependence on imports where the articles could be produced economically in Burma itself, but the programme fell behind. In 1957 gross national product had not regained the level of 1939, and that, Charles

Fisher felt, could not simply be attributed to insurgency and the fall in rice prices. He suggested that Burma's leaders should 'resist the temptation to industrialize for industrialization's sake, and continue to concentrate the greater part of the nation's economic activity on primary production and related processing'.[47] The failure of their policies helped to erode the position of the civilian elite. The military, who took over in 1962, pursued policies that were at odds with those to which other Southeast Asian countries were turning: it embarked on ISI, but in the context of what it called a 'socialist' programme and an emphasis on autarchy. Those policies were to fail, too.

Even where ISI was successful, it clearly had its limits. In the Philippines, George L. Hicks and Geoffrey McNicoll had written in 1971, import substitution 'made it possible for capital goods imports and therefore industrial output to rise rapidly. … an essentially easy process, bringing considerable growth with relatively little learning of difficult skills'.[48] At least from the late 1960s, however, it was clear that a new form of the international division of labour would bring opportunities for export-oriented industrialisation (EOI), and that was now pushed by international bodies like the World Bank and the IMF. Developing countries should concentrate on manufactures that they could produce efficiently, thanks, for example, to lower labour costs, fewer regulations against pollution, and lower tariff barriers in purchasing countries. They should take full advantage of relations with multinational corporations and other sources, and the experience and the know-how they gained would enable them to extend into other fields. Under this pattern of relationships the United States and Japan, and also Korea and Taiwan, began to transfer manufacturing activities to Southeast Asia. Southeast Asian countries could take advantage of the 'product cycles of these investments to establish themselves in new and increasingly higher-value manufactures'.[49] The talk was of 'developmental authoritarian regimes', but it turned out that what was crucial was not in most cases the role of the 'autonomous state' itself, but the alliance between state actors and business sectors, and their interaction with their foreign interlocutors.[50]

Conclusion

When Britain signed the Elgin treaty with Japan in 1858, Marx took it as a sign that 'world trade was taking a new direction'. Bourgeois society, he wrote to Engels,

> has experienced its sixteenth century a second time—a sixteenth century which will, I hope, sound the death knell of bourgeois society, just as the first one thrust it into existence. The particular task of bourgeois society is the establishment of the world market, at least in outline, and of production based upon the world market. As the world is round, this seems to have been completed by the colonization of California and Australia and the opening up of China and Japan.[51]

Making the world market, however, is an endless task, renewed as industrialisation passes through new stages. Here, perhaps, was yet another sixteenth century, and it may not be the end of history.

In Southeast Asia the elite responded to these trends in the way that a study of the Thais might have suggested. In the 1960s Fred W. Riggs had seen Thailand as a bureaucratic polity that served itself alone, discouraged any further modernisation, and kept local capitalists as pariah entrepreneurs: it would continue, he thought, 'as a relatively well-integrated and hence stable bureaucratic polity, ... at a low level of industrialization and economic growth and an intermediate level of power distribution between the democratic and authoritarian extremes'.[52] By contrast, as McVey points out, the Philippines seemed to have a better chance of success, with no overwhelming bureaucracy, fledgling industries, a Chinese mestizo elite, landowners who invested in industry, and a good education system. In the event it was Thailand that went ahead with industrialisation. What Riggs saw as a parasitic relationship was more than that. It contained possibilities for intra-elite collaboration, for which earlier Thai history suggested some precedent. Indeed the bureaucratic polity in a sense invited the pursuit of wealth. The jockeying for office and the factionalism it involved suggested the need to insure against the reversal of political fortunes by the creation of economic: wise investment could 'provide a safe landing in case of political adversity and a guarantee of continuing family fortune'.[53]

State and commercial elites came together elsewhere in Southeast Asia, too, and it was there, as McVey's brilliant article suggests, that the source of Southeast Asia's capitalist energy in the closing decades of the twentieth century was to be found.[54] In New Order Indonesia the bureaucracy made concessions for the sake of business in the 1970s and 1980s that surprised outside observers. The civilian and military elite identified with business and profited from it. While there were anti-Chinese riots in Indonesia in 1974 and 1980, Murdani, a spokesman for the regime, declared in 1984 that the distinction between *pribumi* (indigenous) and non-*pribumi* was no longer desirable. In Malaysia, too, the opportunities for 'profitable symbiosis' between the Malay and Chinese elites, held out in Mahathir's plan for an industrialised Malaysia by 2020, offered a 'sporting chance', as McVey puts it, of Malay–Chinese equilibrium.[55]

Political elites brought one kind of contribution to the alliance: their contacts, their influence, their capacity to secure contracts and licences. The Chinese elites brought another. In the colonial phase, they had not relied on the state, but had developed networks within the territories and the region that depended on trust and group identity. That helped them in the new phase, and so did the cosmopolitan character of their business: they had gained a knowledge of modern trade, but also, unlike Western firms, of the local market. Japanese firms had found them particularly useful interlocutors when re-establishing themselves in Southeast Asia after the war. It is to these factors, rather than to an innate commercial genius, that McVey suggests looking for an explanation of the central role of the Chinese in modern Southeast Asian capitalism.[56]

The alliance was, of course, sustained by the opportunities that globalisation offered. Power-holders and business leaders came together to take advantage of the East Asian boom and the desire of the United States and Japan to invest in Southeast Asia. In turn that meant, in McVey's phrase, that 'the realization of Southeast Asia's capitalist promise depends ultimately on forces which the region has little power to affect',[57] the continued prosperity of the major economic powers and their continued interest in Southeast Asia. Southeast Asian countries were, as she added,[58] dependent in a new way on specialised and labile international markets, and, though they could mobilise cheap and docile if unskilled labour, particularly that of women, they could be overtaken by countries offering still lower labour costs. There were indeed limits on EOI as there had been on ISI.

Some of the limits came from outside. What kind of industrialisation might be possible in Southeast Asia? Multinational corporations, based elsewhere, might limit it, as colonial powers once had, not, as they did, by employing or failing to employ political power, but by employing economic power: setting the terms of investment, only 'transferring very specific segments of their sophisticated production'.[59] The experience of Singapore was indicative. Its extrusion from Malaysia turned the PAP leadership from ISI to EOI, and it looked to direct foreign investment even at the expense of local capital.[60] Its attempt at a 'second industrial revolution' after 1979 was much less successful than that endeavour. The withholding of the latest technology, protectionism, and the consignment of cheap labour sites to a marginal role in world production, 'ensured that the period of NICs expanding their share of world industrial output was shortlived and confined to an intermediate technological level', Chris Tremewan concludes.[61]

The elite partners of international capital found their options limited, too. Yoshihara Kunio described their activities as 'ersatz capitalism': they were 'rent seekers', 'crony capitalists', 'bureaucratic capitalists',[62] securing and benefiting from licences, monopolies, and subsidies, and working with Chinese, Japanese, and American capital to exploit them. In some ways, as Hicks and McNicoll implied, they had it 'too easy': such industry as they set up was 'technologyless'. The example of Singapore suggests, however, that the main limits came from the outside: the opportunity of further development was not readily forthcoming, if it was forthcoming at all. Cutting down the forests and the creation of 'agribusiness' suggested the fate of the tiger cubs. What was at work, actually as well as figuratively, was what John Gray called 'slash-and-burn Anglo-American capitalism'.[63]

It is tempting to recall the first sixteenth century, the age of commerce, as Reid conceives it. The boom ceased in the seventeenth century, but it was not, he implies, all loss. The period of 'less intense engagement' with the outside world preserved the diversity of Southeast Asia.[64] If the boom of the new sixteenth century collapsed, the consequences would be greater. For the economic, social, and cultural changes it set in motion were, despite some similarities, of a different order of magnitude, and took place in a world far more globalised. It seems that Southeast Asian countries must spread capitalism below the 'big business' level and enhance domestic purchasing power. Only Malaysia and Singapore have the infrastructure, skills, and linkages that are the other way to sustained growth, and, if Tremewan is right, their prospects are uncertain. Otherwise it will be seen that Southeast Asia's minerals and forests—and indeed its peoples—have in some sense been sacrificed for purely temporary gains.

The comparison with the first sixteenth century may extend into the political realm. The 'age of commerce' was also an age of absolutism, in the end, Reid argues, a source, because of its arbitrariness, of its decline. The new age of commerce has been marked by the emergence of strong governments, if not strong states, and the amalgamation of elites. The resources of the outside world have been used not only to develop capitalist enterprise and industry, but to transform traditional patron–client ties into forms of the corporatist state. The political process and the political implications are discussed in subsequent chapters of this book. But it may be that a more democratic approach will after all prove economically advantageous, not simply by encouraging the consumer, but by fostering the capacity for innovation that Southeast Asia will need.

The economic crisis of 1997–98 called attention to such issues, particularly as it extended into the political realm. Cronyism had stimulated the economy in the preceding decades. Now it seemed to be the cause of its collapse. There was an opportunity for a democratic thrust that might check 'corruption', enhance 'accountability', and even provide for the 'stability' that authoritarian regimes notably failed to offer at moments of transition. Yet the crisis, and the 'remedies' for it that international organisations put forward, and indeed imposed, suggested the extent to which Southeast Asia's economies yet remained dependent on the economy of the rest of the world and its governments on decisions made elsewhere. The pattern of the 1970s–1990s was now redundant, as earlier the colonial and postwar patterns had become redundant.

Notes

1 *The Philippine Island World*, UCP, 1967, p. 263.
2 A. Kaur, '"Hantu" and Highway … ', MAS, 28, 1 (February 1994), p. 30.
3 *Bridge and Barrier: Transport and Communications in Colonial Malaya, 1870–1957*, Singapore: OUP, 1985, p. xvii.
4 q. ibid., p. 31.
5 q. *Southeast Asia and the Germans*, p. 202.
6 *South-east Asia*, London: Methuen, 1964, p. 490.
7 Murray, p. 173.
8 Fisher, p. 442.
9 Fisher, p. 443.
10 J. Silverstein, 'Railroads in Burma and India', JSEAH, 5, 1 (March 1964), p. 27.
11 Fisher's phrase, p. 444.
12 *Colonial Policy and Practice*, CUP, 1948, p. 77.
13 p. 442.
14 p. 444.

15 H. W. Dick in Lindblad, *Historical Foundations*, pp. 34, 37–8.
16 Kaur, *Bridge*, p. 125.
17 ibid., p. 138.
18 Fisher, p. 301.
19 Fisher, p. 493.
20 q. H. R. C. Wright, *East-Indian Economic Problems of the Age of Cornwallis and Raffles*, London: Luzac, 1961, p. 228.
21 Elson, *Sugar*, pp. 83–4.
22 Tarling, *British Policy*, p. 96n.
23 Deans to Wellington, 26 October 1830, q. ibid., p. 96.
24 q. C. L. M. Penders, *Bojonegoro*, Singapore: Gunung Agong, 1984, p. 28.
25 See Angus Maddison in Anne Booth et al., *Indonesian Economic History in the Dutch Colonial Era*, Yale, 1990, pp. 332–3.
26 q. Megan Cook, *The Constitutionalist Party in Cochinchina: The Years of Decline, 1930–1942*, Monash U, 1977, p. 162.
27 Andrew Hardy, 'The Economics of French Rule in Indochina … ', MAS, 32, 4 (October 1998), pp. 815, 818.
28 Elisa A. Julian, 'Spain's Last Half Century in the Philippines … ', FEU Faculty Journal, 3 (October 1957), pp. 132–3.
29 Ian Brown, *Economic Change in South-East Asia, c.1830–1980*, KL: OUP, 1997, p. 57.
30 P. Kratoska, *The Japanese Occupation of Malaya*, St Leonards: Allen and Unwin, 1998, p. 22.
31 Irene Taeuber, q. in C. Hirschman, 'Population and Society in Southeast Asia', JSEAS, 25, 2 (September 1994), p. 414.
32 Homan van der Heide, q. R. E. Elson, *The End of the Peasantry in Southeast Asia*, Basingstoke: Macmillan, 1997, p. 116.
33 K. Hewison, *Bankers and Bureaucrats*, Yale UP, 1989, pp. 43–45.
34 Ian Brown, *The Elite and the Economy in Siam*, Singapore: OUP, 1988, p. 155.
35 ibid., p. 177.
36 ibid., p. 177.
37 in Craig Reynolds, *National Identity and its Defenders*, Monash U, 1991, p. 61.
38 Hewison, p. 74.
39 q. W. Blythe, *The Impact of Chinese Secret Societies in Malaya*, London: OUP, 1969, p. 251.
40 q. Elson, *End*, p. 48.
41 *End*, p. 59.
42 Amando Doronila, *The State, Economic Transformation, and Political Change in the Philippines, 1946–1972*, Singapore: OUP, 1992, pp. 51–2.
43 Report of First National City Bank of NY, q. Doronila, pp. 54–5.
44 'The Materialization of the Southeast Asian Entrepreneur', in R. McVey, ed., *Southeast Asian Capitalists*, Cornell UP, 1992, p. 11.
45 Robison, p. 45.
46 Fisher, p. 461.
47 p. 467.
48 *Trade and Growth in the Philippines*, Cornell UP, 1971, p. 229.
49 McVey, p. 12.
50 p. 14.
51 q. Dona Torr, introduction to *Marx on China*, London: Lawrence and Wishart, 1951.
52 *Thailand: The Modernization of a Bureaucratic Polity*, Honolulu: East-West Center P, 1966, p. 395.
53 McVey, p. 23.
54 p. 30.
55 p. 25.
56 pp. 20–1.
57 p. 32.
58 p. 12.
59 P. Regnier, *Singapore City-State in South-East Asia*, KL: Majeed, 1992, p. 95.

60 Lawrence B. Krause, 'Thinking about Singapore', in Krause et al., *The Singapore Economy Reconsidered*, Singapore: ISEAS, 1987, p. 3.
61 *The Political Economy of Social Control in Singapore*, Basingstoke: Macmillan, 1994, p. 37.
62 *The Rise of Ersatz Capitalism in South-East Asia*, Singapore: OUP, 1988, p. 3.
63 *Times Literary Supplement*, 8 August 1998.
64 *Age of Commerce*, II, p. 329.

Village and Town

The villages and towns of Southeast Asia vary in origin, size, and character. A history can but give examples. But, although a great deal has been destroyed, a pedestrian can still recognise something of the past.

A description of village and town life in Southeast Asia would have to reflect its diversity in economic function, in structure, and in culture, and presenting it is perhaps an impossible task. To offer also an account of change and continuity over time, as a historian must, adds to the difficulty. Encyclopaedic knowledge and encyclopaedic length would be essential. When both are available only on a much smaller scale, it seems best to attempt generalisation and illustration, and even those are extremely risky. What may make the attempt more worthwhile is the context that the present work may provide. In particular, its account of the development of trade, transport, and industry offers a basis for considering, not only the changes within villages and towns, but also the changes in their mutual relationships. Further aspects of those relationships are considered when the book turns to social structures and politics.

In this as in other sections of the book, the reader is invited to consider the historical experiences of Southeast Asia, not only by comparison within the region, but by comparison between the region and other parts of the world. But perhaps this topic offers a particular opportunity to extend the historical imagination. What can be read in books can be supplemented by what can be seen on the ground. That can, of course, be as misleading as a book. If an author has shaped or selected the evidence, the forces of nature as well as man will have determined what has been preserved in village and town. Roman villas, Norman castles, Loire chateaux, cathedrals, and mosques will remain, but the less permanent dwellings of the mass of the people will not. Perhaps that is even more true in the tropical climates of Southeast Asia. We see Angkor and Borobudur, but not what surrounded them.

There may be another contrast, too. Both the West and the East have destroyed in anger, and sometimes the evidence of that, albeit paradoxically, remains: the ruins of the English monasteries, the ruins of Ayudhya. They have also destroyed in the course of 'progress'. That trend has been stemmed in the West by a conservationist movement that found its origins in a reaction to the extent of destruction that modern technology made possible and in a concern to find some continuity with the past in a period of unprecedented change. Such a movement seems less appropriate in states that focus on economic development, that believe that they have to escape the past, that fear that conservation may even be a device to hold them back. Even so, it can be seen as a means of nation-building and a support for tourism. Then, of course, it becomes clear that it is not only a question of what has been preserved, but how it is presented.

Settlements and villages

Those who write, those who read, and those who look, will always have the problem of recognising change, let alone explaining it. Perhaps that will be especially true in respect of village communities, which do change, but tend to stress continuity. In his masterly book on village Java in the nineteenth century, Elson points out, for example, how small the villages were in Raffles' day, compared with those of the present: they generally ranged from about 50 to 200 persons. That range was itself in part a function of change. Some of the settlements were even smaller, 'especially more recent and isolated ones', and were the product of pioneering. 'Village inhabitants probably had some rough conception of the optimal size of individual settlements, an awareness of the opportunities further afield, and a sense of the relative advantages of staying where they were or striking out towards the forest frontier.'[1] Some of the factors they would consider were environmental—the availability of water and of firewood, the distance from their fields—and some were not: custom, debts, obligations, ties might stand in their way.

At that time, as Elson points out, Java was relatively thinly populated. Indeed most of Southeast Asia was thinly populated at the time, often much more thinly than Java, and the kind of factors that he describes as operating in the early nineteenth-century Javanese village had operated elsewhere and continued to do so. The development of such villages was not, however, merely autonomous in origin. Commercial contacts with the world outside the village might lead it to diversify and to expand. Political leaders might sponsor settlement, as in a people-scarce Pagan or an expanding Nguyen Vietnam, or resettlement, as in the Spanish Philippines, where people were brought within reach of the missionaries. There is a contrast with more drastic interventions in recent times, but there is also a continuity.

'In the period before the British regime [in Malaya] it was the recognized practice for the chiefs to provide the capital with which a village headman financed his new settlers.'[2] After the British intervened, western Malaya in the late nineteenth century did not attract only Chinese miners. Stability and economic opportunity attracted new settlers, escaping the natural disasters in Kelantan in the 1880s, or the pressure of the Dutch on Aceh or of the Thais on Pattani. Others came from Menangkabau and Mandiling in Sumatra. 'They travelled in parties and settled down together.

In this way new villages emerged which, like existing settlements, were communities in which there was cultural homogeneity within the village.[3] State governments, and also some Malay aristocrats, encouraged these immigrants, for example by making loans to the headman. There were thus political pull as well as push factors, to add to the economic.

The same factors are present, but in different combinations, in the Depression, in the Japanese phase, and in the independence phase. The Depression led unemployed Chinese to squatting in the jungle. The dislocation the Japanese conquest caused, and in particular the Japanese animus against the Chinese, extended the practice, adding to the risk of racial tension, and providing postwar a possible base of support for the Malay Communist Party and its terrorism. One of the political measures the British adopted in the Emergency was the creation, under the Briggs plan, of 'New Villages', often done in great and indeed counter-productive haste. 'I recently spent two days in North Johore', wrote the high commissioner, Sir Henry Gurney, in 1951, 'where the machine works so quickly that a piece of virgin jungle becomes a settlement of 200 houses complete with roads, water and police posts and fencing in ten days'.[4]

The concept was to be followed, with far less success, in southern Vietnam in the late 1950s and 1960s, again with primarily political motives. In traditional Vietnam settlements had been compact and villages were stockaded. In more recently—and more sparsely—settled Cochin-China, villages were characteristically more strung-out, and thus, in the eyes of President Ngo Dinh Diem and his brother, exposed to banditry. Agrovilles, or closer settlement areas, were a means of control and pacification.[5] If traditional Vietnam was in mind, and also contemporary Malaya, the historian might remember the pueblo (township) of the Spanish Philippines.

The Philippines of the pre-war period, and even more the postwar phase of struggle with the Huk insurgents, witnessed a programme of resettlement in Mindanao, in which again economic and political factors were combined. The same was true of the programme of 'transmigration' adopted by the Dutch in the Indies and greatly extended by their successors. There were economic push and pull factors, and also political: the integration of the archipelago had to be weighed against the risk of tensions among the *bangsa* (peoples).

Economic and political pressures on other forms of settlement increased over time, and tended to displace them or make them resemble the predominant form. Specialised and distinctive fishing villages were, in any case, not the norm, though fish has always been the main source of animal protein in most of Southeast Asia. Raymond Firth studied the fishing villages of northeastern Malaya, but fishing was more typically 'a supplementary form of agriculture'.[6] In crowded Java, 'the chief interest' in the 1950s centred on 'fish breeding in artificial ponds and flooded rice fields'.[7]

The Bajau fishing villages of Sabah, described by Lee Yong Leng,[8] 'are built over the sea or river on stilt-supported platforms with "cat-walks" connecting each house to the shore and to one another', sometimes to be found now by the imperilled pedestrian as parts of larger towns. 'It is possible', he suggests, 'that with the mountainous,

forested nature and swampy coasts of the country forming obstacles to inland penetration, most of the first settlements of North Borneo may have had their origins in
such villages as these'. That, he adds, is uncertain, but they are relics of the past.

Postulating a historical progression is indeed hazardous. The same may be true
of another mode of settlement, the multiple dwelling-house or longhouse customarily associated with Sarawak, though a feature of life elsewhere in Southeast Asia as
well. Was this a stage in the settlement of not very accessible territories, now left
behind only in certain niches? That seems possible, but perhaps again not certain,
since in the colonial phase Dayak continued to build longhouses and Kadazan
(Dusun) did not. In general, however, the old system has been broken down under
the impact of economic, cultural, and political change, though it may be preserved
as virtual reality for modern tourists.

Dwellings in the early nineteenth-century Javanese villages that Elson recreates
were 'crude and simple structures, easy and inexpensive to construct',[9] built on stilts
in west Java, elsewhere set on the ground, with stamped earth floors. 'They comprised a single room with a framework of timber or bamboo poles, with walls made
of timber or, more frequently, woven bamboo, and roofs thatched with grass or palm
leaf.'[10] There was little or no furniture. 'People ate, sat and slept on the floor on grass
or palm leaf mats with cushions.'[11]

A nineteenth-century Malay house was raised on wooden or brick pillars, and
comprised three parts: the verandah for the reception of visitors, the central part of
the house, and the kitchen, with 'a simple hearth of large stones, a collection of
cooking and water pots, and culinary implements such as a coconut rasp or a mortar
for grinding chillies'.[12] Greater security and prosperity led the better-off to use sawn
timber and planks for the house, and to use tiles on the roof, or corrugated iron,
'which turns the house into an oven at midday'.[13] European and Chinese manufactures began to replace traditional utensils. Candles and paraffin lamps replaced resin
torches, and in 1909 Winstedt wrote that 'cheap Chinese earthenware is common
everywhere now'.[14] A space in front of the house was edged with herbs and flowers,
and on the steps the peasant gossiped with a neighbour. The women pounded the
rice and the poultry scratched for a living. The chief or local magnate would, of
course, have a more pretentious house, and Winstedt found in the houses of school-
masters with whom his work brought him in touch 'crocheted antimacassars and
bentwood Austrian chairs, photos of the owner by a Chinese perpetrator and oleo-
graphs of Queen Victoria or of the Sultan of Turkey'.[15]

In the early-twentieth-century Philippines the gap between the rich and the poor
was perhaps even more demonstrable. The roads radiating out from the pueblos to
the villages or barrios were, James LeRoy wrote, 'quite thickly lined with the cane
houses of the humbler natives, and here and there the stone house of some well-to-
do proprietor'.[16] The aristocracy mingled with the people—at the cockfights, for
example, which LeRoy so much condemned—but their wealth, education, and culture stood them apart, and 'distant readers' could readily construct, 'from stories of

upper-class Filipino balls and banquets, besilked and bejewelled ladies, pretentious theatricals *à la espagnole,* orchestras discoursing Verdi and Bizet, and over all the borrowed circumlocutions of Spanish courtesy, a Filipino society which is really distant from the lives of the people'.[17]

If such a picture demonstrates the results of change over time—both in the accumulation and distribution of wealth and in the way it is expended—it is no difficult matter to project it into contemporary times, when, for example, Malay and Chinese elites in Malaysia join in a cosmopolitan *nouveau riche* consumer lifestyle, 'the high culture model for modern capitalist Southeast Asia', as McVey calls it,[18] while the cultivator and artisan have T-shirt and transistor and perhaps motor-scooter. But while it may represent a gulf between the elite and the masses, it also represents a gulf between the village and the city. In both cases it is a source of resentment and emulation, not less obvious because of the emergence of daily-migrant workers, but more.

Cities of the archipelago

The functions of the city in Southeast Asia have been more diverse than those of the village. The evidence they have left behind is often more permanent. Their builders often made statements of their purpose, even though that might mean change, or even destruction, rather than preservation. And the cities were more often visited by literate observers.

Indeed there is a risk, from which this book is not exempt, that writers, readers and pedestrians may focus too much of their attention upon them, compared to rural and agricultural life. But, as J. E. Spencer writes of early Southeast Asia, '[t]he city was the chief consumer of agricultural surpluses, the point of accumulation of wealth and tradition, and the chief developer of cultural patterns—the centre of civilization. It was the nerve centre of the state and the chief object of attack by an invader.'[19] It continued to be so. Writers and readers may trace the changes in the patterns both by studying cities that represented but a stage or two in the historical process and by studying cities that occupied the same site for centuries. Pedestrians may find relics of old cities of the first kind—say the ruins of Pagan—or modern cities of that type—say Kuala Lumpur itself, a late-nineteenth-century mining town that became a national capital in less than a century. They may also visit cities of the second kind—Hanoi, for example, or Manila—and witness their history in their topography and in the buildings that have been preserved.

Spencer's definition perhaps implies that there was only one kind of city, the consumer of agricultural surpluses. In the archipelago, however, there were entrepot cities, placed on the coast and at river-mouths, living off the commerce of the region and its connexion with the outside world. The agrarian city had a substantial central complex, executed largely in stone, though its palaces were usually in wood. The maritime cities had limited resources of stone and corvée: their religious edifices were usually in wood and little remains of them. Both types were 'a sprawling mass of houses and buildings'.[20] Sri Vijaya can no longer be seen. But the pedestrian need not be confined, so far as early history is concerned, to the cities that consumed agricultural surpluses. Old Brunei still, for the most part, exists, through threatened by fire as well as by development: a city built over the water, rather than on land, but no mere fishing village.

If Sri Vijaya has disappeared, Brunei has, of course, changed. The changes can be followed both in the library and on the ground (and on the catwalks). Then the centre of a trading empire, the Brunei town of 1521 impressed Pigafetta, as he recorded in his account of Magellan's voyage of circumnavigation. 'That city is entirely built in salt water, except the houses of the king and certain chiefs. It contains twenty-five thousand hearths [families].'[21] At the time of the Spanish attack in 1578, the city was, one Spaniard put it, 'very large and rich' and 'had the appearance of another Venice. The buildings were of wood, but the houses were excellently constructed.'[22] By the early twentieth century it was very different, and perhaps seemed even more so. For F. N. Butterworth, writing after World War I, it was less the Venice of the East than the Vienna of the East, 'the biggest Malay city of the world and the capital of a Sultan having only a little bit of country left on which to support its dignity.'[23]

By then, under the influence of the British Resident, the town was developing on land, and downtown Bandar offers evidence of that phase not only in street names but in the preservation of the old palace and, further afield, the former residency. Juxtaposed but extending well beyond the limits of the protectorate city is the city of the oil-rich independent sultanate, with its vast palaces, its stunning mosques, its shopping centres, high-rises, resettlement estates, motorways, university, and fun-fair.

The fate of the neighbouring sultanate of Sulu was very different, and so was that of its capital city, often attacked by the Spaniards, but finally garrisoned only after 1876. It had been built along the banks of a tidal stream, called Suba' Bawang, and at the head of the roadstead, even over the shoal and beach and into the roadstead itself. 'That portion of the town which is not within the stockades is built in regular Malay fashion, on piles', Captain Henry Keppel wrote in 1848–49.[24] 'The houses run in rows, or streets; and outside of them is a platform about 6 feet wide to walk upon. This is supported underneath by a light scaffolding of bamboo.' Forts on the high land to the east offered protection, and other *kuta* (strongholds) defended the approaches.

After the Spanish occupation, Jolo comprised a 'walled town', Tiyangi Sugh; San Remondo, to the south; Tulay, to the west; and Busbus, to the east. The 'walled town' was laid out with broad clean tree-lined streets and parks, with substantial houses for the officers, market, church, theatre, hospital, and schoolhouse, attractive but boring, Ada Pryer found on a visit in 1898: 'it has a half continental half oriental air, a broad boulevard planted with trees stretching away before one with Chinese shops on either side'. The general impression was 'that everyone has just awakened from a lazy sleep and is proposing to take another nap as soon as possible'.[25] A long row of Chinese houses and shops began at the lower point of the Tulay delta and stretched out to sea. There the Chinese had resided for many generations and by the time the Americans arrived they controlled the trade of the archipelago.

In the 1920s Sixto Y. Orosa thought the town 'presented a most cheerful appearance'.[26] The monument to the conquistadores built by Governor Arolas was replaced by one of a uniformed nurse, and a monument to Rizal in the main plaza, also including figures of a Moro with a plough and of a Christian Filipino blacksmith, again testified to American purpose. But Sulu was to be the scene of a major conflict between the Moros and the post-independence government in 1974. 'A whole town was reduced to ashes, tens of thousands of people were uprooted, hundreds killed on both sides', writes T. J. S. George.[27]

The main entrepot at the outset of the age of commerce was Melaka. Ruled by a Malay sultan, it was thronged by traders from across the Straits and across the seas. The sultan's palace was in a walled-off precinct on St Paul's Hill. Immigrant Malays were located on the slopes and on the far side of the estuary, while *orang laut* (men of the sea) were close to the water's edge. The main bazaar was situated on a stone bridge that spanned the river. Wealthier merchants lived to the north and had business offices in the town. It was this city that the Portuguese captured, occupying St Paul's Hill and building the governor's residence, a town hall, and churches; this city that the Dutch took from them, building a new town hall, still in existence, and that in turn the English acquired, stopping short, thanks to Raffles, of destroying it; and it was there that the Tunku chose to proclaim Malaya's independence in 1957. The pedestrian as well as the reader can trace some of that history, preserved partly because the silted port limited redevelopment.

In the Dutch capital, Batavia (Jakarta), the malarial canals of west Java combined badly with the stuffy, tightly packed and multi-storeyed Dutch houses Coen built. In the eighteenth century many Dutch citizens moved to a more favourable location on the outskirts of the city at Weltevreden, an area adjoining the open space later called Koningsplein (King's Square) and later still Lapangan Merdeka (Independence Square). There they built country villas, surrounded by gardens, and enjoyed 'an expansive luxurious life concerned with prestige and the emphasis on social occasions'.[28] The houses the Dutch built in Weltevreden borrowed something from the *priyayi*, and the suburb plan of the streets was, as McGee suggests, imitative of the Javanese *kraton* (palace)-based cities. Java was indeed the home of another kind of city, one associated with agricultural settlement and bureaucratic-patrimonial rule, and emblematic of the ruler's power.

Cities fell into patterns, even if they were not deliberately planned. Subsequent history might overlay or disrupt those patterns, leaving ruins or monuments behind, even customs and trades as well. Singapore has a discontinuous history. The island enters the record, somewhat uncertainly, as Temasek, an outlier initially, it seems, of Sri Vijaya; then it became, as a city to which, according to the Malay Annals, 'foreigners resorted in great numbers', the subject of contest between Majapahit and the Thais. From the late fourteenth century, the name 'Singapore' began to be used of a city that became a dependency of Melaka and, following the Portuguese capture of that city, of its successor-state, Johore. By the early nineteenth century it had perhaps only 1000 inhabitants, most of them *orang laut*.

It was this site that, after the return of Java, Riau-Lingga, and Melaka to the Dutch, Raffles acquired for 'a great commercial emporium and a fulcrum, whence we may extend our influence'. One of a line of scholar-officials, and something of a romantic, he saw Singapore as 'classic ground'.[29] But that did not prevent a ruthless handling of the old site in order to create the new town. 'A new world is being created, the old world destroyed.'[30] The Forbidden Hill, where Raffles said the tombs of the Malay kings were, was partly levelled for Fort Canning, and a large stone at the mouth of the river, allegedly emblematic of Majapahit, was blown up in 1843. In turn, however, Raffles' own town was, though not obliterated, overlaid by the growth of Singapore as a commercial city, an imperial city, and a city state.

For much of the nineteenth century, indeed, it remained a small city, government buildings on the left bank of the river, Chinatown on the right, and enclaves for the Malay rulers at Telok Blangah and Kampong Gelam. It was not without elegance, still apparent, for example, in G. D. Coleman's Armenian Church of St Gregory the Illuminator of 1835. In the 1840s European merchants began to move into what were then suburbs, River Valley Road and Orchard Road. Some of the bungalows and leafy gardens yet remain in Tanglin and the Cluny Road area. The style of Coleman and his successor J. T. Thomson persisted, a kind of tropical Palladianism, with broad verandahs, venetian shutters, high ceilings, interconnecting rooms, chunam stucco, elegant loggias. Convicts from India built the more Gothic Anglican cathedral, completed in 1864.

'A perfect paradise, full of shady avenues of flowering trees', wrote Ada Pryer.[31] Singapore had, however, begun to take on new roles, as the import-export economy expanded. The first tin-smelter was established on Pulau Brani in 1890; it benefited from the rubber trade, to the creation of which it had indeed contributed; and it became a distributor and later a refiner of oil. Singapore also began to see itself as an imperial city, even before it became a naval base. Its hotels began to stake a claim to quality. The Raffles was opened by the Sarkies brothers in 1886: a major renovation created the elegant building of the 1890s. The Raffles Museum was opened in 1887. The Town Hall was renovated and reopened as the Victoria Memorial Hall in 1905. Yet perhaps the characteristic feature of the imperial town was its combination of elegant villa and Chinatown. The latter was the focus of the Improvement Trust, created in 1920. The Post Office of 1928 and the City Hall of 1929 created 'the image of a showcase city', James Warren has written,[32] and he has vividly depicted its 'underside'. Urban overcrowding remained, and the conditions that prevailed in colonial Singapore were a powerful argument for drastic change on independence.

Entrepot, source of the rubber tree, naval base, avenue of Islamic modernism, centre for communist activity, scene of the British surrender in 1942, Singapore did not suffer much destruction in the war. Postwar it remained a British base: it became a garrison town and a university town as well as a commercial and political centre. Patrick O'Donovan decided that it looked like 'some Asian Slough'.[33]

With the breakaway from Malaysia, and its emergence as an independent state, Singapore was to become one of the Four Tigers, an industrial centre as well as a distributional centre, a financial centre as well as a commercial centre, a tourist centre as well as the home of over two million people, with a major airport at Changi and the busiest of seaports, but with no hinterland, an exemplary centre placed among other larger countries, half admiring, half envious. The wonder was not bought without political and psychological costs. It also changed the face of Singapore. Reclamation, a feature of its life since the 1820s, proceeded on an unprecedented scale in the new industrial centre of Jurong in the 1960s, and between Collyer Quay and Changi in the 1970s and 1980s. The skyline changed and with it the way of living. Relocating 87 per cent of the population in thirty years, the skyscrapers of the central city and the Housing and Development Board blocks of the suburbs almost obliterated Chinatown—now but a tourist trap—and literally or figuratively over-shadowed the old European bungalows. Some of colonial Singapore remained, but not much. The Raffles Museum became the National Museum, the Raffles Hotel was refurbished, the Victoria Memorial Hall upgraded as the home for the Singapore Symphony Orchestra. But Raffles Institution, mainly a Coleman structure, was demolished in 1967–68 to make way for the Raffles Centre. Perhaps too much of the old that was good went, along with much that was bad. But attempts have been made to preserve an oral and pictorial legacy, and national pride is a motive for conservation as well as change.

Mainland cities

The older cities of the mainland were, like those in central Java, exemplary cities of a different kind. The irrigation system created by the Khmer rulers from the late ninth century made it possible to exploit the land more efficiently and to create and sustain cities. The city of Angkor Thom was built between 1181 and 1219. 'Unlike our western cities, it was not just a group of houses, a market and a seat of government. It was a replica in miniature of the fabled world of Hindu cosmology, a small model of the universe, a microcosm.'[34] At the centre was the Bayon, a mountain in stone, symbol of Mount Meru, the abode of the gods. Surrounding it was an enclosure, including the king's palace, and round this a wall and a moat, both symbolic and defensive. Outside the royal enclosure was 'a combination of densely-packed villages separated by rice fields and vegetable plots, palms and fruit trees'.[35] Canals from the artificial lakes ran through the city, irrigating the land and providing transport. What Henri Mouhot 'explored' in the nineteenth century and what the tourist may now see are, of course, the remains of the royal city, and not of the whole 'urban' area.

Some towns had a more continuous life, and survived to take on other roles. Hanoi as a city is older than its name. A citadel was built there in 791. Choosing it as the capital of Vietnam in 1010, Ly Thai-to called it Thang-long. A later name was

Dong Kinh, often used in colonial times in a Western transcription as a description for the whole of northern Vietnam. Whatever its name, the city has been the capital of the Vietnamese state for most of its history. Its core was the Red River delta, and the city, known for its lakes, lies on the lower reaches at the confluence with the Duong river. The memory of Le Thai-to, who turned out the Ming in the early fifteenth century, is associated with the Lake of the Restored Sword (Hoan Kiem Ho) in the heart of Hanoi. The Nguyen, who reunified Vietnam in the early nineteenth century, moved the imperial capital to Hué, where its remains, damaged in the Tet offensive of 1968, can still be seen. The French made Hanoi a capital again, but now of what they called 'French Indo-China'. Hanoi greatly changed, but it retained the characteristics given it by its history as a capital of a state for the greater part of a thousand years.

More Confucian than the Confucians, Vietnamese rulers favoured agriculture rather than commerce, and Thang-long had not welcomed foreign merchants. At the time of the clash with the French, Hanoi was indeed an agglomeration of capital, commercial town, and juxtaposed villages. The first comprised the citadel, where the representatives of the Nguyen emperor resided, a Vauban-style structure built under Gia-long. The commercial town lay between river and citadel, divided into a Chinese quarter, including the richer merchants, and a Vietnamese quarter of artisans. To the south lay a number of enclaves, including the temple of Confucius, the examination compound, the mint, and the south fort, designed to protect Hanoi from attacks coming up-river. The villages were scattered amidst the marshes and rice paddies of the delta.

Under the French the ramparts of the citadel, largely destroyed on municipal instruction in the late 1890s, became the outlines of the main thoroughfares. Inside, the royal pagoda was on the site of a palace built by Ly Thai-to. Its central pavilion, built on a sacred knoll, was razed in 1886. The citadel also contained warehouses, stables, a prison, a firing range, temples, and a great banyan tree. The French installed a race track, and watched the races from a tower built by Gia-long. In the examination compound, the site of Garnier's camp in 1874, a palace was built for the imperial representative, later used by the library and archives, and the site was also used by the Gendarmerie and the Ecole des Arts Pratiques. The commercial town was bounded by the Lake of the Returned Sword, the Red River and the citadel, a place of narrow and congested streets protected by numerous gates. Much of it was burned in 1883. Quickly rebuilt under French guidance, it remained a sector with narrow streets, often specialising in particular commodities. The French city lay between the lake and the southern fort, site of the French concession. Fortified at first, it became the site of the Résidence-Général, the University, and the Ecole Française d'Extrême Orient. The French quarter developed more to the west than the south, effectively linking concession and citadel.

It was in the citadel that the Japanese interned the French troops in March 1945, and in Ba Dinh Square that Ho Chi Minh read the proclamation of independence in

September. The capital of the Democratic Republic, Hanoi was first bombed by the United States on 17 April 1966, and several quarters were razed by B52s. 'The evergreen capital … lived in order and combat readiness … the children played cheerfully beside air-raid shelters dug in front of their houses, in public squares or at the cross roads.'[36] The streets 'swarmed with hundreds of bikes—perhaps one out of two cyclists carried a girl gracefully on the luggage-carrier as on a scooter'.[37] The bombing interrupted the reconstruction of Hanoi. That had concentrated on industrialisation in the suburbs, leaving the old centre undisturbed. The 'renovation' (*doi moi*) to which the regime turned after the conflict with the Khmer Rouge and the Chinese threatened it. Adding to the problems of 'red tape' and 'corruption' the developers, however, face 'a burgeoning conservationist movement that is struggling to preserve Hanoi's architectural heritage'.[38]

'The South is Vietnam's California, and Saigon is its Los Angeles', Neil Sheehan wrote.[39] A 'freewheeling spirit' arose from its newness. And that was not eliminated by renaming it—as Hanoi had been renamed in the past—or renaming its streets—somewhat, after all, in the French style—to denote the changing of regimes. Saigon became Ho Chi Minh City. The Rue Catinat of the French, which had become Tu Do (Freedom) under the Diem regime, became Dong Khoi (Uprising).

The distinction between a predominantly politico-administrative city and a predominantly commercial one may be drawn in Burma, too. The capitals of the monarchy, though shifting, were almost all in the dry zone heartland: Pagan, whose ruins may be seen, Ava, Mandalay. The colonial and post-colonial capital was Rangoon, the site of Alaung-hpaya's victory and of a great pagoda, but not the capital of his dynasty.

Like Pagan, Ayudhya can be visited, but what the visitor finds are the remains of its innumerable temples, and little else of the city the Burmans sacked in 1767. The new capital, Bangkok, initially repeated old patterns. A royal enclosure contained the palace, the government offices, the main temples. Across the river were the residences of the Thai, 'rows of floating houses built on pontoons floating on the canals which were the streets'.[40] The commercial city expanded in the nineteenth century along the New Road from the palace walls to the east bank, the major commercial and banking area. Much of it seemed to observers like a Chinatown, and outside the whole city were market gardens largely occupied by Chinese. The changing pattern of the late nineteenth century has been almost overwhelmed by the economic changes Thailand has undergone since the 1950s. The canals have become streets, choked by petrol-driven traffic. Always to a unique extent combining a dominant political and a dominant commercial role, Bangkok has become the epitome of a primate city.

This account can only be a cursory and example-based survey, which the reader may amplify by using other sources, and, it is suggested, by personal observation. Some generalisations may nevertheless be attempted. A frequent feature of the cities was the presence of water, a source of food, of trade, of transport, of defence. Another was the impermanence of much of the building, so that what remains may provide a one-sided image of the past, emphasising the governmental rather than the commercial, the rulers rather than the people. Yet contemporary popular dwellings, now often interspersed with more permanent residential or commercial structures, may resemble those that have not survived. Indeed the cities, greatly changed though they are, may still retain features of the past, or enable one to imagine them. Those that were capitals sought to plan, and so did the colonial powers, as a means of asserting their control. But beyond the centre, the planning was, as it were, by allocation—certain areas for certain peoples, certain streets for certain trades, in a pattern by no means unique to Southeast Asia—and within the great cities that grew up *kampong* (villages) remained, and indeed, at least in Yogyakarta, were marked by 'an overwhelming sense of the importance of propinquity and neighbourship'.[41]

Rural–urban links

Patrick Guinness's comment is made in a discussion of the customs of such a *kampong*: are they survivals of a rural pattern or adaptation to an urban existence? Over the centuries the relationship between the village and the city has undergone a range of changes. That it must always have been diverse in character makes it difficult to generalise, but it is possible to typify. Trade between the *ulu* and the *ilir* established one kind of connexion, often inflected, as Barbara Andaya has shown, by custom, by claims of kinship, by the demonstration of supernatural qualities. The symbolic, as well as the administrative, also played a role in linking settled village and capital city. The economic expansion of the nineteenth century and the development of better transport systems not only facilitated the growth of towns, but it also meant that the migration might not be permanent, and that urban-dwellers might retain village links and renew them in times of crisis. It also promoted a new degree of centralisation, making more real what had been largely symbolic claims.

Besides the villages and the great cities, there had always been a range of smaller towns, and their diversity increased: add to the centres of regional government and market towns of the past the mining towns of the nineteenth and twentieth centuries, the railway junctions, the resort towns. But in Southeast Asia 'the urban population is most clearly associated with the largest cities',[42] and that trend continued in the post-colonial phase. Then, indeed, the great cities became the focus of national aspiration as well, and there was a risk that the elite in the capital would, like the tourist, neglect the countryside.

Notes

1 Elson, *Village*, p. 4.
2 J. M. Gullick, *Indigenous Political Systems of Western Malaya*, London: Athlone, 1958, p. 130.
3 J. M. Gullick, *Malay Society in the Late Nineteenth Century*, Singapore: OUP, 1989, pp. 104–5.
4 q. R. Stubbs, *Hearts and Minds in Guerrilla Warfare*, Singapore: OUP, 1989, p. 102.
5 D. J. Duncanson, *Government and Revolution in Vietnam*, London: OUP, 1968, pp. 313–14.

6 Fisher, p. 608.
7 ibid., p. 336.
8 *North Borneo (Sabah) A Study in Settlement Geography*, Singapore: Eastern Universities P, 1965, p. 94.
9 Elson, *Village*, p. 4.
10 p. 5.
11 p. 5.
12 Gullick, *Malay Society*, p. 182.
13 q. ibid., pp. 183–4.
14 q. ibid., p. 185.
15 q. ibid., p. 185.
16 *Philippine Life in Town and Country*, NY and London: Putnam, 1905, p. 42.
17 p. 67.
18 *Capitalists*, p. 26.
19 q. T. McGee, *The Southeast Asian City*, London: Bell, 1967, p. 31.
20 J. Kathirithamby-Wells, 'The Islamic City … ', MAS, 20, 2 (April 1986), p. 335.
21 q. Robert Nicholl, *European Sources for the History of Brunei*, Bandar Seri Begawan, 1990, p. 11.
22 q. G. Saunders, *A History of Brunei*, KL: OUP, 1994, p. 46.
23 P. Blundell [pseud.], *The City of Many Waters*, London: Arrowsmith, 1923, p. 68.
24 q. N. Saleeby, *The History of Sulu*, Manila, 1908, p. 97.
25 *Diary*, p. 102.
26 *The Sulu Archipelago and its People*, NY: World Book Co., 1923, p. 4.
27 *Revolt in Mindanao*, KL: OUP, 1980, p. 218.
28 McGee, p. 51.
29 q. Turnbull, p. 1.
30 *Hikayat Abdullah*, p. 162.
31 *A Decade in Borneo*, London: Hutchinson, 1894, p. 136.
32 *Rickshaw Coolie*, Singapore: OUP, 1986, p. 213.
33 *For Fear of Weeping*, London: McGibbon and Kee, 1950, p. 13.
34 McGee, p. 37.
35 pp. 37–8.
36 Minxhosi Yoner, in *They Have Been in North Viet Nam*, Hanoi: FLPH, p. 22.
37 Bedrich Kacirek, in ibid., p. 40.
38 FEER, 13 April 1995.
39 *Two Cities*, London: Cape/Picador, 1992/4, p. 100.
40 McGee, p. 74.
41 Patrick Guinness, *Harmony and Hierarchy in a Javanese Kampung*, Singapore: OUP, 1986, p. 170.
42 q. McGee, p. 55.

Part Three

Societies and Commitments

This part of the book is concerned with social and political structures: the organisation of the various types of state that have existed in Southeast Asia; the human relationships, between patrons and clients, among members of associations; the mobilisation and application of force, in particular through armies; religion; and education.

It is divided by topic, but also uses chronological, country-by-country, and comparative approaches.

The Philippines, Maluku, Java, and Dai Viet, sixteenth, seventeenth, and eighteenth centuries CE

State and Society

Pre-colonial, non-colonial, colonial, and post-colonial states shared a number of strategies, though they deployed them in different ways, and their effectiveness varied. Burma, Vietnam, and Mataram may be compared. Mataram may also be compared with Brunei, and Brunei with the peninsular sultanates and with Sulu. The Spanish state in the Philippines may be compared with a non-colonial state, and the Siamese state with a colonial one.

State formation and state-building are not the same, Jim Schiller has suggested. State-building is a directed activity, designed to increase the power of the state by securing for it more resources, material or spiritual, or reducing the power of its opponents. State formation he sees as the consequence of such activities, but also of the activities and responses of others, 'capricious outcomes' rather than intended results.[1] He is writing of contemporary Indonesia, but the concepts are useful in considering Southeast Asia over a much longer period, and indeed in comparing it with other parts of the world.

That requires drawing out two implications. First, it may be argued that over a period of time the two processes interact. A ruler, for example, will adjust attempts at state-building according to the changes that have been brought about in the process of state formation, and the history of the state will become a series of interactions between the two processes, more or less successful. Second, it may be useful to consider the range of options available for the building of states, and to assess to what extent they have been available, or been seen to be available, in different places and at different times.

One consequence of this is to produce a perhaps rather crude general schema, which may nevertheless have a particular value for discussing a region comprising several states and for facilitating a comparative approach within and beyond it. Second, it becomes feasible to adopt a very inclusive definition of the state, and not to confine the application of the word to what we now consider the state has become: indeed it continues to change. That does not mean that there is a progression through which states have to pass, nor that they ultimately emerge in a similar

form. What it does mean, however, is that we can both depict the nature of a particular state and consider in what measure it represents a type of state. That is to be
done by considering the objectives of the state, the resources it has available, and the
uses it makes of them.

In this taxonomy it is possible to include both the rudimentary and the sophisticated, the ancient and the modern. It is possible, too, to include the colonial and the
post-colonial, and to point to their similarities and contrasts. Some states had
resources that were not available to others, potential that those could not release or
could not contain. Some could use, borrow, or transform features of others.

Ronald Robinson and John Gallagher stressed that empire had depended, not
upon force alone, but upon securing collaborators among those it ruled. In this,
however, empires were not after all peculiar. No state has survived merely on the
possession of force. All have needed some other means of securing the support of
the people whom the state purports in some way to comprise. Not all have been able
to use the same means. Some states have been better endowed than other states.
Sometimes some of the means that have been used have conflicted with others.
Sometimes their usefulness erodes with time. Their degree of success may vary, of
course, according to the ends they have set themselves. Their ability to adapt to
'capricious outcomes' may also vary.

One means of binding together state and people that has been particularly strong
in Southeast Asia has been the tie between the patron and client. For most of its history, the region has generally been sparsely populated, and states have tended to
count their strength by population rather than by territorial possession. A monarch
might lay claim to the most absolute power, but in fact would often be no more than
primus inter pares, forever building up a series of patron–client relationships
designed to make his power more real, but always at a cost. Marriage ties were a
favoured device. The distribution of honours was another.

Above all, the monarch needed to be able to reward and win support by distributing wealth, or the capacity to accumulate wealth, like the *anugraha* (favours)
that the ruler of Sri Vijaya bestowed on his supporters.[2] This was the nature of
what Max Weber called the patrimonial state, which has proved a most useful concept in Southeast Asian history. Lacking coercive capacity, the state won allegiance
by distributing fiefs and benefices in return for tribute and loyalty. Centralising
what resources the state had available was clearly important, increasing them, too,
if that were possible. The attempt to capitalise on new resources, if they did
become available, might, however, produce a new imbalance of power, even a
revolt. The main task for much of the history of these states was in fact to guard
against the erosion of those resources and to prevent the emergence of over-
mighty subjects. Spies and informers had an essential role. Weber indeed argued
that patrimonialism worked against production-oriented capitalism. It gave
'free rein to the enrichment of the ruler himself, the court officials, favourites,

governors, mandarins, tax collectors, influence peddlers, and the great merchants and financiers who function as tax farmers, purveyors and creditors'. The ruler's favour created wealth and destroyed it.[3]

Bureaucracy is another means of sustaining the state. It did not necessarily do this in ways that are familiar in the late-twentieth-century West: it might not be actively exerting the state's authority and carrying out its legislation. Indeed it might not be primarily an administrative tool at all, but rather another means of conferring honour and status. It was certainly another means of conferring power over people, and thus offered the prospect of building up patron–client relationships. It was likely, however, to give the ruler rather more control than the patrimonial system. It might, for example, be more open to talent or choice than to the claims of heredity. But it would have its drawbacks, whether or not it was penetrated itself by patron–client or familial obligations. It would tend to take on a corporate status and to encompass the ruler, as well as his subjects, by rules and regulations. Prescribed hierarchy, rigid etiquette, and sumptuary regulations were indeed part of the repertoire of the state. But, generally accepting and endorsing them, rulers might also react by arbitrariness, designed not simply to deal with particular cases, but to demonstrate and sustain their independence of the monster they had created.

In the mandala system Southeast Asian states characteristically mixed these two systems in so far as they were in any case distinct. Within a core part of the realm the ruler might be supported by a bureaucracy; within a second circle by patrimonial relationships; and beyond, shading off into 'inter-state' relationships, by looser ties of vassalage, backed up by occasional displays of force. What was essential in the core and in the patrimonial area was, of course, the link with the population at large, rural and urban. Crucial in the formal as well as the patron–client patterns were the intermediary authorities and their relationships with the tribal or village headman. Often they were ambivalent, but so, too, were the relationships of headman and villagers. The type of the Javanese *jago* (fighting cock) is not peculiar to Java: at one moment bullies who might serve the powers-that-be, at another outlaws who could get away with it, even Robin Hoods. The 'strong men' in the Kedah villages of the early twentieth century, or the *nakleng* in rural Siam, were not dissimilar.[4]

The colonial state adopted a different mixture. It tended to rely more on bureaucracy, and on a more active form of bureaucracy. It was less able to utilise patron–client relationships at the top level, at least in their traditional forms, though British Residents in Malaya might behave like 'squires'.[5] It had to rely all the more on other means of gaining support and compliance. Generally, however, it utilised traditional relationships at lower levels in the hierarchy, though the patron–client patterns came under pressure as the economy was modernised and bureaucratic demands increased. The position of the village headman became still more uncomfortable, though sometimes still more profitable. 'The local elite … is a problematic element in any colonial system', as Jeremy Beckett puts it.

To the extent that it controls the lower orders it may be either an ally of the regime or its enemy. And to the extent that it exploits them it may be either a partner or a competitor. Whichever course it follows there are dangers. If it is defiant it risks destruction, and at the very least jeopardizes the protection given by its masters. If it is compliant it may jeopardize its legitimacy among the common folk.[6]

Pre-colonial and colonial states were similar in other ways. One was the importance attached, as might be expected in a region where for the most part the population was scanty, to corvée labour. Another was the emphasis on indirect taxation. Many traditional rulers engaged directly in commerce, as, of course, did the Portuguese king, the European East India companies, and the Dutch colonial regime, and to a lesser extent that of the Spaniards, too. They also raised funds by creating monopolies and tax-farms. Those became the prime source of colonial revenues, and of the revenues of Chulalongkorn's Siam. 'The colonial regime in Java itself became addicted to opium.'[7] In the Federated Malay States the British needed money to pay allowances to the Malay rulers and build infrastructure, but their administration consisted of a handful of British officials, Asian clerks, and police. The farmer bore the cost of the tax system and policed it,[8] though it also furnished him with capital.

In another way pre-colonial and colonial states deeply contrasted. The former normally drew upon religious sanctions, with the ruler presenting himself in some degree as god-like or as the protector and guarantor of the faith, even if converted to Islam retaining something of the sacred. Again that had drawbacks as well as advantages. The ruler might not live up to the standards his exemplary and intermediary role required, and what was a source of strength could become a source of weakness. A religious order might on the other hand become over-mighty subjects, challenging the ruler to control or reform or discipline them, at the risk of undermining their value as guarantors of the state itself. The practice and the problems were not unfamiliar in the West, and the relationship of state and church indeed continued to be an issue in the twentieth century. In general, however, the colonial state was in no position to draw upon religious sanctions. The major exception was, of course, the Philippines state created by the Spaniards, and that faced problems not dissimilar to those faced by non-colonial states: it relied upon the religious orders and could not control them. For most colonial states the religious factor was quite different: they could not make it a source of support, and the most they might hope to do was to avoid making it a source of opposition. 'Prestige' was a kind of substitute.

Magic and ceremony are another resource of states, old and new, Western and Southeast Asian. Clifford Geertz wrote of the 'theatre state' in Bali. But, as H. Schulte Nordholt suggests, there is a risk that we are led to see the Balinese king as an icon, rather than 'a charismatic leader of flesh and blood who had to overcome constant threats to his position'.[9] The idea that spectacle was not for the state but what the state was for would have seemed odd to Louis XIV, even to Lully. It would, as Merle

Ricklefs suggests, have seemed odd, too, to the courtiers of Sultan Agung or Mangkubumi, 'who thought that the state was for getting rich and powerful while avoiding enemy plots and treasons'.[10]

The colonial state—though not surprisingly perhaps more in India than elsewhere—gave great attention to proper form and ceremony. In Burma it attempted to inculcate the 'imperial idea'. But that was no substitute, say, for the *pusaka* or treasures of the Southeast Asian monarchs, to which rebels paid the tribute of imitation, their crowns, umbrellas, daggers, gongs, drums, cannon, and insignia, or for their *silsilah* or genealogies. The *daulat* of the Sultan of Melaka could not be taken over by the Portuguese, though they could take over his city.[11] It continued to affirm a bond between the successor rulers of Johore and Riau-Lingga and their subjects. Yet, if colonial states did not possess magic, the coronation of their monarchs at home was full of symbolism, and the symbolism not without purpose.

States exist not only in themselves but in relation to other states. From that, too, they may both draw advantage and suffer disadvantage. Successful defence or successful invasion preserves or enhances a state's power, both in terms of prestige and resources, and it was characteristic that in traditional Southeast Asia those resources would be likely to include captives who would become a useful source of support for the state, generally without any sense of 'national' or 'ethnic' tension. A relationship with a larger state could be turned to account, even though it might be at odds with the universalistic pretensions of the ruler: in return for tribute, the state might receive support, both in terms of prestige and in terms of trade goods that could be used to consolidate the relationships with clients and vassals.

A colonial state had a different relationship with the outside world. It might hope to receive support from a distant metropolis, in particular of course by sea, or from another colonial possession within Asia. That was, once more, a strength, but also a weakness. Support was remote and uncertain, dependent, too, on the relationship with other outside powers. Nor could the triumphs of the colonial state, often outside the region anyway, be expected to win it the support a victory might bring a monarch with religious or universalistic claims, who might carry off a sacred image or a white elephant. The colonial state would at best secure the rather more negative benefit of adding to its prestige. It would demonstrate its strength and thus the impracticality of challenging its power.

Violence is, of course, another adjunct of state power. A state seeks, if not to monopolise its use, to enjoy the most sophisticated means of applying it. Its aim is, of course, to employ it sparingly but effectively, and thus in conjunction with the other means at its disposal. The colonial powers came to enjoy a dominance at sea which was, of course, particularly supportive in the archipelago, but their superiority on land was less evident. Technologically, the military equipment and armaments of the Europeans, if superior on their arrival in Southeast Asia, only became more so, particularly in the course of the nineteenth century when, driven by their own rivalry, the Western powers turned to account the potential of their industrial revolution.

Their drill and organisation were also superior, so that in formal struggles they were likely to have the advantage. In less formal struggles, however, that was much less likely to be the case, one reason, indeed, why they preferred the limited but, as they hoped, decisive use of force. Guerrilla struggles were not, of course, peculiar to colonial regimes in Southeast Asia or elsewhere, but it may be that they were especially challenging because it was more difficult for the colonial regimes to constitute the political context without which the military struggle was hard to win. Guerrillas might, by contrast, be headed by a prince or by a figure with traditional charisma.

Another comparison may be made. Colonial armies were not recruited in the metropolis alone: they relied in substantial part on recruitment in Asia, drawing particularly on minority elements or on foreigners. The strategy seems an obvious illustration of classic imperialist divide-and-rule. Yet there were pre-colonial precedents. Kings of Burma made loyal soldiers of their 'foreign' prisoners, while the rulers of Mataram wanted to use Balinese or Bugis. A professional army might, after all, become too bureaucratised to be loyal, and the ruler too dependent on those who were supposed to defend him. The use of mercenaries was a familiar practice in Europe before national armies became dominant in the nineteenth century, and praetorian guards are still common to every kind of personal regime.

It is worth comparing pre-colonial and colonial states in another way. Unable readily to generate additional resources of power, the traditional state was likely, as Schiller suggests,[12] to devote its main energies to survival, to hanging on to power, and to maintaining the checks and balances that required. One condition of its survival was that it did not attempt to do too much. Excessive burdens on its subjects, undue breaches of custom, dislocating the links between the village and the superstructure: those might bring about the fall of the regime. The position for colonial powers was not entirely dissimilar. Too interventionist an approach to government might undermine the relationships on which it so largely depended. They were all aware, though the weaker among them perhaps more than the others, that their security again depended on limiting their objectives. 'Peace and order' and the maintenance of *adat* (custom) the Dutch sought to combine with the expansion of the cultivation system under van den Bosch and his successors.

Pre-colonial regimes fell because they were challenged from within or from outside or both. The same was true of the colonial regimes. From outside they were challenged by Japan, which had replaced a regime deeply oriented to the maintenance of the status quo by one deeply determined on change at home and on abandoning seclusion from the rest of the world. The colonial regimes were also challenged within their Southeast Asian dominions because they themselves, and the increasing demands of the new international order, had brought about changes that made it impossible to maintain the status quo. Their opponents sought to reconstitute the state on a 'national' basis. The colonial powers attempted a series of adjustments, some still recognisably devices from the traditional repertoire, some more novel. The Japanese invaders made a new approach still more necessary. The making of puppets and the search for partners had domestic as well as foreign aspects.

It was indeed difficult for the colonial state to change the pattern of its internal relationships. Those employed a range of devices, but were essentially based on acquiring collaborators, and selectively applying force to create and sustain the relationship. With some the state was more impatient than with others, and some were more compliant than others. A range of answers to the colonial challenge was, after all, possible: compromise, resistance, surrender and a deal after resistance, surrender without resistance and a better deal. The last was the choice of Johore in 1914. 'It is best to surrender instantly to overwhelming odds', as Allen concludes, 'and hope stealthily to recuperate lost advantages during the ensuing euphoria'.[13] The extent to which a state had to unravel also varied. In Johore the ruler was retained, in Burma displaced. Locating collaborators in the social structure was also a differentiated task: the emperor in Annam, social climbers in Cochin-China. Economic and social change threatened the relationships established, since new elite elements emerged, borrowing from Europe a new ideology, but laying claim to a traditional inheritance as well. Winning its collaboration was not necessarily impossible, but it would involve casting the existing elite aside. Such a change any government, but perhaps especially a colonial government, might hesitate to undertake. Could it risk rejecting old collaborators in search of new? or was it better to stick with the tried and relatively true? There was a risk of losing the one without gaining the other.

The answers also depended on the nature of the new elite and its objectives. Its emergence owed something to the modernisation of colonial society through the operation of economic forces and to the provision by government or other agencies of education as an aid to general efficiency but also an avenue of personal advancement. Even the most conservative of colonial states could not avoid these changes. It might, however, survive if it could come to terms with them. A moderate new elite, willing to work with the colonial power rather than overthrow it, could offer the colonial state new opportunities, if it could realise them. They might not be long-term. The new deal, if reached, might be predicated on a further increase in power-sharing, even on the prospect of ultimately gaining political independence, so that all that remained of the colonial state was the borders it created, and, it might be hoped, a new partnership. Moderates, however, might not be a majority among the new elite, and if they failed, they would be displaced by others less complaisant.

In a sense two attempts at state formation were to compete. In the competition, of course, much depended on the allegiance of the people as a whole. They, too, had been affected by the changes that had affected the elite. Government became more interventionist; contacts with the international market prompted economic change. The custom that both bound and supported the peasants was disrupted, and the towns both grew and changed their nature. Could the politicisation of either be avoided? if not, how could it be shaped, and by whom? Even though they maintained a monopoly of organised armed force, and increased the use of spies, informers, censorship, deportation, and exile, the colonial states could not prevent the penetration and spread of new ideas, which the improved communications both with the outside world and within the colonial state tended to encourage.

It is hard in any case to escape the conclusion that the colonial state could not survive, and that the phase of competition was a phase of transition. Though able in some measure to modernise, the colonial state was still oriented to the status quo, and it was certainly unable to focus the loyalty or mobilise the people in the ways that a nation-state could. The Japanese invasion made the transition yet more certain, shorter, and more violent. The overthrow of the colonial regimes, and the involvement in the expansive world economy of the postwar period, opened the way to far greater changes in Southeast Asia in every field of human endeavour. Yet old patterns persisted, sometimes in new forms. Marshal Sarit revived the plough ceremony. 'On the first occasion the bulls, frightened by enormous crowds, broke loose and the auspicious plough had to be drawn by government officials.'[14]

Though the independent regimes that were established were able to build on the new loyalties in a way that the colonial state could not, and were able, too, to draw on economic resources on an altogether new scale, they yet still drew on the old repertoires of power. It was now possible, indeed necessary, to have a national army, though it might still be difficult to control. A bureaucracy was likely to be extended, not only because the role of the state itself extended, but because it offered opportunities for patronage. In some respects, indeed, patrimonialism re-emerged with new opportunities, for the vast expansion of international trade and investment greatly increased the resource available to the new governing elites and their potential for winning clients. What was less certain was the fate of the democratic institutions that colonial powers had sought more or less reluctantly to establish in their later years, in part as a means of attempting to win over the emerging elite, in part as a means of justifying the continuance, at least for a period, of colonial rule.

Pagan and after

Michael Aung-Thwin has entitled his account of Pagan 'the origins of modern Burma', and clearly some of its patterns endured. The great unifier was Aniruddha (1044–77), but the reign of Narapati Cansu (1173–1210) and his successor Natonmya (1200–34) marked the height of Pagan's development. Its structure included a hereditary royal family; a semi-bureaucracy; a populace, partly bonded, partly exempt; a united Buddhist church, its head appointed by the king; and a uniform judicial system. Aung-Thwin describes it as a conical structure, with horizontal categories of difference and vertical links. The layers included the court and the royal family; the upper and lower officials, including township and district heads, probably hereditary, but appointed; and the commoners. The links were at once formal and clientelistic. The commoners included *asan* or *athi*, the unbonded; *kyun*, those bonded to private individuals; *hpaya kyun*, those commended to religious institutions; and *kyun-taw*, those attached to the crown itself, called *ahmudan* from the mid-fourteenth century. Land was granted at the pleasure of the king, or irrevocably, but its value was realised only by the service of the *kyun*. Groups with similar functions resided in particular villages or in sections of towns named after their craft. The priority was on order and on hierarchy.

The king drew strength from Pyu traditions and from Mon scholars and above all from Theravada Buddhism. The term *cakkavattin* was used for great unifiers, and the concept of *dhammaraja,* creator of political and moral order, was deployed to justify the creation of a new dynasty. The king was the protector and benefactor of Buddhism. But what was the strength of the monarchy, Aung-Thwin argues, was also its downfall. Over time, change occurred, with which it was difficult to deal. The building of temples made merit for individuals, stimulated economic activity, and promoted the demographic and material basis of the state. But grants to the sangha (the order of monks) were irrevocable, and increasingly the state lost control of irrigated land and people. By the end of the Pagan period perhaps 63 per cent of the irrigated land had thus become tax-exempt, and the people *hpaya kyun.* The king could act only by reforming the sangha, but there were limits to what that could effect, since it performed an essential legitimating function. Pagan was thus weakened when it faced the new Yuan dynasty in China, though it did not collapse.

According to Lieberman,[15] the first Taung-ngu kings followed the Pagan pattern, but were based not on the traditional dry zone, where a ruler could draw on the Shans, but on the delta, where a ruler could draw on the expanding international commerce and on Portuguese mercenaries. They maintained direct rule over a core area, other parts were held as appanage, and beyond that lay ethnic vassal principalities. The main sub-centres were ruled by *bayin,* relatives of the king, but tending nevertheless to compete with him. What brought the kingdom down, however, was its attempt at maintaining an over-extended empire, including Chiengmai and Ayudhya. That strained the resources of the delta area, despite the settlement of captives there, and other areas withdrew their support. Rebellion against Nan-da-bayin was justified by *acaravipatti,* failure of duty.

The restored Taung-ngu brought the capital back to the heartland. While again settling deportees near the capital, they took steps to counter the disintegration that the previous regime had suffered. Those involved centralisation and bureaucratisation, both designed, of course, to ensure control over the *ahmudan,* those who owed crown service, and the *athi,* those who did not. Relatives of the king now had to live in the capital, and administer their appanages through agents, and under Anauk-hpet-lun more non-royal men were appointed *myo-wun* or governor. Plural appointments were made to the *hlutdaw* (council), where collegial decision-making was designed to inhibit powerful individuals, and there were two subordinate hierarchies, territorial and departmental, checking and overlapping, and spies a-plenty. But, as with earlier systems, virtues were also drawbacks.

The court and its officials became the focus of politics, and ministerial factions reached out into the countryside in patronage networks, gentry and provincial officials allying with one court faction or another for appointments and support for extortionate taxation schemes, while 'chains of patron–client clusters extended all the way ... to lowly headmen—and indeed to cultivators on the subvillage level'. [16] This increased the pressure the state exerted on the nuclear area and prompted many to become *kyun*, exempt from royal tax and service obligations, which in turn tended to lead to further pressure. Factionalism also prevented the emergence of strong rulers who could check these trends. The last Taung-ngu king, an English visitor wrote, was entirely ruled by ministers 'without any other knowledge but a base private Interest, which makes the Country in general wish for a change, because every petty Governour of Towns or Cities, if he can but satisfy the Minister at Court, can at his pleasure oppress the people under him, without any fear of Punishment'.[17] Weakness at the centre also led to loss of control over the periphery, over Chiengmai and over the Shan saw-bwas in the 1720s and 1730s. The revolt in Pegu thus swept away the remnants of the Taung-ngu state in 1751–52.

The Kon-baung state, created by Alaung-hpaya and his successors, failed to avoid the drawbacks the previous kingdoms had faced, the abuse of local office and the erosion of central revenue and services. One traditional device, again employed, was to boost the crown service population in the core area. That was an objective of the periodic raids into Manipur, and also of the intervention in Arakan, not previously a vassal state, in 1784–85. Perhaps as many as 35 per cent of the service people in the capital area were non-Burman. The deportations from Arakan were, however, more or less the last. Subsequent campaigns against the Thais depleted rather than added to the state's manpower resources, and Bodaw-hpaya's irrigation and temple-building projects over-exploited the resources at the state's disposal.

Again one answer was to enter debt bondage or client relationships with members of the royal family or high officials, who thus enhanced their political position; another, to follow the semi-respectable bandit-chiefs. Under the *hlutdaw* of the Kon-baung kings were some fifty departments, many of them concerned with administering the crown demesne and the *ahmudan*, apparently divided into nine *taiks* covering 496 villages. The *athi* were more the responsibility of the territorial authorities. They included the *myo-wun*, some of whom were super-*wun*, those of Martaban, Taung-ngu, Prome, Hanthawadi (including Rangoon), and after its annexation, Arakan. Their tasks were to collect taxes, transmit the crown's share, adjudicate cases, and assist the crown service groups in the area in performing their functions, and a crown representative, *na-khan*, was included in the *myo* administration. Intermediary between the appointed *myo* officials and the village headmen were the hereditary *myo-thu-gyi*, who settled the corvée demands and kept records. At the village level the headmen were hereditary *thugyi* or *myei-daing*. As under the restored Taung-ngu, the non-hereditary appanage-holders, *myo-za*, exercised the crown's powers, but were generally not permitted to live in the district concerned.

Authority was again characteristically incomplete and overlapping, the objective being to avoid undue concentrations of power that might challenge the crown. But all this did not suffice to preserve the status quo. The demands the crown itself made—in part in order to pursue its conflicts with other kingdoms, in part to make merit—were themselves a source of change. By 1820 the crown had lost the service of perhaps 25 per cent of its *ahmudan* and *athi* population compared to that of 1783. Those escaping crown service or tax-burdens boosted the following of appointed officials—a *myo-wun* of Hanthawadi had 5000 followers—while hereditary officials were in a strong position to accumulate land and tenants. Appointment to higher officialdom was by influence, not by examination. The object of office was wealth and following, and the route was faction, the performance of duties being neither so active nor so inactive as to attract the negative attention of the king. The ultimate focus of faction politics was the succession. There, as elsewhere, primogeniture might limit dispute at the price of incompetence. Alaung-hpaya favoured collateral inheritance, but that enhanced conflict, and the potential for intervention from outside that succession disputes offered.

Like their predecessors, the Kon-baung kings developed the style of a universal monarch. Bodaw-hpaya went further: he saw himself as the Buddha Metteyya, ready to propound a new teaching, though he failed to persuade the leading monks. The sangha was by this time treated virtually as another crown service group. In 1787 Bodaw-hpaya had appointed his preceptor as *tha-thana-baing* or chief of religious affairs, and made him responsible for doctrinal instruction and discipline.

Mindon sought to preserve the diminished state from the British and to strengthen it by centralisation and better revenue collection. But that required additional patronage, so as 'to buy off political discontent from officials who were losing their independent sources of income'.[18] The loss of trade revenues from the south meant that other sources were needed, one being timber concessions mainly to British firms. That created new pressures on the centre: concessionaires wanted reduced rates; and political opponents of the current ministers could always accuse them of selling out the country's interests to foreigners. More traditional problems also faced Mindon and Thibaw: control of local centres of power, for example, and of the sangha.

Under the British administration there could, of course, be no relationship between ruler and sangha of the type that had both helped and hindered the monarchy. The approach differed in other ways, too. While the monarchs had relied to a substantial extent on captured aliens to counter the erosion of their power, the British came to Burma with the resources of their Indian empire, and continued to rely largely upon them. They also came to Burma with their Indian experience in mind, and both factors extended the alterations that the change of ruler was bound to bring. Moreover, they acquired Burma piecemeal, taking first those areas where the traditional Burman system was less fully established. The British in Tenasserim and later in Pegu used appointed *taikthugyi* rather than *myo-thu-gyi*, increasingly on a territorial basis, while at the village level after 1876 the *kyedangyi* or largest taxpayer fulfilled the thankless task of man of all work. In Upper Burma, the *myo-thu-gyi* had been a much stronger social force. But of that the British had no experience, and many engaged in resistance or rebellion. Influenced by his Indian background, Commissioner Crosthwaite argued that they were usurpers of village power. In 1888 it was decided, partly as a pacification measure, that the deputy commissioners should designate a headman for each of Burma's 17 000 or 18 000 villages, influential citizens vested with the powers of tax collectors, police officers, and petty magistrates. The system was consolidated by the Village Act of 1907. 'We have no art in our government', said Donald Smeaton, the Financial Commissioner. '... The result ... is ... that the reforms we endeavour to introduce strike no real root.'[19]

The disintegration of the old pattern was completed at the higher level by the development of the bureaucracy and its increasingly specialised agencies, and then by the constitutional experiments of the 1920s and 1930s. Those involved an attempt to share power between the British administration and a partially democratised constitutional system. For that Burma offered no precedent, though India did. But its chances of success were reduced by the conclusion that, as a result, it had to be introduced bit-by-bit, for a potential government has to be able to campaign on the basis of a policy it can plan to implement. The alternative was to rely on corruption, patronage, and paramilitary violence. For those there was plenty of precedent. The Japanese introduced an authoritarian model, with Ba Maw as *adipadi*, while postwar the British determined to renew the effort to create multi-party democracy.

Emperors, mandarins, notables, and Frenchmen

Wresting independence from China in the tenth century, the Vietnamese state was at once embroiled in a struggle between the new central authority and local chiefs. The Former Le dynasty relied initially on Buddhist monks and scholars, but they were strong enough to overthrow it in 1009 and establish the Ly. This dynasty, and the succeeding Tran, sought to set up a mandarin system on the Chinese model, designed to recruit the talented, rather than merely the rich and powerful, though poor boys could make good only with support from a rich family or a village. The first examinations were held in 1075. Establishing and maintaining the integrity of the system over against 'feudal' practices required continued effort. In 1236 the Tran drew up salary schedules and redefined the bureaucratic hierarchy with that objective in mind. The extent to which Dai Viet was a Confucian state was, however, exaggerated by later dynasties and by French scholars. The Ly drew on every resource to sustain their government: 'personal leadership in war, law, and religion, ... more elaborate Court protocol, ... tapping the country's economic resources, and, with the aid of a fledgling bureaucracy, ... seeking to consolidate and even enlarge the territory they had inherited'.[20] Under the impact of the Mongol invasions, the bureaucratic innovations of the Tran faded away. Ho Quy Ly reinstated classical examinations after the Cham invasions of the 1380s, but family and clan loyalty remained a feature of the regime. John Whitmore pictures a royal clan and aristocracy that patronised Confucian studies among others, 'and selected its favorites and its most trustworthy servants to run the state'.[21]

Le Loi's new dynasty was fairly haphazard at first, but, as Nola Cooke puts it, Le Thanh-tong's reforms were 'one of the great watersheds' in Vietnamese history:[22] their object was to expand and consolidate countrywide a loyal elite, its main roots in the central provinces ringing the Red River plains. He offered opportunity to literati families fostered by Neo-Confucianism during the Ming occupation, countering the clannish military groups from Thanh-hoa that had dominated since its overthrow, but excluded active collaborators. In 1462 he revived the examination system; in 1465 he issued regulations restricting Buddhism, Taoism, diviners, and sorcerers; in 1466 he revamped the provincial administration. Perhaps his 'restoration' was too radical and contributed to the dynasty's collapse and the chaos that followed. Some joined the Mac because they were excluded from the new bureaucratic system: Mac Dang Dung himself came from a family compromised by active collaboration with the Ming. Revolts against the Le in the early sixteenth century were also supported by adherents of Buddhism and customary practices.

The Restored Le saw first a renewal of the dominance of the military clans under the Trinh. But as the war with the Nguyen dragged on, the Trinh again looked to literati from the central plains, though they now came from a more contracted area round Hanoi, and there was tension between established literati families who had served the Mac and wished to re-enter the ruling class, and 'southern' military families.[23] Diversified in its sources of power, the Trinh fostered Buddhism and allowed Christianity. The Nguyen regime was more 'Southeast Asian' still. 'Dang-trong's organization and ethos resembled more closely the decentralized, spiritually eclectic Ly and aristocratic Buddhist Tran than it ever did the more Confucian, sinicized Le state, even as modified under the Trinh.'[24] It was based in less sinicised parts of Vietnam. Indeed Buddhism was effectively the state religion: the first act that asserted Nguyen sovereignty in the south was Nguyen Hoang's construction of the Thien Mu pagoda at Hué in 1601.

The Nguyen dynasty's examination system was always to be small-scale. Other routes to mandarin status were more important: military service, inheritance, patronage. Only in the 1830s—when Minh-mang also suppressed the remnants of Cham autonomy—did southern participation begin to rise, and then powerholders mainly from Hué and neighbouring provinces subverted the examination system so as to produce graduates from the Nguyen heartland. The dynasty did not win the loyalty of the northern literati, and Le restorationism resurged. 'In the 1860s, external assaults combined with internal uprisings to send Bac-ky [Tonkin] slowly sliding into the endemic disorder that would so cripple the kingdom's response to the protracted French colonial crisis.'[25]

The French retained the monarchy in Annam, its task 'that of confining the transformation of minds within the limits of prudence and of abating opposition through its words or its deeds, whenever the colonial power deemed it useful'.[26] They hoped it would shore up their protectorate. They wanted a pliant monarch, especially in view of the anti-French revolt in Cambodia in 1884 and of the Can-vuong movement in Vietnam. But they left the monarchy so little power that its collaboration could not be useful. French over-emphasis on its 'Confucian' character only further weakened it. It ignored other traditions of the Vietnamese king: a protector figure, 'part rebel, part guardian of agricultural fertility, and part cultural innovator',[27] less Sinic than Southeast Asian. The postwar 'head of state', Bao Dai, could draw on neither source.

In the Confucianist pattern—though it was honoured in the breach as well as the observance—central government and the village were linked through the *tong* or canton, comprised of two to five villages. The canton chiefs were thus the brokers and mediators between government and village. They were selected by district or prefectural mandarins from lists submitted by the relevant villages. If they served satisfactorily for three years, they could become low-grade mandarins, a device for integrating village and government. Again the village had a tutelary deity, but its guardianship had to be authenticated by an imperial certificate. The village itself was administered by a council of notables, delegating authority to a committee of village officials or *huong chuc,* headed by the village chief, *ly-troung,* the link with the *tong* (canton) officers, likely to be himself a degree-holder or self-made literatus.

In Burma the first acquisitions of the British were in the south, where Burman authority was weaker and less strongly rooted in tradition. The first acquisitions of the French in Vietnam were comparable, and in fact what they called 'Cochinchine' was the only part of Indo-China that was formerly made a colony. The principal mandarins in any case left: few collaborated with the French. French inspectors, representing the governor in the twenty-two arrondissements, relied on interpreters, often missionary-trained, men like Paulus Huynh Tinh Cua and Petrus Truong Vinh Ky. By the late 1870s France had established schools that produced trained Vietnamese, and from 1881 lower-echelon bureaucratic posts were available to them. It was a new elite, and increasingly its 'mandarins' came from the wealthy class that emerged in the colony.

In Tonkin and Annam the administration was initially left more intact than it was in Upper Burma, but it eroded over time. In Annam new agencies were grafted on to the imperial government, and placed under the jurisdiction of the French resident. In Tonkin colonial authority was even more open. In 1886 the emperor delegated all authority to a viceroy, the *kinh luoc,* who was responsible to the emperor and the Résident Supérieur. In 1897, two years after the creation of the Federated Malay States, Governor-General Doumer decided to implement the union of French Indo-China of 1887. The Union government took over and standardised public services, such as civil affairs, education, health, public works, and communications, funded by the revenue of state monopolies, including opium, bought from the Hmong. The *kinh luoc* was abolished, and each of the five divisions had its lieutenant-governor or Résident Supérieur, heading an administration funded by land and head taxes.

Unlike those in the south, northern mandarins could not retreat, and many collaborated. Mandarin examinations were abolished in Tonkin only in 1915 and in

Annam in 1919. By that time young persons had begun to go direct to French schools. Only the existing elite had access to them, however, and some in any case withheld their children from what few there were. Recruitment thus became narrower than ever. 'Our principal support in Indo-China', a French officer wrote in 1945, 'can be found among intellectuals with jobs and of a certain age, attached to French culture; the mandarinal cadres whose destinies are linked with ours; Annamite Catholics; and retired military personnel who have remained loyal to us'.[28] The French stressed the Confucian patterns of the Vietnamese past and haphazardly sought to turn them to account. The regime they built up had in the event a far more heterogeneous backing, insofar as it had any. In some ways, however, that made it more like the previous dynastic regimes, not less.

Nor did links with the village replicate the idealised past. The mandarins were paralysed during the Nghe-an–Ha-tinh rebellion of 1931, prompting the French to unmediated violence. The corrupt village notables were a liability. Though they overemphasised the communist role in the rebellion, the French recognised, in the words of the Résident Supérieur, that 'revolutionary leaders will exploit us for the abuses for which the notables are responsible'.[29] As in other colonial regimes, the traditional authority of the notables was weakened by their assimilation to government. They were tempted to make up for that by exploiting their office. Aside from the opportunities for profit, the job was indeed unattractive. French taxation was higher; individual rather than communal assessment made it more inflexible; and the notables were held responsible for payment. '[T]he prosperous and honourable families show a certain repugnance for these perilous functions', the Lieut.-Governor of Cochin-China wrote in 1902, 'which thus too often fall into the hands of those who are unskilled, and even, sometimes, dishonest'.[30] In 1921 the French re-established communal elections in Tonkin, but the institution was too far gone to recover. In 1941 the French allowed selection by informal consensual authority, but nothing could arrest 'the deterioration in the relationship between villagers and notables'.[31]

Left in control for most of the Pacific War, the French changed their style, perhaps, not altogether paradoxically, in ways that paralleled those of the Japanese elsewhere: a kind of participation and mobilisation that borrowed from Vichy and tried to evoke an Indo-Chinese loyalism. Once they were dislodged, however, their chances of re-establishing their control, already threatened, were, as they recognised, quite limited. It was impossible to find collaborators sufficiently convincing that they could be sustained by a minimum of force. Nor was their regime in any position to restore the crucial relationship between state and village. That failing was to be shared by its American-sponsored successor.

Of it their opponents took advantage in the struggle that finally reunited Vietnam as a nation-state. The use the Viet Minh leadership made of communist ideology perhaps paralleled the use earlier rulers had made of Confucian precepts, partial imitation and innovative re-creation, rather than replication. Stephen O'Harrow suggests that in fifteenth-century Vietnam Confucianism was 'the framework within which events took place, but not necessarily the motor which propelled them'. Vietnam's Marxism was likewise no mere imitation of Soviet or Chinese models, but 'a tool to achieve its own ends'.[32]

Mataram and the archipelago

In the Malay archipelago the colonial and post-colonial states were based far less than the mainland states on the contours of the pre-colonial period. There were, however, some structural similarities, and those were not confined to Java. As might be expected, agrarian states there, like Mataram, possessed features not unlike those of the mainland states, but so, too, did maritime states, like Brunei. Some of these features, moreover, carried over into the colonial and post-colonial states, despite their different configuration.

Javanese kings were portrayed as god-on-earth—or, as Ricklefs puts it, 'all gods to all people'[33]—an identification that survived the advent of Islam; but in practice they had to resort to a repertoire of devices common in other patrimonial states: they demonstrated prowess, they balanced and manipulated, they used spies, they took hostages. They did not tour, but, if in their capital, officials had to attend their court, and sons of officials had to put in compulsory court service. Marriage was an important tie: 'the Javanese elite was tied into a crazy layered network of marriage ties, the main function of which seems to have been to reinforce other networks, patron–client networks for example, or to bind where no other bonds yet existed'.[34] There were other control devices, various punishments, for example: death, sacking, banishment, exile. The ruler was not strong militarily: the peasant levies readily melted away; and the professionals, paid with income from the land like the rest of the administrative elite, were too much part of that elite to be entirely loyal. Slaves and mercenaries, preferably from other countries, were all the more important. Nor did the ruler have a monopoly of force: his *bupati* had professional troops, too.

Like Burma, Mataram divided its lands into core appanage regions (*negara agung*) and outlying territories (*mancanegara*). The former were taxed directly for the court or retainers, or given out as appanage to family members and court officials, with the right to collect taxes (*pajeg*) and to levy some services and corvée. Administration was left to the *bekel* or agent, drawn from *lurah* (headman) families or landowning peasants. Outlying territories were governed by *bupati*, collecting taxes and providing levies for military and construction tasks, and being paid by tax-free rice-fields.[35]

Bureaucracy functioned as an administrative tool, but more important, Remmelink argues, was 'its power-generating and status-defining function'.[36] Holding office gave control over people and office was for the ruler to bestow. Like other bureaucracies, the *priyayi* of Mataram wanted rules and regulations, but an element of arbitrariness was important for the ruler if he was to maintain his authority. The inheritance of Amangkurat I's violent despotism was a help. Much of the manipulation of the elite, its factions, its competing patron–client networks, was left to the *patih* (vizier), so that the king could appear to be above it all, the just monarch. In trade, too, officials had to reckon with the king: he might keep revenue out of the hands of the elite by making over tax-farms to the Chinese. From the late eighteenth century, tax-farmers increasingly replaced *bekels*, and *bupati* used them, too: they were more distant and more exacting.

The basis of this state was the peasant and the village, defended by *adat* or custom, but tied to the men of power, *sekti,* by a network of patron–client relationships. King and official had both to respect and to break the *adat*. The ambivalent figure of the *jago* both resisted them and aided them.

In dealing with Mataram the VOC could take advantage of its weaknesses as well as of its own strengths. One weakness was military, and the VOC was in a position to prevent the ruler's using Bugis or Balinese mercenaries. Succession disputes were an occasion for intervention, and the VOC's assistance came at a high price. The cession of the coastal regencies to the VOC 'might be construed as a lease of gigantic proportion',[37] but it meant that the ruler lost control, and the Regents were backed by its power, given new economic opportunity, and tended to become hereditary. In the 1743 peace contract, the VOC made the appointment and dismissal of the *patih* and the main Regents dependent on its approval, and their appearance at court was no longer required.

Though remnants of the sultanate endured into the twentieth century—and the Sultan of Yogyakarta was a significant figure in the Republic—the VOC's intervention in Mataram increasingly came to be a take-over. Within the territories it thus effectively acquired, however, it retained some of the old structure, but it was modified. The Regent was now backed by the VOC and his position was no longer subject to the Sunan's manipulative whim, and the deliveries of produce the Company sought were a source of profit to both parties. The practices the VOC developed in the eighteenth century were made more systematic by its successor in the nineteenth. Under the culture system the same relationship was retained and indeed intensified. Van den Bosch not only affirmed the hereditary tenure of the Regents: he gave them a culture percentage. Indeed his system, though introducing new crops, relied on old practices. Despite the insistence on *adat*, however, the position of the *priyayi*, and more particularly their relationship with the villagers, changed. They became more closely identified with the government and were more exploitative, while the villagers increasingly turned to Islamic leaders, of whom the colonial regime could not make use. The role of the *priyayi* was indeed the source of much of the criticism of the cultivation system from the 1850s onwards. The state began to curb its abuses, and that effectively brought it to an end. The indigenous elite became 'a beautiful ornament'.[38]

In the 'liberal' period the Regents indeed lost part of their role, but the village headman retained his significance: the village was a source of labour in an economic system that mixed old forms with new capitalism, and dealing with the *lurah* was advantageous. In the 'Ethical' phase the Dutch bureaucracy expanded and made more direct contact with the peasants. However well-meaning its intentions, its actions tended to have an alienating effect. The disturbances of the late 1910s and 1920s were an argument for reviving *adat* and the influence of those whose authority rested upon it. Neither the Japanese regime, nor indeed the Republic, was able to do without the *lurah*.

At the higher levels, the Dutch wavered. Influenced by Ethicism, and apprehensive of Islam, they sought the support of a new *priyayi* elite, offering Western culture, even, in the Volksraad, a limited political participation, but they were nervous about political activity. By 1930 the intelligence organisation, the Algemeene Recherche Dienst, had 800 employees, mostly Indonesian, while the *pangreh praja* or native civil service hounded the nationalists. Officials like the Director of the Department of the Interior welcomed the government's reaction in the 1930s: 'The era in which the praises of Western democracy were to be sung and imitation had to be striven for is happily now past, now it is understood that … it is better to adapt the political superstructure to Eastern attitudes'.[39] In the Japanese phase, the *pangreh praja* were associated with the recrudescence of forced labour and inefficient rationing, and some were overthrown in the early months of the Republic.

In the Outer Islands, over which the Dutch asserted their control in the late nineteenth century, they again looked to traditional chiefs. 'In order to attain good feelings', Governor Goedhart wrote in 1928, 'it is first of all necessary that we remember that our power in Aceh, aside from the force of arms, depends in the main on the *uleebalangs*. Through them and with them we can win over the people. Without them in the long run we will accomplish nothing in Aceh.'[40] They, too, were to be destroyed in the revolution.

The Portuguese in East Timor also sought to build their influence on the chiefs. The chiefs of the *sukus* were incorporated into petty kingdoms, and their *regulos* or little kings coopted by the granting of titles. Those were dissolved, however, at the end of the nineteenth century, and the kingdoms gerrymandered into districts under direct colonial authority. Rebellion followed in 1911–13, and military forces were sent in from Mozambique. The *liurai* or traditional rulers became figureheads, and order was maintained by European and African troops and requisitioned Timorese.

Brunei

Most of the realms in the island region were not, like Mataram and its predecessors, based on fertile rice-growing regions. They were generally based on controlling the traffic between the *ulu* and the outside world through settlements at or near the river-mouths, and in some cases on the creation of entrepots that might cover a wider area. Yet, while the political challenge that faced them was unlike the challenge that faced the Javanese kingdoms, the essential structure of the realms was not wholly different. One of them has survived to the present day, and its nature and the changes it has undergone have been described by Donald Brown and others.

An eighteenth-century English observer, John Jesse, thought that the Brunei government resembled

> our antient Feudal System; for, although there is more respect paid to the Regal Power here, than in any other *Malay Country* I have been in, (for this obvious reason, that the SULTAN has entirely the power of appointing the great Officers of State, and of course can always influence the publick Councils) yet, however, each *Pengiran* has the entire sway over his particular Dependants, whose cause they never fail to espouse, even when he may stand in opposition to the Sovereign Authority.[41]

The Brunei system of offices, of a mixed Hindu and Muslim derivation, included four viziers or *wazirs,* the *bendahara,* the *temenggong,* the *di-gadong,* and the *pamancha,* with not very precisely defined central governmental functions; a number of lesser ministers or *cheteria,* like the *wazirs* men of noble blood or *pengirans,* the most important being the *shahbandar;* and some non-noble officials or *mentiri.* The sultan and the main officers were supported by the assignment as appanages of particular districts generally named after the rivers that flowed through them, or in effect of the occupants of those districts. Those were called *kerajaan* in the case of the sultan and *kuripan* in the case of the *wazirs* and others. In contrast, other rivers, or parts of rivers, were *tulin* or *pesaka,* held by *pengirans* as private and hereditary property. The sultan, as Jesse said, could appoint to the major offices. But *pengirans* with substantial *tulin* could challenge a sultan who was personally weak, or who was by accident of inheritance unable to add the resources of large *tulin* properties of his own to his *kerajaan* holdings. The sultan stood for the integrity of the realm, but his powers, particularly in *tulin* properties, were limited, and what he could do depended in practice on wealth, following, standing, and marital alliance.

A *pengiran* enjoyed the allegiance of followers or *hamba* and the services of slaves, *ulun* or *kawan.* But a large household was a demonstration of influence and prestige rather than a source of wealth, and a nobleman's style of living was sustained by profits from the rivers he inherited or held as the appanage of office. In the rivers he had followers; he also had the right to tax the population in various ways, either in person, in the case of *tulin,* or, through an agent, in the case of *kuripan.* By the late nineteenth century, some paid a poll tax, but most of the taxes were less regular: *chukei dagang* or *chukei serah,* forms of forced trade; *chukei basoh betis* and *chukei bongkal sauh,* paid when the *pengiran* or his agent visited the river; and *chukei tolongan,* paid on important events in the *pengiran's* family.

These descriptions belong to a period when Brunei had lost the larger empire to which it aspired at the time when the Europeans first came to this part of the world, and it is impossible to determine how far its system had been modified by the time it became a merely riverine state. The maintenance of its authority over northwestern Borneo was, however, clearly made easier by the diversity of the peoples over which its rule still extended: it extended the resources of the diplomacy on which in a sense the state largely relied. The direct contacts of the *pengirans* were with the down-river settlements, likely to include Malays, if not Bruneis, and also Islamised Melanaus, Kedayans, or Bajaus. Upstream were normally non-Muslim tribes, Dayak, Kayan, Murut, for example, with whom the Brunei connexions were less direct. Diplomacy and allegiance were not backed by external force, but tribe could be used against tribe if need be. Yet it is possible to exaggerate the sense of 'ethnic' difference. It may indeed have been intensified by utilisation. But people would alternatively, or in addition, see themselves as subjects or followers, Muslims or non-Muslims.

It was this system that James Brooke sought to reform, while his successor sought to replace Brunei rule altogether. Initially the first Raja of Sarawak wanted to regularise taxation and bring an end to a system he considered oppressive. The obstacles he faced, and the failure of the British government to continue its backing, prompted him instead to expand his raj by acquiring the permanent 'lease' of further rivers, compensating the *pengirans* by annual fixed payments, and installing his own system, itself reliant, needless to say, not simply on the use of force, but on combining its effective deployment—using the Sea Dayaks, now identified as Iban, whom the raja had first treated as pirates—with a divide-and-rule approach not wholly unlike that the Bruneis had followed, predicated, too, on avoiding too much 'development' and the wholesale overthrow of *adat*. 'Our population requires an experienced commander', Charles Brooke wrote in 1866, 'but when once the relations of one party with another are properly understood, it is a singularly easy government to carry on,—tribes, one with another, being so well balanced, that in the event of danger arising from any one party, the other may be trusted to counteract evil influences, and act as a balancing medium in the scale.'[42]

The administration, once established, worked through chiefs. Raja Charles borrowed from Malaya when he introduced *penghulu* as intermediaries between the *tuai rumah* (longhouse headmen) on the one hand and the native officers and the European Residents on the other. While the creation of this status 'validated their positions in the community, it also co-opted them as supporters of government policy'.[43] The raja stressed that Residents and their assistants should gain the confidence of the chiefs: they were expected, as Tom Harrisson put it, to behave like 'transplanted English Devonshire Squires',[44] in a sense establishing a patron–client relationship of a type still not entirely unfamiliar in Britain itself. The Council Negri, established in 1865, brought the chiefs together every three years. Charles's style remained personal. His son Vyner had difficulty maintaining it, not simply because he lacked the motivation, but because the government's tasks inter-war became more complex. His brother Bertram was concerned at the growing impersonality of administration and the alienation of the people from the raj.

In North Borneo, even more fragmented than Sarawak, the Company had, as it were, to find chiefs, and the way was open to the compliant and the adventurous. In its penurious early years its administration was spread thin, and it was unable to check the abuses of those it appointed. The unrest of the 1890s focused on Mat Salleh, no 'rebel', nor yet a 'nationalist', but a formidable adventurer, backed in some measure by traditional claims from Sulu. The Company mixed unconvincing force and unconvinced conciliation, at first trying to fit him into its emerging panoply of chiefs, and finally 'really smashing him'.[45] In the interwar period Governor D. J. Jardine, from Tanganyika, sought to give the chiefs a greater role, though his experiment—a Native Administrative Centre at Bingkor—was never replicated.

At the end of the century, the remnant of Brunei had become more difficult to manage. The rivers round the capital became the focus of the *pengirans'* revenue-raising, while they could no longer call in tribes from other rivers to deal with the revolts that prompted. The British installed a Resident before Brunei entirely unravelled. Though his role was to give advice, that advice had to be accepted, and this almost entirely changed the traditional system, displacing the 'feudal' structures of which Jesse had written. Initially power came into the hands of the Resident and the British officials. But it also removed the traditional limits on the sultan, now clearly, moreover, hereditary in the family of Sultan Hashim. The latter days of British protection were not accompanied by an effective attempt to democratise the realm, and the development of the oil and gas reserves still further increased the power of the royal family. The state was by the late twentieth century the only Malay monarchy still in existence, but it was now more absolute than 'feudal'.

The Malay peninsula

The appointment of a Resident in Brunei in 1906 had been based on the precedent established on the Peninsula after 1874. Under the Pangkor treaty, the ruler had to seek and accept advice on all matters save religion and custom, the ambit extending to custom as well under the Federated Malay States treaty of 1895, the model for Brunei. 'No one knew what [the Resident] was to do, there was no precedent for anything, no scheme and nothing to guide Residents in those early days beyond a general instruction that they went to the Peninsula, not as rulers but as advisers.'[46] Their general objective was clear: to bring 'order' and help 'open up' the country. What was less clear was that this might require more than advice in states where traditional patterns prevailed. Even after the punitive action that followed the murder of Birch, his successor, Hugh Low, still had difficulty with the Raja Muda of Perak: 'he has no idea of government, except that the ryots were created to produce revenues for the rajahs... ; if I were only here to advise such a man, ... our hope of restoring peace ... would be vain, and the position of Resident untenable'. The advice given, Governor Robinson replied, was 'authoritative advice and may not be lightly rejected. ... All the same the fiction (if such you prefer to call it) that the Residents are merely advisers must be kept up.'[47] It was in this way that the old systems were altered.

The sultan had controlled a royal district, which he governed like a district chief, but he had not exercised pre-eminent power. He had survived partly by manipulation, by sustaining his *daulat*, by ceremony, by possessing the regalia, and partly because he was needed in 'foreign' affairs. The new circumstances were quite different. The sultan's role changed, though, except in respect of Islam, his power did not increase. Once largely in the hands of district chiefs, power now tended, as a result of the treaties, the development of tin, and the creation of infrastructure, to come into the hands of the Residents and the British officials, while the rulers focused on Islam and intensified its Erastian nature.

Swettenham had nevertheless secured the rulers' assent to the creation of the Federated Malay States, assuring them that they would be more important, and their views more likely to be listened to, should they be at variance with those of the governor/high commissioner or the Secretary of State. In fact their importance seemed less. Power was increasingly centralised on the Resident-General's government in Kuala Lumpur, so much so that the Sultan of Perak protested at the 1903 durbar—he wanted the governments to be 'separate entities'[48]—and Johore and the northern states kept out of the 'federation'.

In the inter-war period the idea emerged that 'decentralisation' might facilitate all-Malayan union in the form of federation, not only meeting the reservations of the Perak ruler, but also overcoming the doubts of Johore and the northern states. A further argument was provided by the belief that it was necessary to support the rulers, not only as a bulwark against the influence the Kuomintang and CCP had on the Chinese, but also to discourage Malays from looking to Indonesian nationalism in part in reaction to that influence. 'But for [the rulers] the Malays would become a mob', wrote the Parliamentary Under-Secretary, Ormsby-Gore.[49] Decentralisation also meant, however, changing the balance between the Chief Secretary in Kuala Lumpur and the governor/high commissioner in Singapore, and it became involved in a bureaucratic dispute, already begun pre-war: would it centralise power in Singapore? would it destroy government in Kuala Lumpur? That issue brought up others: would the economic interests of Malaya be subordinated to the entrepot at Singapore?

On his visit in 1932, Sir Samuel Wilson, Permanent Under-Secretary at the Colonial Office, was 'clear that the maintenance of the position, authority and prestige of the Malay Rulers must always be a cardinal point in British policy; and the encouragement of indirect rule will probably prove the greatest safeguard against the political submersion of the Malays which would result from the development of popular government on western lines'.[50] But after the disputes of the 1920s, Sir Cecil Clementi tried to push the concept through too rapidly, and in face of the various obstacles—including opposition to the break-up of the Federated Malay States—his successor, Sir Shenton Thomas, did not get far. The British attempted a more drastic programme in 1945–46, but quickly abandoned Union for Federation along Clementi lines. It was not surprising that the leading Malays in this period, and in the subsequent struggle for independence, came from unfederated states.

Sulus and pirates

If Dutch inability to come to terms with the sultanate of Aceh was rather excep-tional, the Spaniards had never been able to reach lasting understandings with the Moro sultanates. At the end of the nineteenth century, Sulu was still sufficiently independent to secure a separate treaty with the United States. That sultanate, like Brunei, had a long history, and the accounts of it, dating mainly from the nine-teenth century, may not fully cover the changes to its structure. The general lines are clear, however.

What the early sultanate dealt with was not unlike what Morga found in more northerly islands at the outset of Spanish rule: 'when any one of [the] chiefs was more spirited than others, in war or other occasions, such an one brought round him a larger number of partizans and of men, and by him the others were governed, even though they were chiefs also'.[51] Pre-dating the arrival of the Spaniards, the sul-tanate came to terms with pre-Islamic structures. That tended, C. A. Majul argued, to limit the implementation of the powers normally associated with a sultanate. In theory the land belonged to the sultan, he was the highest political authority, and he was represented in each island by Tausug or Samal *panglima* or governors and sub-ordinate officials. In practice, however, the sultan needed the cooperation of the *datus*, chiefs whose ancestors were possibly pre-Islamic, and whose wealth and standing rested on their followers, or *amba*, their regular and debt slaves, and their property. In theory they owed tribute to the sultan. In practice, Majul suggests, they might refuse it or decline to obey him. Such opposition was modified by kinship ties, custom and tradition, and the sultan's power also depended on possession of slaves and followers, wealth and property. It depended, too, on his capacity for leadership and his ability to defend Islam.[52]

Thomas Kiefer modified the Majul description, preferring to see Sulu as a 'seg-mentary' state.[53] He distinguished the ascribed title of *datu*, given to the aristocracy, and the religious title of *salip*, from the achieved titles, *datu, salip, panglima*. A leader could secure 'influence and political power in a community or region through a combination of legal competence, wisdom, wealth, a deft manipulation of alliance, and perhaps military competence'. The sultan would legitimise the acquisition of power by conferring a title which might also restrain 'potentially recalcitrant lead-ers' and give them a stake in the sultanate. Kiefer's suggestion certainly allows more fully for change and adaptability: it also suggests comparison with other Southeast Asian polities in which rulers struggle to retain control by a variety of devices, including the allocation of status.

It was like other Southeast Asian states, archipelagic or not, in other ways. 'Strictly speaking', Kiefer writes,

> the sultanate of Sulu was a multi-ethnic group state which did not have any recognised boundaries. Territorial sovereignty was recognised however, but only in relation to a

center. Authority was always stronger at the center than at the peripheries. At the further edge there might be only a verbal or ritual hegemony. ... The further a subordinate was from the center, the more likely would he be to shift his allegiance from one superordinate authority to another.[54]

'The influence of the individual chiefs depends chiefly upon the number of their retainers or slaves, and the force they can bring into their service when they require', the US Commodore Charles Wilkes wrote in the 1840s. 'These are purchased from the pirates, who bring them to Sulu and its dependencies for sale.' The slaves, he thought, were better off than the freemen, who were the prey of the datus, and the lower class of freemen put themselves under the protection of particular datus in order to secure protection from others. 'The chief to whom they thus attach themselves, is induced to treat them well, in order to retain their services, and attach them to his person, that he may, in case of need, be enabled to defend himself from depredations, and the violence of his neighbours.'[55]

On piracy Majul and Kiefer again differ. Theoretically, says the former, piratical raids needed the permission of the *ruma bichara*, the sultan's advisory council. That, says Kiefer, was only an advisory assembly. Headmen, datus, factions of young men, could mount raids for slaves and booty without the sultan's permission. The sultan had at least to appear to stand off, though he possibly profited indirectly as the holder of rights over market fees when spoils were sold. He could use influence against it, but rarely command a monopoly of force in external relations.

Over piracy itself, there has been controversy, in respect of Sulu and also other parts of the peninsula and archipelago. That has arisen in substantial part because it is a European word and carries European overtones, and its use tends to obscure the nature of the actions in Southeast Asia it purports to describe. In the nineteenth century, indeed, some of that obfuscation was intentional. To act against piracy was an obligation of civilised governments, and the British and the Dutch specifically committed themselves to collaborating against it in the treaty of 1824. An extended definition of it might extend the role of imperial naval forces in bringing order to the archipelago, of which the suppression of piracy was a part. Penang merchants who objected to the attempts of the Sultan of Aceh to enforce control over the outports described them as piracy. James Brooke described the use of Iban in punitive raids on other Brunei rivers as piratical. Intervention on the peninsula could be justified by invoking piracy, as in the Kurau episode of 1827 or the *Magicienne* voyage of 1832. The use of the word on such occasions was less reasonable than its application to the activities of the Ilanuns, called in by Johore after the Dutch attacks of the 1780s, or of the Johore privateers themselves, following the collapse of its government.

Even so, the fit was not exact. In the Malay world there was often a strong political element to robbery and violence at sea. It was indeed part of the dynamics of the state system: a means by which an entrepot's claims might be built up and sustained and a means by which it might be challenged or overthrown. It was also a means by which change might be avoided or effected within a state: an aristocracy might condone it in its adventurous younger sons; a bold man might seek to increase his wealth and status by plunder and his following by raiding or slave-trading. The first practice could hardly be condemned if there were to be political change, but it did not follow the conventions which the Europeans had developed for the making of war, civil or international. The second practice, again, might have seemed less alien in the Europe of the crusades. But by the nineteenth century the Europeans would characterise it as piracy, which they now defined as mere robbery at sea, unauthorised by regular political authority. The advance of the positivist approach to international law helped to deny Malay states that authority. That was a licence to curb the activities of states, if not to deny their existence. Checking piracy was not, however, a European innovation. China had helped to establish Melaka in order to check it.[56] Rama III of Siam issued regulations against pirates in 1813, together with instructions to the sultans of Kedah, Kelantan, and Trengganu.[57]

The nineteenth-century controversy has extended to twentieth-century historians. Some piracy clearly originated in the labelling of activities that Europeans wished to stop. The piracy of Johore and the Sulu archipelago was of another order, and the main dispute has been about its origins. In the case of Johore, it seemed to result, as a contemporary put it, from 'the breaking down of larger Government',[58] the checks and balances of the traditional sultanate ceasing to operate. A. L. Reber and James Warren have offered a more positive account of Sulu piracy. Its main aim, Warren argues, was to secure labour, so that the sultanate might respond to the China market of the late eighteenth and early nineteenth centuries. Piracy and slave-raiding did, however, exist before that, existed even before the Spaniards arrived, and they had become, and indeed remained, a way of carrying on warfare against the Spaniards. 'Raiding', as Reber writes. was 'a recognized political tool' in Southeast Asia. 'For Sulu it was a combination of political reprisal and slaving. ... a profitable business ... also a means of weakening a rival state by depleting its population.'[59]

Filipinas

To the north the Spaniards had established a regime that was unique in Southeast Asia. The Philippines was a colony long before the other European powers established colonies in the region, and, still more exceptional, its population had been Christianised. Yet the structure of the regime may still be usefully compared with others in Southeast Asia.

What they called Filipinas had been somewhat exceptional even before the Spaniards arrived. Though in commercial contact with China and with Borneo, it was politically fragmented: not only were the coastal peoples divided from those in mountainous regions like the Sierra Madre and the Zambales mountains in Luzon;

but lowland peoples were themselves split into a mass of petty states, *barangay*, ruled by clan chiefs or *datu*, with great men or *maharlika*, free men or *timagua*, and slaves. Though there were Bruneis in the Manila area when Legazpi arrived, the process of state-building, already advanced in Sulu and Mindanao, had not, as Morga recognised, taken place in Luzon and the Visayas. It was this that gave the Spaniards their opportunity. They were able to secure the collaboration of the *barangay* elite on mutually beneficial terms. The comparison is with the Muslim sultans as well as with the European regimes that were elsewhere to displace them.

The conquest had been aided by ships from Mexico, and the government continued to rely on a subsidy, or *situado,* from New Spain. But its military forces were small, and the regime had largely to depend on its own resources. Those it utilised in three ways. An administration was organised on the normal Spanish colonial model, staffed by Spaniards. At its head was a Captain-General and an *audiencia* that checked the power of a chief executive so remote from the metropolis. Initially the territory was divided into *encomiendas,* some retained by the government, most parcelled out to deserving Spaniards, who thereby gained the right to collect a poll-tax and levy statute labour, in return for protecting their wards. The private *encomiendas* were reduced during the seventeenth century and finally disappeared under a cedula of 1721. A more regular provincial government had been organised from the late sixteenth century, headed by the *alcalde mayor* or governor. Below him the *gobernadorcillo* headed the pueblo (later *municipio*), and below the pueblo was the *visita* or barrio, generally comprising one *barangay*.

It was at the level of the pueblo and the barrio that the Spaniards incorporated the native elite into their system. The *datu* and *maharlika* became headmen or *cabezas de barangay,* and magistrates or *gobernadorcillos* in the municipios, and with other office-holders, constables, inspectors of palm-trees and rice fields, notaries and church officials, they formed the local elite, the *principalia,* a substantially hereditary oligarchy which was yet renewed by intermarriage with Chinese immigrant families whose claim to leadership lay in their commercial wealth. The Spanish regime had come to rely on the elite for levying the dues the *tao* or peasant owed the state, and the elite benefited from their role. Those dues, as elsewhere in Southeast Asia, included a government demand for labour, the *polo* or *repartimiento,* and the forced sale of goods or *vandala*. The demands were especially heavy in the formative years of the state, when Spain's control of the Philippines was contested by the VOC. The elite secured a percentage, and had the right to demand personal services.

In their ability to draw on religious sanctions for their regime, the Spaniards, of course, differed from the other European regimes, but in this respect their state may be compared with non-European states. Arriving before Islam had taken hold, the religious orders were able to effect the conversion of the population. Once it was effected, however, the regulars did not give way to the seculars, as would normally have been the case: the regulars all along managed to hold on to the majority of benefices. The reason, it seems, is to be found in the colonial relationship. Few indios or natives were admitted into the orders, none at all into the Society of Jesus, nor any mestizos or mixed bloods, only Europeans and *criollos* or local-born Spaniards. As a result, there was a European in each community, watching over and manipulating the activities of the principalia. 'The experience of two centuries has shown', Pedro Sarrio declared in 1787, 'that in all the wars, rebellions, and uprisings that have broken out, the religious parish priests were the ones who contributed most to the pacification of the malcontents.'[60] From 1835 certification from the parish priest was needed for appointment to local posts.[61]

Yet such Europeans were not entirely under the government's control: their ultimate allegiance was to the head of their order, and they resisted the bishops' claim to visitation. Moreover they built up large landholdings, some as a result of donations by Spaniards 'seeking spiritual benefit',[62] others by Filipinos. The labourers were exempted from *repartimiento*. That affected royal revenue in any case, but the privilege was also abused: 'it is against conscience', the University of Santo Tomas was admonished in 1704, 'to usurp them from His Majesty by giving an excessive number of receipts of exemption'.[63] Claiming exemption from temporal authority, friars had in 1697 refused to present their land titles to the court of Compositiones y Indultos. But the reforms of the later eighteenth century had little impact—'the friar estates emerged unscathed'[64]—and nineteenth-century conservative opinion helped the friars. A parallel can be drawn with the Pagan kingdom.

The Spanish conquest was aided by the divisions among the islanders. It was the same with the continuance of the Spanish regime. The different orders were concentrated in different regions, and the language they used—not Spanish—became the predominant language in those regions, and even came to identify distinct peoples, the Tagalogs, the Ilokanos, the Bikolanos, for example. Those divisions were useful to the regime: the Pampangans, for example, were the source of a native constabulary that could be used elsewhere in the islands. Even the weakness of the regime could be a source of strength. The coastal settlements the missionaries established in the Visayas in order to facilitate their work made the people a readier prey of Muslim raiders from the south. In turn, however, they could look only to the Spanish government for what protection it was able to offer.

The opening-up of the colony to foreign trade in the nineteenth century enriched the elite, still further strengthening its position, and its political ambitions were enhanced. The Spanish government declined, however, to abandon the friars, a particular butt of the emerging nationalists, or to share power at national level. Those moves were left to the United States, which established an even closer relationship with the elite that in effect ensured that it would rule the post-colonial Philippines. The Philippine Commission in its report of 1900 argued that the 'educated Filipinos' would be 'of infinite value to the United States in the work of establishing and maintaining civil government throughout the archipelago. As leaders of the people they must be chief agents in securing their people's loyal obedience to the new government.'[65] Temporising with the Japanese, the elite also worked with MacArthur, and,

half-initiated by the Spanish regime, it was best able to turn the democratic structures that the United States created to account.

The Thai kingdoms

The European powers treated the Malayo-Muslim sultanates in different ways. Their
effect on the Thai treatment of Pattani was indirect. Prosperous in the early seventeenth century—a source of pepper—it had also been a cradle of Islam. The revival
of the Thai state under the Bangkok dynasty, however, renewed its earlier claims
over the peninsula, and Burney, as the British East India Company's emissary, did
not contest those over Pattani. For the rest of the nineteenth century, it was treated
as a dependency that paid tribute to Bangkok, but which retained its autonomy, its
own ruler and nobility. That position changed in the late nineteenth and early twentieth centuries, as King Chulalongkorn consolidated his kingdom in order to ensure
its survival. The administrative reforms of 1902–06 grouped the dependencies north
of what became the 1909 line into a *monthon* or circle. The central bureaucracy took
control from the local nobility and pursued an assimilationist policy.

The process of consolidation in the north caused less tension, since there was no
religious clash, but it did not proceed without violence. In the 1870s and 1880s
Bangkok had brought the northern teak forests under its control, partly in response
to the British, partly in order to secure revenue. The Phraya Phap rebellion in
Chiengmai of 1889–90 was against new taxation, the flow of revenue to Bangkok,
British teak extraction. Another revolt, started in Fang in 1901, continued into 1902,
and crushing it amounted in effect to conquest. Some of the local rulers and officials
were, however, incorporated into the new bureaucracy.

Surrounded by colonial powers, Siam tended to behave like one, incorporating
the peripheral territories that it did not have to surrender more firmly in the realm,
both by administrative measures, and also by the building of railways. '[T]he Thai
official sent from Bangkok to supervise the administration in Chiengmai or Ubon
was only somewhat less "foreign" than the British district officer in Malaya or the
French *résident* in Indo-China.'[66] But the state structure in the core of the realm also
changed, in part as a result of the penetration of the world economy, and in part as
a result of deliberate action by the rulers.

In Thai tradition, the head of a *muang* had authority over people, not territory.
Rulers sought to make *muang* into *ratchaanacak,* the ruler of which is a raja, exer-
cising authority (*ana*) based on identification with sacred power, manifest in public
rites: his throne at the centre of a *cak* (circle) or mandala reflecting the cosmos.
Within the circle lesser rajas recognised the greater as long as he demonstrated that
he possessed authority.

Ayudhya was a collection of *muang*, those near the capital allocated to royal children, while outside the circle there were tributary states (*muang khun, prathet sarat*),
which presented gold and silver flowers, and independent *muang*, which were

potential tributaries. *Muang* rulers had to feel that participation was rewarding. In theory the king had absolute power to appoint governors. In practice they were probably hereditary, sustaining patronage networks into which the king tapped. Each *muang* also had a royal agent or spy, *yokkrabat*. *Sakdina,* or marks of dignity, expressed in terms of land, but probably in effect of manpower, were allocated to *muang* according to their class. Governors of first- and second-class *muang, chao phraya,* had *sakdina* of 10 000 rai (2.5 rai = 1 acre). At the top were the royal families (*chao*), with no limit, while the functionaries of high rank (*khunnag*) had a *sakdina* of up to 10 000 rai. At the bottom, apart from the slaves and debt-bondsmen, were the *phrai,* men with a 10–25 rai entitlement who, as king's men (*phrai luang*) or nobles' men (*phrai son*), owed corvée or, in later periods, payment to their lords or patrons. The essential link was the *nai* or *munnai*, with a *sakdina* rank of 400 rai. To the *nai* the commoners, registered by the state, sometimes by tattooing, delivered the service they owed and paid tax in kind or money, and they could also be called upon for service in time of war. The state was sustained not only by this hierarchy of patron–client relationships, but also by its mutually supportive connexion with Buddhism, and by its control of external trade.

After the destruction of Ayudhya in 1767, Taksin adopted the Ayudhya style in his attempt to rebuild the kingdom round Thonburi, but he had to use force against the outer *muang* and against tributaries, Chiengmai, Laos, Cambodia. His aspiration to proclaim himself *cakkavattin* led to his deposition. Moving the capital across the river to Bangkok, Rama I redistributed *muang* under ministries, extended *muang* over the southern tributaries, and insisted that *muang* officers visit Bangkok once a year.

The system was being modified even before Mongkut made the Bowring treaty of 1855. Competing for the king's patronage, nobles amassed wealth, and the king found it difficult to secure corvée labour. The state thus hired labourers for public works, including Chinese coolies. To increase revenue, particularly following the fall-off in the junk trade after the acquisition of Hong Kong in 1842, the kings extended the practice of tax-farming, again usually using Chinese.

The Bowring treaty, and the closer involvement with the world market it promoted, brought about the virtual dissolution of the old system. Bondage was undermined by extra-territoriality, which foreign consuls defined expansively so as to cover a range of ethnic groups. Rice, prohibited before 1855, now became the major export, not sugar, as Bowring had expected. In the 1860s and 1870s land became a commodity to be bought and sold, and wage labour replaced slave labour. The state itself sought tax in money rather than corvée, and corvée was finally ended in 1899, replaced by a poll tax. Keeping his *phrai* retainers became impossibly costly for the *nai*, and as the delivery of taxes to the state passed to the tax-farmers, the *nai* lost their traditional role, and the *phrai* such protection as it had afforded them. The new bureaucratic state of the late nineteenth and early twentieth centuries reincorporated the *nai*.

After the Paknam incident of 1893 the General Adviser, Rolin-Jaequemyns, reminded Chulalongkorn that 'one of the surest means of consolidating Siam's external autonomy and independence was to improve prudently but seriously its internal administration'.[67] The state was built by the monarchy, not only in response to pressure from the outside, but as a result of a struggle within. The nobility, headed by the Bunnag family, had secured the accession of Mongkut, but was challenged by his successor Chulalongkorn, who had visited British India in 1872. In 1874 he set up the Privy Council, and it took over day-to-day administration, making deals with the tax-farmers, curbing the monarch's rivals. The increase in revenue that resulted made it possible for the monarchy to build up its armed forces, and the decline of the nobility became irreversible. Then a regular centralised bureaucracy began to replace the tax-farmers. From 1886 all revenues went to the Royal Treasury or Finance Office, which became the Ministry of Finance in 1890. Other ministries followed. The models the king and Prince Damrong followed in their reforms were the colonial *beamtenstaaten* of the Indies, British Malaya, Burma, and the raj.[68] At the highest levels foreign advisers were used. But the expansion of the bureaucracy— there were 25 000 civil officials in 1900 and 79 988 in 1918–19—meant that official posts had to be filled by commoners, well outside the old *sakdina* rules.

Local government was also progressively restructured. In the 1890s, the *monthon*, which grouped townships under Bangkok-appointed high commissioners, was the focus of the change; later it was the province. But the most crucial relationship for the regime, as for other Southeast Asian regimes, colonial or otherwise, was that with the village. The old system had been eroded or displaced. The Local Administration Act of 1914 was the culmination of attempts to replace it. Under this the rural population were to be organised in *muban* (village, hamlet), in turn grouped into *tambon* (communes), at which point they were linked with the state structures, *amphoe* (district), *changwat* (province), and *monthon* (circle or county). The village headmen were to elect the commune headmen (*kamnan*). It was these men who had the task of locally articulating what the central government wanted. But that was hard to reconcile with the traditional role of headmen, in Siam as elsewhere, that of representing the village to the outside world. There was no enthusiasm for being elected.

The bureaucracy it had created overthrew the absolute monarchy in 1932. A rule-governed bureaucracy is essentially at odds with arbitrary monarchy, as the Mataram rulers had recognised. Chulalongkorn's successors, moreover, had continued to involve many princes in the administration, provoking the resentment of commoners. The monarchy, itself using stricter descent rules than before, gave the country kings less competent than Chulalongkorn. But though the Promoters acted in the name of the people, they did not implement a democratic system. Absolutism was replaced in theory by constitutional monarchy, but in practice by a civilian-military oligarchy. It was by this that King Prajadhipok justified his abdication in 1935: 'I am willing to surrender the powers I formerly exercised to the people as a whole, but I am not willing to turn them over to any individual or any group to use in an autocratic manner without heeding the voice of the people.'[69] In fact the oligarchy continued to hold power for decades. Arguably Thailand is still working out the implications of the revolution of 1932.

Conclusion

Across Southeast Asia, on the mainland and in the archipelago, the structures that states adopted were often strikingly similar, and so, too, was the repertoire of tactics and strategies employed by rulers. That continued to be true when the Europeans began to establish colonial realms which resembled each other but resembled their predecessors also. The similarities have to be studied as much as the differences. Statecraft was, of course, responding to a number of common conditions, the demographic immaturity of the region, the importance of personal ties, often of a patron–client nature, the challenge communication presented to control. In the nineteenth and twentieth centuries those conditions changed, and the structure of states, and the statecraft of rulers, changed as well. But while Southeast Asia was redivided politically, its regimes pursued strategies and tactics that still had a good deal in common, whether they were colonial regimes or not. They continued, too, to be influenced by and to utilise the practices of the past, even though they had developed in different circumstances. That was to be true also of the post-colonial regimes. Again they can be compared as well as contrasted, across time and across the region, and indeed with a regime that was never formally colonial, though often similar, that of Siam/Thailand. The contrasts and similarities will be evident again in an account of the politics of the states of Southeast Asia.

Notes

1 Jim Schiller, *Developing Jepara in New Order Indonesia*, Clayton: Monash Asia Institute, 1996, pp. 17–18.
2 Wolters, *Fall*, pp. 14–15.
3 M. Weber, *Economy and Society*, ed. G. Roth and C. Wittich, NY: Bedminster, 1968, III, pp. 1099, 1095.
4 Cheah Boon Kheng, *The Peasant Robbers of Kedah*, Singapore: OUP, 1988, pp. 18–19, 58n.
5 cf. John G. Butcher, *The British in Malaya, 1880–1941*, KL: OUP, 1979, p. 54.
6 in McCoy and de Jesus, p. 391.
7 G. William Skinner in A. Reid, *Sojourners and Settlers*, St Leonards: Allen and Unwin, 1996, p. 81.
8 J. G. Butcher, 'The Demise of the Revenue Farm System in the Federated Malay States', MAS, 17, 3 (July 1983), p. 390.
9 *Bali: Colonial Conceptions and Political Change, 1700–1940*, Rotterdam: Erasmus U, 1986, p. 9.
10 'Unity and Disunity in Javanese Political and Religious Thought of the Eighteenth Century', MAS, 26, 2 (May 1992), p. 665.
11 J. Kathirithamby-Wells, 'Forces of Regional and State Integration in the Western Archipelago, c. 1500–1700', JSEAS, 18, 1 (March 1987), p. 27.
12 p. 15.
13 q. Christopher S. Gray, 'Johore 1910–1941 …', PhD thesis, Yale U, 1978, p. 14.
14 D. Insor, *Thailand*, London: Allen and Unwin, 1963, p. 56.
15 *Burmese Administrative Cycles*, Princeton UP, 1984.

16 ibid., p. 85.
17 q. ibid., p. 155.
18 Robert H. Taylor, *The State in Burma*, U Hawaii P, 1987, p. 85.
19 q. J. Cady, *A History of Modern Burma*, Cornell UP, 1958, p. 153.
20 O. W. Wolters, *Two Essays on Dai-Viet in the Fourteenth Century*, New Haven: Yale Center, 1988, p. xxxiv.
21 *Vietnam, Ho Quy Ly, and the Ming*, New Haven: Yale Center, 1985, p. 68.
22 'Nineteenth-century Vietnamese Confucianization …', JSEAS, 25, 2 (September 1994), p. 277.
23 K. Taylor, 'Literati Revival in Seventeenth-century Vietnam', JSEAS, 18, 1 (March 1987), p. 21.
24 Cooke, p. 306.
25 N. Cooke, 'The Composition of the Nineteenth-Century Political Elite of Pre-Colonial Nguyen Vietnam', MAS, 29, 4 (October 1995), p. 764.
26 Nguyen The Anh, 'The Vietnamese Monarchy under French Colonial Rule, 1884–1945', MAS, 19, 1 (February 1985), pp. 153–4.
27 A. Woodside, *Vietnam and the Chinese Model*, Harvard UP, 1971, p. 12.
28 q. D. P. Chandler, 'The Kingdom of Kampuchea, March–October 1945 …', JSEAS, 17, 1 (March 1986), pp. 85–6.
29 q. P. Baugher, 'The Contradictions of Colonialism…', PhD thesis, Wis-Madison U, 1980, p. 412.
30 q. M. Osborne, *The French Presence in Cochinchina and Cambodia*, Cornell UP, 1969, p. 151.
31 Truong Buu Lam, *New Lamps for Old*, Singapore: Maruzen, 1982, p. 57.
32 'Nguyen Trai's Binh Ngo Dai Co of 1428', JSEAS, 10, 1 (March 1979), p. 174.
33 M. Ricklefs, *The Seen and the Unseen Worlds in Java*, St Leonards: Allen and Unwin, 1998, p. xix.
34 W. Remmelink, *The Chinese War and the Collapse of the Javanese State, 1725–1743*, Leiden: KITLV P, 1994, p. 18.
35 Moertono, pp. 116–17. P. Carey, 'Waiting for the "Just King"…', MAS, 20,1 (February 1986), pp. 70–1, 75, 79.
36 p. 22.
37 Remmelink, p. 25.
38 Elson in Lindblad, p. 131.
39 q. Nordholt, *Bali: Colonial Conceptions*, p. 39.
40 q. Morris in A. Kahin, ed., *Regional Dynamics of the Indonesian Revolution*, Honolulu: U Hawaii P, 1985, p. 85.
41 A. Dalrymple, *Oriental Repertory*, London, 1808, II, p. 6.
42 *Ten Years in Sarawak*, London, 1866, II, pp. 308–9.
43 V. Sutlive, *Tun Jugah of Sarawak*, Kuching: Sarawak Literary Society, 1992, p. 78.
44 q. Jon Reinhart, 'Administrative Policy and Practice in Sarawak …', JAS, 24, 4 (August 1970), p. 855.
45 q. N. Tarling, 'Mat Salleh and Krani Usman', JSEAS, 16, 1 (March 1985), p. 59.
46 F. Swettenham, q. P. Kratoska, ed., *Honourable Intentions*, Singapore: OUP, 1983, p. 179.
47 Low to Robinson, 28 May 1878; reply, 9 June. C.O. 882/4, Public Record Office, London.
48 q. Jagjit Singh in Zainal Abidin, ed., *Glimpses of Malaysian History*, KL: Dewan Pustaka, 1970, p. 73.
49 q. K. Ghosh, *Twentieth-century Malaysia: Politics of Decentralization of Power, 1920–1929*, Calcutta: Progressive, 1977, p. 304.
50 *Report on his Visit to Malaya in 1932*, Cmd. 4276, London: HMSO, March 1933.
51 A. de Morga, *The Philippine Islands*, trans. H. E. J. Stanley, London: Hakluyt, 1868, p. 297.
52 'Political and Historical Notes on the Old Sulu Sultanate', *Philippine Historical Review*, 1, 1 (1965).
53 'The Tausug Polity and the Sultanate of Sulu: a Segmentary State in the Southern Philippines', *Sulu Studies*, I, Jolo: 1972, pp. 19–64.
54 p. 50.
55 *Narrative of the United States Exploring Expedition during the years 1838, 1839, 1840, 1841, 1842*, London: 1845, V, pp. 344–5.
56 Hall, JMBRAS, 58, 2, p. 89.
57 L. Gesick, 'Kingship and Political Integration in Traditional Siam, 1767–1824', PhD thesis, Cornell U, 1976, p. 169.
58 q. N. Tarling, *Piracy and Politics in the Malay World*, Melbourne: Cheshire, 1963, p. 53.

59 L. Reber, 'The Sulu World ...', MA thesis, Cornell U, 1966, p. 157.

60 q. de La Costa in Gerald H. Anderson, ed., *Studies in Philippine Church History*, Cornell UP, 1969, pp. 72–73.

61 Dery, p. 134.

62 Roth in de Jesus and McCoy, p. 134.

63 q. D. M. Roth, *The Friar Estates of the Philippines*, Albuquerque: U of New Mexico P, 1977, p. 76.

64 ibid., p. 52.

65 q. David F. Porter, 'Ilokos: a Non-Tagalog Response to Social, Political and Economic Change, 1870–1910', PhD thesis, Cornell U, 1980, p. 110.

66 B. Batson, *The End of the Absolute Monarchy*, Singapore: OUP, 1984, p. 12.

67 q. Tips, p. 225.

68 B. Anderson, *Imagined Communities*, London and NY: Verso, 1991, p. 100n.

69 q. Batson, p. 317.

Obligations and Associations

The sense of hierarchy that marked the societies of Southeast Asia and the states that were built upon them was traditionally accompanied by a sense of mutual obligation. That mutuality was eroded over time, and other forms of association emerged, without entirely displacing the traditional.

State systems drew upon, though they were also challenged by, the sense of hierarchic but mutual obligation that marked Southeast Asian life. It has continued to mark it. 'As soon as Southeast Asians speak', as Anthony Reid has put it, 'they place themselves in a vertical relationship'.[1] The assumption behind their speech patterns is 'that society is naturally hierarchic, like the family, so that comfort and intimacy are best achieved when one can address the other party as an older or younger brother or sister, or as father, grandfather, uncle, boss or lord'.[2] Vertical bonding, as Reid adds, still strikes anthropologists as characteristic of the Southeast Asian societies they study. In the Philippines it is described in terms of *utang na lo'ob*, the debt of gratitude.

'It requires effort for modern Westerners', Reid comments, 'to understand a situation where unequal relationships can be both cooperative and intimate'.[3] Even the nuclear family is now under strain in the West. But a not much earlier history, idealised or not, may offer some basis for comparison and understanding. 'Westerners' might think of the village squire, who was owed deference, but who was expected to help in times of crisis and to take part in times of celebration, and to whom one might be 'obliged' if a son or daughter were found a 'position' or awarded a scholarship. Or 'Westerners' might recall their Shakespeare and their Webster, clearly belonging to a society in which the patron had obligations to his followers, and they might switch allegiance should those obligations not be met. The idea of 'service' indeed persisted into the age of the nation-state, which was owed 'national service' in return for protection and other benefits.

Thus freedom and obligation did not part company in the West, but freedom was inconsistent with one form obligation took. Greek and Roman law came to define the status of 'slave' with greater precision, and 'true' slaves were distinguished from 'serfs' by the perception of them as inferior outsiders, initially from the 'Slav' nations of the Black Sea, and later from the black nations of Africa. Slavery, it was also thought, was contrary to the natural state of man, and the result of some kind of deterioration from it. European observers of Southeast Asia in the phase of 'discovery' found slavery both widespread and mild.

Slaves and dependants

'Slavery', like 'piracy', is indeed a term laden with Western associations that make it hard to use in Southeast Asian history. Since, however, it is also hard to avoid, it is best to take advantage of the comparative possibilities it offers in respect to societies elsewhere. The main contrast seems to lie in the continuity between slavery and other forms of dependency, sustained in Southeast Asia but not in the West. That tended, too, to muffle the concept of 'freedom', even if in the West itself 'freedom' did not imply a total lack of obligation. The words in current use in general do not relate to a distinction between slave and free. Only 'merdeka' took on that character in an earlier period. That itself derived, however, from a term used in Sri Vijaya to describe a chief or leader of a group of subjects or bondmen, in turn derived from a Sanskrit description of a person of great spiritual power or wealth.[4]

The control of men, rather than of land, was the key to Southeast Asian social systems: they were, as Europeans used to say, worth their weight in gold. 'The Raja looks to the number of his following as the gauge of his power', wrote Swettenham in Malaya in 1875, 'and other Rajas will respect and fear him accordingly. Thus he tries to get men into his service.'[5] What was important to leaders and would-be leaders was the men and women whom they could place in a dependent relationship. 'For the poor and weak, on the other hand, security and opportunity depended upon being bonded to someone strong enough to look after them.'[6] The father of Hang Tuah, the folk-hero of the Malays, 'went in search of a living, [and] presenting himself to the Datuk Bendahara, he made himself hamba to him'.[7] The focus was therefore not on the degree of legal freedom a person might possess, but on the object of a person's obligation, and thus of his or her niche in society. The same terms—*kyun* in Pagan Burma, *phrai* in Siam, *hamba* in the Malay world, *ata* in the Bugis world— were used to cover what in the West would be covered by a range of words, subject, vassal, or slave.

These bonds were transferable, 'and it is this', Reid suggests, 'that provides the overlap with slavery'. Bondsmen could be 'presented as a marriage gift, donated to a monastery, offered as tribute, given as security for a loan, sold or inherited'. Yet the imagery throughout was 'that of the extended family', and even a slave was 'permitted a level of intimacy with his master which no one who was not a member of the household could dare assume'.[8]

The origin of this system of obligation commonly lay in debt. Meeting ritual obligation was one source of debt, gambling another. 'Sale or commendation of oneself and/or one's wife and children to a wealthier person' was a way out of 'severe hard-ship'. 'Pawning one's dependants or oneself … , or else entering a very unequal part-nership with the creditor who became the patron if not the master, were the common Southeast Asian means of obtaining capital.'[9] Theoretically the debt could be redeemed, and that was to enable Europeans to draw a distinction between debt slavery and what they regarded as 'true' slavery. In fact labour was not sufficient to redeem the capital, but only to pay the interest. Of the pre-Spanish Filipinos, Morga wrote: 'it is to be understood that they made these slaves during their wars and dif-ferences … : and most frequently on account of loans and usurious contracts, which were current among them, the payment, stock and debt increasing with delay, until they remained as slaves'.[10] The relationship was not seen in terms of cash return. The term for debtor in nineteenth-century Perak, for example, was *kawan* or compan-ion, and in Sumatra *pengiring* or follower. 'Nor has the debtor under this system any means of becoming free, unless some relative or friend comes forward to pay for him; and even in this case the creditor might if he so willed, and if were a Rajah in all probability would, under some pretext, refuse the offer of payment.'[11]

That does not, however, mean that these were slave societies, Reid insists, 'since the legal categories of slave and free were not well defined, obligation and fealty were more central to the Southeast Asian system than status-as-property, while in certain cases serf seems a more appropriate word than slave'.[12] Even this W. H. Scott doubted. The Visayan *oripun* and the Tagalog *alipin* were not slaves but, being bound not to the soil but to other men, they were not serfs either.[13] Nor, Reid adds, did the distinction of 'savage' slaves, captured or bought from the hill people, persist in its initial harshness.[14] The same seems to be true of sea captives. 'A master was liable to neglect a *bangaya* who was remiss in his duties, but their statements and travel accounts of observers reveal that slaves, especially those with knowledge and skills, had good relations with their master and were not easily distinguished among their following.'[15] Harshness certainly existed, but it could be counter-productive. Labour was scarce, and the state administrations were rarely strong enough to enforce a bond challenged by a pull-factor as well as a push-factor. Debt bondage was indeed preferred to state service in Taung-ngu Burma.

Unable to acquire labour for their new urban centres because the free market was limited, and because they lacked the traditional ties that substituted for it, the early Europeans resorted to recruiting slaves, preferably from remote areas, India, Madagascar, Arakan, or New Guinea. They fell into Southeast Asian ways, however. The tyranny in Company Batavia was of the domestic sort. Slaves might be badly treated, but that was true of the lower orders more generally. 'The master has all power over the Slave, except that of killing him', La Loubère wrote of late-seventeenth-century Siam; 'And tho' some may report, that Slaves are severely beaten there (which is very probable in a country where free persons are so rigidly bastinado'd) yet the slavery there is so gentle, or, if you will, the Liberty is so abject, that it is become a Proverb, that the Siamese sell it to eat of a … *Durion*.'[16]

Important in pre-colonial society, these systems were a basis for the pre-colonial state itself: to a great extent it built upon patron–client relationships, offering protection and allocating rewards and status in return for allegiance. The colonial state still used them, but authority tended to become more impersonal. In Laos and Cambodia, for example, the French suppressed slavery and debt bondage, but revived state corvée and made it more efficient. It was argued, not unpersuasively, that Southeast Asians saw wage labour as demeaning. Hugh Clifford's Pahang Malay would not work if he could help it, and would not be tempted 'by offers of the most extravagant wages'. Murmur *kerah* (forced labour) in his ear, 'he will come without a murmur, and work really hard for no pay'.[17] At the same time, the economic changes that coincided with the imposition of colonial rule created a new system that did not entirely differ from the old, but lost much of its meliorative reciprocity.

While colonial rule tended to reduce the autonomy of the village, expansion of agricultural production for sale broke the relative autonomy of local subsistence patterns.[18] Loss of common land, the rise in absentee ownership and use of hired agents, the increase in non-village labourers, the expansion of money-lending, all undermined the network of reciprocity. Previously a local leader could seldom rely on outside force and therefore had to take account of local opinion. With the backing of the state that was now less necessary. The undermining of the village also undermined clientage: the colonial transformation eroded the bargaining position of the clients. Kin and village had limited the patron's power, and so had the capacity to flee, when population was sparse and land a-plenty. Under the colonial system peasants needed patrons more, but patrons needed clients less.[19] And the export economy enhanced the power of elites: the rights to open land, pasture, and free fuel diminished.

In the Philippines the old relationship had, even before Spanish rule, taken the form of share-cropping, and it persisted. 'The share tenant likes a landlord who treats him paternally', wrote Robert A. Polson and Agaton P. Pal in the 1950s, 'and consequently, a paternal landlord is the recipient of many extra services from his tenant. … The fact that a landlord always grants a tenant's request for credit and the fact that the credit is granted at a crisis period in the tenant's life binds him in endless gratitude to his benefactor.'[20] It was, in Taft's words, 'a kind of quasi slavery called caciquism'.[21] But now it was losing the sense of reciprocity. Benedict Kerkvliet contrasts two inter-war hacenderos in Talavera, Bulacan: Manuel Tinio, who was seen to have *utang na loob*, and his son, Manolo, who was 'more strict, businesslike, and impersonal'.[22] Peasants joined the PKM (National Peasant Union). 'We wanted the landlords, but we wanted them to be just. … Getting a larger share was important. But also we wanted landlords to stop treating us as their slaves.'[23]

The same kind of feeling—and the same kind of remedy—Ralph Smith finds in the Vietnamese agrarian discontent of 1930–31. Trouble came not in provinces with large estates, but in those with small. 'On the large estates of the "newer" provinces, the factor of estate patronage probably sustained the existing social structure. It was in areas where this kind of patronage was at a minimum that there was most trouble.'[24]

Labour

Traders and capitalists without access to compulsory labour had used the old system of credit advances in new ways. They were struck by the fidelity of Southeast Asian debtors, who saw the advances in terms of mutual obligation. Indeed, in the case of southern Sumatran states that Barbara Andaya describes, trade had been connected with kinship ties, which were designed to sustain trust, and its expansion was associated with their expansion. A Jambi prince evoked the mutual obligations involved in negotiating with the Dutch: 'As long as we have traded together, we have been brothers'.[25] Chinese traders were drawn into the pattern through marriage with local women, important in hawking and marketing. For the Chinese themselves, kinship was again a source of trust. A contract was 'drawn up to regulate relations between those who could not rely on ties of blood or adoption to ensure fair dealings'.[26]

A contractual approach was applied to immigrant labour on the plantations of the late nineteenth century. Wage labour, as Reid says, became available in nineteenth-century Southeast Asia 'chiefly in the form of immigrant Chinese in the cities'.[27] Finding labour for mines and plantations was more difficult. Not surprisingly, it tended to take on the character of bondage, though without also assuming the patriarchal features that had often had a meliorating effect. The state, too, might be in a stronger position than in the past to enforce the bonds, and to limit the *de facto* ability to challenge them by running away or changing employer.

That was the case, for example, with the plantation labour in the tobacco plantations developed on the east coast of Sumatra by Nienhuys and other pioneers from the 1860s onwards. Initially it was provided by imported Chinese coolies. They were paid some cash at the time of recruitment—in order to pay off their travel debts or meet the needs of family members they left behind—and they worked for at least a year to pay it back. In some ways the system was not unlike the debt bondage so common in traditional Southeast Asia, as its proponents pointed out. 'Malay *adat* gives the planter the opportunity to ensure that his coolie meets his obligations; because he can punish them if they try to evade them.'[28] But there was no sense of mutual obligation. Indeed the system was notorious for its inhumanity, and desertion was common. 'Crimping' was common, too, rather as, in other systems, followers had sought new masters.

The state ideology of the day favoured, at least in theory, a free market for labour. In this case, it was persuaded to make an exception. That could be partly argued for as a means of protecting the coolie. The main reason was the need to ensure a regular labour supply for the industry. Under the Coolie Ordinance of 1880 no labourer–employer relationship could exist without a contract, verified by an official immediately after the coolie's arrival. That covered a minimum of three years, during which the coolie might not leave the plantation without written permission. He was entitled to decent treatment, but could be given a leave-pass to complain only as an individual. If he ran away or refused to work diligently, he was subject to penalisation. Sentences included forced labour on public works, and the time spent on that was added to the contracted period still to be worked out when the coolie was returned to the plantation. The one-year minimum had been abandoned, so that it might be possible 'both to recoup the advances and recruitment costs from the contracted labourer and to obtain the profit yielded to an estate by the initially unskilled work-man after he had been trained'.[29] And not many returned to China, or to Java, a later source of coolies, after three years. 'On the one hand the coolie thinks that he cannot go away as long as he is in the red in his master's books; on the other hand the employer wants to retain him, and as long as the latter can ensure that the coolie remains in debt, it is easy enough to persuade him to sign a new contract.'[30]

In a pamphlet of 1902, *Millions from Deli,* J. van den Brand attacked the system. He saw it as akin to slavery. '[I]t is contrary to the honour of God; it is contrary to humanity. Truly, the lack of freedom cannot be recompensed with a nice hospital and a handful of money.'[31] But neither the coolie ordinance itself, nor the violence it sustained, were destroyed by the Ethici of the new century. A few planters distinguished themselves by attempting to ameliorate the conditions on the estates, however. One was C. W. Janssen of the Senembah company, who set up schools. One of the teachers he appointed was the revolutionary Tan Malaka. 'The class which toils from dawn to dusk; … the class which lives in a shed like goats in a stable; and is arbitrarily flogged or sworn at and damned to hell … . that is the class of Indonesians known as contract coolies.'[32]

When he explained the working of the Coolie Ordinance to a British official, the latter had said: 'We don't want slavery here'.[33] The Coolie Ordinance was allegedly based on Malayan precedent, but the system introduced there, though by no means beyond criticism, was less harsh. Following the second Anglo-Chinese war (1858–60), the Manchu government had formally permitted emigration, and the escalating demand for cheap labour in Southeast Asia had boosted what had already come to be known as the 'coolie trade'.[34] The abuses involved led the Straits Settlements government to set up the Chinese Protectorate in 1877. One of its functions was to supervise the making of contracts. The labourer was normally indebted for his passage, and those and other costs, and the profits of the recruiter and lodging-house keepers, were effectively paid by the employer and recovered from the labourer. The system was not slavery, but indenture. It meliorated the debt relationship, but also sustained it.

The indenture system was formally abolished in 1914. That did not immediately end it. 'Difficulties occurred in the unwillingness of the labourers to complain of "old established customs"', as Victor Purcell, who worked in the Protectorate, put it, 'and they were more or less bound by ties to the contractor.'[35] The system, he added, received a death-blow with the introduction of the Aliens Ordinance of 1933, partly the result of the Depression, and also of Clementi's approach to Malayan politics. Under it the governor was given the power to limit the number of aliens landing in the colony. '[I]t became much cheaper to recruit labour in Malaya where there was already an adequate supply.'[36]

Indian labour was also imported, particularly to meet the demand for cheap labour on the part of the plantation industry in Malaya, and also, as Governor Weld put it in 1887, to counterbalance 'the great preponderance of the Chinese over any other races in these settlements, and to a less marked degree in some of the Native States under our administration'.[37] The Indian government was more protective than the Chinese, and, even when in the hands of the British, was no push-over. An ordinance of 1884 permitted Indians to leave the Straits Settlements to labour in the Malay States, but it prescribed the terms for indentures, and an Indian Immigration Agent was empowered to inspect places where indentured labourers were employed. Under it, however, the supply of labour increased only temporarily, and it fell off in 1889. The indenture system was unattractive to Indian labour and unsatisfactory to the planters. Another system was more successful, the so-called *kangany* system, more or less as used in Ceylon. The *kanganys* were headmen, or 'coolies of standing', in theory senior members of families, who controlled gangs of labourers often, though not always, composed of family units, and also recruited the labourers in India. This system was increasingly adopted in Malaya. Employers paid the *kangany*'s passage to India and a commission for each labourer recruited. Employers also paid the passages of the labourers, but did not require them to enter contracts. They were, however, expected to pay the expenses of their recruitment. The employer relied on reasonable terms and the influence of the *kangany* to keep the labourers on the estate.

The demand for labour prompted by the rapid growth of rubber plantations in the first decade of the new century prompted the Straits government to make the Tamil Immigration Fund Ordinance in 1907. Under this employers contributed to a fund a sum assessed in terms of the number of days worked by Indian labourers in their employ. The fund was used by the Indian Immigration Committee—composed of five planters and three officials, the Superintendent of Indian Immigration, the general manager of the railways, and the government surgeon of Perak—to meet virtually all the costs of transporting a labourer from his home in India to his place of employment in Malaya. The arrangement was superimposed on the *kangany* system. The committee could raise or reduce the number of *kangany* licences, and could thus adjust supply to demand.

Under the dyarchy reforms, emigration was placed in the hands of India's new central legislature. It determined to ensure that indenture was permanently prohibited, and to use the power to halt or restrict emigration so as to obtain better conditions for Indian labourers. An Indian civil servant was appointed as agent in Malaya, and a Malayan Indian added to the committee. In the Depression many Indians became unemployed and returned to India at the committee's expense or their own.

The planters were apprehensive that they might be caught without an adequate labour force if rubber prices improved. India's answer was that wages would have to be restored. The planters accepted this in 1937, but reports of a cut in wages led the Central Indian Association of Malaya—a middle-class federation of Indian associations, encouraged by agents of the Government of India—to appeal to the government of India, and it halted assisted emigration from June 1938. By this time, however, the labour force in Malaya was sufficient to meet the planters' requirements.

Chinese associations

If the Indian government tended to interest itself in the fate of overseas Indians, the Chinese, it was thought, were used to looking after themselves. The Chinese who came to nineteenth-century Malaya and Singapore already possessed dialect and regional affiliations, and 'speakers of the same dialect naturally clustered together socially for security, recreation and mutual assistance'.[38] Family and clan ties marked the village communities from which the migrants came, and these, too, became the basis of associations. Migrants sustained their loyalty to family and clan and demonstrated it by remittances home. The kinship pattern, already strong in the provinces of Kwangtung and Fukien, the source of most migrants, indeed became even stronger overseas. Again the migrants—peasants, lonely, in 'a totally foreign environment'[39]—needed support and protection, and needed, too, to provide for decent burial if they did not return. Third, there were the secret societies, anti-Manchu in origin, particularly important while immigration was male-dominated.

Their role in the Straits Settlements and Malaya Yen Ching-hwang has closely connected to the coolie trade. 'To pursue maximum profit, the coolie traders required an effective control system which would cover supply, transportation and distribution of coolies. This forced them to co-operate with the secret societies in the Treaty Ports and those in Singapore and Penang.'[40] *Samseng,* the secret society thugs, were used for example to 'soften' the resistance of coolies who found that they were being sent to Deli rather than Singapore or the peninsula.[41] Yen notes, as have many observers, the 'monopolisation' of particular jobs and businesses by certain dialect groups, elements of which persist, Cantonese in restaurants and catering for example, Hokkien in trading and banking. That he attributes to the role of dialect and clan associations in placing migrants in employment. 'The power of the secret society was used to maintain or consolidate certain lucrative businesses such as mining, opium and spirit farms, gambling, and prostitution. It would be an exaggeration to claim that secret societies were mainly responsible for the monopolization of occupations.'[42] The two societies most prominent in nineteenth-century Malaya were Ghi Hin and Hai San, identified with Cantonese and Hakka respectively.

Like earlier rulers, Southeast Asian and European, the British initially adopted a system of indirect rule in respect of the Chinese communities, and relied on a Capitan China. Such men were leaders of the associations, and no doubt often secret society leaders, too. Initially the Chinese Protectorate hoped to reform the system rather than replace it. 'The police however, will, I think, bear me out when I say that the Hoeys (Secret societies) are often very useful in assisting the government to deal with the lower classes of the Chinese', wrote the first Protector. '…[S]uch societies when left to themselves, and allowed to acquire power and wealth, are undoubtedly dangerous.'[43] Weld's successor as Governor of the Straits, Sir C. Smith, resolved to suppress them. 'In a Colony properly administered, it is not prudent to have an *imperium in imperio*. The Government must be the paramount power, and it is not so in the eyes of many thousands of the Chinese in the Straits Settlements.'[44] The method chosen in the Straits Settlements ordinance of 1889 was to make all unregistered societies unlawful. A Chinese Advisory Board was set up.

Some Malay states also adopted the ordinance. There Capitans faced a dilemma, resolved as the British tightened their control. As in the Straits leading Chinese severed their links with the secret societies, and strengthened their ties with the dialect associations, which were in any case becoming more relevant with the maturing of the Chinese community. Secret societies became underworld gangs, but the dialect associations became more powerful. In turn, of course, they were to be displaced, as stronger colonial government gave way to yet stronger post-colonial government. 'Today', Edwin Lee writes, 'the dialect group and clan associations are looked upon as relics of a bygone age, reminiscent of the life and struggles of immigrants but out of place in the modern industrialized society that Singapore has become. As they fade into obscurity, the dialect group and clan bodies are regarded as fit subjects to be recaptured in the photographic exhibitions and "dioramas" of the National Archives and the National Museum.'[45]

Trade unions

In modern industrialised societies labour came to be organised in another way, through the creation of trade unions. Their role was, of course, tested in the West. Was its purpose to secure better conditions for the workers? Did that itself require a larger political role? Did that role grow too large? Did it become superfluous in affluent societies? Did trade unionism hinder the response to globalisation? In post-colonial Singapore the government did not entirely reject unionism. It was a way— in succession to earlier ways—in which the workers might be controlled and led. 'The position of secretary-general of the NTUC eventually became a cabinet post.'[46]

Unionism was, of course, a novelty in Southeast Asia when it began to emerge with the growing industrialisation and urbanisation of the early twentieth century. Of its position in colonial Java, John Ingleson has offered a masterly study, and he explains both its origins and its limitations. The workers who came to the cities were in a position not wholly unlike that of migrants from overseas. Kinship and friendship networks linked village and city and helped 'migrants' to adjust. Particular urban occupations were 'monopolised' by 'migrants' from particular regions. 'In a society where no welfare safety net was provided by the state, the only security for the urban majority were ethnic and kinship ties, mutual benefit associations and the sense of community in the kampungs where they lived.'[47] Foremen played a large role in recruitment, looking to the home village with which they retained links. They exploited the workers, but also 'lived in and were part of the kampung communities and were constrained by their communal and social obligations'.[48]

The early urban strikes—to which older workers or foremen usually gave what leadership there was—were, like peasant protests, 'sudden outbursts of pent-up frustrations and longstanding grievances, and lacked class consciousness, class organization or even formal leadership'.[49] The changes Javanese society was undergoing, together with the impact of the Ethical Policy and the emergence of new political movements, heightened the sense of injustice. Those who sought to channel it, and to create a strong labour movement, were, however, beset by the continued challenge of spontaneity, and often found themselves trying to stop strike action, rather than encourage it: 'the unions were more spectators than instigators of strikes, although, of course, when strikes broke out they did publicly and vociferously support them and did try to bring them under their control'.[50] Strike action played into the hands of a government that became increasingly repressive in the 1920s, and so did even *ex post facto* leadership. The government was only too keen to attribute labour unrest, not to poor conditions and low wages, but to the malign influence of communist agitators. In fact the intellectuals had seen the danger in acting too soon and thus inviting repression, but were in no position to prevent it. Given the attitude of the workers on the one hand and the government on the other, together with an over-supply of labour, it was impossible to develop a labour movement.

There was, however, no guarantee that a post-colonial government would favour a strong labour movement. The successes of SOBSI (Central Organisation of Workers in All Indonesia) in the 1950s were unspectacular. Most workers, Donald Hindley observed, were still in small enterprises, and employers still accepted 'a certain fatherly responsibility'. The Indonesian workers, he added, 'are usually not far removed from the peasantry, and retain a strong sense of acceptance of authority or the tradition of open obedience'.[51]

In earlier times trade was facilitated by the trust imbued by the adoption of family relationships. Subsequent associations adopted them, too. The most common one is that of fraternity. Members were brothers. In that, of course, the Southeast Asian experience was not unique. Nor is fraternity in the West confined to American undergraduates and Freemasons. It is, however, a challenge to the vertical values that have dominated society in Southeast Asia.

Notes

1 A. Reid, ed., *Slavery, Bondage and Dependency in Southeast Asia*, St Lucia: UQP, 1983, p. 6.
2 ibid.
3 p. 7.

4 p. 21.

5 q. Gullick, *Indigenous Political Systems*, p. 98.

6 Reid, *Slavery*, p. 8.

7 Hikayat, q. P. Sullivan, *Social Relations of Dependence in a Malay State: Nineteenth Century Perak*, KL: MBRAS, 1982, p. 63.

8 Reid, *Slavery*, pp. 8–9.

9 ibid., pp. 9–11.

10 pp. 299–300.

11 W. W. Birch, q. Sullivan, p. 50.

12 *Slavery*, p. 12.

13 in ibid., p. 153.

14 ibid., p. 12.

15 Warren, *Zone*, p. 219.

16 q. Reid, *Slavery*, p. 24.

17 q. ibid., p. 35.

18 James C. Scott, 'The Politics of Survival …', JSEAS, 4, 2 (September 1973), p. 244.

19 ibid., p. 246.

20 q. Mary R. Hollsteiner, *Reciprocity in the Lowland Philippines*, Quezon City: Ateneo, 1961, p. 8.

21 q. Porter, 'Ilocos', p. 107.

22 *The Huk Rebellion*, UCP, 1977, p. 10.

23 q. ibid., p. 123.

24 in M. Leifer, ed., *Nationalism, Revolution and Evolution in South-East Asia*, Zug: Inter Documentation, 1970, p. 14.

25 q. B. W. Andaya, *To Live as Brothers*, U Hawaii P, 1993, p. 39.

26 p. 54.

27 Reid, *Slavery*, p. 34.

28 Veth, q. Jan Breman, *Taming the Coolie Beast*, Delhi: OUP, 1989, p. 28.

29 q. ibid., p. 41.

30 q. ibid., p. 129.

31 q. ibid., p. 257.

32 q. ibid., p. 285.

33 q. ibid., p. 256.

34 Yen Ching-hwang, *A Social History of the Chinese in Singapore and Malaya, 1800–1911*, Singapore: OUP, 1986, p. 6.

35 *The Chinese in Malaya*, London: OUP, 1948, p. 199.

36 p. 200.

37 q. J. Norman Parmer, *Colonial Labor Policy and Administration*, Locust Valley: Augustin, 1960, p. 19.

38 Yen Ching-hwang, p. 37.

39 Turnbull, *Straits Settlements*, p. 109.

40 p. 112.

41 pp. 114–15.

42 p. 117.

43 q. Yen, pp. 115–16.

44 q. Edwin Lee, *The British as Rulers*, Singapore UP, 1991, p. 137.

45 in Ernest Chew and Edwin Lee, *A History of Singapore*, Singapore: OUP, 1991, pp. 242–3.

46 Tremewan, p. 33.

47 J. Ingleson, *In Search of Justice*, Singapore: OUP, 1986, p. 17.

48 p. 23.

49 p. 63.

50 p. 146.

51 *The Communist Party of Indonesia*, UCP, 1964, p. 155.

Armies and Guerrillas

The nature and purpose of the military forces of the pre-colonial, colonial, and post-colonial states differed, and the role they played also differed from state to state.

The idea that men banded together or sought protection from a patron did not disappear with the emergence of the state. Indeed, while a modern nation-state seeks to monopolise the use of force within its territories, and opposes the existence of private armies and paramilitary groups, it also regards its citizens as potential members of a national conscript army, and in some cases requires them to undergo compulsory military training or service.

The emergence of the state, however, also involved the emergence of more specialised military forces. They had two purposes: to maintain order within the state; and to protect or advance its position in relation to other states or entities. A number of problems also emerged, and states have struggled with them over the centuries, for they endure even amid changing circumstances. How was a military force to be sustained? How was its loyalty to the state to be ensured? How was its effectiveness to be maximised?

The resources available clearly depended on the wealth of a state and its capacity to mobilise that wealth. States that were still relatively weak were likely, like those in medieval England, to rely on the services of a well-equipped knightly class and its followers. Ensuring their loyalty was a matter of personal ties of fealty and of rewards for service, and involved leadership and diplomatic skills, not merely issuing orders. Regional ties might also be turned to account. In that respect the lack of a sense of 'nationality' was an asset. In conducting a 'foreign' war, however, it was a drawback, though mitigated by a similar deficiency on the part of the opponent. Effectiveness was increased not only by technological advance, but also by applying it creatively.

The problems changed their character in subsequent centuries but not their essence. A richer state could afford a stronger army, and it had the option of deciding whether and to what extent it should be a standing army, what the obligations of its subjects or citizens were, and how they should be enforced, and whether it could pay for mercenaries. The tension between civilian and military control became more apparent. And so did the impact and the cost of new technology.

Nineteenth-century Western states were able, both ideologically and organisationally, to mobilise their subjects or citizens en masse, evoking 'patriotism', dispensing with mercenary forces. They still faced immense costs and in World War I only the strongest survived a struggle the scale of which few had envisaged.

Pre-colonial armies

Even the most powerful states in Southeast Asia in the pre-colonial phase were weak. The answers they found for their military problems can be compared with those that early European states found. None could sustain a large standing army. Rulers sought to sustain a relatively small but loyal force that would support the dynasty and give the central government an advantage. Beyond that there were regional forces, which were both necessary in times of foreign war, and difficult to control in times of peace.

Early eighteenth-century Mataram, as Willem Remmelink puts it, was lacking in military muscle. A peasant militia melted away. The professionals, in any case not too good with their flintlocks, as the VOC was pleased to note, were also lacking in loyalty. Other patrimonial rulers were able to rely on slaves or mercenaries, if possible from other countries. That the VOC prohibited, while not giving the ruler a reliable praetorian guard.

The Burman monarchs again relied on the service of obligated followers, generally in the core region of the state, sometimes composed of originally non-Burman peoples settled there for the purpose, and also at times on mercenaries. Anauk-hpet-lun, for example, settled the followers of the Portuguese adventurer de Brito round Ava, and they became, with Indian Muslims, the backbone of the Restored Taung-ngu artillery.[1] The uncertainty of the loyalty of power-holders outside the core led monarchs to impose undue burdens on the core region, and undertaking major wars challenged the continuance of the dynasty itself.

Vietnamese monarchs divided their armies into two categories based, as Greg Lockhart says, on Chinese models, but also affording comparison with systems in other Southeast Asian monarchies. Elite or 'guards' regiments were responsible for the protection of the dynasty, and under the Nguyen were only recruited between Quang-binh and Binh-thuan, 'the regions most loyal to the dynasty'.[2] The far north and the far south provided only 'regional' regiments. Lockhart comments on the size of the military establishment, perhaps over 110 000, readily increased, moreover, in time of war. But he also points out that military units were, as in China, employed on civilian tasks, like repairing dikes, digging canals, collecting harvests, growing their own food, and working on palace and temple construction. Another Chinese model had long existed, the 'military-agricultural colony' (don dien), designed to stabilise frontiers and open up new land, and creating additional regional forces.

Don dien round Gia-dinh were the bases for Gia-long's march north against the Tay-son. They were also used in an attempt to stop the French invasion. The need to ensure loyalty led Minh-mang to insist that 'çivil officials must not consider guns and cannon to be the sphere of responsibility of military bureaucrats'.[3] Bureaucratic ties were not, however, an unequivocal guarantee of loyalty, nor, indeed, did they guarantee efficiency.

Colonial armies

The armies of states like these can be compared with those of early European states, but have much less in common with the citizen armies of the nation-state. It was in the phase in which those were developing in Europe that most of Southeast Asia was brought under colonial control. The Southeast Asian armies of the colonial phase may be compared with both those of contemporary Europe and those of Southeast Asia in the monarchical phase. Several features are at odds with the former but consonant with the latter. Unlike those of contemporary Europe, but not unlike those of the monarchies, they were not national armies. They were small forces, rarely recruited from the majority peoples, mercenary in character. In some respects, therefore, they resembled the monarchical forces. They differed in that they ceased to fight each other. The 'international' wars of Southeast Asia came to be fought or avoided outside Southeast Asia, and Southeast Asian armies increasingly had a 'law-and-order' role.

Southeast Asia did not therefore traverse the path that the Western states followed and that created the Western image of the army. That is of a force the primary task of which is to defend the state from other states, which might or might be thought to be threatening it, backing up or substituting for the diplomacy of interstate relations. At times, it might be called upon to deal with domestic unrest, but generally only as a result of a particular crisis. For the most part its focus was outward. That could, of course, affect its domestic role. A regime might win support at home by concentrating on enemies abroad, and the army might win a corresponding influence at home, and a corresponding share of the budget. In a major international crisis, indeed, the relationship of the government and the armed forces would tend to change. An army normally under civilian control might need greater powers. The English had customarily seen a standing army as a threat to liberty. An army based on conscription gave the modern state enormous power over all its subjects, and the role of the military authorities, and of the values associated with them, was highly contested.

In some sense the colonial world was insulated from this process. Before the colonial powers arrived, Southeast Asia had, of course, known intra-regional conflict, sometimes on a large and indeed devastating scale, particularly, perhaps, in respect of the struggles on the mainland. Those continued into the nineteenth century, in the early part of which states sought to strengthen themselves, less because of a threat from the Western powers than because of inter-state competition among Burma, Siam, and Vietnam.[4] It was for this reason that Minh-mang was anxious to acquire a steamer,[5] and Rama III fell out with the British merchant who sold him one.[6]

Colonial control brought such struggles to an end. It was not itself established without opposition, not only from the states of Southeast Asia, but also from guerrilla movements. Against them mobile rather than static tactics were employed—by van Heutsz in Aceh, for example—while increasingly it was recognised—as by Galliéni and Lyautey in Tonkin—that military operations had to be coordinated with political and socio-economic policies. But once that control was established, military conflict among states ceased until World War II challenged it and enabled Thailand to attack Vichy Indo-China. In a perhaps unprecedented way, Southeast Asian societies had been demilitarised. Their relations with one another were not determined by their relative strength, nor did competition among them prompt military modernisation as it did in Europe. In the aftermath of the Japanese occupation guerrilla war was renewed. Templer's tactics in the Emergency echoed Lyautey's. The Dutch lost 2500 in the war of Indonesian independence, 90 per cent in guerrilla actions. [7]

In the meantime within their territories colonial powers had used force sparingly but tellingly, their aim being to back up the relationship with cooperative elites on which they substantially relied. The role of such forces was rather that of an armed constabulary than an army, since there was no call for an external role. The colonial powers also tended to draw the non-Western element in their forces from peoples who did not form the majority among those over whom they claimed to rule. In that, of course, their actions were not without precedent in Southeast Asia—in Burma or in Mataram, for example—nor indeed in Europe before the emergence of the nation-state. But it meant that the armies of colonial Southeast Asia were in no sense national armies, as those of the West itself had become, and even in Siam, the exception to prove the rule, the army was heavily bureaucratised. It also meant that Southeast Asian armies could play but a limited role in defending Southeast Asia from a new external aggressor in World War II.

The restricted size, nature, and role of colonial armies were indeed made possible not only by the absence of inter-state conflict within Southeast Asia but by the absence also of external threats to all or any part of the region. Pre-colonial states had at times found it necessary to use their armies to defend themselves, in particular from the Chinese. It was, for example, war with the Chinese that compelled the Burmans to withdraw from Ayudhya after they had destroyed its capital and enabled Taksin to create a new Siam. In the colonial period there could be no such apprehension. China was able only to make ineffectual gestures in opposition to the establishment of French control in Vietnam.

For the most part, however, it was their naval predominance that served to protect the position of the colonial powers in Southeast Asia against external rivals. That had been built up over time, and in part as a result of rivalry among the Western states. In the course of such struggles, however, the naval strength of Southeast Asian states had been destroyed. That had the more immediate effect on states whose power had been rather naval than military, those of the peninsula and the archipelago in particular, but in the nineteenth century encompassed the mainland states as well. The impact of external naval threats was further diminished in the nineteenth century by the superior position of one power even among the predominant Europeans, Great Britain. In the twentieth century, when its superiority was threatened, it was able to welcome the United States, now a major naval power as well, to the region, and for a time at least both to conciliate and fend off the Japanese. It was this shield that—supplemented, albeit inadequately, by air forces in the interwar period—made it possible for the colonial powers largely to rely on constabulary-type forces and on local naval forces that had no more than a policing and anti-smuggling role.

Colonial powers were even so cautious over recruitment. In 1876 the Secretary of State asked Governor Jervois to consider the provision of a force to enable troops from India and Hong Kong to leave Perak after the post-assassination expedition. 'On the one hand it may be desirable that it should not appear to the Malays to be that of a dominant power imposed on them from without; on the other a force drawn from beyond the Peninsula may be found most reliable.'[8] A paramilitary force, mostly Sikh, was set up. In 1930 the Volksraad rejected the proposal of a co-operating nationalist, M. H. Thamrin, for creating a native militia. 'It seemed that *sana* [non-Indonesian members] feared a constantly trained *sini* [Indonesian] military far more than they were willing to admit.'[9] The people of Singapore 'built the base with their labour, and provided skilled technicians for the dockyard', McIntyre writes, 'but defence was supposed to be provided by other races'.[10]

Colonial powers indeed hesitated to go further even in face of the growing threat from outside that Japan began to present in the 1930s. Could they build up local forces upon which they could rely? That suggested evoking a national spirit against a national enemy, and it might turn against the colonial power itself. Before World War I military authorities had suggested creating a Malayan defence force, two battalions of Malay infantry to serve alongside one British. 'By taking thought in time', said the Inspector-General of Overseas Forces, Ian Hamilton, 'we may save the stitches nine. A loyal and patriotic Malay nation, trained to arms[,] might well prove in future a fitting guardian for the Western portal to the Pacific [and] a doughty defender of one of the richest and fairest portions of the British Empire.'[11] No such proposal was implemented, for, as Hamilton's own words suggested, it implied a major change in Malaya's political position. As World War II threatened to engulf Southeast Asia, and to give Japan its chance to intervene, a visiting New Zealander commented in Batavia on the limited size of the local force. His Dominion was raising 75 000 men out a population of 1.5 million. Netherlands India ought to raise more than 100 000. The British consul-general referred to 'the uncertain value of much of the human material available'.[12]

When external defences failed, the territories were without effective defence. Indian troops were to fight heroically for the British, as the names on the war memorials at

Kranji and in Labuan testify. In analysing the reasons for the 'fall' of Singapore, Perham and Gent and his colleagues at the Colonial Office recognised that a colonial territory could not defend itself, and associated the future security of the territory with nation-building, the tasks being, as it were, redistributed, with an imperial base in Singapore, and a unified Malaya more capable of defending itself. To elicit the loyalty and the service that a modern army required, the concept of the state had also to be modernised along the lines of the nation-states of the West. Colonial regimes had to be defended by others. If they had to defend themselves, they could no longer be colonial.

Post-colonial armies

The Japanese sought to square this circle. Partly under the impulse of the GEACPS, and partly under the pressure of short-term necessity, they were prepared to create and utilise military forces recruited from the majority peoples and on a patriotic principle, if not always an explicitly national one. They sought to win over the Indians, creating an Indian National Army under leaders who aspired to redeem India from foreign rule. They also welcomed the collaboration of a Thakin-led Burma Army. In Indonesia, though they were reluctant to promote the advance to independence within the Sphere offered to Burma and to the Philippines, they created PETA, a Japanese-led army recruited among the Javanese.

In most territories independence did not, however, come easily: it required a struggle against the colonial powers. In that the forces that the Japanese trained played a role. There was also a role for guerrilla forces, for example in Indonesia, where they picked up some of the locally disposable force that the *jago* could release. The nature and role of the armies in the new nation-states were affected by the ways in which they emerged. The military might assume, formally or informally, a leading role in their government, challenging civilian control. At the same time, it might itself be more unified in appearance than reality, and reflect its heterogeneous origins, and also the regional and 'ethnic' loyalties that were the legacy of the pre-colonial and colonial past and the result of geographical factors. Modern Western-style armies, like modern nations, had to be created by continued effort over time, though their relationship was mutual.

The role of armies in post-colonial Southeast Asia extended beyond their role in colonial Southeast Asia. They were no longer primarily armed constabularies: they were also nation-builders. That meant that their role was larger, too, than that of the armies in conventional Western state in normal times, and it was possible for military leaders both to evoke the precedent of the peasant armies of earlier Southeast Asian monarchies and to draw on the ideology of unconventional Western states. Armies, too, came to be associated with 'development'. Distinguishing it from the 'professionalism' of conventional Western armies, their augmented role was sometimes captured in, if not rationalised by, the term 'new professionalism'.[13]

In another respect, however, their role was more limited than the role of the armies in the West, and even perhaps those of pre-colonial Southeast Asia. It was still more focused on the internal than the external, on preservation rather than defence or attack. Whatever the level of conflict within states in post-colonial Southeast Asia, and whatever the tensions among the great powers, conflict between or among Southeast Asian states was rare. In the Cold War itself the great powers generally respected the frontiers of the new states, seeking rather to influence the governments within them than to alter their colonial inheritance, and membership of the United Nations was a further constraint. The super-powers were aware, too, of their common interests, as well as their mutual antagonism, and there were limits beyond which, particularly after the Korean War, they avoided going. States in Southeast Asia might pursue their security and their interests by aligning themselves with one side or the other. They might also try to increase their leverage by a policy of 'neutrality' and by affirming the Bandung principles.

In Vietnam, indeed, the United States sought the involvement of other states, in Southeast Asia as well as outside, including Thailand and the Philippines, while Cambodia was drawn in, too. But the Bandung principles gained ground as US intervention wound down. The Vietnam–Cambodia conflict of 1978 linked old antagonisms with the Sino-Soviet dimension of the Cold War. But it also prompted attempts to expand the concept of a zone of stability and non-interference. ASEAN sought both to avoid regional conflict and to resolve differences that arose among its members. It was designed to continue the inter-state peace that had prevailed, with the signal exception of the Vietnam–Cambodia struggle, ever since the colonial period. The members have stopped short of integrating their forces: 'they have been far more active and determined in their separate and, usually, secretive arms build-up programmes and acquisition of sophisticated weaponry'.[14] Their aim is, after all, to maintain their national identity. Nor do they wish to provoke the PRC.

The armies of modern Southeast Asia reflect therefore both a commonality and a diversity of experience. Their defence role is generally limited. Their domestic role varies from country to country. It naturally tends to be larger in countries that had to fight for their independence. But there an army may also be more difficult to hold together, both because of its origins, and because of the wider range of interests, options, and arguments that an expanded role in the state involves.

Indonesia

The Indonesian army was put together from a number of sources that reflect phases in the development of the state itself. The VOC had not, of course, relied merely on naval strength, and its intervention in Mataram involved some major campaigns. The Maluku garrison of 1618–20 included soldiers from Scotland and the Shetlands, from Bremen and Hamburg: like the missionary activity of the Catholic church, the

VOC was a European venture, not merely a 'national' one. In the mid-seventeenth century, its officers were exclusively European, though not exclusively Dutch. The soldiery was, as Merle Ricklefs puts it, 'an ethnic patchwork. There were Europeans of various origins, people of mixed ancestry of various kinds and companies recruited from particular Indonesian areas. The VOC seems to have kept companies of Mestizos, Mardijkers [freemen], Ambonese, Balinese and Bugis military on a fairly permanent footing and enlisted more Indonesians when they were needed. In major campaigns the Company always fought alongside local allies with their own commanding officers.'[15]

At the end of the Java war in 1830 the military forces the Dutch kingdom had in the Indies numbered 13 555, of whom 6000 were Europeans. It was in that year that the colonial state formally created its army, KNIL, the Royal Netherlands Indies Army. In 1853 it comprised 1218 officers and 26 678 men, of whom 10 343 were Europeans, 1744 Ambonese, and 14 591 Javanese, Sundanese, Buginese, and Madurese. Where no sense of nation existed, it was possible to use Indonesians against Indonesians. The Dutch recruited from the majority people, but the officers were largely European, and the Javanese were balanced against recruits from other parts of the archipelago. In 1937 the KNIL included 12 700 Javanese, 5100 Menadonese, 4000 Ambonese, 1800 Sundanese, 1100 Timorese, and 400 Madurese, Bugis, Acehnese, and Malays.[16] Recruitment from Maluku had become more significant.

The KNIL, as Ulf Sundhaussen says, was 'originally designed for internal security purposes only'.[17] With the threat of Japanese aggression it began to retrain for external defence as well, and a number of Indonesians were admitted to the new Military Cadet School in Bandung. The Japanese administration transformed the situation in Java, though not elsewhere. It had only 10 000 troops in Java, seen as a resource base. As the overall situation deteriorated it moved in October 1943 to establish PETA (Pasukan Sukarela untuk Membela Tanah Jawa, Volunteer Force for the Defence of Java), which at the time of the surrender consisted of sixty-nine battalions in Java and Bali: at full strength 33 000 men in Java and 1500 in Bali. It was given basic infantry training and 'a *samurai* type of indoctrination aimed at stimulating a high level of fighting spirit (*semangat*) [*seishin*]'.[18] Indonesians served as officers, even as battalion commanders: a few of those commissioned, like Suharto, were former KNIL non-commissioned officers. The Hei-ho, a small auxiliary corps that had been set up late in 1942 mainly for guard duties, was by contrast commanded solely by Japanese officers, but, though not seen as prestigious, it was probably almost as well trained. In addition the nationalists organised the paramilitary Barisan Pelopor (Vanguard Corps) and the Muslim organisation Masjumi the Hizbu'llah (Army of Allah). Youth organisations were also created and given both indoctrination and some military training. Javanese society was, it might be said, re-militarised.

On the declaration of independence, however, the surrendering Japanese disarmed PETA and other weapon-carrying organisations. The Republican leaders, furthermore, hoped to secure independence by diplomacy rather than struggle, and supported the dissolution of PETA, rather than its transformation into a national army. *Pemuda* (youth) groups, however, formed fighting organisations of their own, the *laskar*, and in order to maintain law and order the Republic set up the BKR (Badan Keamanan Rakyat, People's Security Agency) on 22 August, joined mainly by PETA personnel. The readiness of General Christison, the commander of the British and Indian troops in Java, to deal with the Republic dissipated some of the caution of its leaders[19], and early in October the BKR became the TKR (Tentera Keamanan Rakyat, People's Security Army), still concerned with security, its title suggested, but now an army, and better able not only to preserve law and order but also to influence negotiations. Most of fifteen commissioned KNIL officers of Indonesian origin joined it, believing that the surrender of 1942 had terminated their obligations to the Dutch crown, and so, even more willingly, did the Bandung cadets, among them being A. H. Nasution and T. B. Simatupang. So, too, did some of the *laskar*. In the new year, as the political situation again shifted, the force was again renamed, and in a more explicitly national way—it became the Tentera Republik Indonesia (Army of the Republic of Indonesia)—and it was reorganised.

In such reorganisations the better-trained ex-KNIL officers were bound to play a predominant role. That did not, however, mean that they differed from their more numerous PETA counterparts over the role of the army as a whole. Whether or not they were influenced by their Japanese training, ex-PETA officers had no experience of subordination to a civilian authority and were 'accustomed to an existence free from civilian interference or direction.'[20] Ex-KNIL officers, trained differently, were aware, however, that, even in the West, political and military functions were closely integrated in times of crisis. The peril in which the Republic stood argued for a special role for the army, and the attempts of the civilian cabinets to control it only tended to increase its distrust of the *diplomasi* they pursued and its identification with Tan Malaka's demand for full independence. Its commander-in-chief, Sudirman, an ex-PETA battalion commander, identified the army with the nation. Its loyalty was to the revolution. 'The army considered itself to be the guardian of the state ideology', wrote Simatupang. 'This is a position which reminds one of the attitudes among military leaders during the Weimar Republic in Germany, who considered themselves to be the bearer of the idea of the state.'[21]

Defeat in the first police action prompted Hatta's attempts to 'rationalise' the army and make it more efficient. As deputy to Sudirman, Nasution drew up a defence plan, based on the experience of the police action. It called for guerrilla war, or 'total people's war', and the creation of territorial defence forces and fully armed mobile striking forces. The plan was denounced by the PKI and labelled 'Spoor's plan.'[22] The party's allies in the armed forces seized Madiun, and though the revolt was suppressed, the army retained a lasting antagonism to the communists and the left.

The second police action, which the Dutch undertook even though the defeat of the communists had given the Republic a new measure of international support, enhanced the army's role. President Sukarno and other civilian leaders had been made prisoner. 'Whether our Republic will perish or continue to exist at present primarily depends on whether the Republic still lives in the hearts of the officers, non-commissioned officers and soldiers of the Indonesian National Army', Simatupang declared.[23] These were the heroic days of Sudirman, *bapak tentera,* a sick man in a sedan chair but determined to resist. Guerrilla activity indeed played a role in making the Dutch realise that, despite their initial success, they could not win. The army distrusted the renewal of *diplomasi* that followed, and Sudirman was tempted to resign. Unity between Sukarno–Hatta and the TNI must come first, Nasution argued, and the cease-fire went into effect, Sudirman exhibiting the 'disinterested loyalty' that was the first quality of the *ksatria* (warrior).[24]

Sudirman died early in 1950, and the first government of independent Indonesia, led by Hatta, installed Simatupang as chief-of-staff of the armed forces and Nasution as army chief-of-staff. Ex-KNIL officers, not ex-PETA nor ex-*laskar,* they were nevertheless not simply the 'professional soldier' in the Western image. Simatupang was against 'Kuomintangism' and 'Latin Americanism', and did not want a merely military government, often the feature of 'liberated' states. He did, however, see the structuring of the new state as a 'joint effort on the part of both political and military leaders'[25] and, given the existence of armed opposition within the new state, it clearly had an internal security role. The relationship of the partners was, however, difficult to settle. The new army leaders renewed the programme of rationalisation and efficiency. Nasution cut the army down to 200 000, including 26 000 ex-KNIL, while 80 000 *laskar* were still unintegrated. Officers alienated by the programme encouraged political intervention in 1952, and the ex-KNIL leaders were driven out. Early in 1955 a conference at Yogyakarta re-established unity within the army, and it opposed political intervention by reasserting its national role yet more strongly.

That did not amount to a take-over. Restored to his position as army chief-of-staff, Nasution wanted to cooperate with the government as long as it worked for the common good and not merely for sectional interests. The tumultuous events that followed the 1955 elections, however, vastly enhanced the role of the army, even though they began with acts of military insubordination. In March 1957, accepting a proposal from Nasution, Sukarno proclaimed martial law, using the Dutch Regulation on the State of War and Siege of 1939. In the subsequent struggle, Nasution both demonstrated the army's strength and sought to win the rebels back to the fold. He was successful. The seizure of Dutch property helped. So did the interest in opposing communism shared by the army leadership and the rebels. 'For Nasution and the Army the regional rebellion had turned out to be a blessing in disguise.'[26]

In November 1958, by which time the military already occupied a wide range of non-military functions, including the management of former Dutch companies, he redefined the role of the army in terms of a 'Middle Way'. It had to be seen, he said, as 'not just the "civilian tool" like in the Western countries, nor a "military regime" which dominates the state power, but as one of the many forces in society, the force for the struggle of the people which works together with other people's forces'.[27] That, as Salim Said puts it, started 'the long journey of the *dwi fungsi* ("dual function") doctrine, which in essence legitimized the sociopolitical role of the military'.[28] Nasution accepted Sukarno's Guided Democracy. He sought to minimise the role of parties and expand that of 'functional groups'.

He was, however, a critic of the army-dominated regime Suharto created after the abortive coup of 1965. Dwi fungsi had changed again, and Nasution called, not for its abandonment, but for its 'purification'.[29] He argued, indeed, that the mode of its implementation under the New Order put the army in the same position as the colonial army, an army used to implement the government's policy. That, he claimed, was contrary to Sudirman's position: the army should not be a 'dead tool' in the hands of government.[30] Politics was too serious to be left to the politicians. Nasution had, it seems, seen the army rather in the role of monitor than actor, of trustee rather than director. But he had himself concluded that political parties were neither a proper nor a necessary check upon it. That left little else but self-regulation.

Sundhaussen concludes his magisterial account of the role of the Indonesian army by setting it against S. E. Finer's conclusion in *The Man on Horseback* that in unstable Third World polities military regimes are inevitable. It does not, he suggests, justify so fatalistic a view. If the army did not adopt the position of a peacetime Western army, it did in the first twenty years show 'a remarkable degree of restraint'. TNI leaders 'first reacted to provocation and intrusion by politicians into the military sphere, and only gradually expanded their political roles in the face of progressive civilian failures'. The take-over was not inevitable.[31] Once it had occurred, however, it was certainly difficult to undo. Under the New Order, half of the *bupati* were army officers and one-third of the ambassadors. Thousands of officers, active or retired, were appointed or seconded to other posts. The practice was stopped in 1999, one year after Suharto's fall.

Moluccans from KNIL had endeavoured to set up an independent republic in 1950, breaking away from newly independent Indonesia. They were defeated, and many went to the Netherlands. By the 1970s the community there numbered 32 000. Impatient at their treatment, the exiles turned to terrorism. The Dutch government resorted to what might have recalled colonial tactics. 'Dumbfounded, the people watched the television screens, as jets dived over one of their trains and tanks attacked one of their schools.'[32]

Burma

The Burmese army offers some parallels with the Indonesian, though it has not been the subject of such sophisticated study. The military system of the monarchy and its reliance on men assigned to its service were displaced by the British. In their wars, they mainly relied on British and Indian troops. In the Company phase they also raised local forces, such as the Arracan Light Infantry, which fought on the British side in the second war. After the Indian Mutiny of 1857, however, most local forces were disbanded, and the army was recruited from the 'martial races' of India, organised into battalions by 'class companies'. Even so Karen units were raised for active service in the third war. The only regular army unit recruiting Burmans, however, was the Sappers and Miners, formed in 1887.[33]

In World War I four battalions of Burma Rifles were formed—Karens the largest element, but also Burmans, Arakanese, Kachins, Chins, Shans, and Gurkhas—and they served in the Middle East. After the war the number of battalions was reduced, and in 1925 recruitment of Burmans was terminated. The standard composition of a battalion of Burma Rifles was two companies of Karens, one of Kachins, and one of Chins. In 1927 the Sappers and Miners were disbanded, and Burmans could thus serve only in the military police. Ten years later, when Burma's new constitution was inaugurated, Burmans were again recruited into the Rifles, but they found other races occupying the higher ranks. In 1939 only 472 Burmans (including Mons and Shans) were members of the armed forces: there were 1448 Karens, 868 Chins, 168 others. There were four Burman officers, seventy-five from the 'minorities'.[34] Expansion after the outbreak of war in 1939 led to the recruitment of more Burmans, but two whole battalions were made up of Shans, officered entirely by Shans. The new troops were raw and, by the time the Allied forces were retreating towards the Indian border in face of the Japanese, 'most of the newly-raised units had been reduced to their British officers and their Indian clerks', and only the 2nd Burma Rifles remained a fighting unit to the last. About 800–1000 survivors of Burcorps remained. Some 500 volunteered to stay on, the majority of them Delta Karens, 'whose families were even then in mortal danger from BIA tyranny'.[35]

The Burma Independence Army force was created by Aung San and his thirty comrades who had secured Japanese military training in 1940–41, and recruited expatriate Burmans in Thailand. When the Japanese invaded Burma, the BIA entered Tenasserim, recruiting as it went, and about 4000 actually fought against the British. It regarded all Karens as British collaborators, and its actions did much to intensify the Burman–Karen feud. Many of its units were uncontrollable, and on 24 July 1942 the Japanese disbanded it. A smaller and more disciplined Burma Defence Army was formed, recruited in part from the BIA, in part from veterans of the Burma Rifles and the military police, and trained in a military academy set up at Mingaladon. With 'independence', Ne Win became chief-of-staff, and Aung San minister for defence, and the force was retitled Burma National Army (Burma Tatmadaw), but its role remained largely that of national security. Almost entirely Burman, it is said to have added a Karen battalion, thanks partly to Aung San.

After the liberation of Rangoon in May 1945, personnel of the BNA, which had defected to the British side in March, were given the opportunity of enlisting in the regular army, the nucleus of which was the re-formed 2nd Burma Rifles, one-third

Karen, one-third Chin, one-third Kachin. Aung San wanted the BNA battalions incorporated as whole units, but though he argued that the men felt that they had 'lost their soul', and were being made to 'give up an organisation which has already become a nation[al] institution',[36] the British insisted on individual recruitment. They did, however, abandon the 'class company' concept, and in that way BNA comrades were kept together as the overwhelming majority of the Burman units. Many did not join up, but formed the People's Volunteer Organisation (PVO, Pyithu Yebaw Ahphwe), allegedly an old comrades association, in fact a private army for the AFPFL.

Learning of Aung San's political ambitions when a commission for him was being discussed, Mountbatten insisted 'that the choice must be clear cut. Soldiers, throughout the British Empire, were not allowed to partake in political activity.'[37] In the 'fourth Anglo-Burmese war', however, liaison with the Burman battalions was maintained and, with the backing of the PVO, helped to ensure victory. The prospect of early independence, coupled with the assassination of Aung San in July 1947 and the accession of a civilian premier, led on the other hand to a loss of prestige, both in the Burman battalions and the PVO, and 'a tremendous loss of direction'.[38]

The independent government was thus challenged, not only by the communists, but also by the PVO, despite Nu's attempt to retain their allegiance with a 'Leftist Unity' programme of May 1948. About 60 per cent of them resorted to arms, and three of the ex-PBF battalions mutinied, though not the 4th Battalion, formerly commanded by Ne Win. The government was able to rely upon the six battalions of Karen and Kachin Rifles. But some Karens wanted to take advantage of the government's helplessness, while many justifiably feared the rebel PVO, and also the local security forces that the government recruited from loyal PVO. Outright clashes ensued between the newly formed Karen National Defence Organisation and the PVO and ex-PVO forces. Three Karen battalions 'threw in their lot with their brothers',[39] and for a while Rangoon itself was under threat.

The army that, with the aid of the air force, gradually restored a measure of security in the subsequent years and drove the rebels into the hills, had, of course, to be substantially reconstructed. All Karens were at once relieved of their posts, and new battalions were formed. The Kachin Rifles were expanded from three to six battalions, and three new battalions of Shan Rifles were constituted. In the early 1950s the fighting strength was greatly increased, in part by incorporating more of the irregulars. Though it had to deal with the incursion of Kuomintang troops into Kengtung, its main role in the 1950s was, as Tinker puts it, an 'internal security' one, and its disposition seemed to have 'little relevance to the possibility of external attack'.[40]

In the 1960s the army in Burma, like that in Indonesia, assumed a governing role, in which Mingaladon graduates stood out. In part it was responding to the civilians, and in part redeeming what it considered their inadequacies. The concessions Nu offered the minorities, for example, it saw as an attack upon the Union it had fought to maintain. In the subsequent years, the tension took a different form, between those who continued to fight the rebels, and those who enjoyed a semi-civilian life and the perquisites of power, the 'military' faction and the 'party' faction. After the 1988 crisis, its size grew: 170 000 strong that year, it numbered 350 000 in 1997. So did its dominance.

Vietnam

Postwar Vietnam had to fight against external powers far longer than other Southeast Asian states and it also contended with civil war. Such events, of course, shaped the role of the military. Traditional Vietnam, like its Chinese exemplar, asserted civilian control, and it was indeed civilian mandarins who led the disastrous struggles with the French. Under the Nguyen, elite troops, combined with different combinations of regional forces, had sufficed to deal with rebellion, but they could not deal with the French incursion into Cochin-China. They fell back on a defensive strategy and then on a defeatist one. Garnier took the citadel at Hanoi in 1873 with 212 men. Only far too late did the dynasty authorise popular resistance in the north on the basis of *can vuong* (save the king). Breaking its back 'in hundreds of fortified villages was an expensive, bloody and time consuming business', and took 30 000 troops.[41] Galliéni adopted the 'oil spot' technique. 'One only moves into new territory after having completely organised that in the rear. They are the unsubdued indigenes of yesterday who aid us and who serve to prevail over the unsubdued of tomorrow.'[42]

Vietnamese Christians had fought on the French side in the 1860s. Le Myre de Villers recruited the first 1700-strong Vietnamese regiment of *tirailleurs* in 1879. A second one followed in 1903, replacing French and French African troops redeployed elsewhere in the empire. Many 'volunteers' went to war after 1914. By 1930 out of the thirty-one battalions in the Indo-China army, twenty were indigenous, some 20 000 men. In addition there was a militia (Garde Indigène), a paramilitary force based, like the old regional forces, on the provinces, some 15 220 men, with 388 French officers and NCOs. The army was the target of the nationalists in the late 1920s, and in January 1930 a mutiny broke out at Yen-bay, a military post of over 600 troops, commanded by French officers and NCOs. It was a fiasco, and the French were able to deal with the unrest of 1930–31, too, though resorting to air attacks.

The French army, depleted to help defend France itself, was, however, in no position to resist the Japanese. Instead France compromised. Not breaking the continuity of French control till the coup of 9 March 1945, Japan did not create a national army in the months remaining before its surrender, only beginning to create a *giyutai*, more limited than a *giyugun* (volunteer army). The Vanguard Youth movement, developed under the Vichy regime, was, however, allowed to become more political in orientation. But, as law and order broke down, bandits and brigands became more threatening, and the Indochinese Communist Party seized the opportunity to renew a guerrilla struggle, borrowing and adapting the concepts Mao put forward in China.

In the conflict between the returning French and the Viet Minh regime that was finally joined in December 1946, the latter were aided by the recruitment of perhaps 10 000 ex-colonial officers and troops, and by training received from some Japanese officers. With the initial French successes, however, the war once more became a guerrilla struggle. Victory eluded the French, and their military efforts were costly to them in terms of both lives and what a British Foreign official called the 'drain of treasure'.[43] They had raised thirty-three Vietnamese battalions by December 1948, but those were incorporated in the French Expeditionary Force. France found it difficult to set up an alternative regime and to give it its own army: 'few Vietnamese would join the army unless they had a real incentive to do so'.[44] On the other hand, encouraged and supported by the triumphant CCP, Vo Nguyen Giap was able to proceed to the 'war of movement' and finally to inflict a major defeat on the French at Dien Bien Phu. Now, as Lockhart puts it, 'everyone knew that the French had been defeated'.[45]

Creating a rival army was, of course, a major task for the Ngo Dinh Diem regime, supported by the United States. Indeed not only Chinese and Vietnamese precedent but also the state-building requirements of the present led the President to assert a direct control over the army. Once he was certain of its loyalty, he used it 'as an instrument to consolidate and extend government control'.[46] Of twenty-two chiefs of province in Cochin-China in April 1957, fourteen were army officers, and of these nine were at the same time commanders of military subzones. Insofar as the ARVN was prepared for war, however, its American advisers had not prepared it for the kind of war it was to face. Instead they had conceived of a Korean-style war. The crisis that ensued led to the collapse of the Diem regime and a military take-over.

The United States, however, pushed the ARVN into the background, resorting to a bombing campaign in the north and then to introducing its own troops in the south. Like the French, the Americans resorted only belatedly to 'Vietnamisation', and to building up the ARVN, the object being, according to a critic of US policy, Senator W. Fulbright, to keep 'our punchy protégés in Saigon staggering around the ring for a few years longer'.[47] Armies are, of course, an opportunity for individual advancement as well as a provider of common defence. In this one, it seems, the former objective predominated. It was not, says Alexander Woodside, 'a major channel for satisfying nationalist aspirations. But it was a major channel for satisfying upward-mobility aspirations, especially ... the career dreams of sons of the landowner and bureaucratic classes'.[48] But it is possible that the failure of the whole venture may have meant that the ARVN's qualities have been undervalued.

Under Vo Nguyen Giap, the army of the DRVN developed into 'a cohesive, disciplined, thoroughly professional fighting corps'.[49] Army and government were closely integrated through the communist party. 'The units of the Lao Dong Party in each section, and in each company, are the backbone of the Army. They discuss every phase of the coming battles, and the political commissar is the key officer. Except in actual combat, his position is as important as the military commander's.'[50] It was the Politburo's task to integrate the policy of the government and the strategy of the army. The faction that leaned towards the Soviet Union, led by Le Duan, tended to prevail, and Giap, stressing armaments and professionalism, leaned that way.[51]

The People's Army was over one million strong in the mid-1980s, the second-largest army in Asia. The nature of economic reform in Vietnam in the 1980s and 1990s led to growing tension between the army and the civilian leadership. If ARVN officers had fled or been re-educated after 1975, now victorious veterans were neglected and current pay rates lowered. The impact of the changes in the Soviet Union on the Seventh Party congress in 1991 prompted an increase in military influence. 'This heavy concentration of military men', Michael Williams wrote in 1992, 'is likely to find reflection in opposition not only to cuts in the size of the armed forces but to any move towards pluralism or multi-party democracy'.[52] Aware of its historic role, the army tended also to identify itself with the 'socialist system', and to criticise those who, while seeking to retain party dominance, were pursuing privatisation and free market initiatives. In 1995 it suggested that those were the goals of American imperialism, and that the market line was a decisive precondition for 'the final victory—the victory in peace—[that] will belong to the United States'.[53] The army flexed its muscles, and its chief political commissar, Le Kha Phieu, became party chief in 1997.

Thailand

The trajectory of military development in Siam/Thailand offers comparisons and contrasts. Unlike Indonesia, Burma, and Vietnam, it did not undergo colonial rule. It could thus make an easier transition from royal army to national army. Yet after 1932 the army assumed a major role in the revolution that Siam did undergo, not one that overthrew a colonial power, but one that ended an absolute monarchy. It thus staked a claim to a share in government, even at times to a dominance over government, and assumed some kind of guardianship role. Though an independent state, Siam/Thailand fought no major wars in the modern period. Its army's duties were therefore mainly domestic. Even earlier than the army in Indonesia, it became heavily bureaucratised, and then heavily involved in 'development'.

The modern Thai army may be traced back to the establishment of a military pages' corps, trained by English officers on loan from India, under Mongkut. In 1870, his successor, Chulalongkorn, organised a European-style military troop among his pages, the king's Guard Regiment, and other specialised military corps followed. In 1886 all land and sea forces were brought together in the Military Affairs Department, and a military cadet school was set up. After the creation of the cabinet in 1892, military matters were gradually concentrated in the Defence Ministry. At the other end of the scale, the old system of service was replaced by conscription in the non-British European style.

In 1905 the position of Commander-in-Chief was created. The Crown Prince was appointed, and under Chulalongkorn most of the highest officers were princes trained in overseas military academies: 'in the process of reorganizing and strengthening', as David A. Wilson puts it, he was 'careful to keep control of this powerful instrument in the hands of loyal princes'.[54] It did, however, assume a rather special position. Rama VI created a Council of National Defence, 'a sort of military cabinet', which 'put military affairs on a governmental footing approximately equal to all civil affairs combined'.[55] The special position the armed forces secured under the absolute monarchy helped to determine their position under subsequent regimes.

Modernisation made it possible to send the small expeditionary force to France in World War I, and unlike modernisation in other spheres, it was carried through without foreign advisers. The army was thus a source of national pride. The main role was still domestic. 'As a school of training and as a safeguard of internal peace and order', wrote W. A. Graham in 1924, 'the maintenance of armed forces sufficient adequately to reinforce the gendarmerie and police is not only desirable but absolutely necessary whatever may be the nature and extent of their foreign political value'.[56] Its foreign role had indeed been limited. But that, too, had to be seen through a domestic prism. The army, made up of Thais and led by them, was an emblem, if not a guarantee, of Siam's independence.

In the coup that overthrew the absolute monarchy in 1932, civilian and military Promoters worked together in opposition to the dominance of the princes and the budget cuts applied both to armed forces and civilian bureaucracy as a result of the Depression. But proceeding by coup almost guaranteed the subsequent dominance of the military. 'Civilians might have continued to rule if they had stuck together', Wilson observes. 'But they did not.'[57] A second coup in 1933 re-emphasised that the proponents of constitutional government depended on the military. In the coming years the army increased its share of the budget, and it became very much the constituency of the minister for defence, Pibun, who became prime minister in 1938.

The onset of international conflict further enhanced the role of the military, and it even engaged in conflict with neighbouring Indo-China. The ties between Pibun and the Japanese gave the civilians an opportunity to overthrow him when the tide of war turned in favour of the allies. The civilians now sought constitutional limitations on the role of the military. The coup of November 1947, carried out almost entirely by army officers, was, by contrast, designed to 'exonerate the honor of the army which had been trampled underfoot'.[58] Aware of the corruption of the postwar governments, the military leadership also assumed the role of saving the nation from 'the dishonesty and evil of various kinds in the government circle'.[59]

Army leaders were able, too, to invoke the special connexion of the military forces with the long-standing independence of the Thai state. 'Thailand is a country which is independent and fully sovereign', Field Marshal Phin Choonharan declared in 1955, 'and it must have an army to shield, defend and maintain its independence and sovereignty undivided. ...' As commander-in-chief of the army, he said, he 'tried fully to have our army go ahead speedily into a state of development greater than that of our neighbors which have just recently joined the ranks of independent nations'.[60] Virtually unchecked in the 1950s, however, the military forces became themselves a focus of corruption and factional strife. Sarit's coup of 1957 was in turn designed to 'clean up the mess'.[61] His regime was also 'development'-oriented.

'Politics is government service and government service is politics …', General Arthit Kamlang-ek was to declare. 'If the military is also responsible for government service, how can it be separated from politics?'[62] Recent decades have witnessed a series of attempts to accommodate the position of the armed forces in a Thailand at once more developed and more democratic.

The Philippines

Though Filipino troops took part in the Franco-Spanish expedition against Nguyen Vietnam in 1858, the colonial army of the Spaniards was primarily a constabulary force, and was indeed often needed to back up the municipal, provincial, and regional police forces.[63] From the beginning of their regime, the Spaniards had drawn on the local population, and there was no European garrison 1570–1828. They found the Pampangans notably loyal.[64] 'Common soldiers were recruited from the indigenous population by military conscription though unit commanders had to be of European or Mestizo origin', Bankoff writes of the nineteenth-century Philippines.[65] Otherwise the European component included just 1500 artillerymen.

Within the Philippines the US regime relied on the municipal police and on the armed Constabulary, successor to the Spanish Guarda Civil. 'The general purpose of the constabulary was to serve as the enforcement arm of the civilian government, acting as a combination-state police and FBI.'[66] Its officers initially came from the US Army, but Filipinos soon came to join the upper ranks. 'Prior to 1934, the only American official responsible for Philippine affairs who sought to include any preparations for national defense as a part of the education for self-government was Gov. Gen. Leonard Wood.'[67] Governor-General Murphy vetoed a bill for the creation of a bureau of national defence in 1934. A Philippine National Guard, set up in World War I, had been abolished.

'All these many years we have helped you in education, sanitation, road-building and even in the practice of self-government', General MacArthur told Quezon. 'But we have done nothing in the way of preparing you to defend yourselves against a foreign foe.'[68] With the establishment of the Commonwealth in 1935 and the fixing of a date for independence, the old policy became outdated, and the change in the policy of Japan, marked by the Manchurian adventure, underlined the need for the Philippines to build up a defence force of its own. 'Self-defense is the supreme right of mankind no more sacred to the individual than to the nation', Quezon told the inaugural session of the National Assembly in November 1935, 'the interests of which are immeasurably of greater significance and extent'.[69] MacArthur was

Quezon's choice as miltary adviser. '[H]is appointment as Field Marshal of a State and an army, neither of which has, as yet, an independent existence, was', General Pershing thought, 'more or less ridiculous'.[70]

Initially incorporating the Constabulary, though that was separated from it again in 1938, the army grew in size. Quezon envisaged a total force of only about 10 000 enlisted men, roughly equivalent to the military strength of the US army in the Philippines at the time, including Filipinos in American service. But men over twenty-one were liable to serve, and a reserve force was also trained at the rate of some 30 000 a year. Such a force offered no security against a Japanese attack, however, and critics like Camilio Osias, editor of *Philippine Forum,* argued that, since defence could not be adequate, it would be better to have none, but to have independence earlier, plus neutralisation. The uncertainty of the American commitment was only resolved in July 1941 at the time of the Japanese move on southern Indo-China. The Philippine Army became part of the US armed forces, and Roosevelt named MacArthur as commander of the US Army Forces in the Far East (USAFFE). They were, however, in no position effectively to resist an attack on the scale or of the scope of that the Japanese launched in December.

The inability of the colonial power to defend the Philippines was mainly determined by its other priorities. Of some effect, however, was the tension that arose because of the colony's advance to the semi-autonomous status of the Commonwealth government. F. B. Sayre, the US high commissioner, shared with other Americans in Manila, and also with critics like Aguinaldo, the fear that an army would encourage Quezon to act like a dictator. It was indeed true that the concept of national defence in the Philippines, set out by L. Siguion Reyna of the department of the interior in May 1935, gave the army, not only a defence role, but a civilian one. It would engage in other activities, like road construction and agricultural colonisation in Mindanao. It would thus not only defend the nation and train its youth. It would also engage in civic action. That would help to justify military expenditure, at the cost, however, of obscuring the division of responsibilities between the civilians and the military.

In the Philippines the Japanese did not create an army till December 1944, when they set up Makapili, Patriotic League of Filipinos, nominally led by Artemio Ricarte, a nationalist who had gone to Japan years before, but drawing also on the Sakdal resistance of the 1930s. In the postwar phase the Americans assumed the role of defending the Philippines more definitely than they had in the Commonwealth phase, though Filipino nationalists could argue that their bases exposed the Philippines to attack. The armed forces of the Philippines were focused on domestic tasks. Those, however, were extended by the need to control paramilitary violence during the elections, and the need to deal with Huk insurgency. As a result there was 'a high potential for intervention by the armed forces'.[71] With the knowledge of US authorities, and the approval of Nacionalista politicians, Magsaysay seriously considered a coup in 1953, when there were fears that President Quirino would 'steal the election through wholesale fraud'.[72] His overwhelming victory made it unnecessary.

Under Magsaysay, nevertheless, the military became more involved in civil affairs. He appointed military officers to key civilian positions, and he deployed military personnel in civic action projects, including, as Quezon had envisaged, resettlement projects in Mindanao. In his first term President Marcos expanded the military's role dramatically and linked it to the developmentalism of the 1960s. The Four-Year Economic Programme for 1967–70 argued that the AFP, 'with its manpower, material, and equipment resources plus its organizational cohesiveness', possessed 'a tremendous potential' for implementing plans that required 'the total mobilization of the nation's manpower and material resources'.[73] US aid was obtained as a *quid pro quo* for sending an engineering battalion to Vietnam, and the civic action brigade was expanded in 1967 to fifteen battalions. That accustomed Filipinos to an expanded role for the military.

Taking power in September 1972, Marcos was nevertheless careful to shroud his action in the legality of martial law. In this way, however paradoxical it was, he could hope to ensure the support of the AFP, which was still committed to the US doctrine of civilian supremacy. Marcos characterised the military in various terms like 'catalyst of social change', 'training institution for national leaders', 'defender of the seat of government', a 'nation builder', and 'model of national discipline and self reliance'.[74] In 1972 the total force, including the PC, was 50 674; in 1977–78, 164 000, including the local self-defence forces; by 1986 it numbered 230 000. Its task expanded with the increasing level of disorder, to which its violence and its employment of vigilantes arguably contributed. The line between the civil and military became increasingly blurred. Marcos was not content with the traditional loyalty to the civilian regime: he sought to make the army part of his system. Fabian Ver, head of the Presidential Security Command and from 1981 chief of staff, was a relative, and so was Fidel Ramos, head of the PC, both of them, like Marcos himself and Enrile, the defence minister, Ilocanos. Ver was particularly noted for his fanatical loyalty to Marcos. But younger officers, frustrated by its failures, came to resent the politicisation of the army, and the assassination of Benigno Aquino further alienated them from Ver, widely thought to be implicated, and from the President.

The overthrow of Marcos nevertheless required the involvement of the military, thus helping to rehabilitate it, and General Ramos succeeded Aquino's widow as president. The AFP retained its development role. The AFP, he declared, could 'anticipate an expanded role in our country's journey to development. Philippines 2000! Political stability has been restored and enhanced, and a climate conducive for economic take-off is now in place. We likewise foresee an armed forces more relevant and attuned to our national goals and aspirations.'[75]

Malaya/Malaysia

The Malaysian armed forces also expanded in the 1970s. British Malaya had relied on the navy and on limited British and Indian imperial forces based in Singapore. It also recruited soldiers from India and Nepal, Sikhs, Punjabis, Gurkhas. After the creation of the Federated Malay States, the Malay States Guides were set up, stationed at Taiping, one artillery company and seven companies of Jat Sikhs and Muslims, under British and Indian officers. The Malay Regiment was started in 1933 with twenty-three recruits being taken into an 'experimental company'.[76] Late the following year it was decided to make up a whole battalion, 793 men, but a second battalion was authorised only in March 1941. Banning the radical KMM movement, the Japanese made its leader Ibrahim bin Yaakub commander of a giyugun started early in 1944, called PETA in Malay, but it had no role after the war. Indians joined the INA. No Chinese were recruited, but some joined the communist-led MPAJA.

The main burden of struggling against the guerrillas after 1948 was carried out by British forces, including Gurkha troops. Extensive use of the Malay Regiment in the Emergency would no doubt have exacerbated the inter-communal tension the British sought to limit. The army of independent Malaya/Malaysia was predominantly Malay: in 1969, 64.5 per cent of army officers were Malay. After the inter-communal crisis of that year, the army expanded rapidly, especially the Malay Regiment, which was entirely Malay, and grew to twenty-six battalions by the mid-1980s. 'The government backed the army as an overwhelmingly Malay force to back up the government in the event of further communal conflict.'[77] Even the multi-ethnic ranger battalions tended to be largely Malay. Here was a constabulary force with a difference. At the highest levels the links between the civilians and the military were close. In 1987 the prime minister appointed his brother-in-law commander-in-chief. But, even in the 1969 crisis, there was never any suggestion of a military take-over.

Singapore and Brunei

The British had also been responsible for defending Singapore. That they had characteristically attempted largely by naval means, and on land by a mix of British and British-led Indian troops. The mutiny of the Indian troops in 1915 had been a demonstration of their wartime weakness in the East, but there was no real threat from an outside power. In the next war Japan's interest turned to antagonism, and, without adequate naval and air forces, the British and their Commonwealth troops were unable to retain Singapore.

Precipitated into independence in August 1965, the new Republic had at once to create a defence policy and a defence capability. Singapore sought to maintain its security by making a defence arrangement with Britain, Malaysia, Australia, and New Zealand, encouraging the United States to stay in the region after it lost its Philippines bases, and developing relations with its neighbours through ASEAN and in other ways. Somewhat inconsistently, it turned to Israel for a model for its own army. Israel sent a small team of advisers, who recommended the creation of a national service army with a nucleus of officers and NCOs. The Singapore Armed Forces Training Institute was set up, and in 1967 compulsory conscription was introduced, with two to two and a half years' service being followed by service in the reserves till age forty. Nation-building was in mind. 'Nothing creates loyalty and national consciousness more speedily and more thoroughly', said Goh Keng Swee, the first minister for defence, 'than participation in defence and membership of the armed forces'.[78] But by its army and its air force the Republic was also indicating to others that it would not be easy to eliminate: the metaphor was that of the 'poisonous shrimp'. Goh Chok Tong preferred the analogy of a porcupine.[79]

Brunei's approach was also deterrent. It had relied on its British protector till 1984. When it then attained full independence, it joined ASEAN. But Gurkha soldiers were retained, both as part of the British army and the Brunei forces.

Guerrillas

Guerrilla forces featured in Southeast Asian history, before, during, and after the colonial period. Their structures were necessarily different, and so, of course, was their mode of operation. Yet in one sense they resembled more regular forces: in both cases it was a question of demonstrating your strength and thus your opponent's weakness. The guerrillas used persuasion, intimidation, and violence. A distinctive feature of guerrilla activities is a motivation that keeps them going in face of superior forces. Organisation and indoctrination play a role. The strong vein of millennialism in Southeast Asian societies can also be significant, but that may be short-term in duration. A long-term struggle may require a deeper level of indoctrination. If you could sustain continued operations, you might, as Vo Nguyen Giap saw, outlast an outside power, even the most powerful state on earth, if, a democracy, it could not effectively mobilise its people.

Notes

1 Lieberman, p. 53.
2 *Nation in Arms*, Sydney: Allen and Unwin, 1989, p. 18.
3 q. Woodside, *Model*, p. 149.
4 cf. A. Reid, *The Last Stand of Asian Autonomies*, Basingstoke: Macmillan, 1997, p. 19.
5 Woodside, *Model*, p. 283.
6 Tarling, *Imperial Britain*, p. 138.
7 H. L. Wesseling, 'Post-Imperial Holland', *J Contemp Hist*, 15 (1980), p. 126.
8 q. Sadka, p. 237.
9 Bob Hering, *M. H. Thamrin*, Kabar Sebarang, 1996, p. 105.
10 *Naval Base*, p. 228.
11 q. Nadzan Haron, 'British Defence Policy in Malaya, 1874–1918', in K. M. de Silva et al., eds, *Asian Panorama*, New Delhi: Vikas, 1990, p. 443.
12 q. N. Tarling, 'When the Old Lady Dies', *Southeast Asian Review*, 3, 1 (August 1978), p. 72.
13 q. J. Soedjati Djiwandono and Yong Mun Cheong, eds, *Soldiers and Stability in Southeast Asia*, Singapore: ISEAS, 1988, p. 17.
14 Chandran Jeshurun in Chin Kin Wah, ed., *Defence Spending in Southeast Asia*, Singapore: ISEAS, 1987, p. 12.
15 Ricklefs, *War, Culture and Economy*, p. 17.

16 H. L. Zwitzer en C. A. Heshusius, *Het Koninklijk Nederlands-Indisch Leger 1830–1950*, 's-Gravenhage: Staatuitgeverij, 1977, p. 10.

17 *The Road to Power*, KL: OUP, 1982, p. 1.

18 ibid., p. 2.

19 Salim Said, *Genesis of Power*, Singapore: ISEAS, 1991, p. 25.

20 Sundhaussen, p. 19.

21 q. ibid., p. 33.

22 ibid., p. 39.

23 q. ibid., p. 42.

24 L. M. Penders and U. Sundhaussen, *Abdul Haris Nasution*, St Lucia: UQP, 1985, p. 50.

25 Sundhaussen, p. 53.

26 ibid., p. 111.

27 q. Salim Said, pp. 135–6.

28 p. 136.

29 Said, p. 143.

30 ibid., p. 144.

31 Sundhaussen, pp. 272–3.

32 Wesseling, *J Contemp Hist*, p. 137.

33 H. Tinker, *The Union of Burma*, OUP, 1957, p. 314.

34 A. Selth, 'Race and Resistance in Burma, 1942–1945', MAS, 20, 3 (July 1986), p. 489.

35 Tinker, p. 318.

36 q. Tarling, *Anglo-Burmese War*, p. 162.

37 ibid., p. 164.

38 Tinker, p. 322.

39 ibid., p. 40.

40 ibid., pp. 334–5.

41 Lockhart, p. 34.

42 q. Lockhart, p. 36.

43 q. N. Tarling, *Britain, Southeast Asia and the Onset of the Cold War, 1945–1950*, CUP, 1998, p. 302.

44 Hammer, p. 288.

45 p. 263.

46 W. C. Klein and M. Weiner, in G. Kahin, ed., *Governments and Politics of Southeast Asia*, Cornell UP, 1959, p. 347.

47 q. Sam C. Sarkesian, *Unconventional Conflicts in a New Security Era*, Westport: Greenwood, 1993, p. 102.

48 A. B. Woodside, *Community and Revolution in Modern Vietnam*, Boston: Houghton Mifflin, 1976, p. 281.

49 in Kahin, p. 399.

50 q. ibid., p. 399.

51 Thai Quang Trung, p. 35.

52 Michael C. Williams, *Vietnam at the Crossroads*, NY: Council on Foreign Relations Press, 1992, p. 37.

53 q. G. Kolko, *Vietnam. Anatomy of a Peace*, London and New York: Routledge, 1997, p. 138.

54 *Politics in Thailand*, Cornell UP, 1962, p. 169.

55 p. 170.

56 q. Wilson, p. 171.

57 p. 174.

58 q. Wilson, p. 177.

59 pp. 177–8.

60 q. Wilson, p. 187.

61 ibid., p. 180.

62 q. Soedjati and Yong, p. 23.

63 G. Bankoff, *Crime, Society, and the State in the Nineteenth-century Philippines*, Ateneo de Manila P, 1996, p. 137.

64 John A. Larkin, *The Pampangans*, UCP, 1972, pp. 26–7.

65 p. 137.
66 Larkin, p. 166.
67 Gopinath, *Manuel L. Quezon: The Tutelary Democrat*, Quezon City: New Day, 1987, p. 139.
68 q. ibid., p. 143.
69 q. ibid., p. 146.
70 q. Carol Morris Petillo, 'Douglas Macarthur: The Philippine Years', PhD thesis, Rutgers, 1979, p. 343.
71 A. Doronila, *The State, Economic Transformation, and Political Change in the Philippines, 1946–1972*, Singapore: OUP, 1992, p. 139.
72 ibid., p. 139.
73 q. ibid., p. 140.
74 F. Celoza, 'The Rise of an Authoritarian Regime in the Philippines', PhD thesis, Claremont, 1987, p. 252.
75 q. Daniel Lucero in David Dickens, ed., *No Better Alternative ...* , Wellington: CSS, 1997, p. 41.
76 Dol Ramli, 'The Malay Regiment, 1933–1942', JMBRAS, 38, 1 (July 1965), p. 205.
77 H. Crouch, *Government and Society in Malaysia*, Sydney: Allen and Unwin, 1996, p. 135.
78 q. E. Chew and E. Lee, eds, *A History of Singapore*, Singapore: OUP, 1991, p. 163.
79 in Chin Kin Wah, ed., *Defence Spending in Southeast Asia*, Singapore: ISEAS, 1987, p. 201.

3.4 Religion

The major world religions all established themselves in Southeast Asia, though inter-playing with local and popular cults and practices in the pre-colonial, colonial, and post-colonial periods.

To write about religious experience is no easy matter, particularly if the writer has no sense of having shared it. An historian, moreover, is likely to focus on the role of religion in society and politics. Yet it is necessary at least to assert the autonomy of the religious experience, in the sense that it is felt, if at all, by the individual, and even an historian who does not feel it recognises that it exists. Describing religious movements or their role in the state will be necessary but not sufficient. Indeed the description will be foreshortened if this dimension is not borne in mind. What gives such movements their power, and what makes the state interested in them, is ulti-mately their ability to offer individuals some kind of meaning to their lives, some kind of understanding of their place in the world, some guidance as to the way of handling its incomprehensibilities. That is also the basis of conversion. It intensifies the religious experience, offers better answers, prescribes new ways of behaving.

To stress individual experience is not, of course, to omit the sense of community that the religious also share. Through a community individuals may indeed hope to attain a deeper experience and secure a fuller guidance, while those who leave it, temporarily or permanently, may still not only seek a yet deeper experience, but offer an example or an inspiration to those who remain. Yet once a community exists, others exist. Religious feeling, like other forms of identity, both binds and divides. Those it binds may feel the need not only to strengthen their own religious experience, but to give others the opportunity to share it. Others may accept, per-haps compromise: conversion is a process, not a single event, both for the individual and the community. But others still may resist, and in their very resistance find a new strength in their own religious experience and their sense of community.

Both the religious experience of the individual and the sense of community among the religious have made religious communities powerful supports, but also powerful enemies, of other kinds of community. Religion could reinforce them but also rival them. Within a tribe or a village a tension might be felt between chief and priest. At the state level, a ruler might welcome, but also fear, the support of a church or a religious hierarchy. Religion could also inspire opponents—old believers, for example, who believed that change was endangering religion itself; or reformers, who, sharing something of that belief, concluded that reform was necessary, if need be breaking with the state to secure it.

These general remarks are included both to suggest what Southeast Asians shared with the common experience of humanity and what differences their history brought them. One difference applies, perhaps, particularly to the study of early Southeast Asia. 'In Western societies religion is generally felt to be clearly separated from other fields of social and political life', as J. G. de Casparis and I. W. Mabbett point out, 'so that it can be studied for its own sake. This is also the case with modern Southeast Asia. In pre-modern Southeast Asia, however, it is hardly possible to separate religion from other fields of socio-economic and cultural life, with which it is closely interwoven.'[1] That task is, however, a test historians and their readers have to face in other 'pre-modern' societies. Treating religion as a topic may be a helpful means of analysis, even if contemporaries did not see it as a separate sphere of human activity. In modern times, after all, religious experience and affiliation are closely intertwined with social and political behaviour. And in recent times, especially but not solely in the Islamic world, the state has tended to reassert a role.

A second distinctive feature of Southeast Asian history is the incursion of the Western powers from the sixteenth century onwards, and the subsequent establishment of colonial rule over almost all the region. Religion came to be identified both with the Western cause and with its opponents. In this, however, Southeast Asia was not unique, though the diversity and complexity of the process were characteristic. Indeed it ought to be seen in the longer term as part of a sequence of changes in which a region, for the most part very much open to the outside world, borrowed from, adapted, and reacted against the religions of other regions and other peoples, while those religions themselves were changing as a result of reform or revival. In the late nineteenth and early twentieth centuries, it might be said that the two kinds of change became more closely linked and that they speeded up.

That process was related to the major shifts brought about by imperialism and by economic development. But, just as the relationship between imperialism and economic change was a complex one, operating more at the micro than the macro level, so was their relationship with religious change. It was influenced by and influenced the imperialist thrust and the reaction to it. It was a response to economic disruption and a refuge from it.

The major religions

The idea of reincarnation is not peculiar to Asia, still less to India, but there it took a particular form with the concept of karma (deeds). Those determined one's lot in a future existence, and in Hindu India that was tied into the caste system, positioning *kshatriyas* (nobles) and brahmins (priests) as contending heads of an increasingly complex system. But this world was after all but illusion (*maya*), from which deliverance might be sought by austerity, knowledge, and faith. A trio of great gods coexisted with village godlings and spirits, Brahma the creator, Shiva the destroyer, and Vishnu the preserver. Shiva and Vishnu in particular were taken up by sects and their writings, *puranas* and *tantras*. Shiva stood for life, creating, sustaining, destroying: his consort is Kali, terrifying, but to her worshippers kindly; his son Ganesha. Vishnu stood for love. His consort is Lakshmi, her festival Diwali. His avatars or incarnations include Rama, the story of Rama and Sita being told in the *Ramayana,* and Krishna, part of the *Mahabharata,* the *Bhagavad-Gita,* being devoted to a discussion between Krishna and the warrior Arjuna. The influence of Hinduism in Southeast Asia is not confined to immigrants from India. Much earlier it played a role in the creation of Southeast Asian states. Rulers could be seen as avatars of Vishnu, brahmanic ritual sustained their courts, their capitals replicated the cosmic Mount Meru.

Its arrival in the region was, however, preceded in India by the emergence of Buddhism, *dharma* or *sasana,* the Buddhist path. Like Jainism—from which Gandhi was much later to borrow *ahimsa* (non-violence)—it was an attempt to escape the overbearing burden of karma, in its case by offering the prospect of nirvana. It thus grew up in the Hindu world—Buddha Gautama was the scion of a *kshatriya* family—and Hinduism indeed sought to assimilate the Buddha as another avatar of Vishnu. In fact Buddhism shared many of the assumptions of Hinduism, such as the belief in the cycle of rebirth, and the belief that animals as well as men have souls. The doctrine that the Buddha taught, or that has been handed down as his, is 'centered on the belief that suffering and pain are the outstanding traits of this world'.[2] The Four Noble Truths tell us that the painfulness of man's existence is caused by his desires, and his suffering will cease only when desire has ceased. The route to that end, the 'eightfold path', is righteous social behaviour and enlightened self-discipline. By that means we may reduce our desires 'and eventually escape completely from the passions of the world and thus end the cycle of existences in which all living beings are caught'. The doctrine requires no gods, nor even prayers: chants and formulas, statues and pagodas, are aids to meditation. Monks are not priests, 'and do not stand between the individual Buddhist and the road to salvation'.[3] 'The organisational goal of the Sangha [order of monks] is primarily to facilitate the individual attainment of *nirvana* through disciplined secluded life and meditation.'[4] The other task is to preserve the teachings of the Buddha.

Buddhism fell into two schools. Mahayana envisages 'the gradual rise to perfection of Buddha-hood through a long succession of existences as a Bodhisattva'.[5] 'The prospective attainment of complete enlightenment was conceived as affording opportunity for the emergent Buddha to lend a helping hand in vicarious concern for less-favored folk on the way.'[6] In Theravada Buddhism, everyone is on their own, and pretensions to Bodhisattva status tend to seem sacrilegious. It did allow the

monarch a role, however. The purpose of kingship was to repress anarchy and promote righteousness (*dharma*). The king also had to improve the karma of his subjects, and so ensure their happy rebirth. Giving alms to the monks was the most
efficacious method, and so the sangha had to be kept pure. Kings associated themselves with the myth of the *cakkavattin*, the World Ruler, supposed to act by example, but often acting by conquest, and Bodaw-hpaya of Burma even saw himself as
the Buddha Metteyya, ready to propound a new teaching. But rebels could claim that
they had karma, and that rulers had lost it.

Mahayana gained acceptance in post-Han China, in Sri Vijaya, in eighth-century
Java, in Vietnam and Champa, in pre-Aniruddha Pagan, in twelfth-century Angkor.
The consecration of Iskandar of Palembang, the founder of Melaka, employed
Saivite-Buddhist rites. But Theravada, of which Sri Lanka became the centre, came
to dominate mainland Southeast Asia, particularly after it was reformed in the
twelfth century. Even so it was mixed with Hindu legacies and overtones.

In India itself great religions coexisted with small. The same was true in Southeast
Asia. Buddhism was assimilatory, but it was also, like other religions, accommoda-
tory: it took over and moulded earlier cults, turned burial mounds into stupas, tree
spirits into protectors. 'Multitudes of spirits and gods have been worshipped and
honored, tolerated along with Buddhism.'[7] A rather rarefied doctrine did not entirely
satisfy the needs of all, and people sought the shield of supernatural powers. 'Amulets,
talismans, portents, the whole panoply of apotropaic magic pervaded the religious
life of everybody, high or low, monk, ascetic or layman.'[8] In Vietnam Mahayana lay
alongside Confucianism at one level, and at another, particularly in the south, the folk
religions characteristic of a more remote Southeast Asian past. The *nats* or spirits of
Burma were sanctioned by Buddhist orthodoxy. Melford E. Spiro indeed suggests
that there were two religions in Burma, one, Buddhism, for the next world, and one,
the *nats*, for this world.[9] When a Burman 'wants to build a house, launch a boat,
plough or sow his fields, start on a journey, … or even endow a religious foundation',
J. G. Scott wrote, 'it is the spirits he propitiates, it is the nats whom he consults'.[10] Java
offers the experience of *kebatinan*, often said to be the core of Javanism, 'the traditional Animistic-Hindu-Buddhist magical-mystical religious complex'.[11] Its mysticism—designed to establish a direct relationship between the individual and the
sphere of that which is almighty—can include or exclude occultism, magic, and esoteric practice. In the *abangan* way of life, it implies a belief in prophecy, an acceptance
of the power of amulets (*djimat*) and of the role of *dukun* (healers).

Islam had to replicate the process of assimilation, accommodation, or condemnation in regard to both great religions and small. It was to make little inroad upon
Theravada Buddhism, but it had much more success in opposition to the Hindu-
Buddhist cults of the archipelago. Sociologists have suggested that it was accepted in
part as a means of throwing off the caste system associated with Hinduism and
influential especially in the non-rural areas. 'This explanation is supported by the
facts', adds C. A. O. van Nieuwenhuijze, 'inasmuch as Islam spread [in Indonesia]

inland from the harbour towns and coastal areas, whilst in the interior of the islands the courts remained the last strongholds of Hinduism'.[12] The caste system was more theoretical than real. But there is certainly a sense that all Muslims are equal as members of the same community holding the same faith, the *ummat Islam*, the community of Islam, and that clearly had an appeal, particularly in the age of commerce. 'The commercial ethos of Islam, its identification with economic success, the authority of its written texts, and its eminent portability in an age when people seeking new livelihoods were obliged to leave ancestral shrines and territorially-based spirits for long periods—all these factors, [as] Reid suggests, attracted indigenous traders, mariners, and perhaps cash-crop producers.'[13] The concept of ruler shifted from god-king to God's representative, but any decline in a cosmic role was compensated for by increased functions as local head of the *ummat*. Islam also established links with foreign states, and empowered rulers against Hindu kingdoms and animist tribes. At the same time, it is clear that Islam compromised. Even today the Javanese is likely to observe customs and act according to ideas that belong to earlier traditions or to Hindu-Buddhist culture.

The community—living according to the Koran, and to the deeds and sayings of the Prophet or *sunna*, that jointly make up the *sharia* or law, and to *hadith*, the traditional record of the Prophet's words—was an ideal, rather than an actuality. For it was intended to be universal, as well as at one with the one God. In fact, of course, the Islamic world was divided into separate states from its early years. The concept of a united community, in which religious affiliation supersedes other forms of affiliation, remained, however, as Clive Christie says, 'an unchanging ideal'.[14] Linked to that was the concept of the Islamic state.

Linked, too, an aspiration to universality: humanity is divided between the Darul Islam, the abode of Islam, and the Darul Harb, the abode of conflict—that is, the non-Islamic regions. It is an obligation on Muslims to protect the Darul Islam and to help expand it by conversion. These tasks might involve *hijra*, separation, or 'emigration', Muhammad's response to the initial rejection of his teaching in Mekka: an Islamic community should withdraw from persecution if that persecution endangers its survival. Another possible response to adversity, but also a means of undertaking missionary work, was *jihad*, or endeavour in the cause of God.

It was with Islam that Christianity had joined battle in Europe and the Mediterranean, and the advent of the Europeans in Southeast Asia extended the conflict. Christianity had a message of salvation, sustained by the record of Christ's life and teaching. It differed inasmuch as its followers developed from a persecuted community into a powerful and hierarchically organised church, for which neither Buddhism nor Islam had parallels. The Papacy indeed contested the leadership of 'Christendom' with the Holy Roman Empire. By the time of the voyages, other states were emerging, at times at odds with the Papacy as well as with each other. Some took up the cause of 'reformation', others took up the cause of 'counter-reformation', designed to counter the growth of Protestantism. The voyages in some sense assumed the task of Christendom's crusades, extending the struggle with Islam beyond the Holy Land. In addition they were not only a response to the determination to build up modern states in Europe and to acquire the wealth that made essential. They were also to take on some of the fervour of the Counter-Reformation. The aims were at times in conflict. Commercial contact and religious conversion, the Portuguese found, were at odds, and the Dutch Calvinists were to heed the lesson. The incursion of the Europeans indeed prompted a strong Muslim reaction and strengthened the hold of Islam on most of the island world. Only in the Philippines—where the hold of other major religions was less than anywhere else—was conversion successful on any scale.

The pre-colonial phase

The elites of the early archipelagic states adopted and adapted elements of Indian civilisation where they were useful and inspiring. Those included Brahmanic Hinduism—Saivism more than Vaisnavism—and later Buddhism—Mahayana rather than Theravada. Modified forms of Hindu ceremonies were employed in the old Javanese courts, in, for example, the ceremony of royal consecration (*abhiseka*) and in funerary rites (*sraddha*). Temple deities surrounded Siva with Durga, a spouse, Ganesha, and a sage or guru, perhaps symbolising the worldly figures of king, queen, prime minister, and spiritual guide. The great Siva complex of Roro Jonggrang, east of Yogyakarta, paralleled the heavenly king who ruled the cosmos with the earthly king who ruled his kingdom, conceived of as a mandala of concentric circles representing diminishing degrees of allegiance, with the king as the centre, and also as a hierarchy, with the king at the peak. But, while sustaining the heart of the kingdom, symbolically and administratively, brahminism also influenced the life of contemplation, in the case of those who became hermits, or those who joined an *asrama* or religious community.

'Its influence on the agricultural communities was probably confined to those elements of Saivism that were consistent with popular beliefs', de Casparis and Mabbett tell us.[15] Vishnu's mount, the heavenly bird Garuda, was quite popular, and it remained so. The tourist, flying on the Indonesian airline or not, is sure to see when visiting Indonesia the Javanese shadow theatre, *wayang kulit,* with its plots based on the great Indian epics, *Mahabharata* and *Ramayana,* and telling of heroes like Bhima, one of the five Pandawa brothers in the former, with whom Sukarno was able to identify himself. Brought to life by a *dalang,* the puppets assume a peculiar shape in order to avoid the Muslim prohibition on the representation of living beings.

Mahayana Buddhism developed a new pantheon, different kinds of Buddhas, iconographically distinguishable by the position of their hands; many different Bodhisattvas, and their female counterparts, Tara; together with some Hindu gods. In Java it flourished in the Sailendra period and in the Singosari–Majapahit period. Its greatest monument is Borobudur. It may mark the origin of the Sailendra. It may also have been an 'encyclopaedia of Buddhism', its reliefs depicting basic Mahayana texts with which a teacher might instruct a student. Tantric Buddhism, in which rituals are employed to shorten the long road to Buddha-hood and nirvana, influenced Kertanagara and his kingdom.

Mahayana Buddhism flourished more consistently in Sumatra, but left fewer monuments. The rulers of Sri Vijaya were great patrons, but the nature of their empire, and its weak population base, meant that they left behind no equivalent of the Javanese or Khmer monuments. Their successors, the rulers of Melayu, maintained links with Javanese Buddhism, and the spiritual father of Menangkabau, Adityavarman, followed a type of Tantrism. That esoteric form had little popular appeal, unlike the Theravada Buddhism of the mainland. No doubt that helped to leave the way open to Islam in the archipelago.

Islam had only established itself in Southeast Asia six centuries after its foundation. Though there were Shi'ite influences, it was Sunni Islam that was established, together with one of its four schools of law, the Shafi'i. The earliest Muslim kingdom, Pasai, near Lho Seumawe, dates from the late thirteenth century CE. The spread of Islam was first inhibited by the existence of strong Hindu-Buddhist kingdoms, and then facilitated by their decline in the fifteenth century. A significant stimulus was the conversion of the ruler of Melaka, who thus linked his realm with the ocean-wide Muslim commercial network. It became the greatest entrepot of Southeast Asia, and Islam spread to other centres with which Melaka had commercial ties. The ruler of Melaka assumed new titles, *sultan* and *syah,* and claimed to be the deputy of Allah, to whom obedience was due as a religious obligation. Other Muslim kingdoms or 'sultanates' emerged, and in turn became the focuses of further expansion. Islam also established itself in northern Java, and Giri, near Surabaya, became an important Muslim centre. A strong vein of the mysticism propounded by devout *sufis* existed alongside orthodox Islam, and they 'presented Islam in a style which may have been more readily acceptable to the mystics of the Javanese court than might have been true of a more legalistic variation of the faith'.[16] The tradition of the asrama was taken up by the *pesantren* or *pondok.*

The arrival of the Portuguese and the Spaniards, whose monarchs were the 'patrons' of Christianity, was a challenge to Muslims, but also a goad. They had to oppose the Christians, but also to spread Islam, and, though conversion from Islam to Christianity was rare, to intensify its hold upon those who were no more than nominal Muslims. Except in the Philippines and parts of eastern Indonesia, the European incursion strengthened, rather than weakened, the position of Islam, and the triumphant Turkish empire of the sixteenth century was a source not only of inspiration but of assistance. 'To some extent', as Barbara Andaya and Yoneo Ishii put it, '... there was a "race" between Islam and Christianity, and adherents of each tried to confirm their commercial, political and spiritual hold over particular areas'.[17] In the Indonesian archipelago the destruction of Melaka was followed by the creation of new sultanates, and Aceh became a leading Islamic centre. Only Bali stood aside, reshaping the heritage of Majapahit and developing an invigorated Saivism. The successors of the Portuguese and the Spaniards, the Dutch and the English, were more cautious, generally dissociating themselves from missionary activity, and striving to put their relationships simply on a politico-commercial basis. In the two centuries of the VOC's existence, fewer than 1000 *predikants* left to serve in the East. They concentrated 'on the "blind heathen" and on the Roman Catholic communities which they had conquered from the Portuguese'.[18] Their success in setting religious and other interests apart was bound to be limited, but as their power grew, Islam 'emigrated'.

In the Philippines the Spaniards, though interested in the trade of Maluku and of China, adopted a different priority. There, it might be said as a result, Christianity won the race, though the struggle with the Muslims, joined in Manila, continued in the form of piracy and marine warfare throughout the islands and beyond for three centuries. An Augustinian accompanied Legazpi, his task to preach to the inhabitants and to baptise those who accepted Christianity. Franciscans followed in 1578; Jesuits, a creation of the Counter-Reformation, in 1581; Dominicans in 1587; Recollects in 1606. By 1594 there were 267 regulars (those living under rule, members of religious orders) in the Philippines; by 1655, 254 regulars and sixty secular clergy (those not under rule, but, if parish priests, under episcopal control). Using particular Filipino languages, each order was entrenched in particular regions, where those languages prevailed or came to prevail. The bulk of the Tagalog provinces, the citadel of Spanish power, thus went to the Augustinians and Franciscans. The Augustinians obtained Pampanga and Ilocos, the Franciscans Camarines. The Dominicans obtained Pangasinan and Cagayan and divided the Visayas with the Jesuits, who also settled in Mindanao. Coming late, the Recollects collected little.

Through these men, the indios were converted to Christianity, and it became a bulwark of Spanish rule, as the 'friars' were never slow to point out. 'An important factor in the success of Christianity', Andaya and Ishii observe, 'was the fact that many aspects of worship struck a familiar chord in Filipino culture'.[19] Communion recalled ritual feasting, holy water had been important in animist rites, rosaries and crosses were taken for talismans. Baptism, too, extended the patron–client system through securing *compadre*, or godparents, generally of a higher status, and linking them with the family as a whole. Like other religions, Christianity indeed makes many compromises, and in the Philippines it took on a distinctively Filipino character. It was the continued task of the friars to eliminate irreconcilable practices like the propitiation of spirits.

Under canon law secular clergy should replace regular once conversion has been effected. That did not take place in the Philippines. The religious orders were essential to the colonial administration: in 1622–34 there were only sixty lay Spaniards outside Manila and Cebu. Seculars would be less reliable, even if trained, because, unlike the regulars, they would not be Europeans, but indios or mestizos. The Council of Trent had decreed that the regulars engaged in pastoral care were subject to the jurisdiction of the bishops. That conflicted with privileges granted to the orders by Pope Adrian VI. It also met the same obstacle: the Philippines government depended on the regulars, whatever might be said by the king, who had as patron the exclusive right to present candidates to the bishoprics. The result was a continued struggle. The 'enlightened' monarchy of Carlos III expelled the Jesuits in 1767, and a court prelate, Don Basilio Sancho de Santa Justa y Rufino, was sent as archbishop to Manila to assist in the expulsion, and to make the example clear to others. In 1774 Governor Anda secured—'that the king may be lord of those dominions'—a royal decree requiring regulars to submit to episcopal visitation, and providing for the secularisation of curacies held by regulars when they became vacant.[20] But Sancho's hasty ordinations of indio seculars were counter-productive. He referred to the 'black jealousy' of the orders.[21] '[T]here were no oarsmen to be found for the coasting vessels', the Manila joke ran, 'because the archbishop had ordained them all'.[22]

On the mainland neither Islam nor Christianity made much headway in the face of Theravada Buddhism. It seems first to have taken hold among the Mon states in Burma and Thailand, like Thaton and Dvaravati, and then been taken on by the kingdoms that overran them from the eleventh century onward. The tradition is that Pagan's 'great unifier', Aniruddha, was converted to Theravada after conquering Thaton, and also established links with Sri Lanka. A successor, Kyanzittha, who completed the famous Shwezigon, was probably more significant. The building of temples was closely integrated into the life of the kingdom, though also a source, despite royal attempts to reform the sangha, of its ultimate collapse.

Before the advent of Theravada on the mainland, brahmanic cults of Siva and Vishnu had coexisted, and brahmins were to retain astrological and ritual functions at the Buddhist courts. With access to sacred texts, lawbooks, and other literature in Sanskrit, they had been priests, teachers, ministers, and counsellors. Cults of Siva and Vishnu were strong in the ancient kingdoms of Chen-la/Cambodia and Champa, and the outer galleries of the great monument at Angkor emphasise Vaisnavite myths. As late as the thirteenth century, Angkor witnessed, after the 'ostentatious display' of Mahayana under Jayavarman VII, a temporary revival of Hinduism. The spread of Sinhalese Theravada followed in the thirteenth century. The Thai kingdoms that succeeded Angkor also supported Theravada, establishing links with Sri Lanka, building stupa, paying respect to the sangha.

Mahayana had taken root in what became Vietnam in the late second and early third centuries. The prosperity of the province of Giao-chi coincided with 'the first flowering of Indian civilization in Southeast Asia', and benefited from it.[23] 'Buddhism, Confucianism and Taoism all flourished in varying degrees. Buddhism … captured the imagination of the common people by attaching itself to the indigenous spirit cults. … Ruling-class people were predominantly Confucianist by virtue of their education. Taoism lay between Buddhism and Confucianism.'[24] In subsequent centuries there were Vietnamese as well as Chinese pilgrims to India and Ceylon.

On the assertion of independence from China, 'Vietnamese Buddhism helped foster stable dynastic institutions that gave political shape to the new Vietnamese identity'.[25] But Confucianism—itself, if not a religion, giving men a view of their place in the world, offering a code of ethics, and furnishing rituals that supported a sense of identity—was in some sense in competition, and it was actively promoted by later rulers, particularly after Vietnam had destroyed the Ming attempt to re-establish Giao-chi. There remained not only a strong allegiance to Buddhism, especially but not only in the south, but also 'a religion of small sects', often innovative and eclectic, and seen as 'potential centres of political revolt'.[26]

Though Muslim gravestones dating from the eleventh century have been found in Champa, Islam was to make only a limited impact on the mainland. The Cham king became Muslim in the seventeenth century, and most Chams became nominal Muslims. Exposed politically, they were exceptional. Andaya and Ishii adduce as explanation 'the entrenched position of Theravada Buddhism and its widespread integration into local culture, forming an all-encompassing belief system which seriously addressed questions regarding the afterlife as well as the problems of this one'.[27]

Nor, of course, was there any sense that a battle with Christianity was being joined, as in the archipelago and the Philippines. The Europeans at first made relatively little impact on the mainland. Only in embattled seventeenth-century Vietnam did Christian missionaries enjoy substantial success: first Jesuits expelled from Tokugawa Japan, starting at Da-nang in 1615, and then at Cachao (Ke-cho), the Trinh city, in 1627, and later priests sent by the Societé des Missions Etrangères, sponsored, despite Portuguese protests, by the French crown. In 1650 Alexandre de Rhodes reported that there were already 300 000 converts in Vietnam.[28] It was a time of civil war, and, though there were intermittent 'persecution' and 'martyrdom', outside contacts were welcomed by Trinh and Nguyen. Missionary activity was, however, seen by both regimes as essentially subversive, and even before the civil war ended, Christianity was banned.

Following the truce between the regimes, and particularly after the French intervention at Bangkok, the SME headquarters, persecutions became more regular, though missionary activities did not stop. After 1738 Clement XII gave the north to the Jesuits who fled from China following the Rites controversy, while the French Society concentrated on the south. Missionaries, as one of them put it, made the day night and the night day.[29] Nor did Christian communities die. After one edict ordering Vietnamese to remove crosses, images, and rosaries, Rhodes tells us, 'God … put a provincial governor on our side … , who … gave us time to caution our neophytes to keep all emblems well hidden'.[30] The Jesuits, who stressed the importance of using the local language, also left behind another legacy, Rhodes' romanisation of Vietnamese into *quoc ngu*.

The colonial phase

In the colonial phase the continued existence of Christian communities was to provide a rationale for French intervention in Vietnam. So, too, was the Nguyen 'persecution' of the Catholic missionaries, fired with a new zeal by the post-Revolution revival within the Catholic Church in France. In the task of reunifying the kingdom, Nguyen Anh had sought the help of France through the SME missionary Pigneau. After he had succeeded, he reduced the number of Frenchmen in his service, and his successor, Minh-mang, sought their total exclusion. He identified Christianity with the subversion of a realm he increasingly based on a reassertion of Confucianist values, in the pursuit of which he also attacked popular Buddhist and animist practices. Though the Nguyen came from the south, they found the south intractable, 'culturally different. … more Cambodian, more Buddhist, less Confucian, less Sino-Vietnamese than the center and the north', and 'more pragmatic, more concerned with geography, medicine, fortune telling, and astrology than that of the rest of Vietnam'.[31]

The French and American naval interventions of the 1840s did not reverse Nguyen policy towards the missionaries, and Tu-duc's execution of a Spanish bishop in 1857 enabled Napoleon III to secure Spanish collaboration, and Filipino troops, for the joint expedition of 1858. Its seizure of Tourane (Da-nang) did not result in a revolt in Tonkin such as the missionaries had forecast, and the expedition turned to the south. In the colony of Cochin-China that the French subsequently built, they did, however, rely to a substantial extent on the collaboration of Christian converts, and in a sense the indigenous nature of Vietnamese Catholicism was undermined by a tendency to identify it with the colonial power.

In Cochin-China syncretist sects, known as Cao Dai (Great Palace) began to emerge in the 1920s, involving belief in spiritualist revelation, directed by a Supreme Being, and an attempt to unite the religions of China and Christianity. Cao Dai tapped veins of nativism and millenarianism, and Tay-ninh became the centre of a mass movement. A new sect appeared in the Trans-bassac in 1939, the Hoa Hao Buddhists. The sects, attacked by Decoux, were cultivated by the Japanese, and remained a factor to be reckoned with till a state-building Ngo Dinh Diem destroyed them in the 1950s.

In Siam the Chakri monarchs both reformed Buddhism and centralised their control over the sangha. The reforms began with Mongkut, a monk before he became king Rama IV, and, in their emphasis on rationality, have been compared to those of the Protestant Reformation. His successor, Chulalongkorn, created a unified sangha under a patriarch, as well as setting up a department of religious affairs within the new ministry of education.

In Burma the American Baptist mission had begun work before the first Anglo-Burma war, but success came after 1825, and especially after 1852, above all among the Karens, for whom Christianity was a link with the British, their deliverers. The British, as in India, adopted, however, a policy of religious neutrality, affirmed after the Indian Mutiny: Queen Victoria's proclamation of 1858 thus enjoined 'all those who may be in authority under us that they abstain from all interference with the religious belief or worship of any of our subjects on pain of our highest displeasure'.[32] That, of course, was entirely inconsistent with the role of the Burman monarchy which had always had a close relationship with the sangha, had appointed a *thathanabaing*, and enforced discipline through royal commissioners. Taking over Lower Burma after 1852, the British could neither recognise the authority of the *thathanabaing*, now in Mandalay, nor appoint a substitute. Overthrowing the king himself in 1886, the British provided no substitute so far as the sangha was concerned. Though after a break in the late 1890s, a new *thathanabaing* was recognised, his jurisdiction was limited, and the enforcement of his orders depended on the civil courts, not on commissioners. 'The unity, discipline, and dedication to religion of the Buddhist monks declined alarmingly during the 1920's', largely as a result of 'the disruption of the traditional system of ecclesiastical authority'.[33] The British had been apprehensive lest a well-disciplined sangha under a strong primate might challenge their rule. Instead they faced political *pongyis* 'quite free from the discipline of the hierarchy'.[34] After 1938 the office of *tha-thana-baing* lapsed.

Non-interference in religion and custom was a clause in the treaties the British made with the rulers of the western Malay states when they abandoned non-intervention in the 1870s. The traditional relations between the ruler and the people had, of course, comprised both the 'secular' and the 'religious', though they were more formal in some of the Malay states than others. In Rembau there was apparently a state *kathi* in the 1830s, with a general oversight of all the mosques, and in Perak there was an Imam Paduka.[35] In other states, or at other times, the responsibilities of the ruler as defender and arbiter of the faith might be fulfilled more informally or less piously. There was no 'distinct or organised class of *ulama*'.[36]

While British 'advice' in fact interfered with custom, and indeed the Federated Malay States treaty dropped that limitation on it, non-interference prevailed in respect of Islam. The British did not fear the influence of *ulama* as the Dutch did, and encouraged rather than restricted the haj. Christian proselytisation among the Malays was prohibited, and special Koranic teachers were appointed to the vernacular schools. As Bill Roff pointed out, non-interference did not, however, mean no change. Restricted in their political role, the Malay elite emphasised the roles that remained to them. The treatment of Islam in the states became as a result much more authoritarian, hierarchical, and Erastian. 'By the second decade of the twentieth century Malaya was equipped with extensive machinery for governing Islam.'[37] Haji Abbas b. Md Taha once remarked: 'To become a State Mufti in Malaya is a great glory. You have an official uniform, with a whole banana-comb of epaulettes on the shoulder, a *jubbah* embroidered with a gold thread, a silk turban, and your own car.'[38]

The 'orthodox' Islam of the 'kaum tua' which was thus sustained the reformists or 'kaum muda' thus sought to criticise. Those reformists drew upon their knowledge of changes in the Islamic world as a whole, with which Southeast Asia was put in closer touch after the opening of the Suez Canal. More Muslims undertook the haj, and Singapore, the centre of the pilgrimage trade, largely in the hands of the Arab community, became an entrepot of ideas as well as commerce. That role expanded when publishing facilities, mainly owned by Jawi Peranakan—offspring of South Indian Muslim-Malay marriages—were set up from the 1870s onwards. *Al-Imam*, a new periodical in Malay that appeared in Singapore in 1906, drew on the Egyptian modernist movement, and assisted in setting up a madrasah, later imitated on the peninsula. Its call for a system of education that would at once purify Islam and incorporate modern secular knowledge was a challenge to Malay society in general, but to the state religious elites in particular. 'The Kaum Tua', wrote *Al-Ikhwan* in 1929, 'behave as though it was obligatory to believe all the law books of the *ulama*, and every word in them, as though they were the Kuran itself ... while the Kaum Muda hold that the Kuran and *hadith* alone have this authority, and that as none of the *ulama* are free from error, God has given us reason, or intelligence, with which to examine what the *ulama* say.'[39]

The Dutch were much more concerned about the political influence of Islam than the British. They hardly needed the Java War to remind them, nor the influence of the Wahhabi reformers in stimulating the Padri War. Their empire was large, and, despite their avoidance of missionary activity, the growth of their power tended to identify Islam with opposition, whether in open revolt or war, or more passively within the village. That was a further reason for collaboration with the *priyayi* and *adat*-based elites, who were also concerned at the increased influence of *kiyayi* and *ulama*. Their collaboration in the economic field, particularly after the introduction of the cultivation system, tended, however, to associate the *priyayi* with the colonial oppressor, to undermine their traditional power, and to encourage the peasants to look to the Muslim leadership. They looked, moreover, not to the leadership associated with the 'secular' authorities, but to the more independent teachers and scribes, who found their authority in their knowledge of the Koran and their more distinctly Islamic or *santri* (pious) way of life. An increasing number of Muslims went on the haj after 1869—11 700 in the peak year, 1896—stimulating the struggle of orthodoxy against the long-standing Sufism of the archipelago, and adding to the long-standing Dutch concern over 'fanaticism'.

Against this background Christiaan Snouck Hurgronje, appointed to the newly created office of Adviser on Arab and Native Affairs in 1889, developed a new Islamic policy for the Indies. The political threat of 'fanaticism', and that of a pan-Islamic movement centred in Constantinople, could, he argued, be diminished by toleration of Islam as a religion: no barriers, for example, should be placed in the way of the haj. Officials should avoid 'hajiphobia'.[40] The government should not, however, 'platonically envisage all those trends that bear, or tend to bear, a political character'.[41] It should couple vigilance with a continued association with the *priyayi* and the *adat* chiefs. It should, moreover, place that association on a new basis, the extension of Western education and culture, taken, too, beyond the nobility. Snouck was thus a representative of the Ethical era.

In his brilliant account of Dutch policy on Islam, the late Harry Benda pointed to the weaknesses in Snouck's analysis. It relied in substantial measure on a separation of religion and politics, 'at best a temporary phenomenon of Islam in decline'[42]

—a *hijra*, perhaps—and not a permanent feature that would survive an Islamic awakening. Snouck also failed to realise that Islam could modernise itself and point the way to modernity. That the reformists in Egypt and India were determined to show, and their ideas stimulated the Indonesian Islamic leaders who created Muhammadiyah in 1912. Its schools taught a modern curriculum and its missionary activity copied the methods of the Christian missionaries who had become active among non-Muslims—competing with Islam in the Batak lands from the 1860s, for example—and were given greater scope under the Ethical Policy. 'Where the nineteenth century had witnessed the rise of a rural *santri* civilization of Islamic orthodoxy, the twentieth saw the emergence of its urban, reformist and dynamic counterpart.'[43] That meant tension, if not conflict, not only with the colonial ruler and its allies, but also with more orthodox ulama, particularly in rural Java, organised in Nahdlatul Ulama from 1926. Sumatra and Java gave reformism a different reception, too. Twentieth-century economic change in the Outer Islands helped to produce a middle class for which Islamic reformism had a special appeal. In Menangkabau in particular, it was a means of struggling against a matriarchal and communalistic *adat*. Merantau meant for some young men the opportunity to become respected Islamic scholars.

Islamic 'fanaticism' stimulated Spanish action against the sultanates in Mindanao and Sulu and also the opposition to it. Spain's 'blockade' of Sulu tested the readiness of the British to associate with another colonial power. 'When I consider what has been the course of events in this unhappy group of Islands', wrote Robert Meade of the British Colonial Office in 1874, 'and the spectacle afforded to orientals of a Christian Power murdering, pillaging and burning with no adequate excuse—and that Power so weak that the slightest intimation from us that proceedings must cease, would no doubt be attended to—I think a more vigorous course might well be adopted'.[44] Though they ruled more Muslims than any other power, the British did little. They did nothing when the United States adopted a still more violent, though more effective, policy in the early twentieth century.

Spain's struggle with Sulu coincided with a growing challenge to Spanish rule in Luzon. Its initial focus was within the church, and the government's reaction to the Cavite mutiny of 1872 was the garrotting of three secular priests. Frustration among the seculars had increased in the nineteenth century, particularly after the Jesuits, expelled under the Enlightenment rule of Carlos III, were allowed to return in 1859. They were placed in Mindanao, and the Recollects shifted to the Manila-Cavite region, just where the seculars were strongest. In 1893 seculars administered only 150 of the 967 parishes.

The revolution of 1896–98 was partly directed at the friars, and they were driven from their parishes, which seculars sought to fill. That still left Spanish bishops with jurisdiction over church and people, and whatever the influence of freemasonry among the revolutionary leaders, they were clear that it could not continue. Their answer was to recognise as *vicario general castrense*, or military vicar-general, Gregorio Aglipay, an Ilocano who had studied at San Juan de Latran in Manila as a working student, and at Vigan, and after being ordained had served as a coadjutor to a regular in the Tagalog provinces, and become Aguinaldo's military chaplain in July 1898.[45] 'If we continue to acknowledge the spiritual leadership of the Spanish prelate', he told the Filipino clergy in a manifesto of October 1898, 'the Revolutionary Government, by political necessity, will have to withdraw its support from us. Without such support, we shall not be able to exert to the full our moral influence upon the people, or stop the advance of pernicious doctrines.'[46] The following year an Ecclesiastical Assembly in Paniqui, Tarlac, in effect set up a Filipino National Church. In face of the American advance, it never got off the ground. But, given Aglipay's excommunication, it might in any case have lost the support of what John Schumacher calls the 'revolutionary clergy', rather than kept it.[47]

The US government reached an agreement with the Vatican that envisaged the sale of the friar estates, but not the immediate withdrawal of the friars. In this context an impulsive Ilocano nationalist, Isabelo de los Reyes, launched the Philippine Independent Church in August 1902, with Aglipay as Supreme Bishop. The schism spread. The strength of Aglipay's movement, Governor Wright told President Theodore Roosevelt, lay 'in his appeals to the Filipino as a race to form an independent church of their own and also in the fears which many men, naturally inclined to be good Catholics, have that the regime of the American Bishops is but a continuation of that of the Friars'.[48] With the final resolution of the lands issue, and the diminution in the number of friars, however, upper-class participation fell away. A decision by the Philippines Supreme Court that the church buildings were the property of the Catholic Church was a severe blow to the Aglipayan church which had occupied them. Its strongholds thereafter were Ilocos Norte and Zambales. The church, too, had fought back. In the apostolic constitution *Quae mari Sinico* Leo XIII recognised the end of the *patronato* and reconstructed the church. A provincial Council was held in 1907.

Though often enlisted as the support of government, religion by no means guaranteed it. To the extent, indeed, that it gained a hold upon the people, it could also be a vehicle of opposition, identifying subversion with heresy as much as the orthodox was identified with the established. Inasmuch, moreover, as millenarianism was a strong feature of Southeast Asian societies, the chances of such an identification increased. An old order should be restored, or a new one created, in order to realise the promise that religions so often held out, or to avoid the catastrophe they predicted. The popular movements in the Philippines so well described by Reynaldo Ileto are only examples.

The case of the Philippines also suggests that, if the relation of ruler and religion can be ambiguous, so, too, is the relation of religion with those who would supplant the ruler. They may indeed secure popular support on a religious basis, but that support is likely to be at an angle to their main thrust, particularly as politics and religion became more distinct. That was true of Filipino nationalism, and it was to be true also of Burman and Indonesian nationalism.

The post-colonial phase

Independent states had to review the question. At the same time they faced major economic and social change at home that conduced to religious revival, and they were also exposed, particularly as communications expanded, to the impact of revivalism among religions abroad. At the end of World War II, K. P. Landon saw Southeast Asia as 'a crossroad of religions'. At the end of the century, as Paul Stange has commented, 'the region remains a site of encounter between deeply held and widely divergent world-views', though, as he wrily adds, 'pragmatic utilitarianism may be the most powerful missionary force and the communities of that faith are expanding'.[49]

Aung San espoused a secular nationalism. 'We must draw a clear line between politics and religion. ... If we mix religion with politics, then we offend the spirit of religion itself.'[50] The independent Burma of U Nu, however, recalled the pre-war association of *pongyi* and nationalists, and it renewed links between Buddhism and the state. The Ecclesiastical Courts Acts of 1949 and 1951 were intended to strengthen the sangha's organisation and discipline, depleted under foreign rule, and the government sought also to restore the tradition of scholarship in the Pali scriptures. Though Marxism was not renounced, the task of the Buddha Sasana Council, as Nu saw it, was 'to combat anti-religious forces which are rearing their ugly heads everywhere'.[51] His government sponsored the Sixth Great Buddhist Council, held in Rangoon between May 1954 and May 1956. At its close monks pressed that Buddhism be made the state religion. Nu's support of this—of a kind of spiritual welfare state—helped to win his faction the 1960 election, and in August 1961 the legislation was passed.

The philosophy of the Burma Socialist Programme Party, set up by the military after it seized power, drew on several Buddhist concepts and used the appropriate Pali terminology. But *The System of Correlation of Man and his Environment*, published in January 1963, was in fact at least incipiently totalitarian rather than Buddhist. It was, it claimed, 'a philosophy that meets both material and spiritual needs'.[52] The socialist state had to plan for the improvement of the people's spiritual life, but that life was defined without using the word religion.

The Revolutionary Council had promptly abolished the Buddha Sasana Council. When all parties other than the BSPP were dissolved in 1964, the government also ordered Buddhist and other religious organisations to register with their local Security and Administration Committee, but the order was rescinded when a monk immolated himself in protest. In 1965, Ne Win called an All-Sangha All-Sect Convention at Hmawbi in order to purify the hierarchy, but though that recalled the action of a monarch, his aim was rather to constrain the political action of *pongyi* than to tighten the links between Buddhism and the state. In 1974 monks were involved in large-scale demonstrations associated with the burial of U Thant, a Burman who been UN Secretary-General. In 1980 the state at last secured fuller control. The First Congregation of the Sangha of All Orders for the Purification, Perpetuation and Propagation of Sasana, held in Rangoon in May, adopted a constitution that paralleled that of the state, and provided for the township People's Council to take action against monks or monasteries violating the Buddhist code of behaviour.

The regime had attacked *nat* worship, though its claim to 'rationality' was modified by the patronage that General Sein Lwin afforded astrology. That indeed became increasingly popular. With increased economic pressure, 'and the diminished opportunity for individual ambition to express itself', Sarah M. Bekker observed, Burmans increasingly resorted to supernatural support and relied on magical forces. At the same time, there was 'an attempt to "Buddhify" the supernatural, even those traditional non-Buddhist practices, which were always accepted before'.[53]

Self-immolation—barbecuing, as the President's sister-in-law called it[54]—had struck the world's imagination when Thich Quang Duc had carried it through in Saigon in June 1963. That was part of the growing Buddhist protest against the regime of Ngo Dinh Diem, pro-Catholic and, still more significantly, deeply clientelistic. The sangha in Vietnam was relatively small, but it had begun a revival in the 1950s, and its spokesmen believed Buddhism could contribute to a national revival. Yet the regime, which had attacked the syncretic Cao Dai and the folk-Buddhist Hoa Hao sects, offered the Buddhists no recognised role. 'Barbaric as they must seem to any Westerner', as the Australian journalist Denis Warner wrote, 'the repeated suicides struck a deep emotional chord in Vietnam. People who had forgotten they were Buddhists started to pray again.'[55] That the Buddhist leaders exploited to the full, as they did the international publicity that the suicides secured. The regime's attack on the Xa Loi pagoda on 21 August sealed its death warrant. But under Diem's successors Buddhist activism gradually fell away. 'The appeal to Buddhism as a basis for nationalism was undermined by Cao Dai dominance of Tay Ninh Province, Hoa Hao power in the western Mekong delta and the semi-autonomy of the Montagnard animists, Khmer border people, and Muslim Cham remnants.'[56] Only a million joined the United Buddhist Association set up at the Xa Loi pagoda to unite South Vietnam's Mahayana and Theravada followers.

Socialist Vietnam compromised with Buddhism. 'Support has even extended to the establishment of a High Level School of Vietnamese Buddhist studies.' The syncretic sects in the south, long shorn of their political role, flourished in the 1990s. The regime was, however, 'actively hostile to anything representing popular millenarianism, which it sees as representing a throwback to definitely outdated superstitions'.[57] In that, however, it is not different from other independent governments, nor they from the regimes that preceded them.

The Thai government both patronised and utilised Buddhism. 'The Nation will remain prosperous and stable as long as the Religion provides the pillar for the national culture and morality', Prime Minister Pibun declared in 1943. 'Conversely, Buddhism can only maintain its strength and endurance if the Nation is stable and unified.'[58] The post-coup government had reformed the sangha under an act of 1941, and undertaken a project for the translation of the Pali text, the Tripitaka, into Thai. Seeing Buddhism as a national religion, it also expected its citizens to become Buddhist.

Pibun's post-1947 government was less aggressive. For it Buddhism was, however, a bulwark against communism, and for Pibun it was a source of legitimacy in his struggle with his political rivals. The government undertook the restoration of temples. Pibun attended the synod in Burma, and Nu, visiting in 1955, acknowledged that Thailand under Pibun had 'become a state enriched with great merits'.[59] He played a major role—too large a role in the king's view—in the celebrations of the 25th Centenary of the Buddhist Era in May 1957. His successor, Sarit, drew monarchy and religion together in support of 'development', and monks were used in community development programmes.

At the same time, Sarit increased central control over the sangha under an act of 1963, with the avowed object of reducing sectarian rivalry. Phra Phimonthan, abbot of the Mahanikay order, more 'populist' than the Dhammayut, was persecuted, and conservative elements in the sangha remained dominant, even though it was polarised, like the wider society, in the 1973–76 phase. The hierarchy thus tended to seem out of touch. Outside the sangha, Buddhism was dynamic. Santi Asoke, founded in 1975 by Phra Phothirak, and supported by Chamlong Srimuang, Governor of Bangkok, insisted that moral authority came from the individual, and the founder fell out with the sangha. The Dhammakai sect, founded in 1970, saw no contradiction between spiritual growth and material accumulation, and like some American fundamentalist groups, became fabulously wealthy. By contrast 'development monks', Phra Nakphatthana, coming mostly from the north, led community projects in the villages.

Most of the population of independent Indonesia were Muslim, but it did not become an Islamic state. Its politics were as a result deeply affected by the tension between those who wished it to be one and those who did not, a tension itself acted upon, as in the past, but now, at a time of Islamic revival, even more intensely, by outside influences. Sukarno was against an Islamic state, and Suharto against Islamic politics. But belief in God is one of the five principles on which the state has rested since Sukarno enunciated Pantjasila as its basis in 1945, and a Ministry of Religion became a stronghold of Islamic influence in the bureaucracy and a support for Muslim educational and other organisations. Over the position of *kebatinan*, the mainly Javanese mystical sects, the government was ambivalent.

Under Malaya's *merdeka* constitution of 1957, Islam became the official religion of the federation. The ruler remained the head of the Muslim religion for his own state, while the new king became responsible for the non-Malay states, Penang and Melaka. Everyone had the right to practise his religion, but state law could constrain the propagation of religious doctrine among Muslims. When Malaysia was created and Sarawak and Sabah were incorporated, it was agreed that this provision would not apply in those states. Subsequently, however, 'Islamization has been intensified through its role as a vehicle of Malay cohesion', and the *dakwah* or missionary movements represented 'a reinvigoration of Malay identity through strengthening of a pure Islamic commitment'.[60]

For many of them, however, the attempts of the UMNO-dominated governments to meet the challenge of the Islamic resurgence of the 1970s did not go far enough: the establishment of an Islamic Research Centre and a Missionary Foundation, for example, were seen as merely symbolic acts. Prime Minister Mahathir sought to 'ride a tiger', but also to shape an Islam that would endorse learning, thrift, and hard work. Students overseas, he suggested, were radicalised for or against the West. What was needed was a balance, 'accepting what was good from the West but continuing to hold firmly to Islamic values'.[61] The Islamic University, opened in 1983, was designed to provide that balance. Bank Islam, launched the same year, was designed to refute 'the idea that Islam is not compatible with progress'. No such bank existed in the time of the Prophet, but that did not mean 'there cannot be one in this time'.[62]

Securing what it saw as 'full' independence in 1984, Brunei Darussalam declared itself with the blessing of Allah to be now and forever 'a sovereign, democratic and independent Malay Muslim monarchy, committed to the teachings of the Sunni sect, and based upon the principles of justice, public service and freedom'.[63] The foundations of the concept Melayu Islam Beraja were laid by the Director of Information, Ustaz Badaruddin, the previous year. Islam, it has been suggested, countered the doubtful legitimacy of absolutism in the modern era, and also the dangers of Brunei nostalgia for the past. But it required a correction of the image of the regime in terms of fundamentalist criticism of its secularism in the late 1980s.

In Singapore, on which in some other respects Brunei models itself, the government actively concerned itself with religious life. In the early 1980s it promoted Confucianism, and at the end of the decade it tabled a white paper on the maintenance of religious harmony. Religious organisations had retained some autonomy under the PAP, and the young were attracted to them. The spread of English made Christianity more attractive, and it was seen as modern. In 1994, 40.6 per cent of Chinese university graduates were Christian, as were four cabinet ministers, and one-third of MPs. It was also a focus for progressive social thinking. The role the Catholic Church played in the Philippines precipitated a PAP move against community workers in 1987, and it forced the church to close its Justice and Peace Commission by threatening to put church organisations under the Societies Act. The Maintenance of Religious Harmony Act of 1990 gave the government extensive powers to repress the activities of religious groups.

In the Philippines the martial law regime borrowed the rhetoric of Popes John XXIII and Paul VI and the Second Vatican Council (1962–65), but 'any similarities between the stated goals of the Marcos government and the social action of the Catholic and Protestant churches in the 1960s and the 1970s were overshadowed after 1972 by periodic military raids on church institutions, the gaoling of priests and pastors engaged in social justice work, and the deportation of foreign missionaries ministering to the needs of the poor'.[64] The conservative majority of the Catholic Bishops Conference concentrated on defending specific church interests, but moderates, engaging in what Jaime Cardinal Sin, Archbishop of Manila, called 'critical collaboration', were prepared to criticise specific injustice. In reaction to martial law, the National Secretariat for Social Action, Justice and Peace (NASSA), established in 1966, was reinvigorated, and it linked the Latin American ideas of consciousness-raising, pioneered by Paolo Freire among the poor in Brazil, with the concept of the basic Christian community, members of which were to become agents of their own liberation. The programme was endorsed by the CBCP in 1977. A Ministry of Defense report singled out the basic Christian community movement as a 'dangerous form of threat from the religious radicals'.[65] Organising such communities the government tended to see, in Mindanao and elsewhere, as synonymous with supporting the communists.

The regime's Crisis Papers of 1983 advocated winning over the conservative elements in the hierarchy and undercutting critics like Sin. After Marcos's re-election in 1981, church–state relations had deteriorated markedly: authoritarian rule continued, and the government contended that the church was infiltrated by communists. In the run-up to the snap presidential election of February 1986, Sin declared that participation was an act of Christian faith, requiring honesty and integrity. His views were endorsed by the CBCP, and when it became evident that Marcos intended to stay in power despite the outcome, the bishops recommended a 'non-violent struggle for justice'.[66] Undermining the old constitutional structures, the Marcos regime had not only given the army an influence unprecedented in the independent Philippines: it had also pushed the church, including the hierarchy itself, into a social and political role that was, in both senses of the word, more critical. There were no parallels elsewhere in Southeast Asia.

Except in Brunei Darussalam, avowedly secular regimes remained in control in Southeast Asia in the 1990s. Yet, if the region had in 1945 been a crossroad of religions, that crossroad was by the end of the century still busier. As ever—even more so in an age of air travel and improved communications—it was open to influence from outside, from Islamic fundamentalism or Christian liberationism, for example. But the new age of commerce in Southeast Asia was also an age of dramatic economic and social change, in which men and women were ever more inclined to seek solace or understanding in religious experience. Nor did they find that solely in the mainstream. Not only consumerism, but magic, mysticism, and millenarianism had a hold on the urban middle classes, duplicating their traditional hold on the villages.

Notes

1 *CHSEA*, I, p. 276.
2 R. Birling, *Hill Farms and Padi Fields*, Englewood Cliffs: Prentice-Hall, 1965, p. 81.
3 pp. 81, 83.
4 H.-D. Evers, 'The Buddhist Sangha in Ceylon and Thailand', *Sociologus*, 18, 1 (1968), p. 22.
5 *CHSEA*, I, p. 318.
6 J. F. Cady, *Thailand, Burma, Laos, and Cambodia*, Englewood Cliffs: Prentice-Hall, 1966, p. 42.
7 Birling, p. 83.
8 *CHSEA*, I, p. 286.
9 *Burmese Supernaturalism*, Englewood Cliffs: Prentice-Hall, 1967, p. 268.
10 q. Spiro, p. 271.
11 J. A. N. Mulder, 'Aliran Kebatinan as an Expression of the Javanese World-view', JSEAS, 1, 2 (September 1970), p. 105n.
12 *Aspects of Islam in Post-colonial Indonesia*, The Hague and Bandung: Van Hoeve, 1958, p. 36.
13 Lieberman, MAS, 1993, p. 543.
14 *A Modern History*, p. 132.
15 *CHSEA*, I, p. 311.
16 Ricklefs, *Seen* p. xx.
17 *CHSEA*, I, p. 521.
18 Boxer, *Dutch*, p. 143.
19 *CHSEA*, I, p. 532.
20 D. D. Parker, 'Church and State in the Philippines, 1565–1890', BD diss., U Chicago, 1936, p. 79.
21 q. de la Costa in Anderson, p. 93.
22 p. 95.
23 K. W. Taylor, *The Birth of Vietnam*, UCP, 1983, p. 84.
24 ibid., p. 83.
25 ibid., p. 264.
26 Smith in Leifer, p. 5.
27 *CHSEA*, I, p. 525.
28 Micheline Lessard in Taylor and Whitmore, eds, *Essays into Vietnamese Pasts*, p. 142.
29 q. Adrien Launay, *Histoire de la Mission de Tonkin*, Paris: Maisonneuve, 1927, p. 464.
30 q. S. Herz, trans., *Rhodes of Vietnam*, Westminster, Md: Newman, 1966, p. 53.
31 Woodside, *Model*, p. 220.
32 Donald E. Smith, *Religion and Politics in Burma*, PUP, 1965, p. 42.
33 ibid., p. 52.
34 p. 55.
35 W. Roff, *The Origins of Malay Nationalism*, Yale UP, 1967, p. 68.
36 p. 71.
37 Roff, p. 73.
38 q. Roff in Tregonning, p. 172.
39 q. Roff, pp. 77–8.
40 q. F. von der Mehden, *Two Worlds of Islam*, Gainsville: U Florida P, 1993, p. 3.
41 q. H. Benda, *The Crescent and the Rising Sun*, The Hague and Bandung: Van Hoeve, 1958, p. 24.
42 p. 29.
43 ibid., p. 48.
44 Minute by Meade, 12 August. C.O. 144/4[9188A], Public Record Office, London.
45 Porter, 'Ilokos', pp. 65–9.
46 q. Pedro S. de Achutegui and Miguel A. Bernad, *Religious Revolution in the Philippines*, Ateneo de Manila, 1960, I, p. 52.
47 *Revolutionary Clergy*, Manila, 1981, pp. 272, 270.
48 q. Achutegui and Bernad, p. 239.
49 *CHSEA*, II, pp. 529–30.

50 q. ibid., p. 118.

51 q. ibid., p. 126.

52 q. ibid., pp. 293–4.

53 in J. Silverstein, ed., *Independent Burma at Forty Years*, Cornell SEAP, 1989, pp. 51, 52.

54 J. Buttinger, *Vietnam: A Dragon Embattled*, London: Pall Mall, 1967, p. 995.

55 *The Last Confucian*, Penguin, 1964, p. 222.

56 *CHSEA*, II, p. 546.

57 *CHSEA*, II, p. 564.

58 q. Kobkua Suwannathat-Pian, *Thailand's Durable Premier*, KL: OUP, 1995, p. 130.

59 q. ibid., p. 143.

60 *CHSEA*, II, p. 566.

61 q. Khoo Boo Teik, *Paradoxes of Mahathirism*, KL: OUP, 1995, p. 176.

62 q. Khoo, p. 179.

63 *Pelita Brunei*, 4 January 1984, in Malay, q. G. Braighlinn, *Ideological Innovation under Monarchy*, Amsterdam: VU UP, 1992, p. 87n.

64 Robert L. Youngblood, *Marcos against the Church*, Cornell UP, 1990, p. 64.

65 q. ibid., p. 93.

66 q. ibid., p. 200.

3.4

Education

The nature and purpose of education in Southeast Asia, and the extent of its availability, varied from regime to regime and from time to time.

Education can be compared with religion. It offers individuals kinds of understanding of themselves and others, means of perceiving their place in the world, ways of developing personality and shaping character. Yet it is a matter for the community as well as the individual, and not merely because the individual may seek the support of the community or seek to share enlightenment. The community may want, through education as through religion, to determine its membership, to increase its cohesion, to secure support in a world that may be threatening or incomprehensible. Individual and community may at times be at odds. Heresy may have to be suppressed, and ideology to be imposed. The studious layman and the over-educated may be troublesome. Books may be burned or banned.

The written word indeed provides another link. The major religions are scriptural, as well as experiential. To gain a deeper understanding of them, and thus both to develop one's capacity to serve the cause and enlighten others, it is necessary to be literate. It is not surprising that, as states became more sophisticated, their rulers might seek the service of priests, possibly less encumbered by kinship ties than a secular bureaucracy, certainly possessed of skills other than their knowledge of the other world and of the ritual that invoked it.

Religion and education share the concept of levels of access and attainment. Religious understanding may come in a moment of enlightenment, though only as a result of study or meditation, or as a result of preaching that interprets scripture in an apposite way or that casts a previous experience in a new light. More characteristically, religious learning came to be associated with a period of study—sometimes in close association with an avowed master, sometimes in individual withdrawal from the world, sometimes in a monastic community—and access might be affected by an acceptance of poverty or a supply of wealth or support from family or patron. The recognition of such study was more or less formal. Magic powers or miraculous deeds might be one sign of attainment. At another pole, strongest where religion was backed by an ecclesiastical hierarchy, attainment would be measured by the award of degrees.

Education shares some of these concepts, and, inasmuch as its purpose was or came to be separated from the enhancement of religious experience, it yet retained some of the earlier associations and utilised structures that were parallel or similar. Skills might be acquired through apprenticeship or through institutionalised training. A wider education might involve full-time participation in formal study in schools that might be based on those created by religious communities or that might indeed be otherwise the same institutions. Colleges and universities reflected their ecclesiastical origin.

Important as the content of religious learning was to church, community, and state, so, too, was the content of the curriculum in education. Was it what the individual and the patron sought? Did it conflict with what the religious authorities taught? Did it serve the state by providing appropriate expertise? The answers to those questions remain in contention. Different responses are offered at different times and in different places, and that is true of Southeast Asia as of other regions. What the colonial powers wanted was not what the monarchs had sought. Nor did the nationalist movements accept an education that they saw as either too destructive or insufficiently liberating, even more limited than the education offered in the metropolis. The independent states saw education as an aspect of 'nation-building' and as an agency of development. Perhaps it was not surprising that the concept of an education that was there, as it were, for its own sake, gained little purchase on the makers of policy. But at the end of the century they were by no means alone in their emphasis on utility since, as it became more 'universal' elsewhere, education became more utilitarian.

Burma

In the Burman monarchy, pagodas 'dotted the countryside … , and each village had a monastery school, or *kyaung,* adjacent to it'.[1] To these males were sent at around the age of eight. There they waited on the *upesins,* those who had passed formal examinations in the scriptures at age twenty or above, and on the *pongyis,* those who had spent ten further years of self-denial. 'They also learned to read, write, and cipher, to memorize the Buddhist commandments and the Pali formulas used in pagoda worship.'[2] Students were supposed to remain at the *kyaung* until at the age of 12–15 they were initiated by the *shin-pyu* ceremony into the status of *ko-yin* or novice. A young Burman would serve as a *ko-yin* for a minimum of one lenten season. Those who stayed longer sometimes became difficult to discipline. Most, however, had abandoned the *ko-yin* life before twenty, and probably married a woman who would not have been to school, but been trained by her mother in domestic tasks. 'A knowledge of letters is so widely diffused', Michael Symes wrote in the 1790s, 'that there are no mechanics, few of the peasants, or even of the common watermen … who cannot read or write'.[3]

Western education was initially provided primarily in Christian missionary schools in Tenasserim and Arakan and later in Pegu. In 1866, however, a Department of

Education was established in Rangoon, and the government began to take a larger role. At first it attempted to use the *pongyi kyaung* as a medium, 'but the monkhood was by and large uncooperative', and it turned to fostering secular schools under its own or missionary or private management. *Pongyi* education also 'lost out … because it came to lead nowhere vocationally or professionally'.[4] Well-to-do Burmans sent their children to government and mission schools where English was taught and competent students might aspire to a place in the new bureaucracy. That education was, however, 'an alien affair',[5] and it did not, and in missionary schools could not, combine subject teaching with moral and civil training. The standards of the Buddhist schools, on the other hand, were not high, and religious and moral instruction consisted of 'perfunctory memorization'.[6] In 1936, on the eve of the parliamentary system, out of 1.6 million children aged 6–11, 0.4 million went to recognised schools, 0.2 million to others.

In World War I Governor Butler had appointed a committee 'to ascertain and advise how the imperial idea may be inculcated and fostered in schools and colleges in Burma'.[7] It recognised the impulse the struggle had given towards the creation of a commonwealth of nations, among which Burma, under British tutelage, would come to play its part. But nationalists in Burma—represented, for example, in the Young Men's Buddhist Association—also saw the importance of education in shaping the future of Burma, and those that aspired to or had secured higher education connected their personal hopes with their hopes for their country. Would the colonial government give them the employment for which they had made themselves competent and the influence they believed they were qualified to exert?

Part of India, Burma shared in the development of Western university education strengthened by the Universities Act of 1904. By 1919, 875 Burmans were enrolled at the University of Calcutta. In the meantime a government committee in Rangoon was working out the guidelines for a university there. It favoured a residential university with a relatively high standard of entry, and the act of August 1920 adopted its approach. Already concerned that Burma was not sharing in India's political reforms, nationalists argued that the object was to restrict the number of graduates so that Burma could never govern itself. Somewhat unenthusiastically, since they had met the entrance requirements, the current students were persuaded to strike. The strike spread to schools, and *pongyis*, editors, and politicians called for a 'national' system of education. Most of the national schools that were set up did not long survive, and no national university was created. The agitation had, however, not only enlivened Burman nationalism: it had also stressed the political centrality of the university, in turn putting at risk the centrality of learning on the campus.

Independent Burma's future leaders were the leaders of the university strike of 1936. The president of the student union, Nu, denounced a lecturer for immorality and called for his dismissal. The student newspaper, edited by Aung San, published an inflammatory article. When the student leaders were disciplined, a strike was called. Examinations were at hand, and that ensured cooperation in the university and in schools at least from the less well-prepared students. The post-1937 government amended the act so that it met many of the demands of the students and the politicians who had taken up their cause. It even provided for 'legislative review of examination results'.[8]

Ironically Nu, as premier in the 1950s, and also chancellor, was to be deeply concerned over political activities on the campus and over the low level of learning. The caretaker Ne Win government 'effectively restored discipline … at the expense, however, of free discussion, even in the classroom'.[9] Universities were, however, to be a focus of opposition to the BSPP government and to its military-dominated successors.

Malaya, Borneo, and Singapore

In Malaya, not part of India, the British established no university till after World War II. Some tertiary institutions had been set up, however. The Straits and Federated Malay States Government Medical School, opened in 1905, was renamed the King Edward VII College of Medicine in 1920, and Raffles College, conceived in 1918 as a means of celebrating Singapore's centenary, was finally launched in 1928. Chinese leaders had wanted a university, but Richard Winstedt, who had been appointed principal, endorsed the views of the Chief Justice: 'disabuse your minds of such hope. There are not in Singapore and the Straits sufficient boys who would be thought proper for university education. … It is very much better that a few boys should go home to get a proper education.'[10] It was not until 1949 that the two institutions were combined to create the University of Malaya.

A residential Malay College, designed to prepare the young members of the Malay aristocracy and royalty to take part in the modernising administrations of the Malay states, had been opened at Kuala Kangsar in 1909, an Eton of the East. The training of teachers for Malay schools, begun at Malay College, Melaka, in 1900, was from 1922 provided in the Sultan Idris Training College at Tanjong Malim.

Though these institutions came to play a large part in the creation of Malay nationalism and the leadership of independent Malaya, the government's educational purpose was far more limited. 'The aim of the Government', a report of the Federated Malay States Chief Secretary, George Maxwell, declared in 1920,

> is not to turn out a few well-educated youths, nor yet numbers of less well-educated boys; rather it is to improve the bulk of the people and to make the son of the fisherman or peasant a more intelligent fisherman or peasant than his father had been, and a man whose education will enable him to understand how his own lot in life fits in with the scheme of life around him.[11]

Before the British intervention of the 1870s, 'formal' education had been provided in the Koran schools. When a boy approached puberty, he was handed over to a teacher from among the village *ulama*, themselves pious products of the system. In the village, he was likely to be taught in the teacher's house, or in the *surau*, a building used for religious purposes, or on the steps of the mosque. In the Straits Settlements, and also in Kedah, Kelantan, and Trengganu, there were *pondok* schools.

In these, like the schools in Buddhist countries, the students lived and studied with a well-known teacher, tending his fields in between. Much Malay education was informal, or based, as R. J. Wilkinson put it, 'upon a sort of apprenticeship'.[12]

The British Residents did not take over the Koran schools, which were 'not', in their view, 'a suitable base on which to build an educational system'.[13] Instead they sought to establish Malay vernacular schools alongside the Koran schools. A secular elementary education was, however, a novelty, and it seemed to have little to offer the villager. Attendance was, therefore, a problem. But the energetic and influential Resident of Perak, Frank Swettenham, adopted a policy of expansion, and, though he had doubts about educating the Malay woman, four Malay girls' schools were established in 1890–91. Instruction in English, however, or any kind of 'higher' education, he thought dangerous. 'I do not think we should aim at giving Malays the sort of higher education that is offered by the Government of India to its native subjects.'[14] That was left to the Malay Eton, and its graduates were recruited to a new Malay Administrative Service, founded in 1910.

For the most part the Residents and the Federated Malay States government adopted a *laissez-faire* attitude to education in the Chinese community. The migrants sought, however, to transplant the age-old system of their homeland, though the schools that were set up were 'only approximate, often even faint, replicas'.[15] Both the reformists in China and the revolutionaries took an interest in education among the overseas Chinese, and the growing influence of the Kuomintang prompted a change in British policy. In 1920 the School Registration Enactment was passed, and subsidies were subsequently advanced as a means of extending government control. Clementi sought to limit the use of Chinese-born teachers and Chinese-produced texts. But there was no enthusiasm for attracting Chinese away from Chinese schools by extending English-medium education.

If the Chinese could rely for a time at least on the resources of their relatively tightly knit communities, the Tamils, employed by planters or by the government, were, as Loh says, dependent on them for their educational needs.[16] Only the shortage of labour for the rapidly expanding rubber industry prompted action. To encourage immigration, the Federated Malay States decided to establish Tamil schools 'with the object of making the F.M.S. from the point of view of the Indian immigrant, an outlying province of India like Ceylon'.[17] Tamil schools were also provided by plantation managers, often in a makeshift way. The Labour Code of 1923, a response to the Government of India's Emigration Act of the previous year, included a requirement for estate schools as well as day-care facilities. But Tamil education was the Cinderella of the plural system, and few Tamil children had the chance to secure English education.

The ambitious aim of the Malay-led Alliance governments that secured independence for Malaya in 1957 was to create a national system that would have a Malay emphasis, and yet not alienate the other communities. Following the Razak report of 1956, the first national Malay-medium secondary schools were set up. Alongside them were national-type schools, fully assisted but permitted to use a language other than Malay. Under the report of the Rahman Talib committee, set up after the 1959 elections, there would, however, be no government-sponsored examinations in Tamil or Chinese beyond the primary level, an arrangement that 'effectively forced the closure of all or most Chinese secondary schools'.[18] Many shifted to English-medium schools. Towards English the government's attitude was somewhat ambivalent. The schools were of high standard, and they had created the common educational experience that enabled the community leaders to work together in the Alliance. But further steps followed the 1969 crisis. In 1970 the government announced that English-medium schools at the elementary-primary level would be phased out by 1983, so that the whole system would come to use Bahasa. In the same year Universiti Kebangsaan was opened, and the vice-chancellor of the University of Malaya announced that it, too, would use the national language.

The Chinese reaction to its education policy had been one factor in boosting the opposition to the Alliance in the 1969 election. In turn the crisis that followed prompted the introduction of the New Economic Policy, designed to advance the economic role of the Malays more rapidly. Quotas increased their participation at university level. A very large number of Chinese students, however, sought tertiary education overseas. Nor did the ambivalence over English quite vanish, particularly when Prime Minister Mahathir set Malaysians the target of becoming an industrial nation by 2020.

The Company spent little on education in North Borneo. 'Educational progress has been far too rapid in the Philippines during the American Occupation', Governor Jardine said, 'but it can hardly be denied that it has hastened far too slowly during fifty-five years of the British Occupation of North Borneo'.[19] He himself did not advocate education in English. He echoed Maxwell: 'We hope to make the boys good citizens and good cultivators'.[20] A government vernacular school for sons of chiefs, founded in 1915, closed in 1930. Only in the 1930s did vernacular schools become popular. Mission schools used English, the key to advancement. The government left the private Chinese schools alone. Postwar the pattern did not greatly change, though education expanded. Even so, only 35 per cent of children were at school in 1956.

In Sarawak the Brookes, ruling through the Malays, opened the first Malay school at Kampung Jawa in 1883. They left the education of the non-Muslim Dayaks to the missionaries, though offering them some financial support. The mission schools—the first opened by the Society for the Propagation of the Gospel in 1847, others later opened by the Catholics, the Seventh Day Adventists, and the Borneo Evangelical Mission—accepted all races, however. Chinese education was provided by the clans and associations with some government support. The system was thus fragmented and urban-biased, but major steps were taken after 1937, when R. W. Hammond reported that the state of education, other than Chinese, was 'behind that of most British Colonies or Protectorates comparable' in wealth or 'the educability of its people'.[21] By 1941 the fifty-four district primary schools catering for Muslims had

4831 pupils; the Chinese operated 158 schools with 13 416 pupils; and the forty-five mission schools, using English, had 4097 pupils.

Colonial Sarawak set up the Batu Lintang teachers college in 1948. The main thrust was establishing rural primary schools, run by local authorities. The government struggled to control the curriculum in the Chinese schools, which were penetrated by communism. Financial grants were one means, but success was incomplete, and Chinese secondary schools resisted conversion to English in 1961, the basis for an expanded national system. By the time Malaysia was set up, about half Sarawak's school age population was at school: 78 per cent of the Chinese, 45 per cent of the Malay; 33 per cent of the Dayak. Those in secondary education rose from 1050 in 1948 to 17 727 in 1963.

In Singapore an English-educated elite had gained access to state employment in the 1930s. But the Chinese community had built up a complete school system, often antagonistic to the colonial government, and postwar it added the Chinese-medium Nanyang University (1956). The People's Action Party began by linking a socialist-oriented English-educated elite and communist-oriented Chinese-educated leaders. In power the PAP sought to dissociate itself from its earlier partners, finally achieved in the Malaysia process. It did not, however, wish to provoke a 'chauvinistic' reaction by a direct attack on Chinese education. It ostensibly pursued a policy of bilingualism, arguing indeed that 'Asian values' were best taught in Asian languages. English, however, became more important as post-Malaysia Singapore internationalised its economy. Chinese-medium schools ceased to be viable by the late 1970s, and in 1980 Nanyang, already under attack, was merged with the University of Singapore, the successor of the University of Malaya, to form the National University of Singapore.

Its aims are 'becoming an international hub for learning, scholarship and research' and providing that 'special engine that will keep the country growing, prospering and maturing'.[22] Secondary, vocational, and university education all expanded. At the same time they were highly regulated by a government keen to define the national purpose.

Indonesia

Colonial governments, better able to do without advanced education, sought to constrain more than regulate. That was the case with the Dutch in Indonesia. Even that could, however, be counter-productive. Higher education was offered at the Engineering College at Bandung (1919), the Law College (1924) and the Medical College (1926), at the University of Batavia (1941), and, for fewer still, in the Netherlands itself. Yet so limited a provision hardly fulfilled the aims of the Ethical Policy or countered the threat of Islam. Coupled with a dearth of employment opportunities, it tended to create an oppositional rather than an assimilationist leadership. Moreover the institutions, mostly in West Java, tended to bring students from various parts of the Indies together and to create a sense of being Indonesian, a sense even stronger among the few who studied in the Netherlands itself: 'young Javanese were for the first time meeting not only Europeans but also Sumatrans, Ambonese and Sundanese. The effect was both confusing and electric.'[23] Even this limited provision marked an advance on the pre-Ethical Policy phase.

Indonesian males were traditionally educated in Islamic schools, *madrasah* and *pesantren* (boarding school), according to a pattern that, as in Malaya, recalled that of the pre-Islamic period. They attended on, and indeed served, teachers and scribes, *ulama* and *kiyayi*, who were held in awe because they could read the sacred books, and commanded even more respect if they had performed haj. After the founding of Muhammadiyah in 1912, they were to face the competition of a network of schools that reflected the objectives of Islamic reformists, and offered a modern curriculum alongside teaching concerned with matters Islamic. That was a development which Snouck had scarcely foreseen. But the competition the Ethical Policy offered was not extensive.

In the nineteenth century the Dutch government had not seen Western education as a priority. Its use of the *priyayi* elite in the cultivation system drew on their traditional status and a modern education would have been more hindrance than help: in 1900, it seems, only four out of seventy-two *bupatis* knew Dutch. In the 'liberal' period, the Dutch established chiefs' schools (*hoofdenscholen*) for the sons of the higher elite, and from the 1890s gave them an increasingly vocational character. But the demoralisation among the higher *priyayi* in a phase during which they had lost many of their old privileges meant that the Dutch had to recruit from the sons of lower officials or even from non-*priyayi*.

Even under the cultivation system there had, of course, been at least a minimal need for Western-educated Indonesians, for, almost literally, bean-counters. In 1851 the government set up a teachers training school (*kweekschole*), and in the same year it sought to solve its need for semi-skilled medical workers by establishing the 'Dokter-djawa' school for training vaccinators in Weltevreden: two wandering Menangkabauers arrived in 1856. In the liberal period employment also became available in the irrigation, forestry, railway, telegraph, and other services. In this way a semi-*priyayi* elite began to emerge, tending to resent its subordination to their often less well-educated *priyayi* superiors.

Education was a plank in the Ethical programme, but different Dutch officials gave it different emphases. Snouck and the director of education between 1900 and 1905, J. H. Abendanon, focused on the elite, seeking to modernise it and secure its support. In 1900 the *hoofdenscholen* were reorganised as Training Schools for Native Officials (OSVIA), open to any Indonesian who had completed the European lower school. In 1900–02 the Dokter-djawa school became STOVIA, the school for training native doctors, and Abendanon abolished the fees for the less wealthy. Only in his hopes for increasing educational opportunities for upper-class Javanese women was Abendanon defeated. But he published the moving letters of Raden Ajeng

Kartini, the daughter of the Jepara *bupati*, in 1911, and the government was later to subsidise the schools set up by a private Dutch fund, the Kartini Fonds.

In 1892–93 the government had revamped primary education, establishing First-Class Native Schools for *priyayi* and those going on to the semi-professional schools, and more rudimentary Second-Class Native Schools, designed to meet an urban need for basic secular schooling. In 1907 the First-Class Schools were reformed so that they taught the Dutch language, and in 1914 they became Dutch Native Schools (HIS). That relieved the pressure on, and preserved the character of, the European schools (ELS), otherwise the only schools, aside from mission schools in the Outer Islands, 'where an Indonesian could learn Dutch adequately and proceed to OSVIA and STOVIA',[24] or proceed to Hoogere Burgerschool (higher middle-class school), which provided secondary education in Dutch. In 1914 MULO schools, offering more extended lower education, were set up for those, European, Indonesian, and Chinese, who had completed primary education, and in 1919 AMS, general middle schools, were established to carry students to university entrance level.

It was only in the 1920s that university-level education became available in Indonesia with the founding of the technical and law colleges and, out of STOVIA, the medical college. Hitherto the only way for Indonesians to enter tertiary education was by joining the European system, going through the HBS, and proceeding to the Netherlands. In 1905 only thirty-six Indonesians entered HBS. In 1913 Hoesein Djajadiningrat, from a distinguished *bupati* family, became the first Indonesian to gain a doctorate.

If Snouck and Abendanon favoured an elite approach, van Heutsz and Idenburg looked to a more basic and lower-level approach. To provide even Second-Class schools for the masses would, it was estimated, cost more than the colonial government's total expenditure. Instead, at the governor-general's instigation, village schools (*desascholen,* also called people's schools, *volkscholen*) were to be set up, the villagers themselves unenthusiastically bearing much of the cost. In 1915 *Inlandsche Vervolgscholen* (native senior schools) were created to take students to a higher level. The old Second-Class schools first became *Standaardscholen,* intended for those engaged in trade, but were later assimilated to the village school-*vervolgschool* pattern. To allow village school students to proceed to secondary education, link schools (*Schakelscholen*) were opened in the 1920s, offering a course that allowed entry to MULO, but they did not flourish. Vocational education was provided by mission schools in Java, as well as in the Batak lands and Minahasa, and after 1909 by the government. Most of the graduates became employees of European firms.

The system was elaborate, but it was not well-resourced, nor did it deal with large numbers. In 1930–31, 1.66 million Indonesians were in the vernacular primary schools designed for them, 8 per cent of the relevant population group. In the Dutch-Native system there were 84 609 Indonesians. Some 7000 were in Dutch-medium secondary education in 1941, mostly in MULO. In vocational agriculture and forestry schools there were 392, and at university level 178. By 1941, 230 had graduated from the engineering, law, and medical schools. In addition there were those who attended mission schools, those who attended Muslim schools, which the government sought to regulate, those who attended the Taman Siswa schools, set up by Ki Hadjar Dewantara in the 1920s in an endeavour to combine modern education with Javanese tradition, and those who attended Chinese schools. By number, as against percentage, there were more illiterates in Netherlands India in 1940 than in 1900.[25] 'The educational legacy bequeathed to independent Indonesia was … an extremely meagre one.'[26]

The relatively small educated secular and Islamic elite that governed independent Indonesia not surprisingly put an altogether different priority on education, in keeping, indeed, with its commitment to constitutional democracy. 'State and private (mostly religious) high schools and university-level institutions sprang up everywhere, but especially in Java, and many achieved high standards.'[27] The adult literacy rate, only 7.4 per cent in 1930, rose to 46.7 per cent in 1961, and the use of Bahasa Indonesia throughout the system established it firmly as the national language. The New Order after 1965 adopted an approach to politics and development that in some ways recalled that of the colonial regime. But it could not dispense with modern education, even though it might find itself at odds with student youth.

The Philippines

In the colonial Philippines there was no such disjunction as in Burma and Indonesia between the government and the traditional providers of education. There was, however, some tension, and that increased in the nineteenth century when liberal governments emerged in Spain. In fact, however, friar dominance continued, and neither the government nor the religious orders welcomed the challenge they faced from the members of the elite who gained high-level Western education, the *ilustrado*.

Their missionary endeavour led the Spaniards to establish an all-level European-style education system in their first decades in the Philippines. The friars established schools that taught the rudiments—reading and Christian doctrine, more rarely writing and arithmetic—and despite the injunction of the Council of the Indies in Madrid tended not to use Spanish even for teaching Christianity. The Jesuits pioneered secondary education, starting with the College-Seminary of San Ignacio in Manila in 1585, and Pope Gregory XV raised it to university status in 1621. It closed in 1768, when the Jesuits were expelled. The Dominicans established a secondary school in 1611. That began to offer degrees in 1626, and became a royal and pontifical university in 1645. Santo Tomas, as Filipinos will tell you, is thus twenty-five years older than Harvard.

The nineteenth-century reforms were set out in the 1861 report of a commission on public education established by Governor-General Crespo and in the subsequent decree of 1863. This established a normal school for men in Manila, and one for women followed in 1871. The law also provided that there should be one primary school for boys and one for girls for every 5000 inhabitants in towns and one in every barrio with a population of over 500. Spanish was to be used; attendance was to be compulsory; expenses were to be met by the municipality. The change that followed was less dramatic than these moves implied. The normal school was supervised by the newly returned Jesuits, and the local schools by the local friars. Attendance was not enforced, the curriculum remained rudimentary, and local languages continued in use. At the end of Spanish rule, there were no more than 2167 primary schools, attended by some 200 000 boys and girls. But the American author, Frank C. Laubach, said they 'compared favorably with the schools of Spain of the same period'.[28]

Secondary schools were covered by a decree of 1867. The first-class ones offered a five-year course, with an emphasis on Latin grammar and the classics, others less than the full five years. They were in two categories, public and private, the latter, the majority, including many religious foundations, numbering 90–100 by 1895. The Moret plan of 1870, designed to secularise secondary education, was never carried out, owing to the opposition of the orders.

Moret also wanted to turn Santo Tomas into a secular University of the Philippines. A compromise retitled it for a brief period the Royal and Pontifical University of the Philippines. In 1875 the government secured considerable supervisory powers over the university, and there were laymen as well as Dominicans on the staff. A total of 242 degrees were awarded between 1865 and 1870; 952, 1870–82; 193, 1882–86; 540 ,1886–98. Though some who were not well-off succeeded, generally only the well-off could access university education, even in Manila. You needed preparation that was not available in ordinary parish and convent schools, obtained from paid tutors or private schools with teachers called *latinistas*. Then you went to a first-class secondary school, and then to Santo Tomas. And, if wealthy enough, perhaps on to Madrid, to Barcelona, or another European city.

The graduates could not get the posts for which they were fitted, the university pointed out in 1887: they could go into ill-paid professional jobs, but the government preferred men educated in Spain. The university urged a change of policy in order to avoid political disturbances.[29] As in other colonial territories, indeed, graduates who could not secure positions for which their education fitted them were to spearhead opposition. That happened earlier in the Philippines than elsewhere in Southeast Asia, since Western education was more readily available, and a wealthy mestizo class had access to it.

Those who went to universities outside the Philippines, in Spain or elsewhere, made contact with European thinking—even if Spain itself was not at the forefront of change—and there, too, they were less trammelled by censorship. Those men included some of the most famous of the leaders who advocated a new colonial policy and, disappointed, sought independence, foremost among them the great polymath José Rizal, others, too, such as Antonio Luna, Pedro A. Paterno, and Graciano Lopez Jaena. Tertiary education helped to draw 'Filipinos' together, as it did Indonesians. Tagalogs predominated, but Jaena was a Visayan, and Aglipay and de los Reyes were Ilocanos.

The educational policies of the short-lived Republic reflected the experience and aspirations of the revolutionaries. Education should be secularised, a common language should be used (the Biaknabato constitution of 1897 declared Tagalog the official language), and popular and vocational education should be stressed. The government also created a state university, based first at Malolos and then in Tarlac.

As at home, so also in its newly acquired colony, the US government did not aim at reconstructing society, but rather at creating opportunity for individual advancement. Education thus had a key role in its policies and it was also seen as a means of preparing the masses for effective citizenship and for democracy. But in the event American educational policy did not do much to relieve the tao from conditions of extreme dependence, though it raised the literacy rate to 49 per cent by 1939. Instruction was now in English, a foreign tongue, and poverty permitted only 48 per cent of schoolchildren to go beyond third grade and 3 per cent to high school. By 1948, 59.8 per cent over ten years of age could read and write in some language, and 37 per cent were literate in English. But education was still elite rather than popular.

It was, however, more secular and more public. After the Philippine Assembly passed the Gabaldon Act in 1907, the central funding of barrio schools was increased, and enrolments rose from 150 000 in 1901 to 1 059 987 in 1929. A law of 1902 placed the financial responsibility for secondary schools on the provinces, but the insular government paid the salaries of the teachers. In 1903 the enrolment was 450; in 1929, 74 463. Boys predominated. The Assembly set up a state university in 1908, the University of the Philippines.

Alongside the public system, the private system continued and extended. Increasingly it came under government supervision, but it represented the continuance of the long-established connexion between religion and education into the new age of secular education. The private elementary and intermediate schools, predominantly Catholic, enrolled some 45 000 in the late 1920s, and the secondary schools some 20 000. At the tertiary level Santo Tomas and the Jesuit-founded Ateneo fell into the private category. They were joined by Protestant foundations like the Silliman Institute in Dumaguete (Oriental Negros), and by non-sectarian institutions, like the University of Manila and Far Eastern College.

These endeavours expanded still further in the independent Philippines. Yet as in the Spanish period, and again, though in a different way, in the American period, the provision of education and the overall orientation of the state did not coincide. That was, of course, not necessarily a disadvantage, for a state can undermine the purposes of education as well as support them. A system that produces unemployable graduates can, however, be a source of frustration to them, as well as of concern to the government. In the late twentieth-century world, the Philippines has in its educated citizenry and its substantial use of English extraordinary advantages it has yet fully to turn to account. The belief that it can do so is, however, important to those who take a liberal view of education, just as the hope that it can carry out 'development' is important to those who do not accept that an authoritarian government is essential.

Thailand

In Siam, Chulalongkorn's reforms of the 1890s extended into education. In alien-ruled Burma, the traditional monastery-based schools were unwilling to accept a modern syllabus, but in Siam they did. In 1921 Vajiravudh's government enacted a compulsory primary education law, though it did not at first apply to the whole kingdom. In 1935, 1 756 233 should have been at primary school: 1 026 547 were. The governments of the 1930s increased expenditure on primary education, and in 1937 a national scheme was introduced, requiring four years' compulsory education. By 1939 there were 429 government schools at various levels; 10 768 primary schools aided by local bodies and monasteries; 304 municipal primary schools; and 1308 private schools. Literacy in 1937 was 31.11 per cent overall; 47.02 per cent of the male population was literate. The Sarit 'development dictatorship' committed itself to lengthening compulsory primary education from four to seven years, and the numbers in secondary schools rose by 63 per cent between 1958 and 1962. They were to triple between 1965 and 1975.

Sarit's government also expanded vocational education and opened universities in Chiengmai and Khon Kaen. Hitherto university education had been available only on a limited scale—one of the reasons why the army offered an attractive career—though the royal foundation, Chulalongkorn University (1916), created by amalgamating the Royal Medical College and the Civil Service College, had been joined after the 1932 coup by Thammasat University (1934), created from the Law School, more open and drawing on somewhat lower social strata. Other universities were established in Bangkok and the regions, and an open university, Ramkhamhaeng, in 1971. In the early 1980s more than 200 000 were enrolled in higher education, though vocational schools tended to come a poor second choice after universities, and to draw more students from less elite backgrounds. That had had its political hazards in the 1970s. But it also suggested that in Thailand, as in the Philippines and Malaysia, there was a mismatch between development objectives and educational provision, though it was a different one. It was not that education was valued for its own sake, but that it was thought to offer good bureaucratic prospects.

Vietnam

In traditional Vietnam bureaucrats were recruited—frequently more in theory than in practice—through periodic public examinations Chinese-style. Such examinations made access possible, though affected by family circumstances, but, because their goal was government service, and because the government was anxious to ensure the loyalty of its bureaucrats, the curriculum was rigid. 'In Vietnam as in China', as Woodside puts it, 'the graduate of the system who entered the bureaucracy after passing these examinations was unlikely, in later official life, to offer unique or eccentric interpretations of organizational problems'.[30] From Minh-mang onwards the Nguyen emperors re-adopted the system as part of their attempt to guarantee the unity of the kingdom after the disruption of the Tay-son phase. But it did not help in dealing with the problems with which the West presented Vietnam.

According to the curriculum inaugurated in 1826 the lectures in all schools treated the Chinese classics and their commentaries on the odd days of the month, and on the even days they treated the Chinese histories. The teachers, as Dao Duy Anh put it, lectured 'with their eyes shut'.[31] At the Thanh Hoa regional site in 1825 one scholar ignored the issued topics, and wrote in his examination book: 'If examinations and their topics are for choosing scholars, you ought to revive the elegance of good literature and abolish the vulgarities of learning for the purpose of public service'.[32]

Villages chose their own teachers. They might be scholars who had failed the examinations; or who had passed but had no desire to be officials, like some of the Le loyalists; or officials who had retired. They might teach in their own homes, or in classrooms set up in the homes of the wealthy. A father would bring his son to the teacher and the household head who sponsored the teacher, and they might confer on a new and auspicious name for the boy. The students would collect money from the villagers to pay the teacher, who received no official pay. Girls remained at home, learning the four virtues from primers.

'Colonial educational policy', Woodside writes, 'was characterized by a tension between cultural expansionism and racial elitism'.[33] French cultural influence was to be brought to bear on the Vietnamese, but not too much of it. The colonial regime, and particularly the French in the colony, 'feared that the colonial schools might produce an unmanageable army of French-speaking Vietnamese intellectuals who could compete with native Frenchmen living in the colony for positions in the colonial administration'.[34]

'Franco-Annamite' primary schools and colleges emerged in Cochin-China, mainly in the urban centres, with secondary or lycée education developing only after 1910 and in a few institutions. In Tonkin traditional examinations continued till 1915 and in Annam till 1918. That year Governor-General Sarraut revamped the system on the Cochin-China model, cutting back the traditional schools. His reforms were, however, themselves pruned by Governor-General Merlin, and by 1930 only 323 759 children were at public schools, about 60 000 at government-approved private schools, and 3000 in lycées. Like that in Netherlands India, the system in Vietnam was elaborate but not extensive. In the inter-war period 827 qualified for the baccalaureat.

In Cambodia at the end of the protectorate 120 000 were in French-Khmer primary schools, and 77 000 in 'unreformed' pagoda schools. The first high school, Lycée Sisowath, opened in 1935. In 1950 there were 1500 secondary students of all races. In Laos in 1946 there were only 175 elementary schools, and the first lycée was opened in 1947. There was no higher education in Laos or Cambodia, and only a few could afford to go to Vietnam, fewer still to France. One Cambodian obtained a medical degree in France before World War II: he had stayed on in France after enlisting in World War I. Cambodia's only pre-war graduate engineer was his son.[35]

The University in Hanoi, opened only briefly in 1907, was reopened in 1917. From all Indo-China it enrolled 3000 students in twenty-five years, the maximum numbers being in the Vichy period. There had been twenty-five graduates in 1925, nine in 1926. In 1921–22 students at Hanoi University had included 268 Vietnamese, thirty Chinese, five Laotians, nineteen Cambodians, and three Frenchmen.

The tasks of the DRVN government were in a sense obvious. They involved substituting Vietnamese-language textbooks for French ones; expanding provision; and introducing practical science. By 1966 there were more than 3 million students in the primary and middle-school programme, six times as many students as in all Indo-China in 1939. The number of primary-school teachers rose from 20 000 to 180 000 between 1956 and 1971. The system was closely associated with politics: every school had its management cadres, principal, assistant principal, party cell secretary, youth federation cell secretary.

Teachers had been prominent among the revolutionaries. They were also prominent in the politics of the southern Republic. Their role was, however, limited by the predominance of the military and by a legacy of the past that the regime had failed to dislodge. Woodside suggests 'the persistence, throughout the war years of the 1960s, of a southern upper class, effectively detached both from science and manual labor, whose children continued the diploma-hunting individualism of the upper-class families of the colonial period'.[36] American intervention provided only an alternative focus. The 1969 government budget for overseas study was six times that for the one National Technology Center in Vietnam. Only in 1973 did Saigon set up the Thu Duc polytechnic university, modelled on Massachusetts Institute of Technology.

Conclusion

'Development' revealed educational deficiencies throughout Southeast Asia. In Thailand, it seemed that lack of technicians would prevent advance to 'tiger economy' status. In Malaysia, national language policy was in tension with the need for English, and many students went overseas, in part for political reasons, in part for lack of places. Some of the deficiencies could be attributed to the colonial phase, but not all. Almost everywhere colonial regimes had educated small numbers. The same was, however, often true in the metropolises. In 1902 only 9 per cent of 14-year-olds in Britain were receiving any full-time education. In 1903 the Philippines claimed 44.2 per cent literacy; 40.7 per cent was the average for Spain in 1910. The gap opened up in the late colonial period, when colonial governments were cautious over political advance, and indeed over economic change. The boom in education belonged even in the West to the postwar phase. By then the Southeast Asian countries, emerging from the Japanese occupation, were engaged in post-colonial struggles, and in often premature or ill-conceived plans for industrialisation. They were thus poorly prepared for the economic expansion of the 1970s and 1980s, the conditions for which were not in any case conducive to take-off. What they did, however, tended, perhaps excessively, to echo the narrow utilitarianism of colonial educational policy.

Notes

1 Cady, *Burma*, p. 49.
2 p. 59.
3 q. ibid., p. 63.
4 ibid., p. 170.
5 q. Taylor, p. 113.
6 Cady, p. 196.
7 ibid., p. 195.
8 ibid., p. 383.
9 R. Butwell, *U Nu of Burma*, Stanford UP, 1963, p. 210.
10 q. K. Tregonning, *A History of Modern Malaya*, Singapore: EUP, 1964, p. 229.
11 q. Philip Loh Fook Seng, *Seeds of Separatism*, KL: OUP, 1975, p. 29.
12 q. Rex Stevenson, *Cultivators and Administrators*, KL: OUP, 1975, p. 17.
13 Stevenson, p. 31.
14 q. ibid., p. 61.
15 Loh, p. 36.
16 p. 44.
17 q. Loh, p. 45.
18 Tham Seong Chee, 'Issues in Malaysian Education…', JSEAS, 10, 2 (September 1979), p. 326n.
19 q. Sabibah Osman, 'The Role of Governor D. J. Jardine in Improving the Welfare of the Indigenous People of Sabah, 1934–37', JSEAS, 20, 2 (September 1989), p. 207.
20 q. p. 209.
21 q. Ooi Keat Gin, 'The Attitudes of the Brookes towards Education in Sarawak, 1841–1941', JMBRAS, 70, 2 (1997), p. 54.
22 q. Edwin Lee and Tan Tai Yong, *Beyond Degrees: The Making of the National University of Singapore*, Singapore UP, 1996, p. 234.
23 S. Abeyasekere, *Jakarta: A History*, Singapore: OUP, 1987, p. 97.
24 M. Ricklefs, *A History of Modern Indonesia*, London: Macmillan, 1981, p. 150.
25 J. M. van der Kroef, 'Dutch Colonial Policy in Indonesia', PhD thesis, Columbia U, 1953, p. 222.
26 Anne Booth, *The Indonesian Economy in the Nineteenth and Twentieth Centuries*, Basingstoke: Macmillan, 1998, p. 274.
27 Ricklefs, *History*, p. 226.
28 q. Gregorio F. Zaide, *Philippine Political and Cultural History*, Manila: Philippine Education Co., 1957, II, p. 96.
29 E. Alzona, *A History of Education in the Philippines, 1565–1930*, Manila: UPP, 1932, pp. 143–4.
30 *Model*, pp. 169–70.
31 q. ibid., p. 188.
32 q. ibid., p. 210.
33 *Community and Revolution*, p. 82.
34 p. 82.
35 M. F. Herz, *A Short History of Cambodia*, NY, 1958, p. 67.
36 *Community and Revolution*, p. 297.

Part Four

Protest and Politics

The relationships of Southeast Asian states with their peoples, with each other, and with other states were described in the first part of the book. The second dealt with the economic and environmental relationships of states and peoples, and the third with social and state structures. The fourth part takes up the question of domestic politics.

Like the first part of the book, the chapters of the fourth adopt a topical emphasis, but seek to combine it with a chronological approach. Within that framework each chapter proceeds largely country-by-country and comparatively.

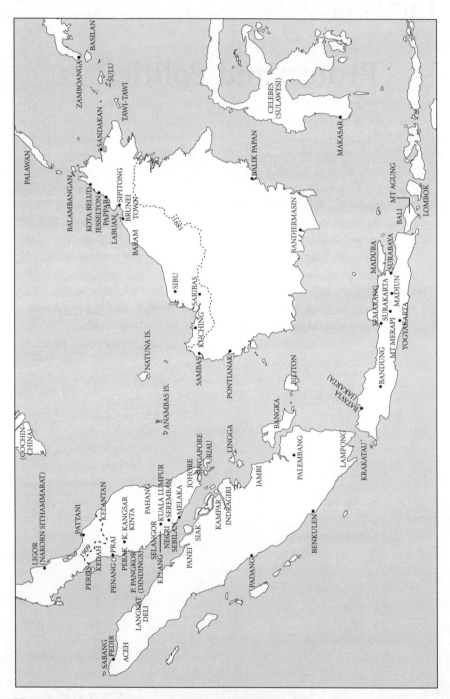

Malaysia and Indonesia, nineteenth and twentieth centuries CE

Millenarianism and Court Politics

Court politics are not peculiar to monarchical regimes, nor is millenarianism peculiar to colonial regimes. Indeed the history of Southeast Asia is in general strongly marked by millennial movements, though they have taken various forms.

Adopting an inclusive definition of the state has risks and advantages. It risks what historians have called 'presentism', the assumption that the past was like the present, preventing our comprehending what it was actually like, and it risks in our particular case what historians have called 'Euro-centrism', inhibiting our understanding of countries, as well as times, in which 'they do things differently'. It also offers the opportunity of comparison over time and between types. By adopting a broad, if crude taxonomy, this book attempts to take advantage of the opportunity, while minimising the risk, and, trying to show what various regimes had in common, also to seek a better understanding of their differences.

The book proposes to deal with 'politics' in the same way. Again there are risks. In his book *The Invention of Politics in Colonial Malaya* (1994), Tony Milner suggests that, just as the life of the 'mediaeval European' was 'saturated with religion', 'we in the late twentieth century possess a fundamentally political outlook. We tend to attribute a political significance, often a political motivation, to virtually every action no matter in what type of society or in what period of history that action may have occurred.' The anthropologist Louis Dumont complains, Milner says, that we take for granted that all communities have politics, 'in the sense that they consist of individuals maximising their advantages and manipulating their situations. We assume that each polity represents the sum total of the "rational" political manoeuvrings of its individual citizens.'[1] 'The term "politics" carries assumptions about individualism and motivation which are not relevant to the practices of all communities.'[2]

So narrow a definition is indeed unhelpful, but it is not essential. It is, perhaps, a description of one kind of politics, a kind that may be prevalent among 'us' in the late twentieth century. But to adopt it runs the risk of depriving other societies of their politics because they do not fit the definition. In discussing politics, as in discussing the structure of states and statecraft, it is possible to adopt a broader view, and to look for comparisons and contrasts. If indeed 'our' politics are emphatically individualistic, that does not mean that there cannot be other kinds of politics, nor that such have not existed in the past. 'Our' present concern may invite us to look for individual motives, but it should not presume either that they have the same strength, or that they are absent, or that they may not express themselves in the same way.

Even a brief account of the structure of Southeast Asian states and their statecraft suggests the presence of politics, though not necessarily in the forms or with the emphases that 'we' give to them. A patron did not build up an extensive clientele merely because 'that was the way things were done', but because he wanted to do something: to win influence or wealth or power, to protect or reward his clients, to make merit. A ruler did not build temples or make marriage alliances merely in fulfilment of the dictates of established custom. Politics were conducted in ways that are foreign to 'us', but only an over-simplified individualistic model would preclude our using the word in such cases.

'Our' individualism has another drawback. Even in our own times—perhaps especially in our own times—it tends to reduce the role of ideas and ideals: men and women are on the make, and ideas and ideals no more than ploys or means of attacking opponents. The relationship is, of course, more complicated, and it always has been. Individuals determine their views as a result of a mixture of motives, and the policies they adopt, or seek to have adopted, may combine, more or less inextricably, what is good for them, and what is thought to be good for others too. But, if that is true of 'our' politics, it may be true of other kinds of politics, too. A 'faction' or a 'party' at a Southeast Asian court advanced its cause, not simply in terms of seeking royal favour or patronage, but in terms also of the direction of policy. At Brunei a 'piratical' party opposed the faction that James Brooke supported. In Bangkok, the Bunnags pushed their candidate for the throne on the death of Rama III, and committed Siam to a new treaty with the British. Faction struggles in Mandalay prompted the disastrous policy decisions of 1885.

Nor, of course, was factionalism confined to the great issues of the colonial confrontation. The Cambodian court of the late seventeenth and early eighteenth centuries saw the pro-Siam king Neak Sor set against the pro-Nguyen faction, represented by his cousin, Neak Non. There were what Ricklefs calls 'lethal feuds' among the courtiers in the Kartasura of Pakubuwana II.[3] Factionalism, he points out, was normal in Java, as it was in Europe, India, and China. One of the ruler's tasks was to manipulate factions, to form alliances, to reach *mufakat* (consensus). Factions were also the key to implementing court decisions throughout the realm, since, as in Burma, court factions represented the peak of the patron–client networks. Succession was a focus. Factions at the Nguyen court divided over the succession of Tu-duc, and Hong Bao's supporters were to rebel in 1854 and to revolt at Hué in 1866. As Ralph Smith suggests, 'political improprieties' may be 'glossed over' in the court records, and the realities of political conflict and court intrigue obscured.[4]

Too narrow a definition of the past politics of Southeast Asia may also fore-shorten the understanding of the politics of the contemporary phase in another way. For they adopt practices from the past in a combination with those of other countries and more recent times. In many cases they have been usefully described, in Weberian terms, as 'neo-patrimonial' systems. Patrimonial states had politics, though not simply of the individualistic kind. 'Neo-patrimonial' described ways of running modern states that drew on past political practice, though combined it with modern practice, modern ideas, and modern techniques, and also with an unprecedented level of economic opportunity. Court politics are not absent, though they cannot be mere replicas of the past.

If these remarks are designed to suggest the advantage in a broad approach, they suggest also the need for caution. They suggest that we do well to regard the Southeast Asian political elites of the past as thinkers and actors, acting within a cultural and political context, not simply as automata fulfilling cultural norms. They were rational beings, though they cannot be presumed to be acting according to the rationality according to which 'we' are supposed to act, nor, indeed, according to an entirely different rationality. If that is the case with the elite, it is just as necessary to understand the motivation of the masses. They, too, have been subjected to great change in the past century and a half. Their approach may mingle elements of the past and elements of contemporaneity. They, too, will help to determine the nature of modern politics, and indeed the fate of the states in which it operates.

Some may see the peasant approach to politics as irrational. In *The Moral Economy of the Peasant* (1976) and *Weapons of the Weak* (1985), James Scott has described low-level forms of peasant resistance, small deeds that limit the exactions of landlords, or frustrate the excesses of the powerful. But if it extends beyond that, it tends to go in the direction of the millenarian. And yet that may be better seen, not as irrational, but as proceeding according to a different rationality. Millenarian protest belongs to societies and polities in which there is, or seems to be, no other way of seeking change, or seeking to reverse the adverse effects of change: it belongs to non-participatory polities, tending to appear 'in regions where relevant political institutions are lacking or undeveloped, or inaccessible, so that the distressed can find no institutionalized way of expressing their grievance and pressing their claim'.[5] So it is found among peasants in traditional societies, or in isolated areas of modern societies, among marginal elements of the working-class, among recent immigrants, among minority groups. The movements try to recapture an apparently better past or to pre-empt a happier future or both. Those who participate are clear that change cannot be effected in any other way than by inspired action, by trust, by faith, by following a charismatic leader, by a kind of magic. It is not an irrational approach, but it does not follow the rationality of participation. That is not available, or not seen to be available. '[M]illenarian movements, even though religious in a sense, were not other-worldly. They were concerned with rational goals pertaining to this world even if the goals were not rationally perceived. Or, to put it differently, they were concerned with goals which were rational within the framework of an existing world-view.'[6]

The movements are not peculiar to colonial societies or to colonial times, though colonial officials might record them more thoroughly than their predecessors. The Little Tradition in China comprises a strong element of millenarianism, and so do the *yonaoshi* or 'world renewal' movements in Japan. Millennial attitudes are, after all, familiar in European societies, too, particularly, though not exclusively, in peasant societies. Arguably, however, colonial structures are conducive to them. In them, after all, the prospect of other, more 'rational', forms of political action seems remote indeed.

In Southeast Asia they are certainly not confined to the colonial phase. In opposition to ruling elites, peasants turned to leaders with prowess—social bandits, former priests—strengthened themselves with amulets, tattooed themselves in rejection of the tattooing to which regimes sometimes subjected them. 'It ... can be argued', David Marr suggests, 'that the Vietnamese elite—sometimes unconsciously, often more openly—utilized Chinese learning against the mass of their own people. ... Their heated denunciations of "heterodox" creeds and attitudes among the people doubtless were motivated in part by insecurity and the fear that somewhere in the villages things were going on, thoughts were being propounded, over which they exercised little control, either moral or coercive.'[7] At times of crisis, the Little Tradition might challenge the Great. One case was the Tran Cao rebellion of 1516, prompted, perhaps, by the Le's intense Confucianisation in the preceding years. Tran Cao claimed descent from the Tran, declared himself the incarnation of Indra, and also claimed to be fulfilling a popular prophecy. His forces reached the capital and destroyed the Le dynastic temple.[8] Peasant rebellions in Vietnam were usually local, and governments had time to organise their response. Tay-son began like this, and, but for the Trinh invasion, forcing the Nguyen to fight on two fronts, it might have failed.

Nor were such events confined to Confucianising Vietnam. The Kha 'rebellion' against Siamese authority in Champassak in 1819 was led by a renegade monk who claimed magical powers.[9] The enforced submission of Cambodia to reunited Vietnam, along with increased corvée and colonisation, prompted rebellion in the eastern provinces in 1820–21 led by a monk called Kai, using what the Vietnamese called 'superstitious means'. He 'washed the heads of his soldiers, reciting *sutras* to give them strength, and shaking drops of water on to them to keep the Vietnamese from dispersing them in battle. If the Vietnamese fired guns, the power of the Khmer would keep the bullets from going far or coming close to them. When Kai's blessings were over, his soldiers lost their apathy, and went out to battle the Vietnamese.'[10] To 'us' it may seem incomprehensible. Yet reading about those who went away to war in 1914 makes it less so.

If millenarianism belonged to the pre-colonial as well as to the colonial phase, the records belong mostly to the latter. Probably, too, millennial movements then increased in number, particularly during the nineteenth and early twentieth centuries, when economic and political changes greatly affected the position of the peasantry. The colonial structure that came to predominate in the region certainly left little room for a participatory approach: there were 'no effective ways *within the colonial system* to influence policy decisions or stimulate much-needed reforms'.[11] There could be little sense that change can be brought about by political action of a 'modern' kind when the rulers were demonstrably of another race and backed by outside power, and the Golden Age became associated with their expulsion.[12] The old patron–client systems were under threat, or were ceasing to deliver the expected level of protection. And that perception, and the need to protest, extended, significantly enough, to Siam, where the rulers were not alien, but where the changes they introduced were, and the political system that they operated was becoming more absolute in deeds, not merely words.

The movements could generally still be characterised as localised and short-term. Their inspiration was religious in form, for life was perceived in that way, and religion not seen as a thing apart. Religion, indeed, can both support and subvert the status quo. Indeed, inasmuch as the state may seek to control it, and to use it for purposes of control, it may also be used, in different forms and with different leaders, to challenge the state. That may be the case at the elite level, when the ruler has to regulate the sangha or the religious orders; but it is also the case at the village level. One reason for regulating the former was, indeed, to avoid losing control over the latter. There was always the risk of doing too much, as well as too little: of alienating the masses from religious leaders who became too elite-oriented, and prompting them to turn to soothsayers, magicians, holy men, hermits, mystics, and heretics of one form or another.

Netherlands India

In late nineteenth-century Java the Dutch were particularly apprehensive about the impact in the countryside of the increasing numbers of haji. They returned to the archipelago, not only more critical of the colonial order, but also more critical of 'official Islam'. The expanded network of *pesantren* and *tarekat* (mystical brotherhoods) brought their message to a rural population affected by 'diminishing welfare' and increasing bureaucracy. That message was, as Ileto puts it, received in the context of 'older expectations and traditions'.[13] Returning to Banten in 1872, Haji Abdul Karim established a village school in his home village, but also travelled through Banten, stimulating a religious revival in which he came to be regarded as a saintly figure with the power to cure and the capacity for invulnerability. He predicted the imminent arrival of the Mahdi and the Last Judgment. In 1888 a rebel army, composed largely of followers of the *kiyayi*, attacked the government officials in Cilegon, wearing *djimat*, convinced that in their holy war they were invulnerable. They were 'crushed in less than one month'.[14]

Not all the peasant movements in colonial Java were millennial—the non-violent Samin movement was more associated with kebatinan—and not all millennial movements were inspired by Islamic teaching. Central and eastern Java possessed the older tradition of the just king (*ratu adil*) and the west that of the Ratu Sunda, and Javanese messianism was strengthened by the *Pralambangan Djajabaja* or Djoyoboyo prophecies, which were attributed to a twelfth-century king, but possibly originated with the humiliation of Mataram at the hands of the Dutch. Resistance to the Dutch on Lombok in the early twentieth century often took the form of messianic *datu an* movements, centred on charismatic individuals who claimed to reincarnate or have a special relationship with a past ruler.

A century earlier Dipanegara had embodied 'the widespread millenarian expectations of the time, and made himself the focus for the ideals and longings which had gripped the Javanese countryside before the outbreak of the war' in 1825.[15] The background, well analysed by Peter Carey, was characteristic as well as specific. One feature was the growing burden of taxation in Yogyakarta. The opening-up of new lands in the late eighteenth century and the expansion of cash crops had enriched the 'landowning' peasants, and the rulers reacted by rackrenting the tollgate and market farms and reducing the cadastral unit. Annexations by the British conquerors of 1812 worsened the situation: courtiers and officials who lost out had to be provided for elsewhere in the appanage regions; while peasants in the annexed regions had to pay land-rent, and found as well that old demands were still enforced unofficially. The demands of the restored but cash-strapped Dutch made the tollgates even more of a burden. They also alienated the elite. The Resident had allowed appanage holders to lease estates to individual Europeans and Chinese, and then the governor-general had cancelled the leases, leaving the appanage-holders to reimburse the planters for the capital they had invested meanwhile. This was no Golden Age, but a Time of Wrath, and the eruption of Merapi in 1822, like the appearance of cholera the previous year, surely heralded the reign of the *ratu adil*. Adopting elements of the Muslim messianic tradition as well, Dipanegara ordered the restoration of the old level of rice-field tribute. And he sought to drive out the Europeans, who captured him only by stratagem.

The Philippines and Malaya

In the Philippines, where the combination of earlier traditions and the Catholicism brought by the Spaniards was more complete than the combination of Islam and earlier Javanese practices, millennial movements invariably took on Christian overtones. The popularisation of Catholicism gave it a life outside the institutions that the Spaniards set up, and to that the *tao* turned in protest against the demands of government and the vagaries of economic change. Outside the pueblo there were hermits, curers, and heretics, as well as bandits and wanderers, and in the mountains one might escape the oppressive life of the lowlands. The propagation of Christ's teachings, through hymns, poems, and dramas, and, as Ileto has convincingly shown, the dramatised epic of His passion, death and resurrection, helped to reshape the popular view of the world so that it fused elements of the remote past and elements of the introduced. A Kristo was a man of power, lowly and humble, but superior in knowledge to the priests of the establishment. To die for his cause was to see heaven. In the teachings of the church, so presented, lay the basis for millennial protest movements.

Such movements often in fact emerged from sodalities and confraternities that the church had at first officially approved, but which changed their character as a result of catastrophic events or under the impact of charismatic leaders. Under the leadership of Apolinario de la Cruz—an indio lay brother from Tayabas, unable to enter an order—the Cofradio de San José was transformed in the 1830s from a normal sodality devoted to good works to a kind of alternative church. The Tagalog Christ and his movement were suppressed only with considerable violence and loss of life: 300–500 of his followers were killed, his body cut up, and his head displayed on a pole on the road to Majayjay. But even so his movement was not by any means the last, though its numerous successors, the Colorum sects, were not on such a scale.

The American regime brought popular resistance—which, like other colonial regimes, it called banditry—to an end, or at least down to manageable proportions. Underground organisations proliferated, however, and, after 1923, 'a new generation of potential redeemers' emerged.[16] Some were Rizalista, prophesying the second coming of the great nationalist leader. Some, like Pedro Kabola, associated the coming of 'independence' with the millennium. Pedro Calosa's rising in Tayug, Pangasinan, in the Depression of 1931 was colorum in style. It sought independence and the end of tenancy, invoked magic and used *anting-anting* (talismans). Caciques played down its economic origins.

In Malaya millennialism and peasant revolt were often associated. The resistance of *penghulu* Dol Syed in the 'Naning war' with the Melaka authorities of 1831–32 indeed evoked magic and mystique more than millennial aspiration.[17] By contrast the Trengganu revolt of 1928—which followed the undermining of traditional relationships—had messianic overtones: an Imam Mahdi would restore the true faith. The Director of the Malayan Security Service, J. D. Dalley, was concerned over the revival of the cult of invulnerability in 1946–47: even educated Malays had a 'sneaking regard for it'.[18] 'Much lies dormant which we must desire shall remain so', Clementi warned.[19]

Siam

Millennial movements were not confined to the colonial territories in the colonial period. Phraya Phap's rebellion in Chiengmai was directed against the enforcement of Bangkok's control in the north. A petty official linked to the Chiengmai royalty, he was able to mobilise some 3000 peasant followers by articulating their discontent in a popular religious idiom. Invulnerable, a man of extraordinary powers, 'he was expected to reign as the ideal Buddhist king of a revitalized Chiengmai that was independent of Bangkok and free of taxes'.[20] The Holy Men Phu Mi Bon rebellion in Udon and Isan in 1902 was messianic in form. The disconcerted Chulalongkorn concluded: 'we have misused a foreign model of administration'.[21]

Mobilisation

In almost all these cases both the peasants, and those they followed, looked, in millennial style, for an alternative society and an alternative polity. Such might be expressed in terms borrowed from the currently established and be designed to bring them to life in a purer form. They might be expressed in terms that evoked an idealised past: the Tangerang disturbances of 1924 sought to bring back the gloried sultanate of Bantam, while Hsaya San's rebellion in depression-ridden Burma looked for 'a Burman Buddhist King'. Neither leader nor followers could find a place in the society or polity that existed, and it did not offer them the means of effecting change in a 'rational' way.

The development of a different kind of politics would be slow and spasmodic. It depended in part on the economic and political changes that helped to create a new elite and to offer it new ways of formulating and propagating political aspirations. It depended also on the attitude of the state, colonial or otherwise, which would, to a greater or lesser degree, contemplate a growth in participation, opening up opportunities, opening up, too, the prospect of winning further opportunities by exerting pressure in one form or another. It depended, third, on the attitude of the masses, whose support would be necessary in that endeavour. Would governments and collaborating elites permit it to be sought? On what terms could it be acquired? How secure would it be? Would it involve a commitment to more radical change? The answer to these questions would help to determine the success of the elite. It would also help to determine the policies it would follow if it were successful in securing power. Would politics become more participatory? Would the millennial alternative still be attractive?

Securing the backing of the masses was made possible by the disruptive effects of economic change and of the expansion of the role of government. When European rule became more active—even for what could be described as worthy purposes—it became more alienating. The Ethical Policy, for example, brought the Dutch administration into closer contact with the village, and the peasants felt that they were being pressed by alien forces to do alien things, albeit in the colonial rulers' view for their own good. If modernisation made it difficult to secure continued loyalty from the elite, it also dislodged the traditional allegiance of the masses. They became more open to mobilisation. Stepping up the activities of police and intelligence services would delay and impede the changes, but it would not stop them.

That did not, of course, mean that the villagers were empty of ideas, ready to have new ones inscribed upon blank minds. Modernising governments produced incomprehensible, if not alienating, policies. What the new elites had to offer was also novel and might also be alienating. How could they secure the popular support they needed if they were effectively to challenge the powers-that-be? They had in fact to present their views in different ways, and indeed often to compromise them. Their objectives and their support were at times irreconcilable: the end justified the means, but the means could qualify the end. The legacy carried over into the independence period. Elites created expectations they could or would not meet: their politics reflected that.

In power, new elites were tempted to adopt new forms of patrimonial politics. On the way to power, they often sought to appeal to the millennialism that was so strong a tradition among the peasantry of Southeast Asia. The 'rational' aims of the leaders were thus tied to the 'irrational' aims of the followers. The Filipino nationalists fought Spain, and later the United States, in the name of an independent republic, and in the hope of setting up a kind of politics based on the premises and promises of the European enlightenment. Their followers joined them in part perhaps because they were clients, but also because they believed that a new era was at hand, in which the kingdom of Christ would be realised on earth, and the promise of the resurrection redeemed.

A strong vein of millennialism not surprisingly penetrates the modernising politics of Indonesia, too. Tjokroaminoto, the leader of the first mass movement, Sarekat Islam, was identified as the *ratu adil*, the just ruler of Javanese tradition, while the *djoyoboyo* prophecies appeared not only to envisage the reunification of Mataram, but to foretell the departure of the Dutch. Millennialism helped but also hampered the Indonesian communists.

Marx himself had to contend with utopianism. It was, he believed, a main enemy: it conduced to action that was bound to be ineffectual, revolutions that were sure to be disappointed. He urged a 'scientific' approach that took account of historical trends and practical realities. Yet even he retained a residue of utopianism. 'He had simply thrust the happy consummation a little farther off into the future.'[22] Marxist activists had to work their way through this contradiction. The most successful were those who insisted on patient political work, indoctrination, organisation, coupled with planned violence, and discounted rapid results.

To hold to that stance was difficult in China, and it was difficult in Indonesia, too. The attempt to create a mass movement built on its strong millennialist aspirations, and the leadership failed to counter the risks by patient political work. More than once the Indonesian communist party was prompted to act prematurely and in the short-term manner of a millennialist movement. More than once it was virtually destroyed as a result: in 1926–27, in 1948, in 1965.

In Vietnam, at least after the French brutally suppressed the uprisings of the early 1930s, the communists learned their lesson more thoroughly. Mass movements were not enough: 'the assumptions and the aims of secular politics must be well understood if the popular base is to remain cohesive for any length of time. The cadres had to teach the peasants not only how to form committees of action and how to draw up lists of grievances and demands, but also why this type of activity was different from joining sect-organizations and participating in undirected millenarian violence.'[23]

The government's report denied that Hsaya San's rebellion, which began in Tharrawaddy in December 1930 and spread to the delta, was 'purely an economic uprising'. It pointed to the role of some of the village-level nationalist organisations, to the part played by the *pongyis*, and to 'the fact that the Burman peasants ... are still amazingly superstitious and extraordinarily ignorant and credulous', resorting to charms and amulets and absorbing prophecies.[24] The rebellion was not simply traditionalist. Hsaya San was a district nationalist leader frustrated over the failure of the elite politicians to alleviate the condition of the peasants. That was a lesson for post-colonial elites.

It was not only in the Philippines of the late 1890s that 'independence' came to be associated with millennial hopes. 'Independence' was a magic word for the Sakdalistas, who sought to turn mass discontent to account in the 1930s. In Indonesia, too, the long-prophesied overthrow of the Dutch was accompanied by millennial aspirations which nationalists evoked, but the new Republic would not be able to realise. Even if the new elite had wanted to develop a more participatory system—and that was the logic of the struggle they had led—the high expectations that had been aroused were bound to make it difficult. The elite, there as elsewhere, came to be content with a manipulatory approach that set participation at the level of a safety-valve.

Notes

1 p. 1.
2 p. 11.
3 *Seen*, p. 209.
4 'Politics and Society in Viet-Nam during the early Nguyen Period', JRAS, 1974 (2), p. 154.
5 Yoneo Ishii, 'A Note on Buddhistic Millenarian Revolts in Northeastern Siam', JSEAS, 6, 2 (September 1975), p. 126.
6 Sartono Kartodirdjo, *Protest Movements in Rural Java*, Singapore: OUP, 1973, p. 17.
7 *Vietnamese Anticolonialism*, UCP, 1971, p. 20.
8 Cooke, JSEAS, 25, 2, p. 29.
9 D. Wyatt, 'Siam and Laos, 1767–1827', JSEAH, 4, 2 (September 1963), p. 28.
10 1869 poem, q. D. Chandler, 'An Anti-Vietnamese Rebellion in Early Nineteenth Century Cambodia ...', JSEAS, 6, 1 (March 1975), p. 21.
11 M. Adas, *Prophets of Rebellion*, CUP, 1979, p. 91.
12 Sartono in Claire Holt, ed., *Culture and Politics in Indonesia*, Cornell UP, 1972, p. 99.
13 *CHSEA*, II, p. 224.
14 Sartono Kartodirdjo, *The Peasants' Revolt of Banten in 1888*, The Hague: Nijhoff, 1966, p. 261.
15 Carey, MAS, 20, 1, p. 65.
16 D. R. Sturtevant, *Popular Uprisings in the Philippines, 1840–1940*, Cornell UP, 1976, p. 141.

17 Emrys Chew, 'The Naning War …', MAS, 32, 2 (May 1998), p. 376.

18 q. A. J. Stockwell, 'Imperial Security and Moslem Militancy …', JSEAS, 17, 2 (September 1986), p. 326.

19 q. C. M. Turnbull, 'British Planning for Post-war Malaya', JSEAS, 5, 2 (September 1974), p. 253.

20 Ileto, *CHSEA*, II, pp. 214–15.

21 q. Bunnag, p. 154.

22 Edmund Wilson, *To the Finland Station*, London, n.d., p. 332.

23 Hue-Tam Ho Tai, *Millenarianism and Peasant Politics in Vietnam*, Harvard UP, 1983, p. 108.

24 *The Origin and Cause of the Burma Rebellion*, Rangoon: Superintendent Government Printing, 1934, pp. 38–44.

4.2

Nationalism

Nationalism emerged in the Philippines in the late nineteenth century, and in Indonesia, Burma, and Indo-China in the early twentieth century. In each country it had distinctive features. In Malaya it was 'communal' in character. In Siam, still independent but resenting the loss of territory to the colonial powers, it took a different form again.

In introducing his account of the rise of nationalism in Vietnam, William J. Duiker suggests that 'nationalism is the result of a gradual process which begins with a primitive awareness of shared destiny and of ethnic or cultural distinctiveness. Only gradually does national consciousness expand into an awareness of the modern concept of nationhood, rooted in the mass of the population.' Through the process 'a people become conscious of themselves as a separate national identity in the modern world, ... willing to transfer their primary loyalty from the village, or the region, or the monarch, to the nation-state'. Duiker suggests stages in the process: patriotic movements that might be labelled 'protonationalist'; 'modern nationalism', beginning when 'the elite leadership of such movements becomes increasingly sophisticated about the nature of the world beyond the borders'; and 'mature nationalism', which 'makes its appearance when a substantial portion of the local community begins to be aware of its society as a definable national community in the world, as a body of citizens linked together by a common destiny, and not simply as the patrimony of a ruler or of an aristocratic class'.[1]

Stage by stage, a people becomes conscious of a sense of community as a nation, and of its position as a nation among nations, in what becomes a world of nation-states. Duiker's suggestion encompasses the shift in loyalties and identities that has to occur. It distinguishes the articulation of those loyalties among the elite and among the masses. It points out that nationalism distinguishes one community from another. It argues that the general aspiration of nationalists is to independence in a world of nation-states. In all these ways it is useful, though, as he would be the first to admit, incomplete, a 'working definition', as he puts it. It is particularly useful for the present book. The approach of the book to the history of Southeast Asia is regional, and such models are a helpful basis for a regional and in some measure comparative approach. But it also seeks to place the history of Southeast Asia in a context of world history that yet avoids both an Euro-centric and an Asia-centric approach. It thus seeks 'working definitions' that are as neutral as possible, and uses models that, albeit crude, encourage the perception of both similarity and difference.

The concept of nationalism is, of course, European in origin, but even in Europe the Duiker model suggests comparisons and contrasts, variants in the working-out of the process, as they might be called. In Western Europe, for example, the sense of national community arises within a monarchical state that over several centuries has built a larger sense of unity. A shift to a sense of nationality might or might not involve the abolition of the monarchy, although its position would certainly change. In other parts of Europe the sense of distinctiveness from others to which Duiker draws attention plays a larger role. The German romantic nationalism of the early nineteenth century was a reaction to the post-revolutionary French version, associated both with invasion and the rationality of the Enlightenment, and the state it envisaged was more corporatist as a result. Nor did the Bismarckian Reich quite fit the model: it did not, as the 'Pan-Germans' lamented, include all those who spoke German. Italy, too, was divergent. Nationalists had laboured both to unify it and to free it from alien control. But what brought success was intervention against Austria from outside, and indeed a shift of power among other European states, coupled with the skilful diplomacy of the Piedmontese leadership. Yet the new state seemed to disappoint the high hopes of the Risorgimento. Unification, it seemed, had been brought to Italy: the state had preceded the nation, and now the state had to build the nation; Italians must no longer look just to the *paese*. Yet even in France not all would share Prosper Mérimée's intense loyalty. Victor Hugo had called the motherland 'an idea'. 'The motherland an idea!' Mérimée burst out. '... It is the living amalgam of our ancestors, of our fathers, of ourselves.'[2]

Applying the Duiker model in Europe brings out elements of congruence and exception that make its value more evident rather than less. That consists not merely in the opportunity it offers for comparing the emergence of nationalism and the nation-state among the Europeans. It also suggests its value in considering those developments in Southeast Asia. For some Indonesian political thinkers at the end of World War II, for example, the 'corporatist' approach of the Germans was more attractive than the 'liberal' approach of the French. In the case of Indonesia, again, but perhaps also of some Filipinos, the aspirations of the Pan-Germans may be a useful basis of comparison, and they were surely an example to the Thai leaders of the 1930s and beyond. Nor is it possible to ignore the comparison that may be made between the destruction of the Austrian empire in Italy and the destruction of the European empires in Southeast Asia. To what extent did the nations achieve independence? To what extent was it thrust upon them? What was the result of struggle, what the result of diplomacy?

In central and eastern Europe, in other parts of the Habsburg dominions, the 'working definition' seems a more exact fit than in the west. There an elite conceived a nation, an 'imagined political community', in Benedict Anderson's phrase,[3] and sought to bring it into existence, both by calling up a justificatory past, and by building up the understanding and support of the people in whose name it purported to act. Yet here, too, there is an element of antagonism upon which the 'working' definition perhaps places too little emphasis. There were rulers who were, or who now seemed, alien; empires that had to be broken up; oppressors who had to be overthrown. That could distort the 'process'. The elite might be tempted to compromise: elements in it, perhaps apprehensive of the longer-term implications of enlisting mass support, and of the possibility of social as well as political revolution, might hesitate, or at least conclude that more 'nation-building' had to be done first. Others might attempt premature revolution, despairing of change in any other way, pressed perhaps by the enlarged hopes of the followers they had enlisted. A nationalist movement might fail, but it might also achieve 'premature' success as a result, perhaps, of external factors. Nationalisms, after all, existed in a world of states, if not yet a world of nation-states. The leaders of even such states might intervene, and, as was the case of Napoleon III in Italy, not necessarily in favour of the status quo.

Again, the 'working definition' is helpful in regard to Southeast Asia, both in respect of comparing the nationalist movements there, and in comparing them with nationalist movements elsewhere. The concept of an 'imagined political community' was indeed put forward by a leading authority on Indonesia and Thailand. The appropriation of the past, evident, for example, among Palacky and the Czech intellectuals, is paralleled in Indonesia and Cambodia. Moderate, even collaborationist, forms of nationalism were evident in Cochin-China as in the Philippines. Nervousness about the masses was a feature of Rizal's thinking. The attitude of the ruling power is again part of the story, perhaps even a more significant part: not only helping to create the conditions under which nationalism might emerge and the borders within which it might act, but shaping the development of the movement by affording or denying opportunities to collaborate or participate or resorting to repression. '[A] nation was born', as the Indonesian journal *Tempo* put it, 'because of our efforts to give meaning to the fruit of history that fell into the garden of our experience'.[4]

Significant, too, is the attitude of other external powers. They offer examples. Will they do more? Will they help to sustain a colonial regime, if not by direct intervention, then at least, say, by denying sanctuary to its opponents or even arresting them? or will they intervene to overthrow it, intentionally or otherwise thereby offering the nationalists new opportunities, if also new challenges? In this respect nationalisms in Southeast Asia, at least as the twentieth century advanced, found themselves in a broader international context than those of nineteenth-century Europe. In general information about other parts of the world was now far more widely diffused, and that contributed to the creation of 'public opinion' on international affairs, within countries, but also among them, so that it became possible to speak of 'world opinion'. Heavily inflected by national interest, that opinion was at the same time bound to recognise the wider applicability of the national concept with which it had grown up. The emergence of 'international' organisations pointed the same way.

So, too, did two other changes apparently, but not in fact, at odds. First, as more nation-states secured independence, more still were likely to do so: not only did it come to seem the norm; they could in a measure support each other. Second, two super-states appeared, the United States and the Soviet Union, who became rivals. Their rivalry was, however, expressed in part by competing for the allegiance of lesser states. That gave nationalists yet more leverage, but it also introduced a complication. For after the revolution of 1917 Russian internationalism was associated with social revolution, and with an ideology that at least envisaged the ultimate withering-away of the state. Working with that internationalism could thus divide nationalists as well as help them. It could also complicate their relationships with others: with the colonial rulers, with their neighbours, with the United States.

Applying Duiker's 'working definition' involves taking account of changes over time as well as in geographical context. In two other ways, perhaps, the 'working definition' itself needs to be supplemented, in respect to Europe as well as to Southeast Asia. First, nationalism is a disintegrative as well as an integrative force. It was not merely that nationalism might undermine or overthrow an alien or imperial regime. Nationalisms might themselves contend. Even in the established states of the West, there were nationalisms that countervailed that of the majority. The French revolutionaries faced that in Brittany and the Spanish state has to accommodate the Catalans. Whether or not the United Kingdom reconciled the Welsh and the Scots, it failed to reconcile the Irish. In inter-war Europe, new nation-states were challenged from within as well as from without: to some extent they inherited the problems of the Habsburg empire that the Great War had helped them to displace. In Southeast Asia aspirant nationalisms were challenged or stimulated by rival aspirant nationalisms. The successful creation of an independent state might face its new rulers with the kind of problems the successors of the Habsburgs faced. Not every nation could indeed have a state. Could a nation-state accommodate other nationalisms? It was hard even to accept other kinds of identity.

The other drawback in the 'working definition' perhaps results simply from its employment of historiographical shorthand. It speaks of 'process'. Yet, like other changes, it cannot be understood without a full account of the personal factors involved. Pointing to the existence of opportunity or the presence of challenge is insufficient on its own. They require a response or demand an initiative. What happens depends in part on the nature of the response and the quality of the initiative. Judgment and leadership, for example, have to be part of an account of the winning of Indonesian independence, stamina and determination part of an account of the regaining of that of Vietnam.

The final comment Duiker prompts is a reminder. So much of Western history, and of the modern history of Southeast Asia, is taken up by the nation-state that it is hard to conceive of a world in which nationalism and the nation-state did not exist, but allegiance was given to king or priest, to patron or clan, and identity so found. It is hard also to do justice to those who seem to us to act against a 'national' interest, or in ways that seem to take no account of it, accepting 'alien' rule or serving in 'foreign' forces.

Filipinos

The first nationalist movement in Southeast Asia was that in the Philippines. That it was the first suggests at once that economic change was a necessary but not a sufficient condition for its emergence. The opening-up of the Philippines expanded international trade, but also reduced its isolation. It also brought unprecedented wealth to the mestizo elite, and so was likely to upset the established hierarchies upon which the regime depended: the 'brutes' were now 'laden with gold'.[5] But the formulation of the challenge presented to the regime also owed a great deal to the educational facilities that it had provided, initially in the course of the process of Christianisation, and more generally to the degree of Europeanisation to which the Spanish colonial endeavour exposed at least the elite of the Philippines. In the nineteenth century a more critical elite element emerged, the *ilustrados*, the enlightened. Spanish colleges in Manila and elsewhere opened access to new worlds of thought, new potentialities, even if, like Spanish liberalism itself, they tended still to be cast in the categories of the eighteenth-century Enlightenment. Such elite elements were bound to be restive in a colony dominated by friars, caciques, and Spanish officials.

The crisis of opportunity was first felt within the church. The return of the Jesuits disappointed the seculars and contributed to the unrest that found a more open outlet after the 1868 revolution had brought more liberal officials to the Philippines, headed by Carlos Maria de la Torre. Filipino liberals, led by lawyer-professor Joaquin Pardo de Tavera and by José Burgos, formed the Comite de Reformadores, and welcomed the new governor-general. He released Felipe Buencamino, gaoled because he had led students at Santo Tomas who sought the use of Spanish not Latin. His successor, Izquierdo, cut off reformist discussions. Reactionaries assumed power again in the colony even before they did in Spain itself, and this precipitated the Cavite mutiny of January 1872. Allegedly implicated, three seculars, Burgos, Gomez, and Zamora, were garrotted, and other priests and lawyers were deported to the Marianas.

Governor-General Primo de Rivera was to write in 1896:

> the native priest, having the Christian spirit, educated in the seminary, enlightened by the friar ordinarily living with him, is probably the most hostile and most dangerous of those who confront us. And this is as it should be. When you instruct a man and give him a superior education; when you ordain him, train him in the gospels … that man can be no man's servant. …[6]

But the regime did not attempt to win over the seculars. On the contrary, it resorted to what it hoped would be seen as exemplary use of violence. Writing back in 1842,

Sinibaldo de Mas y Sanz, the Catalan littérateur and traveller, had offered his government the choice: to preserve the colony or 'to decide on its emancipation and prepare it for freedom'. He preferred the latter: 'how can we combine the pretensions of liberty for our own selves and desire to impose our own law on distant people?' If that course were chosen, he envisaged 'a popular assembly of representatives in Manila', and a Spanish withdrawal, leaving behind 'a constitutional form of government', perhaps headed by an Infante.[7] Spain would thus have attempted the kind of policy the British were later to adopt and enjoin: working with a new elite, and offering it a growing share in government, in the hope that it would preserve ties with the metropolitan power even after securing independence. Perhaps the example of the Latin American revolutions was in Sinibaldo's mind. His government did not, however, choose the option he preferred. Indeed it made no choice, in effect therefore simply falling back on the first option, but in a very negative form. In 1893 there were but three Filipinos in the governor-general's cabinet. Their colleagues were the archbishop, the commander of the navy, the vice-governor, the president of the Audiencia, the intendant of the treasury, the director-general of civil administration, and the provincials of the six religious orders.

Others besides the seculars were challenging the regime, too, above all the growing numbers of *ilustrados*. Attending private schools or colleges under priestly direction in Manila, Iloilo, or Cebu, some went on to Hong Kong or to Europe, and the opening of the Suez Canal made this easier. 'If you can do no better, study in Spain, but preferably study in freer countries', Burgos had recommended.[8] Those who went to Spain, however, certainly enjoyed a freer life than they could in the colony. Even so the aims of the so-called Propaganda movement were strikingly moderate at first. In 1888 Spaniards and Filipinos in Spain founded the Asociacion Hispano-Filipino, which was reformist in tone—it wanted, for example, the compulsory teaching of Spanish, hitherto limited by the friars' utilisation of various Filipino languages— and began *La Solidaridad* in Barcelona. The following year Marcelo H. del Pilar of Bulacan became the driving force behind the journal, and transferred it to Madrid: it sought the expulsion of the friars, representation in the Cortes, a prohibition on deportation without sentence. The movement was backed by Spanish Masonry, and in 1891 the Filipinos were allowed to set up lodges in the colony. But the government was generally unresponsive, and the reforms of the 1880s—the abolition of the tobacco monopoly in 1881 and of tribute in 1884, the reduction in compulsory labour, the reorganisation of the provincial governments, and the revision of the legal codes—did not touch the real grievances of the *ilustrados*. '[A]ll those … who among normal civilized people are considered good citizens, friends of progress and enlightenment, in the Philippines are *filibusteros*, enemies of order', as Rizal put it, 'and, like lightning rods, attract on stormy days wrath and calamities'.[9] Revolution became more likely.

That belief, and doubts about it, are evident in Rizal's thinking. Scion of a well-to-do family from Laguna, educated at Santo Tomas University and in Spain, but also in Berlin and Heidelberg, he espoused a reformist programme, aiming at the reduction of abuses and the secularisation of parishes, his marvellous novel, *Noli me Tangere* (published in Berlin, 1887) unsparingly criticising the friars but also the old elite. There was more than a touch of millennialism about it. 'Our people slept for centuries', declares Elias, one of the characters, 'but one day the lightning struck, and, even as it killed Burgos, Gomez and Zamora, it called our nation to life. God has not failed other peoples; He will not fail ours, their cause is the cause of freedom.' But Ibarra replies that 'wrongs are not righted by other wrongs'.[10] The frustration of Rizal's hopes did not destroy his fears about the consequences of adopting a more violent course, and his second novel, *El Filibusterismo* (published in Ghent, 1891), presents the arguments in dramatic form. Padre Florentino tells the dying Simoun (Ibarra) 'that we must secure [liberty] by making ourselves worthy of it ... and when a people reaches that height God will provide a weapon, the idols will be shattered, the tyranny will crumble ... and liberty shine out like the first dawn'.[11] The Liga Filipina that Rizal founded in 1892 still did not aim at separation. What it seems he hoped to do was to confront the regime with so strong a movement that it would feel compelled to make concessions without the need for violence.

He was arrested and deported to Dapitan in Mindanao. '[M]y crime consists solely in having desired for my equals the exercise of political rights, a most just aspiration which any man possessing self-respect should have.'[12] That left the way open for the less patrician leadership of Andres Bonifacio: less patrician, but, as Glenn May has argued, still not proletarian. Son of a tailor in Tondo, Bonifacio might better be thought of as a Manileno on the make. He was a Mason, and he joined the Liga. But about the same time he founded the Katipunan, a secret society with Masonic and traditional overtones, which sought the overthrow of the regime, while its newspaper was called *Kalayaan,* independence. Its discovery in August 1896 precipitated a crackdown by the Spaniards, apprehensive lest the *ilustrado* should join the movement. They executed Rizal. In turn that precipitated the Filipino revolution.

In Manila Bonifacio's forces were beaten, but outside it the Tagalogs continued to resist, particularly in Cavite. One reason was the effective leadership of Emilio Aguinaldo, *capitan municipal* or mayor of Kawit, who had not had the schooling of an *ilustrado*, but who had experience of leading the police against bandits. After the expulsion of the Spaniards from the province, it was administered by two municipal consultative bodies, one, Magdalo, also the Katipunan name of Aguinaldo, at Kawit, and the other, Magdiwang, at Novaleta, associated with Mariano Alvarez. The latter invited Bonifacio to Cavite, but that stimulated tension between Magdiwang and Magdalo, which only helped the Spaniards. In March 1897, therefore, the revolutionaries met at Tejeros, and replaced the Katipunan with a revolutionary government headed by Aguinaldo as president. That Bonifacio could not accept: he was executed by his fellow revolutionaries on 10 May 1897. The Spaniards recaptured the province by the end of that month, and Aguinaldo moved his government north, eventually to Bulacan. At the end of the year he reached a truce with the Spanish authorities, mediated by Pedro A. Paterno, son of an 1872 exile. Aguinaldo and others went into exile in Hong Kong. The Spaniards hoped the revolution would fizzle out. For the revolutionaries it was a time for regrouping and spreading unrest outside the Tagalog provinces.

Embarrassed though Spain was, the inglorious compromise seemed, however, to bear out the comment Rizal's correspondent Blumentritt had made. The Philippine revolution, unlike colonial revolutions in the mid-twentieth century, had secured no overseas aid. The revolution had no precedent in Southeast Asia itself, and no 'world opinion' espoused its cause. Only some of the wilder nationalists in Japan were able to offer a little unofficial help. The revolutionaries now placed their main hope in the United States. It did indeed intervene, fending off the Germans as well as the Japanese. But, defeating Spain, it did not accept the Philippines Republic. In November 1899 Aguinaldo had to disband his troops, but a long period of guerrilla war ensued. Aguinaldo was captured only in March 1901 and Malvar, the last general, surrendered only in April 1902.

Bringing this guerrilla war to an end, like others, was achieved not merely by force, but by political means. The revolution, strongest in the Tagalog provinces, had built up its strength there partly because it had been joined by members of the elite. Whatever their patriotic motives, they had an interest in supporting an effective government, such as—at least at first—Aguinaldo's promised to be, and thus securing internal stability and perhaps international recognition. When the prospects of that eroded, they turned to the American alternative, and in so doing further eroded the Republic's diminishing chances. At the same time, they could argue that the American option would offer not only stability but autonomy. Indeed, while McKinley's re-election as US President clearly affirmed annexation, the Americans came to talk of self-government.

The nature of the struggle and of its termination is not, however, best understood merely in terms of the elite that appropriated the word 'Filipino' and sought, against tremendous odds, to create an independent state in the unpropitious circumstances of Southeast Asia at the end of the nineteenth century. The elite had an ambivalent relationship with the masses, whose strength was needed against the colonial power, but was itself a source of concern. The 'masses' indeed saw the struggle in a different way. That was evident, even before the rebellion broke out, in the case of Rizal. Like other nationalists in Southeast Asia and elsewhere, he sought to create a 'usable past': in his edition of Morga's *Sucesos* he had documented the lost Eden, as Ileto puts it.[13] That privileged the *ilustrado*. But he became himself implicated in the different thought world of the '*pobres y ignorantes*': like Apolinario, he was hailed as a Tagalog Christ King. Returning to the Philippines in 1887, he had been persuaded to leave again in 1888 for his own safety's sake, but his absence only intensified the 'popular textualisation' of his career. 'Alas, José!' a townmate wrote to him in 1889. 'All the people here ask about you and pin their hope on you. Even the poorest people of the mountains are asking about your return. It seems that they consider you the second Jesus who will liberate them from misery!'[14] On his again returning to his homeland, it may even be that he began to play the role in which, *Pasyon*-like, he was thus cast: his poem, 'My Last Farewell', suggests as much.

It seems likely that *taos* kept up the struggle, not so much because their patrons went to war, as because they characterised the struggle in a different way: it was for them not a struggle for independence but for the realisation of the kingdom of God on earth. Aguinaldo was seen as a liberator sent by God. Even the doubt that Glenn May has cast upon Ileto's interpretation of Bonifacio's role does not, as he admits, dislodge his argument that the Philippines revolution is connected with the millenarian tradition.[15] But for that, indeed, the struggle could not have been carried on for so long or with such desperate intensity. Yet at the same time the popular association of independence with social revolution, with turning society on its head, gave the elite caution. It was a further reason for ending Rizal's ambiguity in a different way, collaborating with the United States in setting up a more stable government.

The tension had been present throughout. The Republic, set up in June 1898, had to show foreign powers that it could govern. It therefore needed the elite, 'despite lower class reaction against its continued predominance'.[16] It indeed needed peasant support, too, but there was no chance that peasant expectations could be met. The Republic demanded labour and services just like the old regime, and the peasant reaction began to frighten the elite, to seem in some cases 'radical' and 'communistic', as Modesto Joaquin, a prominent Pampangeno, put it.[17] American firmness was therefore welcomed. By contrast Malvar kept going by affiliating his guerrillas with the colorums. '[N]ot only those within the towns constitute the people; the lowest laborers are included, and they are the ones who act with greater honesty of intentions and are more sincere in their aspirations.'[18]

Though recruiting itself to the ranks of the colonial powers, the United States was a colonial power with a difference: challenged at home, its imperialism was from the start seen as transitional, even though that involved depreciating the current achievements of the Filipinos. Among the early allies of the Americans was a group of upperclass Manilenos, led by T. H. Pardo de Tavera, who in 1900 formed a Federal Party that aimed at making the Philippines a state of the Union, and who were at first much patronised by Governor William H. Taft. It offered the Americans advantages, in particular helping to bring resistance to an end: it mobilised 'a very large number of Filipinos who have been at heart friendly to the American cause', as Dean C. Worcester put it.[19] For the Filipinos statehood offered tutelage and protection, but without colonial inequality or second-class citizenship. The party gave the *ilustrados* some leverage with the Americans and helped to ensure that their policy, unlike Spain's, was reformist, but they rejected statehood. Under the Organic Act of 1902, the President ordered the setting-up of a Philippines Assembly, with a national election to be held in 1907, and for that the Federalistas organised themselves as Progresistas. A Nacionalista party was also formed, aiming more openly at independence, led by Sergio Osmena, a Chinese mestizo from Cebu, and Manuel L. Quezon of Tayabas. The party triumphed, securing over one-third of the approximately 100 000 votes cast by an electorate restricted by property and literacy in English and Spanish.

The elite indeed strengthened their position under the new colonial ruler. They secured the lion's share of the monastic lands and after 1909 free access to the US market, and while the free admission of American products into the Philippines limited industrial growth, the government also discouraged the setting-up of big American corporations that might have competed with the large-scale Filipino estates. The elite also benefited politically. The United States offered what the Spaniards had denied, the opportunity to participate in policy-making at national level, though confining that offer to the advantaged. It did not at once promise independence. But the demand and American opposition to it helped the elite, too. Though in fact the Filipino leaders did not want it too soon, independence became the major political issue, if not the only one, and social issues did not enter politics.

The Democrat victory in the US elections of 1912 brought in an administration devoted to early independence for the islands. Somewhat ambiguously, however, the Jones law of 1916 provided for independence when a stable government had been set up. A senate was created, the franchise extended, the legislature's powers increased. President Wilson's wartime advocacy of self-determination as a principle of politics led in 1919 to a mission from the Philippines aimed at persuading him to set a date. The Democrat Governor-General F. B. Harrison meanwhile speeded up the filipinisation of the public services and gave the legislature exceptional latitude in this and other matters. That gave Osmena great influence, prompting Quezon to organise a new party, which won the elections of 1922. But he faced a Republican governor-general, Leonard Wood, and the Republicans took a rather different stance on independence for the Philippines.

In 1908 Taft had declared that 'we wish to prepare the Filipinos for *popular* self-government'. It was not Congress's purpose 'that we were merely to await the organisation of a Philippine oligarchy or aristocracy competent to administer the government and then turn the Islands over to it. ...' Early independence for the Philippines would 'subject the great mass of their people to the dominance of an oligarchical and, probably, exploiting minority'.[20]

Whatever its ideals, Democrat rule had made that more likely. Wood inherited the Taft policy, but his attempts to implement it, coupled with his wish to encourage more foreign investment in the Philippines, could only provoke a reaction from the elite which it could base on nationalist arguments. The chief effect of Wood's programme was indeed to unify the nationalists, reconciling Osmena and Quezon, and prompting their collaboration with the Democrata opposition of men like Claro M. Recto. Politics focused yet more intensely on the issue of independence. Wood's Republican successor, Henry L. Stimson, backed away from his programme, and restored the 'cabinet' system that Wood had abandoned. The Nacionalistas were stronger than ever, and the Democratas dissolved in 1932.

In the United States the Democrats' idealism was rekindled by a minor and perhaps misguided economic interest. US beet and cane interests had tried to prevent competition from the Philippines by limiting the land purchases and leases corporations might make. That, however, had not discouraged the Filipinos. The Depression strengthened the agitation against alleged Philippines competition in the US sugar market with the domestic producers of sugar-beet, though in fact it mainly competed with the Cuban product. That gave a new spur to the programme for independence in the 72nd Congress, which had a Democrat House and equality in the Senate, and it passed the Hare–Hawes–Cutting Act. Under that the Philippines was to be given independence after a ten-year interim phase of government by a commonwealth with limited powers. Tariff privileges were to end with independence and be reduced in the interim. American bases might be retained after independence, but meanwhile the President, with whom the conduct of foreign policy would continue to rest, was to negotiate with other powers for a treaty neutralising the islands. President Hoover found this confusing—'We should honestly and plainly declare our intentions'[21]— but his veto was unavailing, for the 1932 election installed the Democrat F. D. Roosevelt as President.

The act had not only resulted from the activities of American lobbyists, but also from a mission from the Philippines led by Osmena and his aide Manuel Roxas. Quezon opposed some of the provisions in the act his rival brought back, and, with his aide, Elpidio Quirino, headed a new mission to Washington. That secured the Tydings–McDuffie Act. It involved only minor modifications—Quezon was prepared 'to settle for anything different enough to call his own'[22]—but enabled him to generate sufficient support to win the 1934 elections. A convention drew up a constitution for the Commonwealth, and this was submitted to the electorate in 1935, in a referendum in which the non-Christians voted for the first time. Later that year Quezon, Aguinaldo, and Aglipay stood for President. Quezon again triumphed. Osmena became Vice-President. About one million voted out of a population of 13 million.

This was hardly, to use Taft's phrase, 'popular self-government'. Among the *taos*, indeed, popular movements tended to reflect the persistence of older ideas rather than the penetration of new. A communist, Jacinto Manahan, organised the Tenants Union in 1919, and in 1924 it became the National Union of Peasants in the Philippines. But the Communist Party founded in 1930 by Crisanto Evangelista, was, though Manahan was involved, an urban movement. It was put down in 1931, so that it was Pedro Abad Santos' Socialists who capitalised on the Depression, and the Communist Party merged with them in 1938. But probably more significant among the *taos* were a revival of the Colorum sects, and, as in Kabola's case, the continued association of independence with a relief from oppression.

The most famous of the popular movements aiming at independence was the Sakdal ('Accuse') movement of the 1930s. This, however, was not simply a peasant movement, for its leader was Benigno Ramos, a petty officeholder who had fallen out with the ruling groups and sought to rally popular support in the Depression. Nor did it rule out participation in the political system. In 1931 Ramos advocated non-cooperation, borrowed from Gandhi in India, but in 1933 he formed a political party, which did quite well in the 1934 elections, especially in Laguna. But the oligarchs reunited, and the movement had no chance of securing power by such means. Early in 1935, after Ramos had tried to secure arms from Japan, it chaotically attempted to seize power. The Constabulary suppressed the resulting disorder, the bloodiest affair being at Cabuyao, where fifty Sakdalistas were killed and four constabularymen. The timing was significant: the uprising was a protest against the establishment of the Commonwealth, representing for Ramos the triumph of the elite politicians, and for the *tao* a semi-independence without social change. 'The rank and file of the radical wing of the Sakdal party ... believe that the establishment of the Commonwealth Government is a move to establish and maintain in power a group of Filipino leaders who represent the upper classes who will oppress the lower classes', a government report stated.[23]

Indonesians

Comparing nationalist movements on the basis of a 'working definition' is likely to show up differences as well as similarities. The differences, already geographical, cultural, and historical, will be intensified if the movements occur at different times. They will, for example, occur in different contexts, so far as the development of communications is concerned, so far, too, as international political factors are concerned. Yet the comparison may still be worthwhile, and indeed help to pin down the characteristics of nationalist movements in general and in particular. The Indonesian nationalist movement emerges later than the Filipino movement, as well as in different circumstances. But it has common features.

One was the relationship to the provision of Western education. That had long been available in the Philippines, even though it was in the hands of the religious orders rather than the state. The Dutch began to provide it in the Indies only in the latter half of the nineteenth century, and their main focus was on the elite. The economic expansion of the closing decades of the century, coupled with improved communications with Mekka, enhanced the role of Islamic education and Islamic leaders, and the Ethical Policy took the shape it did partly in order to counter that. It sought to create elite elements that would have a deep appreciation of Western culture and form an enduring link between the Indies and the 'mother country'. Such an elite was, however, bound to seek greater participation in the governance and political affairs of the Indies, and the colonial power would have to face the kind of dilemma that Sinibaldo de Mas outlined in the Philippines half a century and more earlier.

In handling this the Dutch had to reckon with the changes that were taking place in the metropolis and in the world at large. In part as a result they accepted what the Spaniards had never accepted, the creation of a central institution, the Volksraad. Yet they remained unwilling to give it a substantial role, and rejected even the proposals of its more moderate members. Their position differed from that of the Spaniards in another way, not tied to the chronological difference: they had a more genuine case for working with nationalisms rather than nationalism. Spanish government had depended in part on divide-and-rule, but, even though the revolution was largely

Tagalog in leadership, neither they, nor indeed their American successors, sought to stimulate rival nationalisms in the other regions of Luzon and the Visayas, while the aspirations of the Moros, religious and separatist in nature, could not be turned to account, once at least that they were no longer a source of fear. The Dutch, by contrast, could find substantial differences among the peoples included within the frontiers of Netherlands India, and at times they sought to utilise them. There was, however, an unresolved, perhaps unresolvable, inconsistency in their approach.

Perhaps indeed there were two inconsistencies. One was, of course, that between the pulling-together of their empire and the possible devolution of power. The other was between the two principles of any decentralisation. Should it be based on 'ethnic' difference or administrative convenience? In the Dutch answers to these questions political considerations predominated. Devolution was risky, but in a federal structure it could provide a means of retaining power, as Hendrik Colijn, its advocate, saw: 'in a unitarian state it is certain that the various nationalities—in the absence of a positive community of interests—will unite themselves into a common front against the foreign ruler', but in a federal structure the Dutch government would be able 'to retain for a long time to come its moral role of disinterested arbiter in the ever-sharpening struggle for national and economic dominance between the various territories'.[24] Such a structure, even if it nodded to ethnicity, would be more effective if it broke up the largest of the possible units. The Indonesians, particularly in the Outer Islands, might have responded to devolution on either basis, or to federation. Dutch moves were, however, slow and limited—the provincial system, started in Java in the 1920s and extended to the Outer Islands in the 1930s, was merely bureaucratic—and were overtaken by a Java-led nationalism all the more determined to keep the inheritance of empire together.

At the start of the century Japanese residents had been given European status, and a Chinese Association was organised in Batavia, the Tjong Hoa Hwe Koan. Was there 'some kind of abacus', the hero in Pramoedya's novel asks, to 'use to calculate how many dozens of years it will take the Javanese to reach the same level as the Japanese?'[25] With the Japanese victory over Russia in 1904–05, however, '[w]e started to feel that we, Orientals, indeed did have a chance', as a student put it.[26] The first nationalist movement was Javanese in origin, and at first aimed at the restoration of a Javanese kingdom. Boedi Oetomo (Glorious Endeavour) was started by a retired medical subordinate, Dr Djawa Wahidin Soedirohoesodo, and Prince Notodirdjo, son of Pakualam V, and supported by members of the *priyayi* elite and of the princely families. In 1915 it founded a youth organisation, called Jong Java (Young Java) from 1918. Its Javanese focus was emphasised by the founding of similar organisations elsewhere in the Indies: Sinar Budi, the first modern social organisation in Gorontalo (Sulawesi), was set up in 1912, inspired by Boedi Oetomo. No doubt to the gratification of the Ethici, Boedi Oetomo aimed at a fusion of European and Javanese values, influenced by Tagore and Gandhi. But it entered politics in 1915, as a result of a debate about the creation of a wartime militia, and joined in petitioning for a parliament. Faced by competition from other organisations, the chairman, R. M. A. Woerjaningrat, became more radical, and stressed the need to contact the masses.

The leadership of the first political party in Java, the Indische Partij, was substantially in the hands of Eurasians, including E. F. E. Douwes Dekker, great nephew of Multatuli. No doubt again to the gratification of the Ethici, it was based explicitly on the principle of association, though it was more vehement than the government anticipated, and it was declared illegal in 1913. Some of its members were gaoled and exiled. Others joined Insulinde, founded at Bandung in 1907, based at Semarang from 1911. In 1919 it became the Nationaal-Indische Partij, or Sarekat Hindia, aiming at independence and non-cooperation.

Sarekat Islam (Islamic League) had never taken the associationist path, from which these groups diverged. The penetration of Chinese merchants into the interior of Java after the relaxation of the pass system in 1904 threatened the Indonesian batik merchants, and in reaction Haji Samanhoedi founded the league in 1912. Initially there was again a connexion with the court at Surakarta, the centre, 'at least symbolically, of all authority and power in Java'.[27] That was shunted aside, in part by the Dutch, in part also by a new leader, a Surabaya merchant, Tjokroaminoto, son of a former *wedono* (district chief) of Madiun, an 'unrivalled orator'.[28] Learning from Dekker, he held his first big rally at Surabaya in 1913, attended by 10 000 people. At the 1916 SI congress, he looked forward to the establishment of the Volksraad as a step toward self-government in ten years.[29] Under his leadership SI soon became a vast and generalised mass movement, with over two million members by 1919, and with representation in the Outer Islands, too.

In some sense nation-wide, SI was not, however, simply or even predominantly nationalist. Its rapid growth indeed reflected the wide range of the membership it acquired, and it had great difficulty in defining its objectives. The central leadership was further weakened by the fact that in March 1914 the government, nervous about a mass movement, and hoping that local branches could be tamed by local authorities, while it contained the centre, conferred legal status only on the branches. Above all, however, it represented opposition to the threats to Islam presented by the Dutch colonial government, Chinese traders, capitalism, and the alienation of the *priyayi* from the people. It was, and remained, 'a coalition of groups, associations, and sects varying according to local and regional circumstances'.[30] What excited the elite, and worried the government, was the extent of its support among the people. That had been secured on a traditional rather than a modern basis. The peasants looked to Tjokro as the *ratu adil* and expected SI to remedy their grievances. Its following would collapse if it failed.

Its acquisition of mass support led to competition for its leadership from more radical elements, all the more difficult to deal with because only branches had been granted official recognition. In Java, by contrast to other colonial territories, there was a lower-class European element that formed an avenue for the direct entry of

European radicalism and of Marxism, carried by men like Hendrik Sneevliet, and subsequently stimulated by the Bolshevik revolution and the activity of the Comintern. In that indeed Sneevliet played an important role, guided by his experience in Java. He had been employed as a journalist in Semarang, one of the more liberal and open cities, and as secretary of the Commercial Association, then founded the ISDV in May 1914. It was linked with the labour movement, especially the railway and tramworkers union. But the need for wider support drew it to the SI, in respect of which it developed a 'bloc within' strategy. That it sought to continue, even after becoming the PKI in 1920.

The competition among the parties, and their search for mass support, tended to radicalise them, and the government began to react more strongly, particularly after Fock replaced van Limburg Stirum as governor-general. The radicalism should not, however, be seen as a result of the penetration of Marxism. It resulted rather from the pressure of peasant grievances, on which the elite wished to capitalise, and the Marxism of the day itself reflected its aspirations. The Garut affair of June 1919, implicating, or used to implicate, the SI in the disturbances in eastern Priangan, horrified the Ethici—they had 'opened up a Pandora's box'[31]—and led native officials, also affected by the government's harder line, to desert the movement. In 1921 the central leadership broke with the communists. Tan Malaka rightly feared the schism would spread to the locals, 'which would be extremely dangerous for the people and … make much easier the work of the reactionaries'.[32] Their grievances unredressed, the peasants turned back to more traditional forms of protest, the formation of secret societies, oath-taking.

Finding it difficult to organise the unions, and facing government repression, the communists turned to the countryside, organising Sarekat Rakyat. The PKI leaders were themselves seized by utopianism: the *djoyoboyo* prophecy was now identified with the Soviet Union, and the revolution was 'often compared with the coming of the *Ratu Adil*'.[33] Arrests dislocated the leadership in 1925, making the party more confused about its direction and more dependent on terrorism to retain support. The Comintern insisted that revolution was impossible but, with no other outlets, the PKI turned to it.

In Banten the PKI secured the support of the old Bantenese nobility, of some of the *ulama*, of the *jawara* (*jago*), and of the peasants whose taxes they promised to abolish, generally not the landless, therefore, but property-holders who brought their followers in too.[34] But at the village level there were also overtones of '*ratu sunda*' and holy war and, as the leadership fell into disarray and its followers became more impatient, increasingly millenarianism took over. Arrests in August and September left *ulama* and *jawara* in control, and they led the armed revolt of November. The other centre of revolt was West Sumatra, scene, too, of 'a strange sort of Communism indeed' as Sjahrir put it.[35]

'Come Comrades, forward, close ranks. We shall not be able to reach our goal if we wait till the world has come to an end.'[36] The desperate endeavour failed. About

13 000 were arrested as a result of the disturbances of 1926. The process was marked by extortion on the part of spies, the paying off of old scores, and excesses by Ambonese soldiers. The trials resulted in a few executions and numerous sentences of imprisonment. Others, included many against whom there was insufficient evidence to press charges in court, were exiled to Boven Digul. The colonial government was not simply abandoning the liberal spirit of the Ethical Policy. It was reading the people a lesson it was not to forget.

Certainly the PKI had brought destruction on itself. Tan Malaka had opposed the adventure, as against other leaders like Alimin and Musso—'we must … avoid a defeat which would paralyze our organization for a long time to come'[37]—and when the Comintern adopted the Stalinist line of 1928, he broke with it and turned to 'national' communism. For the rest of the inter-war period the communists were at most an underground movement; and those who thought of themselves as communist did not present themselves as such. The government's repressive policy was intensified in the Depression. It became more traditionalist in focus, concerned to uphold *adat*, re-establish *priyayi* prestige, restore peace and order. It sought to seal off the peasantry against outside agitators, to confine them to the cities, and to keep them within bounds by surveillance, police warnings, trials, and imprisonment. Arguably, however, these steps helped to create an Indonesian nationalist movement.

The limits the Dutch had placed on tertiary education had helped to bring the few who benefited from it together. In Batavia or Bandung, or in the Netherlands itself, young men from Menangkabau or elsewhere met Javanese, and increasingly all saw themselves as Indonesians. 'Those who studied abroad figured particularly strongly in the leadership of the early Indonesian nationalist movement.'[38] In the metropolis, indeed, nationalists felt freer than at home. Hatta echoed Rizal and his colleagues: 'It is as if another sky is arching out over their heads. They become aware here of the feeling of freedom. … The truth is that we have been set free from the colonial hypnosis. … From here we can see the *colonial* truth clearly.'[39]

A somewhat similar process affected the development of nationalism itself: the constraints the Dutch placed upon political activity, particularly after 1926, in a sense made it easier for a small educated leadership to conceive of the future in more particularly Indonesian terms and to work out its implications, undistracted by pressing calls for action from a popular following and from communist rivalry. Meanwhile the colonial government, apprehensive about any political activity, took no steps to promote region-based nationalisms. There was, as Lance Castles says, little basis for 'Sumatranism', for example. Identity was likely to focus on the *sukubangsa*, the sense of being Menangkabau, or Sundanese, or Javanese. That could be coupled with a sense of being Indonesian.[40]

The intelligentsia formed 'study clubs', like that in Bandung which a young graduate of the Engineering School there, Sukarno, helped to found in 1926. Witness to the decline of SI, and of the vain attempts of his mentor, Tjokroaminoto, to maintain its unity, he argued for a clear focus on Indonesian independence, and sought to play down the differences among Indonesians, religious, cultural, and social, and to defer arguments about the nature of the state that would be created. Nicknamed '*jago*' in his youth, he became the 'necromancer of unity', setting *sini* against *sana*, pitting the Pendawas against their opponents, the Kurawas.[41] The object was 'an independent Indonesia in the quickest way possible. This entails that we do not strive for independence by means of improving miserable living conditions in our country, but we must strive for independence *in order* to improve these living conditions.'[42] Though students returning from the Netherlands—where Perhimpunan Indonesia had been organised in 1922—played a significant role, Sukarno became chairman of the PNI, founded in Bandung in July 1927. At the end of that year he also took the initiative in creating PPPKI (Permufakatan Perhimpunan Politik Kebangsaan Indonesia or Unanimous Consensus of Political Organisations of the Indonesian People), a federation of the various groups that were striving for independence.

The Indonesian Student Union (Perhimpunan Peladjar-peladjar Indonesia) had been founded in 1925. In 1928 it held an All-National Youth Congress which pledged the young to one nation, Indonesia; adopted as its language Bahasa Indonesia, in fact Malay; and sang a national anthem, 'Indonesia Raya', first played on a violin-ukelele-guitar combo.[43] Though taken by a small group, those were crucial decisions. The word 'Indonesia' had first been used in the nineteenth century— by J. R. Logan, a writer, and by Adolf Bastian, an ethnologist—but not, as now, for 'Netherlands India'. The first organisation that used the word was the Indonesisch Verbond, founded in 1917, ancestor of the PI. The PKI used it in 1924 and the PNI in 1927. With the work of the PI, the study clubs and PNI, it helped to bring about fusion with other organisations, and Jong Java and other youth organisations— including Jong Sumatra, which had been founded in 1925—merged in Indonesia Moeda (Young Indonesia) in 1930. Malay was the lingua franca of the archipelago, and almost all the 200 indigenous newspapers were in Malay by 1925. Making it the national language was convenient to the Menangkabau, and avoided the use of Javanese, which was entangled in an hierarchic society. By the 1920s Javanese nationalists had 'ceased to object' to its new status,[44] while non-Javanese could welcome the fact that the national language was not the language of the putative majority which 'minorities' would have to learn.

Sukarno was arrested in 1929 and imprisoned after a major trial. Governor-General de Graeff used the courts rather than internment: his aim was to play by rule. '[I]t made an excellent impression in native circles', he said,[45] though it also gave the nationalists an opportunity to put their case, of which Sukarno made the most. Released at the end of 1931, he was arrested again in August 1933, and exiled to the island of Flores. In 1934 Hatta was arrested, and also another Menangkabauer, Sjahrir, and they were sent to Boven Digul. 'Backstage', de Graeff had written, 'I try desperately to promote a native middle-of-the-road party ... , a party which the government will need and which is indispensable to the normal development of parliamentary life in this country'.[46] Colijn, he thought, was wrong to think that revolutionary nationalism could be checked 'with a few words and acts of power'.[47] But his successor, de Jonge, took a different line. Under him politics were yet more clearly confined to those who would cooperate and focused on the Volksraad. The cooperating nationalists gained experience and were not entirely ineffective. The creation of Parindra (Partai Indonesia Raya) in 1935 indeed tested Dutch toleration: its goal was 'Indonesia Mulia', Glorious Indonesia, implying, but not stating, that the aim was independence. By 1941 it had 121 branches and perhaps 20 000 members, double the PNI at its peak.

Among its founding groups was BO. Its course illustrated a continuing trend in Indonesian politics in this phase. In 1931 it had opened itself to all Indonesians, changing its spelling from Oetomo (Javanese) to Oetama (Malay/Indonesian), and in 1932 it changed its stated objective from promoting 'the harmonious development of the country and people of Java and Madura' to 'Indonesia Merdeka'.[48] Nor were such names merely camouflage. Parindra's support, for example, extended to the Outer Islands. There the elite was increasingly coming to terms with an Indonesian nationalism. It was essential that it should not be a cloak for Javanese dominance.

Noted earlier for its 'loyalism', the distinctive region of Minahasa had a genuine interest in decentralisation, displayed when the Dutch finally created a Government of the Great East in 1938. Its increased support for the national cause was indeed coupled with a federalist approach. The Minahasa leader, G. S. S. J. Ratulangie, restated that in 1938, when Parindra and the Sundanese party Pasundan sponsored rival candidates for a city council election in Bandung: 'our leaders must understand the absolute necessity of political solidarity against anything which lies outside the ideology of Indonesian unity. On the other hand, it is equally necessary that they recognise the right of every ethnic group to retain its autonomy within its own ethnically defined region.'[49] Even a limited measure of political participation clearly opened up such issues.

It could also be expected to revive the question of the Islamic role in politics. The events of the 1920s had weakened the more politically oriented Islamic leaders, and drawn more attention to the Muhammadiyah. The Nahdlatul Ulama, founded in East Java in 1926, was also non-political. That did not prevent the government's renewing the pre-Snouck controls on the haj, nor its tightening controls over Islamic as well as secular education. The government also strengthened the supervision the Regents exercised over the *penghulu* (religious judges), and in 1937 sought to remove inheritance matters from their purview. Those moves brought Islamic reformists and the more conservative NU together, and in 1937 they formed the Islamic Federation or MIAI. The following year Agus Salim and others formed the Partai Islam Indonesia, and it sought representation in the Volksraad, where the cooperating nationalists had so far displayed little sympathy for the Islamic cause. Here again was a rift which would challenge the unity of the nationalist movement.

The negative attitude of the colonial power—its 'Colijnnial' policy[50]—helped, however, to promote unity. In 1936 it had rejected the Soetardjo petition—of which

Ratulangie was a prime mover—which had called for a ten-year transition to autonomy within the Dutch constitutional framework. F. B. Harrison thought the petition reflected the Philippines plans. Quezon had indeed visited Surabaya in October 1934, and he had aspirations to lead the 'Malay' peoples.[51] Dutch officials thought him 'more subversive ... than Marx, Lenin, Trotsky and Stalin rolled into one'.[52]

Nor did the government respond to the creation in 1937, perhaps influenced by the Comintern's shift to popular front policies, of Gerindo (Gerakan Rakyat Indonesia or Movement of the Indonesian People), hostile to fascism and designed to counter the right-wing Parindra, even though it was suspicious that the latter was under Japanese influence. No concessions were offered even in 1940, when the majority of the nationalist groups declared their loyalty to the cause of the Western democracies. Governor-General Tjarda had 1918 in mind: van Limburg Stirum's declaration had aroused expectations which the government could not promise to fulfil. Finally in September 1941 GAPI, a federation of mostly secular nationalist parties, joined MIAI to form a Council of the Indonesian People. Soetardjo asked about the Atlantic Charter, just signed, and got an evasive answer. Only in January 1942, when the Japanese were conquering Malaya, did Tjarda agree to a conference. The Wiwowo bill of February 1940—seeking more autonomy, more power for the Volksraad, the creation of an imperial council—became the basis for the queen's broadcast in December.

Malays and Malayans

In Netherlands India, the elite 'imagined' an Indonesian community, allegiance to which tended not only to displace older loyalties but to pre-empt new loyalties to 'Java' or 'Sumatra' or 'Minahasa'. No such process was taking place in the territory that the British called 'Malaya'. There ethnic divisions were stronger, intensified by recent and rapid economic change and immigration from India and China. The migrant communities, though becoming more settled, focused on the nationalist movements in their land of origin. Malays increasingly thought of themselves as a community rather than simply as subjects of their rulers. Constituting a political allegiance to Malaya was more problematical. Such a state would not only be an alien creation: it might be dominated by aliens. Some indeed looked to Indonesian nationalism for an answer: reconstituting the Malay world in a new context might protect the Malay way of life. The colonial power itself was in a dilemma. A more modern state would have to be Malayan rather than Malay. Yet it felt bound to protect the Malays. It tended to pursue a rather negative policy of limited decentralisation, not so much because 'divide and rule' was a colonial maxim, as because the way forward was uncertain and contentious, and it was possible to put off seeking a 'solution'. The British did not 'divide and rule'. 'More correctly, their policy was "*laissez-faire* and let rule".'[53]

Even in British hands, the Indian government had displayed an interest in the fate of Indians overseas. That increased as nationalism intensified in India. Three stimuli thus acted on Indian nationalism in Malaya in the inter-war period: the Indian Government agency attached to the Labour Department after 1923; Indian journalism; and the Central Indian Association in Kuala Lumpur, founded in 1936 partly in reaction to the pro-Malay measures of the decentralisation programme, and stimulated by Nehru's first visit to Malaya in 1937, which promoted a solidarity hitherto lacking between the professional class and the Tamil labourers from whom it was not recruited.

Chinese nationalism had long interested itself in the Malay Chinese community. That was true of the reformers, like Kang Yu-wei, and of the revolutionaries, like Sun Yat-sen. Their heir, the Kuomintang, also recognised the political and economic importance of the community in Malaya. Teachers from southern China spread Chinese nationalism in schools and outside them, even among Straits Chinese, using moreover the 'national' language that helped to counter the linguistic divisions that the largely illiterate immigrants had brought with them. Politically the Kuomintang used both traditional secret society techniques and also semi-Western types of mass organisation designed to counter the appeal of tribal and other associations. Often at odds with the Kuomintang in China in the 1920s, the British suppressed it in Malaya in 1925. Clementi affirmed that in 1930, but it continued to exist. With the opening of the undeclared war of 1937, the Kuomintang renewed its efforts to stimulate Chinese national feeling and to collect money, and the colonial government, now anxious to discourage Japanese aggression, was as lenient as possible.

Communism was mainly supported by the Chinese, especially the Hainanese, though Singapore was a centre for the movement in respect of Indonesia as well. Following the split between the Kuomintang and the CCP in China in 1927–28, the Nanyang Communist Party was created early in 1928. Using Ho Chi Minh, the Comintern tried to seize the initiative the CCP had so far enjoyed in Malaya by founding the Malayan CP in 1930. It still concentrated on the Chinese, focusing its activity on the Chinese schools, among both teachers and students, and on the immigrant labourers affected by the Depression. But, like the Kuomintang, it, too, gained a new task and a new opportunity with the onset of the war of 1937, and its front organisations, the Anti-Imperialist League and the Anti-Enemy Backing-up Society, gained a new importance. Not all favoured this Asian version of the popular front policy, and Lai Teck was sent from Hong Kong to deal with the extremists.

The identification of the immigrant communities with the nationalist cause in their land of origin could be misleading. It did not mean that they saw themselves, or that they should have been seen, merely as ephemeral elements in Malaya. It was a sign rather that they were becoming more settled and more permanent. Inter-war Malaya, however, offered them few opportunities for identification, still fewer for political participation, and the perception that their interests were elsewhere seemed, perhaps paradoxically, to justify that. Their presence undoubtedly promoted an emergent 'Malay' consciousness. Where that could or should lead was less clear. One Kelantan intellectual, Abdul Kadir Adabi, responded to the renewed talk of decentralisation under Clementi by saying that the unfederated states wanted to enter the federation: before that, however, 'raise the dignity of the Malays and teach them; appoint more Malays to government posts, limit the Malayan Civil Service to only Malays and Englishmen'.[54] But one reason the British developed their intelligence service was their concern lest Malays were looking to Indonesia.

One of the earliest influences on the Malay community was Islamic reformism. It penetrated in the early years of the century to a relatively small middle-class group, sometimes local-born non-Malays of Arab or Menangkabau origin, who had been to Mekka and to Egypt. They reacted against the Erastian character of Malayan Islam, which had been brought about by the concentration of the sultans and their governments on the religious matters left to them under their treaties with the British. They published books and journals and established madrasah, but took no direct political role.

The first Malay association with political aims was the Kesatuan Melayu Singapura (Singapore Malay Union), founded in Kampong Glam in 1926 and designed to encourage a greater Malay role in government and to make representations on behalf of the Malays. The leadership came from English-educated Malay journalists, government servants and merchants. Eunos Abdullah, the first president, had been given a seat on the Straits Settlements Legislative Council, and it was designed to support him. There was no parallel organisation in the Federated Malay States. But all kinds of cultural and literary societies emerged, led by vernacular schoolteachers, religious teachers, and government servants. They included Sahabat Pena, Pen Friends, the outcome of a twice-weekly journal *Saudara*, started in 1928. Its first conference, held in Taiping in November 1934, was the first pan-Malayan gathering of a non-official kind.

At the Sultan Idris Training College at Tanjong Malim all the teaching was in Malay, and students read the vernacular and Indonesian press. Four students became members of the PNI in 1929. The same year the group also played a leading role in setting up a student union, and in 1938 they began Kesatuan Melayu Muda, joined also by students from the School of Agriculture at Serdang and the Technical and Trade Schools at Kuala Lumpur. Their 'solution' was radical, vaguely Marxist, anti-colonial, aiming at Indonesia Raya, and 150 of them were behind bars when the Japanese arrived. The other Malay Associations of the 1930s, more associated with the aristocracy, called Pan-Malayan Congresses at Kuala Lumpur in August 1939 and at Singapore in December 1940. They believed that the British were still a necessary balance against the Chinese. But now the Japanese overthrew them.

Burmans and Burmese

Some of the nationalists in Burma joined the Japanese, but there nationalism had taken a different course. Like other states on the mainland, and by contrast to those in the peninsula and archipelago, it had a long history to which it could recur, even though it was not the history of a nation-state. Indeed, though it had lost parts of its kingdom earlier in the century, the monarchy had finally been displaced only in 1886, and while its heirs, unlike the Mataram and Nguyen princes, played no role in the nationalist movement, the monarchy remained a living memory, and in that sense a permanent challenge to the legitimacy of the British monarch. Nationalism in Burma, as elsewhere, was to develop in part as a result, substantially unintended, of the policies of the colonial power, and in part as a reaction to them. That was no less true, perhaps more, because in a way two colonial powers were involved. Burma had been conquered from India, and Indians benefited from the opportunities the conquest opened up. In Malaya and in Indonesia nationalism was prompted in part by a reaction to the Chinese presence. Burman nationalism reacted still more strongly against the Indian presence. There was a major difference, however. Nationalism was astir among the Chinese as among the Indians, but the Indians were also struggling against their British rulers. India offered the Burman nationalists not only an example, but also assistance.

In Burma, as in Indonesia and the Philippines, elite and masses articulated their objectives in different ways. The Western-educated minority took the lead in attempts to revitalise and modernise Buddhism, and there was no equivalent in Burma of the tension between 'secular' nationalists and Islamic modernists in Indonesia. In 1906, stimulated by the success of the Japanese, educated Burmans founded the Young Men's Buddhist Asssociation in imitation of, but also in rivalry with, the YMCA. Their interest in the fate of Buddhism did not, however, enable them to forge a direct link with the peasantry. Popular Buddhism still focused on the sangha, even though its monarchical protector had been overthrown, and the *pongyi* enjoyed the respect of the villagers, who pinned on them their hope that alien rule would be displaced and monarchy restored. To create a mass movement, the Western-educated had to take account of the aspirations of the *pongyi* and their followers.

The constitutional experiments of the British invited them to make the attempt, but could not promise them success, nor themselves succeed. Those experiments were more advanced than the experiments in Malaya, more advanced, indeed, than those elsewhere in Southeast Asia, even, in some respects, the Philippines. One reason was that Burma was treated as part of India, and experiments in the latter suggested that the equivalent should at least be considered in the former. The other reason was that Burman nationalists pressed for equal treatment. The British thus set out on a far bolder course than in Malaya. They kept to it in the 1930s, when Burma in effect moved ahead of India: the status quo policies Britain followed in that decade meant, rather paradoxically, continued political advance where that had already got under way, as well as continued 'political sleep'[55] where it had not. But the results satisfied neither Burmans nor British.

In 1917 Montagu had envisaged 'the gradual development of self-governing institutions, with a view to the progressive realisation of responsible government in India as an integral part of the British Empire'.[56] Of India Burma was a part, and here were new opportunities for Burman nationalists. In December 1917 the YMBA sent

a delegation to Calcutta, pressing for separation from India, and then a separate settlement over the future of Burma. As a result the Governor of Burma recommended
increased self-government at the district level on the pattern of developments in
India since 1882; and a majority of elected representatives on the Legislative
Council, which had been predominantly a nominated and non-Burman body since
its creation in 1897. The YMBA was alarmed lest separation should mean less
advance than in India, and sent two delegates to London. The Secretary of State
agreed to include Burma in the Indian 'dyarchy' proposals after an inquiry. During
the delay the YMBA organised a mass protest against the University Act of 1920.
That, the subsequent strikes, and the founding of national schools imparted a new
intensity to Burman nationalism, and the General Council of Burmese Associations,
as the council of the YMBA now called itself, boycotted the dyarchy inquiry of 1921.

Dyarchy was nevertheless introduced in 1923. It provided for a legislature of 103,
with seventy-nine members elected on a household suffrage, fifty-eight of them
Burman, and two Burmese ministers, responsible for 'transferred' activities, education, local government, public works, public health, cooperation, and forests. The
British presented dyarchy as a preparation for self-government, not simply as a minimum concession to nationalism, and some Burmese joined in, but as a preparation
it was deficient. It required Burmese ministers to take account of non-Burman interests, but, by providing for their separate representation, appeared to envisage a communal approach. Burmese ministers, furthermore, had no control over finance, and
they were therefore not being offered experience in handling such crucial issues as
allocation and prioritisation, and weighing the political and practical factors involved
in those processes. Nor, of course, could ministers offer a programme to the electorate in the manner of the democratic forms of government the British had in mind.

At the same time, however, they had brought an electorate into existence.
Moreover, the struggle over education had created a new context for dyarchy. In that
the *pongyi* had played an important part, stimulated by U Ottama, a monk who had
visited Japan in 1910 and returned from India in 1921. He insisted that Buddhism
was threatened by an alien government, and he built a mass movement on the basis
of non-cooperation. Aided by the weakness of the headmen, his *pongyi* followers
gained control over many of the local nationalist organisations or *wunthanu athins*
formed by the GCBA. In August 1924 he precipitated a riot in Mandalay, and disaf-
fection was widespread in 1924–25, though unlike that in contemporary Indonesia
it was not influenced by communism, perhaps because Burma lacked the direct links
with the European movement that Sneevliet and others provided.

Those who sought to appeal to the electorate had to take account of popular feeling, but under dyarchy they were in no position to offer a political programme that
would counter the insistence of the *pongyi* that Buddhism was in danger. Affected
by the disturbances, however, the GCBA split, some breaking away to enter the
Legislative Council in 1925, including Ba Maw, a lawyer. But it was not possible to
pass legislation that effectively dealt with popular grievances, and the local boards

and councils, established under the Rural Self-Government Act of 1921, were also viewed with apathy and became very corrupt. Elections did not lead to real power, and could do little to win popular allegiance to the system, or to those who were prepared to attempt to make it work.

The split took a new form, however, when the Simon Commission reviewed dyarchy in 1929. A 'Burma for the Burmans League' advocated separation from India and curtailment of Indian immigration. This was above all a secular group, a Rangoon intelligentsia—vernacular editors, minor officials, and so on—aiming at freedom from *pongyi* domination. But mass backing lay with the *pongyis* and their associates, immediately less affected by Indian competition for official posts, and able to advocate non-separation and cooperation with the Indian Congress in fighting for the freedom which it was alleged the British wished to deny; they were, it was said, trying to rescue Burma from 'the Lost Dominion' and making it 'Safe for Capital'.[57] The Commission was widely boycotted. But following the Hsaya San disturbances of 1930–31, a faction of the Westernised leadership entered the Legislative Council, led by U Chit Hlaing.

The Simon Commission reported in favour of early separation, with guarantees for the status of the new government. Following a Burma Round Table Conference in 1931, Ramsay MacDonald, the British prime minister, spoke of an election on the issue of separation. In the ensuing campaign, an Anti-Separation League was formed out of the boycotting GCBA groups and the supporters of Ba Maw, and it made the most of the popular suspicion of the British. The Separationists, on the other hand, tried to arouse popular hostility to Indian labourers and money-lenders. Wealthy Indians tended to support the Anti-Separationists, nationalists though they were. They triumphed. Once elected, however, some of them, though not Ba Maw, quailed before the prospect of inclusion in the Indian Federation: joining the Congress's struggle had been designed to expedite Burma's political advance, not to bring about its permanent inclusion in India. No clear decision emerged from the Legislative Council, therefore. The British government resolved the Burmans' dilemma by deciding on separation.

The new constitution of 1935, which came into effect in 1937, made Burma all but a self-governing dominion. It discarded dyarchy in favour of a cabinet responsible to an elected House of Representatives of 132 members. The suffrage was on a taxpayer basis, effectively covering about one-third of the male population and one-tenth of the female, and was effected in ninety-two general, twelve Karen, and eight Indian constituencies. There were also representatives, for example, from business groups, six of the eleven being British. The House was checked by a Senate, half elected, half appointed, and the governor, assisted by Counsellors, retained extensive powers in the field of defence, foreign relations, and monetary policy. In addition, under section 139, he could assume special powers in the event of an emergency.

The elections held in 1936 gave three seats to a new faction, the 'Thakins'. In 1931 the All Burma Youth League had been founded, aiming to revive the national school organisation of the early 1920s and extend its contacts with non-national schools. Associated was a student group, and from 1935 they called themselves Thakins as an affirmation of their nationalism. Their inspiration was fluid, drawing on Sun Yat-sen, Sinn Fein, Nietzsche, Upton Sinclair, and Palme Dutt. Some Marxists were among them, like Soe, Than Tun, and Thein Pe, drawing their communism not direct from the Comintern, but from India and from the British party. The younger and more radical Thakins distrusted the older lawyer politicians and their reliance on xenophobic *pongyi*-led mass support, but at this stage themselves had no support in the countryside. Support came initially from students at the University of Rangoon. Their clash with the university authorities led to the strike of February 1936, led by Nu, the president of the Union, Aung San, editor of the student news-paper, and Kyaw Nyein. The Thakins also sought to work among urban labour groups, mostly in fact Indian. They also took part in the elections. That was, per-haps, a sign that they were prepared to use the constitution promulgated by the colo-nial power, even though struggling against it. Their success was, however, limited, and another prospect was soon to appear more attractive.

The new constitution offered much more scope for the development of a parlia-mentary system and for the carrying out of a legislative programme. But a minister relying on Burmans needed support from sixty-five out of the ninety-five Burman members. Factionalism persisted, too, and the lack of a dissolution mechanism gave it scope. Leading Sinyetha, Poor Man's Party, Ba Maw managed to initiate legislation to benefit the agriculturist, such as the Tenancy Act, but his rival, Saw, was able to use the anti-Indian riots of 1938 to embarrass him and he was overthrown early in 1939. In the succeeding Pu ministry, Saw was the strong man, enjoying mass support from the All-Burma Pongyis Council and the para-military Galon. The system, as Governor Dorman-Smith was to put it, did not break down, but it 'creaked very badly'. The House of Representatives was 'of poor quality'; parties were 'hopelessly corrupt'; and the electorate 'ill-educated'.[58] But those were judgments made after the Japanese invasion had destroyed the system, and when an alternative was being planned. The 1935 constitution had been in operation for only a few years, and a longer trial might have produced a different judgment.

Politics in Burma were affected by the opening of the war in Europe. The possi-bility that it could be used to advance Burma's political development at once put that at the top of the political agenda. Late in 1939 the British agreed that the goal for Burma was 'the attainment of Dominion status'. Even in the crisis of mid-1940, how-ever, they declined to promise that it would be reached at the end of the war. As the situation in the Far East deteriorated late in 1941, Saw, as premier, tried again, and, despite the Atlantic Charter, again in vain. 'We were engaged in a struggle for our very lives', Churchill told the premier, 'and this was not the time to raise such con-stitutional matters'.[59] Saw was quite unsatisfied, and distributed a pamphlet, 'Burma's case for full self-government'. Before he got back to Burma, the Japanese had bombed Pearl Harbor. It was then that he allegedly contacted the Japanese through their consul in Lisbon.

The fate of the Thakins was rather different. In May 1940 the Japanese had sent Colonel Suzuki Keiji to Burma. Under the alias Minami Masuyo, he succeeded in attracting Aung San, Ne Win, and others to his cause, and he also says he contacted Saw, who asked if Japan would give Burma military aid in its struggle for freedom. He was deported, but Aung San was not apprehended and left Burma for Amoy. The aim of the Japanese, the British thought, was to recruit agents who would 'try to stir up trouble in the event of our going to war with Japan'.[60] The war, when it came, was of course more catastrophic than the British anticipated. Aung San and his Thirty Comrades—Thakins brought to Japan for guerrilla training by the Minami Kikan, nucleus of the BIA in December 1941—expanded their aspirations. Independence had somehow to be secured from the struggle among the colonial powers.

In the Philippines, Indonesia, and Malaya, the newly 'imagined' nations adopted the frontiers of the colonial state without, for the most part, alienating other potential nations within those frontiers. The particular risk was that one dominant group would capture the national cause and impose its prescriptions on the others. The Filipinos did not entirely avoid that in the case of the Moros. The Malays proceeded with caution, since their majority was slight. The Indonesians avoided adopting a merely Javanese nationalism, even though non-Javanese were apprehensive of it. The frontiers of royal Burma had fluctuated. Those accepted by the colonial power did not include all that the greatest Burman conquerors had at times appropriated, but did include, not only the Mon but also most of the Shan territories, and it was this state that Burman nationalists 'imagined' as their patrimony. That was indeed a major source of tension with the colonial power. It believed it had obligations to the non-Burman peoples, the 'Burmese' more generally. Those were hard to reconcile with its commitment to political advance in Burma.

Economic, social, and political change had also altered the perceptions non-Burman peoples had of themselves and of their proper relationship with others. Their old relationship with the monarchy could not, of course, continue: what was their relationship to 'Burma' to be? The most dramatic changes occurred amidst the Karens. Never assimilated by Burmans or Buddhism, they were liberated by British conquest from handicaps suffered under royal rule. Many also moved into the lowlands. In other cases, it was easier to divide Burmans and other peoples in 'Burma' on a geographical basis: the Shans, Kachins, and Chins continued to dwell almost entirely in the hill areas. The constitutional developments of the inter-war period provided for Karen representation in parliamentary Burma. The 1935 Act left the peoples of the 'Scheduled Areas'—the Shan states, administered through their chiefs, and the hill tracts, inhabited by Chins, Kachins, Nagas, and Karens—under the direct control of the governor. Burman nationalists resented the special provision for minorities in parliamentary Burma. They also opposed the territorial limits upon it, which seemed like colonial divide-and-rule. The British certainly recruited

Karens and other minorities to the police and the army, but their policy was probably less purposive, more expedient: concessions to Burman nationalism were necessary now; the relationships with the non-Burman peoples were a matter for the longer term. Attempts to solve them were perhaps unlikely to succeed and were not urgent. In hindsight, of course, the issue looks different. Over time the peoples became more distinct, not less, while both Burmans and non-Burmans felt betrayed by the colonial power.

Vietnamese

Opposing colonial rule, nationalist movements in Southeast Asia were likely, where they could, to turn the generally royalist legacy of the pre-colonial past to account. That was not merely a matter of appropriating its history as a backing for their imagined nation. The royal system had over the centuries established a strong link with popular tradition. Even where royal families no longer existed, ideas about the just monarch might still be current and potent. In some cases monarchies still existed. Their position was likely to be equivocal. Often they were kept in being because the colonial ruler found them a useful instrument for securing collaboration and compliance. But, wittingly or not, they could be a focus for nationalist leaders, not all of whom insisted on seeing them merely as feudal remnants. In some cases a younger son or a pretender had a particular interest in a link with those opposing the colonial power.

In Netherlands India, for example, some of the Mataram princes connected themselves with the nationalist movement. Malay sultans appeared to be defenders of Malay culture, and a member of the Kedah family was to be the first prime minister. In Burma, the British dislodged the monarchy, but its hold on the popular imagination was demonstrated in the Hsaya San rebellion, and in their wartime planning the British gave some consideration to the idea that monarchy might be reintroduced. In Vietnam the French retained the Nguyen dynasty. They did not make effective use of it, administering Cochin-China separately as a colony, and never allowing the royal court sufficient power for it to act as a viable collaborator. But those they installed as emperor had some sense of their potential as national leaders, and a pretender, Cuong De, a descendant of prince Canh, closely identified himself with a conservative wing of the nationalist movement.

The earliest nationalist movement indeed emerged as a transformation of the mandarin-led opposition that the French faced in the protectorate of Tonkin, provoked in part by Doumer's consolidation of French Indo-China. On Ham-nghi's capture and exile, the Can-vuong loyalists accepted Cuong De as their leader, and Phan Boi Chau, a man born to a relatively poor scholar gentry family in Nghe-an, at this time associating monarchy with the national cause, secured his patronage. Then, having formed the Duy Tan Hoi (Modernisation Society), Phan sought assistance from Japan, a monarchy identified with successful imitation of the Europeans, and opposition to them, later illustrated in their 1905 victory over Russia. 'The strength of Japan has been felt in the Northwest, all the way to the Ch'ing and to the Russians', he wrote to Okuma. 'Why then has Japan allowed the French to trample over Vietnam without trying to help us?'[61]

Though assistance was not forthcoming, he built up a nucleus of Vietnamese students in Japan, where there were many Chinese as well. In 1906 he arranged for the pretender to go there via Hong Kong, and in 1907 he joined a League of East Asia. Following the 1907 Franco-Japanese treaty, however, the Japanese government expelled Phan Boi Chau and Cuong De in 1909, and dissolved the organisations set up among Vietnamese students in Japan. After the Chinese revolution of 1911 overthrew the Manchus, Phan abandoned his insistence on restoring monarchy, and with some of the Vietnamese who had gone to neighbouring China, he organised the Quang Phuc Hoi (Restoration Society) on the model of the Kuomintang. But in Vietnam he had been able only to inspire revolutionary acts, like the attempted revolt in the Hanoi garrison in 1908, and he now vainly organised the assassination of Sarraut in 1912.

'Violence is death.'[62] Those were the words of Phan Chu Trinh, who came from a wealthy scholar gentry family in Quang-nam, and led another wing of the nationalist movement. It sought concessions from the protecting power on the basis of the principles of its revolution of 1789, but its strategy did not evoked a positive response. The reformist manifestations that followed the deposition of emperor Thanh-thai in 1907 indeed met with repression: the Dong Kinh Nghia Thuc (Free School of Hanoi) was closed down in 1908, and after his alleged involvement in the tax riots in Annam that year, Phan Chu Trinh was first sentenced to death, then imprisoned on Pulau Condore, then exiled. The French authorities tended not to distinguish reformist activities from revolutionary ones.

The removal of French troops in the war led in 1916 to plans for an insurrection fostered by the emperor Duy-tan himself. It failed completely. The emperor was exiled to Réunion and was to die in 1945 as a French major and Companion of the French Liberation. Phan Chu Trinh was allowed to return to Vietnam in 1925, and there he died the following year. In 1925 Phan Boi Chau had been arrested by the French in Shanghai. Living on in Hué, he was to declare that, had the French offered collaboration, the Vietnamese would have forgotten the word independence. He wanted to offer 'loyal collaboration',[63] but the French authorities did not believe him. Despite the eloquence of Governor-General Sarraut, they had also rejected the approach of emperor Khai-dinh, who went to Paris in 1922 to advocate a proposal put forward by the moderate Pham Quynh, revitalising the protectorate treaty of 1884.

In the protectorate the nationalist movement had an early start, in part simply because it derived so immediately from the traditional mandarin class, which reacted against the French, but secured access through its wealth and education to new ideas and new overseas contacts. In the colony of Cochin-China social change was more profound, and it was only with World War I, and in part as a result of its ideological stimulus, that a new nationalist movement appeared there, marked for instance by the founding of the Parti Constitutionaliste about 1917. Made up of civil servants, teachers, merchants, and landlords, it showed a 'moderate and pro-French orientation'.[64]

It was to this social group that Sarraut had looked when he found his reforms, modest though they were, opposed by the governor of Cochin-China and the French colons (settlers). The Colonial Council, established in 1880, had by 1910 still only six Vietnamese members in a total of eighteen, selected by delegates chosen by village notables. The political reforms of 1922 finally expanded the electorate from 1800 to 20 000—in a population of some three million—while the Vietnamese members now numbered ten out of twenty-four. The French were also exceedingly cautious over the other route to participation, naturalisation, though it was provided for in 1881. In 1914 there only some 360 naturalised French citizens in Cochin-China. Nor was there any intention of applying the criteria that would have allowed those who served in the world war to gain citizenship.[65]

In such a context, the Constitutionalists, like the moderate mandarin movements, received little positive response, and some colonial circles began to see their leader, Bui Quang Chieu, as a radical. Another admirer of the French, Nguyen An Ninh, was disappointed by their failure to put their ideals into action. Sarraut had seduced the youth of Vietnam, and they preferred reform to revolution: 'if in two or three years they see the futility of their efforts, they will tire and cede a place to those who will be more useful to the Annamite race'.[66]

The arrival of Alexandre Varenne, appointed governor-general by a leftist government in Paris, revived optimism among the nationalists. A speech he delivered in December 1925 indeed made a guarded reference to the possibility of independence. 'Her mission achieved, it is possible to believe that [France] will leave nothing in Indochina but the memory of her labour, that she will demand no role in the life of the peninsula, either to direct or to advise, and that the peoples who will have profited by her tutelage will have no other ties with her but those of gratitude and affection.' Indo-China 'could aspire to a fuller and higher life, to become one day a nation'.[67] The nationalists looked for deeds, not words. Varenne hedged. In Paris Bui Quang Chieu warned that Indo-China would be lost in fifteen years if it was not given reforms. In Saigon Nguyen An Ninh told a demonstration on 21 March 1926 that Varenne would give nothing. 'There is no collaboration possible between French and Annamites. The French have nothing more to do here. Let them give us back the land of our ancestors.'[68] He was arrested. Varenne indeed gave little. Pham Quynh was denied recognition for his Progressivist Union, though it was collaborationist.

The new contacts with the outside world provided by the war—including the Vietnamese soldiers and war-workers sent to France—helped to stimulate a post-mandarinal nationalist movement in the north. So, too, did the frustrating policies of the colonial government, offering few employment opportunities for educated Vietnamese, and no prospect of political participation. In December 1927 a new revolutionary organisation was established in Hanoi, the Viet Nam Quoc Dan Dang

(Vietnamese Nationalist Party): 'the aim and general line of the party is to make a national revolution, to use military force to overthrow the feudal colonial system, to set up a democratic republic of Vietnam'.[69] The model was the Kuomintang and the strategy was based on Sun Yat-sen's: military take-over, followed by political tutelage, then constitutional government. In 1929 its leadership was decimated by arrests that followed the assassination of a French official. In some disarray, and pressed by the onset of the Depression, the VNQDD planned a series of uprisings at military posts in the Red River delta early in 1930. 'It is better to die now and leave behind the example of sacrifice and striving for later generations', Nguyen Thai Hoc declared. 'If we do not succeed, at least we will have become men.'[70] Mutinies at Yen-bay and elsewhere were, however, suppressed. Forty-three bombs were dropped on Co Am, a village to which Nguyen Thai Hoc had fled, '*une solution radicale, le retour définitif de l'ordre*', as Patrice Morlat somewhat ironically describes this colonial 'frightfulness'.[71] Most of the VNQDD leaders were executed.

'Really, we should do something else here than repress', wrote the secretary to the Résident Supérieur of Annam in January 1931.[72] Fear, Milton Osborne suggests, 'drove the French to reject any significant liberalization of their rule ... the middle ground of genuine constitutional opposition of the sort which emerged in India was not available'.[73] The policies of the French tended to destroy rather than boost the prospects of the moderates. Yet those who turned to revolution had little chance of success, not merely because of the effectiveness of the Sûreté, but because of their lack of popular backing. That the Can-vuong movement had enjoyed, albeit on a traditionalist basis, but its successor, the mandarinal movement, had failed. Neither the middle class in the south, nor the frustrated intelligentsia in the north, were in a position again to evoke that kind of support. Confucianism, always an elite movement, could hardly be the focus of mass nationalism. Nor were the nationalists in a position, like the movements in Burma and Indonesia, to evoke support on a religious basis. If they turned to violence, it was even more likely to take the form of self-defeating adventurism.

These lessons were not lost on the communists, though even they were, as elsewhere, tempted by adventurism. Thus while the repression of the French tended to push nationalism in a revolutionary direction, it was the communists who were best able to secure popular support. To what extent their objectives were merely 'national' or also 'international' became a question the significance of which could only increase in the absence of effective rivals. French policy continued to do nothing to build those up. The attempts to carry out Pham Quynh's policy after the return of emperor Bao Dai in 1932 were half-hearted. Though they had retained the monarchy, the French continued to deprive it of any power.

Communism had been slow to penetrate into Indo-China, and it was among the exile community in France itself that it first took hold. The leading figure was Nguyen Ai Quoc, later known as Ho Chi Minh. He was born of a mandarin family in Nghe-An, and educated at the Lycée Quoc-hoc at Hué. That was a nationalist school founded by Ngo Dinh Kha, a minister to Thanh-thai who resigned when he was deposed, and father of Ngo Dinh Diem, also a pupil, as were other future communist leaders, Vo Nguyen Giap and Pham Van Dong, himself the son of a mandarin involved in the Duy-tan affair. In 1912 Nguyen Ai Quoc left Vietnam as a ship's cabin boy. He was cook's help to the great Escoffier at the Carlton Hotel in London during the war, joined an Overseas Workers Association that supported Ireland's struggle for independence, haunted Versailles in the hope that the peace negotiations would reflect Wilson's Fourteen Points, read the Lenin theses, became a founder member of the French Communist Party, went to Moscow in 1924, and finally joined the Comintern mission in Canton. There in 1925 he founded the Viet Nam Thanh Nien Cach Menh Dong Chi Hoi, or Revolutionary Youth League of Vietnam.

Its aims were broad: national revolution, overthrow of the French, restoration of independence through the organisation of an anti-imperialist front. Emphasising nationalism rather than communism was in keeping with the Lenin theses, which the Comintern was currently following. Ho Chi Minh did not even set up a communist party, though within the league the Communist Youth Group (Thanh Nien Cong San Doan) was intended to be its nucleus. It was a sign that he believed that the revolution needed patient preparation and had to avoid premature action. About 300 young Vietnamese were trained in Canton, and by the end of 1925 the first trainees were beginning to return. 'Unlike its predecessors, the new movement was strongly determined to grow roots among the masses. … Ho emphasised that the proletariat and the peasantry, the most alienated elements in society, were the key to the success of the revolution.'[74]

Organising an anti-imperialist front was more problematic. In Cochin-China Trotskyism appealed to southern individualism and had spread among the urban workers. In northern Vietnam the VNQDD preferred armed insurrection to Marxism. Outside Vietnam the Kuomintang broke with the CCP in 1927, and the Comintern abandoned the Lenin theses. In 1929 the league broke up into two rival communist parties, the Communist Party of Indo-China and the Annam Communist Party. Urged by the Comintern to promote unity, Ho convened a meeting in Hong Kong early in 1930 which decided to found the Communist Party of Vietnam (Viet Nam Cong San Dang), changed again later in the year at the insistence of the Comintern to Indochinese Communist Party (Dang Cong San Dong Duong). The Yen-bay adventure had meanwhile more or less destroyed the VNQDD.

What turned out to be an adventure now virtually destroyed the ICP. Worsening economic conditions prompted an increasing number of strikes in the urban areas of Vietnam and on the plantations, and in May 1930 peasant riots began in Nghe-an. No doubt infiltrated party activists had a role, encouraged by Comintern rhetoric. But, despite the customary analysis of the French, the ICP was 'barely managing to keep up with events'.[75] Concentrated in the traditionally rebellious provinces of Nghe-an and Ha-tinh, the peasant unrest reached its height in September. The

French bombed a crowd advancing on the provincial capital, Vinh, but their authority had collapsed in the countryside. That was an opportunity for the communists which they could hardly ignore, but it was also a danger. The regional committee organised soviets in the form of peasant associations, and encouraged the restitution of communal land, though not the general confiscation of landlord holdings. To destroy the movement the French, seeking on this occasion the collaboration of the imperial court, tried to set up a loyalist organisation. But they also declared martial law and called in the Foreign Legion, and managed to arrest most of the leadership. Ho Chi Minh was gaoled in Hong Kong in June 1931, though not surrendered to the French. The events of 1931 provided a heroic legend. But they also reminded the communists of the perils of adventurism, while reaffirming the revolutionary potential of the peasantry.

The programme of the Popular Front government, formed in May 1936 by the French Socialist Party led by Léon Blum, made one reference to the colonies: it promised a commission of inquiry. Early in August it announced the establishment of a Colonial Inspection Commission, and nationalists in Vietnam began to prepare for its arrival. The idea of an Indo-Chinese Congress that would prepare a list of demands made the colonial government nervous, however, and the Vietnamese reaction to a visit by the minister for labour early in 1937 led conservatives to predict disturbances if the inspection team itself came. 'As was so often the case with French policy toward Indo-China, the Popular Front government then caved in to colonial opinion and cancelled the inspection trip.'[76] If the Dutch had rejected Soetardjo the previous year, at least there had been a means of presenting a petition. The year 1937 itself was the one in which Burma got its parliamentary government going.

Though a Popular Front government had not fundamentally changed French policy in Indo-China, its policy being 'very little different from that of other French governments',[77] and there was still no opportunity for a moderate nationalist movement, it had permitted the revival of communism. That was, of course, made easier by the Comintern's new policy of 1935, designed to seek a common front against the menace of fascism. The right to form political parties was recognised in Cochin-China, and the communists in fact took a leading role in the Congress movement. But that movement had also shown moderate distrust of communist dominance. The communists were themselves divided: not only by the struggle between Trotskyists and Stalinists, but also by their ambivalence over the importance of the peasants.

Early in 1939 Cuong De, who had left Japan for Hong Kong when the undeclared war began in China, formed Viet Nam Phuc Quoc Dong Menh (the Alliance to Restore Vietnam), designed to evict the French with Japanese support. He gained support from Cao Dai and from some members of the Constitutional Party, but generally nationalists did not want to trade one colonial power for another. The ICP was bound by Comintern policy, which was more supportive of the French than other nationalists were, and it was attacked by the Trotskyists. The Nazi–Soviet alliance invalidated the policy, while the opening of the European war led to wide-spread arrests and banning of both communists and Trotskyists. Those who remained fled into China or into remote areas of Tonkin.

In other parts of Southeast Asia nationalists generally accepted the frontiers established by the colonial powers. Contesting those powers' control might involve suppressing or denying other nationalisms, and taking up their cause could be condemned as an imperialist ploy. 'Nations' were forged in a three-way conflict, at times, indeed, a four-way one, given the role of international factors. 'Indo-China' was a colonial creation, designed for administrative convenience, but also consolidating the division of Vietnam into three regions, Tonkin, Annam, and Cochin-China. On occasion, the French seemed to envisage that it would be this entity that would gain independence, as Varenne's veiled language suggested. For that to have had any chance of success, however, the French would have had to adopt a far more positive policy towards political development. The policy they in fact adopted allowed the development of nationalism only by reaction, and it drew on the sense of Vietnamese unity enjoyed in the pre-French past. The Comintern adhered by contrast to the French pattern: it insisted that the communist party be 'Indo-Chinese'. The predominantly Vietnamese leadership accepted that, at least as a strategy, and the communists in Laos and Cambodia were certainly going to need their help. They would not, however, be willing to submerge their own nationalism.

Khmers

Nationalism was slow to develop in Cambodia. There was, indeed, a strong sense of identity, maintained in part by popular Buddhism, 'a symbolic assurance of eventual liberation'.[78] In that the monarch, retained by the French, found a source of strength that the Vietnamese monarchs lacked. While, moreover, the sense the Burmans and Vietnamese had of their identity was sustained by their expansive relationship with their neighbours, the sense of identity Khmers felt was sustained by the sense that their continued existence was threatened by their neighbours. The protectorate 'kept Cambodia in being as a nation',[79] but it was at the price of incorporation into an Indo-China manufactured by the French and opening Cambodia to the penetration of the Vietnamese, employed on rubber plantations and in the federal services.

The limited nature of economic change, and the limited provision of education, meant that the potential for a nationalist movement took time to realise. In 1930 the French founded the Buddhist Institute in an attempt to isolate Cambodian Buddhists from potentially disruptive influences from Siam, but it exposed Khmer intellectuals to some of the political currents affecting monks in Cochin-China. With French approval three young Cambodians affiliated with it, Son Ngoc Thanh, Sim Var, and Pach Choeun, published a Khmer-language newspaper between 1936 and 1942. It was called *Nagara Vatta* (Angkor Wat). The contrast between the current situation of Cambodia, and the glories of Angkor which the French had uncovered, weighed deeply on Khmer nationalists, however. Like others they were inspired by a past they appropriated, but they were also burdened by its immensity. Pach Choeun had been a volunteer in World War I. In 1942 he was arrested for his role in an anti-French demonstration and Son Ngoc Thanh fled.

Laos

Their move into Laos had not given the French control of all the old kingdom of Lan Xang. Those parts of Laos they did control they saw as a collection of *muang*, of which the kingdom of Luang Prabang was the largest, not as a political entity, and its development, they thought, could only be the work of Vietnamese migrants. At the opening session of the Consultative Assembly in Vientiane in 1923, Résident-Supérieur Jules Bosc declared that this was the first time since the division of Lan Xang that representatives from throughout Laos had met together. But such an assembly could, as Martin Stuart-Fox says, do 'nothing to promote representative government or mass political interest, and contributed little to a sense of Lao national identity'.[80] The limited Western-educated elite that emerged mainly from the princely families and the heirs of the higher mandarins included men like Prince Petsarath, who studied at the Ecole Coloniale in Paris, and his half-brother, Prince Suphanuvong, who studied at the Lycée Albert Sarraut in Hanoi and then the Ecole Normale des Ponts et Chaussées in Paris. They were to play a role in the united Laos created only at the end of World War II, and that did not include those parts of Lan Xang that, as Bosc had not mentioned, formed part of the modern Thai state.

Thais

By the 1930s, indeed, Thai nationalists were seeking to regain control over what they had lost earlier in the colonial phase. In Siam, of course, nationalism followed a trajectory that was unique in pre-war Southeast Asia, since it was not a question of struggle against a colonial ruler. It certainly reflected, however, the impact of economic change and of Western ideas, common experiences in late-nineteenth- and early-twentieth-century Southeast Asia. But the course it followed, while not without parallels in Europe, may also be usefully compared with that followed by the newly independent regimes of the postwar period. Nationalism was employed by domestic elites in their struggle for power and popular support, even at times at the risk of conflict with neighbours.

Concerned to preserve as much as possible of their dominion in a colonial world, the Chakri kings had engaged in diplomacy and established bureaucracy. They had also given it a name: it was Mongkut who made the foreign-derived word 'Siam' official, and thus created the concept of the state, though Thais referred to their state as Muang Thai or Prathet Thai. It seemed less necessary to build a national identity. 'The administrators did not need to mobilize the populace to their cause', McVey suggests, 'and the king could not rally them to his because he had no means of reaching them save through the bureaucratic apparatus'.[81]

Rama VI's attempt to create an official nationalism indicates that he was restive with a situation that at once seemed out of date and confining. His ideological formulation—derived both from the Sukhotai period and from Edwardian Britain—was Chat, Sasana, Phramakakasat (Nation, Religion, King). There was another component, too, anti-Chinese sentiment: the state no longer depended on Chinese tax-collectors, and the Chinese had overthrown their own monarch in the revolution of 1911. Finally there was a historical component. Rama VI extolled King Naresuen. He also strengthened the National Library, and when Siam entered the war replaced Dr Frankfurter by the French epigraphist Georges Coedès, who published the inscriptions of Sukhotai.[82] The troops had a new flag, 'the symbol of Siam joining in harmony with the Allies in order to suppress the evil in world', said the king.[83] Its colours were red (nation), white (religion), and blue (king).

The revolution of 1932 that ended the absolute monarchy was carried through largely by the official class it had created. Increasingly dominated by military elements, the ruling elite articulated a new Thai nationalism, and its propagandist, Luang Vichit, citing Goebbels, echoed Rama VI.[84] The state was renamed Thailand in 1939. Pro-Thai policies were pursued at home, directed against the Chinese and designed to assimilate the Muslims, and pan-Thai policies were pursued abroad, at the expense of the colonial powers, but also of those who expected their protection.

Notes

1 William J. Duiker, *The Rise of Nationalism in Vietnam*, Cornell UP, 1976, p. 15.

2 q. A. W. Raitt, *Prosper Mérimée*, London: Eyre and Spottiswoode, 1970, p. 315.

3 *Imagined Communities*, London, NY: Verso, 1991, p. 6.

4 q. R. William Liddle, *Leadership and Culture in Indonesian Politics*, Sydney: Allen and Unwin, 1996, p. 90.

5 S. M. Borromeo, 'El Cadiz Filipino: Colonial Cavite, 1571–1896', PhD thesis, Berkeley, 1973, p. 148.

6 q. C. A. Majul, *The Political and Constitutional Ideas of the Philippine Revolution*, Quezon City: UPP, 1967, p. 115.

7 *Report on the Condition of the Philippines in 1842*, Manila: Historical Conservation Society, 1963, pp. 191–2, 194.

8 q. L. Y. Yabes, ed., *Jose Rizal: On his Centenary*, Quezon City, 1963, p. 221n.

9 q. J. N. Schumacher, *The Propaganda Movement*, Manila: Solidaridad, 1973, p. 42.

10 trans. L. Ma. Guerrero, London: Longmans, 1961, pp. 320–1.

11 q. Majul, p. 25.

12 q. ibid., p. 47.

13 in David K. Wyatt and A. Woodside, eds, *Moral Order and the Question of Change*, Yale UP, 1982, pp. 275–6.

14 q. Ileto, p. 313.

15 Glenn A. May, *Inventing a Hero*, Manila: New Day, 1996, p. 162.

16 Milagros C. Guerrero, 'Luzon at War ...', PhD thesis, Michigan U, 1977, p. 69.

17 q. Guerrero, p. 178.

18 q. R. Ileto, *Pasyon and Revolution*, Quezon City: Ateneo de Manila UP, 1979, p. 199.

19 q. R. J. Sullivan, *Exemplar of Americanism*, Ann Arbor: UM, 1991, p. 122.

20 q. C. A. Grunder and W. E. Livezey, *The Philippines and the United States*, Norman: U Oklahoma P, 1951, pp. 85, 101.

21 q. Grayson L. Kirk, *Philippine Independence*, NY, 1936, pp. 227–34.

22 T. Friend, 'The Philippine Sugar Industry and the Politics of Independence', JAS, 22, 2 (February 1963), p. 188.

23 q. E. H. Jacoby, *Agrarian Unrest in Southeast Asia*, Bombay: Asia Publishing House, 1961, p. 213.

24 q. C. L. M. Penders, ed., *Indonesia Selected Documents*, St Lucia: UQP, 1977, p. 138.

25 *This Earth of Mankind*, trans. Max Lane, Melbourne: Penguin, 1982/1991, p. 315.

26 q. J. Ingleson, *Road to Exile*, Singapore: HEB, 1979, p. 7.

27 George D. Larson, *Prelude to Revolution*, Dordrecht: Foris, 1987, p. 29.

28 Takashi Shiraishi, *An Age in Motion*, Cornell UP, 1990, p. 53.

29 S. L. van der Waal, ed., *De Volksraad en de Staatkundige Ontwikkeling van Nederlands-Indie*, Groningen: Wolters, 1964, I, p. 174.

30 Michael C. Williams, *Communism, Religion and Revolt in Banten*, Athens: Ohio U, 1990, p. 115.

31 Takashi, p. 113.

32 q. R. McVey, *The Rise of Indonesian Communism*, Cornell UP, 1965, p. 107.

33 McVey, p. 179.

34 Thommy Svensson and Per Sorensen, eds, *Indonesia and Malaysia …* , London and Malmo: Curzon, 1983, pp. 109–11.

35 q. B. Grant, *Indonesia*, Melbourne UP, 1964, p. 21.

36 Surakarta party organ, q. S. Stromquist, 'The Communist Uprisings of 1926–7 …', JSEAH, 8, 2 (September 1967), p. 191.

37 q. Stromquist, p. 191.

38 J. A. Scholte, 'The International Construction of Indonesian Nationhood, 1930–1950', in H. Antlov and S. Tonnesson, eds, *Imperial Policy and Southeast Asian Nationalism, 1930–1957*, Richmond: Curzon, 1995, p. 206.

39 q. Mavis Rose, *Indonesia Free*, Cornell U, 1987, p. 18.

40 'The Political Life of a Sumatran Residency: Tapanuli, 1915–1940', PhD thesis, Yale U, 1972, pp. 176–8.

41 A. Reid, *The Indonesian Revolution*, Melbourne: Longman, 1974, p. 7.

42 q. C. L. M. Penders, *The Life and Times of Sukarno*, London: Sidgwick and Jackson, 1974, p. 35.

43 Ingleson, *Road to Exile*, p. 66.

44 H. van Miert, 'The Jong Sumatran Bond …', MAS, 30, 3 (July 1996), p. 608.

45 q. Eduard J. M. Schmutzer, *Dutch Colonial Policy and the Search for Identity in Indonesia, 1920–1931*, Leiden: Brill, 1977, p. 96.

46 q. ibid., pp. 95–6.

47 q. ibid., p. 107.

48 Larsen, pp. 140–1.

49 q. D. E. Henley, *Nationalism and Regionalism in a Colonial Context*, Leiden: KITLV P, 1996, p. 132.

50 B. Dahm, *Sukarno and the Struggle for Indonesia's Independence*, Cornell UP, 1969, p. 173.

51 N. A. Bootsma, *Buren in de koloniale tijd*, Dordrecht: Foris, 1986, p. 107.

52 q. Friend, *Between Two Empires*, p. 170.

53 Milne in Wang Gungnu, *Malaysia*, London: Pall Mall, 1964, p. 328.

54 q. Khoo Kay Kim, 'Sino-Malay Relations in Peninsular Malaysia before 1942', JSEAS, 12, 1 (March 1981), p. 100.

55 Lau, p. 23.

56 q. T. G. P. Spear, *India*, U Mich P, 1961, pp. 342–3.

57 Furnivall, pp. 166–7.

58 q. Tarling, *Fourth Burmese War*, p. 7.

59 q. ibid., p. 4.

60 q. Tarling, *Pacific War*, p. 276.

61 q. Marr, *Vietnamese Anticolonialism*, p. 113.

62 q. Duiker, p. 53.

63 q. ibid., p. 93.

64 Duiker, p. 136.

65 Hue-Tam Ho Tai, 'The Politics of Compromise…', MAS, 18, 3 (July 1984), p. 383.
66 q. Duiker, p. 143.
67 q. ibid., p. 145.
68 q. ibid., p. 148.
69 q. ibid., p. 156.
70 q. Hue-Tam Ho Tai, *Radicalism and the Origins of the Vietnamese Revolution*, Harvard UP, 1992, p. 222.
71 *La Répression Coloniale au Vietnam*, Paris: L'Harmattan, 1990, p. 122.
72 q. Tai, *Radicalism*, p. 248.
73 in W. F. Vella, ed., *Aspects of Vietnamese History*, U Hawaii P, 1973, p. 167.
74 Duiker, p. 204.
75 ibid., p. 221.
76 ibid., p. 248.
77 Hammer, *Struggle*, p. 92.
78 David J. Steinberg et al., *Cambodia*, New Haven: HRAF, 1959, p. 95.
79 M. Herz, p. 66.
80 *Buddhist Kingdom, Marxist State*, Bangkok: White Lotus, 1996, p. 35.
81 q. Chai-anan Samudavaija in Craig Reynolds, ed., *National Identity and its Defenders*, Clayton: Monash U, 1991, p. 60.
82 W. F. Vella, *Chaiyo!*, U Hawaii P, 1978, p. 206.
83 q. Nuttannee Ratanapat, 'King Vajiravudh's Nationalism and its Impact on Political Development in Thailand', PhD thesis, Northern Illinois U, 1990, p. 113.
84 J. Stowe, *Siam becomes Thailand*, London: Hurst, 1991, pp. 102–3.

4.3 | Democracy

The adoption of Western-style democracy in Southeast Asia was associated with the ending of Western rule. Its fortunes varied from country to country, but everywhere it took some hold. Compare the experience of the first countries to gain independence, the Philippines and Burma, with that of Indonesia and Malaysia. Compare the experience of the Indo-Chinese states with that of independent Thailand.

Nationalism was designed to transform or to supersede other loyalties, and so great a hold has it gained that it is now hard to admit the extent of their validity, even in the past, and to avoid pre-dating or over-emphasising its role. Its ideology had an additional implication. Articulated by an elite, it had also to encompass the masses. Indeed members of the elite endeavoured to strengthen their cause by speaking for them. In due course, as the 'working definition' suggests, their loyalties had to be transformed, too. In the meantime the support of the masses might be offered or secured on a different basis—on the basis, for example, of older loyalties, of xenophobia, of a millennial hope or the appeal of traditional or charismatic figures, of a religious cause or a guerrilla struggle, or in the twentieth century of the mixture of education, organisation, and selective use of violence that avowed communists came to develop.

There was another long-term implication. If the national cause were the people's cause, on what basis was it to participate in the nation-state which it should win? Like other states it would link elite and masses; it would be a means of distribution. On what basis? Nationalism could be utilised to sustain an authoritarian regime, monarchical, dictatorial, even communist. It could also justify a democratic approach, in which, in one way or another, the citizens selected their leaders, and made them more responsive. It proved hard even for authoritarian regimes altogether to avoid an element of participation, though they could often turn it to account. Napoleon III offered the powerful precedent of a plebiscitary dictatorship. Bismarck called in the masses against the politicians, evoking parties he could hardly cope with. It was his constitution that appealed to the Meiji reformers in Japan, though they modified the example, and universal male suffrage was not introduced till 1925. World War I indeed gave a powerful impulse to the democratic cause in

Japan and elsewhere. The empires of east and central Europe had collapsed or been defeated, and the United States, the United Kingdom, and France were victorious. Particularly in the US case, they had articulated their cause in democratic terms.

The concept of a world of nation-states encompassed the notion that those who had secured that status would be joined in due course by others who were yet dependent or 'undeveloped'. Were they not also actually or potentially 'nations'? That was a notion seized upon by the new elites that government policy and economic change helped to create, and they pressed for its implementation, even in territories that had no proto-national history. It was also taken up by those who pursued a more ethical colonial policy. It might indeed justify a continuance of colonial rule until a nation could govern itself, perhaps in a remote future. Democratisation in the metropolis did not necessarily make it easier to abandon colonial territories, but it did make it harder to rationalise an old-fashioned colonialism based simply on dominance, profit, and extraction. A different rationale had to be offered. That could be expressed, like the Ethical Policy, in assimilationist terms. But, particularly in a democratic polity, it was hard to deny that other peoples should also advance politically, and thus also enjoy some kind of participation. The idea was connected with that of the nation-state. Colonial powers that took this stance could, however, still argue in terms of preparation for self-rule, perhaps, indeed, even more vigorously. The concept of an advance to democratic self-government became the paradoxical rationale for continued imperial rule, for how long it was rarely stated.

In a sense additional qualifications were added to the criteria for a nation-state, one indeed that not all Western states met themselves: the existence of a franchise, political parties, civil liberties, a range of non-state organisations. The humourist Will Rogers imagined a conversation between President Hoover and Patrick Hurley after his visit to the Philippines in 1931. 'I asked Pat, "Pat, are they ready for independence?" He says, "No", I say "how can you tell when a Nation is ready for independence?" He says, "I don't know. I never saw a Nation that was."'[1] Paul McNutt told Douglas MacArthur that an independent Philippines would not hold honest elections. 'Paul, you're absolutely right', the General replied, 'but ... the Filipinos will hold as honest an election as you ever had in the state of Indiana'.[2] The criteria were indeed unclear, open to interpretation and contestation. Taft had looked for popular self-government in the Philippines, not oligarchy. Harrison told the Filipinos that the Americans 'eagerly await convincing proof that you are capable of establishing a stable government of our own',[3] and the Jones Act echoed the phrase. He later defined a stable government as one elected by the people, capable of maintaining order, and able to discharge international obligations.[4]

To the extent that self-government would involve popular participation, the preparation might take a long while: if power was not to be transferred only to an elite, the masses had to be educated so that they might take a real part in a really democratic system. The chance that a colonial autocracy could in fact produce a post-colonial democracy was, of course, slim. '[S]overeignty is external to the colonized territory and in such a circumstance, there can be no democracy. Any attempt at the development of democratic institutions in circumstances so constitutionally antithetical to their prosperity can only produce a distorted experience for the colonized.'[5] Even a staged process was unconvincing . The point that Robert H. Taylor made about inter-war Burma is a valid one: 'British policy-makers failed to note that in order to allow an indigenous political elite to govern the country, that elite would have to be able to respond to the problems of its electorate'.[6] A similar point lent validity to Colijn's comment on the Volksraad: it would not enable the educated native 'to take his place in the administration in such a way as to be able to cooperate on the basic principle of responsibility'.[7]

Quezon was frustrated by the constraints of the Commonwealth government of 1935. He was alleged to have declared that he would prefer 'a government run like hell by Filipinos to one run like heaven by Americans'.[8] 'Independence seems like a marriage', Sukarno declared. 'Who shall wait until the salary rises, say to 500 guilders and setting up house is complete? Marry first!'[9] A trial marriage was impossible. The impracticability of the whole concept, and the impatient response to it, could only further reduce the possibility of intermediate stages between colony and nation-state, reduced, as they already were, by international change.

The concept of preparation for self-government, and in particular for popular self-government, was problematic at best, and its element of self-serving the source of cynicism at home and abroad that helped to lead to attempts to fix a timetable. Yet there was a point that the criticism missed. If the criterion of democratic participation was not met in the period before self-government was granted or independence secured, it could hardly be enforced afterwards. An outside power would be seen as interferingly neo-imperial. Only a population made conscious of its rights could check an elite that, perhaps borrowing other Western traditions or appropriating past Asian experience, was disposed to ignore them. An outside power might, after all, prefer to support a collaborative elite as colonial powers had. The rationale could be offered that 'Asia' was not 'ready' for democracy, and that a 'strong' government was necessary to avoid a communist take-over and facilitate 'development'.

That, however, missed another point, the experience of the late twentieth century suggested. A democracy did require experience, though it could not be provided without independence. It required, as Rizal had recognised, a conscious effort: it required 'economia', the husbanding of resources, and 'transigencia', give and take.[10] That might mean that decisions were disrupted or deferred by contention. Yet that was not an argument for abandoning the process. There were, after all, good reasons to think that, as Harrison said, democracy and stability were connected, and even that 'development' would be more soundly based, and more 'accountable', if afforded the transparency of a democratic process rather than confined to a new version of the court politics and patrimonialism of the past.

World War II, like the first, gave an additional impulse to the democratic cause: the Fascists and the Nazis and the Emperor system had been defeated. Though the Soviet

Union was among the victors, the United States was certainly the most significant of the Allies in Asia. Its anti-imperialism was a factor the colonial powers and their opponents had to take into account, its advocacy of democracy, too. Independence movements realised that they had a better chance of winning outside support if they emphasised their democratic nature. In that respect, their struggle enhanced the identification between the national and the democratic cause. In the early years of the American regime, the *ilustrados* adopted American not Spanish models in the new assembly, knowing that Americans were watching: '[t]hey felt that it would be easier for the latter to judge their performance, and their growing capacity for democratic self-government, if they adopted procedures familiar to Americans'.[11] At the end of World War II the Indonesians were keen to show that their government was orderly and that it was democratic.

The independence movements had, however, also been affected by the Japanese occupation, which had promoted a different approach to politics and a different way of mobilising the masses. It had, too, created new elements within the elite, including in some cases a military leadership that tended to distrust civilian politicians, democratically inclined or otherwise. Yet another source of leadership emerged in the course of guerrilla struggles against the Japanese or, later, the colonial powers. The guerrilla leadership was, of course, bound to be populist. That did not, however, necessarily commit it to a democratic approach, and its position was sufficiently ambiguous to alarm those who were.

Oligarchy in the Philippines

In World War II the United States pledged itself to return to the Philippines, but also to carry out its promise to grant independence according to schedule. Such a programme would demonstrate American success in the war. It would also renew the example the United States had set other colonial powers in the new context created by the war and its ideological dimension. In that programme, independence was closely associated with democracy, as it had been throughout American rule. What had been at issue was the nature of that democracy, the extent to which it offered choice, the numbers of those to whom it offered participation.

Spain's legacy was equivocal. It allowed a very limited kind of democracy, only at the local level. In 1758 the governor-general had deprived the *alcalde* of the power to appoint the *gobernadorcillo*. Instead twelve electors selected by lottery selected three of the *principalia*, one of whom would be recommended to the governor-general by the *alcalde*. The electors had to be able to read and write and to speak Spanish, and so were bound to be wealthy. In the electoral competition bribery, patronage, kinship, and clan or family rivalries played their part. Though Filipinos wanted to show the Americans that they could manage a democracy, many of these practices now emerged on a national scale.

American rule, moreover, tended to strengthen the power of the elite, both by offering it expanded economic and political opportunity and by making it struggle for more. The democratic institutions it set up were, partly as a result, run in an oligarchical manner. Essentially there could only be one political issue, the securing of independence. Politics focused rather on the sharing of power and its promises, and their shift to the national level extended the patron–client relationships that marked Philippines society in the Spanish phase. The setting-up of the Commonwealth government did not alter the position. Independence was at hand, but not yet granted. President Quezon consolidated his position by his extraordinarily adroit use of patronage, coupled with a populist programme of 'Social Justice', designed to meliorate post-Sakdal peasant discontent. In 1934 E. D. Hester had forecast 'an irresponsible autocracy'.[12] 'Our President has more power than Mussolini', General Paulino Santos, an admirer, declared.[13] But, while in some sense the Philippines was naturally a one-party state, it was not a fascist one. Quezon dominated by translating an old style of politics into a new dimension. He was 'the first Filipino politician with the power to integrate all levels of politics into a single system', McCoy points out. At the provincial level he sought to maintain two equally balanced parties at a peak of conflict that facilitated his intervention and manipulation.[14] The limited size of the electorate no doubt made for oligarchy. Expansion would challenge its political style. Would a real party system emerge? or would it resort to Bonapartism?

In the Philippines, as elsewhere, Japan was able to secure collaborators. The exiled revolutionary Artemio Ricarte was brought back, but the collaborators came from the elite in the islands. Reluctantly departing for Corregidor, Quezon made a last-minute and vain appeal for the United States to grant independence, with the idea that the United States would withdraw and guarantee that independence jointly with the Japanese.[15] He told the secretary of justice, José Laurel, and Jorge Vargas, his deeply trusted executive secretary, 'jack of all trades and master of them all',[16] to stay behind and 'deal with the Japanese',[17] adding MacArthur's warning that they should not take an oath to Japan. The Japanese made it clear to Laurel and his colleagues that the alternatives were 'a government of iron backed by military force' or a '*gobierno-muñeco*', a puppet government.[18] They chose the latter. As in the previous invasion of 1898–99, the elite sought order rather than upheaval because, as Grant Goodman suggests, of 'their intense desire to sustain the political, social and economic status quo as far as possible'.[19] It was not after all certain that the Americans would return, whatever MacArthur said—they had planned to go in any case—and they had let the Filipinos down. The elite's position was consolidated by the grant of independence in 1943, when Laurel became president. The political structures that the conquerors set up were, moreover, not without their relevance or their appeal. They were designed to mobilise but control the population, and included the Neighbourhood Association, the Liaison and Public Assistance Service, and the Kalibapi, the Association in the Service of the new Philippines, headed by Vargas and Benigno Aquino, one of those who thought the United States would not return.

At the same time the elite was 'politically astute enough to maintain a foothold among key non-revolutionary guerrilla organizations and thus protect themselves in the event of a Japanese defeat'.[20] It was Ramos, the ex-Sakdal leader, who in 1944 organised the Makapili to fight against the United States and its guerrilla affiliates. In southern Luzon the position was different again. There the landlords fled to Manila, and the Hukbalahap, emerging in part from the pre-war peasant movement, took over control. Resisting repression by the Japanese and the PC, they were seen as 'communist-inspired' by Edward Lansdale, chief of US military intelligence.[21]

Collaboration was to become an issue in the postwar Philippines, and indeed to contribute to the emergence of a two-party system. But reality changed less than rhetoric. Collaboration was indeed not the main issue, but reconstruction. Like Burma, the Philippines was fought over twice, and the destruction had been very great: 'without question the most completely destroyed and dislocated battle ground of the war'.[22] The United States was expected to help towards rehabilitation in a substantial way, and that prospect, with apparently immense opportunities for 'pork-barrel', refocused Philippines politics along non-ideological lines. Members of the two parties that emerged did not greatly differ: they were aggregations of factions that the leaders tried to hold together. In fact the two-party system was, in O. D. Corpuz's telling phrase, a one-and-a-half party system.[23]

The analysis the acting British consul offered in May 1945 was cynical but not invalid. Accustomed to thinking that they were in a different category from other colonial peoples, D. F. MacDermot wrote, the Filipinos looked for 'a shower of gold'.

> This belief in Santa Claus reduces Filipino political interest to two questions: how much is America going to pay, and who is going to control the money? … Independence … is seen as an advantage in that it will limit outside interference with the disposal of the loot; as a disadvantage by those who fear that even a generous America may not adequately cushion the shock of separation from American economic protection. … Collaboration … is regarded not so much as having been a reprehensible action in itself … but as a stick with which one clique may belabour another when the time comes to scramble for the gold.[24]

While Osmena had been saddled by the United States with the task of punishing collaborators, MacArthur supported Roxas's bid to be President. He was seen as the best guarantee of a stable and pro-American government. Backed by the deceased Quezon's old financiers, he was also joined by other factions, because Osmena was thought to be harder on collaborationists. At the same time, he was supported by the conservative USAFFE guerrillas, anti-Huk and anti-communist, partly because MacArthur supported him. Osmena tried to postpone the presidential election till after independence, to avoid an anti-collaborationist stance, to obtain material aid from the United States, all in vain. Under the Commonwealth he had deferred to Quezon, and now he had even stronger reasons for preferring a monolithic kind of government based on intra-elite compromise. He could not get it, and he blamed Roxas' competitive approach for undermining elite hegemony.

Finally Osmena turned to the nascent Democratic Alliance, which included Manila reformers and ex-Huk guerrilla elements, and backed anti-collaborationism with anti-establishment feeling. He lost the election by a slight margin. Roxas now tried to consolidate his position with pork-barrel and patronage. The resources had to come from the United States, and he deferred to its interests. But nothing like what he wanted was forthcoming. Under the leadership of the wartime leader Laurel opposition factions were solidified on a 'nationalist' basis—directed against the 'parity' of treatment for its citizens the United States had required when granting an independence privileged by trade concessions and rehabilitation—though Laurel avoided open opposition until he secured amnesty early in 1948.

That hardly meant the creation of a second party. At the same time the defeat of Osmena cut out the element of popular participation he had been forced to contemplate. To get the parity amendment through Congress and thus benefit from the Bell Trade Act, Roxas and his Liberals had denied three Senators and nine Congressmen their seats. Six of the nine were from the Democratic Alliance and one other sympathetic, and the move effectively denied the radicals and Huk affiliates entry into a non-violent political process. Taking over on Roxas' death, the Vice-President, Quirino, allowed Luis Taruc and his followers to take their seats, and they took part in the 1949 presidential election, vainly supporting his rival, the now openly active Laurel. But, failing to provide effective participation, the regime also failed to offer effective land reform. The violence of the army and the constabulary completed the alienation of the peasantry in Central Luzon, who had already faced the returned landlords and renewed repression, and the Huk movement revived. At first the Communist Party opposed rebellion. Only after May 1948 did it endorse armed struggle.

It was this that, in the growing Cold War of the early 1950s, drew US attention to the land reform issue, and indeed prompted it to play a more active role than it had pursued before it had granted independence: Robert Hardie's report of 1952 pointed out that 'officially constituted bodies have been recommending remedial action since the time of Taft'.[25] The United States responded promptly to Quirino's request for an economic mission. The object of the Bell mission of 1950 was 'to see what could be done to make of the Philippines a reliable ally and a secure base in the Pacific'.[26] Under the subsequent Quirino–Foster agreement of November 1950, the Philippines agreed to initiate reforms in return for American technical and economic assistance. Hardie recommended vast changes that would substantially eliminate tenancy. The agrarian problem became a major issue in the 1953 presidential campaign.

That was won by Ramon Magsaysay, Secretary for Defence under Quirino, but now candidate for the Nacionalistas. The support of Laurel's party was not his only advantage. He had carried on an effective campaign against the Huks, making the army and constabulary less abusive, but also offering education and resettlement to those who were captured or surrendered. That also won him the approval of the Americans. His proposals for agrarian reform indeed in some respects resembled those Hardie put forward. He won, too, the support of the smaller Democrata Party which, representing the sugar interests of the Visayas, needed good relations with the United States, but also hoped to confine agrarian reform to the rice areas of Luzon. Once elected, however, Magsaysay was, partly for this reason, to find it impossible to carry through the effective programme of land reform to which he had committed himself. The Land Tenure Bill was pushed through Congress only in face of extensive opposition, some of it from middle-class elements that were in fact substantially dependent on income from rice estates, and from intellectuals, who saw it as a guarantee of continued dependence on the United States.

The Huk leader Taruc had surrendered in 1954, and Jesus Lava sought to negotiate and emerge into the politics of coexistence. There was indeed a great deal of popular support for Magsaysay. He had set a precedent by carrying his campaign to the barrios, engaging in stunts, as Quirino called them, to appeal to the people. His failure to deliver the reforms he promised can be explained in the context of the regime within which he worked: the kind of elite support that he needed to become President prevented his meeting when in office the expectations he had aroused in the barrios. That interpretation has generally influenced the judgment on his presidency. But the subsequent history of the Philippines, and in particular of the Marcos phase, may modify an earlier point of view. The campaign in the barrios suggests a Bonapartist answer to the problems of the regime, rather than a democratic one. Instead of strengthening the democratic system by popularising it, it ran the risk of by-passing it, and of rendering it, not responsive, but redundant.

In hindsight it is, of course, too easy to discount the democratic features of the regime and to dismiss its potential. The separation of church and state was maintained; the press was strikingly free and keen to expose corruption; the civilians were clearly in control of the military, even if it played a more substantial role than used to be thought. Nor did the country fall apart, as Quezon had feared. 'What shall we do when the Americans are gone', he had asked at the Letran college in 1937, 'when that stimulus to be united no longer exists? We shall have strife such as that which existed when we were students here ... and when the Tagalogs used to fight with the Ilocanos, the Pampangos with the Visayans, the Visayans with the Tagalogs'.[27] The practice was to balance Luzon with the Visayas on the presidential/vice-presidential ticket.

The electorate expanded, partly as a result of the spread of literacy, and then also as a result of an easing of the qualification; and, though the president even in 1964 could not reach more than one-third of the population in any one language, the turn-out was respectable. In 1953, the electorate was 5.25 million: 78 per cent voted. In 1961 the figures were 9 million and 70 per cent. The Magsaysay campaign had indeed clearly had an effect. So, no doubt, did patron–client pressures. The system was certainly still based on factions rather than parties, and changing sides was not uncommon: in 1961, indeed, patronage and pork-barrel transformed the Nacionalista majority that the election had produced in Congress into a Liberal one. Even so, the system tended to produce an alternation in power, the strongest evidence being that no president was ever elected for two terms. That made it a relatively effective distributor of goods and services. 'We have a two-party system all right; abuses are checked by regularly throwing the abusers out of power.'[28] What was missing was an active attempt to modernise the way the population was increasingly participating in the electoral institutions and to realise their democratic potential. '[W]e must learn to make democracy more than a word, a slogan, a fetish', Senator Claro M. Recto declared in 1952, 'and to look upon it as a dynamic thing, a practical business'.[29] Instead new elements in the elite were to look to a stronger executive, and President Marcos was to write old Bonapartism very large.

Postwar exchange controls helped to promote import-substituting industrialisation. In that the landed elite showed only a limited interest, and they opposed the continuance of controls that reduced the competitiveness of their exports. In 1962 Macapagal offered a compromise. He devalued the peso, thus helping the exporters, but used tariffs to protect the industrialists. The latter—by origin Chinese merchants, Filipino traders, civil servants, and professionals—needed access to capital and also to government favour, the means to secure import permits and licences. That contributed to corruption, and also to the growth of executive power. Increased political participation, meanwhile, transferred some power from the landholding factions to professional politicians, dependent on national party funds to mobilise voters at the local level.

Those changes did not suggest that the development of Philippines democracy was impossible. In some sense, indeed, they suggested the reverse. But, as Gary Hawes argues, the economic dynamism of import substitution industrialisation, and of the 'Filipino First' policies followed since Magsaysay, was exhausted by the late 1960s.[30] The technocrats therefore wanted to open up the economy and they looked for structural reform. Even that did not necessarily mean an end to democratisation, though US policy-makers were increasingly taking the view that development required, at least in the initial stages, an authoritarian regime. Nationalists were after all critical of the influence the United States still exerted in the Philippines. What the constitutional convention of 1971 proposed was a new system, fundamentally changing the role of the presidency, and introducing a prime minister. The framers moved to prevent either Marcos or his wife from taking that office, and that prompted his seizure of power.

Elected President in 1965, Marcos had been demonstrating the inadequacies of the old system, but also increasing them. In the former role, he seemed like a new Magsaysay, making direct contact with the barrios, and using the army in civic action. But, while popularising President and army, that tended to weaken existing political structures and civilian leaders, while technocrats were tempted to think that a 'strong man' might be the means of the restructuring they sought. At the same time, Marcos made change more necessary by abusing the old system. He determined to break the precedent that had helped to sustain it by winning a second term of office in 1969. That he achieved, and indeed he won all ten regions, even Cebu, his rival's home province, though at such a cost to the economic position of the Philippines that restructuring seemed more urgent. '[T]he vanquished Liberals managed to secure enough popular backing to sustain their hope of eventually recovering from their defeat, rallying disaffected majority leaders and alienated citizens for a return to Malacanang', wrote José Abueva in 1970. 'It is this realistic chance of recouping lost public favor and political favor ... that makes the "outs" persevere within the constitutional framework and that promotes political stability in a country where poverty and inequalities abound.'[31] But succession in office added to the tension in another way: it reduced the distributive effectiveness of the one-and-a-half-party system still further.

The crisis was not in itself an argument for abandoning democracy: it was indeed seen as an argument for reconstructing it. It was certainly not an argument for putting more power into the hands of Marcos. His coup, however, ensured that reconstruction led that way. He presented himself as a reformer, and for a while many were convinced, inside the Philippines and outside. But though he was readily able to destroy the old political structures, his authoritarianism did not really attempt to create the New Society of which he spoke. His aims were political.

The postwar experience of the Philippines underlines the wisdom in Will Rogers' humour. What countries were 'ready' for self-government? None. To develop a democratic system needed continued commitment and patient effort, and it was never likely to be perfect. It was not something easily taught, certainly not something a colonial power could easily teach, but it was something that had to be learned. Tied to the notion of independence in a world of nation-states, the idea could not be simply jettisoned. Its future depended on the extent to which the elite was able and willing to use it, and, though much less, and sometimes to its disadvantage, the extent to which it was encouraged or enjoined by other nation-states. To expect it to operate in newly independent Asian countries even with the kind of efficiency it demonstrated in some at least of the Western countries was quite unrealistic.

A democratic system took hold in the Philippines partly because it suited the elite and partly because it suited the colonial powers. '[T]o the extent that there was [now] a failure of democracy, it was a failure not of the institutions per se, but rather of the commitment of the political elite to make those institutions work.'[32] The Filipinos were to reject the Bonapartism that Marcos introduced, but even he sought to present his regime in terms of participation, arguing, in an echo of Taft or Wood, that the New Society would be less oligarchical than the old.

Past and present in Burma

Parliamentary democracy in Burma had no real links to history or reality, Michael Aung-Thwin has argued. It was 'a current fad (democracy had recently triumphed over fascism), adopted for a variety of (usually non-indigenous, non-autonomous) reasons', 'a foreign system', imposed on Burma and with little to support it. The 1962 military take-over turned this around. The year 1948 saw the paramountcy of a small, 'middle', capitalist class, concerned with economic development. 'The place of the military and bureaucracy … has always been paramount in Burmese history. …' The post-1962 economic systems were 'modern versions of the pre-1886 indigenous form, rather than of the colonial and post-1948 form'.[33] 1948, Aung-Thwin insists, was not a watershed. It was significant for the Westernising elite, but for most it was 'meaningless'. It was followed by chaos and disorder. But 1962 also involved 'a collective psychological desire to establish "real" independence, which necessarily included purging one's colonial past'. The Burmese were concerned with 'a meaningful and ordered society that preserved traditional patterns, and with finding some way to recover a lost identity', reacting less to the few years after 1948 than to the many years of colonial rule.[34]

The analysis seems over-emphatic. What the military did could certainly be presented and perhaps understood in this way, but it was also clearly selective and self-serving. It is possible to see continuities with the tradition that Pagan established and that succeeding dynasties sought to emulate. But that another approach had also taken root was surely only emphasised by the recrudescence of the democratic movement in the late 1980s, even though that, as Aung-Thwin has recently argued, owed a great deal to intra-elite struggle.

Prior to the declaration of independence on 1 August 1943, the Japanese had set up an Independence Preparatory Committee, which prepared a constitution, and then, as a state assembly, ratified it. During the discussions Tun Oke, Ba Sein, and Kodaw Hmaing advocated restoring the monarchy. In the event Ba Maw became *adipadi*, or head of state, but used royal forms and, though himself a Christian, patronised Buddhism. A privy council, appointed by the *adipadi*, was entirely advisory. 'In an address to it in November 1943 Ba Maw made it clear that the Privy Council is organically different from a popular assembly or legislature and that it is not intended to represent the people but to give private counsel to "the sovereign" (Ba Maw).'[35] The monolithic structure favoured by the Japanese was not unlike their own Meiji constitution. As in Japan, too, the minister for defence was a serving officer. The structure, however, took on traditional features, but, as indeed in the Meiji case, they were transformed in the process. They were to be a means of mobilising the masses, coupled with a single party, Maha Burma, and a range of national organisations. Members of the elite worked within this new structure for a mixture of reasons, as in the Philippines. It related them to the masses, but not on a democratic basis. Whatever the legacy of monarchy, the occupation superimposed a legacy of authoritarianism that mixed the old and the new.

The colonial power had under pressure from the elite offered some experience of a more democratic process. Its wartime plans involved going back on that and reinstituting direct rule, partly in order to rehabilitate a Burma which, like the Philippines, had been fought over twice, but also for the somewhat paradoxical purpose of creating a more effective democratic system. Suspending popular politics was, however, unrealistic, as the returning governor quickly realised, but he was unable to come to terms with the AFPFL. At the core of the dispute was the nature of democracy in Burma. Backed by both wartime planning and the policy of the new Labour government, Dorman-Smith wanted to institute a multi-party system, seeing the AFPFL, despite its name, in the image of the one-party regimes against which the war had been fought. He failed, but the struggle at least made AFPFL more insistent on gaining a popular backing and adopting constitutional practices, whatever the extent of their de facto mobilisation of power. The British government shifted its policy and, as Mountbatten had earlier advocated, worked with the AFPFL.

The break between Aung San's leadership and the communists, first the Red Flags of Soe, and then the White Flags of Than Tun, did not represent the triumph of a middle-class leadership, but rather a dispute over strategy within a middle-class leadership. The question was whether the communists would work or be allowed to work within the system, or challenge not the government of the day but the system itself. In fact Soe chose overthrow, and Than Tun chose mass opposition. Then, with the threat of arrest, he went underground in March 1948, a decision that coincided with the new 'struggle' line.

The assassination of Aung San in July 1947 was brought about by Saw, an old-time politician not prepared to work within the system—which he thought had consolidated AFPFL dominance—and use what was being set up as a means of challenging those who had played a leading role in setting it up. 'To stay in Burma longer, to clear the place up, to create the conditions for at least something approaching a responsible democracy—an Augean stables of a job—would have required more nerve and sinew than we seemed to have available for this forgotten satrapy in 1946 and 1947, after men had died in their thousands to retrieve it', the late Louis Allen remarked.[36] Even if Britain had been in a stronger position, however, it is doubtful that it could have done more to create the 'conditions' for a democracy. Such endeavours, questionable pre-war, were even more likely to be counter-productive postwar. The attempts to create a multi-party system had themselves been disastrous, strengthening AFPFL resolve, and reviving Saw's ambition without offering any prospect of its realisation. In any case Aung San's death not only ensured that his successors fought for complete independence. It also seemed that in death, as much as or even more than in life, he stood for a democratic approach to Burma's politics.

Beset in its initial years by communist-led and ethnic unrest, the government of independent Burma sought to win popular support by programmes couched in terms both of left-wing socialism and of popular Burman tradition: the object was a welfare state, Pyidawtha (Happy Land). 'Our heritage is proud and strong, but our true history lies ahead.'[37] A measure of the political success of the system was electoral participation: 3.9 million voted in 1956; 6.6 million in 1960. The divisions that appeared within the ruling AFPFL were not an indication that the system had failed, but they were a challenge to develop it so that it might accommodate them. The challenge was not met.

The prosperity of the Korean War phase had helped to keep the league together, but from 1955 capital was in shorter supply. That encouraged tension among the leaders. Struggling for independence had in general been a unifying factor: deciding on the future of an independent country raised ideological issues about the nature of the state and the policies its government should pursue, issues, too, of allocation and priority, connected in turn with issues of power and patronage, potentially divisive and likely to promote factional rivalry. The aim, it had been agreed, was a welfare state. Not all the elite were agreed, however, on the emphasis given to industrialisation. When the economic position deteriorated, the disputes became more serious, especially as AFPFL leaders had based their political support on promoting particular programmes and on the patronage that offered, on pork-barrel and log-rolling, as Frank Trager put it.[38] The divisions were the more intense because, as Prime Minister Nu was to admit, the civil service itself became politicised: 'we appointed party adherents as civil servants. … We came dangerously close to creating a party civil service of the kind that exists in totalitarian states.'[39] Whatever the impact on efficiency in times of prosperity, that magnified the difficulties in times of adversity.

The differences among the Thakins over the role of industrialisation to some extent reflected the different levels of Westernisation among them and among the popular elements to which they appealed. The socialist core of the AFPFL was divided by 1953, Thakin Tin and Kyaw Tun, who were not graduates, concerning themselves above all with the agricultural programme, as distinct from the 'college set', led by Kyaw Nyein and Ba Swe. Without an organisation of his own, Nu was jealous of Ba Swe and Kyaw Thein, and sought support among the minorities and, somewhat contradictorily, among Buddhists, his initiative lying behind the Sixth Theravada Synod in 1954–56. The curbs on the development programme brought out the differences within the leadership, articulating differences among Burmese more generally. That brought about the crisis of 1958.

The elections of 1951 had witnessed a complete triumph for the AFPFL, except in Arakan. Those of 1956 saw the growth of an opposition group, the National Unity Front, more left-wing, reflecting popular disappointment with the achievements of the welfare state programme, as well perhaps as the new orientation of international communism. In the split that occurred mid-1958 Nu and the Tin faction turned to the Front for support, and to the Shan and Arakanese minorities, Nu coming out openly for an Arakanese state. In face of their opponents, Kyaw Nyein and Ba Swe, they survived a no-confidence motion in the Chamber of Deputies. Nu's faction, the 'Clean' AFPFL, prepared for elections by seeking support from the minorities, Nu now holding out the prospect of a Mon state, and from the left, offering generous amnesty terms to surrendering communists, PVOs and other rebels, hoping thus to defeat the other faction, the 'Stable' AFPFL. In September, however, the army stepped in, prompted, it is said, by younger pro-Stable officers, concerned at the advance of communism, the decline of security, and the threat to the Union itself involved in the promises to the minorities. Indeed Brigadier Aung

Gyi had close relations with the Stable faction, though it was Nu who formally asked Ne Win to intervene.

Divisions within the ruling party had led to the creation, it might be said, of one-and-a-half parties, faction-ridden, but with the potential, perhaps, of a more effective articulation of the aspirations of the Burmese electorate. That this was not the route that the development of the Burmese system followed does not prove that the system was irrelevant or that the Burmese were not fit for democracy. There is, however, a clear indication that politicians were prepared to step outside the system, initially at least, however, with the idea that the military, almost Dorman-Smith-style, might put it right.

Though prolonged beyond its constitutional limit, the military intervention of 1958 was indeed temporary. Ne Win assumed the premiership on a caretaker basis. His regime worked against Nu, of whom Ne Win was a long-standing rival. Its objective was, however, still to create conditions in which the democratic system could work more effectively, though it has also been suggested that one of the reasons the army returned power to the civilians was it had experienced its own factionalism and feared the damage to its unity.[40] In any case the new elections, finally held in 1960, were a triumph for Nu and Tin, and in that sense the army leaders had to judge that their intervention had failed. They were, however, given another opportunity.

The elections had again turned partly on patronage. Nu's Pyidaungsu party itself split, a rural faction, calling itself the Thakins, overcoming its urban-based components. They wanted the cancellation of import licences, though they were important to the businessmen who financed the party, and the setting-up of government companies which they hoped to dominate.[41] Nu's electoral success owed much not merely to left-wing and minority support and to popular dislike of the army's authoritarianism, but also to his charisma and to his association with Buddhism. He also ordered the construction of two national *nat* shrines. The promises he held out, however, could not all be realised. In a constitutional amendment of 1961, he carried out a pledge to make Buddhism the state religion, but that produced opposition from a National Religious Minorities Alliance, representing three million non-Buddhists. Even Buddhist minorities were alienated, because Nu had promised them more political autonomy than he could now offer: the hopes of the Shans had been raised, and the attitude of the caretaker regime had produced open rebellion. But Nu could not satisfy them.

Opposed to Nu's religious and federalist policies, Ne Win carried out a second coup in 1962. This time the army's intervention was not temporary: the aim was not caretaking, but revolution. Utilising left-wing concepts and initially winning NUF support, it set up a Revolutionary Council, comprised of seventeen self-chosen military officers led by Ne Win, which formulated a programme, *The Burmese Way to Socialism,* announced on 30 April. It constructed the Lanzin or Burma Socialist Programme Party, and subsequently, in 1964, outlawed the remnants of all the other parties. The ideology of the party was expressed in a paper mostly drafted by U Chit

Hlaing, *The System of Correlation of Man and his Environment,* a rehash of Marxism and a dash of Buddhism. Initially Aung Gyi set Burma on the track of economic growth, as perhaps the earlier connexion with the Stable suggested he might, but in 1963 Ne Win removed him, and turned to Ba Nyein, Tin Pe, and the Thakin leftists. They intensified the policy of nationalisation and promoted the cooperative movement. But in 1971 income per capita was still below 1938–39 levels, and in 1972 the Lanzin's new programme accepted the concept of foreign assistance and re-emphasised agriculture.

Ne Win, says Badgley, came to govern like a tyrannical king, drawing his ministers from the military, especially the 4th Regiment he had commanded in the Japanese phase.[42] He demanded discipline from the Sangha, calling the All-Sangha All-Sect convention at Hmawbi in 1965 in order to purify the hierarchy, also forcing through a limited registration of monks. While there were parallels with the past, however, they are not exact. 'Although I have argued', Wiant writes, 'that the most powerful political symbols of the Burmese revolution have their genesis in the past, the revolution in Burma is anything but an attempt to recreate the past. ... its aspirations are projective ... an attempt to forge a society which has no historical analogue.'[43] The regime, like its predecessor, offered a mix of the old and the new: if it echoed the old monarchy, it also echoed European socialism. But it abandoned the democratic commitment that its predecessor had included.

The concept of democracy survived. Anti-dictatorship had, after all, been the main theme of Nu's speeches in 1960, insists Chao Tzang Yawnghwe. 'The Burmese voters may be many things, even superstitious and unworthy of democracy, but they nevertheless chose democracy and U Nu in 1960.' Western thought, he adds, has a basic contradiction: democracy is an 'alien transplant'; but the nation-state, also a transplant, has a sanctity in Western eyes.[44] 'The kind of commonwealth that can prosper within Burma's current boundaries', Badgley added, 'has yet to be devised'.[45] Persisting with a democratic approach might have led the Burmese to it.

Parliamentary and 'guided' democracy

Concerned lest they indicated that the United States would leave Southeast Asia, the Dutch had also thought that its reforms in the interwar Philippines were too precipitate: even Governor-General de Graeff, who extended the powers and membership of the Volksraad, thought that the Americans had given the Filipinos too much too quickly.[46] The Dutch were characteristically ambivalent about the Volksraad. The result of expanding its role, Idenburg had told van Limburg Stirum in 1918, would be 'an oligarchy of the worst kind, that is, of incapable people'.[47] The Indies were 'unripe': a parliament 'with responsible government powers' would lead to their total loss.[48] But though the Volksraad's powers and its electorate remained limited, it did offer nationalists who were prepared to collaborate—Thamrin, Soetardjo, and Ratulangie, for example—a limited democratic experience. Most nationalists declined to collaborate, however, and following the 1934 crackdown by de Graeff's successor, de Jonge, many leaders were in internal exile. After the disturbances of the 1920s, and given the risks of the Depression, the Dutch were indeed determined to isolate the elite, cooperating or not, from the masses.

The Japanese occupation changed that. The Japanese did not, of course, directly contribute to the creation of a multi-party democracy: democracy was 'a declining form'.[49] Their policy throughout Southeast Asia was to mobilise support for the war effort. Nowhere was democracy their chosen route, and in Indonesia they did not need till late in 1944 even to make the gestures towards independence they made in Burma and the Philippines. Like all regimes, they did, however, need collaborators, and that was particularly the case because they needed to hold their conquests with a minimum military force. They needed, too, a level of popular mobilisation beyond that the colonial powers had sought. Their policies tended therefore to give the elite greater opportunities and to transform its political and administrative experience. They tended, too, to transform its contact with the masses. What the Japanese did thus had unintended outcomes, and those in turn affected the prospects for a democratic system of politics when their occupation came to an end.

The transformation of the position of the non-collaborating secular nationalists was only the most obvious of the changes: it was far from being the only one. Parindra members were prominent in the Triple-A movement, started in March 1942. Once the Japanese administration had been built up, however, it turned to non-collaborators. Though Sukarno and Hatta failed to get it openly to acknowledge 'Indonesia', they were prominent in Poetera (Poesat Tenaga Rakyat, Centre of People's Power), inaugurated by the Japanese in March 1943. It operated, however, mainly among the urban intellectuals. For the mobilisation of the masses the Japanese relied rather upon the native administrator corps. The *pangreh praja* were all the more necessary because the Japanese were themselves poorly prepared to administer Java and interned the Dutch. Particularly below the national level, they were the main element in the Jawa Hokokai (Himpoenan Kebaktian Rakyat, People's Loyalty Association), intended to be an all-inclusive mass organisation similar to the Imperial Rule Assistance Association (Taisei Yokusankai) in Japan itself, and announced in January 1944.[50] The aim, as with other organisations, was to reinforce the administrative machinery by juxtaposing an all-embracing mass organisation.

The secular nationalists attained a national role that the Dutch had denied them, but their contacts with the masses were still limited. The Japanese aimed at 'mobilization without politicization',[51] and had no wish to pay the price of the latter for the limited amount of the former that the nationalists were in a position to offer after the crackdown of the 1930s. That, however, was not entirely to their disadvantage. For the *pangreh praja* accumulated not only the advantages of collaboration, but also the disadvantages, which increased as the conditions in Java grew harsher. The same was true for the *uleebalang* in Aceh: '[t]hey were between the frying pan and the fire'.[52] The secular nationalists avoided so substantial an identification with an oppressive regime. They still inherited a problem when the opportunity came to assume power. Was the new state to be built on a 'social revolution' or was it too to rely on a traditional elite, now more discredited?

Under the Dutch alienated peasants had tended to look to Islam and to Islamic leaders. Maximising its influence by reversing Dutch policy, the Japanese government gave them a greater role, establishing an overall Muslim organisation, Masjoemi, in 1943, and a religious affairs section (*shumuka*) in each residency after April 1944. The aim was to win over the *ulama*, and to use them to help the occupation forces 'grasp men's minds', as the Japanese put it. In his pioneering work, *The Crescent and the Rising Sun*, Harry Benda depicted this change of policy in terms of divide-and-rule. In fact, Aiko Kurasawa suggests, the Japanese wanted the *pangreh praja* to guide the *ulama*, and the *ulama* and their *santri* were often set to work within the framework of the Hokokai. The Japanese emphasis was on eliminating rivalries and eliciting cooperation. The *ulama* were not given power: they were propagandists. The military administration 'never relaxed its caution towards Moslem leaders'.[53] But, as she says, Muslim leaders were brought into national-level politics and recruited into government agencies. Their experience secured them the basis for political advancement in postwar Indonesia.

Though their aim was to eliminate rivalries and elicit collaboration, the Japanese created other organisations that under a different political system could contend for leadership. If it changed the role of the *ulama*, their popular mobilisation also changed the role of youth. In some sense that was the Japanese move with the most revolutionary potential. Not only in Indonesia, but elsewhere, it challenged traditional deference on the widest scale, and others were to utilise the social and political energy that could be released. Seinendan (*barisan pemoeda*) (youth corps) were introduced, again on the model of an organisation in Japan, on the Emperor's birthday, 29 April 1943. 'In order to convince the youth of Java to work actively with the government and to support the construction of the Co-Prosperity Sphere in Greater Asia, it is necessary that they be given guidance and education.'[54] The Japanese authorities wanted to channel the energies they released: they sought to keep *seinendan* under the control of the *pangreh praja* and avoid ties with the nationalists and Poetera. The major impact, Kurasawa suggests, was on village youth, bringing it contact with urban society, enhancing self-confidence and status. But the movement set off in directions that had not been anticipated, particularly after the surrender.

In reorganising the army, the Japanese again broke the colonial pattern, in part in response to the short-term necessity of maximising support, in part guided by their tendency, in the absence of any developed plan for the Southeast Asian conquests, to follow precedents set by their own model of modernisation, exemplar for the nations of the Sphere. The major change was the creation of PETA, with officers recruited from the majority community, and trained in a style that differed from KNIL's. After the surrender, they, too, were to claim a political role, as well as a military one.

In face of the various contenders for power, the position of the secular nationalists was boosted by the preparations for independence that belatedly followed the Koiso announcement. Perhaps partly prompted by the Blitar mutiny of February

1945, the military authorities, albeit reluctantly, began to imitate the pattern set in Burma and the Philippines, and set up an investigatory committee in March, to be followed only on 7 August by a preparatory committee. The most famous product of the first session of the former was Sukarno's articulation of the state ideology, the Pantjasila, which endorsed nationalism, humanity, popular sovereignty, social justice, and faith in one God. A second meeting discussed religion again and also the boundaries of the state.

The skills of the secular nationalists added to their influence. Those present did not, of course, include Indonesians who conceived that the new state should be based on democratic forms of participation. It would be a mistake, however, to conclude that the forms of government devised in 1945 were designed to offer the occupiers the flattery of imitation. Yet it would also be a mistake simply to see them as a reflection of an Indonesian or Javanese tradition that compelled the rejection of any Western model. Like the Meiji leaders, the Indonesians looked rather to a different Western model, that shaped by German, rather than French or English or American, experience. That enabled them to evoke tradition, but the result was, of course, to create something new. Western philosophy had become part of their discourse on the nature of the state. If it was an invitation to invoke other values, it was bound to shape them.

In the debates of the investigating committee on 31 May Raden Supomo had, as David Bourchier tells us, outlined his vision of the integralist state. Indonesian village communities, he said, were characterised by attachment to communal harmony, social solidarity, a feeling of oneness with the leaders. The only appropriate *staatsidee* was one that put the highest value on social harmony and the preservation of time-honoured bonds between the ruler and the ruled. That, as J. H. A. Logemann was to point out, corresponded to the organic state of the continental philosophers, in which the state is synonymous with organised society and embodies the *Volksgeist.* Indeed Supomo quoted Hegel, Spinoza, and Adam Müller, and had been introduced to National Socialist ideology in the Netherlands. What he wanted, however, was not a fascist state, but one that mirrored the village community in mutual help (*gotong royong*) and familyness (*kekeluargan*).[55] These ideas were reflected in the constitution that the committee proposed, though, at the instance of Hatta and his supporters, it also provided, rather inconsistently, for political rights.

In Indonesia, by contrast to the Philippines, there was no guerrilla struggle, and, by contrast to Burma, there was no Force 136. No substantial underground group contended with the collaborating elite led by Sukarno and Hatta. There were, however, dissident elements, including the ex-Gerindo group led, until his arrest in 1943, by Sjarifuddin, leader of the illegal PKI founded by Musso on his visit to Surabaya in 1935–36, pursuant to the Comintern popular front line; the group led by Sukarni, an associate of the non-Stalinist Tan Malaka, and by Chaireul Saleh; and the group led by the Socialist Sjahrir and by Roeslan Abdulgani. It was the last whose fortunes were to be boosted by the attempts of the Republic to win international support after the surrender.

The Republic was proclaimed on 17 August, after the Japanese surrender but well before the Allies, let alone the Dutch themselves, were ready to take over. In the interim it sought to strengthen its position, partly, indeed, so that it might appear, as the Philippine Republic had hoped to appear in 1898, as a fait accompli. The 'top priority' of the first cabinet 'was to demonstrate its authority over an orderly population'.[56] That committed it, too, to using the *pangreh praja* and to limiting the prospects of social revolution, stirred up by the harshness of the occupation, the association with it of the *pangreh praja*, the activities of the *pemuda* and of the *jago* and *jawara*. But it also committed it to adopting a more democratic approach to political participation. Its strategy was 'one of going over the heads of the Dutch to appeal directly to the Allies for recognition'.[57] Obsessed with the issue of collaboration, the Dutch condemned a Republic nurtured and led by Sukarno, a 'puppet regime', a 'last-minute organisation'.[58] The Republic showed its more democratic side in order to counter their influence on the Allies, particularly the British, who led the occupying forces.

Late in August it had set up a Central Indonesian National Committee (KNIP), including members of the preparatory committee and 135 other nominees, representing a variety of opinions, though de-emphasising Islamic and *pemuda* elements. Early in November it was decided to encourage the formation of competing parties, 'because with such parties every current of thought which exists in society can be guided into an orderly path'.[59] They were soon set up, including a Socialist party led by Sjahrir and Sjarifuddin; a re-established PKI; a Masjumi party and a new PNI. Sjahrir published his pamphlet *Our Struggle*. 'Indonesia's fate ultimately depends on the fate of Anglo-Saxon capitalism and imperialism', he declared. Its power must not be mobilised behind the Dutch. Indonesians should aim to increase the world's confidence 'that we are capable of disciplined ordering of our state and nation'.[60] A Sjahrir cabinet was installed, and, though elections were not held, the multi-party system gave expression to a wide variety of the political interests created before the war and in the occupation.

Not all accepted this form of politics. Men like Tan Malaka looked to social revolution and to a struggle with the Dutch. In Java unrest was contained with difficulty, and in Sumatra the Republic had to accept the killing of the East Coast rajas. Indeed the initial failures of the Sjahrir policy of *diplomasi* also tested the political approach adopted within the Republic, while the communist leaders were influenced by the shift in international communism late in 1947. The premature communist insurrection of 1948—which Sjarifuddin and his rival Muso, just back from Moscow, could not but join—was, however, defeated, and that won the Republic the decisive support of the United States. Moreover, while the Dutch had sought to counter the Republic by revivifying federalism, they had to commit themselves to forms of participation, time-serving though some of those involved may have been. The sovereign Indonesia of 1950 began its political life with a parliament that included both federalists and Republicans. Though its members, all appointed, were apprehensive of the outcome, and slow to act, it was committed to a further step towards democracy, the creation and operation of an electoral system. Elections for a parliament and for a constituent assembly were finally held in 1955.

The difficulties the new state had faced in the interim added, to an unrealistic degree, to the hopes attached to the elections. Once independence had been secured in 1949, it became necessary to decide on the kind of state it was and the kind of policies it should adopt. It was quickly decided that Indonesia should be a unitary state, not a federal one, since federalism was associated with the Dutch and their struggle against the Republic.

> Although a federal system is, in fact, suitable for such a far-flung archipelago as Indonesia, and might be expected to strengthen the feeling of unity, the manner and timing of the move by the Netherlands Indies Government had aroused such antipathy towards ideas of federation that it was found necessary to make the change from a federal to a unitary state before a constituent assembly could be formed to draw up a definitive constitution,

as Hatta, the vice-president, a Sumatran, put it.[61] Only one attempt was made to secede: the Republic of the South Moluccas was proclaimed in April 1950. But though the inclusion of the federalists in the appointed parliament reduced the possibility that the unitary state would be dominated by the largest single group, the Javanese, its ideology shaped by their views, and its policies by their interests, it did not eliminate it. Would all the Javanese share the same interests and ideology or would they be differentiated? To what extent would they share interests or ideology with the Outer Islands? There was a risk that politics would focus not simply on the sense of national union that the struggle for independence had tended to create, but on so-called 'primordial' allegiances, on the sense of belonging to a *suku*, Javanese, Sundanese, Acehnese, or identifying with an *aliran* or way of life, *santri* or *abangan*.

The unitary state was also a centralised one. That made the decisions about its nature and about its priorities more important, but also more difficult to resolve. The parties that had been created or recreated since 1945—cliques or collections of cliques that sought to win power at the centre—tended to focus on such issues, and their struggles deepened their differences. One of the main differences was over the role of Islam in the state. Back in 1945 some had sought the creation of a Islamic state, but the secular nationalists had opposed it. No advocate of an Islamic state, Sukarno had sought unity by compromise. The constitution would incorporate the Pantjasila he had enunciated, but add to the principle 'belief in one God', put first, the so-called seven words or Jakarta charter, 'with the obligation of the adherents of Islam to practise Islamic law'. But the secular leaders had taken advantage of the urgency of August to get the compromise dropped, as also the provision that the president should be a Muslim. It was thus an unresolved issue and a source of tension. The other main division was in the economic sphere. Most were agreed that foreigners should not play a dominant economic role in the post-colonial state. To define their role more specifically, however, required further decisions about the nature of the state, deferred during the struggle with the Dutch.

The attitudes of the parties towards these two issues were complicated, and there were differences within them as well as among them. For example, the modernist leadership of Masjumi, supported by traders and well-to-do peasants, took a down-to-earth view of the role of foreign, even Dutch, capital. By contrast, the PNI, iden-tified with Sukarno, opposed an Islamic state, but favoured the continuance of the revolution in the form of a continued struggle against colonialism. Indeed it tended towards a bureaucratic view of the state rather than a capitalist one. It found some-thing in common with Nahdlatul Ulama, which, under a more conservative Islamic leadership, broke away from Masjumi in 1952, and even with the PKI when it sought to make a post-Madiun comeback. The ideological divisions were interleaved with regional ones. The modernists in Masjumi came largely, like Hatta, from Menangkabau. NU found its support more among the rural *ulama* of Java. PNI, too, was predominantly Javanese in character.

In the 1950s it was generally thought that state-building required economic plan-ning, and new states readily assimilated the concept. The UN expert Benjamin Higgins found Indonesia incapable of doing it.

> Back of the long delay in completion of the development plan is the fundamental problem which confronts all aspects of Indonesian economic policy: the lack of reso-lution of the basic political conflict concerning economic and political goals and the relationship of Indonesia to the outside world. Indonesia has not yet decided what kind of economic and social organisation it wants, nor whether or to what extent it wishes to rely on foreign experts, foreign aid, and foreign investment in achieving its development objectives.[62]

'The lack of economic progress', Higgins suggested, 'heightens tensions between the center and the regions, strengthens extreme nationalist sentiments, and causes general dissatisfaction with whatever government happens to be in power'.[63] For a while, in Indonesia as in Burma, the prosperity brought by the Korean War allevi-ated some of the tensions, though also making it easier to defer the harder decisions. The collapse of the boom reduced the prices of Indonesia's exports and destroyed the favourable balance of trade. Foreign exchange problems emphasised regional rivalries. Most of the exports now came from the Outer Islands, but government expenditure concentrated on Java, where the majority of the population was. Sumatra received only one-eighth of the foreign exchange earned by its exports, Kalimantan less.[64] Java came to seem a parasite on the Outer Islands.

This was the context for contention among the parties before the elections. The cabinets headed by Hatta, Natsir, Sukiman, and Wilopo put their emphasis on eco-nomic rationalisation, 'administrators', as Feith describes them.[65] The end of the

boom, however, contributed to the creation of a cabinet without Masjumi participation, led by Ali Sastroadmijojo, and supported by PNI, NU, and PKI, and also by
the President, 'solidarity-makers' in the Feith categorisation, building support by
nationalist and anti-colonialist campaigns, but also by a heavy emphasis on patronage. Campaigning for the election heightened the tension, for it became essential for
the parties no longer to concern themselves mainly with the politics of Jakarta. They
had to build their popular support by extending their patron–client ties at lower
levels, winning over the village headman, the *ulama*, the *dalang*. Some villages went
over wholly to one party. Others tended to divide according to the lines of tension
within the village, in Java in particular along the *aliran*. The parties indeed adopted
appropriate symbols. Since suffrage was universal, but the electorate substantially
illiterate, that was, moreover, technically useful. The result was, however, to identify
the parties even more closely with differences about the nature of the state, and to
risk what Geertz called 'sacralized bitterness'.[66]

'Elections were regarded by the newspaper-reading public as a way out of a
highly unsatisfactory general political situation', Feith tells us. 'This situation was
seen in terms of recurring cabinet crises, army challenges to government authority,
corruption, political nepotism, party bickering, and above all the impotence of governments in the face of the enormous tasks facing it in every direction. Thus a very
great deal was expected of the elections.'[67] Elections, it was hoped, would make parties
less factious, and give governments more stability and moral authority. In retrospect
that optimism seems surprising, since elections were bound to intensify divisions and
extend political rivalry outside the capital. Certainly it made the outcome all the
more disappointing. 'Keen disappointment is felt in many Indonesian groups
because the 1955 elections have not created political stability', Feith commented.[68]
High expectations contributed to undue despondency, and indeed to an impatience
with the system. For it to work it had to be made to work. The Indonesians had to
give themselves the experience that their colonial rulers had denied them. It is hard
to argue that democracy was ineffective in the Philippines because there were too
few divisions and in Indonesia because there were too many.

Disappointment was not confined to the elite. The elections were an astounding
success, not only in technical terms, but in terms of popular participation. A very
large proportion of Indonesians voted, enough to shame other democracies where
voting was not compulsory. In the parliamentary elections in September some 39
million voted, 91.54 per cent of the electors, and of the 39 million 87.65 per cent cast
valid votes. The people turned out a second time to elect the constituent assembly
in December, when 89.33 per cent voted. By contrast to the Philippines, Indonesia
saw little disorder or open intimidation. No doubt villagers were following their
leaders. But the elections seem also to have had a ritual, almost a religious, character, and an element of millennialism was involved. Independence had heightened
popular hopes. Participation in the elections would surely realise them.

In the Indonesia of the 1950s a stable government could not be created by single-
party dominance. Before the elections, indeed, it had been widely thought that

Masjumi, the leading Islamic party, would, despite the NU breakaway, be clearly victorious, and that had prompted concern, not only from its rivals, but from the President himself. In fact the outcome was quite different. Masjumi's hopes were dashed. NU did well. So did PNI and PKI, with which it had been working in its search for popular support, while PSI did badly. The first cabinet, the second formed by Ali Sastroadmidjojo, was thus a PNI–Masjumi–NU coalition under PNI leadership. To many, it seemed the mixture as before, 'just another Cabinet', as Feith puts it,[69] no more able than the pre-election cabinets to tackle major problems or carry out bold policies. The fact was that there was no consensus that would permit such an approach. A stronger government might have destroyed what there was, and risked the continuance of the new state. An electoral process could not in any case produce such a government in the Indonesia of the 1950s. That did not mean that it had to be abandoned. Only over time and with continued effort could the system have helped to build and respond to a growing consensus. But time was offered neither by opponents of the system, nor even by its supporters.

The dynamics of the system had not after all been left unchanged, as Feith suggested.[70] The elected parliament revealed a danger that the appointed parliaments had tended to conceal. Those, especially that of 1950, had over-represented the Outer Islands by comparison with the more populous Java. The elected parliament, more closely reflecting population densities, did not do so. It was now possible that the greater numbers of the Javanese would make them politically predominant, and that government policies, mirroring this, would severely prejudice the Outer Islands. That possibility was increased by the fact that PNI, PKI, and NU were shown to be Java-based parties, drawing their strength from East and Central Java, while Masjumi's main strength was in West Java and the Outer Islands. In the September election 24.8 per cent of the votes in East and Central Java went to PKI, 27.6 to NU, 28.3 to PNI; and 10.8 to Masjumi. PKI was the most Javanese of all the parties and Masjumi the least. Governments that failed to include a Masjumi element would be deeply suspect in the Outer Islands and subject the system, if not the state itself, to great strain. Moreover, at the end of 1956 Hatta, seen to stand for the Outer Islands, resigned as vice-president.

That stimulated army-led revolts in the regions against the Jakarta government: Husein took over in Central Sumatra on 20 December; Simbolon announced martial law in North Sumatra on 22 December; in January 1957 Barlian formed a Garuda Revolutionary Council in South Sumatra; and early in March Sumual declared martial law in Sulawesi, issuing a Permesta (Perjuangan Semesta, Total Struggle) Charter, demanding more autonomy for the regions and a restoration of the Dwi–Tunggal (Sukarno–Hatta) leadership.

Against this background Masjumi, which had been calling for a Hatta-led cabinet, withdrew from that led by Ali on 9 January, leaving its PNI–NU collaborators to depend on PKI. The parties would not accept a four-legged cabinet, as proposed by Sukarno. He formed an emergency one under Djuanda, but Masjumi men who joined it were expelled by their party. In a National Council Djuanda formed as

Sukarno wished more than half the members were Javanese, and it was dominated by PNI, PKI and the national communist Murba. The rebellious colonels attended a *Musyawarah Nasional* (national deliberation) convened by Djuanda, but basic differences remained. Conflict deepened in November when the UN motion on West New Guinea failed, and take-overs of Dutch enterprises followed. Three Masjumi leaders left for Central Sumatra. A meeting at Padang on 10 February issued an ultimatum to Jakarta: a new government must be headed by Hatta and the Sultan of Yogyakarta. When that was rejected an alternative government was proclaimed, PRRI (the Revolutionary Government of the Republic of Indonesia). It did not indeed aim to break up Indonesia: it was 'a movement for the change of national policy, not for separation from the Indonesian state'.[71] What it wanted was to change the direction of the government in Jakarta. But, supported by Masjumi and PSI leaders, it suggested that they had abandoned the electoral process they had favoured. Despairing of their prospect of a share of power, they had turned to military leaders who had challenged Jakarta on a different basis and at least in part for different reasons. Their success would have strengthened the role of the military. Their failure strengthened the role of an army, against Nasution's centralisation of which the local leaders had been reacting.

The defection of the Masjumi leaders, and the failure of the Padang venture, have to be seen in another context. They withdrew from a system in which they had been taking part. Others had not taken part, and had challenged it almost from the outset. One was Kartosuwirjo, a pre-war PSII leader who became secretary of the new Masjumi political party in November 1945. But he was unhappy when the party accepted Renville, and after the conclusion of the Roem–van Roijen agreement, proclaimed an Islamic state in West Java. His Darul Islam movement retained a hold on the countryside throughout the 1950s, despite the efforts of the army's Siliwangi division. By 1955 the government in Jakarta was confronted with a rival Government of the Islamic State of Indonesia. Its other components included Kahar Muzakkar, leader of the ex-guerrillas in South Sulawesi, unhappy with the prominent role the Jakarta government gave Minahasans like Kawilarang and Warouw after it had dispersed the ex-KNIL troops. Kartosuwirjo was also joined by Daud Beureu'eh, leader of the *ulama* who had destroyed the Acehnese *uleebalang* at the end of the occupation. They had sided with the Republic in the struggle with the Dutch, but saw the 1950 government as no more than a continuation of colonial rule. The formation of the first Ali cabinet had been the signal for Beureu'eh's insurrection.

One reason for the failure of the Padang venture was that those that supported it did not all agree, and Barlian did not in fact support it. Much of the opposition in Menangkabau was on an Islamic basis, of little appeal to the rebels in Sulawesi or Tapanuli. Moreover, the rebels could not readily link up with the earlier opponents of the Republic. In Sulawesi the leaders were Menadonese, antagonists of Kahar Muzakkar, though he joined forces with them on 17 April 1958. In Aceh Djuanda made concessions, not sufficient to win over Daud Beureu'eh, but sufficient to persuade his followers to topple him in March 1959. In February 1960 the unsuccessful rebels set up the United Republic of Indonesia, but they remained disunited, and they could not restore their position. In April 1961 Simbolon dissociated himself from them, and in August Sjafruddin Prawinegara, the President, urged his followers to lay down their arms.

Outside support for PRRI had been limited. What there was risked being counterproductive by identifying the rebels with foreign-sponsored disunity. But if the United States had persisted, it would have been supporting a movement in which the most democratic elements in Indonesia had already compromised themselves. The Java-based parties had failed to recognise Masjumi's apprehensions. Masjumi, however, looked first to Hatta; then left Ali's government; and finally turned to the colonels. 'The conclusion that can be drawn from Indonesia's experience is that in a plural society, democracy can take root if there exists a mechanism which allows the important minorities to share the powers of government and to regulate and reconcile their differences. In the last analysis, however, it is not the mechanism but the men operating it who will ensure that democracy does not break down.'[72] 'Constitutional democracy was both overthrown by its opponents and abandoned by those who had earlier upheld it.'[73] Masjumi and PSI were discredited, and in August 1960 banned.

In the crisis President Sukarno did not abandon 'democracy', but he renewed his criticism of the party mechanism that formed part of it. 'We made a great mistake in 1945 when we urged the establishment of parties, parties, parties.'[74] He wanted a 'Guided Democracy' (*demokrasi terpimpin*). On 21 December 1956, shortly after the seizure of power in Central Sumatra, he announced his *konsepsi*. A multi-party system was 'imported', based on conflict, party against party, majority against minority. The aim should be consensus, reached through deliberation and leadership, and, putting this in an Indonesian phrase, he called for a *gotong-royong* (mutual help) cabinet, and a national council that would represent not parties, but functional groups. It was a new version of his anti-Dutch programme, and was indeed coupled with an intensified insistence on the struggle for West New Guinea. The PRRI rebellion and its suppression seemed to put him in a position to carry out the *konsepsi* he had continued to develop during 1957. Early in 1959 he and the Djuanda cabinet sought to persuade the constituent assembly to readopt the 1945 constitution, which, with an amendment to the electoral law allowing for functional groups, they considered would be an effective means of introducing Guided Democracy. Muslim politicians in turn recurred to the Jakarta charter, but could not get it adopted. In July Sukarno dissolved the assembly and brought in the 1945 constitution by decree. In that he simply acknowledged that the charter inspired the constitution and formed a unity with it.

Sukarno had deemed constitutional democracy irrelevant to Indonesia, only sharpening the differences among the Indonesians that he had devoted his life to reducing. The politicians who had supported it had themselves lost patience with it as a means to accommodate those differences, attempting a pronunciamento, and then engaging, counter-productively, in civil war. The way was open to Sukarno to propose a system such as he had favoured in 1945 before constitutional democracy was introduced. It had the advantage that it could represent, through the 'functional groups', a wide range of opinions, including those of minorities, an advantage, indeed, that the appointed parliaments had in fact shared under the constitutional regime. But was it now itself relevant? A constitutional democracy required patience, practice, give-and-take. Even a Guided Democracy required a degree of trust, and that was harder to secure after the crises precipitated by the elections and the subsequent civil war.

The weakening of the party system as a result of this process also, perhaps paradoxically, weakened the prospects of Guided Democracy. Without himself having an organisational base, Sukarno perceived himself as the Guider. 'After hearing the general views and contra views, The Guider summarizes the points into a compromise palatable to each faction. No one side wins totally to the exclusion of others.'[75] Whether this was ever a practical approach, it was not by the late 1950s. The President's role as Guider was confined by the diminution of those he sought to guide.

In the phase of so-called Guided Democracy, he was in fact able to do no more than balance between what had become the two most important holders of political power, the army and the PKI. Nor was it possible to take policy initiatives. The President displayed little interest in economic policy: 'I am not an economist. ... I am a revolutionary.'[76] The political system provided no other means of dealing with the issues that the old system had failed to deal with. More and more, it focused on an external campaign, the regaining of West New Guinea, and, when that was successful, on *konfrontasi*. For a while such campaigns provided a focus for agreement between the army and the PKI and a source of presidential leadership. But *konfrontasi* failed to stop Malaysia.

Attempting to re-establish itself after the Madiun disaster, PKI had taken a nationalist line. 'The basic principle we must adhere to ... is to subordinate the class struggle to the national struggle', D. N. Aidit declared.[77] PKI was conscious that it must avoid repeating the pattern of 'intensive enthusiasm' and 'complete disillusionment'.[78] It needed a more assured commitment than it had secured through its earlier association with millennial aspirations. Again, however, it took what Ho Chi Minh and the Vietnamese would have condemned as short cuts. Its cadres it found among those who could not otherwise get ahead in the new Republic, without good connexions or education, the patronage of political leaders or military commanders: petty bourgeois, middling peasants. As the elections approached, it looked also to village notables, encouraging an overlap between the socio-economic leadership at that level and the local peasant front. It tended to rest on the wealthier strata, attracted by its *abangan* emphasis or its modernist image. The combination was strikingly effective in the electoral phase and certainly alarmed the PKI's opponents. The Guided Democracy phase was, as Ruth McVey has pointed out in a brilliant article, another matter.

Aidit had telegraphed Sukarno after he dissolved parliament in March 1960: 'seriously endangers democratic life in our country'.[79] Some PKI leaders, as McVey says, argued that it would be better to give up a legal existence, as Masjumi did, and wait for better times, lest the party should be destroyed or discredited. In Aidit's view, that would be 'to avert disaster by committing suicide'.[80] The President's need to balance the army still offered an opportunity. PKI bolstered the Guided Democracy regime, driving it to the left, strengthening the position of leaders and officials ready to accept it, pressing for the 'retooling' (exclusion) of those opposed, aiming still for a share of power at the top. In this context the party took up land reform. It did not expect that to be as controversial as it turned out to be: an act had been passed in 1960, there were few great landowners, and martial law had been ended in 1963. In the event there was violent opposition, particularly from larger landholders, often *santri*, and Islamic youth. Notables and their clients left the PKI, while the peasants, fearing that the party would not be able to protect them against landlord and bureaucratic reprisals, hesitated to join in the campaign for 'direct action' (*aksi sepihak*). A minority, however, went further than the leadership wanted, trying to commit it to a radical course, but in fact damaging its attempts to join the elite. The leadership concentrated on anti-foreign campaigns, demonstrating its usefulness, and working towards breaking the army's monopoly of arms by seeking the creation of a Fifth Force to help carry through the national struggle against Malaysia. It did not want conflict, but the inculcation of a radical mood. But '[t]he danger grew that the PKI's constituency would lose patience with its leaders' collaborationist course, or conversely, that its growth would alarm the ruling elite into uniting to destroy it'.[81] It seems that both happened in sequence.

Over the origins of the attempted coup of 30 September 1965 there has been substantial controversy, and it seems likely to remain controversial. After it the army took power, and it was unwilling to accept an interpretation that ascribed the coup in part to the army. It nevertheless seems that the coup began as an internal army matter. Officers of the Dipo Negoro division, inspired by a mixture of traditional Javanese viewpoints and a revolutionary idealism, based both on leftist ideology and PETA-style training, were antagonistic to general staff officers, corrupt and comfortable in the capital, unwilling to press *konfrontasi* hard enough. Striking down the top brass could thus free the hands of the President, in whose name the officers claimed to act. Though several generals were killed, the coup failed: perhaps indeed the killings were unintended; they were certainly counter-productive. The army, under the leadership of Suharto, the commander of the strategic reserve (KOSTRAD), now had the opportunity to seize power, even at the expense of Sukarno. It was also able to smash PKI. That, indeed, does not seem to have been preparing for a coup, and events appear to have caught its leaders unawares. Their aim, after all, was, as Leslie Palmier puts it, 'to float to power on a tide of popularity'.[82] It is possible, however, that elements in the PKI, discontented with the leadership and apprehensive of the generals, especially in view of Sukarno's illness, were more adventurous.

The results in any case were, once more, a disaster. Indeed the disaster was unimaginably bloody: at least 500 000 died. Encouraged by the army, civilian vigilantes engaged in an orgy of killing, not simply related to antagonism to the PKI. The coincidence of local and national factors in 'the unusual absence of restraining forces, unleashed deep antagonisms in a fury of murder', as Robert Cribb puts it.[83] 'The failure of national politics to provide workable and working institutions to fulfil the promises of independence threw the Indonesian people back on loyalty to older social divisions which became polarized around Islam and Communism.' Indonesia, he adds, had no established rules for the conduct of politics: there had been constant experiment since 1945. Under Guided Democracy the absence of conventions of political behaviour, coupled with the habit of lip-service, made political judgment more difficult just when, in conditions of economic decay and 'naked political rivalry', it became more necessary.

The coup might at first appear just as another political manouevre. The army presented it as a PKI attempt to seize power. On the basis of the violence that followed it built a new regime that preserved democracy in a form that sought to combine an electoral process and even the continuance of a party system with an approach that recalled the integralism of Supomo and that appropriated the Pantjasila of Sukarno and his concept of functional groups.

The Alliance

So far from preserving Sukarno's Guided Democracy, *konfrontasi* had destroyed it. In that sense the resolute defence of Malaysia by the British had achieved an additional goal, though the enormous cost contributed to their determination to withdraw from Southeast Asia in the subsequent decade. The struggle had also helped to consolidate the new state, at least to the extent that it made it easier for the government to win the election of 1964. The threat from outside, however, only obscured internal tensions that were in fact increased by the crisis. The real test for the democratic system Malaya had adopted on becoming independent in 1957, and that Malaysia had taken over in 1963, was still to come.

In Malaya the colonial and protecting power had been reluctant to take any steps towards a more democratic system in the 1920s and 1930s. In India and in neighbouring Burma the British introduced electoral and ministerial systems. Their reforms in Malaya were much more cautious, and their initial aims, in any case confined to decentralisation and unification, were more than they could manage. A sense of obligation to the Malays enhanced their caution. No mandate had been 'extended to us by Rajas, Chiefs, or people, to vary the system of government', Sir Hugh Clifford, governor and high commissioner, declared in 1927: 'the adoption of any kind of government by majority would forthwith entail the complete submersion of the indigenous population'.[84]

Wartime planning, paradoxically enough, envisaged a bolder policy. Again the initial focus was on the constitutional structure rather than on participation, though the ultimate aim was to provide for a democratic Malaya on the basis of a common citizenship. Perhaps that was never put strongly or immediately enough to appeal to the Chinese and Indian communities. The prospect in any case so alarmed the Malay community that the constitutional policy was itself revised and the citizenship proposals curtailed. The outbreak of the Emergency in June 1948 seemed further to reduce the prospect of democratic advance: the left-wing groups vanished from politics. And yet, in another somewhat paradoxical development, it came to seem that such might indeed offer a way of bridging the communal divisions that the war and postwar events had intensified.

The Emergency prompted new political initiatives based on elite collaboration among the communities. The emergence of the Malayan Chinese Association in February 1949 revived a scheme that Tan Cheng-lock, an influential leader drawn from the 'Baba' (long-settled) Chinese community, had once before envisaged. The British welcomed it, and encouraged Dato Onn, the UMNO leader, to welcome it, too. Malcolm MacDonald, the commissioner-general, used the Communities Liaison Committee, begun informally in December 1948, to promote their collaboration. The MCA was intended at once to work with UMNO and to seek organised support within the Chinese community. The crucial question was the compatibility of those two objectives: on that depended the effectiveness of the MCA and the approach on which it was based. In turn that depended on what UMNO was prepared to offer. There it was a question of reconciling a mass following with what an elite leadership advocated. The basis of the elite compromise took account of the economic strength of the Chinese and the political strength of the Malays: the Chinese would gain in the political field and the Malays in the economic. Would UMNO leaders be able, without sacrificing their political support, to offer MCA leaders sufficient for them to consolidate theirs? Would the latter have to ask more than the former could give?

To combine such a compromise with a democratic system seemed problematic. Competitive politics was likely to put the position of moderate leaders at risk and to bring forward those who articulated larger demands or evoked so-called primordial allegiances in their attempts to secure mass support. Surprisingly, however, it seemed to work, partly because its proponents were determined to make it work. In 1951 Dato Onn formed the Independence of Malaya Party in order to crystallise the cooperation of the CLC, but he failed to win the Malays from UMNO or the Chinese from the MCA. Instead the two communal parties collaborated in the Kuala Lumpur municipal elections of 1952, each placing candidates where its community had most voters, and the Alliance enjoyed a triumph. The prospects of political advance consolidated it, and the Malayan Indian Congress (MIC), which had been set up in August 1946 with John Thivy as first president, leaned towards the IMP, and then wavered, finally joining in October 1954, its weakness indicated by those who suggested that MIC stood for 'May I Come'.[85]

In the first elections for the Federal Legislative Council, held in 1955, the Alliance secured fifty-one out of fifty-two constituencies, thus dominating a council of ninety-eight. There were no communal seats, and a different principle of collaboration had been followed. The scope of citizenship had been widened in 1952, but many Chinese had so far failed to register, and the delineation of constituencies had produced fifty seats with a Malay majority, only two with a Chinese, none with an Indian. But fifteen Chinese and two Indians were elected on the Alliance ticket, Tunku Abdul Rahman, the UMNO leader, having insisted on a substantial number of 'immigrant' nominations, and the electorate having voted for them, on the platform of *merdeka:* 'the voters did not vote communally: they voted for a team'.[86] 'The result ... is the first step towards racial harmony in this plural society country', the Tunku declared.[87] In the future, he saw, the Chinese element in the electorate would increase. He was offering experience in communal collaboration.

The *merdeka* constitution retained the states in a federal system and wrote in other safeguards for the special position of the Malays, though also further expanding the citizenship qualification. There were now two main questions. One was the continued success of the Alliance. Could that continue once independence had been gained? In the 1959 elections it secured 74 out of the 104 seats in the House of Representatives. 52 of its 69 Malay candidates were successful, 19 of its 31 Chinese, 3 of its 4 Indians. It won 24 of the 40 constituencies in which Chinese now predominated. 13 seats went to a predominantly Chinese combination of the Socialist Front and the People's Progressive Party, and 14, all on the east coast, to the Pan-Malayan Islamic Party. Its position still seemed secure. The other question was a related one. Had the success of the Alliance so strengthened a communal approach to the electoral system that other alternatives were impossible? That would constrain the development of democratic politics. The position was complicated by the assumption of a new task, so soon after *merdeka*, the creation of the wider federation of Malaysia.

The creation of Malaysia was itself conceived in terms of communal bargains and compromises effected at elite level, the Borneo territories as a counterweight to the inclusion of a predominantly Chinese Singapore. In the 1964 election campaign the PAP leaders from Singapore argued for a different approach, a 'Malaysian Malaysia'. That struck at the deal on which the Alliance was based. Confrontation helped the government to win the 1964 elections—'something like a referendum' on the government's policy[88]—but winning them on the basis of an external threat obscured the need to deal with internal strains. The Alliance directorate was 'mesmerized' by 'a spectacular electoral victory'.[89] Now the Tunku was criticised by the MCA elite for treating the PAP threat too lightly, a criticism echoed from a different direction by sub-elites in UMNO and the Islamic-oriented PAS. His answer was to expel Singapore from Malaysia in August 1965. On this basis he hoped to preserve the inter-communal bargain. The chances that some other approach to democratic politics would develop had been reduced by this succession of events, the creation of Malaysia, the electoral victory, the PAP challenge.

The bargain had already been under some strain. 'Young bloods' in the MCA had demanded a better bargain in 1958, but their leader was driven to resign, and replaced by Tan Siew Sin, more acceptable to an UMNO worried about its position on the Malay-dominated east coast. Education and development plans favoured the Malays, and the MCA lost its role in seat allocation. The essential bargain had remained, however, as William Case argues.[90] The events of 1964–65 increased the strain. The aspirations of the Chinese were heightened, while Malays began to demand that only Malay should be used in official transactions and schools, 'Young Turks' and 'Ultras' like Mahathir and Musa Hitam criticising the Tunku's ethnically accommodative policies. The campaign for the 1969 election strengthened chauvinistic claims and the results led to violence. The Alliance did not suffer a major defeat, though it lost ground, but 'the apparent "victory" of the non-Malay opposition parties in terms of seats had a great impact',[91] and the Alliance lost or nearly lost several state assemblies. In Selangor youthful DAP supporters marched on the residence of the *mentri besar*, Harun Idris. A counter-demonstration on 13 May turned into major riots. In the crisis the Tunku failed to exercise leadership, and his deputy, Tun Razak, used the military to restore order.

In 1960, the year the Emergency officially ended, the government had even so passed the Internal Security Act, institutionalising the British practice of preventive detention. Tun Razak's National Operations Council recalled the Emergency itself. But, though his programme was designed to win back the UMNO constituency, it did not abandon accommodation with the Chinese: it placed it on a new footing, marked in particular by the adoption of the New Economic Policy. It did, however, signal that the democratic system, though, again, not abandoned, would be operated in a yet more idiosyncratic way. The Alliance treated opposition parties, as Case puts it, with a mix of 'cooptation, pre-emption, grudging tolerance and repression'.[92] The constitutional provisions could not be questioned even in parliament.

The PAP

Their strategic interests and their postwar political experiments in Malaya had encouraged the British to treat Singapore separately, but, since it was assumed that such a small state could not survive on its own, the ultimate objective had to be 'merger'. In the meantime they maintained a colonial government, but sought to democratise it by holding elections on an increasingly wide franchise and by instituting a form of dyarchy. That envisaged large-scale participation by the mostly Chinese-speaking population in Western-style politics. Mobilising its support required a popular appeal that would outbid traditional loyalties to clan and dialect associations, and that was, of course, readily found in anti-colonialism. In the 1955 elections the Labour Front, led by David Marshall and Lim Yew-hock, working on a platform of independence and a welfare state, won the largest number of seats, but not a majority. That prompted Marshall to emphasise his anti-colonial credentials. 'One cannot defend democracy by refusing it to those who are anxious to support it. We have been taught to admire the British Constitution and British traditions of administration; Britain cannot now deny the implications of its own lessons.' He claimed that '*merdeka* will rally the majority of the people against Communism'.[93]

In the subsequent talks in London Marshall sought independence, ceding back defence and external relations, and proposing a defence and security council for a transitional period of up to six years. Britain would be able to suspend the constitution if internal insecurity threatened the defence installations or the government of Singapore acted against the constitution, but would not be able to do anything short of that. Alan Lennox-Boyd, the Colonial Secretary, would not agree: Singapore had insufficient experience of stable democratic government; and the British wanted powers that were less drastic than suspending the constitution, and could therefore be more readily used. The British government had lost its base at Trincomalee, and that made it more intractable over Singapore: it did not deal with Marshall as it had with the Tunku. 'Alan has given me the Christmas pudding', Marshall complained to Eden, 'but he insists on the arsenic sauce'.[94] A proposal that Britain should retain powers that it would exercise only on the advice of the defence and security council Marshall would contemplate only if a Malayan chaired it, not the British high commissioner. His successor, Lim, settled for less, while the British accepted that Malaya would have the casting vote on the council.

In the 1959 election the PAP triumphed. The Rendel constitution of 1955 had provided for a Legislative Council with twenty-five elected members out of a total of thirty-two. The 1959 constitution provided for a fully elected 51-seat assembly and compulsory voting. That meant 'politics on a mass scale'.[95] Such was likely to throw power to left-wing politicians who could appeal to the Chinese-educated and to trade union members. They and the British would, however, be at odds. This was an opportunity for English-speaking moderates like Lee Kuan Yew. 'We, the returned students', he had told the Malayan Forum in England in 1950,

> would be the type of leaders that the British would find relatively the more acceptable. For if the choice lies, as in fact it does, between a communist republic of Malaya and a Malaya within the British Commonwealth led by people who, despite their opposition to imperialism, still share certain ideals in common with the Commonwealth, there is little doubt which alternative the British will find the lesser evil.[96]

The object was now to ally with the left, while yet building relations with the British.

In power the Labour Front had sought to break the communist hold upon the Chinese secondary schools and the trade unions. It had incurred an unpopularity of which its opponents made use, while the PAP moderates yet benefited from the arrest of Lim Chin Siong, a left-wing colleague. The PAP programme was independence through merger. Singapore could not survive on its own nor, without Malaya, could it build a socialist economy. 'Without this economic base [the Federation], Singapore would not survive', said Lee.[97] '[I]mpelled by the imminent danger of a *very* left wing or pro-communist government coming to power in Singapore',[98] the Tunku now dropped his opposition to merger. Perhaps persuaded by changes in the international situation, including the crisis in Laos, perhaps persuaded, too, by the defeat of the PAP candidate in a by-election by a former mayor who sought complete independence, the UMNO leader came to feel that the PAP was a guarantee against something worse that might come about when the constitution was revised in 1963. That conclusion was reinforced when the PAP's English-speaking leadership broke with its left-wing allies, who formed the Barisan Sosialis.

Merger, however, proved to be only temporary, and in 1965 Singapore became an independent Republic. Almost the same size as the Isle of Wight, Patrick Dean had put it in 1956, '[i]t cannot exist effectively as an entity on its own'.[99] That view had been shared by the PAP itself. Now circumstances had changed, and it was able to disprove its own prognostications. Its leadership, however, stressed, even more than its critics thought necessary, that it was essential to avoid political division. The Barisan had been destroyed in the Malaysia phase by the creation of community organisations that undermined its control of the party, by a referendum in 1962, and by Operation Cold Store, in which Chin Siong and 112 activists were arrested on 2 February 1963, following the Brunei revolt. Singapore became in effect a one-party state. There was no opposition in parliament for fifteen years.

The Alliance-type in Borneo

Malaysia included Sarawak and Sabah as well as Singapore. By 1961, when it was proposed, neither had advanced very far along the road to democratic participation, which was one of the objects of British policy when they were made colonies fifteen years earlier. The prospect of incorporation in Malaysia prompted a rapid mobilisation of popular support. Not surprisingly the parties tended to stress communal or ethnic loyalties, to utilise traditional leaders, and to give influence to those who could deploy wealth and acquire clients: 'the parties are more like retinues', Margaret Clark Roff was to write in 1974.[100] Once Malaysia was created, the central government sought to create a Peninsular pattern in Borneo. The fit was inexact: parties were multi-'racial', 'communities' were divided, there was no strong Malay party. But the power of the Kuala Lumpur government was ruthlessly exerted to create Alliance-type politics. In Sarawak the pattern of outside dominance, exerted by the Bruneis in the 1830s, seemed to be repeating itself in a new form.

In 1961 Sarawak was more 'advanced' than Sabah. The colonial government had inherited the raj's Council Negri, through which the governor sought advice. In 1956 it began elections at the district level, with indirect elections to the Council. The system led to the creation of parties. The Sarawak United Peoples Party, formed in 1959, was intended to be multi-racial, but led by Chinese, especially Hokkien businessmen, while attracting left-wing support. In reaction the Datu Bandar formed PANAS (Party Negara Sarawak), multi-racial, but increasingly under the control of pro-cession Malays. 'Ethnic' loyalties were not the only ones, however, and the parties, coming from divided communities, were prompted to seek alliances outside their community. An Iban party followed in April 1961, the Sarawak National Party (SNAP), headed by Stephen Ningkan and led not by traditional leaders, but by self-made Iban, especially from Saribas, often Shell workers. Party Pesaka, a more traditional group led by Tg Jugah, was set up in July 1962. Barjasa (Barisan Ra'ayat Jati Sarawak), predominantly Melanau and non-Kuching Malay, had preceded it at the end of 1961.

SUPP attracted support from Kedayans and Bruneis in Limbang, opposed to the status quo, and it made contact with Azahari and the PRB. But the Brunei revolt, the reaction to it, and the subsequent Indonesian attacks, harmed SUPP, and the 1963 elections were won by the Sarawak Alliance of Pesaka, SNAP, Barjasa, and the Sarawak Chinese Association. Ningkan became chief minister. What the federal government wanted, however, was a more amenable Iban-Islamic government, comprising Pesaka and Barjasa. In June 1966 the Tunku displaced Ningkan, declaring that he had lost the confidence of the Council Negri. When the High Court ruled that unconstitutional, the federal government declared an emergency, and the governor dismissed Ningkan. Government came to be led by Barjasa and Panas, merged as Bumiputera Sarawak.

In Sabah there had been no electoral politics by 1961. The Legislative Council, set up in 1950, included nine official members, and ten nominated non-officials. From 1956 the latter were chosen by the governor from names put forward by the Conference of Native Chiefs, the Chinese Chamber of Commerce, the North Borneo Chamber of Commerce, and the Planters Association. By 1961 there was an unofficial majority, but the members were not elected.

Several parties emerged when the Malaysia proposal stimulated political activity. They included the United National Kadazan Organisation, set up in August 1961, led by Donald Stephens, a man of mixed Dusun-Australian parentage, and the United Sabah National Organisation, led by Dato Mustapha, appealing especially to Muslims. 'Dusun' was a census-based categorisation that laid the basis for group identification: Stephens campaigned for the use of 'Kedazan'. Both he and Mustapha were helped in their party-building by timber concessions.

Early in 1962 the Murut leaders, including two sons of Gunsanad, who had helped the Company in the Mat Salleh rebellion, broke with UNKO to form the United National Pasok Momogun Organisation, based particularly in Tambunan and Keningau. The breach was soon, however, healed, and all, including the urban Chinese parties, joined the Sabah Alliance, which triumphed in the first elections, held at local level, in December 1962. In the indirect Legislative Council elections of July 1963, USNO got eight members, UNKO five, Pasok Momogun one, and the

Chinese party four. Stephens became chief minister. With federal government help, however, Mustapha worked against him. Though it did well in the 1967 elections, UNKO was not included in the government, and it dissolved, many joining USNO to avoid losing their concessions. Government was now, as in Sarawak, oriented to the Malayo-Muslims.

Sangkum

In Indo-China the French colonial and protecting governments had throughout been unresponsive to the kind of appeal Marshall put to the British in Singapore, and had in fact offered little experience in democratic politics. At the same time the elites had to struggle to win or to preserve their independence, and could, perhaps even more than Marshall's successors, justify an approach that emphasised leadership and unity rather than participation and diversity.

After the return of the French, the kingdom of Cambodia became an autonomous state, and elections were held for a constituent assembly on 1 September 1946. The pro-independence Democratic Party, headed by Prince Sisovath Youtevong, took fifty of the sixty-seven seats; the Liberals, more pro-French, fourteen; the conservatives none. The king finally accepted the constitution, under which the National Assembly would be dominant, in July 1947, and further elections were held. Two new parties appeared, one being the Khmer Renovation of Lon Nol and Sirikmatak, conservative though pro-independence, but it got no seat. The Democrats were in a majority, but their prince had died, and the party fell apart, some members concerned simply with their own advancement, others openly sympathising with the Issarak, 'anti-French *maquis* cum bandits who controlled much of the countryside'.[101]

The Assembly was dissolved in September 1949, and a new government set up, responsible to the king, led by Yem Sembaur, a conservative Democrat. In new elections the Democrats still secured a majority, but they were on the defensive, and the French, with whom they were negotiating independence, accused them of being pro-Issarak and therefore pro-Viet Minh. Sihanouk intervened on the conservative side and, heading a new government, asked for full powers to rule for three years, promising to secure independence. The Assembly declined to agree, but the Democrats virtually suspended activity. In January 1953 Sihanouk dissolved the Assembly, and he and the right-wing ruled alone. To this government, however, the French were ready to transfer power, while government forces, now headed by Lon Nol, acted against the Issarak and the Viet Minh in Battambang with a barbaric degree of violence.

The absolute monarchy seemed to be re-emerging. But for the elections promised by Geneva for 1955, the Democrats resumed activity, strengthened, but also radicalised, by Cambodians returning from France. Khmers who had fought with the Viet Minh also seized the new opportunity for electoral politics, and formed the Pracheachon (Citizens). The followers of the wartime nationalist, Son Ngoc Thanh, re-emerged to create the Khmer Independence Party. The conservatives got together to form the Sangkum Reastr Niyom (People's Socialist Community), with Sihanouk, who had his father named king in his place, as its supreme councillor. Coercion and violence were deployed to help secure its victory, and in fact it secured all the seats, with 82 per cent of the vote, the Democrats coming a poor second. Lon Nol became minister for national defence. In 1957 the Democratic Party was dissolved, its leaders having been beaten up. Pracheachon feebly contested the 1958 election, which gave Sangkum 99.6 per cent of the vote. Its leaders were arrested before the 1962 contest, and soon after Saloth Sar, Ieng Sary, and Son Sen, deciding that gradualism would not succeed, fled to the maquis. Sihanouk had, as David Chandler puts it, 'killed any possibility of political pluralism'.[102] 'I was over confident I knew all the answers', he confessed in 1998.[103]

Politics now concentrated within Sangkum, and they were a contest for wealth and power. What counted was winning Sihanouk's support or inciting him against your enemies. The system, if Bonapartist, recalled the old kingdom. Its socialism was Royal Buddhist Socialism—one without class conflict—with the sovereign providing for his people's welfare, and its state industries and nationalised enterprises were like appanages. Periodic scandals occasioned turns at the trough. An element of redistribution helped to preserve the system, while aid from the United States, the Soviet Union, and China helped to provide something to redistribute. The system was also sustained by Sihanouk's traditional appeal.

His overthrow in 1970 Michael Vickery has suggested should be attributed to clique differences. 'Socialising' reforms in 1963 had turned the economy over to a group friendly to Sihanouk, at the expense of another right-wing group which would have preferred a more rational capitalist approach. Those who took over were in any case not new men: Lon Nol, Yem Sembaur, Sim Var. Son Ngoc Thanh, who had drifted to the right, got no support from his old enemies as prime minister. Nor, of course, were the circumstances favourable to a renewal of the democratic approach, even if the men had been.

Though the struggle for independence had been as elsewhere associated with a more democratic approach, that had not been sustained. The elite had been divided, the Democrats themselves at times irresponsible, the right-wing apprehensive of participatory politics. Concerned at the Viet Minh connexions of the former, the French had preferred the latter; and putting himself at the head, Sihanouk had secured the country's independence but also placed it under a Bonapartist regime. It provoked opposition while also in the end failing to reward its supporters.

Throughout, it must be added, Cambodia's struggles took place in the context of the conflict in Vietnam. Their connexions with the Viet Minh made the Democrats and the left-wing particularly unpalatable and particularly vulnerable to the French and to the right-wing. Yet, while the repression to which the latter felt more justified in resorting only intensified the alienation of their opponents, those who were driven towards the Viet Minh had no wish to remain permanently under its control.

The elite was in fact united on one thing: the need to preserve Cambodia. About the strategy for doing so, it was deeply divided, and it did not use a democratic system for resolving those differences.

Royal Government and Pathet Lao

Anxious to make up for the loss of Lao territories in 1940–41, Decoux implemented a policy of Lao Renovation, one of the executants being Charles Rochet. His pro-tégés, Katay Don Sasorith and Nhouy Abhay, were to play a prominent part, along-side the princes, after the coup of March 1945. When the French returned a constituent assembly was set up, and a national assembly was elected in November 1947. Elections were again prescribed at Geneva. Laos, however, had the additional challenge of the Pathet Lao, regrouping in Phongsali and Samneua. Indeed the Pathet Lao refused to take part in the 1955 elections, when the Royal Government refused its demand that the candidate age be lowered from thirty to twenty-five and women be allowed to vote. Following the coalition agreement of November 1957, additional seats were to be contested. Though they were scattered through Laos, nine out of thirteen Pathet Lao-backed candidates were successful, and the conser-vatives began to take alarm. After the Phumi Nosavan coup of December 1959, the government dealt a blow at the Pathet Lao candidates by gerrymandering and by revising the qualifications for candidates. The results were a travesty, while the guer-rillas extended their control in the villages by coercion and persuasion. An electoral system with which the elite had at first been comfortable could not cope with the post-Geneva tensions.

Elections in Vietnam

Vichy had mobilised youth in Vietnam, but in a Petainist not a democratic way, and the Grand Federal Council of 1943 offered no electoral representation. The Japanese supported the Dai Viet government of Tran Trong Kim, but also, rather contradic-torily, worked with the sects in Cochin-China. Their coup also gave the Viet Minh an opportunity, and Ho Chi Minh proclaimed independence on 2 September. 'All men are created equal. They are endowed by their Creator with certain inalienable rights. …' Ho quoted the American declaration of independence partly with the hope of winning American support against colonialism: 'if we enlarge the sphere of our thought, this statement conveys another meaning: All the peoples on the earth are equal from birth, all the peoples have a right to live, be happy and free.'[104] Though the minister for the interior, Vo Nguyen Giap, added in his message that same day that Vietnam was 'a democratic republic',[105] its leaders did not, like those in Indonesia, endeavour to extend their appeal to the United States by adopting a more democratic approach. Like other communists, they felt obliged to use the word, but they gave it a special meaning. In any case their appeal was vain.

Indeed the United States was to oppose the holding of the elections in Vietnam proposed as part of the Geneva settlement in 1954, and it encouraged Ngo Dinh Diem to avoid carrying them out. The fear was that the Viet Minh would win. The Americans urged Diem to accept the principle of elections, but to insist on guarantees of fairness. In fact he declared that the southern regime was not bound by the Geneva agreements. The way was thus prepared for a contest between two regimes, the Democratic Republic of Vietnam, and what became, after Diem defeated Bao Dai in a referendum on options for setting up a 'democratic regime'—in Saigon getting almost 200 000 more votes than there were registered voters[106]—the Republic of Vietnam. Unable to secure unification by electoral means, the DRVN was to encourage and support guerrilla activity in the south, finally adopting Le Duan's policy early in 1959. In turn the United States expanded its support for the RVN, but for which it would have been overthrown in months.

The struggle was above all for the control of the countryside, as it had been in the French phase. In Vietnam, as much as elsewhere, if not more so, the links between village and regime were crucial. The communists began *tru gian* (killing tyrants) in mid-1957. Village support was easily lost in any case. Resorting to violence could be counter-productive. A more positive approach was difficult to pursue. Diem's 'agrovilles' were followed by the Americans' 'strategic hamlets'. But reconcentration had to be accompanied by reconstruction and guarantees of security, lest the guerillas were simply to be given greater opportunities. Buying time to carry out this massive task became a reason for US attacks on the north from late in 1964. Buying time was also necessary for the task of building up an army for the Republic, even though it could be bought only by giving American troops a combat role, and thus making the struggle seem more like a colonial war than a national or civil one.

Political developments were marked by a similar paradox. The United States lost confidence in Diem and supported his overthrow late in 1963. Yet it hesitated openly to install a successor. Its part in the overthrow seemed to be a gamble, and it took some time before a clear winner emerged. He was, of course, bound to be a military 'strong man'. But some kind of democratic system was necessary to validate the government the Americans were supporting in southern Vietnam. Diem himself had created Can Lao (Personalist Labour Party). Personalism was derived from the philosophy of the French Catholic Emmanuel Mounier. Its rationale is suggested by Diem's message to the constituent assembly in 1956: 'democracy is neither material happiness nor the supremacy of numbers ... [but] is essentially a permanent effort to find the right political means of assuring to all citizens the right of free development'.[107] It could later perhaps be seen, as Duiker suggested in 1994, as 'a shrewd if imperfect attempt to blend traditional and modern ideas ... an approach that is being applied with varying degrees of success throughout the region today'.[108] It was seen at the time as a source of corruption, dictatorship, and alienation. Indeed, like others, the Diem regime, backed by US aid, built support on personal and familial ties. It also won support from the army and the Catholic refugees from the north. It got little cooperation from the mandarins.[109]

The subsequent military regime, headed by the Catholic Nguyen Van Thieu and the Buddhist Nguyen Cao Ky, was committed to an electoral process. An election law was promulgated in June 1966. Neutralist and communist candidates were excluded, but otherwise anyone over eighteen could vote. The elections, held in September, were observed by foreign diplomats and newsmen, and they found no significant evidence of manipulation or malpractice. In some sense that was a success, though it had been pointed out that 'few peasants are likely to risk offending officials by refusing to vote'.[110] 80 per cent voted, returning thirty-three Catholics and forty-four Buddhists.

In the north the struggle could only confirm the leadership of the communist Lao Dong party. A new constitution was promulgated in January 1960, and elections were held in May. There was no secret ballot, and there was little choice: 458 party-selected candidates contested 362 seats; 99.85 per cent voted.

Strong men in Thailand

The involvement of the United States in the struggle in Vietnam deeply affected the prospects of democracy in Siam/Thailand. There the attitude of the ruling elite had, in this as in other respects, resembled that of the colonial rulers elsewhere. Jit Poumisak, the radical critic of the 1950s, maintained that Rama VI's ideology was designed as a diversionary move in defence of the 'sakdina system':

> in the Sixth Reign when the pungent smell of democracy began to spread everywhere the Sixth Reign ruler tried to mobilize the People and intensify their hatred of the Chinese by showing them that the poverty and troubles they experienced stemmed from the Chinese in Muang Thai. ... The solution was not to change from sakdina to democracy but to rally together and strike out at the Chinese. So everyone lay around in bed dangling his feet and hating the Chinese![111]

Rama VII, by contrast, spoke the language of gradualism: 'if it is admitted that some day we may be forced to have some form of democracy in Siam', he wrote in 1927, 'we must prepare ourselves for it gradually. ... We must try to educate people to be politically conscious, to realise their real interests so that they will not be misled by agitators or mere dreamers of Utopia.' At first he looked to local government. It seems, however, that Prajadhipok thought of granting a constitution, otherwise 'the inevitable result would be a coup d'état and a military dictatorship',[112] and a draft was prepared early in 1932, advocating gradualism, as in Burma.

The coup of 1932 pre-empted him. He was, however, critical of the oligarchy that took over: his 'main thesis' was 'that he had given up his absolute power to the whole Thai people and not to any group'.[113] The Promoters adopted a feature of the gradualist approach in their constitution, drafted by Pridi, allegedly borrowing from Sun Yat-sen: the nomination of half the members of the assembly. Full representation would follow after ten years, or when half the population had completed primary education, whichever was the sooner. That seemed merely likely to rivet the Promoters' control. The government refused the king's demands that the nominated members should be elected by all the officials, active and retired, and not simply appointed by the government, and that army and navy officers on the active list should not take part in politics. It also refused his demand that his veto should be overridden only by a two-thirds majority or by plebiscite. He abdicated, his letter making a strong statement of his desire for 'true democracy'.[114]

In 1943–44 Sir Josiah Crosby, the pre-war British ambassador in Bangkok, argued that, at the end of the war, the Allies should take steps to diminish the role of the Pibun-led military in Thailand, so as to allow democracy a fair chance. He argued for 'some form of tutelage', reviving the old system of advisers backed by one of the UN 'as a quasi-tutelary authority'.[115] Such a colonialist approach was not adopted by the British, and it was still less acceptable to the Americans, the authority he had in mind, who did not even accept that Thailand was at war. The cause of democracy could not be advanced in this way. But, as the war drew to a close, Pibun had resigned, and the Thais, not unlike the Indonesians late in 1945, had seen the advantage of displaying their more democratic image. The civilian leader, Pridi, though once seen as a communist by king Prajadhipok, had collaborated with the Allies, and stood behind or himself led the first governments of postwar Siam.

Though they did not intervene in the way Crosby had advocated, the British did not, however, help Pridi to consolidate civilian rule. Indeed their insistence on a free delivery of rice embarrassed him, and exposed his governments to nationalist criticism. The Americans opposed the British demand, hoping thus to sustain their interests and strengthen a friendly government, but they did not prevent it. Their policy thus contributed to a long wrangle, which, along with corruption, the mystery of the young king's death in June 1946, and the loss of the Indo-China territories, damaged the civilian cause. That helped the military, temporarily deprived of power but not destroyed, to plan their return, and they could find allies in the conservative-royalist clique led by Khuang Aphaiwong.

Early in 1947 President Truman referred to the 'internal stability of a democratic Siam' and the need for a strong leader. That seemed like support for Pibun, who was returning to politics with a Right is Might party pledged to preserve the dynasty, to hold free elections, to uphold press freedom, and to cooperate with the United Nations. It was 'an insult to the intelligence of the outside world for the Marshal to prate about his attachment to democracy', declared Crosby's successor, Geoffrey Thompson. Subsequently, however, he was to advocate acceptance of Pibun's coup in November 1947, and the government that was subsequently set up under Khuang was recognised after elections—in which 22 per cent of the electorate voted—had confirmed its position in January. Indeed, when Pibun himself took over in April 1948, Thompson favoured recognition. Siam needed a strong man, and he had come to power by 'comparatively speaking constitutional means'.[116] The Americans for their part had, Frank Darling suggests, become 'less interested in assisting the evolution of constitutional democracy and more concerned with opposing the spread of Communism'.[117]

Pibun was not, however, the strong man that he had been. The November coup was led by Phin Choonhavan, who had commanded the Thai troops that occupied the Shan states in the war, with his son, Chatichai; Sarit Thanarat, commander of the Bangkok-based first regiment of the First Division; Praphat Charusathien, commander of the first battalion of the first regiment; Thanom Kittikachorn of the Royal Military Academy; and Phao Siyanon, son-in-law of Phin. Those men and their associates boosted their power in the following years in a number of ways. One was the removal of rival sources of power: the failed 'Manhattan' rebellion of June 1951 led to the destruction of the navy as a political factor. The constitution was modified. In 1946 an upper house had been added, elected by the lower. The coup group introduced a provisional constitution in 1947, the 'Under the Red Giant Water Jar Constitution', making the upper house a nominated body. In turn the royalist-democrats had in 1949 brought in the so-called permanent constitution, providing for it to be nominated by the king and not the premier. In November 1951, just before the young king returned from Europe, the 'Silent Coup' replaced the 1949 constitution and brought back that of 1932, alleging as reasons 'Communist aggression and widespread corruption'.[118] The people, said Pibun, 'needed a further period of tutelage'. Phao, the police chief, declared that a stable government needed the support of the king, of the armed forces, and of the people, by which he meant not 'the masses in the sense used in the West', but the civil servants.[119]

Above all, the coup group increased their wealth and influence through the control of state or semi-state enterprises, and through the acquisition of aid from the Americans, whose policy, as it developed under Dulles, the Thai government was all the more ready to endorse. 'Thailand's security requirements had not made alignment with the United States inevitable. ... Rather, military politics—and the lure of military assistance—made alignment with the United States compelling.'[120] Politics became factional. Two competing cliques emerged, Soi Rajakru, including Phin and Phao, and Sisao Deves, including Sarit, Thanom, and Praphat, the Phao clique favoured by the CIA, since it was prepared to support clandestine operations in support of the Kuomintang, and the Sarit clique preferred by the Pentagon.

Rivalry between the factions opened up some scope for alternative views. Lacking organisational support, Pibun himself—no democrat indeed, but more willing to make a pretence than Phao or Sarit, men from the provincial towns, wholly educated in Thailand—promoted a democratisation campaign, and to the concern of the United States the factions all competed for leftist or neutralist support in the run-up to the elections of 1957. Secretary-General of the ruling party, Seri Manangkhasila, Phao, already exceedingly corrupt—'a sort of local Beria', as C. L. Sulzberger put it[121]—made sure it won. But his 'no holds barred' methods—bribes, omission of names from the lists, the use of hooligans, illegal voting—produced a level of public discontent which gave Sarit, who dissociated himself from them, his opportunity. He carried out the coup of 16 September and overthrew the government. The coup group of 1947 had finally destroyed itself, and Sarit had emerged as 'the outright winner'.[122] More elections were held in December: the turn-out was 13 per cent.

Ruling with an entirely appointed assembly after his further coup in October 1958, Sarit invoked a new version of Rama VI's nationalist ideology—Nation, Religion, King—coupled with a programme of 'development' heavily influenced by the West and a continued orientation towards the United States. Ambassador U. Alexis Johnson tried to make Thailand a 'pilot plant': it presented, he declared, 'an opportunity for American capital to demonstrate what private enterprise can accomplish in the development of a country'.[123] After Sarit's death in 1963—two weeks after President Kennedy's assassination—his colleagues, Thanom and Praphat, took over. In 1968 they experimented with a new constitution, and in 1969 they added an elected lower house to an appointed senate. Development had, however, changed Thailand, and the ageing dictators found it slipping out of their control. The shift in US policy also worked against them. In November 1971 they carried out a coup against their own creations, but they could not restore Sarit-style absolutism. The new middle-class and its offspring undermined them: in October 1973 a movement to restore constitutionalism, stimulated by a small group of academics, politicians, and students, 'snowballed' into huge demonstrations, and the dictatorship fell.[124] The monarchy's position had changed, too. Under Rama IX it became not simply something for dictators to manipulate: its popular support gave it a political role of its own. King Bhumibol became the citizen king that Vajiravudh had contemplated, but used his power to curb the excesses of dictators and also democrats.

In 1959 Sarit's foreign minister, Thanat Khoman, had suggested that immature democracy meant instability. Should Thailand try once more to 'revamp the imported institutions, adapt them to our needs and replant them with the hope that they will be able to take root and prosper?' He thought it 'preferable to fall back on ourselves and forget about these institutions for a time. It is immaterial if in this process some voices from abroad may clamour that democracy experiences a setback in Asia. ... It is of no avail to try to ape those who, after all, are different from us in many respects.'[125] But Darling rightly questions whether 'the democratic ideas accepted by the growing middle class were any longer Western or "alien"'.[126]

Conclusion

The colonial powers had more or less half-heartedly sought to develop democratic politics, and the war on the whole strengthened its hold. No kind of regime could entirely free itself from the concept. How positively it would be used and whether it would be given real meaning were other questions. It had the potential to offer stability and to resolve conflict, but that would certainly require the give-and-take of which Rizal had spoken. That was experience which the colonial powers, even if willing, could never provide. But the post-colonial elites were perhaps too ready to resort to other methods.

Notes

1 q. L. Gleeck, 'President Hoover and the Philippines', *Bulletin of the American Historical Collection*, 9, 4 (October–December 1981), p. 39.

2 q. Friend, *Between Two Empires*, p. 254.

3 q. L. Gleeck, *American Institutions in the Philippines (1898–1941)*, Manila: Historical Conservation Society, 1976.

4 *The Cornerstone of Philippine Independence*, NY: Century, 1922, pp. 200–1.

5 Paredes in Ruby R. Paredes, ed., *Colonial Democracy*, Yale UP, 1988, p. 65.

6 'The Relationship between Burmese Social Classes and British-Indian Policy on the Behavior of the Burmese Political Elite, 1937–1942', PhD thesis, Cornell U, p. 207.

7 Schmutzer, p. 73.

8 q. R. Paredes, 'The Partido Federal, 1900–1907: Political Collaboration in Colonial Manila', PhD thesis, Michigan U, 1989, p. 182.

9 q. T. Friend, *The Blue-eyed Enemy*, PUP, 1988, p. 110.

10 H. de la Costa, 'Nascent Philippine Nationalism, 1872–1896', *Philippine Historical Review*, 3, 1 (1970). p. 166.

11 B. S. Salamanca, *The Filipino Reaction to American Rule, 1901–1913*, Shoestring P, 1968, p. 63.

12 q. Friend, *Between Two Empires*, p. 152.

13 q. Gopinath, p. 46.

14 in Paredes, ed., p. 120.

15 Mahajani, pp. 432–3.

16 q. Gopinath, p. 67.

17 Friend, *Between Two Empires*, p. 212.

18 ibid., p. 214.

19 'The Japanese Occupation of the Philippines: Commonwealth Sustained', *Philippine Studies*, 36 (1988), p. 102.

20 ibid., p. 103.

21 Kerkvliet, p. 147.

22 Paul McNutt, q. K. T. Carlson, 'The Twisted Road to Freedom', MA thesis, U of Victoria, 1990, p. 16.

23 *The Philippines*, Englewood Cliffs: Prentice-Hall, 1965, p. 95.

24 MacDermot to Eden, 31 May 1945, 17. F.O. 371/46463 [F 3822/1127/23].

25 *Philippine Land Tenure Reform*, Manila: US Mutual Security Agency, 1982, p. 8.

26 Grunder and Livezey, p. 284.

27 q. Andrew B. Gonzalez, *Language and Nationalism*, Quezon City, 1980, p. 46.

28 Teodore M. Locsin, q. J. R. E. Waddell, *An Introduction to Southeast Asian Politics*, Sydney: Wiley, 1972, p. 248.

29 q. David G. Timberman, *A Changeless Land*, Singapore: ISEAS, 1991, p. 27.

30 in R. McVey, ed., *Southeast Asian Capitalists*, Cornell UP, 1992, p. 151.

31 'The Philippines: Tradition and Change', *Asian Survey*, 10, 1 (January 1970), pp. 56–7.

32 Timberman, p. 70.

33 in J. Silverstein, ed., *Independent Burma at Forty Years*, Cornell UP, 1989, pp. 29, 27.

34 pp. 24, 25.

35 I (45) 1, 3 January 1945. L/PO/238, India Office Library.

36 Louis Allen, '"Leaving the Sinking Ship". A Comment on Burma and the End of Empire', in D. K. Bassett and V. T. King, eds, *Britain and South-East Asia*, Hull, 1986, pp. 73–5.

37 *Pyidawtha*, Rangoon, 1954, p. 10.

38 'The Political Split in Burma', *Far Eastern Survey* (October 1958).

39 q. Silverstein, *Forty Years*, p. 37n.

40 F. K. Lehman, ed., *Military Rule in Burma since 1962*, Singapore: Maruzen, 1981, p. 6.

41 John Badgley, 'Burma's Military Government ...', *Asian Survey*, 11, 6 (August 1962), p. 25.

42 in Silverstein, p. 70.

43 in Lehman, p. 71.

44 *The Shan of Burma*, p. 108.

45 in Silverstein, p. 78.

46 Bootsma, p. 70.

47 q. Penders, *Documents*, p. 129.

48 p. 130.

49 q. Shigeru Sato, *War, Nationalism and Peasants*, St Leonards: Allen and Unwin, 1994, p. 62.

50 Aiko Kurasawa, 'Mobilization and Control: A Study of Social Change in Rural Java, 1942–1945', PhD thesis, Cornell U, 1988, pp. 498–9, 495.

51 p. 483.

52 q. Reid, *Blood*, p. 126.

53 pp. 461, 470–3.

54 q. Kurasawa, p. 478.

55 David Bourchier, 'Totalitarianism and the "National Personality": Recent Controversy about the Philosophical Basis of the Indonesian State', in Jim Schiller and B. Martin Schiller, eds, *Imagining Indonesia: Cultural Politics and Political Culture*, Athens, Ohio, 1997, pp. 159–61, 168.

56 Lucas in A. Kahin, p. 41.

57 R. Cribb, 'A Revolution Delayed...', AJPH, 32 (1986), p. 77.

58 q. Tarling, *Cold War*, p. 88.

59 q. Reid, *Blood*, p. 172.

60 Cornell, 1968, pp. 21–2, 24–5.

61 *Portrait of a Patriot*, The Hague: Mouton, 1972, p. 555.

62 *Indonesia's Economic Stabilization and Development*, NY: IPR, 1957, p. 46.

63 p. xv.

64 D. W. Fryer, 'Economic Aspects of Indonesian Disunity', PA, 30, 3 (September 1957), p. 197.

65 H. Feith, *The Decline of Constitutional Democracy in Indonesia*, Cornell UP, 1962, p. 113ff.

66 q. ibid., p. 357.

67 *The Indonesian Elections of 1955*, Cornell UP, 1957, p. 5.

68 ibid., p. 91.

69 *Decline*, p. 471.

70 *Elections*, p. 91.

71 B. Harvey, *Permesta: Half a Rebellion*, Cornell UP, 1977, p. 152.

72 Goh Cheng Taik, 'Why Indonesia's Attempt at Democracy in the Mid-1950s Failed', MAS, 6, 2 (1972), p. 244.

73 Feith in R. McVey, *Indonesia*, New Haven: HRAF, 1963, p. 322.

74 q. Feith, *Decline*, p. 517.

75 *Autobiography*, Indianapolis, 1963, p. 279.

76 q. Legge, p. 331.

77 q. D. Hindley, *The Communist Party of Indonesia*, UCP, 1964, p. 58.

78 McVey phrases, in McVey in D. S. Lev and R. McVey, eds, *Making Indonesia*, Cornell UP, 1996, p. 101.

79 q. Hindley, p. 288.

80 McVey in Lev and McVey, p. 110.

81 ibid., p. 112.

82 'The September 30 Movement in Indonesia', MAS, 5, 1 (1971), p. 14.

83 in R. Cribb, ed., *The Indonesian Killings*, Monash U, 1990, p. 27.

84 q. R. Emerson, *Malaysia*, NY: Macmillan, 1937, pp. 174–5.

85 R. Vasil, *Politics in a Plural Society*, KL: OUP, 1971, p. 35.

86 Irene M. Tinker, 'Malayan Elections: Electoral Pattern for Plural Societies?', *Western Political Quarterly*, 9, 2 (June 1956), p. 279.

87 q. ibid., p. 280.

88 K. J. Ratnam and R. S. Milne, *The Malayan Parliamentary Election of 1964*, Singapore: UMP, 1967, p. 110.

89 Karl von Vorys, *Democracy without Consensus*, Princeton UP, 1975, p. 161.

90 *Elites and Regimes in Malaysia*, Clayton: Monash, 1996, p. 101.

91 Crouch in H. Crouch, Lee Kam Hing, and Michael Ong, eds, *Malaysian Politics and the 1978 Election*, KL: OUP, 1980, p. 3.

92 p. 115.

93 Marshall's memorandum, April 1956. GBPP, *Singapore Constitutional Conference*, Cmd 9777, Appendix 4.

94 q. Chan Heng Chee, *A Sensation of Independence*, Singapore: OUP, 1984, p. 171.

95 Ong Chit Chung, 'The 1959 Singapore General Elections', JSEAS, 6, 1 (March 1975), p. 63.

96 q. Tremewan, p. 17.

97 q. Turnbull, *Singapore*, p. 274.

98 Milne in Wang, p. 332.

99 Minute, 9 March 1956. F.O. 371/123212 [D 1052/4] Public Record Office, London.

100 *The Politics of Belonging*, KL: OUP, 1974, p. 75.

101 M. Vickery in B. Kiernan and Chantou Boua, *Peasants and Politics in Kampuchea, 1942–1981*, London: Zed, 1982, p. 92.

102 *Brother Number One*, Boulder: Westview, 1992, p. 49.

103 *New Zealand Herald*, 2 November.

104 q. Allen B. Cole, ed., *Conflict in Indo-China*, Ithaca: Cornell UP, 1956, p. 19.

105 ibid., p. 22.

106 David L. Anderson, *Trapped by Success*, NY: Columbia UP, 1991, p. 128.

107 q. Bernard B. Fall, *The Two Viet-Nams*, NY: Praeger, 1963, p. 249.

108 William J. Duiker, *U.S. Containment and the Conflict in Indochina*, Stanford UP, 1994, p. 246.

109 Roy Jumper, 'Mandarin Bureaucracy and Politics in South Viet Nam', PA, 30, 1 (March 1957), pp. 153–5.

110 Charles Mohr, q. Kahin and Lewis, p. 268n.

111 *The Real Face of Sakdina*, in C. Reynolds, *Thai Radical Discourse*, Ithaca: Cornell UP, 1987, p. 142.

112 Johns to Simon, 29 June 1932, 137. F.O. 371/16261 [F 5918/4260/40], Public Record Office, London.

113 Chula Chakrabongse, *The Twain Have Met*, London, n.d., p. 185.

114 q. B. Batson, ed., *Siam's Political Future*, Ithaca: Cornell UP, 1974, pp. 101–2.

115 q. N. Tarling, 'Atonement before Absolution', JSS, 66, 1 (January 1978), p. 22.

116 Minute by Palliser, 12 April 1948. F.O. 371/69991 [F 5435/21/40], Public Record Office, London.

117 *Thailand and the United States*, Washington: Public Affairs P, 1965, p. 67.

118 Darling, p. 92.

119 q. Kobkua, p. 60.

120 Daniel Fineman, *A Special Relationship*, Honolulu: U Hawaii P, 1997, pp. 124–5.

121 q. Darling, p. 179.

122 Kobkua, p. 212.

123 q. Darling, p. 172.

124 Anderson and Mendiones, p. 37.

125 q. Insor, p. 110.

126 p. 197.

4.4

Authoritarianism

It seemed possible by the mid-1990s that the political systems of the nation-states that converged in ASEAN would themselves converge in what Clark Neher was prepared to call 'Asian democracy'. Such regimes were markedly authoritarian, often affording the army a special role, but were tempered by the long-standing practice of patron–client relations, and by a residual democracy. In the late 1990s that convergence seemed less certain. The economic crisis of 1997–98 challenged the various regimes, and they reacted in different ways. Was convergence on a more democratic approach possible?

In the postwar phase a democratic approach to politics in Southeast Asia had been promoted by international trends. In the course of winning independence, or in the case of Thailand of ensuring its continuance, the democratic elements in domestic politics had been thrust to the fore, and the association between independence and democracy brought out. It contended with more authoritarian approaches, looking for justification in the pre-colonial past, inheriting colonial absolutism, recalling the practices of the Japanese occupation. The problems the new states faced in the economic and political field could be presented as arguments for such approaches. Was it possible to hold the new states together without them? Without them how could they handle the economic expectations that independence had raised, but which the Korean War boom could only temporarily satisfy? Democracy had, of course, the potential for dealing with such issues, perhaps more effectively, and in some cases at least its defenders did not make the most of it. Though the concept was domesticated in Southeast Asia, its practical hold on Southeast Asian politics diminished in the 1960s. Already the Sangkum dominated Cambodia, Sarit had seized power in Thailand, and Ne Win had taken over in Burma for a second time. By the end of that decade the Suharto regime was installed in Indonesia, Malaysia was under the National Operations Council, and Marcos had been re-elected.

These changes were also promoted by international trends. Southeast Asia's location expanded the political significance of what happened there. It thus became a focus for the Cold War, and it was particularly affected by the means the United States adopted to deal with the implications for the struggle of the communist victory in China and the consequent changes in the role of Japan. Its increasingly direct involvement in the Vietnam War was accompanied by a less direct involvement in Thailand, which yet contributed to the military take-over. US policy was disposed to support 'strong men', leaders less noted for their endorsement of democracy than for their opposition to communism. Its policy towards development also changed. It was argued that economic advance was a question of take-off. For that a strong government was needed, such as Japan had possessed after the Meiji restoration.

These arguments neglected the disadvantages of such a change of approach, and the potential of democracy for dealing with those disadvantages. One problem was recognised, that 'strong men' had to establish their political legitimacy. There was another limit on their capacity to supply the leadership and stability that were sought: they were mortal. Whatever its intrinsic advantages, a democratic regime has the practical advantage that it offers a means of resolving the problem of political succession without coup or conflict. In the economic field, it was not merely a matter of take-off, but of ensuring that economic advance was maintained. That, after all, the Japanese had themselves discovered. If it was not to depend entirely on the continued involvement of foreign investors, and the continued application of foreign know-how, it might require a more dynamic approach to intellectual activity than 'strong men' tend to find politically convenient.

Whatever their strengths or weaknesses, authoritarian concepts were not attractive only to American policy-makers, but to those in Southeast Asia, too. Like other ideas in Southeast Asia's past, like democracy indeed, the concepts were domesticated, but given their own inflection, differing indeed from country to country. Those technocrats trained in the United States themselves might have no domestic power-base, but, believing that they had answers to the problems their countries faced, looked for patrons. They found them in army leaders or in 'strong men' like Marcos, however much their longer-term aspirations might differ. The model itself might be deficient. Its application in these circumstances might have quite unexpected results, strengthening strong men, but also placing development under their patronage, or making the stability it required depend on their wisdom or longevity. Such a system also risked reducing the flexibility and responsiveness a 'developing' economy required if it were not to become entirely reliant upon the great corporations that came to dominate the global economy. The local elite might come to resemble the collaborators of the colonial period. But, whereas colonial powers had difficulty in changing their collaborators, multinational corporations, for which Southeast Asia was but one area of activity, found them more easily disposable.

The colonial relationship overlaid traditional patron–client relationships without displacing them. So, too, did the relationship between international capital and the political systems of independent Southeast Asia. The democratic approach had been inflected by them: parties were often aggregations of factions, and pork-barrel a means to distribute favours and privileges. Shifting away from that approach only emphasised their role: patron–client relationships were a fundamental support for the 'neo-patrimonial' regimes of Southeast Asia. They inflected their authoritarian-ism, too. But the regimes were deprived of the openness or 'transparency' that democracy could better provide, and that came to seem a necessity.

New Order

The 'New Order' in Indonesia was to be welcome to the outside powers, concerned at the threat to Malaysia and the advance of communist influence. It was also to owe a great deal to outside sources of aid and investment. But its nature can only be understood in terms of the way it came to power. It did not simply originate in the growing strength of the army and the weakness of its opponents. It originated also in the massacres that followed the failed coup of 30 September 1965. They not only eliminated the communists. They also created a sense of complicity with the new regime, and at the same time a sense that the crisis thus resolved was caused by others, by dabbling in democracy and left-wing politics, by experiments that must not be repeated. Though the army played a role in stimulating the massacres, it was able to present them as the result of Old Order chaos.

The colonial state had been held together by a military-bureaucratic apparatus, interleaved with long-standing practices of cooption and manipulation. Forging a participatory policy had partially reduced particularism, but at the cost of polaris-ing differences on the basis of nationalism, Islam, and communism. President Sukarno's answer was no better. His mass campaigns, as Ken Young puts it, 'deep-ened divisions as much as they superseded them'.[1] If the old military-bureaucratic restraints were removed, violence was likely to be very great, violence that would reflect both the particularism of the colonial past and the polarisation of the phase since independence. Moreover, the army did not merely remove its restraints. It encouraged violence.

In both the electoral and Guided Democracy phases, mobilisation had extended ideological differences to village level, consolidating what some have seen as 'primor-dial' loyalties, and *aksi sepihak* had shown the potential for conflict. Even so the scale of the violence that now ensued seems disproportionate. For that there may be two reasons. One comprises the local factors that were still very much part of Indonesia's social and political life. The other is the role of the army, which was prepared to risk unleashing violence in the belief that it could thereby consolidate its position.

Certainly there was a range of local factors, as Robert Cribb has shown. In Lampung local Muslims killed Javanese migrants. In Indonesian Timor, Protestant clergy who had allied with poor peasants were an easy target. In western Lombok, Muslim Sasaks attacked the traditional Balinese ruling elite. In Bali itself land had increasingly come into the hands of the old elite, but it resented its absence of polit-ical power. It had looked to the PNI, while in face of that the Sukarno-appointed regional head, Anak Agung Bagus Suteja, had looked to the PKI. Intervillage rival-ries led whole villages to declare for the PKI, and thus to condemn themselves to extirpation, along with members of the ruling house of Jembrana, from which Suteja came. If in Bali the PKI was antipathetic to Hinduism and its upholders, in East Java it was associated with Hinduism, and exposed to attack by Muslim vigilantes. In Java, indeed, the ferocity of the killings was associated with the old *santri–abangan* rift, polarised by more recent events. The Muslim youth group Ansor, affiliated to NU, played the main vigilante role. Indeed the unleashing of youth was a powerful energiser of the bloody purges.

The army, particularly KOSTRAD and RPKAD, played a direct role in the killing, but also armed and encouraged the vigilantes. Widespread killings did not generally begin until elite military units arrived in a locality and sanctioned violence by instruction or example. Where the army opposed the use of auxiliaries, as in West Java, deaths were fewer. The violence was 'more than the climax of years of internal struggle within Indonesian society. It was a political choice deliberately taken by the military commanders who controlled perhaps the only instrument of State policy that could be relied upon—the army itself.'[2] Geoffrey Robinson questions Sarwo Edhie's remark that, while in Java 'we had to egg the people on to kill Communists', in Bali 'we have to restrain them'. Killing had begun in Bali before RPKAD arrived, but it increased thereafter. The army, it seems, wanted to control the violence, not prevent it.[3] From outside Indonesia came expressions of support rather than restraint. US officials made it clear that their government was 'generally sympathetic and admiring of what the Army [was] doing'.[4] The embassy helpfully provided lists of communist cadres. But, totally unprepared and often resigned to their fate, followers were eliminated too.[5]

This provided the background for the dissolution of the Old Order, and the installation of the new. The army hesitated to take direct action against Sukarno because of his revolutionary role, and because of the sympathy for him among Javanese officers. His position was, however, greatly weakened by the destruction of the PKI, and his attempts to point out that it had had a major share in the national struggle were counter-productive. In January 1966 students demonstrated in Jakarta against rising prices and called for the dissolution of the PKI. Sukarno tried to reassert his power. He announced a new cabinet, dropping Nasution, retaining Subandrio. Massive demonstrations followed, and on 11 March troops surrounded the palace. Suharto insisted that full powers be conferred on him (Supersemar), the PKI was dissolved, and Subandrio arrested. Appalled at the massacres and unwilling to compromise, Sukarno saw the remnants of his authority removed bit by bit. The provisional MPR (People's Deliberative Congress) elected Nasution chairman and revoked the life tenure that Sukarno had been granted. Its study committee sought an explanation of his role in the coup. Deeming it unsatisfactory, the MPR deprived him of his functions in March 1967, and made Suharto Acting President. Only a year later did Suharto assume the title as well as the functions.

Enjoying political support from outside, the New Order also tapped into the economic resources of the world system, as the United States increasingly stressed the importance of building strong regimes in Southeast Asia, rather than undertaking direct intervention, and the Japanese tried to set a larger economic role in the framework of a more acceptable political rhetoric. Central to the New Order's policies, as Jim Schiller has put it, was a 'state project' of economic growth and state-building in conjunction with foreign and domestic capital, and unlike previous Indonesian regimes it was able to 'borrow' power from states and classes in the world system by way of extra-systemic resources of capital, technology, and skills.[6] The oil boom of the 1970s was turned to account. Technology enabled the government to gain expanded access to oil and minerals and to monitor local and provincial governments more effectively. The 1984–85 budget was forty times the budget of 1967–68.

The 'state project' was shaped by those who led it. As David Brown has pointed out,[7] the New Order regime was frequently cited when the concept of a 'neo-patrimonial' state was developed in the late 1960s. In the traditional patrimonial state fiefs and benefices were distributed in return for tribute and loyalty. Then resources were limited and so was the power of the state. In the modern version of such a state, the ruler behaves in a not dissimilar way, but has more patronage and greater coercive power, provided he can sustain conditions acceptable to international capital and the leaders of the major world states.

The army in Indonesia presented a technocratic face and the regime employed technocrats. Suharto brought back Sumitro Djojohadikusomo, who had been in the PRRI cabinet, as minister for trade and commerce. His protégés at the University of Indonesia had developed links with SESKOAD, the Army Staff and Command School, encouraged by Guy Pauker, part of a Ford-funded MIT team in Indonesia, who had argued in 1959 that soldiers would be a better counter to communists than socialists would be. In 1966 Suharto asked Widjojo Nitisastro, recently returned from Berkeley, to form a team of advisers. He rejected Sarbini Somawinata, also an economics professor, who wanted a democratic approach, countering the economists he chose, not with democrats, but with 'nationalists' like B. J. Habibie, who adopted 'unorthodox' approaches, partly designed to escape the limits imposed by the multinational corporations. Technocrats after all operated in a political context, whether or not it was a democratic one.

'The problem the competing groups have to face is not how to mobilize the masses to change decisions, but how to influence the President's decisions by manipulating the factional balance within the top levels of the military and bureaucracy.'[8] The New Order completed the displacement of the parties that Guided Democracy had begun, and they could no longer be the means of competing for power and patronage. It developed the corporatist structure, already started under Guided Democracy, 'a system of functionally based organizations acting as conduits between societal interests and the state'.[9] The competition now took a factional form. It was not reduced by the increased availability of resources available, but it became easier to regulate, because of the lack of public exposure, and, so long as it could be sustained, because of economic growth. '[P]atrimonial largesse and efficiency proceeded hand in hand', Amal says.[10] The system was, of course, bound to produce favouritism, nepotism, and corruption. It also produced a further Javanisation of the political and military elite. At the same time it seemed to put at least the leading Chinese in a privileged, if dependent, position: they were important to the military, but could not be allowed to feel too secure.

The New Order was, as Liddle puts it, 'a political desert'.[11] But it 'depoliticised' the management of the state only in the sense that it retreated from the mass participation in politics that had in different ways marked both electoral democracy and Guided Democracy. Even so it did not entirely abandon participation. By contrast to the colonial regime—which in some respects it resembled—the New Order felt bound to seek democratic legitimation. It was *negara pejabat*, the *Beamtenstaat*, in McVey's phrase.[12] But merely relying on army or bureaucracy, supplemented by deference and patronage, was no longer sufficient. The answer was not to abandon participation altogether, but to control it, so that it would help to contain frustration and to limit repression. The idea was indeed not entirely foreign to the experience of the colonial regime in its latter days. The New Order differed inasmuch as it was not directly responsible to a metropolitan government, and could indeed depict expressions of outside opinion as interference. It also differed inasmuch as it manipulated the parties it allowed and set up its own. Participation runs the risk of activating discontent, not alleviating it. The options for participation have to be prescribed, but not in too alienating a way.

In such a system elections are not designed to change governments but to endorse them: they are rituals rather than competitions. Indonesians were thus urged to make the election 'successful' (*siaksekan Pemelu*) and to celebrate a 'festival of democracy' (*pesta demokrasi*).[13] In such elections, however, it was not clear how the government should define an impressive victory. Nor, therefore, was it clear how much it was worth spending, either in terms of resources or in terms of the goodwill that might be lost by too repressive an approach. That left the opposition some room for manoeuvre. It could not hope to win power at the national or regional level, but it might challenge the government at the local level, building on factions not attracted by the rewards the state offered and not dependent on it, and finding a mass support that could resist state pressure. The NU, as Schiller points out, maintained a viable alternative in Jepara, which he has studied in such an illuminating way.

The government moved against the PKI after the 1965 coup, but other parties were also emasculated. It was in a strong position to intimidate them after the massacres, and it sought to maintain an atmosphere of fear. Opsus, the army's special operations group, subverted their conventions. Though Muslim groups and Muslim students played an important role in the founding years of the New Order, the government did not permit the revival of Masjumi, associated with the regional revolts, and it intervened in Parmusi (Partai Muslimin) as well as in PNI. In 1973 the government further limited the parties by compressing them into two groups, PPP (the Islamic groups) and PDI (the others). 'With one and only road already mapped out, why should we then have nine different cars?' Suharto asked.[14] It also changed the electoral rules. It developed the concept of the 'floating mass', implying that partici- pation was limited to a vote in the elections: there were to be no politics at village level between elections, and party branches below the *kabupaten* level were closed down.

Not content with the manipulation of other parties, the government set up its own. Sekber Golkar (Joint Secretariat of Functional Groups) had been started in 1964 to counter PKI influence. In 1969–70 it was restructured as the government's election machine as it moved towards the second national election in 1971. Officials, already made to join KORPRI (Corps of State Officials), hastened to join Golkar, for they had no wish to share the fate of the left-wing officials, many from the PNI, who had been declared inactive after the coup. More widely Golkar worked by campaigning, even between elections. Above all, however, it worked by employing patron–client networks, coopting rather than coercing leaders and helping them to build their followings. in 1971 it secured 62.8 per cent of the vote; in 1977 it was to secure 62.11 per cent; in 1982, 64 per cent; in 1987, 73 per cent; in 1992, 68 per cent. Half the seats in provincial and *kabupaten* assemblies were reserved for Golkar appointees, and military commanders and their civilian counterparts at district and sub-district level were involved in securing the government's victories. Village heads were told that their loyalty was being tested. Their position was indeed crucial for the New Order as for previous regimes. They were rewarded by the assignment of land, as in the past, and they were given incentives for tax collection. But above all they now became a funnel for funds and supplies under government development programmes: they had 'power of disposal over the torrent of resources which flowed into the village'.[15] Golkar did not win over the *santri* elements, and it remained, as Brown says, an alliance of communal groups—locality-based, ethno-linguistic and religious in character—in which resource allocation was always threatening to pro- voke rivalries.[16]

'The crucial foundation of the New Order's ideology lies in its discourse of a vio- lent genealogy', writes Ariel Heryanto.[17] The state was, however, not without an ide- ological underpinning, whatever it meant to the mass of the people. It adopted Pantjasila, articulated by Sukarno in 1945 in rather different circumstances and for a rather different purpose: it became not a political compromise, but 'the ideologi- cal expression of an indigenous culture'.[18] In his national day speech of 1982 Suharto described it as *asas tunggal* (sole foundation) for all parties. A decree of 1984 required all parties to adopt it, and NU withdrew from active politics, returning to 'the commitment of 1926'.[19] Under Guided Democracy Sukarno had distilled out of *adat* traditions the concepts of deliberation (*musyawarah*) and consensus (*mufakat*), which became 'cultural-ideological instruments' of the New Order, too.[20] Added in was an emphasis on development that Sukarno could never have endorsed: Suharto's title, *Bapak Pembangunan*, Father of Development, suggested some of the paradoxes involved.

In the late 1980s the integralist ideas associated with Supomo resurfaced, and were incorporated in P4, the ideological sessions millions of Indonesians attended each year, and in school and university courses. That, David Bourchier suggests, was probably the regime's answer to the trend towards greater democracy elsewhere in the Third World. Indonesia was not to be judged by Western standards, the government was saying: the collective well-being came first. 'We are indeed moving towards greater freedom', Moerdiono, the state secretary, declared in 1990, 'but the rhythm must be arranged (*diatur*). It is like an orchestra, where each of the instruments had its own particular function to perform in accordance with the melody.'[21] The regime, Bourchier thinks, perhaps overplayed its hand. Critics of the New Order were prompted to revive interest in Sjahrir and Hatta, and Adnan Buyung Nasution, a human rights lawyer, pointed to the commitment to political rights and freedoms of the members of the constituent assembly of 1956–59. That discourse was not dead after all.

There was a widespread feeling that the system had to be changed. But Suharto was re-elected in March 1998, and only the intensifying economic crisis prompted his overthrow in May. The revolution was driven by students, campaigning against *korupsi, kolusi, nepotisme.* The middle class, who had 'ceded their political rights in exchange for social stability and economic growth',[22] were pushed into action by the crisis. Getting rid of Suharto offered the political establishment a way out. Would the revolution go further? The fear of chaos checked the radicals, but also those in power. The attempt at an orderly procedure, with the Vice-President Habibie taking over, was not merely time-serving. It allowed Indonesia to restore a measure of democratic practice as well as discourse, despite some outbursts of violence, and to give some reality to its democratic commitment by redeveloping institutions of civil society that authoritarianism had destroyed or aborted.

'Apart from one burnt polling station, a shortage of ink and ballot papers, and a few other glitches based on inexperience, Indonesia's first free elections in 44 years were almost a model of decorum and transparency.'[23] The Indonesian Democratic Party (PDI), heir to PNI and led by Sukarno's daughter, Megawati, won 34 per cent of the votes in June 1999, Golkar came second with 22 per cent, and the National Awakening Party (PKB), offspring of NU, won 13 per cent. In October the MPR elected the head of PKB, Abdurrahman Wahid, as president, rather than Megawati. She, however, became vice-president, and it seemed possible that, after all, democracy was again offering Indonesians a legitimated government and a chance to create the stability and unity which, as Geoff Forrester suggests, they have long craved.[24]

New Society

In the Philippines Marcos had been overthrown by 'People's Power' in February 1986, and the democratic system had been restored. All the more, perhaps, because of his attack on it, it reappeared substantially in its old form, though with a renewed determination to make it work, and a wider sense of identification with it. It was true, too, that, despite his announced intentions and his long tenure of office,

Marcos had not created a 'New Society'. He had only distorted the old, in some sense already incipiently authoritarian.

At the outset of the martial law regime in September 1972, the prospects had seemed rather different. It was possible to see the creation of an authoritarian regime in the context of the development literature of the 1960s, and to take it as a means of establishing the strong government that was now held to be required. The United States accepted the coup because it might produce a more effective government in a region in which governments were now expected to take more responsibility for their defence, and in a country where it based forces it would use to provide the overall shield it still promised. The United States also accepted the take-over because it was in keeping with the new emphasis in development theory. The World Bank and the International Monetary Fund indeed welcomed the new regime. The role of outsiders in the Marcos coup must not, however, be exaggerated, nor must the fact that it initially opened up new opportunities for American investors be alleged as evidence that they promoted it. The coup had domestic origins.

To some extent they indeed lay with Filipinos who had in a sense internalised current development theory, the so-called technocrats, influenced by foreign advisers, trained in the United States or in the American-funded Colleges of Business Administration and Public Administration at the University of the Philippines or at the Asian Institute of Management. They had concluded that the old system obstructed development and that Marcos, who had after all enlisted their talents in his first administration, was the strong man they needed. The business community had been divided by the changes of the 1960s which had removed controls and permitted devaluation, and thus weakened the fledgling import-substitution industrialists and helped the traditional agricultural export sector. Some industrialists moved towards the nationalists, but the majority preferred the development strategy espoused by the technocrats. What the technocrats—men like Rafael Salas, Alejandro Melchor, Cesar Virata, Vicente Paterno, Jaime Laya—depended upon, however, was the favour of the President.

> Under the Bonapartist regime the intelligentsia—or at least a section of it: the technocrats—never had it so good. Great opportunities for fabulous incomes ... [had] suddenly been opened to them with the entry of multi-national corporations and the proliferation of new government agencies. Furthermore, the suspension of political institutions previously dominated by the traditional oligarchy [had] immensely enhanced their influence in the making of public policies and programs.[25]

But that influence was subject to the priorities that Marcos imposed, and they were political in nature. However much the theory of development might envisage 'depoliticisation', that was, of course, impossible in practice. The New Order in Indonesia turned from a participatory form of politics to a bureaucratic form of politics. In the New Society again regime politics oriented around the President. Despite the rhetoric, his aims were fundamentally political. The technocrats had been enlisted for a political purpose, and in the end men like Virata and Laya could not speak out. Freed from Congress interference, they were now subject to crony interference.

Marcos aimed, as Hawes puts it, at 'preservation' not 'transformation'.[26] He can perhaps be best understood by placing him in the succession of previous presidents. The office had always possessed a vast potential for power. Compared to the dictators of the 1930s, Quezon had realised it, not only by campaigning for independence and social justice, but by aggregating patron–client relationships on an unprecedented scale. Magsaysay had uncovered another possibility that could only extend as the electorate expanded, the power to undercut the oligarchy and the institutions it supported by direct presidential contact with the barrios. Marcos outdid Quezon and reinterpreted Magsaysay.

The more Marcos changed Philippines society, the more it was the same. The emphasis on 'development' persuaded investors and international bankers to part with their money, but the inflow of capital was intended to create a yet stronger system of patronage and clientelism. Outside resources were acquired to extend the old system, not to replace it. The economy was placed in the hands of 'cronies', who owed their position to him. Cronyism, as Hawes puts it,[27] was an exaggeration of, not a deviation from, the existing relationship of economic and political power in the Philippines. But it proved counter-productive. Accompanied by mismanagement, it helped to destroy the economy, not to develop it, and in turn that undermined the government itself. 'There has been a profound loss of confidence in President Marcos and his ability to govern', declared a US Senate Committee on Foreign Relations report in October 1984. '… There is a sense of despair when people in the provinces speak of the government's ability to understand, let alone address effectively, the range of problems besetting the country.'[28] The regime was notorious for corruption on a scale hitherto undreamed-of. It was a 'kleptocracy', as Stephen Solarz put it,[29] designed to make Marcos the ultimate patron, and to prevent others piling up wealth.

The regime was, in Nemenzo's phrase, Bonapartist. In other words, it envisaged popular participation in terms of plebiscite, securing popular sanction for government policies rather than promoting debate about them. The constitution, for example, was 'ratified' by show of hands at citizens' assemblies. Marcos cloaked his regime with legality, or legalities: it was 'constitutional authoritarianism'. He was indeed unwilling to set up instruments for the control of public participation, such as are commonly found in corporatist states, perhaps because he feared the strength of the old political culture.

For the elections he finally scheduled for the Interim National Assembly in 1978, however, he created a government party, the Kilusang Bagong Lipunan (New Society Movement), based on the old Nacionalista party. Amid accusations of fraud, the opposition won only fourteen seats, thirteen in the Visayas and one in Mindanao. In January 1980 Marcos called snap local elections, in which KBL won 95 per cent of all the seats. By 1981 he felt able to dispense with martial law. He was still re-elected President in 1981. What tended to provoke active opposition was, not simply economic decline, not all of which could be blamed on the regime, but the regime's excess. Subsidies, monopolies, and cheap loans substituted a 'ruthless elite for a merely inefficient one'.[30] The government destroyed the press, one of the checks in the Philippines system, once perhaps too free, now certainly unduly subservient. What finally undid the regime, however, was its apparent resort to high-level assassination, unprecedentedly escalating the violence that had long marked Philippines politics and that the regime, despite its pretensions, had only expanded. Now it was no longer a question of low-level 'salvaging', the Filipino version of right-wing government-sponsored terrorism.

With an eye on international criticism and a view to portraying himself as a defender of democracy, Marcos had allowed the Liberal leader, Benigno Aquino, detained since 1972, to stand for the Interim Assembly in 1978. He chose as his campaign theme Lakas Ng Bayan, People Power (Laban). Even in such an election, his charisma was powerful. 'Marcos won the election but Ninoy won the hearts and minds', as Napoleon Rama, who had been vice-president of the constitutional convention, put it.[31] Released after pressure from the Carter administration in 1980 and allowed to go to the United States for medical treatment, he was shot at Manila airport on his return on 21 August 1983. Like Rizal, he was seen as a martyr: the Philippines was 'worth dying for', he had said.[32] The assassination, as the Senate Foreign Relations report put it, 'changed the political scene fundamentally. It has galvanised the political centre of Philippine society into active opposition, as evidenced by the National Assembly elections on 14 May 1984, and has proved a rallying point for the Left.'[33]

Marcos had seen those elections as 'an opportunity to refresh his mandate' before the presidential elections in 1987. It was also 'the litmus test of his government's willingness to open up the country's political process by allowing genuine participation of a democratic opposition'.[34] An authoritarian regime once more sought legitimacy in democracy. But, if it was to serve that purpose, it had to be controlled. The Marcos methods—martial law, now dropped; cronyism, a yet more exclusive patron–client system, now all too blatant; and now also, it was believed, assassination—did not ensure that. The opposition parties—UNIDO and the combined Philippine Democratic Party–Lakas Ng Bayan (PDP–Laban)—did far better than Marcos or US observers expected. Of the 183 seats contested, the opposition parties won fifty-nine, including sixteen out of Metro-Manila's twenty-one. A citizen watchdog group, Namfrel (National Movement for Free Elections), limited harassment on the part of Marcos's supporters. But some believed that, had the vote been fairer, the opposition would have won 100 seats.

Though the spread of communism was an argument for martial law, it expanded further under the Marcos regime. 'As people's livelihoods worsened, traditional loyalties, social relationships, and patron–client ties have disintegrated', Larry Niksch wrote. 'The government has been unable or unwilling to fill the vacuum, but the communists have keyed their efforts towards these socially displaced people.'[35] In the 1960s the old Moscow-line PKP had been challenged by José Ma. Sison and other student leaders at the University of the Philippines, who admired Mao and the cultural revolution he had set going in the People's Republic. Expelled by the PKP leadership in April 1967, Sison and his supporters formed the CPP the following year. He secured the army he needed when he was joined by Bernabe Buscayno (Commander Dante), a leader of the Huks in the 1950s, now disaffected by their collapse into indiscriminate plundering as a result of the successful operations against them. The New People's Army was formed in March 1969. When martial law was proclaimed the NPA disappeared into the hills. Initially the guerrillas were ineffective. But better training enabled them to take advantage of the opportunities the failures of the regime offered them. The frustration among the anti-guerrilla forces prompted them to acts of violence that only helped the guerrillas, not only to win community support, but to cover their own violence by a public relations campaign against that of the government forces. Their growing success in the 1980s was a reason why the Reagan administration bluntly warned Marcos late in 1985 that reforms were urgently needed and threatened to cut off aid. It was soon after this that Marcos announced a snap presidential election. 'I want to settle once and for all these silly claims that my government is inept.'[36]

At this point, as he knew, the opposition parties were divided, with neither an agreed programme nor a single leader. The two most prominent candidates were the widow of the assassinated Benigno Aquino, Corazon (Cory), and Salvador (Doy) Laurel, leader of UNIDO. The former, though not a politician, had become a rallying-point of the opposition, and given it moral authority. The latter was the son of José P. Laurel, the wartime collaborator, and was a former associate of Marcos, but, though he lacked the popular appeal of Mrs Aquino, he was a shrewd politician. Cardinal Sin, the archbishop of Manila, brought them together. Marcos had the fanatical support of the Iglesia na Cristo sect. The attitude of the Catholic church itself was another matter. Cardinal Sin had advised 'critical collaboration', and the majority of the Catholic Bishops Conference of the Philippines were 'moderate'.[37] The assassination of Aquino prompted a change of approach.

'We are learning to bring our problems within a political framework instead of within that of irrationality, authoritarianism and violence', the archbishop declared from his pulpit. On behalf of Manila's bishops, he issued guidelines on the elections and warned against a plot to frustrate the expression of the people's will. 'If a candidate wins by cheating, he can only be forgiven by God if he renounces the office he has obtained by fraud.'[38] Fraud and intimidation marked the elections on 7 February. But what counted was the counting. Marcos attempted to falsify the results. Despite the indications from Namfrel, with 68 per cent of the returns counted, that Aquino was ahead by 7 318 552 to 6 657 195, the National Assembly declared Marcos the winner with 10 807 197 votes to Aquino's 9 291 716. Mrs Aquino announced a civil disobedience campaign. Tension increased, together with speculation that Marcos intended to silence his critics. It was then, on 22 February, that two of the most significant figures in the armed forces rebelled, Juan Ponce Enrile, the just resigned defence minister, and the vice chief-of-staff, Fidel Ramos.

Reformism in the AFP, though much discussed, had surfaced only in March 1985, when a group of Philippine Military Academy graduates demonstrated at a ceremony attended by the President. A 'Statement of Aspirations', drawn up in February, and a further statement of 'Common Aspiration', issued a month later, set out the aim of the reformists, 'an effective, efficient and fair-minded armed forces in the service of the country and the people'. 'Promotions and rewards should be on the basis of merit. The overall aim is to improve the morale of a military which has become largely alienated from the people, particularly in the combat areas.'[39] There was support at higher levels, from the board of the Association of AFP Generals and Flag Officers, from Enrile, and from Ramos, a critic of Ver, who took over as acting chief-of-staff during the investigation of the assassination, and who had a clean reputation.

Before the election Ramos met Enrile and several of his senior advisers, including reformists like Colonels Gregorio Honasan, Eduardo Kapunan, and Victor Batac. The assumption was that Aquino would win, and the plan was to force Marcos to concede. In the regions reform officers would neutralise the loyalists and prevent their moving support to Manila. In Manila there would be a 'surgical' strike, based on Camp Aguinaldo and Camp Crame. Carrying out the plan was foreshortened by intelligence reports that Marcos and Ver had ordered mass arrests. Enrile and Ramos began their rebellion on 22 February within Camp Aguinaldo, moving along the highway to Fort Crame, the PC headquarters, next day. They were exposed to air attack, but shielded on the ground by a human wall on Edsa Avenue. That Sunday morning Cardinal Sin had broadcast an appeal to 'all followers of Christ' to join the display of 'People's Power'.[40] Tanks from the loyalist Fort Bonifacio came to a halt before nuns kneeling before them. They turned back. Loyalist support crumbled, and the US government offered Marcos, not support, but asylum. On 25 February Corazon Aquino was sworn in as President.

These astounding and moving events captured the imagination of the world. Indeed the involvement of the media was part of their success, not only in mobilising People's Power in Manila, but in convincing the United States that continuing to support Marcos was out of the question. People's Power indeed encouraged the opponents of other authoritarian regimes, so that, as with the earlier opposition to colonial regimes, it might be catching. Like the revolution of 1896, however, the events of 1986 were unique to the Philippines. What had happened in Bangkok—as well as what was to happen in Beijing and Rangoon—was quite different, though comparisons may help with explanation.

The events of 1986 were, of course, an exceptional combination of military coup and popular protest. In any other circumstances the coup would surely have failed, for it was weakly organised, and its leaders had to act before they were ready. A more ruthless government could have put it down, particularly if it had acted promptly. Perhaps that is to the credit of Marcos and Ver. It also suggests their sense of a special relationship between the Philippines and the United States: in its old colony, whatever was the case elsewhere, the former colonial power would not continue to endorse the kind of regime it would have had to be. But the collapse of the regime was also evidence that it had never been organised with the method and elaboration of either the corporatist or the communist state. Though he talked of a New Society, Marcos was an old-fashioned kind of dictator, and a Filipino one, relying on extending traditional practices rather than modernising them. Corruption, familism, patronage, and clientelism were not enough. Pushed too far, they could indeed undermine, not only the prosperity that was supposed to be the outcome of the new regime, but also the efficiency and modernity that it had promised.

That perception came to be common in the armed forces. Without the national mission that the Indonesian army believed that it had been given by its role in the revolution, the AFP had shared the technocratic aspirations of the 1960s. Yet its military opponents seemed only to expand, while its civic action programmes seemed only to corrupt. The reform movement bears some comparison with the 'Young Turks' in the Thai army. Like them, they faced a paradox. If they acted, they would be increasing the politicisation of the army, not diminishing it. Supporting an avowed reformer, like Ramos, reduced the paradox, but did not eliminate it. Acting to defend an electoral outcome removed it at least for the time being.

People's Power itself was a Filipino phenomenon. Yet, while it had special features, it also had elements in common with popular movements elsewhere in Southeast Asia. It is an argument of this book that, at least since World War II, there was widespread acceptance that democracy was legitimate and legitimating and not, or no longer, merely an alien import, though it might still appeal to outsiders and be advocated by them and be a means to win their support. In the Philippines, participation had long been practised, and Marcos's Bonapartism had not displaced it. Indeed, he wanted to show that he could win. At the same time, it can still be argued that participation had an element of ritual obligation, and People's Power itself seemed to validate an older kind of politics that had trusted to spiritual power.

One result was to heighten the expectations of the Aquino regime. 'Mrs Aquino rode high on the people's devastation of the Marcos regime along with the antifascist line', as Sison put it. Now she took responsibility, 'and with democratic rights and processes being promoted, more and more people would make higher demands'.[41] Robert H. Reid and Eileen Guerrero suggest, rather contradictorily, both that her presidency 'gave the Philippines time to begin healing the wounds of the Marcos era', and that she 'squandered a unique, historic opportunity to correct the injustices of Philippine society'.[42] Whatever her own talents, she, like Marcos himself, faced the fact that he had not created a New Society. Turning him out brought back the old type of politics. Aquino could not but be disappointing, and the restlessness of the reformists in the army would, but for Ramos' loyalty, have destabilised her regime still further. But it is possible to underestimate the amount of change that took place after 1986.

The extreme left Bayan had boycotted the election and the extreme right had been defeated. Power returned to 'the undeniably elite-led center', as James Rush put it, 'with its complex democratic vision of itself and its fervent belief that elections can bring things aright'.[43] The new constitution returned to the presidential system and the bicameral Congress of the pre-martial law phase. The national elections of May 1987 'took on a traditional cast', while the local elections of 1988 revealed 'the persistence and vitality of traditional politics. ... Voting ... was heavily influenced by direct or indirect personalistic ties, promises of patronage or other benefits, and explicit or implicit threats of punishment'.[44] At the same time the army was unwilling to return to barracks: it believed it had a political role both in Manila faction politics and as a result of its counter-insurgency struggle. RAM (Reform the Armed Forces Movement) criticised negotiations with the NPA, and though Ramos defeated attempted revolts in 1987, it edged the cabinet in a conservative direction. The government did not have 'a reliable military, a unified national political party, or competent civil administration'.[45]

Yet if the role of the army was one novelty, the approach to development was another. Aquino and Ramos, who succeeded her in 1992, were helped by the fact that it was Marcos who had had to carry through the harsh IMF programme of 1984. They recognised that development could now be pursued, not by authoritarian methods, but by liberalisation and privatisation, with a touch of 'nationalism'. Ramos established a new degree of stability and a strong civil society. His successor, Joseph Estrada, elected by due process in 1998, played with some of the cronies, but they were, it seemed, tamed.

Barisan

In Malaysia, meanwhile, a programme of dramatic economic expansion was associated with a more authoritarian approach. Such an emphasis had been increasing at least since 1969. Malayan democracy had throughout presented some non-democratic features. As elsewhere, the advance towards independence had been associated with an advance towards democracy. That, however, took a particular form. It had to take account of the 'communal' divisions which had seemed an insuperable bar to political advance. That it sought to do by deals among the communal elites, made sufficiently acceptable to their followers to ensure success at the polls. As David Brown points out, features of the system included secret negotiations and decision-making among the leaders of the 'grand coalition'; limiting public debate on issues of concern to particular communities; and maintaining elite cooperation 'primarily by the existence of an imminent threat of instability'.[46] Those features seemed indeed to limit the prospects of a fuller democratisation, and the chances that it would become the means of resolving or transcending the differences and conflicts potential and actual among the 'communities'.

After the 1969 crisis, indeed, Malaysian democracy moved in the other direction. The Malay leadership responded to the crisis by adopting a more ethnocentric stance, committing the government to the New Economic Policy, and thus to a reconstruction of the pre-1957 deal between the communities, but still to be effected at the elite level. Razak's NOC was succeeded by a reconstruction of the Alliance into the Barisan Nasional, coopting the opposition parties. 'Although UMNO was the dominant party in the Alliance, it is even more hegemonic in the Barisan.'[47] Politics focused on UMNO, rather than on parliament, and the election of its leaders determined the leadership of the government. The state adopted an ideology, the Rukunegara, and further abridged democracy by prohibiting the public discussion of the special privileges of the Malays, of the status of Islam, and of that of the Malay language. 'Let us remember', said Razak, 'that the democratic system which we are working has to bear the stresses and strains of a multi-racial society'.[48] '[B]etter to have less than 100 per cent democracy than no democracy at all', said Tan Siew Sin.[49]

Accommodation was, however, not abandoned. Instead the government sought to shore it up, and make the new package palatable, by an expansionist programme. While NEP would promote the economic and social advancement of the Malays, there might be enough for the Chinese to benefit, too. NEP paved the Malays' way into the modern economic sector by government intervention on their behalf, continuing a trend begun in the 1960s. Malay bureaucrats and politicians were the main beneficiaries, and in the 1980s UMNO became 'an avenue for wealth expansion', licences, contracts, finance, concessions, being awarded in its interest or in the interest of individuals associated with it. Chinese businessmen shared through 'Ali Baba' arrangements, and MCA set up a company, Multi Purpose Holdings, which cooperated with *bumiputra* organisations.

In 1981 Mahathir Mohamed—one of the Ultras who called for the Tunku's resignation after 1969, later redeemed by Razak—had become prime minister. His appointment as deputy prime minister in 1976 had alarmed the Chinese in the Barisan. His emergence, however, is not to be seen, William Case suggests, as a 'slide into disunity', but 'within a framework of regenerative, accommodative elite attitudes and behaviour'.[50] His plan was to establish Malaysia's status as a newly industrialising country (NIC) by a programme of state-led heavy industrialisation. Minister of trade and industry from 1978, he organised the Heavy Industries Corporation of Malaysia. He wanted the country to reduce its dependence on commodity production and to acquire an industrial base, breaking the colonial pattern, 'Buy British Last' and 'Looking East' being associated concepts. He planned to accelerate Malay participation in the growth process, but he realised that Chinese capital and know-how were essential.

The Barisan governments did not merely depend on mobilising local resources, savings and expertise. Their policy, and above all Mahathir's dramatisation of it in the 1980s, depended also on the buoyancy of the world economy in general and in particular on attracting foreign investment. International downturns would threaten not only the realisation of the grand vision, industrialisation by 2020, but also the maintenance of the system of politics with which it had become connected, since they were likely to reduce the amount of patronage available and intensify rivalry both within and between the elites. The prime minister began to speak in terms of Bangsa Malaysia, as if he hoped that the communal differences of the past would no longer be accommodated but transcended. The New Development Policy of 1991 indeed seemed to alleviate the quota-led approach of the NEP. But, if much depended on overseas trends, much also depended on the masses at home.

Whatever their effects on the elites, the Barisan's economic policies did not reduce the economic disparities within the communities. The poorer Chinese got poorer, and there was a growing disparity within the Malay community. The government sought to reduce peasant poverty, but without alienating the landowners in UMNO. It thus stressed infrastructural change, and subsidised the green revolution. UMNO was also tempted to play up the *bumiputra* myth, and also to make gestures towards Islam that would both coopt and constrain it. Constituents were mobilised in election campaigns by ethnic appeals, then demobilised afterwards, the government, as Case puts it, 'pre-empting the emergence of most voluntary associations with a continuous distribution of development programs, projects and spending'.[51] The intra-elite conflicts that marked both UMNO and MCA in the late 1970s and 1980s tended to arouse communal tension. In October 1987 Mahathir ordered 106 persons detained under the ISA.

In his long tenure as prime minister, he seemed indeed to become increasingly authoritarian. The role of the Agong (king) was truncated, and the Lord President suspended for 'gross misbehaviour' in the course of the conflicts within UMNO in 1987–88. Electoral campaigns were short, rallies limited, investigative journalism discouraged. UMNO dominated the media. But the royal families have benefited from economic opportunities, and Tun Abbas was allowed to publish his account of what happened.[52] In Malaysia there were no pronunciamentos, no massacres, no salvagings, no vigilantes, and the state was clearly in the hands of civilian authorities. What was missing was a sense that the democratic system would be made to work in a more positive way, rather than as a kind of safety valve.

In Case's terms the elites in Malaysia entered 'accommodative relationships'[53] and, as he shows, they maintained them. The result was a stable, semi-democratic regime, in which Malay dominance was tempered by accommodationist elements, and democratic politics limited but meaningful. But it may be that Case underestimates the extent to which Malaysian politics changed over time. He stresses that, even after major political crises like that of 1987–88, accommodative practices were renewed. Less emphasis is put on their changing nature, and less consideration accorded the extent to which each marked a diminution in democratic practice rather than an expansion, either as a result of the intensity of communal feeling, or of the political aspirations of the prime minister, or both. That only made it even more difficult to analyse current and future trends in this unique polity. Would a succession of intra-elite deals suffice to guarantee stability? To what extent would democracy be eroded or expanded? Was politics to be modernised or was the communal approach to persist? The Bangsa Malaysia concept suggested that Mahathir saw the problem. But it involved more than an emotional appeal, more, too, than the assumption of challenging roles in international affairs.

The 1990 elections seemed to witness a 'new competitiveness', but in 1995 the opposition coalition broke up, and the Barisan recorded 'its greatest victory in decades'.[54] The real competition was still within UMNO, and there Mahathir faced his deputy, Anwar Ibrahim. It was contained in 1996, but the 1997–98 crisis precipitated a break, and Anwar was arrested. 'By dismissing Anwar from UMNO, Mahathir displaced the party struggle into the public sphere, with unexpected consequences.'[55] Critical of Mahathir's system, Anwar's supporters called for *reformasi*. But whether that would lead to a re-emphasis on democracy was not clear. Mahathir engaged in repression, but also offered a 'nationalistic' economic policy which had wide appeal. Nor did Anwar's supporters, invoking Islam, secure much non-Malay support, whereas Mahathir's endeavours to overcome the downturn did. The November 1999 election gave him a victory. Large numbers of Malays abandoned UMNO, however, and the Islamic opposition party, PAS, registered major gains.

The NEP gave little attention to the problems of Sabah and Sarawak. Only after Bangladesh's secession in 1971 did Kuala Lumpur recognise the parallel, and then it replaced 'East Malaysia' by Sabah and Sarawak, and called West Malaysia 'Peninsular Malaysia'.[56] Otherwise it relied on the policies it had been pursuing. '[T]he pattern of politics within Sabah', wrote Margaret Clark, 'was essentially that of incorporation of the inland, tribal peoples of the state into union (of interests and identity) with the coastal Muslims, on terms laid down by the latter, strengthened by the support (both implicit and explicit) of the Federal Government in Kuala Lumpur'.[57] The USNO-dominated alliance ruled till 1976, when it was overthrown by Berjaya. That had the support of Kuala Lumpur, which found Mustapha had become too autonomous, and, though it claimed to be multi-racial, it became, under the leadership of Harris Salleh, another Malayo-Muslim ally of the federal government.

It was in turn overthrown in 1985 by the Partai Bersatu Sabah (PBS, United Sabah Party), led by Joseph Pairin Kitingan, a Kadazan who had left Berjaya the year before. Forced to hold another election in 1986, PBS won it by a landslide. In the Malaysian system the federal government provided development funds and controlled internal security, and so a governing party needed to be in the Barisan. PBS was admitted in June 1986, but its relations with Kuala Lumpur were a 'cold war'. In October 1990, when Mahathir called national elections, Pairin joined the opposition. When Mahathir won, Sabah was deprived of development funds, the chief minister was charged with corruption, and his brother Jeffrey arrested under the Internal Security Act. Even so PBS won in 1994. But UMNO-led opposition led Jeffrey and others to cross the floor, and the PBS government fell.

A similar process Clark saw at work in Sarawak. Elections there had been deferred by the 1969 crisis on the Peninsula. When they resumed in June 1970, SNAP,

Bumiputera, and SUPP each secured twelve seats. Unable to deal with SNAP, Bumiputera made an alliance with SUPP. The new chief minister, Abdul Rahman Yakub, was a confidant of Razak, and the federal prime minister had indicated that the emergency would not be lifted if the government included SNAP or excluded Bumiputera. 'SNAP leaders have not shown loyalty to the state. … It was important for the people of Sarawak to think carefully and vote for the party supported by the Federal Government. … The people here have the choice—to vote for a strong Government or to suffer.'[58] In 1974, however, SNAP secured eighteen seats, the same number as Yakub's party (Partai Pesaku Bumiputera Bersatu, PBB), which now included Pesaka as well, while SUPP had twelve. The chief minister therefore wooed SNAP, gaoling its main Chinese member, and it joined the Barisan. The pro-Malay policy of the government did not prevent a recurrence of the old breach between the Kuching Malays and the Melanaus, and a new party, PAJAR (Sarawak Native People's Party), based on the former, denounced Yabub's corruption and nepotism. But the SNAP–SUPP–PBB coalition continued till 1983, under Yakub till 1981, then under his nephew, Taib Mahmud, and he continued as chief minister into the 1990s.

Singaporeanness

Some at least of the thrust behind Mahathir's development policies resulted from comparison with his nearest neighbour, relations with which had elements of tension which a degree of mutual envy tended to exaggerate. In a sense the position of the two states had been reversed since Singapore became independent in 1965. Then it had even seemed doubtful that it would survive, and its leaders themselves had after all insisted that merger was essential to the island's future. Their very apprehension, however, contributed to their success. The sense of threat also helped them to consolidate popular support, their main rivals already having been destroyed during the struggle to enter Malaysia. The emergence of the new state also occurred at a time when not only had small states come to appear politically more viable, or no less viable than others, but when changes in the international economy offered new opportunities to those who accepted the current concept of the international division of labour. Singapore after all had a long history of adaptation, in which alarms about the future were followed by a new level of prosperity. It seized the new opportunities, as it had seized old ones. What was striking under the new regime was its emphasis on leadership.

In the past the entrepot's future had largely depended on the responsiveness of private enterprise, alive to change and opportunity, and the government since colonial times had been a non-interventionist one. Now that changed. The PAP leaders were socialists in origin. Their socialism was no longer relevant, but their interventionism persisted. The Republic's survival seemed to depend on the wits of a small elite. Yet at the same time it needed to encourage an enterprising spirit, rather than a merely compliant one. That was to lead at times to a rather paradoxical approach, in which the government both sought to encourage innovation, and yet also in a measure feared it.

The paradox was evident in the political sphere, and politics indeed enforced it in other spheres. The threat from the outside had sustained the initial dominance of the PAP, and it found justification, even amidst its successes, in uncovering further threats in subsequent years. It promoted a garrison mentality, as Brown puts it.[59] The threats were not merely economic: there was a threat from 'Western' culture, blamed for drug abuse and youth alienation. Nor were the threats merely external. Singaporeans were reminded of the tensions of the 1960s, and of the risk of 'unleashing communal passions'.[60] Religious revivalism, in some part a function of social change, was also seen as a threat: it would generate 'liberation theology' and promote intolerance. In the 1980s the government put increasing emphasis on 'Singaporeanness', and in 1988 Goh Chok Tong, the future prime minister, articulated a National Ideology, including multi-racial tolerance, consensus, putting society above individuals, placing the family as its core unit. 'Confucian' values were endorsed, not associated with the Chinese context in which they had been developed, but with a modernisation of which the sage could have had no conception.

The political structure of the state was a corporatist one. The state and the party were closely linked, and the resources of the one used to ensure the success of the other. Elections were held, but the role of the opposition was limited by a range of devices, constitutional and extra-constitutional, including the Societies Act and the Printing Presses Act, the retention of the Internal Security Act, and controls on housing and education. The PAP indeed aimed at a high level of public endorsement, and the function of the elections was to demonstrate that: 'the legitimacy derived from periodical general elections is central to the PAP's claim of the right to govern'.[61] In Malaysia success was demonstrated by securing the two-thirds majority necessary to pass a constitutional amendment; in Singapore, as in New Order Indonesia, it was based on a historical share of the popular vote. There was no fear of losing an election, but rather of losing the continued indication of success. Yet such a political approach did little to recognise the view that Singapore's survival required the use of all of its wits, and not merely those of the ruling elite.

We want, said Goh, to 'involve Singaporeans in discussion of major policies, and create avenues for them to express their views'.[62] That, it seems, was, however, only to be done through a more 'inclusionary' version of the corporatist model. 'If we have good people, we will try to co-opt them into the PAP and make them part of the system', said Brig. Lee Hsien Loong, the deputy prime minister, in 1994. 'If good people are forced to join the opposition then I think we have already failed.'[63] If democracy was to offer legitimacy, however, voting for the opposition could not be made illegal. Opposition was allowed, therefore, but harassed. It might also be forestalled. In 1984 the government decided that, if fewer than three opposition candidates were elected, up to three non-constituency seats would be offered to losing candidates with the most votes. The new Group Representation Constituencies of

1988 diluted the chances of an elected opposition, and then in 1989 non-elected MPs were introduced, 'a reversion to the British practice of appointed members of the colonial legislature'.[64]

Thailand Incorporated

In the 1980s and 1990s Thailand approached the ranks of NIC that Singapore had attained. It was under a very different political system—one, indeed, that seemed to be subject to continual change, both in the short term and in respect of coups, and in the long term and in respect of the relative significance of its main elements, prime minister and assembly, bureaucracy, monarchy, and army. In the sense that this process represented an attempt to modernise the politics of an independent state, it was shared with other Southeast Asian states. One difference was, of course, that Thailand, never a colonial possession, had been facing the task for a longer period. A second difference was that it had also adopted sooner than its neighbours the model of 'development' that insisted that it required a 'strong' government, insulated from politics. The model had been taken up by Sarit in the dictatorship he assumed after 1958, and fostered by his US supporters, anxious for a firm base for the growing conflict in Vietnam. The Thai armed forces, whatever their technical competence, were no mere technocrats. As elsewhere politics did not cease when they lost their parliamentary character. Their nature became more factional rather than less, and more focused on the leaders of the armed forces.

There were other changes. The long-standing tendency to locate wealth and power in Bangkok increased, alienating outlying regions that now lost even the voice that the electoral system had offered them. A second change was newer, though not entirely novel. Under the Pibun regimes, the state had intervened to reduce the role of 'aliens' in the economy and, somewhat haphazardly, promoted import substitution industrialisation. Now the scale of this enterprise was transformed and, to the extent that foreign enterprise was welcomed, its character. The process continued under Sarit's successors, during whose rule Thailand, like other Southeast Asian countries, received an increasing amount of Japanese investment. In turn that brought wider changes, which the political system found it difficult to accommodate. As a means of so doing, Thanom and Praphat returned to constitutional rule, and then in vain they tried to throw it out again.

Their overthrow was followed by an affirmation of Thai democracy. A new constitution was promulgated in 1974, and the two freest elections in Thai history were held in January 1975 and April 1976.[65] Parties proliferated. They included the Democrats, led by the veteran Seni Pramoj, with experienced politicians as his deputies, Chuan Leekpai and Phichi Rattakun, and they also included the Social Action Party, led by Kukrit Pramoj, allied with Boonchu Rojanasathien, a banker.

There were leftist parties, the Socialist Party, New Force. There was also a military-backed party, Chat Thai, suggesting the possibility that the army might be less disposed to overthrow the party system than to take part in it.

In turn, however, the regime was overthrown by the right wing in October 1976. The communist triumphs in the Indo-Chinese states in 1975 alarmed Thai conservatives, and their alarm was increased by the abolition of the monarchy in Laos. During 1975 and 1976 university student activists were intimidated and beaten up, and in March 1976 the secretary-general of the Socialist Party of Thailand was gunned down in Bangkok. A counter-insurgency expert had organised the Red Gaur as paramilitary mercenaries, drawing on vocational students in the Bangkok area. Coming from very different backgrounds and acquiring qualifications of much less value, they were readily divided from the university students with whom they had been allied in 1973. Thanom's return from exile on 19 September 1976 proved the catalyst of the bloody events of the following month, when the Red Gaur formed a vanguard for the police in their violent attack on the Thammasat students.[66]

The military installed as prime minister the ultra-conservative Thanin Krai-wichian, a friend of the Queen. But while the investor confidence that had fallen away during the 1973–76 phase then returned, it did not last. Thanin, it seems, was too dictatorial, and the military leaders feared that he would provoke civil war. A more conciliatory approach was followed by the military men who replaced him, Kriangsak Chomanan and Prem Pitsulanon.

Under their governments Thailand found a new measure of stability. It was boosted by economic policies that confirmed a shift from import substitution to export-oriented industrialisation. In 1980 Boonchu Rojanasathien announced 'Thailand Incorporated': the state was to be run like a business, with a comfortable niche for foreign capital, but plenty of scope for local capital, Chinese as well as Thai. Boonchu was soon shunted aside, but the strategy remained, exemplified in the eastern seaboard project. Foreign companies were a major force, but 'domestic capitalists retain a dominant position in many key sectors, most notably finance'.[67]

At the same time the parliamentary system became more open—though the 1979 constitution was more like that of 1932 than that of 1974—and it became more functional. 'Political parties ... became political institutions in which Chinese businessmen could identify themselves without having to show their ethnic identity.'[68] The political parties also offered an opportunity to the mafia-type *chaopor* of the Sarit period, fixers who now became local party bosses. In turn that led to attacks on plutocracy (*thanatthippatai*) and a yearning for power to be given to the people. Such might lead to a revival of Pibunism, but it might also lead, patiently handled, to an increasingly democratic form of participation. There was a risk, however, that its involvement with patronage and corruption would prompt destruction of the system rather than modification. In the process the provinces would again lose to the capital, the villages to the cities.

The regime had managed to eliminate many of the threats from the left, not merely by military action, but by social action: fighting the communists made the military aware of the plight of the poor farmers. In the Thanin phase many of the urban and student left went underground, or joined the CPT in the north, the northeast or the south. The CPT was then relatively weak, many becoming members to pursue ethnic rather than ideological causes. The advent of the young idealists strengthened the party, but also divided it: the followers of Jit did not accept its Maoist orientation. The Vietnam–Cambodia and China–Vietnam Wars of 1978–79 shattered the young idealists, while the CPT's adhesion to China led to its expulsion from Laos and Cambodia, even as China itself sought to improve relations with Thailand. But Kriangsak did not benefit merely from good luck. Good judgment prompted an amnesty policy that in these circumstances encouraged defectors.

In 1977 the army leadership was so divided that the Revolutionary Council was headed by an admiral. Kriangsak had a narrow power base and, lacking support from the king, he handed over to Prem, whom he had appointed commander-in-chief of the army, in 1980. With the king's backing, Prem was able to survive two attempted coups, in 1981 and 1985. The source was the so-called Young Turks. Their inspiration was not unlike that of the RAM in the Philippines. Their ideologue was Sanchai Buntrigsawat, a lecturer at the army staff college, who had studied politics at the University of Kansas, and in 1978 published *Why Do Soldiers Stage Coups?* His answer was influenced by a reading of Samuel P. Huntington's *Political Order in Changing Societies* (1968). Social and economic justice must precede democracy. The military could act where the civilians were weak. Young officers who fought against the communists in Thailand, and knew about the conditions of the peasants, found such concepts acceptable. The Young Turks had opposed the corruption of the 1960s and the polarisation of the Thanin regime. They had lent support to Kriangsak and Prem, but now protested against their lack of leadership and the priorities of Thailand Incorporated. Yet, as with RAM, there was a paradox. A faction was striking against factionalism. A coup was trying to change the direction of a stable regime. A political move was undertaken with a view to depoliticisation. Prem gradualism was a better option; 'although undemocratically appointed …, he promoted democratic thinking and behavioural patterns'.[69]

In 1988—when the king became the country's longest-reigning monarch—Prem refused the invitation again to become prime minister. Chatichai, Phin's son, became the first elected prime minister in twelve years. His Indo-China policy was hopeful: turn a battleground into a trading market. But corruption gave the army the opportunity for a coup, and in February 1991 one was carried out by Sunthorn Kongsompong, the supreme commander, backed by the commander-in-chief, Suchinda Krapayoon. A caretaker prime minister, Anand Panyarachun, was installed, but after the 1992 election Suchinda himself, supported by the 'devil' parties, took over. Major demonstrations followed in May. The king intervened, Suchinda resigned, and Anand was recalled to arrange a new election. As he put it, his task was 'returning sovereignty to the people', 'demilitarising the political process and decommercialising the armed forces'.[70] New elections were held in September. The Democrat Chuan Leekpai formed a government. It was another government led by him that had to deal with the crisis of 1997–98.

The Khmer Rouge

The changes within Thailand took place in a context of international change, and in particular change in the policy of the United States, to which Pibun and Sarit had so closely attached its fortunes. The US focus was on Vietnam, but it was always clear that a conflict there could not avoid affecting Thailand's immediate neighbours, Cambodia and Laos. Though from 1968 the United States had begun to seek a means to extricate itself from Vietnam, the process was to have a catastrophic effect on Cambodia.

There is evidence that the United States knew about, without necessarily supporting, the plans to overthrow Sihanouk that Lon Nol and Sirikmatak were developing from 1968. They did not involve his assassination. Lon Nol doubted 'that either he or the United States Army would be able to control the popular uprising he felt would develop from an attempt to assassinate the Prince, successful or otherwise'. Instead he proposed

> to lead a coup when Prince Sihanouk left the country on one of his periodic rest cures … in the south of France. [It] was felt by the General and his advisers that by confronting the Prince with a *fait accompli* when he was cut off from direct access to his resources they could discourage him from attempting to mount a counter-coup, to them a very real and frightening possibility based on their assessment of the profound support he enjoyed among most Cambodians, excepting themselves.[71]

Whether a regime that overthrew the prince could win support in any case must surely have been doubtful. In the capital, indeed, Sihanouk was readily criticised. But, despite the harsh suppression of the Samlaut disturbances of 1967–68, Sihanouk had not lost his appeal to the peasants. A regime in the capital that ignored them would do so at its peril.

The coup, if what was in the event so peacefully carried out can properly be so termed, took place on 18 March 1970. That morning the Assembly voted to dismiss Sihanouk as head of state, and under the constitution its chairman, Cheng Heng, succeeded him. Prime Minister Lon Nol broadcast an endorsement, while armoured cars took up positions in Phnom Penh. Yem Sembaur became foreign minister, and In Tam president of the Sangkum central committee. Lon Nol was disposed to bring the monarchy itself to an end. That Sirikmatak resisted, not simply because of his princely status, but there were newspaper attacks on Sihanouk, and his fury made it certain that he would not retire quietly. Instead he set up a Royal Government of

National Union in Beijing, including a mixture of old opponents and current supporters. Phnom Penh, meanwhile, was supportive of the new regime, but rural discontent was manifest. That helped the Khmer Rouge, but it was also a hindrance to them. Their aim was a Cambodia without either Sihanouk or Lon Nol. 'The Khmer Rouge leaders said that important cadres like us were communists', as one of them put it, 'but the people believe in Sihanouk'.[72]

On 9 October 1970 the Khmer Republic was proclaimed and celebrations in Phnom Penh continued throughout the day. The urban middle class was 'buoyed with a new sense of patriotism and national identity'.[73] The coup had been preceded by attacks on the DRVN embassy, and also on Vietnamese shops in Phnom Penh. There were more positive aspects to a sense of resurgence, though, given Cambodia's position, they, too, were dangerous. One was identification with the Khmer Krom in South Vietnam. Lon Nol, Peang Meth wrote, 'always nurtured a dream of reconquering Cochinchina ... [and] felt an affinity with the ethnic minorities he believed had been robbed of the land rightfully theirs, particularly the Khmer Krom and Cambodians of Cham descent'.[74] The old Democrat Party enjoyed a revived popularity.

About all this, however, there was an air of unreality. The prospects of a pluralist kind of politics had been destroyed by Sihanouk. The state was in the midst of a civil war, in which outside states were also involved, and in which, despite the youthful enthusiasm the regime at first evoked, it was enjoying little military success. Its leadership was inept, partly because Sihanouk had never accepted rivals. The support it had it indeed tended to alienate and, like that of other regimes that come under pressure, its leadership was at odds with itself, particularly after Lon Nol suffered a stroke in February 1971.

In March 1972 he nevertheless assumed the presidency, and installed Son Ngoc Thanh, the old Democrat leader, as premier. In June presidential elections were held under a new constitution which had been endorsed in a referendum at the end of April. Those Lon Nol won only by vote-rigging. The defeated included In Tam, who now became a bitter enemy, and Keo Ann, an urban intellectual who drew on his perceived support for Sihanouk. In the parliamentary elections, neither the Democrats, associated with In Tam, nor the Republicans, associated with Sirikmatak, were prepared to take part. The Socio-Republican Party, a creation of Lon Nol and his brother, thus emerged rather like a new Sangkum. Political infighting continued, even as the real fighting approached the capital. Beleaguered, the remnant of the regime survived longer than expected. On 1 April 1975, however, the president left Phnom Penh, perhaps hoping that his departure would facilitate a compromise.

There was to be no compromise of any kind. Many had fled the harsh discipline already operating in the zones controlled by the Communist Party of Kampuchea (Pak Kommunis Kampuchea, PKK), nicknamed Khmer Rouge by Sihanouk, but some thought the PKK would change once it was victorious. Its association with Sihanouk led prominent families in Phnom Penh to think that he would protect them. War-weariness blinded them, and they misread the United States. In the event,

17 April, when the Khmer Rouge entered the capital, marked the beginning of Year Zero. Its population was driven out. And that marked the start of a regime of violence and genocide, the enormity of which is still hard to grasp. Perhaps from 800 000 to 1 million died, maybe more, many more. About 100 000 were executed without trial, and about 20 000 'smashed' in Tuol Sleng. It is possible, however, to offer something of an explanation, and it after all reveals some continuities with the past.

One source of the Khmer Rouge's ruthlessness was its dramatic success. Phnom Penh fell before Saigon. That was, of course, not solely the result of the PKK's efforts, tough and resolute though it had made itself. Sihanouk had not only helped to isolate the Republic diplomatically: he had also been a drawcard within Cambodia. The DRVN army had provided a shield in eastern Cambodia, behind which the PKK built its army and infrastructure. Its opponents were weakly led, and while it was backed by the PRC and DRVN, they lost their US backing. The PKK's success, however, encouraged a belief, already nurtured in its leaders by their knowledge of the Great Leap Forward and the Cultural Revolution, that anything was possible. At the same time, the PKK did not have the experienced cadres to control the towns. So they had to be emptied.

In the eyes of the small elite that controlled the PKK, the cities were indeed centres of foreign influence and control, sources of opposition to the revolution and of cultural perversion. Their inspiration came partly from their experiences in Paris, to which the Sihanouk regime had driven or sent them. The ideologue, Khieu Samphan, drew on Samir Amin's dissertation of 1957: the traditional economic system had been destroyed by its integration into the world system, it was argued, and the centre dominated the periphery. Like the Martinique ideologue Fanon, he inveighed against wily intellectuals, privileged urban proletarians, and suspect townsmen, and called for violence. Only the peasants were revolutionary.

In Cambodia it was possible to take this literally. The tension between the cities and the countryside had been enhanced in the colonial phase. The cities were the centres of administration, of educational opportunity, of commercial growth. Bureaucrats were often Vietnamese and trade was in the hands of Vietnamese and Chinese compradores. Officials were increasingly recruited through diplomas, rather than drawn from the rich, and felt no sense of local obligation. These attitudes persisted. 'The absence of a true anti-colonial struggle against the French had the effect of prolonging the foreign cultural influence well past the time of independence.'[75] At the same time, the Sihanouk regime had not provided ways of integrating cities and countryside. Intermediary structures were lacking, and the regime depended on Sangkum and Samdech (the prince).

In the countryside the bourgeois radicals felt regenerated by the contact with the peasantry. The patriotism of Phnom Penh itself seemed alien. If it thought of itself, like Lon Nol, as bearing the legacy of Funan, the hinterland bore that of Chen-la, the name indeed he gave his major offensives. Against corruption the radicals could exalt the noble savage. Certainly they were able to unleash the extreme violence of youth. 'Youth is the future of the nation', Lon Nol had declared.[76] But the youth his opponents so terrifyingly mobilised were not the students of Phnom Penh. They were those who were deprived of their advantages. The leaders, often schoolteachers, empowered illiterates.

The aim of the regime was not, however, to return to a pastoral society. Instead it planned to modernise by a different route, by the same kind of 'storming attack' as seemed to have brought victory in the civil war: by 'forced-draft industrial and agricultural modernization'.[77] 'If we have rice, we have everything. ...'[78] Under Pol Pot's four-year plan 'to build socialism in all fields', production was to be expanded by 'political will', and by a ruthless expenditure of those without rights, the 'April 17 people'. That would create an export surplus, in turn to finance industry.[79] There were no Lenin-style plans for a transitional phase. Instead the regime destroyed the elite whose training and talent it needed, still further reducing the prospects of a programme that was unreal in international as well as national terms.

'If our people were capable of building Angkor, we can do anything', Pol Pot declared in 1977.[80] The revolution, like Lon Nol's, had after all nationalist roots as well: Angkor was not a sign of irreversible decline, as the French had said, but of enormous potential. Indeed that seems to Karl Jackson a more important factor than Fanon-style ideology: 'the Khmer Rouge's concept of total national independence springs primarily from the centuries-old fear of foreign invasion rather than from any twentieth-century foreign ideology'.[81] The sense of threat from outside, and the consciousness of weakness, redoubled the regime's extremism. It also led it into a disastrous conflict with its erstwhile allies.

The long-standing distrust of Vietnam had been limited during the struggle against Lon Nol. Empowered by revolutionary triumph after the capture of Phnom Penh, and allied to China, Pol Pot gave vent to his hatred of the Vietnamese and encouraged others to do so. The regime sought to realise objectives of which its predecessor could only dream. Early in 1977 it intensified its attacks on southern Vietnam. Vietnam and Laos signed a treaty in July. Pol Pot visited China in September–October, hoping that the People's Republic would help to strengthen his forces and constrain the Vietnamese. At the end of the year Democratic Kampuchea broke off diplomatic relations with Vietnam. Probably the Vietnamese hoped to prompt negotiations. Instead they provoked purges, and further attacks early in 1978. Now Vietnam not only strengthened its ties with the Soviet Union, but began to encourage Pol Pot's opponents, and the fantasies that Deuch and his torturers had been concocting in the torture chambers of Tuol Sleng began to come true. Following the Vietnamese attack on 25 December, Sihanouk, though virtually under house arrest since April 1976, left on 6 January to plead the cause of the regime at the United Nations, while the following day Pol Pot fled by helicopter.

The Vietnamese invaders established the People's Republic of Kampuchea, based on the DK cadre that had fled Pol Pot in 1977–78, on Khmers in exile since the

1950s, and later on some non-communists from the Pol Pot era. Until 1989 it was kept in being by 200 000 Vietnamese troops, and overseen by Vietnamese cadres. In the jungle a rival 'government'—from 1982 a 'coalition' dominated by the Khmer Rouge, but also including factions led by Sihanouk and by Son Sann, a pre-Lon Nol prime minister—was supported by the Chinese, the Thais, and the United States, and retained the UN seat. With Thai cooperation, arms came from the PRC, including the landmines that maimed thousands of 'enemies'. Financial and political support came from the United States. The UN High Commissioner for Refugees helped to construct border camps, which housed and fed all Cambodians, including the Khmer Rouge. The camps were controlled by the factions and provided man-power for their military forces. Once more the fate of Cambodia depended entirely upon foreign powers. Fear and hubris had destroyed a million people, and in a sense the state itself.

The fortunes of the two parties were affected by the changes in the international situation in the late 1980s. Pol Pot's patrons dropped him, as Chandler writes in his biography.[82] In Thailand the role of the military diminished. Vietnam was increasingly anxious to focus on development. The Soviet Union gave Cambodia less support, while the PRC turned to the 'market'. The unravelling of the Cold War permitted the diplomatic solution that Australia and Indonesia had been seeking. That involved a new kind of foreign intervention, in which, under UN auspices, an attempt was made to rebuild the state on a democratic basis. It was, of course, a difficult task in a country where Sangkum had been succeeded by Angkar (the Organisation), and where the remains of the elite were deeply divided. Real power lay, not with Sihanouk, who became king again in 1993, but with those who had built up their control under the Vietnamese-sponsored regime, and had never surrendered it.

In the 1993 elections FUNCINPEC, headed by Sihanouk's son Rannaridh, and based on the royalist faction in the resistance to the Vietnamese-sponsored regime, secured a majority. The CPP, headed by Hun Sen, former prime minister in that regime, came second, and contested victory. Sihanouk brokered an agreement: there would be two prime ministers and two ruling parties. In a head-on collision in July 1997—which delayed Cambodia's accession to ASEAN till April 1999—Hun Sen destroyed his rivals. The king intervened again in 1998, when the elections yet failed to give Hun Sen complete victory.

The Lao People's Revolutionary Party

The Pathet Lao–Royal Government ceasefire of February 1973 reflected developments in Vietnam rather than in Laos itself. A 'coalition' was established in 1974. During 1975, as South Vietnam collapsed, the Pathet Lao took power, though without great violence, and then it adopted a tougher line. In December Laos became a republic, Suphanuvong became president, and Kaison Phomvihan, secretary-general of the Lao People's Revolutionary Party, became prime minister. The creation of a DRVN-style socialism was pushed ahead, then modified. Decisive moves away from it began in the mid-1980s. The regime became more clientelist and more corrupt. But while Laos was opened up to foreign investment after 1989, the party was determined to maintain its monopoly of power.

Commerce and cadres

After their triumphant capture of Saigon in April 1975, the communists carried out what Le Duan called 'socialist transformation', and in March 1978 Do Muoi, the vice-premier, abolished private commerce. Such moves contributed to an exodus of refugees, especially ethnic Chinese, particularly after the war with China. The 'boat people' alone numbered 46 871 in 1977; 150 398 in 1978; 270 882 in 1979; 119 402 in 1980; and 103 168 in 1981. But, though Le Duan and Le Duc Tho committed Vietnam to Comecon, the regime abandoned 'socialist' policies in the 1980s. It did not, however, abandon party control. The regime became what Thai Quang Trung called a 'nepotistic-dictatorial' system on the Albanian model.[83]

The invasion of Cambodia and the war with China had imposed immense economic costs and involved a world economic boycott. The regime turned not to a plan but to free market economics, particularly after Nguyen Van Linh and Vo Van Kiet—who, assisted by Nguyen Xuan Oanh, a former IMF and Saigon functionary, had encouraged local Chinese to revive the Saigon economy—took over the direction of the national economy in 1985. After 1986 the party evoked Marx, Lenin, and Ho Chi Minh, but followed IMF doctrines. Its policy statements became extraordinarily contorted. '[W]e have completely eliminated the antipathy, prejudice and prohibition against private capitalist and individual sectors', a spokesman declared in 1994, 'thus creating the conditions for all production forces to develop for the sake of the country and the people'.[84] The party endorsed acquisitiveness, but also revolutionary morality: in 1995 Vo Van Kiet called the cadres 'revolutionary mandarins'.[85] In fact corrupt rural cadres enriched themselves, taking land for their own use, so that rural society became 'significantly more like the one against which the Communists first mobilized the masses'.[86] The wealthiest men were in Saigon, but access to political and bureaucratic power compensated for the north's poverty. Allegedly the richest *busiman* in 1996, Le Van Kiem was a crony of Vo Van Kiet and Phan Van Khai, his key deputy and successor.

Vu Oanh, a senior Politburo member in charge of mass work, said in August 1995: 'A mechanism must be built so that the people can participate in criticizing the party organizations and party members. ... Democracy must be expanded even more with respect to politics, the economy, and society.' In September he went further, urging '*representative* democracy, *direct* democracy, and *self-management* democracy at the grass-roots level'.[87] Though he was probably calling for a revival of mass organisations in order to counter calls for 'democratisation', he was dropped. The army, however, aligned with those who took socialism seriously.

SLORC

The analysis Robert Taylor offers in his book, *The State in Burma*, published in 1987, calls to mind Jim Schiller's discussion of the 'state project' in Suharto's Indonesia. In that case the ruling elite looked outside the country for resources that would enable them to realise their objectives. The Ne Win regime, Taylor argues, sought to avoid this. The colonial state in Burma had collapsed, and the growth of mass mobilisation movements, 'not themselves highly institutionalized', created a power vacuum. 'The reassertion of the predominant position of the state after 1948 was attempted initially by recreating the pattern of the colonial state and increasing its representative quality.' It remained weak, unable 'to penetrate society and regain control over rival institutions'. Those who wished 'to resurrect the dominance of a state' in such circumstances had two options. 'One is to open the society to external institutions and forces such as the world economy and military alliances with more powerful states. In that way the state … is able to use outside resources to establish its position within the country', at the cost of some loss of sovereignty. 'The alternative is to force the state upon the remainder of society with the few weapons at its disposal', eliminating its rivals, and 'ensuring that the institutions permitted to exist are dependent upon the state'.[88] It was the second option that the military leaders of Burma chose after 1962.

In the early 1970s the military began ostensibly to appear as civilians, and a new constitution was adopted in 1974, formally giving power to a People's Assembly, with Ne Win as president. Its preparation had been a long process, during which the drafting commission had solicited popular opinion and comment, the argument being 'that the 1947 constitution had been drafted by lawyers and conservative politicians without the participation of the people, and therefore had been incapable of achieving socialism and national unity'.[89] In the process, however, it did not greatly change. The constitution, as Taylor wrote, was 'the logical consequence of the structures of the Party and state created after 1962'. The state was now 'in form not dissimilar from any other one-party socialist state', and the communist insurgents could not now 'claim that they uniquely desire to create a socialist state structure in Burma'.[90]

While it sought to organise support mass peasant and workers *asiayone* (associations), the regime also repressed its opponents. Immediately after taking over, the army occupied Rangoon University, blowing up the students association, cradle of the Thakin movement, and there were further massacres in 1974. The economic failure of the regime, and the encouragement offered by the events in the Philippines and elsewhere, encouraged the pro-democracy activists, however. Demonstrations developed on the Rangoon University campus in March 1988 spread to the centre of the capital, but were put down by special police and the military with excessive force. New clashes followed in June, and in July Ne Win resigned. Sein Lwin, the new leader, had, however, led the troops in 1962 and 1974, and his appointment was a direct challenge to the students. More violence followed. He was replaced by a civilian, Maung Maung, a close friend of Ne Win, and then by Saw Maung, the minister for defence and chief-of-staff, under whom the State Law and Order Restoration Council seized power. It continued repression, but, as a piece of strategic liberalisation, promised elections.

The elections were held in May 1990. Politicians were not allowed to speak or rally against SLORC, but even so the National League for Democracy won a landslide victory, capturing 87.7 per cent of the seats. SLORC then refused to transfer power. The League's leader, Aung San's daughter, Suu Kyi, was kept under virtual house arrest, and NLD members were persecuted and terrorised, though allowed to hold a meeting at her house in September 1997. At the same time, SLORC began a laborious attempt to draft a new authoritarian constitution through a largely appointed constitutional convention, 'the world's slowest-operating rubber stamp body', as a Bangkok newspaper called it.[91]

In terms of Taylor's analysis, however, the regime no longer relied merely on eliminating opposition. It looked for support from outside. Indeed in December 1990 SLORC declared that its legitimacy did not come from the people, but from the fact that it was accepted as the government of Burma by the United Nations and by the world at large.[92] Its repressive policies limited support from the West, but gave the Chinese an opportunity to become a source of arms and a major trading partner. That, perhaps, was the best argument that ASEAN had for the positive relationship it maintained with the regime. The establishment of a Western-style democracy seemed unlikely, despite the endorsement the Burmese gave it in 1990. It remained to be seen whether the regime would move towards the 'soft authoritarianism' that marked other ASEAN countries. 'A quasi-democracy is not as unlikely as it might seem.'[93] It was more likely to come from internal negotiation than from mass mobilisation or foreign intervention, if it came at all.

Michael Aung-Thwin has argued that the struggle between SLORC and Suu Kyi was not between military and civilian rule, nor between authoritarianism and democracy. Rather it was a struggle within the elite, in which personal and generational ties were significant and patron–client patterns 'still paramount'. The ideological factor was 'probably the least important to those living in Burma'.[94] Yet it is possible to be too reductionist, and it was at least significant that factions put their case in those terms. What is striking is the extent to which the democratic discourse, however foreign in origin, survived the authoritarian phase, in Burma as elsewhere. The first generation of postwar leaders in some sense abandoned the struggle to make democracy work. The authoritarianism that followed did not eliminate its ideas, nor even all its forms. Could they be reactivated?

Notes

1 in Cribb, *Killings*, p. 98.
2 K. Young, in Cribb, p. 86.
3 'The Post-Coup Massacre in Bali', in Lev and McVey, *Making Indonesia*, pp. 136–7.
4 q. ibid., p. 127.
5 McVey in ibid., p. 115; Cribb, p. 35.
6 *Developing Jepara*, pp. 18–19.
7 *The State and Ethnic Politics*, London and NY: Routledge, 1994, p. 117.
8 Ichlasul Amal, *Regional and Central Government in Indonesian Politics*, Gadjah Mada UP, 1992, p. 124.
9 Andrew MacIntyre in R. J. May and W. J. O'Malley, eds, *Observing Change in Asia*, Bathurst: Crowhurst, 1989, p. 225.
10 p. 138.
11 q. Schiller, p. 21.
12 q. Schiller, p. 24.
13 Schiller, p. 192.
14 q. Adam Schwarz, *A Nation in Waiting*, St Leonards: Allen and Unwin, 1994, p. 32.
15 Elson, *End*, p. 224.
16 pp. 134–5.
17 in G. Rodan, ed., *Political Oppositions in Industrialising Asia*, London and NY: Routledge, 1996, p. 260.
18 Douglas E. Ramage, *Politics in Indonesia*, London and NY: Routledge, 1995, p. 18.
19 q. ibid., p. 55.
20 The phrase is Bourchier's, p. 158.
21 q. Bourchier, p. 174.
22 Ed Aspinall, in G. Forrester and R. J. May, eds, *The Fall of Soeharto*, Bathurst: Crawford, 1998, p. 141.
23 *Far Eastern Economic Review*, 17 June 1999.
24 cf. Geoff Forrester, ed., *Renewal or Chaos*, Leiden: KITLV P; Singapore: ISEAS, 1999, pp. 11–12.
25 Nemenzo, q. in Benjamin N. Muego, *Spectator Society*, Athens: Ohio U, 1988, pp. 167–8.
26 Hawes in McVey, *Capitalists*, p. 153.
27 p. 159.
28 q. John Lyons and Karl Wilson, *Marcos and Beyond*, Sydney: Kangaroo, 1987, p. 114.
29 q. Timberman, p. 104.
30 q. Timberman, p. 108.
31 q. Lyons and Wilson, p. 110.
32 q. Timberman, p. 128.
33 q. Lyons and Wilson, p. 71.
34 Lyons and Wilson, p. 134.
35 q. Timberman, p. 113.
36 q. Lyons and Wilson, p. 132.
37 Muego, p. 159.
38 q. Lyons and Wilson, p. 48.
39 q. Lyons and Wilson, p. 102.
40 q. Lyons and Wilson, p. 22.
41 q. Lyons and Wilson, p. 95.
42 *Corazon Aquino and the Brushfire Revolution*, Baton Rouge: Louisiana State UP, 1995, p. 249.
43 q. Timberman, p. 155.
44 Timberman, pp. 185, 220.
45 Overholt, q. Timberman, p. 195.
46 Brown, p. 228.
47 Diane Mauzy, q. Brown, p. 244.
48 q. von Vorys, p. 419.
49 q. Gordon P. Means, *Malaysian Politics*, London: Hodder, 1976, p. 403.
50 *Elites and Regimes*, p. 156.

51 p. 122.
52 *The Role of the Independent Judiciary*, KL: Promarketing Publications, 1989.
53 p. xi.
54 W. Case, 'Malaysia: Still the Semi-Democratic Paradigm', *Asian Studies Review*, 21, 2–3 (November 1997), p. 80.
55 E. T. Gomez and Jomo K. S., *Malaysia's Political Economy*, CUP, 1998, p. 202.
56 K. S. Jomo, *Beyond the New Economic Policy*, ASAA J. C. Jackson lecture, 1990, pp. 4–5.
57 *The Politics of Belonging*, p. 128.
58 q. M. Leigh in James C. Jackson and Martin Rudner, eds, *Issues in Malaysian Development*, Singapore: HEB, 1979, p. 353.
59 p. 84.
60 p. 86.
61 Chua Beng-Huat, 'Still Awaiting New Initiatives …', *Asian Studies Review*, 21, 2–3 (November 1997), p. 125.
62 q. Brown, p. 91.
63 q. G. Rodan, ed., *Political Oppositions in Industrialising Asia*, London and NY: Routledge, 1996, p. 106.
64 Tremewan, p. 171.
65 Anderson and Mendiones, p. 38.
66 B. Griffiths in Hunsaker, pp. 77–8, 87–8, 68.
67 Hewison, p. 115.
68 Chai-Anan in Reynolds, *National Identity*, p. 76.
69 Donald F. Cooper, *Thailand Dictatorship or Democracy?*, London: Minerva, 1995, p. 297.
70 q. Cooper, p. 352.
71 Allman, q. J. Corfield, *Khmers Stand Up!*, Monash U, 1994, pp. 57–8.
72 q. Corfield, p. 98.
73 Corfield, p. 106.
74 q. Corfield, p. 173.
75 François Ponchaud, in Karl D. Jackson, ed., *Cambodia, 1975–1978: Rendezvous with Death*, PUP, 1989, p. 157.
76 Corfield, p. 108.
77 Jackson in Jackson, p. 58.
78 q. ibid., p. 60.
79 David P. Chandler, *Brother Number One*, Boulder: Westview, 1992, pp. 120–1, 123–4.
80 q. ibid., p. 13.
81 p. 249.
82 p. 186.
83 p. 92.
84 q. G. Kolko, *Vietnam: Anatomy of a Peace*, London and NY: Routledge, 1997, p. 38.
85 q. ibid., p. 74.
86 ibid., p. 96.
87 q. ibid., pp. 85, 86.
88 pp. 11–12.
89 p. 307.
90 Taylor in Chandran Jeshurun, ed., *Governments and Rebellions in Southeast Asia*, Singapore: ISEAS, 1985, p. 115.
91 *The Nation*, May 1995, q. David Bradley, 'Democracy in Burma?', *Asian Studies Review*, 21, 2–3 (November 1997), p. 26.
92 Jalal Alamgar, 'Against the Current: the Survival of Authoritarianism in Burma', PA, 70, 3 (Fall 1997), p. 350.
93 Bruce Matthews, 'The Present Fortune of Tradition-bound Authoritarianism in Myanmar', *Pacific Affairs*, 71, 1 (1998), pp. 22–3.
94 *Myth and History in the Historiography of Early Burma*, pp. 158–9.

4.5

Separatism

Most of the Southeast Asian nation-states faced one or more separatist movements within the borders they inherited from the colonial powers, and their success in dealing with them was limited. Indonesia added to its problems by acquiring a territory it had not inherited from the Dutch, then surrendered it.

In the systems that preceded the world of nation-states 'separatism' was not, of course, unknown. What is distinctive in that world is its 'ethnic' content. Under other systems breakaway movements might arise from dynastic strife or civil war, from the ambitions of over-mighty subjects or the desire of merchants to control trade, from the desire to escape or to impose religious conformity. In the world of nation-states opposition may come to take the form of 'ethnicity', even of the right to set up a rival nation-state.

The 'process' by which nationalism and the nation-state emerged indeed implied that possibility. Through it, and as a result of economic, social, cultural, and political change, people sought a new sense of identity and a new focus for loyalty. About that, however, there might be differences. Was there to be Javanese nationalism or Indonesian? The concepts that lay behind the world of nation-states involved an unavoidable contradiction. 'The greatest adversary of the rights of nationality is the modern theory of nationality', Acton had written back in 1862. 'By making the state and the nation commensurate with each other in theory, it reduces practically to a subject condition all other nationalities that may be within the boundary.'[1] Wilson's Fourteen Points endorsed both self-determination and nationality, building in an implicit conflict that might easily become explicit.

The application of the ideal at Versailles indeed proved impractical and its outcome unsettling. In the world after World War II, the process of decolonisation sought to avoid the contradiction by being just that: unlike the new nations in Europe at the end of the first war, the new nations in the post-colonial phase were to be successors of the colonial states. It was a matter, as the British liked to think, of the 'transfer of power', and though it was in one sense a revolutionary process, in another it was deeply conservative. The new states joined the United Nations, and they were united within as well as among themselves. UNGA resolution 1514 of December 1960 supported self-determination, but also declared: 'Any attempt at the partial or total disruption of the national unity and the territorial integrity of a country is incompatible with the purpose and principles of the United Nations'.[2] It was a view that ASEAN endorsed.

The monarchies of Southeast Asia endeavoured to assert their control by a number of devices. Even in the case of Vietnam, it would be as anachronistic to attribute to them as it would be to the old European monarchies the ideological stance that was to be associated with nationalism, or to confuse the role of citizen with that of subject. Their attitudes to 'minorities' also differed. Their power over them was limited and their difference accepted. It was sufficient for them to owe a limited allegiance spasmodically enforced by armed intervention and acknowledged by the payment of tribute. Indeed the relationship might be seen as a step beyond the closer allegiance, but still limited control, that a monarch could assert and effect in the core and the more central parts of the kingdom.

In the colonial phase economic, social, and cultural developments could promote a sense of identity distinct from that formulated by nationalism, though akin to it. The breakdown of the old system opened the way for other changes, for new economic opportunities, for access to education, for religious conversion. But the colonial and pseudo-colonial governments also shaped those changes. Whether or not they sought to divide-and-rule, they certainly sought to categorise and to characterise. The old colonial powers, the Spaniards and the Dutch, set out legal categories for their subjects, while the British, imbued with the 'historicism' of the early nineteenth century, believed in 'national character' and myth. There were 'lazy natives' and there were 'martial races'. Colonial powers tended to recruit their soldiers from particular 'communities', if not from other parts of their empire. If, like the British, they began to move to a more participatory form of politics, they sought to provide for 'communal' representation, either by nomination or by special constituencies. The Japanese interregnum still further sharpened the differences that resulted. In some cases the Japanese supported the 'majority', and the Allies were supported by the 'minorities'. In other cases, their reversals of colonial practice prompted a recognition of the possibilities of change. The chaos that followed their surrender unleashed 'communal' strife in Malaya.

In the nationalist struggle against the colonial powers, it was possible to call for, and even to elicit, a sense of common struggle that might subsume other loyalties. Throughout, however, there was an undercurrent of tension, and sometimes more than that. The very fact that the colonial powers were involved tended to mean that the nationalists dismissed the difficulties they faced. The Dutch attempts to create a federal Indonesia damned it, yet in a sense Linggadjati was an attempt to square the circle of self-determination and nationality, and it failed in part because of the contradiction: even with goodwill how could you in practice ask people to what state they wanted to belong? In Burma it was difficult for the Burman nationalists to accommodate the Karens and difficult also to believe that their subsequent armed opposition was not promoted by the British.

Once independence was gained, it had to be secured. In their determination to build states, the nationalist elites were tempted to centralise, and not merely to modernise. The same was after all the case with Thailand, never formally colonised. Inheriting the frontiers of the colonial period, the new rulers sought to consolidate the new states by pursuing the creation of national languages, national education systems, and national histories. The risk was that they would screw up the tensions to such an extent that they would provoke opposition, and prompt it to take the separatist road. Many of the states indeed subsumed earlier states, and their history could be used to validate the claims of what had become 'minorities'. In the postwar world, marked both by Cold War and by the extension of the United Nations, open intervention on their behalf from the outside was unlikely, though covert support all the more probable.

The ASEAN states came together partly to limit it, both from outside the region and, by a self-denying ordinance, from inside. Their domestic approach had much in common, too. In varying mixtures they adopted both force and cooption, in new versions of the old monarchical and colonial styles. They were less ready to attempt 'devolution'. That was a programme that a European 'nation-state' like the United Kingdom might attempt, in some sense in counterpoint, not only with an increased sense of diversity, but also with the growth of globalisation. It was not clear whether it was a step towards disintegration or a means of averting it, and in Southeast Asia it seemed unlikely that the ruling elites would experiment.

The Karens

In monarchical Burma, as in other Southeast Asian monarchies, personal bonds were more significant than 'ethnic' bonds. Even before the arrival of the colonial regime, however, civil strife seems to have sharpened 'ethnic' distinctions. The leader of the Mon revolt of 1740 aspired to create a polyethnic following, and he probably had support from the Karens. Many of them were already moving from the hills to the plains, and they played a prominent role in the Pegu kingdom. The Kon-baung dynasty, by contrast, emphasised its 'Burman' aspect, and the Karens were seen as an internal threat, and also despised as animists.[3] 'We are the eggs, other races are rock; the egg fell on the rock and was broken; the rock fell on the egg, and it was broken.'[4] For the Karens the British attack in 1824–25 was a promise of deliverance.

In Pegu, which the British did not acquire in 1826, the monarchy punished the Mons and Karens who collaborated with them. In Tavoy and Tenasserim, which they did acquire, the Karens gained new opportunities, responding, too, to the American Baptist missionaries who, led by Adoniram Judson, had come to Burma in 1813. Karens in Pegu, particularly the oppressed converts, welcomed the second British invasion in the 1850s, and Christianity became a link with the new rulers. A new leadership developed, particularly drawn from the Sgaw Karens, and in 1881 a Karen National Association was formed, largely under Sgaw and Christian leadership, to promote a sense of unity and political entitlement. The link with the British was affirmed during the third Burma war, when Burman rebels attacked Karen villages, and the British used a Karen levy. Karens, Kachins, and Chins came to monopolise the indigenous security force.

The constitutional developments of the 1920s and 1930s did not extend to the 'hill peoples'. 'Parliamentary Burma' included Arakan, Pegu, and Tenasserim, as well as the old core zone, but the governor retained the control of the Scheduled Areas, Karenni, the Shan states, and the Kachin and Chin tribal regions. In parliamentary Burma, there were 'communal' as well as general seats, one object being to ensure the representation of the plains Karens, of whom there were some 500 000 by 1941: five for the Karens in 1923, twelve in 1935. The Karen leaders had attacked the extension of the Indian reforms to Burma as 'premature', and their experiences in the 1920s prompted them to seek the creation of a separate state in Tenasserim, federated to Burma, but run by Karens with British assistance. Their loyalty, they believed, justified their claim. '"Karen Country," how inspiring it sounds!' San C. Po, an American-educated doctor appointed to the Legislative Council in 1916, exclaimed in 1928. 'What thoughts, what manly feeling, what wonderful visions of the future the words conjure forth in the mind of a Karen.'[5] They were, however, to remain visions, misleading, indeed, and unrealistic. But, though Karen volunteers helped in the suppression of the Hsaya San rebellion, Karen–Burman relations appeared to improve in the later 1930s, and Ba Maw included a Karen in his privy council.

Just as the creation of the British regime had sharpened the tensions between the Burmans and the Karens, however, so did its replacement. During the Japanese invasion, the violence between the communities was renewed, and the Burma Independence Army engaged in anti-Karen pogroms, ended only by Japanese interposition. Under the Japanese, Karen guerrilla resistance persisted, despite attempts to win them over. Two Shan states were made over to Thailand in 1943, but the rest were included in Burma, with the home minister as high commissioner. The Shans were indeed to collaborate, while the Kachins and Chins remained loyal to the allies. Not surprisingly, the returning British forces utilised Chins and Kachins and made contact with Karen guerrillas. That raised their hopes for the future: Andrew Selth compares their position with that of the Arabs in World War I.[6] For both military and political reasons, however, Mountbatten determined to accept the proffered cooperation of the renamed Burma Defence Army and the Thakin-led AFPFL.

If the military struggle created conflicting obligations for the British, their proposals did nothing to reduce the political dilemma they had already faced before the war. The White Paper of 17 May 1945 concentrated on economic reconstruction and political advance in parliamentary Burma. Policy for the Scheduled Areas, Dorman-Smith had suggested, should be framed with a view to ultimate union or federation with ministerial Burma, though it should be made clear that 'we have no intention' of 'forcing' that on the peoples there.[7] The White Paper finally alluded to 'a special regime under the Governor'. But that had little appeal. Neither the AFPFL nor the Burmans outside the AFPFL, like Paw Tun or Saw, could accept the separateness of the hill regions as the country renewed its political advance. And even if the paternalistic approach could satisfy some of the less politically sophisticated frontier peoples, it certainly could not satisfy the Karens, who in any case did not dwell only in the hills.

The Burmese made us slaves, the Karen memorial of September 1945 declared. 'Then came the British, not only as a liberator, but also as a Guardian Angel, maintaining law and order, and preserving Peace and giving Protection.'[8] Now the British had come again, and the Karens sought a role in determining their political fate. They sought, for example, to send a mission to London.

> Discussions … which will affect the whole future of the Karen race, have been going on both in England and in Burma for some time, without reference to the Karen viewpoint as expressed by Karens. The Karens feel very deeply that they have the right to place their views directly on the basis of the fact that, of all the peoples in Burma, they produced the greatest and most sustained effort against the Japanese.[9]

Their aim, as the interim governor, Sir Henry Knight, put it in 1946, was a Karenistan. He doubted if the British government would agree to 'any such fission in these days when the voice of the majority is considered as the voice of God'.[10] The mission, which reached London in September, argued for a separate state, including Tenasserim and the Nyaungglebin sub-district of Pegu. The Burma Office thought that they might 'in due course … amalgamate with self-governing Burma, provided that, and so long as, Burma remained in the Commonwealth'.[11] In this way, perhaps, Britain might reconcile the dual obligations it had undertaken.

Time, however, ran out. At the end of 1946 the British Government agreed to receive a delegation from the AFPFL-dominated Executive Council on terms that envisaged an early advance to independence, with the right to leave the Commonwealth. 'It should be possible to work out some form of local autonomy, under which we retained perhaps certain rights of intervention', hazarded the Cabinet committee, but that could not apply if Burma left the Commonwealth. 'It was important that the Frontier Tribes should not be pressed to join the rest of Burma against their will, if it was about to leave the Commonwealth.'[12] Its answer, to which the delegation reluctantly agreed, was a commission of inquiry.

In the meantime Aung San met representatives of the Shans, Kachins, and Chins at Panglong. He said he was 'ashamed that some of his brethren should still be so far behind the Burmese when the Burmese themselves had been kept so far behind the world by the imperialists',[13] and readily reached an understanding that virtually ended the special regime. That might, as L. B. Walsh-Atkins put it, suggest that their alleged reluctance to join ministerial Burma was a fabrication on the part of British officials. More likely, he thought, the frontier areas representatives, realising that Britain's pledges had no 'effective backing', had quickly adopted what they thought the Burmans wanted, and the British, 'at the cost of looking a little foolish, have preserved our reputation in the eyes of the outside world and avoided the overt denunciation of promises and obligations we were unable or unwilling to meet, by the expedient of securing the free consent of the Frontier Areas to a course to which we had, in effect, arranged that there should be no alternative'. Britain had made promises 'very nearly mutually incompatible'.[14]

The Frontier Areas Commission of Enquiry also went ahead, commenting both on representation in the constituent assembly, and on the possible structure of a federal Burma. 'No one out here among the Burmese or the frontier peoples has even thought of the problems leave alone the answers', as D. R. Rees-Williams, the chairman, put it.[15] One problem was similar to the one that the Dutch and the Indonesians had faced, the chicken-and-egg process by which the states might be delineated. 'What is desirable is surely that a decision as to the formation and delimitation of a potential unit would be taken by the majority of the representatives of areas potentially within that unit', as A. F. Morley put it.[16]

The Panglong agreement, whatever its other limitations, had not dealt with the Karens. The Karen Central Organisation protested against the London agreement, an inadequate quota of twenty-four in the constituent assembly, and the failure to give cognisance to the claim to a separate state. At the Burma Office Sir David Monteath was anxious that the Karens should not be 'let down'. But 'there is not in the Burma case even the card of entry surviving in the India case, of a requirement that the new constitution shall adequately provide for the interests of minorities, before it, or the action necessary to give it effect, is recommended to Parliament'.[17] A conciliatory approach on Aung San's part won over some members of a fractured leadership, but the rest boycotted the election.

The constitution provided for a Union of Burma. It had some federal elements, including a chamber of nationalities, but Union legislation was to override state legislation. There were three states, Shan, Kachin, and Karenni, and two special districts, Chin and Karen (Kawthulay). The Shan and Karenni states had the right to secede after ten years. In such a way the Burmans sought to recreate in a modern state the historical relations with the other peoples within what had become international frontiers. The constitution also made provision for a future Karen state, to include Karenni, Salween, and 'such adjacent areas occupied by the Karens as may be determined by a Special Commission to be appointed by the President'.[18] Twenty seats were reserved for Karens in the lower house.

For no agreement had been reached. Even the AFPFL's Karen allies had joined the demand for a substantial Karen state. AFPFL feared, as Bernard Ledwidge put it, 'that concessions to the Karens will be followed by fresh demands from the Mons and Arakanese and that the fissiparous tendency now manifesting itself in Burma will escape all control and reduce the Burma Union to a loose and powerless federation'.[19] The Karens, on the other hand, were not prepared, as the hill peoples appeared to be, simply to accept what AFPFL had offered. Their growing sense of insecurity, but also their determination, was increased when it became quite clear that Burma would leave the Commonwealth.

In 1948, its first year of independence, Burma faced, as did other Southeast Asian countries, a challenge from the communists. It also faced increasing unrest among the Karens, which its government was only too willing to attribute to support from British interests. Early in 1949 the Karen National Defence Organisation began an open rebellion, and most of the Karen regiments in the regular army defected. The Union government 'hovered on the brink of disaster'.[20] Anxious that it should not collapse, the British government offered help. It did not want its aid used against the Karens, but attempts to link it with the promotion of a conciliatory policy only extended what Bevin called 'Burmese nationalist prejudices'.[21]

In the core districts of the old Burma the capital city might not have survived such onslaughts. Rangoon did. Not only were its opponents divided. 'It afforded direct diplomatic and commercial relations with the outside world and substantial emergency income from the government's monopoly of the export of rice.'[22] The insurrections were contained, but they were not suppressed. Indeed they extended. The incursion of Kuomintang troops into the Shan state, initially in order to attack the PRC, diverted the attention of the military, while creating the conditions under which large-scale opium smuggling and warlordism were to emerge. But insurgency in the Shan state had other sources, and so did that in the Kachin state: 'a growing sense of frustration, expressed by virtually all the minority peoples in Burma, with the progressively more centralised and Burmanised form of government in Rangoon, which they protested was taking too little account of their opinions or needs', as Martin Smith puts it.[23] Loyal adherents of Panglong abandoned it because they concluded that the AFPFL had already done so, and their grievances were now articulated by leaders who, like the Thakins themselves, owed much to their education at Rangoon University. There was also a religious dimension. The Kachins were predominantly Christian. Nu's pushing of Buddhism as the state religion was resented.

While the long military campaigns against the insurgents brought only partial success, however, they made the military leaders even less disposed to compromise than the civilians. Their restructuring of the army along non-ethnic lines after the 1949 mutinies led the same way. 'One Blood, One Voice, One Command' was the Tatmadaw slogan.[24] Nu's readiness to create Mon and Arakanese states, and to enhance Shan autonomy, was a factor in the decision to overthrow him in 1962, along with a growing federalist movement. 'Federalism is impossible; it will destroy the Union', Ne Win declared.[25] The Revolutionary Council abolished the separate state governments and minority administrations. The states remained, not as 'agents of the majority ethnic community of their region but of the central state'.[26] A real attempt was made, however, to recruit minorities into the central committee of the BSPP.

The leaders, Smith suggests, espoused a military tradition 'dating back across the centuries from the founder of the modern *Tatmadaw,* Aung San, to the all-conquering Burman monarchs, Alaung-hpaya in the 18th century and Aniruddha in the 11th'.[27]

Again the historical comparison is apt, but it is not a parallel. Ne Win's army aimed at a union, not merely at control of the core and command over the periphery. It also used modern weapons and modern methods. Pya Ley Pya, its Four Cuts strategy, borrowed its approach to insurgency from the West, owing much to the 'New Village' tactics adopted for dealing with the Communist Party in Malaya, and to the 'strategic hamlet' programme employed in South Vietnam. In the mid-1980s the regime was able to improve relations with its increasingly trade-oriented neighbours, the PRC of Deng Xiaoping, and Thailand, and particularly its army leaders, like Chaovalit Yongchaiyudh, in the hope of cutting the remaining insurgents' supply lines. Late in 1988, however, they were joined by students fleeing SLORC's repression.

'The forty-year history of [ethnic] relations has been a chapter of misfortune verging on the tragic', declared the official programme of the National League for Democracy in 1989.

> Along Burma's extended borders from the extreme north to the far south there are no less than thirteen groups of insurgents—a situation which is sapping the strength and resources of the nation ... we must seek a lasting solution to the problems of the ethnic minorities. ... It is the aim of the League to secure the highest degree of autonomy consonant with the inherent rights of the minorities and the well-being of the Union as a whole.[28]

Some thought that the new links the students forged might be the basis of it. But the NLD was never given the chance to try, despite, or because of, its victory in 1990.

SLORC reverted to a new version of its previous policy, a long-drawn-out attempt to set up a new constitution, coupled with further military action, now even more clearly supported by the Chinese. It secured peace agreements with the Kachin Independence Organisation and most groups in Shan State, many of them drug armies, and in 1995, under extreme military pressure, the Mons also agreed. SLORC continued to batter the Karens, but the students lost all their bases.

The Montagnards

Clive Christie has compared French policy towards the Montagnards in the Central Highlands of Vietnam with Britain's policy towards the minorities on the peripheries of Burma.[29] Though the French sought to make the area a hub of economic activity and drew heavily on corvée labour, they also sought to promote Montagnard identity, to codify Montagnard law, and to develop writing systems. Montagnard units were included in the Garde Indigène created in 1921, and the Bataillon Montagnard du Sud-Annam was formed in 1931.

The Central Highlands and their people became a focus for the struggle between the French and the Viet Minh that was joined in 1946–47. In a letter sent to a Congress of Southern National Minorities at Pleiku in April 1946, Ho Chi Minh stressed that all the 'nationalities' of Vietnam should unite against French attempts to exploit their divisions. For d'Argenlieu, on the other hand, the development of the Montagnards offered the possibility of interposing a barrier between the north and the Mekong region. In May 1946 he announced the creation of a special administrative region, comprising five Montagnard provinces, the Commissariat du Gouvernement Fédéral pour les Populations Montagnardes du Sud Indochinois. When French policy changed, and the Bao Dai regime was set up, the area became a crown domain. In it, however, the French were privileged, and corvée benefited their plantations. Undermining them, on the other hand, was Viet Minh infiltration.

The nationalism of Ngo Dinh Diem's regime involved not only breaking links with the French, but also eliminating the special regime in the Central Highlands. They were incorporated in the new Republic and their people subjected to a programme of Vietnamisation. In response Montagnard leaders sought autonomy, and set up a united organisation, Bajaraka, in May 1958. It also provided the Viet Minh with an opportunity to build a Montagnard base that would help in the infiltration of South Vietnam. In addition Bajaraka made contact with the irredentist movements among the Cham and the Khmer Krom that the Cambodian government was encouraging, partly in response to its belief that South Vietnam and the United States were trying to destabilise it. In September 1964 the Front Unifié de Lutte de la Race Opprimée (FULRO) was set up in Cambodia. Itself in fact distrustful of the links between the US forces and the Montagnards, the South Vietnamese leadership made concessions that stopped short of the autonomy the French had once offered, though intermittent negotiations continued with some FULRO leaders till 1968.

'Montagnard society was to pay a terrible penalty for its peripheral status and its position on the front line in the confrontation between communism and the West.' American involvement became increasingly direct. In a region of crucial strategic significance, the North Vietnamese for their part built up support in the northern sector and targeted the Stieng people in the south. In the subsequent conflicts 'an entire society' was disrupted. Nor did the victorious communists fulfil their promise to create autonomous zones. The unification government was soon fighting against FULRO guerrilla units in the Central Highlands.[30]

A not dissimilar fate befell minorities in Laos. The mountain areas were important to the DRVN in its struggle with the southern regime, and to the Pathet Lao with its struggle with the Royal Government. Meo (Hmong) forces led by Vang Pao were supported by the CIA in the mid-1960s, attacked by the Lao and the Vietnamese in 1977–78.

Isan and Pattani

In neighbouring Thailand the centralisation by which from the late nineteenth century the absolute monarchy replaced the looser relations with the periphery of an earlier period was intensified by the postwar 'development' dictatorships. The northeast was neglected and its inhabitants seen as inferior. Migration to the south, though it could reduce frustration, added to that perception. 'Isan' people began in the 1960s to identify themselves as such. They did not, however, aim to be part of Laos, from which the frontier settlement of 1893 had separated them: they wanted to be distinctive within Thailand.

The parliamentary system had offered them some opportunities. Northeastern MPs were characteristically associated with the opposition, with Pridi, with the Free Siamese movement, and with the opponents of the 1947 coup. Prevented by the Sarit regime from legitimate articulation of its demands, the northeast supported the Socialist parties in 1975. It was a base for the CPT in the late 1970s, but the reopening of democratic politics in the early 1980s enabled it to express its discontent in another way. In the absence of regionalist leaders and organisation, as David Brown points out, the people of the northeast sold their votes to canvassers for the wealthy military-backed parties, and in 1992 they provided the main support for the 'devil' parties.[31] One of the risks in the reforms of 1996 was that the revamped parliamentary system would fail to take account of northern needs.

In the south, too, the absolute monarchy had sought to tighten its control in face of the advance of the colonial powers and of the economic changes of the late nineteenth century. Prince Damrong wanted to make Pattani as prosperous as Kelantan. But, on its integration as a *monthon* in 1902, the ruling Malay families were displaced, and the assimilationist legal reforms were bound to cause the kind of offence to Muslims that, further south, the British sedulously sought to avoid. Resisting Thai authority, Raja Abdul Kadir was gaoled in Phitsanuloke. Released after serving less than three years of a ten-year sentence, he left for Kelantan, with the royal family of which he was closely related. From there he encouraged opposition to the Thais, and the Namsai rebellion broke out in 1922. The following year King Vajiravudh issued new guidelines for the bureaucracy in Pattani, enjoining a greater respect for Islam. But the king was himself an assimilationist, and the officials were Thai.[32]

The constitutional monarchy promoted compulsory education, and that was associated with Buddhism. The elite in Pattani yet felt that the parliamentary system offered them more opportunities than the absolute monarchy. They resolved to take part in the elections, though Abdul Kadir's son and heir, Mahmud Mahyuddin, was to stand aside and keep alive the hope of restoring Pattani's autonomy. Treasuring the same aspiration, the *ulama* helped the candidates, however, and in 1937 Yala, Pattani, and Navathivat returned Malayo-Muslim representatives. But parliament had little power, and the results were disappointing. The Pibun government was, moreover, assimilationist. Siam became Thailand, and patriotism was identified with Buddhism. Tengku Mahyuddin, who had returned to Bangkok, left for British Malaya in 1939.

In the Japanese invasion he escaped to British India. There he played a leading role in helping to recruit Malays for Force 136. He hoped that, by working with the British in the war, he would persuade them to alter the 1909 boundary in the peace settlement. Though the Japanese were cavalier with the boundary, of that there was little chance. The Colonial Office saw no special political or administrative advantage in adding any Siamese territory to postwar Malaya, though Malay-populated areas could 'without difficulty be taken into the Malayan political grouping if that course were required for defence or other reasons'.[33] In any case the war ended without a struggle with Thailand, and with the United States disposed to take its part.

The Free Thai governments were more moderate than the pre-war Pibun regime. Even they, however, aimed at a kind of assimilation. The Patronage of Islam Act of 1945, promoted by Pridi and Cham Phromyong, a Muslim senator drawn from the Muslim community established in Bangkok since the earlier attempts to control the Malay states, was designed to extend the king's protection to Islam, and created regional and central Islamic committees. But it was also designed to redesignate the Malayo-Muslims as 'Thai people who profess Islam', and the role of the Thai bureaucrats in fact increased. Traditional leaders having failed, *ulama* took over, led by Haji Sulong bin Abdulkadir bin Md al-Fatani, chairman of the Pattani district council. In April 1947 he submitted a petition to the Thai government on behalf of the Malayo-Muslims of Greater Pattani, calling for an autonomous entity under a high commissioner. That was unacceptable in Bangkok: the state would fall apart. The return of Pibun dashed his remaining hopes. In January 1948 he and many of his followers were arrested, while others fled to Malaya. Unrest increased when Pibun became premier, and over 100 Malays were killed at Dusong Nyor in Narathivat on 26–27 April 1948.[34] There was concern in the Federation. But on the outbreak of the Emergency there, the Thai government took the opportunity to declare an emergency in the south, while Britain, anxious for its collaboration, discouraged local support for the separatists across the border.

Sarit and his successors renewed the assimilationist policies of the past amid the new emphasis on 'development'. One object was to recruit a new elite among the minority, who would become government officials and carry out government policy, countering the influence of the Malayo-Muslims who sought education in Muslim lands: in 1977 the Thai Student Association in Cairo had 600 members. Such officials, however, found it difficult both to serve their people, and to be part of the Buddhist-oriented state bureaucracy. Sarit and his successors also tried to turn the *pondok* into 'private schools for Islamic education', and to secularise the curriculum. The reactions included attempts to raise Islamic consciousness through the *da'wah* movement; terrorism, partly designed to discourage settlement of Buddhists from the northeast; and separatism.

The main organisation was the Pattani United Liberation Organisation (PULO), founded in 1968, led by young intellectuals trained in the Middle East and South Asia. Its most spectacular act took place on 22 September 1977, when two bombs were exploded during the visit of the king and queen to Yala province. In the 1980s a relationship of convenience developed between Muslim and Thai and Malayan communist rebels, and the tendency of Thai officials to label any opposition communist enhanced it. The future of the movement remained unclear. Its only hope was, however, an improved status for the Muslims within Thailand. That, Ruth McVey suggested, would be difficult to achieve, given Thailand's 'extreme centralization' and the authoritarian relationship between officialdom and populace. Unrest would continue as 'an open, debilitating, but not fatal sore upon the Thai body politic'.[35] Andrew Forbes was more hopeful, though, as he said, any return to assimilationist policies 'would inevitably lead to a resurgence of Malay separatism in south Thailand'.[36] Early in 1998 it was reported that the Thai government was preparing an amnesty bill, designed to treat secessionists in the way communists had been treated seventeen years earlier.

W. K. Che Man has compared the position of the Muslims in southern Thailand with that of the Moros in the Philippines.[37] Over a long period of struggle, they have both developed a sense of identity. In both cases, the leadership has been divided, in part by the very intractability of the problems it faces. That weakens the movements, and also exposes them to manipulation by their opponents. Pattani, however, provided a clearer focus for the Muslims in southern Thailand than either Sulu or Mindanao offered the Moros. Their relationship with what came to be the majority peoples in modern nation-states also differed. Though pressured by colonial powers, the kingdom of Thailand was not under colonial control. No colonial power determined or backed the policies it adopted, and none interposed to develop or protect the peripheral peoples. The latter was the case in Burma. The former was the case in the Philippines. Over a long period the Spaniards had in effect been engaged in a war with the Muslims to the south, whose incorporation in the Philippines was for the most part merely nominal. In that war Christian Filipinos were incorporated in the Spanish forces, and their settlements were the prey of the pirates and slave-traders. In this 'national' history there was plenty to remember and to forget.

The Moros

The destruction of Spanish rule in the Philippines, and the intervention of the Americans, briefly raised the possibility that the sultanate of Sulu might be separated from the rest of the Philippines, perhaps being associated with North Borneo.[38] In fact the United States asserted its claim by making a separate treaty with the sultan in 1899. Once it had subdued the north, however, it proceeded to establish the Moro province in 1903, and the following year it abrogated the treaty with a ruler Gen. Leonard Wood described as 'degenerate, dishonest, tricky, dissipated, and absolutely devoid of principle'.[39] Inspired by Islam, and by the legacy of centuries of struggle, the Moros put up a fanatical resistance to American 'pacification', resulting in the massacres at Bud Dajo in 1906—600 Moros dead, 21 Americans—and at Bud Bagsak in 1913. Moros distrusted the policy of 'attraction' that followed under Governor-General Harrison and Governor Frank Carpenter. Its aim was 'political integration'. The Jones law provided for two appointed senators to cover the 'non-Christian' people, and nine appointed representatives in the otherwise elected House of Representatives. But it seemed to go further. Would not American-sponsored education imply Christianisation?[40]

If colonial rule offered few guarantees, the prospect of inclusion in an independent Christian majority-ruled Philippines seemed still worse. Moro leaders preferred the continuance of American rule. In 1926 the US Congress put on record a Declaration of Rights and Purposes by the Moro leaders: in the event of independence without provision for 'our retention under the American flag', they would declare themselves 'an independent constitutional sultanate to be known to the world as the Moro Nation'.[41] It was, T. H. Haynes, an old Sulu hand, suggested, 'the height of folly to think of subjecting a race like the Sulu Islanders to the domination of Filipino officials or a Filipino parliamentary majority'. The American assertion of sovereignty was questionable: 'Subservience to a Filipino parliament would be the last straw.'[42]

In March 1935, 120 Lanao *datus* wrote to Roosevelt opposing Philippines independence and expressing their wish to remain under American rule. Like the Pattani elite, however, the Moro elite thought it worthwhile to take part in elections. In the 1935 assembly elections in Sulu and Cotabato, victory went to the candidates less identified with Filipino nationalism, and in Lanao Moros for the same reason supported a Christian, Thomas Cabili, though one who spoke Maranao.[43] But the actions of the Commonwealth government more than justified the apprehensions of those who had feared majority rule. Compared to Mussolini, Quezon could be compared to Pibun, too. He was determined to assimilate the Moro population into the mainstream, and he was also determined to promote national unity and security by resettling Christian Filipinos throughout Mindanao.

On the death of Sultan Jamal-ul-Kiram in 1936, Quezon declined to recognise a successor: 'he was fully determined not to have anybody in this country occupying a position of privilege'.[44] '[T]he Sultans have no more rights than the humblest Moro.'[45] In fact he seemed to be concerned with the development of Mindanao rather than the advancement of non-Christian Filipinos. Commonwealth Act 691 declared all lands within the areas occupied by Muslims public lands, open to the first claimant who could produce a 'legal' title. The way was thus opened to land-grabbers, and to the displacement of the Muslims. No programme helped them to legitimise their holdings or make them more productive, and the datus, though in a position to lead, were tempted to work with outside interests. The best arguments for the policy were the pressure on land in Luzon, and the apprehensions about the Japanese that their settlement in Davao could not but arouse. But, if designed to solve current problems, the policy, and its implementation, created new problems for the future, and in fact diminished national unity and security.

The Japanese conquerors offered the idea of Moro self-government no sympathy and saw Mindanao as a strategic stronghold. There, as elsewhere in the Philippines, they secured collaborators, some hoping to limit the impact of the conquest, some to make gains. The collaborators, who included pre-war rivals like Datu Ombra

Amilbangsa and Gulamu Rasul, were not discredited after the war, but had to give way to a new generation that had gained prominence as guerrilla fighters. The guerrilla struggle had produced an unusual level of Moro–Christian–American cooperation. For the Moros participation was a way to demonstrate their prowess and 'consolidate their respective constituencies'.[46] In the war the Moros thus acquired new leaders, and they also acquired arms. Guerrilla back-pay gave them the means to undertake the haj and to build mosques, contributing to a Muslim resurgence, also funded by the smuggling promoted by postwar economic controls.

The new Republic of Roxas and Magsaysay continued, however, the policies of Quezon. The programme of resettlement, interrupted by the war, was renewed, though migrants came from the Visayas rather than Huk-penetrated southern Luzon; and it was expanded, so that migrants increasingly impinged on Muslim and tribal customary land. In Cotabato's Koronadal Valley, the Christian population rose from 18 in 1939 to 30 000 in 1960, and by the late 1950s there were more Cebuano speakers in Mindanao than there were in Cebu. Moro alienation was demonstrated by the rebellion of Haji Kamlun, a Tausug, whose defiance of government made him a kind of hero. It prompted Congress in 1954 to establish a Special Committee to investigate the 'Moro problem', headed by Domocao Alonto, son of the Sultan sa Ramain of Lanao. The 'problem', it concluded, was the integration of the Muslim population in the body politic. In turn that led to the creation of the Commission on National Integration (CNI), designed to assist the economic and social development of the National Cultural Minorities. Its achievements were limited. Its most notable function was to award scholarships to 'minority' students, though only 16.7 per cent of the 8300 grantees between 1958 and 1967 completed their courses.[47] Macapagal's claim to Sabah was in part at least a gesture to the Muslims, but again he failed to deliver.[48]

The 'Jabidah' massacre early in 1968 marked a new stage in the growing conflict. At least twenty Moro trainees were killed in the course of a mutiny on Corregidor. The purpose of their training was unclear: was it, perhaps, to infiltrate Sabah? Whatever it was, 'the imbecility of its execution spilled into criminality', as T. J. S. George put it, and it made 'all sections of the Muslims—secular and religious, modern and backward alike—concerned about their future'.[49] All the accused officers and men were, furthermore, acquitted.

In May 1968 Datu Udtog Matalam, a resistance veteran, five times Governor of Cotabato, proclaimed the desire of the inhabitants of Mindanao, Sulu, and Palawan to secede and establish an Islamic state, calling the secessionist organisation the Muslim Independence Movement (MIM). In that there was a measure of opportunism— indeed Jabidah had affected Samals and Tausugs more than Maguindanaons—and Matalam subsequently accepted the post of Presidential Adviser on Muslim Affairs. But the idea of secession, as Ortiz says, took on a life of its own.[50]

These events, moreover, both reflected and intensified the growing violence that migration was prompting in Mindanao. In Cotabato and northern Lanao groups of

Ilonggo settlers from the Visayas and tribal Tiruray, calling themselves Ilaga (Rats), fought with groups of Muslim Blackshirts and Barracuda, whose violence MIM tended to legitimise. In such a context electoral contests only expanded the violence. In the 1971 local elections Christian politicians challenged traditional Muslim leaders for the first time. If the Muslim groups were linked with Matalam and other Muslim politicians, the Ilaga were backed by Christians, and, it appeared, by the PC commander in Cotabato, an Ilonggo. 'It is virtually a free-for-all', one observer wrote in 1972. 'Muslims fighting Christians; government troops fighting Muslims; political private armies fighting Muslim or Christian farmers, private armies or hired goons fighting army men.'[51]

The situation in Mindanao was cited as a reason for Marcos's proclamation of martial law in September 1972, but it escalated the struggle. The first major act of defiance came a month later, with the seizure of the Mindanao State University campus in Marawi City. Martial law centralised power in Christian hands, cutting out legitimate political activity even for the moderates. It also required the surrender of arms, leaving the Moros exposed to the Ilagas, the army, and the PC. The newly formed Moro National Liberation Front came out into the open, together with its Bangsa Moro Army.

Those were the creation of a young Sulu, Nur Misuari, formerly a scholarship student at the University of the Philippines, and then an instructor. In 1967 he was the moving force behind the creation of the Philippine Muslim Nationalist League and editor of its official organ. In the aftermath of Jabidah he both sought and secured support from the datu bosses with whom he had connexions for the training of a guerrilla force. The training was provided at Pangkor in Malaysia, where it was thought that destabilising Mindanao might lead Manila to drop the Sabah claim.[52] In mid-1971 Nur Misuari called a meeting at Zamboanga, including his ninety recruits, and, breaking with his erstwhile old-style patrons, he established the MNLF. He did not see 'independence' as 'secession': Moroland had never been part of the Philippines.

In the aftermath of martial law, the MNLF gained many recruits, perhaps peaking at 20 000. Rebellion spread throughout southern Mindanao, but the centrepiece was Sulu. That was not a focus for migration, but young Tausug identified themselves with the struggle against the Ilaga elsewhere. Sulu, too, was not only Nur Misuari's home territory. It was where Tun Mustapha of Sabah, already 'a vital prop of the MNLF',[53] had his roots. A major rebellion broke out in February 1974. The government reacted in ways that could recall those of the Spaniards, though utilising vastly greater force. Sulu was bombarded by three naval vessels and by air force jets, and the commercial centre, and the densely populated area of Tulay, were 'completely gutted'.[54] Between 400 and 1000 civilians were killed, and 150–200 rebels.

Other nineteenth-century comparisons might be made. The Sulu conflict attracted international attention, not, as in the 1870s, from rival imperial powers, but from the Muslim states, in particular Libya, where Colonel Quddafi took up the cause. As earlier, however, international support, never in any case likely to endorse secession because of its precedental effect, was counter-productive. Outside intervention made the government more determined to crush the rebels. In this, again like its colonial predecessor, it did not rely on force alone: it used and fostered the divisions among its opponents, between old-style leaders and new, between Sulu and Mindanao. 'Moro' had become a proud badge, rather than a derogatory term, but Moros were not united. The drawback of the government's strategy was that, while it might reduce the cohesion of opponents in a war, it also made it difficult to find a coherent group with which to make peace.

In 1975 Mustapha was overthrown, while Marcos conducted a diplomatic campaign among the Islamic nations and elsewhere. He now felt confident enough to declare that the government was ready to offer autonomy to Muslim Mindanao. The Tripoli ceasefire agreement followed in November 1976. Nur Misuari had not, however, dropped the objective of a Bangsa Moro state declared in 1974. Marcos kept the initiative by proclaiming autonomy in the thirteen provinces listed in the Tripoli agreement, establishing a provisional government, and calling for a referendum. The last proposal was crucial, for by this time Muslims were in a majority in only three, Sulu, Tawi-Tawi, and Lanao del Sur. The result was a rout for the MNLF.

That did not bring peace to Mindanao, where martial law was continued after it was dropped elsewhere in 1981. Crony-promoted 'development', tribal dispossession and the penetration of the NPA indeed only added to the turmoil in what Corazon Aquino described in a campaign speech as 'a land of unfulfilled promises, a war zone, a land forced into fratricidal strife, a land where every day Filipino kills brother Filipino, a land of avaricious exploitation'.[55]

Even before her installation as President, Aquino began negotiations with the MNLF. The split among the Muslims, however, made negotiations difficult, while they were criticised by the military. The promise of an autonomous 'Muslim Mindanao' in the draft constitution of 1986 alarmed sections of the Christian population. In the event, however, Republic Act 6649 provided for a plebiscite. In that, held in November 1989, only four provinces voted for autonomy, and not a single city. 'Like Marcos', Nagasura Madale wrote, 'Aquino has used "the people" as an excuse for explaining why genuine Muslim autonomy is not possible'.[56] In 1996, however, Ramos concluded a peace agreement with the MNLF. Nur Misuari became governor of the Autonomous Region in Muslim Mindanao, formed by the plebiscite, and also chaired the Supreme Philippines Council for Peace and Development.

Aceh

In Aceh, by contrast to Pattani and to Moroland, the people shared the religion of the majority of the population of the nation-state, though their interpretation of it might differ. The people, again by contrast to Pattani and to Moroland, had also shared with the majority a struggle against the colonial power. Aceh had, however, a strong sense of identity, focused in part on a single sultanate, as was the case with Pattani, but not with Moroland. That did not preclude other differences. Indeed the

Acehnese elite was deeply divided between the *ulama* and the *uleebalang*, the territorial chiefs with whom the Dutch had come to terms in order to end the Aceh war. In independent Indonesia the central government was able to secure support, but it was not able to prevent the emergence of secessionism.

Like the Dutch, the Japanese used the *uleebalang*. In 1946 the ulama, organised since 1939 into the All-Aceh Ulama Association (PUSA) led by Daud Beureu'eh, had both prepared the region against the return of the Dutch, and led a 'social revolution' against the *uleebalang* with whom they had been identified. The Republican leaders appointed Daud Beureu'eh Military Governor in July 1947. More controversially, the head of the temporary government after the second police action, Sjafruddin Prawinegara, made Aceh a province. That the Republic government would not recognise, and the Natsir cabinet dissolved it at the end of January 1951.

'While it would not be appropriate to say that the Central Government was purposefully backing the *uleebalang* elements, it was at least true to say … that its policies created a situation in Aceh which worked to the advantage of the uleebalang elements.'[57] The central government's neglect of Aceh, coupled with the psychological impact of the abolition of the province, helped their opponents, however, and gained them popular support. So, too, did the reaction to the speech Sukarno made at Amuntai early in 1953, which insisted that Indonesia was a national state, not an Islamic one. The installation of the Ali government in Jakarta prompted Daud Beureu'eh to proclaim the Islamic State of Indonesia on 21 September. 'We do not want to separate ourselves from our brothers and sisters in other regions … but at the same time we refuse to be treated as stepchildren or left to live like slaves.'[58]

The regional revolts that followed the 1955 elections gave Aceh some leverage. Nasution looked to the subordinate Aceh regiment for support against the rebellious Simbolon. At the end of 1956 Aceh was again granted provincial status, and Ali Hasjmy was appointed governor, a former supporter of PUSA, but rival of Daud Beureu'eh. The latter aligned himself with the PRRI rebellion, but his former associates negotiated with the government to create the Daerah Istimewa Aceh. Daud Beureu'eh insisted on Aceh's right to implement Islamic law. Again the government responded. In April 1962 a decree from Aceh's martial law administrator authorised implementing 'elements of Islamic law'.[59]

Under the New Order regime, however, the hopes of the *ulama* were not realised. A regulation to enable the implementation of Islamic law, enacted by the provincial assembly in 1968, did not get Jakarta's approval. Nor did an attempt to promote the madrasah schools by integrating them with the primary schools under the control of the Ministry of Education and Culture. The prospects became still worse as the New Order adopted a more restrictive stance towards *santri* Islam. The activities of Daud Beureu'eh himself were curbed or manipulated.

At the same time the expansion of secular education in Aceh, and access to it in Jakarta and overseas, was producing a new elite. It was to that elite that the New Order technocrats looked. In other parts of Indonesia it relied on traditional groups or on resource patronage. In Aceh the position was different. The *uleebalang* were too weak to revive, while with the development of the massive gas reserves discovered by Mobil in 1971, Aceh was more likely to be a source of wealth than a grateful recipient. The new secular-educated elite were thus to constitute a 'new *uleebalang*'.[60] But the perception that the central government took rather than gave undermined this strategy. The Lhokseumawe Industrial Zone—occupying the same area as Samudra–Pasai—was an enclave, and few of the rewards of development, as distinct from its pollution, were spread among the Acehnese. Golkar's share of the vote declined in Aceh, while it rose elsewhere. That was reversed only in the 1987 election, which followed the appointment of an Acehnese, Ibrahim Hasan, as governor, and the adoption of a more conciliatory approach, both in respect of Islam and of development. But, as the governor said, the villagers tended to see the regional government, because of its association with the centre, as 'just the same as the Dutch'.[61]

On the other hand, opposition also took a secessionist form. The Free Aceh Movement (GAM) was founded in October 1976 by Tengku Hasan M. di Tiro, a businessman descended from Teungku Chik di Tiro, a *ulama* hero of the long war against the Dutch. 'During the last thirty years', his Redeclaration of Independence asserted in December 1976, 'the people of Acheh, Sumatra, have witnessed how our fatherland has been exploited and driven into ruinous conditions by the Javanese neo-colonialists'.[62] 'Indonesia exists on the principle of territorial integrity of the colonial empire: and an empire is not liquidated if its territorial integrity is preserved. Thus Indonesia is still an unliquidated colonial empire with Javanese replacing Dutchmen as conquerors.' Jakarta was itself in thrall to the Westerners, Indonesia 'their best neo-colony'.[63] The activities of the movement in the 1970s were limited, and so was its support. ABRI was able to break it up. But it re-emerged in 1989, and its insurgency reached a peak in 1990, with some 750 men, perhaps 250 of them trained in Libya, with funding from Acehnese in Malaysia, also a place of sanctuary, and with local support mainly from lower social strata. They were no match for ABRI's programme of terror and resettlement. But the root cause of the rebellion remained unresolved.

West Irian

Netherlands India had extended from Sabang to Merauke. That was the main basis for Indonesia's claim to West New Guinea, although the need for a secure frontier, one of the Dutch reasons for taking it over, was an argument with the leaders of the successor state, too. There were arguments the other way. How would a transfer affect the security of others? Over that the Australians were sensitive, despite their support for the Republic in the struggle with the Dutch. The inhabitants, it could also be argued, had had limited commercial contacts with the Indonesians, and had much less in common with them in terms of culture, language, or custom than with those of Papua and New Guinea, then under Australian administration.

The two parties had been unable to reach agreement during the 1949 negotiations, and the RTC agreement had prescribed further negotiations that would determine the political status of the territory within one year. They failed. While the Republic, and in particular the President, became more determined to add West Irian to its territory, the Dutch became more determined not to hand it over. Increasingly they emphasised the issue of self-determination: their purpose, they claimed, was to prepare the Papuan people to make a choice. 'The application of the Netherlands concept of self-determination with regard to West Irian would mean in fact that we should accept also the same concept with regard to the other islands or regions of Indonesia and consequently accept the disintegration of the Indonesian state',[64] Subandrio told the UN Political Committee. But the argument, though likely to appeal to other successor states, assumed that West Irian was already as much or as little a part of Indonesia as other regions, several of which were then indeed in a state of revolt. The real risk of conflict between those complementary but antagonistic principles, self-determination and nationality, lay in the possibility that a Papuan state would be created that would attract international support.

The conflict contributed to the radicalisation of Indonesian politics in the 1950s. The Indonesian government sought to rally international opinion, and also implemented a limited military campaign of pressure and infiltration. The Dutch for their part began to take steps to implement the provision for a Volksraad, laid down in their 1949 decree for the administration of New Guinea, setting up a number of regional councils, and then, in 1959, the first elected one, in the Biak–Noemfoor region. Slow as the process might be, the Dutch, as Paul Hasluck put it, 'were inclined, against their better judgement, to introduce self-government before the proper time had arrived in the hope that world opinion would be against any attack by Indonesia on a newly independent, self-governing West New Guinea'.[65] In April 1960 the minister for the interior announced the creation of an elective New Guinea Council, and early in 1961 elections were held. Though the Dutch broke up a pro-Indonesian youth organisation, pro-Indonesian parties took part, supported by migrants, but also by some Papuans, particularly from Biak. Most parties, however, favoured Dutch rule, followed by Papuan self-determination. At the end of the year the Council agreed to name the state West Papua and on 1 December 1961 the Morning Star was raised beside the Dutch Tricolour.

Joseph Luns, the Dutch foreign minister, had vainly sought to head off the Indonesian reaction by reversing Dutch policy and seeking UN involvement: in September 1961 he proposed an interim administration under international supervision, with a view to transferring rule to the Papuans. It was not a question of interests or rights, says Gabriel Defert: it was a question of Dutch *amour propre*.[66] The Dutch had sent out their aircraft carrier, the *Karel Doorman*, the previous year. Emboldened by India's take-over of Portuguese Goa, Indonesia now stepped up the military action which KOSTRAD had been preparing under Suharto's command. But more important than military action in itself was its diplomatic context. The United States was not prepared to back the Dutch. 'Inevitably West Irian will go sooner or later to Indonesia', wrote Robert Komer, the White House staffer. 'The only question is will it go with our help, and in such a way that we get some credit for it, or will this issue be left on a silver platter for the [communist] Bloc?'[67] The Dutch capitulated, agreeing to transfer the administration to an interim UN Temporary Executive Authority (UNTEA) from 1 October 1962. Dutch New Guinea was to become Indonesian West Irian on 1 May 1963.

The agreement made a gesture towards self-determination by providing for an Act of Free Choice. That took place in 1969, and the Indonesian authorities ensured that it was no more than a gesture. 'In realistic terms, by ignoring the fact that New Guinea is ethnically and geographically an entity and that all the "musyawarah" in the world cannot turn Melanesian Papuans into Indonesians, we are helping to prepare the ground for a Papuan irredentist movement. ... Where else in today's world would the dictum be accepted that a people was too primitive ever to be free?' asked the *Sydney Morning Herald*.[68] In fact resistance was already under way. Its standard-bearer was Organisasi Papua Merdeka (OPM), and its founders Arfak people, many of them trained in the Dutch-created Papuan Volunteer Corps. But the guerrilla group, Tentera Pembebasan Nasional (TPN), was formed by an alienated Indonesian-trained intelligence officer from Biak, Seth Rumkorem. It was he who proclaimed independence in 1971.

Divided like other such movements though it was, the Papuan opposition was kept alive by the policies of the Indonesians, more colonialist than the colonialists themselves. To exploit the resources of the area the Suharto government again looked to foreign capital. The most striking example was Freeport's exploitation of 'Copper Mountain' under an agreement of 1967. 'An overriding profit motive and a centralist government policy have resulted in a classic situation of colonial exploitation', as Robert Mitton, an Australian geologist, put it.[69] Timber was exploited for trivial rewards, while transmigrants from other parts of Indonesia, in a programme vastly expanded on that of the pre-war Dutch, took the employment opportunities new resource-based industries created. The developments did not surprise Garfield Barwick, a leading architect of the 1962 deal. He had, however, underestimated the ability of the West Papuans to fight back, despite the high level of ABRI violence, and the reluctance of the PNG government, independent from 16 September 1975, to seal the border. 'It is', he said, 'the new "Ulster" in our part of the world'.[70]

Two months after PNG became independent, Indonesia invaded East Timor 'with a degree of brutality that alarmed PNG leaders and angered many citizens'.[71] Students burned the Indonesian flag. It became more difficult for the government in Port Moresby to justify a policy of cooperating with Indonesia along the border at the expense of the OPM. Arguably it became more necessary.

Fretilin

Indonesia's incorporation of East Timor indeed marked a change of policy. The frontiers of the new state, like those of other successor states, had been the frontiers of the colonial state. It was indeed primarily on that basis that the Republic had argued its claim to West Irian. In the 1940s and 1950s some Indonesian nationalists, like Muhammad Yamin, had on occasion gone further, claiming Australian New Guinea, East Timor, and British North Borneo, but they had not received official support. Clashes on the Timor border were reported in November 1962, following India's incorporation of Portuguese Goa the previous year, but Sukarno turned to *konfrontasi*. In that he did not claim North Borneo, but argued its right to self-determination. Moving on East Timor was a break with the past, scarcely justified by the appeal of some of the East Timor leaders. A desire for security had lain behind the claim to West Irian and behind *konfrontasi*. Used by OPSUS, headed by Ali Murtopo, and his protégé, Benny Murdani, it seemed the only justification for the acquisition of East Timor, and, at a time when the communists had won their extraordinary victories in Cambodia and Vietnam, it certainly helped the Indonesians once more to win the support, or avoid the opposition, of the United States. The violence with which ABRI acted, however, helped the Timorese opposition to internationalise a cause that, unlike that of the Acehnese, was in any case never merely domestic, nor, unlike that of the West Papuans, formally abandoned by the United Nations.

After the fall of the Caetano regime in the Carnation revolution in Portugal of April 1974, three political groups emerged in East Timor. The Uniao Democratica Timorense (UDT) was supported by higher civil servants, landowners, some chiefs, and some Chinese, and aimed at progressive autonomy within the Portuguese empire. The Frente Revolucionaria de Timor Leste Independente (Fretilin) advocated the 'right to independence', and drew much wider support from lower civil servants, teachers, students, workers, and immigrants to the north coast towns. A third party, Associacao Popular Democratica Timorense (Apodeti) emerged at the end of May. Much smaller, it wanted to join Indonesia, and it received economic support from Indonesia.

In the first half of 1975, encouraged by a Portuguese administration now oriented towards the Movement of the Armed Forces in Lisbon, UDT and Fretilin collaborated on the basis of a planned advance to independence. Apprehensive of the weakness of Apodeti, the Indonesians sought to undermine the coalition by arousing UDT's concern over Fretilin's left-wing orientation. In August an attempted UDT coup precipitated civil war. The Portuguese withdraw to the island of Atauro, and, after considerable bloodshed, Fretilin emerged in control. 'Many in East Timor now believed that Indonesia would annex the territory, if necessary by military means.'[72] Other countries would not intervene, and Portugal itself was in no position to act. Indonesian raids began in September. The major attack started on 16 October. In the second half of November the pressure increased. Fretilin declared independence on 28 November 1975, while the now allied UDT and Apodeti declared it part of Indonesia. A full-scale Indonesian invasion followed. 'How is it possible to betray a glorious past, the principles of the Bandung Conference?' Ramos Horta asked the Security Council.[73]

On 7 December Dili was, as the Indonesians reported, 'liberated' by troops that, as in *konfrontasi*, they sought to describe as 'volunteers'. The aim was to avoid UN condemnation. In this they did not succeed. Nor was the United Nations convinced by the argument that the UDT–Apodeti alliance, allegedly representing the majority of the people, had sought Indonesian help. UN resolutions were, however, ignored. The Indonesians proceeded with an Act of Free Choice, borrowing from West Irian precedent, and in fact administered by the same man, Ali Murtopo, and in the same way. The result was that East Timor was incorporated into Indonesia on 17 July 1976, becoming its twenty-seventh province, and without the so-called special status of Aceh and West Irian.

Opposition persisted, despite the desperate conditions the guerrillas faced. Perhaps 200 000 people died. ABRI's violence was so great that, through Amnesty International and other organisations, it attracted international attention. A shift in government policy in 1988, moreover, led to renewed civil resistance, and in turn to more violence, such as the Santa Cruz massacre of November 1991. '[T]here is nothing in the Pancasila about slaughter, annexation or violence', said Fernando de Araujo in 1992.[74] Though UN resolutions were ineffective, it was still true that the United Nations had not approved what Indonesia had done. In the case of East Timor, there were, therefore, still some grounds for international action.

That, together with continued resistance, modified the policy of post-Suharto Indonesia. Habibie's interim government, perhaps surprisingly, agreed to a referendum, held on 30 August 1999. Not surprisingly ABRI disliked the result, and contributed to the violence that followed and that led to the intervention of an Australian-led UN force. In October Indonesia formally accepted East Timor's independence, its last troops leaving on the 31st. Arguably that increased, rather than reduced, the chance of sustaining the integrity of a state based on the Dutch inheritance.

The Andamanese

Other parts of the Portuguese empire in Asia were disposed of without a process of self-determination. 1999 also saw the 'return' of Macao to China. '[F]ew bothered to ask what the wishes of the population of Goa were'[75] when India annexed it. As successor to Britain India retained the Andaman and Nicobar islands without question, too. Indeed, my earlier history of Southeast Asia has so far been the only one that sought to treat those islands as part of Southeast Asia. If they are, they are also part of a colony of settlement. Commenting on the 1951 census report, the deputy commissioner pointed to differences between 'local borns' and 'new settlers', but also to the dropping of caste and other distinctions. 'These islands are witnessing perhaps the birth of the organic essence of Indian humanity.'[76] There was also a Karen settlement, originating with forest workers who had come in 1925, and some Burmans, unwilling to become Indian citizens. The 'ruin' of most of the Andamanese, 'both physical and spiritual', was 'almost complete'.[77] Later Tamil repatriates from Sri Lanka came to the islands, and Sikh ex-servicemen from the Punjab were settled in Great Nicobar in the late 1960s.

Conclusion

In writing a history an author, though divergent at times, cannot avoid responding to interests shared with contemporaries. That may indeed make the history not, as many think, less true, but more true. As a result of writing a history, an historian may also, not inconsistently, offer some comment on contemporary interests. These sections of the present book some may think have gone too far down that track. An armchair scholar can be too impractical or too idealistic.

The present author is indeed concerned with the questions that contemporary discussions of human rights have raised. He is entirely sceptical of the attempts to list, as if in opposition, a schedule of human responsibilities. Nor does he consider that such endeavours are made more credible by attempts to set them in an East–West framework. 'To say that freedom is Western or unAsian is to offend against our own traditions', Anwar Ibrahim wrote in *The Asian Renaissance*, 'as well as our forefathers who gave their lives in the struggle against tyranny and injustice'.[78] It is not simply with a view to pre-empting critics, however, that the author admits that they are political and practical issues, and not merely questions of rights.

In his view, taking fuller account of these rights is not simply a moral obligation, and still less an acceptance that Western values have won, but also a practical step towards political stability and economic development. The account he has given of the development of democracy in Southeast Asia suggests that the concept has come to stay. More than that, it is not best used merely as a safety-valve, but has a positive contribution to make to the problems the nation-states of Southeast Asia face. More hazardously, perhaps, he offers a similar conclusion to his discussion of separatism.

In the Philippines Moros have tended to interpret integration as assimilation, and many Christians probably saw it that way. A Maranao CNI commissioner, Mamintal Tamano, saw it differently: integration was for him 'a process which, though seeking to prevent the creation of cultural islands, does not seek to obliterate the tribal groups' distinctive traits. Rather it aims to bring about *unity in diversity*—a oneness of all the different groups found in these islands by reason of a common government, ancestry, and history'.[79] The phrase he italicised is the motto of the Indonesian state. Yet it has been tempted to seek for unity without diversity. And so have the mainland states, Burma, Vietnam, and Thailand.

Whatever the case in the early days of the new state structure in post-colonial Southeast Asia, it is surely now clear that the states are not going to fall apart, and they have made it plain that they will not support claims on each other's territory. It is thus possible to pursue a more pluralist approach. That may not only help to bring destructive conflicts to an end, and with them the risk of foreign intervention in humanitarian causes that are no longer seen as merely internal matters. It may also facilitate a fuller participation in national life and economic and cultural development on the part of all the peoples in each state.

The economic impact of globalisation is equivocal. It will require talent and leadership to take advantage of it. The same is true of its political impact. Globalisation is not against the nation-state, but it can strengthen the politics of cultural identity. It could be used not to destroy identities, but to promote them. The peoples of Southeast Asia have shown their ability to accept more than one sense of identity. That could be turned to account.

Notes

1　q. Peter Lyon, *War and Peace in South-east Asia*, OUP, 1969, p. 213.

2　q. Christie, *History*, p. 122.

3　Koenig, p. 64.

4　q. Cady, p. 43n.

5　*Burma and the Karens*, London: Elliot Stock, 1928, p. 81.

6　'Race and Resistance in Burma, 1942–1945', MAS, 20, 3 (July 1986), p. 502.

7　q. Tarling, *Cold War*, p. 17.

8　q. Christie, p. 55.

9　H. N. Stevenson, q. Tarling, *Fourth Anglo-Burmese War*, p. 265.

10　q. ibid., p. 266.

11　Minute by Walsh-Atkins, 24 September 1946, q. ibid., p. 266.

12　IB (47) 3rd, 8 January 1947, CAB 134/343, Public Record Office, London.

13　q. Vum Ko Hau, *Profile of a Burma Frontier Man*, Bandung: privately printed, 1963, p. 83.

14　Minute, 15 February 1947, M/4/2811, India Office Library.

15　Tel, 24 March 1947. M/4/2853.

16　Minute, 6 May 1947. M/4/2854.

17　Minute, 15 February 1947. M/4/3023.

18　q. Cady, p. 563.

19　Minute, 7 July 1947. M/4/3023.

20　Cady, p. 593.

21　q. Tarling, *Cold War*, p. 347.

22　Cady, p. 595.

23　*Burma: Insurgency and the Politics of Ethnicity*, London and New Jersey: Zed Books, 1991, p. 192.

24　ibid., p. 196.

25　q. ibid., p. 196.

26　p. 115.

27　p. 197.

28　q. Bertil Lintner, *Burma in Revolt Opium and Insurgency Since 1948*, Boulder: Westview, and Bangkok: White Lotus, 1994, pp. 334–5.

29　Christie, *History*, p. 87.

30　ibid., pp. 104–5.

31　*State and Ethnic Politics*, p. 200.

32　Surin Pitsuwan, *Islam and Malay Nationalism*, Bangkok: Thammasat U, 1985, pp. 57–8, 68–9.

33　Draft in Monson to Broad, 15 June 1943. F.O. 371/35979 [F3088/222/40], Public Record Office, London.

34　Surin, p. 161.

35　in 'The Muslims of Thailand', *South East Asian Review*, 14, 1 & 2 (1989), p. 52.

36　ibid., p. 182.

37 *Muslim Separatism: The Moros of Southern Philippines and the Malays of Southern Thailand*, Singapore: OUP, 1990, pp. 70–2, 113–14.

38 Tarling, *Sulu*, pp. 293–4.

39 q. P. G. Gowing, 'Mandate in Moroland …', PhD thesis, Syracuse U, 1968, p. 404.

40 cf. A. T. Ortiz, 'Towards a Theory of Ethnic Separatism …', PhD thesis, U Penn, 1986, pp. 198–200.

41 q. ibid., pp. 204–5.

42 Haynes to Chamberlain, 30 May 1927. F.O. 371/12050 [A 3239/586/45], Public Record Office, London.

43 P. G. Gowing, *Muslim Filipinos—Heritage and Horizon*, Quezon City: New Day, 1979, p. 174.

44 Foulds to Jardine, 28 July 1936. C.O. 874/942, Public Record Office, London.

45 q. N. M. Nisperos, 'Philippine Foreign Policy in the North Borneo Question', PhD thesis, Pittsburgh U, 1969, p. 110.

46 Ortiz, p. 230.

47 Gowing, *Muslim Filipinos*, pp. 184–5.

48 Ortiz, pp. 256, 258.

49 *Revolt in Mindanao*, pp. 125–6.

50 p. 268.

51 Glang, q. R. J. May, in May et al., *Mindanao: Land of Unfulfilled Promise*, Quezon City, 1992, p. 129.

52 Ortiz, p. 280.

53 George, p. 209.

54 George, p. 216.

55 q. May, p. 135.

56 in May, p. 181.

57 Nazaruddin Sjamsuddin, *The Republican Revolt*, Singapore: ISEAS, 1985, p. 52.

58 q. Brown, p. 143.

59 Brown, p. 146.

60 q. Brown, p. 150.

61 q. Tim Kell, *The Roots of Acehnese Rebellion*, Cornell UP, 1995, p. 58.

62 q. Brown, p. 155.

63 q. Kell, p. 62.

64 q. Robin Osborne, *Indonesia's Secret War*, Sydney: Allen and Unwin, 1985, p. 21.

65 q. ibid., p. 23.

66 *L'Indonesie et la Nouvelle-Guinée Occidentale*, Paris and Montreal: L'Harmattan, 1996, p. 216.

67 q. Osborne, p. 27.

68 q. ibid., p. 47.

69 q. ibid., p. 120.

70 ibid., p. 189.

71 ibid., p. 60.

72 Hiorth, p. 28.

73 q. H. Krieger, ed., *East Timor and the International Community*, CUP, 1997, p. 67.

74 q. Schwarz, *A Nation in Waiting*, p. 221.

75 Hiorth, p. 40.

76 Appendix A, p. xliv.

77 p. xlvii.

78 p. 28.

79 q. Gowing, *Muslim Filipinos*, p. 211.

Part Five

Historiography

Mainland Southeast Asia, nineteenth and twentieth centuries CE

Historicism and Presentism

The development of a sense that the past differs from the present is essential to present-day historiography. Some societies in Southeast Asia and elsewhere have been or are more favourable to it than others.

Writing a history of Southeast Asia presents challenges some of which are obvious, some less so. The range of the task and the diversity of talents required even to begin to meet part of it have been ever-present in the mind of the author, borne down, too, by the depth of his obligation to other scholars. Less obvious, perhaps, are the problems that historians generally face, which writing about Southeast Asia only makes more extreme. The author writes in a tradition and for a readership that accept change and seek explanation. But he is also writing about societies that often took quite a different view of the past, and in a phase in which that tradition has itself, though flourishing, been challenged. He is writing, too, about a region where the implications of that historical tradition may have a political significance that matches the implications of its emergence in the West, and indeed more than matches them, given its association with the West. Yet, in this as in other parts of this book, the author finds it helpful, not only to deal with Southeast Asia as a whole, but also to treat the region in a larger context. The commonalities and differences within the region are then better understood, and its experience is seen as part of the larger human experience.

The sense of change among humankind was itself of slow growth, and its acceptance reluctant and qualified. 'All dynastic history moves in circles', Ibn Khaldun believed.[1] The idea that change was a question of decline and restoration was itself recalled from the past in the European Renaissance. Machiavelli came to 'the conclusion that the world always remains very much in the same condition. The good and the bad balance one another, but each varies from region to region'.[2] The sense of the passage of time was accompanied by attempts to segment it into lengths of measurable duration and to name them, and the practice continues, as Tony Reid's identification of an 'age of commerce' in Southeast Asia suggests. Unhappy with a merely vertical division in time, some have suggested horizontal ones. Things changed at different paces, Braudel argued.[3]

However much change is accepted or rejected, and however difficult it is to capture or characterise, it seems clear that the invention of the written word was a powerful inducement to recognise it.

> People in so-called traditional societies confidently assert that things are (and should be) the way they have always been, for oral transmission accumulates actual alterations unconsciously, continually readjusting the past to fit the present. Literate societies less easily sustain such fiction, for written—and especially printed—records reveal a past unlike the present: the archives show traditions eroded by time and corrupted by novelty, by no means faithfully adhered to.[4]

Once the concept of change is accepted, it is not merely a matter of determining its extent, but of understanding its source. That interests those who would 'make' history, and those who want to know how it was 'made'. It is also, of course, crucial to the 'historian', who has to fashion an account from a set of past events and situations. What is involved in that has been much debated, particularly since the development of the 'critical' historiography associated above all with Leopold von Ranke.

Explanation has commonly been offered in terms of 'cause', though, as Michael Oakeshott argued, the word cannot be used strictly in the vocabulary of historical discourse. 'When it appears there it should be allowed to be … no more than an expression of the concern of an historical enquiry to seek significant relations between historical events and to distinguish between those antecedent conditions which are significant for the understanding of a subsequent and those that are not.'[5] A further step is to find a regularity among those relations, and thus to establish expectations or suggest hypotheses. 'The past is most characteristically invoked for the lessons it teaches.'[6] If indeed history repeated itself, or its laws could be established, men could learn from it, and act accordingly.

The concept of change indeed prompted a consideration of the relationship of present and past. The latter could be invoked to 'justify' the former, as with what Herbert Butterfield called the Whig interpretation of history.[7] In the historical account structured accordingly, men are valued for their 'contributions' or recognised as supporting 'lost causes', subject to the 'verdict of history'. The past can also be used to make judgments on the present. Has it fallen away? Have we ignored its 'lessons'?

The issue was at the core of Ranke's approach. In the preface to his *Histories of the Latin and Teutonic Nations* (1824) he wrote: 'To history has been assigned the task of judging the past, of instructing the world of today for the benefit of future years. The present attempt does not claim such an exalted function; it merely wishes to state what actually happened (*er will bloss sagen, wie es eigentlich gewesen*).'[8] 'Showing the past as it had actually been meant not only establishing the facts as correctly as possible, but also placing them in their contemporary context in such a way that the past would come to life again.'[9]

The notion that history should establish this kind of relationship between past and present, often called historicism, was widely shared. 'The main task of the historian became to find out why people acted as they did by stepping into their shoes, by seeing the world through their eyes and as far as possible judging it by their standards.'[10] But was it possible? 'In the alteration of our own character', J. A. Froude wrote, 'we have lost the key which would interpret the characters of our fathers'.[11] If that were so, should the historicist approach be abandoned? Nearly a century or so later some Western historians thought that unavoidable.

In their search for new sources and better explanations, historians had been drawing on other disciplines, such as anthropology and sociology. The emphasis on 'structures' in the work of the French *Annales* school was welcomed by Geoffrey Barraclough as displacing a bankrupt historicism. Barzun and Graff, by contrast, could find 'no convincing argument' why the historian should be 'bound to give up the recital of events and the portraying of participants in favour of the analysis of problems, the comparison of social forms, and the description of institutional or individual essences'.[12]

The implications of the 'linguistic turn' again seemed to some historians exciting, and to others destructive. Abandoning cause and effect—or, as in *The Order of Things,* setting it 'to one side'[13]—and 'the formless unity of some great evolutionary process', Michel Foucault searched, not for structures, but for forms. 'Instead of consciousness and continuities, the stuff of the new social history, Foucault's new cultural history countered with discontinuities, groups of notions, series, discourses.'[14] State, society, sex, the body and the soul, were not stable objects, but discourses, truths as it were for the time being established by a number of power relations.

Foucault cast out too much of what history had to be concerned with, but he offered historians some strategies they could turn to account. His works called attention to a range of topics they had neglected, and he reminded them in a forceful way of the need to pay close attention to the language of the past. Some went further: not only was there no single correct view of a 'fact', there were several correct views. Gertrude Himmelfarb argued, by contrast, that historians were already aware of 'the frailty, fallibility and relativity' of their enterprise. Their discipline had in a sense been created 'to forestall the absolutistic relativism of post-modernism'. They knew there was no absolute truth, but that did not mean that there were no partial, contingent truths. The aim of their discipline was 'a maximum exertion of objectivity'.[15]

A striking feature of past historiographical debates was their concentration on Europe: even more strikingly, that has continued into recent times. Yet a wider range could have enriched them, and could still enrich them. Historians of Southeast Asia, for example, have been testing out the approaches developed in the West, and exploring the implications of their application to the non-Western past. And their contributions have gone beyond the application of the ideas of others.

In many parts of Southeast Asia the sense of change was not readily felt and may still not be so. That relates in part to the strength of oral traditions. Yet in this, as in so many other matters discussed in this book, there is 'neither East nor West', but rather similarities and contrasts over time between parts of the East and parts of the West. It was left to an history-minded anthropologist to juxtapose the two, Donald

Brown, an expert on Brunei. That endeavour added an important dimension which the Western debate seemed to have by-passed.

'[N]o hereditarily stratified society would have developed sound historiography', he argued.[16] The qualities of such an historiography include, he suggested, a precise orientation in space and time, accurate chronology, ability to detect anachronism, access to trustworthy sources, logical coherence, and minimal resort to the supernatural. Its concomitants are a concept of the individual, a concept of the unity of mankind, a concern to predict, interest in education, biography, praise and blame and moral lessons, and the expansion of secularism. All aspects of social placement, they are more readily found in societies 'where social inequalities are substantial but where birth is not perceived as deciding who will be placed high or low'.[17]

Some Western historiography is not 'sound', and some Asian is. For Brown, Florentine historiography is sound, 'rooted in human affairs, and ... inclined to see history as the unfolding of the consequences of human will, impulse and action'.[18] He finds the same qualities in some of the Southeast Asian writings he discusses. In Vietnam, for example, popular scholar poets 'expounded the idea that men, all men, have the potentiality of changing themselves, and then external reality'.[19] Other societies were less favourable to 'sound' history. Soedjatmoko called attention to the 'ahistorical' view of the Javanese, who perceive 'life and the flow of events as a process beyond human control and therefore beyond human responsibility'.[20] The sense of active participation in change is missing.

'Sound' history in Brown's terms was not the same as, though it was a necessary prerequisite of, 'critical' history in Rankean terms: after all it encompassed the Florentines whom Ranke criticised. In that sense, as Sir John Plumb suggests, 'critical history' was a peculiarly European phenomenon, which even the Chinese failed to achieve.[21] Applying the Rankean approach to the Asian past was therefore bound to be explosive, though it was clearly more alien to those societies without a 'sound' historiography than to those with one.

The effect of historicism was the more controversial in that it had developed in the West coterminously with imperialism. The year of Ranke's preface was also the year the 'exclusive Lords of the East' made the treaty of 1824. That meant, on the one hand, that there was little attempt to apply it to the history of Asia itself: instead the main focus was on the Europeans in Asia. It also meant, on the other hand, that, when it was applied, it seemed itself to be a piece of imperialism that ought to be questioned. What kind of history should be written? On what topics should it focus? Who should write it? The debates were the more intense because the questions were not simply for the historians: they had political implications.

Notes

1. *The Muqaddimah*, introd. by F. Rosenthal, p. lxxxiii.
2. cf. R. J. B. Bosworth, *Explaining Auschwitz and Hiroshima*, London and New York: Routledge, 1993, p. 105.

3 *Discorsi*, preface to book 1.

4 D. Lowenthal, *The Past is a Foreign Country*, CUP, 1985, pp. 40–1.

5 *On History and Other Essays*, Oxford: Blackwell, 1983, p. 88.

6 Lowenthal, p. 46.

7 London: Bell, 1931.

8 q. F. Gilbert, *History: Politics or Culture: Reflections on Ranke and Burckhardt*, PUP, 1990, p. 19.

9 ibid., p. 37.

10 John Tosh, *The Pursuit of History*, London and New York: Longmans, 1984, p. 14.

11 q. Lowenthal, p. 233.

12 *The Modern Researcher*, 4th edn, NY: Harcourt Brace, 1984, p. 268.

13 Preface to English edition, Tavistock, London, 1970, p. xiii.

14 P. O'Brien, in L. Hunt, *The New Cultural History*, UCP, 1989, p. 33.

15 *Times Literary Supplement*, 16 September 1992.

16 *Hierarchy, History and Human Nature*, Tucson: Arizona UP, 1988, p. 5.

17 p. 5.

18 p. 248.

19 Marr in A. Reid and D. Marr, eds, *Perceptions of the Past in Southeast Asia*, Singapore: Heinemann, 1979, p. 318.

20 in Soedjatmoko, ed., *An Introduction to Indonesian Historiography*, Cornell UP, 1965, pp. 409–10.

21 *The Making of an Historian*, Hemel Hempstead: Harvester, 1988, p. 293.

Euro-centric and Asia-centric Approaches

Historians writing about Southeast Asia struggled with some success to make their writings take proper account of both the Asian and the European elements in its history.

If it is accepted that change takes place, that there can be no 'truth-full' account or explanation of it, but that such is still worth pursuing, then 'presentism' has its advantages as well as its drawbacks: it is not merely unavoidable but advantageous. The discipline or self-discipline of history, even post-Ranke, may not in itself be sufficient to prompt a challenge to or a re-testing of existing interpretations. Even new 'evidence' may not lead that way. More often, perhaps, reappraisals have reflected shifts in viewpoint which historians have shared with their contemporaries, and have been part of a wider repositioning of the relationship of the past and the present. That was particularly the case with the emergence of 'new nations' after World War II, as the case of Southeast Asia shows, since the historiography developed in the West had been so Western in its preoccupations. Indeed the challenge that offered historians sometimes seemed to be a challenge to their method itself. It was not merely a matter of content or even of perspective, it was argued. The Western approach to history was itself brought into question.

The theoretical view was, it is true, to some extent confused with a debate about content. In the year after Malaya became independent, K. G. Tregonning, an Australian who was then Raffles Professor of History at the University of Malaya, advocated a new approach to the history of Malaya. 'Asia, and not the European in Asia, must be our theme, and suddenly, if you think of that, it makes the Portuguese and the Dutch most insignificant, and almost extraneous.'[1] Another Australian, John Bastin, attacked this view in his inaugural lecture as Professor of History at the branch of the university established in Kuala Lumpur. The role of the Portuguese and the Dutch was far from insignificant. 'Surely the plea for reinterpreting Southeast Asian history from an Asian point of view means something more than the convenient removal of Westerners from the historical narrative?'[2]

What did it involve? Here Bastin moved on to more controversial ground. He quoted Pieter Geyl's attack on writing history from a universal point of view: how can a human being 'allow his mind, shaped in his own cultural environment and its centuries of sustained action, to be dissolved in an unorganic and anarchic *world* without losing hold of his most fertile life-principle?' How, Bastin asked in turn, 'can the Western historian allow his mind to be dissolved in the strangely different, and frequently confusing, Southeast Asian world? … it does seem to me to set severe limitations to the possibility of Western historians ever successfully interpreting [Southeast Asian] history from an Asian point of view.'[3]

European historians, and Asian historians trained in Western historical methods, brought to their study of Southeast Asian history, Bastin claimed, 'the concepts and categories and periodizations of Western historiography', and

> they can hardly succeed in producing the new sort of history for which there is apparently so great a need. The type of Asian and Southeast Asian history which is being written today, even by Asian historians themselves, is history in the Western tradition; for the kind of history with which we are all familiar is indissolubly tied to the whole Western cultural base. … If a different sort of Southeast Asian history is ever to be written, then what is required is a revolutionary reappraisal of existing historical methods and techniques, and of existing concepts and periodization.[4]

But surely here, in his impatience with a revision of history that simply reversed the role of the leading players, Bastin was himself adding a confusion to the discussion. Concepts, categories, and periodisation could be revised without 'a revolutionary reappraisal of existing historical methods and techniques'.

The most sophisticated discussion of the issues was offered by John Smail in a paper presented at the Singapore conference of Southeast Asian historians early in 1961, published soon after in the new *Journal of Southeast Asian History*, and subsequently reprinted.[5] He called attention to a possible interpretation of Bastin's remarks: that there might be 'an Asian thought-world' to which the historian would have to belong who wished to replace 'Europe-centric' history—the term J. G. de Casparis had used—by 'Asia-centric'. To that, however, the Asian historian, as Bastin said, did not belong: though his ancestors might have thought differently, and 'the man in the street' might still do so, 'he belongs in all that is most important to the same thought-world as the Westerner'.[6] The change in perspective that was being sought, Smail argued, could not be seen as a change to a different thought-world, but as a 'shift which takes place within a single (universal) thought-world'.[7]

What should be its nature? He distinguished between a shift in value judgments and a shift in emphasis. The controversy over 'centricity', he thought, added little to the discussion over 'systematic moral bias' in history-writing, one of its 'besetting evils'.[8] Inasmuch, however, as it was not a problem peculiar to writing on Asia, it was not the change of perspective on which to focus. Much of the rest of Smail's paper was thus devoted to the question of emphasis. He approached it through considering the work of J. C. van Leur, whose pioneering work, influenced by his study of

Max Weber, though written pre-war, had become widely known only in the 1950s. Van Leur had argued that historians had exaggerated the role of the Europeans in Indonesia in the sixteenth and seventeenth centuries, and even the eighteenth, but implied that, with the changes of the nineteenth and twentieth centuries, there was 'less and less reason to want to look at things from an Indo-centric point of view'.[9] Van Leur also spoke, however, of the 'autonomy' of Indonesian history. That idea suggested, Smail thought, that historians might put their emphasis 'not on the criteria of visible power but on the underlying social structure and culture', and thus 'establish the basis for a continuous Indo-centric history of Indonesia'.[10] Smail concluded that 'Asia-centric' history had to mean, not simply a revised history of Asian–European relations, but the 'domestic history' of Asia, for which he adopted van Leur's term 'autonomous history'.[11]

Writing about Southeast Asia, earlier generations of Western historians had not in fact merely focused on the Europeans. Many of them were, however, officials, anxious to know more of the people with whom they were in contact, and over whom their influence was increasing. The way they wrote reflected the preoccupations of the period, but also established understandings that endured. Before Ranke published his work on the Latin and Teutonic nations, the future founder of Singapore had conceived of a 'Melayu' nation and renamed the major Malay text as *Sejarah Melayu, Malay Annals,* as it was called in the 1821 translation. Europeans of this period shared a sense of the past as the history of nations, and that shaped their view of Southeast Asia.

The development of Southeast Asian historiography continued to owe a great deal to scholar officials, to Sir Arthur Phayre, for example, in respect of Burma, and in the twentieth century to G. E. Hervey, B. R. Pearn, and, of course, J. S. Furnivall, who developed the influential concept of the 'plural society'.[12] A student of British Malaya at the end of World War II would still be reading the works of the man who popularised the term, Sir Frank Swettenham, while MCS officers, such as M. C. ff. Sheppard and Walter Linehan, had published state histories, and Sir Richard Winstedt a history of Malaya. Victor Purcell, who spent much of his career in the Chinese protectorate, was, after the war, when he became a lecturer at Cambridge, to publish *The Chinese in Malaya* (1948) and *The Chinese in Southeast Asia* (1951). Van Leur himself was, of course, an official of the Netherlands Indies government in the 1930s, working as a *controleur*, and then in the general secretariat at Buitenzorg (Bogor), before his ship was torpedoed in the battle of the Java Sea.

Postwar a number of changes helped to build up a segment of the historical profession that concerned itself with Southeast Asia. D. G. E. Hall, previously at Rangoon University, became the first professor of the history of Southeast Asia in the University of London, and a number of specialist centres were set up in countries outside the region, especially Australia and the United States. University education expanded in the region, too, and new journals, notably the *Journal of Southeast Asian History,* later *Studies,* were added to a list that already included the journals of the Malayan Branch of the Royal Asiatic Society and the Burma Research Society and the *Bijdragen tot de Taal-, Land- en Volkenkunde*. Some major publishers played an important role in publishing research monographs, particularly Oxford University Press.

What was written and published reflected not only the new interest in Southeast Asia's past, but also the new developments in Western historiography that were taking place at the same time. Though those took limited account of what was happening in a little-known field, historians in that field were very conscious of them. So far as the employment of sociological concepts was concerned, van Leur had shown the way, and of him, indeed, Geoffrey Barraclough took account in *Main Trends in History*.[13] B. Schrieke, too, had offered a pathbreaking account of the political structure of seventeenth-century Mataram, revealing, as W. F. Wertheim pointed out,[14] the relevance of the Weberian concept of the 'patrimonial' state, now almost a commonplace of Southeast Asian historiography. A former MCS man, John Gullick, combined his experience and his training at the London School of Economics to produce *Indigenous Political Systems of Western Malaya*,[15] presenting the institutions of Perak and Selangor on the eve of British intervention 'as a working system of social control and leadership in the same fashion as an anthropologist uses material obtained by contemporaneous field work'.[16] Donald Brown, then a doctoral student at Cornell, produced a study of Brunei that combined evidence and perspectives drawn from both his own discipline and that of history, so as to 'trace and clarify' the 'processes of change and continuity in Brunei's social structure'.[17]

Juxtaposing what were often seen as separate disciplines proved remarkably productive. It helped, for example, to reconceive the purpose of written material left behind by states and societies that, in Brown's phrase, did not provide the conditions for 'sound' historiography, and it led, too, to reconceiving the ways in which such material might contribute to a 'critical' historiography. Initially the change of approach was controversial. Old Javanese texts, C. C. Berg argued, could not be read in the way texts were commonly read: 'some Javanese texts are unintelligible unless we suppose the author to have practiced magic, and ... many other texts are easier to understand and fit better into a framework of facts if interpreted on the basis of that supposition'.[18] The results of such an approach might not be politically palatable: Majapahit could turn out to be no more than a myth. But it was also historiographically challenging, not merely to N. J. Krom, editor of the 1919 edition of the *Nagarakrtagama*.

The task, as P. J. Zoetmulder commented, was clear: 'attempt to penetrate into the heart of a culture in order to understand its outward manifestations.' That meant, as Berg saw, 'reading the sources the way they were meant to be read and therefore viewing them as specific cultural manifestations and as component parts of that culture'. The risk of the 'vicious circle' to which Zoetmulder pointed was a familiar one to post-Rankean historians: 'we should read the sources using our knowledge of the cultural pattern, yet how can we comprehend that pattern if not from the sources?' His answer was 'trial and error'.[19]

In respect of later periods, it was possible not simply to call on the resources of other disciplines, but to juxtapose different kinds of written materials. In her book, *To Live as Brothers: Southeast Sumatra in the Seventeenth and Eighteenth Centuries*,[20] Barbara Andaya drew on indigenous sources, chronicles, literary romances, and religious texts, all to be approached with care, since they were composed or copied in the nineteenth century. The focus, too, seemed removed from that of European archives: legendary rulers, ancestral heroes, the animal kingdom, the love affairs of courtiers. But these sources conveyed, in Jan Vansina's term, 'cultural messages' of enduring importance, and certain themes persisted not peculiar to southern Sumatra, the *ulu–ilir* (upstream–downstream) relationship, the ruler–subject tension, the significance of kinship. Those preoccupations were also expressed in the Dutch records, though in a different idiom, appropriate to a more commoditised and depersonalised society, less conceptualised by kinship relations or typified by orality.[21]

Historians, of course, have recognised that European sources are also to be read with their purpose in mind. Those of the VOC, as Graham Irwin pointed out, had no need to make propaganda, since it did not publicise its affairs, and the tradition continued till 1848. What its officials might omit or falsify related rather to their fear of censure from the Directors than from the public, and turned therefore mostly on Dutch activities. 'Where "Indonesian" questions were under review, an official did not need to misrepresent the true situation since he could not normally be blamed if things had gone wrong.' So, Irwin concludes, for this period 'official Dutch accounts of Indonesian customs, institutions, and manners, and of Southeast Asian politics and trade, are as free from distortion and inaccuracy as they well can be'. Furthermore, the Dutch interest at this time was in trade. 'They did not propound theories of colonization; they had no doctrine of a master race. ... they were businessmen, not crusaders.' Their attitude was 'matter of fact', and their descriptions of Indonesian life 'correspondingly free from bigotry and racial antagonism'.[22]

Even if that be the case, it is still profitable to juxtapose European records with other kinds of evidence, and the need to do so perhaps increases just at the phase in history when it becomes more difficult. In the colonial phase, European records tend not only to focus on European activities, but to reflect attitudes of which Irwin found the VOC archives happily free. Harry Benda welcomed William Roff's *The Origins of Malay Nationalism*[23] as 'the first history of the *Malays* in modern times': he had shifted his 'observation post ... to Malays'.[24] He had also drawn on sources other than the British 'colonial' records, countering their 'seductiveness through the use of another, Malay, category of documentation', as Tony Milner was to write in 1986.[25]

Milner argued that historians of British Malaya who relied mainly on colonial records ran the risk, not simply of focusing on British activities, but of over-emphasising their importance. 'In these studies, the British administrators are not merely the principal actors but it is also they who are seen to generate change.' The 'colonial records historians' of British Malaya had been less successful than specialists on Indonesia, he claimed, who had found, say, in sociological models, 'vantage points from which to question the colonial records'. That material, he argued, had to be read 'against the grain'.[26] Yeo Kim Wah, author of a major work on 'decentralisation' in inter-war Malaya, Milner described as 'the exponent par excellence of the "colonial records" style'.[27] He suggested in reply that Milner wanted the rulers and their subjects to supplant the British as the principal players, 'thereby transforming the British lion into a toothless bulldog ahead of its time'.[28] The debate seemed to revive the earlier 'centricity' controversy. But, Yeo argued, the perspective of the British Malayan historian had already shifted, as a result of 'the interplay between the British perspective, the historian's training and critical faculty, and different values nurtured by time and place'.[29]

In his book, *The Invention of Politics in Colonial Malaya*,[30] Milner utilised an 'interrogative' approach to a number of selected Malay texts. In one sense, again, that broke new ground. But, just as his call for reading colonial documents 'against the grain' was falling not on stony ground, but on ground that was already being tilled, so this approach had in some measure been anticipated. 'Deconstruction', insofar as it can be used by historians, had been used by historians of Southeast Asia, as it were *avant la lettre*. 'Deconstruction of early Southeast Asian history ... probably made its effective appearance with C. C. Berg', as Michael Aung-Thwin has written.[31]

If writers in the field of historiography and its theory have been unduly Euro-centric, a few major contributors to the history of Southeast Asia have been recognised as themselves adding to more general historiographical and theoretical debates. Among them, of course, were Clifford Geertz, the pioneer of 'thick description', James Scott, with his work on the 'moral economy' of the peasantry, and Ben Anderson, whose concept of 'imagined communities' made a major contribution to the study of nationalism.

The most recent attempt to 'transcend' the 'East–West dichotomy' has been made by Vic Lieberman, a pioneer in the study of the Burman monarchy. He was apprehensive lest the study of Southeast Asia became so regional that it obscured the differences within it or the similarities with other parts of the world. We might have to 'lay aside our recent distaste for colonial, as opposed to indigenous, history', he suggested, since the closest analogies to the integration of the mainland monarchies in the late eighteenth century might be found in the history of the Dutch and Spanish colonial territories.[32] He also advocated a 'Eurasian' approach, comparing the 'early modern' mainland states with 'early modern' France and Tokugawa Japan.[33] The present author's ambition has been to offer comparisons across time as well as space.

Notes

1 *Straits Times*, 21, 24 November 1958, q. J. Bastin, *The Study of Modern Southeast Asian History*, UMKL, 1959, p. 6.
2 pp. 8–9.
3 p. 9.
4 pp. 11–12.

5   2, 2 (July 1961), pp. 72–102; reprinted in L. J. Sears, *Autonomous Histories, Particular Truths*, Madison: U Wis, 1993.

6   p. 74.

7   p. 77.

8   p. 76.

9   p. 84.

10 p. 88.

11 p. 100.

12 R. H. Taylor, 'Disaster or Decline? J. S. Furnivall and the Bankruptcy of Burma', MAS, 29, 1 (February 1995), pp. 45–63.

13 London and New York: Holme, 1979.

14 Soedjatmoko, p. 347.

15 London: Athlone, 1958.

16 p. 1.

17 *Brunei: The Structure and History of a Bornean Malay Sultanate*, Brunei, 1970, p. vii.

18 in Soedjatmoko, p. 89.

19 ibid., p. 329.

20 Honolulu: U Hawaii P, 1993.

21 pp. xiii–xiv.

22 in Soedjatmoko, pp. 236–7.

23 New Haven, 1967.

24 p. viii.

25 *Kajian Malaysia*, 4, 2 (December 1986), p. 9.

26 pp. 8, 9.

27 p. 4.

28 ibid., 5, 1 (June 1987), p. 25.

29 p. 3.

30 CUP, 1995.

31 'The "Classical" in Southeast Asia: The Present in the Past', JSEAS, 26, 1 (March 1995), p. 90.

32 'An Age of Commerce in Southeast Asia? …', JAS, 54, 3 (August 1995), pp. 804–05.

33 'Transcending East–West Dichotomies …', MAS, 31, 3 (July 1997), pp. 463–546.

National History

National history is a requirement of a world of nation-states. How it should be written, by whom, for whom, are more controversial matters, as the Southeast Asian experience exemplifies.

The emergence of independent states in Southeast Asia stimulated the writing of history both through the provision of facilities, such as universities and national archives, and through the development of new perspectives. But it also provided a new political context, of which historians outside the region, as well as those inside, had to be conscious. The nation-state, as Ruth McVey put it, became, along with modernisation, part of the 'regnant paradigm' in the writing of Southeast Asian history.[1]

Philippe Ariès pointed to the impact of the nation-state on historiography in the West. Heralded by the revolution of 1789, the nation-state came to dominate the world, and, he argued, historians commemorated its ascendancy, displacing earlier concepts of community. 'Just as nation-states colonized territories overseas, so their apologists colonized the past.'[2] Historians gave too little attention to 'those small and intermediate-size communities that had dominated traditional European society'. The demands of the nation-state upon its 'citizens', as the French revolutionaries called them, were not only novel, but perhaps unprecedented in their intensity. If they too were citizens, historians might find their loyalties divided. What should they render to the state? What did they owe the discipline of history, particularly as it took shape under Ranke in the years following the revolution? And if they were not citizens, upon what basis did they comment?

The nation-state was then new, and so was the Rankean concept of history. Reconstructing the past in the name of the state was not, however, new. For earlier European states had sought to strengthen their present position by increasing their control of the past. In Renaissance England, for example, the Tudors saw themselves as heirs, not of classical Rome, but of classical Britain: they looked to its antiquity. Later, England's story was structured, as Butterfield saw, about liberty, not monarchy. Before their revolution colonial Americans had taken British history as their own. 'After the revolution', as Tosh puts it, 'it gradually became clear that the consolidation of a national identity among the thirteen colonies required a distinctively American past'.[3]

'*Qu'est-ce qu'une nation?*' Ernest Renan asked in 1882. The essence of a nation, he answered, was that the individuals in it had many things in common, and also that they had forgotten many things. They must have forgotten the Albigensian massacres and the massacre of St Bartholomew's Day. But, as that most percipient of commentators on nationalism, Benedict Anderson, has pointed out, Renan was assuming that Frenchmen remembered what they were also required to forget.[4] The explanation lies, Anderson suggests, in the historiographical requirements of the nation-state. It must have a past, but the past was not that of a nation-state. The massacres become, not conflicts between enemies, but conflicts, as it were, within the national family, part, as Anderson puts it, of 'a new form of narrative, a narrative of reassuring fratricide'.

If there is strong evidence of a 'Whig interpretation' in the national histories of established nation-states, it is not surprising to find those who wished to found such states seeking support from the past. Often they were contending with rulers who appealed to other loyalties, more likely dynastic rather than national, and it was, for example, in face of the Habsburg rulers, though also in face of the German hegemony with which those rulers associated themselves, that the Czechs built up their claim to national existence, and that Palacky recovered the Czech past. It was a piece of legerdemain, as A. J. P. Taylor recognised:[5] the nationalists were appropriating the achievements of dynasts and peoples of the past, and projecting back into the past the concept of the nation that they now wished to create. Adopting a powerful metaphor, they often wrote indeed of national 'awakening'.

'If this book succeeds in awakening in you the consciousness of our past, which has been blotted out from our memories, and in rectifying what has been falsified by calumny, then I shall not have laboured in vain.' So Rizal wrote in dedicating to 'the Filipinos' his edition of *Sucesos de las Islas Filipinas* (1609) by Antonio de Morga, who, as he puts it, had 'witnessed the last moments of our ancient nationality'.[6]

In Southeast Asia nationalism became the basis of opposition to colonial rule, and the objective was to create a nation-state, often adopting for a new purpose the frontiers the colonial powers had created to avoid disputes among themselves. Nineteenth-century Europe offered some parallels to that endeavour, and there was an attempt to secure historiographical backing for the 'new' nations by the same kind of sleight-of-hand. Again the Europeans unintentionally offered help. Sri Vijaya was 'rediscovered' by George Coedès in 1918, for example, just at the time when an 'Indonesian' nationalism was taking shape, and the evidence of past greatness was welcome.

Gaining independence for a nation-state was no guarantee that a nation-state had been created. The unity created by a struggle for independence could be undermined by success. Minorities would be threatened by majorities. The determination to create a sense of nationality within the nation-state could lead to policies that stressed assimilation to the majority culture, and denied others, not only the right to national independence, but the right to cultural autonomy. What could be unifying could also be divisive.

For historians the writing of 'national' history was clearly a duty. But what form should it take? The problem was more complex than it had been for Palacky, for the Southeast Asian nations had emerged in a different context, not only politically, but also historiographically. The history should, of course, not be 'Europe-centric', but 'Asia-centric'. That was, however, only a partial answer to the question. What emphasis should it have? Which 'Asians' were to be at the centre of it? One option was the 'nationalitarian' one, which would make history fulfil the task of nation-building as the ruling elite tended to see it. That risked, however, not only doing violence to historiography as it was now conceived, but doing violence, too, to the history of the minority elements now within the nation-state. The task Palacky had set himself had been fulfilled, but not perhaps as completely as he envisaged, since independence had in most cases come more quickly than expected. Now the task Renan set out lay ahead in addition. The past had not merely to be remembered and 'forgotten'. It had to be recaptured and 'forgotten'.

The Hindu-Buddhist empire of Majapahit is a case in point. Prapanca's poem of 1365 depicted its prosperity and its glory. But for the Dutch expedition against Lombok in 1894, it would not have become widely known: the philologist Dr J. Brandes was sent with the expedition in order to preserve objects of cultural interest from destruction, and the Nagarakrtagama was one of them. Translated by Kern, it was utilised in N. J. Krom's *Hindoe-Javaasche Geschiedenis,* and its account of the empire found its way into school texts. It was at this time that a nationalist elite was emerging in Indonesia, and Prapanca's account was an inspiration.[7] Yet it was an ambivalent one. Sukarno suggested that the imperialism of Sri Vijaya and Majapahit was not different from the other kinds of imperialism that he rejected. In other parts of the archipelago, Takdir Alisjahbana wrote in 1930, 'conquered peoples did not like the conquerors at all'.[8] Muslim writers were particularly reluctant to see Majapahit as the symbol for the new Indonesia. 'Did not the Sultanate of Demak and the Sultanate of Mataram under Sultan Agung resist the Dutch: is that not one of the proofs of the greatness they have left for our people?'[9] Evoking the greatness of the Hindu-Buddhist empire of Majapahit might divide as well as unite, while at the same time preventing the historian from ascertaining its true nature and from giving due weight to the activities of its opponents.

Merely making opposition to the colonial power a common theme was, perhaps, politically more viable, but it was still insufficient historiographically. To see Lapu Lapu, who killed Magellan, as a national hero, as did Usha Mahajani,[10] is unconvincingly anachronistic. Nor can those commemorated by the Heroes Monument unveiled in Kuching in 1993 be seen by historians, or indeed perhaps by others, in the way the chief minister asked his audience to see them: 'many of the so-called "rebels" killed, executed or imprisoned in the olden days [of Brooke rule] were nothing more than the early nationalists who dared to defy the White Men's rule'.[11] Six of the eight commemorated died opposing Brooke rule, though not in the name of nationalism. One died leading Brooke forces against the Skrang Iban. One, the assassin of the first colonial governor, rebelled with the object of restoring the Brooke regime.[12]

The determination to produce an Indonesian National History prompted the most interesting range of arguments. The concept was put forward soon after the 1955 elections had, instead of promoting a new sense of unity, led to a series of regional challenges, and the notion that a national history needed to serve the cause of nation-building was inescapable. Yet it was just at this time, too, that the works of van Leur and Schrieke were becoming available, inviting not a simple reversal of colonial history, but a more sophisticated way of viewing the past, and the new scholarly strategies that C. C. Berg was adopting were arousing controversy.

The first Indonesian history seminar was held in Yogyakarta on 14–18 December 1957.[13] Though it was organised by Gadjah Mada University and the University of Indonesia, the initiative had come from the minister for education, Sarino Mangoenpranoto, and his successor stressed the role of history in nation-building. The main debate on the philosophy of history was set out by Muhammad Yamin, another former minister, and by Soedjatmoko, a publicist and diplomat. Yamin evoked Ibn Khaldun in advocating a 'synthetic' approach, in which the nationalist interpretation he advocated became the means of organising and presenting the facts.[14]

Most of the participants followed this line rather than Soedjatmoko's, but he set out his view again in a collection he edited, *An Introduction to Indonesian Historiography*.[15] The myth of Majapahit had been exploded by research, he said, alluding to Berg, yet nations seemed to need their myths, and 'for quite some time the Indonesian historian will be confronted with demands for corroborative evidence for existing myths or for new myths'.[16] At the same time, he would not enjoy 'the comparative isolation of his nationalist colleagues of earlier times in other countries', and his history would have to 'stand up to other, non-Indonesian accounts of what has taken place'.[17] 'While in Western historiography the question of historical subjectivity and objectivity became an issue only at the end of a long period of development, modern Indonesian historiography, in its infancy still, is already possibly too familiar with the subjectivity of man's thought and vision.' The Indonesian historian would have, too, 'to reconcile or transcend the different regional historical traditions, in a way that is acceptable not only to most modern Indonesians but also to those from the regions concerned'.[18]

There was, Soedjatmoko thought, yet another problem for the Indonesian historian: 'he is trying to establish the study of history as a scholarly discipline in what is, to a large extent, still an ahistorical culture'.[19] In Java, as Donald Brown later argued, and even in Makasar, 'life and the flow of human events' were seen 'as a process beyond human control and therefore beyond human responsibility'.[20] The problem did not, however, paralyse the historian, Soedjatmoko insisted. Instead he is forced into 'a consideration of the philosophical implications of his discipline and the question of the significance of what he is doing in relation to his own society and the situation in which he finds himself'.[21] The historian then understands 'that the study of history can only be meaningful and is only possible if the historical process is seen as being essentially indeterminate and open to man's deliberate participation in it'.[22] He finds that 'he is leading a breakthrough to a new vision of life and society for his nation, based on man's willing assumption of his freedom and responsibility in relation to history'.[23]

The second national seminar on history was held on 26–29 August 1970. By then the regime had changed, and the thrust of the seminar differed from the first: it was less concerned with a discussion of fundamental issues than with practical activity that would prepare the way for writing the proposed national history as a collaborative work. The main expertise of the central figure in the enterprise, Sartono Kartodirdjo, lay in socio-economic history. In approaching national history, however, he concluded that the socio-economic focus was insufficient on its own. He offered what he called an 'integrationist' approach.[24]

'Even though the plurality of Indonesian society is quite tangible, the national history which is to be constructed is definitely not just an aggregate of regional and local histories; but rather an *amalgamation* of those histories which function interdependently as parts of a coherent whole or system.' The historian, Sartono later told a seminar in Brunei, had to pay 'special attention to interconnections between the parts, as well as to the networks built up by social, economic, political and cultural processes through the ages … the integration process gradually created a unity which is manifested in its ultimate form in present-day Indonesia'. The 'tracing of the process of integration will form a meaningful unity to Indonesian history'.[25]

The reception of the national history when it appeared in 1975 was, as Taufik Abdullah pointed out in Brunei, somewhat critical. How, he asked, should it be viewed twenty years later? More research had been done, new historiographical approaches had been adopted, and better information was available. Several 'silenced historical voices' had begun to be heard again.[26] A national history had to give attention, not only to them, but to 'shared experiences and commonly remembered events'. In a somewhat Renan-esque vein, Taufik suggested that a national history,

> a symbol of integration and unity, which ought to satisfy the requirements of critical academic scrutiny, … should also be an intellectual lens through which the nation can 'make its peace with the past'. A national history should be a lesson on how the nation has dealt with the many conflicts and tragic events of the past, as well as a vision of how it continues its march towards an ever-renewed noble dream.[27]

Thai historiography did not have to reckon with a phase of colonial rule. As part of the modernisation of the state, however, a Western-style historiography superseded the *tamnan* or legendary accounts and *phongsawadan* or royal chronicles: *wong wong cak cak,* Chulalongkorn called them, 'dynasties and battles'.[28] One school, associated with Prince Damrong, emphasised the role of the monarchy. A second emerged after 1932, associated with Vichit, and emphasising the concept of the nation. The more radical discourse stimulated by the upheaval of the early 1970s did not entirely displace these approaches, but contributed to the lively historiography of the 1980s and 1990s. A political emphasis remains. One of the leading figures, Nidhi Aeusrivongse, insists that he is writing Thai history, for Thais and in Thai.

At the Brunei workshop some participants indeed argued that, as national history was most important to the nation concerned, and best understood by it, the involvement of foreign historians was 'both unnecessary and undesirable'.[29] Ferdinand Llanes outlined the development at the University of the Philippines of the *pantayong* school associated with Zeus Salazar. It criticises what it terms *pangkaming pananaw*, the traditional way of writing Philippine history, as 'a discourse that defensively reckons with the view of the foreigner'.[30] An apologia, it is more concerned 'with proving the existence of our civilization or justifying our country's state of development than inquiring into the internal dynamics of Philippine society as it evolved over the centuries'.[31]

Properly conceived, however, that was not an argument against the involvement of foreigners in the enterprise, and members of the UP school themselves embarked on a study of neighbouring countries. It was rather a restatement of the need for a change of perspective, called for in the writings of Smail, for example. The cultural pressures of 'globalisation' made the restatement comprehensible, even timely, though it was perhaps somewhat ironic, but not discreditable, that it coincided with the global proliferation of discourse analysis.

Ruth McVey, by contrast, predicted 'a continuing internationalization' of Southeast Asian studies. 'Eventually, we should expect the emergence of a planetary system in which various foreign centres of research orbit around a Southeast Asia which is their powerful source of analysis as well as of study material.' That, however, might take a long time, she added, given the 'regnant paradigm'. But no alternative vision had emerged, and the very lack of it might leave the way open for creative scholarship.[32]

Her hopes have been supported, perhaps, by the writings which have appeared in the field of what in the West has been called 'history from below'. What has been written in respect of Southeast Asia has again been no mere imitation of what has been done in Europe, though sometimes inspired by it. It has, too, contributed to a critique of an elitist national historiography perhaps even more significant in Southeast Asia than in Europe.

'History from below' was concerned with topics to which historians might have given too little attention in the past, but it did not adopt methods or strategies that would be alien to them or even novel. It was a change of point-of-view that might be compared with that which van Leur advocated towards Indonesian history, and could be seen, not as a shift from the Rankean approach, but as an extension of it that made new demands on the historian, perhaps even more stringent, but not essentially different. The evidence the historian needs may be more difficult to find;

it may need to be read 'against the grain'; and the imaginative leap that has to be taken may be more athletic.

The purpose of writing it was in some part the result of an ideological interest, in some part the result of developments in the discipline. In any case those involved wanted to show that the 'common people' were not simply 'problems' for governments to 'handle', but themselves historical 'actors'. But that might not suffice. 'History from below' would indeed have lost much of its social purpose, as well as its historiographical value, if it were not integrated in some way into what Sharpe calls 'mainstream history', and if it did not alter the perspectives of 'mainstream historians'.[33] An equal and opposite danger is that it would assert itself by denying others and come to regard itself as the 'mainstream', if not the whole river system. The roles of those above and those below would simply have been reversed, rather as a nationalist history might have altered the role of the colonialist.

In Indonesia Sartono was at once pushing ahead with Sejarah Nasional, and writing his major book on the peasantry, *Protest Movements in Rural Java*,[34] and he clearly found these endeavours complementary rather than contradictory. He saw his book as 'a contribution to the reconstruction of Indonesian history from an Indonesia-centric point of view'. An analytical approach, he hoped, would 'shed more light on the whole matrix of social, economic and political structures forming the background of the great events of national history. This approach will in part eliminate the Neerlandocratic bias of Indonesian history on the one hand, and will make possible the reconstruction of historical patterns within an Indonesia-centric frame of reference on the other.'[35]

Like many other Filipino historians, Reynaldo Ileto studied the revolution of the 1890s, but, in his *Pasyon and Revolution*,[36] he studied it in a new light. How did the 'masses'—to borrow a word from the title of Teodoro Agoncillo's earlier account of the revolution—perceive the ideas of nationalism brought from the West by the *ilustrado* elite? Their concept of 'freedom' was in fact not the same. For them the revolution was associated with a this-worldly version of the redemptive message of Christ, so often received through the passion plays of the Tagalog Easter Week. Ileto was influenced by a contemporary clash between the police and a militant sect in Manila, and by reading Hobsbawm's *Primitive Rebels,* as well as Benda and Sturtevant. The most novel feature of his work was its juxtaposition of Spanish sources with Tagalog ones. 'To write history "from below" requires the proper use of documents and other sources "from below".'[37] Some of the documents Ileto used have proved unreliable, Glenn May has argued,[38] but that does not destroy his basic argument: the peasants and the revolution are connected through the millenarian tradition, and not through an alien one, such as the use of the word 'masses' implies.

'It seems incredible to present a history of Singapore without the coolie', James F. Warren declared in the introduction to *Rickshaw Coolie: A People's History of Singapore (1880–1940)*.[39] Supported, too, by oral evidence, his account of the rickshaw coolies was largely based on the coroner's records, several hundred volumes of which he found in the storeroom of a subordinate court. 'A passion for a forgotten past of people who have stood outside history and recovery of a whole set of social relations have been a central preoccupation running through my work', Warren wrote. The book, part of a trilogy on the road to completion, he hoped would 'contribute to a revision of South-East Asian Modern History', and 'to the notion of what is "historical"'.[40] But he did not integrate his history with the 'national' history of Singapore: he placed his people's history, as it were, alongside. Nor, in Hong Lysa's view, did he succeed in giving a history back to the coolies: 'he ironically ends up stereotyping them as helpless victims of circumstances. ... In fact, they did fashion their own forms of submission, resistance or adaptation.' Warren's tendency, she suggests, was 'to romanticize the rickshaw coolies, thence to stress his empathy with them and his role in giving them a history'.[41] Though rather cruelly put, the remark points to a danger in 'history from below'.

Notes

1 'Change and Continuity in Southeast Asian Studies', JSEAS, 26, 1 (March 1995), p. 1.
2 P. Hutton, *History as an Art of Memory*, Hanover and London: U New England, 1993, p. 97.
3 p. 4.
4 *Times Literary Supplement*, 13 June 1986.
5 *The Habsburg Monarchy*, London: Hamilton, 1948, p. 29.
6 q. John N. Schumacher, *The Propaganda Movement*, Manila: Solidaridad, 1973, p. 198.
7 Supomo in Reid and Marr, pp. 180–1.
8 p. 183.
9 p. 184.
10 *Philippine Nationalism*, St Lucia: UQP, 1971, p. 16.
11 q. R. Reece in Putu Davies, ed., *Constructing a National Past*, UBD, 1996, p. 404.
12 ibid., pp. 404–6.
13 H. A. J. Klooster, *Indonesiers schrijven hun geschiedenis*, Dordrecht: Foris, 1985, p. 75.
14 ibid., pp. 77–8.
15 Cornell UP, 1965.
16 p. 405.
17 p. 406.
18 p. 407.
19 p. 409.
20 p. 409.
21 p. 412.
22 p. 412.
23 p. 415.
24 p. 111.
25 in Putu Davies, p. 197.
26 p. 217.
27 p. 218.
28 q. David K. Wyatt, *Studies in Thai History*, Chiangmai: Silkworm, 1994, p. 21.
29 Davies, introduction, p. 23.
30 p. 315.
31 p. 315.
32 p. 9.
33 in P. Burke, ed., *New Perspectives in Historical Writing*, Oxford: Polity, 1991, p. 37.
34 Singapore: OUP, 1973.

35 p. xiii.
36 Quezon City: Ateneo de Manila P, 1979.
37 p. 13.
38 *Inventing a Hero*, Manila: New Day; Madison: U Wis Centre for SEAS, 1996.
39 Singapore: OUP, 1986.
40 p. xi.
41 in Mohammed Halib and Tim Huxley, *An Introduction to Southeast Asian Studies*, London and NY: Tauris, 1996, p. 60.

5.4

Global History

A world of nation-states involves a perspective on world history as well as on that of nation-states. What is the role of regional history?

The 'globalisation' of the late twentieth century is an invitation to write 'world history'. Not many modern historians have been prepared to undertake work on so grand a scale. Most have found 'world history' overwhelmingly challenging in its range and dimension and in its demands upon expertise. They have indeed come to distrust it, not simply because it cannot attain the accuracy of the research-based monograph or journal article, but because it seems to afford too great an opportunity to idiosyncrasy, and not merely to over-simplification. Yet world history has its readers, and if they are not served by the professionals, they may be served by propagandists.

The first to make the world conscious of its unity, the Europeans saw the world through European eyes and wrote largely of European activities. World history was in some sense European history, and that prescribed its focus, its structure, its selection of topics. A different approach to imperial history, stressing the 'imperialism of free trade' and 'collaboration' came about not only as a result of decolonisation and the debates on 'centricity'. It was also prompted by a recognition of Europe's changed place in the world. That was explicitly the case with Ronald Robinson and John Gallagher, who were apprehensive of 'the colonial possibilities of the Marshall plan'.[1]

The theory they developed, however, also accommodated the possibility that the relationship between a colonial power and its colony did not terminate with independence, and that in many cases dependency simply took a 'neo-colonialist' form. Writers about Latin America, the political independence of which had of course been achieved more than a century before, offered a not dissimilar analysis in their '*dependencia*' theory. But while these perceptions offered the possibility of a fuller account of the relationships among states in the imperial and post-imperial phase, they did not clearly show how a new kind of world history might succeed the one created by the Europeans.

A number of Dutch historians developed the category of 'overseas history'. In 1979 P. C. Emmer and H. L. Wesseling published *Reappraisals in Overseas History*.[2]

They admitted that the phrase was in many respects 'an unfortunate one. It resembles a somewhat clumsy attempt to replace the term "colonial history", which has unpleasant political connotations, by another more neutral one.' Overseas history was still 'a Western concept.' Indeed the histories of Asia, Africa, and America, it implied, were 'to be tossed into a heap', with nothing in common but their 'non-European' character.[3] But it was worth retaining the concept 'for the time being'. The European sources were similar, and so were the challenges presented by the search for non-European sources. Another issue also added coherence to the subject: the countries concerned mainly belonged to the Third World.[4]

The contributions Emmer and Wesseling collected raised a number of problems not surprisingly shared by historians of particular parts of the world who struggled with the 'centricity' issues. Did the Western science of history itself contain or represent 'the well known disparity of power'? If it were applied, could it encompass 'event history', given the lack of event-related materials in other cultures, or was one 'condemned' to structural history? What, if any, were the differences between Western scholars and non-Western scholars in the post-colonial period? 'The most extreme answer holds that African history can only be practiced by blacks.' That the editors rejected: it would 'rob history of its scientific pretensions'. They concluded by stressing the opportunities 'overseas history' offered to a comparative approach. Did *dependencia* also function in Africa? Might the concept of the 'dual economy' encountered in Indonesian history also apply in the Caribbean?[5]

In a contribution to Peter Burke's *New Appraisals on Historical Writing*, Wesseling reappraised the reappraisals. He and his colleague had indeed suggested that 'overseas history' was a useful category 'for the time being'. Now he no longer wished to equate it with so-called Third World history: 'the very idea of a "Third World" is … disintegrating, as it no longer reflects reality. In retrospect it even seems strange that countries like India and Indonesia were supposed to form one world with Sudan and Mali for the sole reason that they were all former colonies and are still relatively poor.'[6] Was 'overseas history' still a subject of study? Colonial history had been succeeded by national history. To survive 'overseas history' would need 'some kind of reconceptualization'.[7]

That Wesseling was disposed to find in 'world history'. Everybody now accepted, he argued, 'that Africans and Asians have their own history, as rich and interesting as that of Europe. The question, however, is whether we can stop here and simply consider world history as the sum of a great number of autonomous regional histories.' Historians should study 'how, in one way or another, these various civilizations have become interconnected, how today's world situation has come into being. The real challenge of overseas history is to offer a modern form of world history.'[8]

In that field Wesseling detected two approaches at work. One he called the social-science approach. It analysed a particular topic or phenomenon—state formation or revolution or dictatorship—in various historical contexts. Another was more traditional, 'in so far as it tries to distinguish a certain pattern in the development of modern history and considers the writing of history as the description of concrete historical approaches and events'.[9] Its conceptual framework was that of 'the unification of the world as a consequence of the expansion of Europe and the rise of the West'.[10]

The attempt to write 'world history' that Wesseling appears to have in mind may be related to the kind of history of Indonesia that Sartono sought to create. It needed to take an 'integrating' view of the past. It could not ignore those areas of the world which had a part in the history of the world, but not a part in world history. But it had to put an emphasis on those trends that were to make for a unified world, on the interconnexions among its various regions and civilisations. The risk was that, as a history of Indonesia might overplay the Javanese or the Dutch, 'world history' might, like its imperial predecessor, overplay the role of the West.

Wesseling looked for a 'world history' that would link the history of regions. Purely regional history, he thought, was insufficient, and it may indeed be politically as well as historiographically risky if it sets region against region and 'civilisation' against 'civilisation'. Yet regional history is worth doing, as Tony Reid's *Southeast Asia in the Age of Commerce* has masterfully shown. He himself suggested that 'treating Southeast Asia as a whole makes it possible to describe a number of areas of life which would otherwise remain in the shadows'. For each cultural area sources are fragmentary; but studying them together offers 'a coherent picture … of the life-styles of the region as a whole'.[11] The region is also the context for his more recent studies of 'nationality' and 'ethnicity'. If 'world history' is to be attempted, it has also to allow, to borrow a phrase from one of its practitioners, 'plenty of room for human diversity in all its complexity'.[12]

It is possible that the history of Southeast Asia has a special contribution to make. So Denys Lombard suggested of the Javanese case.

> Since there was little 'metamorphism' here, our orientalists were unable to forge the idea of a 'great East Indian civilization'. Instead of an imposing edifice whose internal workings we could study piece by piece … , we were forced to accept the geographical diversity and take change as our starting point. Yet the question that arises is this: Are the civilizations that seem 'great' to us today in fact those which, at the dawn of their evolution, had the good fortune to overlap several different worlds and to find themselves, like the Indian Ocean islands, at a cross-roads?[13]

This debate is another context for Lieberman's thinking. It was possible to over-emphasise the 'regional' in writing the history of Southeast Asia, he argued, missing some of its diversity, and ghettoising the treatment of its past. A study of the 'early modern' period promised 'to modify the received emphasis on European exceptionalism. … Especially curious are the parallels between the chronologies and multi-state dynamics of Europe and of mainland Southeast Asia, at the far ends of the Eurasian land mass.'[14]

None of the historians native to Southeast Asia has attempted a history of Southeast Asia. The task is indeed a formidable one, in view of its diversity and complexity, and the calls for national history are insistent. Indeed it may be that the 'region', dating only from World War II, may yet remain an outsider's concept, and that to write with it in mind risks renewing an outsider's perspective in succession to the imperialist perspective of earlier historians. '[T]he identity of Southeast Asia as a region and Southeast Asian studies as a field of knowledge are newly imported into Southeast Asia itself', Craig Reynolds writes.[15] The position is likely to change, Hong Lysa has suggested. In Southeast Asian countries today, she wrote in 1996, the official talk was of 'economic complementarity, regional growth and stability. Southeast Asians may well find impetus, and indeed sponsorship, to master a second Asian language and to research the history of their neighbours—for the same reasons that the Japanese, the region's leading investors, have done so.'[16]

The present history is yet another outsider's one. Apprehensive lest it be an imperialist one, the author has endeavoured to reckon with the historiographical issues he has outlined, as well as to tackle some at least of the substantial historical literature now available. Assembling a history of the nation-states seemed inadequate: they are, as a regional history reminds us, recent. At the same time, influenced, too, by a wish to balance narrative and analysis, he sought to avoid entrenching regionalism by discussing issues faced in the region, but not in the region alone. In that, of course, he still ran the risk of 'Westernising' through his choice of issues. That he sought to avoid by presenting them as tasks and interests common to humankind, though viewed in different ways at different times in Southeast Asia, in the West, and in other parts of the world, too. In that endeavour, though abandoning Lieberman's concern for synchronisation, he hoped to make some contribution to 'world history' in the age of 'globalisation'.

Notes

1 Robinson in F. Madden and D. J. Fieldhouse, *Oxford and the Idea of Commonwealth*, London: Croom Helm, 1982, pp. 45, 47.
2 Leiden UP, 1979.
3 pp. 3–4.
4 pp. 4–5.
5 pp. 14–16.
6 p. 68.
7 p. 69.
8 p. 72.
9 p. 88.
10 p. 89.
11 Preface, p. xiv.
12 William H. McNeill, *Mythistory and Other Essays*, Chicago UP, 1986, p. 17.
13 *Le Carrefour Javanais*, Paris: Ecole des Hautes Etudes, 1990, III, pp. 156–7.
14 'Local Integration and Eurasian Analogies …', MAS, 27, 3 (July 1993), p. 570.
15 'A New Look at Old Southeast Asia', JAS, 54, 2 (May 1995), p. 438.
16 in Halib and Huxley, p. 66.

Select Bibliography

General

Brown, David, *The State and Ethnic Politics in Southeast Asia*, London and New York: Routledge, 1994.

Brown, Ian, *Economic Change in South-East Asia, c. 1830–1980*, Kuala Lumpur: OUP, 1997.

Christie, Clive J., *A Modern History of Southeast Asia: Decolonization, Nationalism and Separatism*, London and New York: Tauris, 1996.

Elson, R. E., *The End of the Peasantry in Southeast Asia: A Social and Economic History of Peasant Livelihood, 1800–1990s*, Basingstoke: Macmillan, 1997.

Fisher, C. A., *South-east Asia: A Social, Economic and Political Geography*, London: Methuen; New York: Dutton, 1964.

Furnivall, J. S., *Colonial Policy and Practice*, CUP, 1948.

Hurst, Philip, *Rainforest Politics Ecological Destruction in South-East Asia*, Kuala Lumpur: Abdul Majeed, 1991.

McVey, Ruth, ed., *Southeast Asian Capitalists*, Cornell UP, 1992.

Mohamed Halib and Tim Huxley, eds, *An Introduction to Southeast Asian Studies*, London and New York: Tauris, 1996.

Reid, Anthony, *The Last Stand of Asian Autonomies: Responses to Modernity in the Diverse States of Southeast Asia and Korea, 1750–1900*, Basingstoke: Macmillan, 1997.

—— ed., *Slavery, Bondage and Dependency in Southeast Asia*, St Lucia: UQP, 1983.

Reid, Anthony, and David Marr, eds, *Perceptions of the Past in Southeast Asia*, Singapore: Heinemann, 1979.

Scott, James C., *The Moral Economy of the Peasant Rebellion and Subsistence in Southeast Asia*, New Haven: Yale UP, 1976.

—— and Ben Kerkvliet, 'The Politics of Survival: Peasant Response to "Progress" in Southeast Asia', JSEAS, 4, 2 (September 1973), pp. 241–68.

Tarling, Nicholas, ed., *The Cambridge History of Southeast Asia*, 2 vols, CUP, 1992.

Early and Early Modern History

Bellwood, P., *Prehistory of the Indo-Malaysian Archipelago*, Sydney: Academic P, 1985.

Boxer, C. R., *The Dutch Seaborne Empire, 1600–1800*, London: Hutchinson, 1965.

Coedès, G., *Les Peuples de la Péninsule Indochinoise*, Paris: Dunod, 1962.

Glamann, K., *Dutch–Asiatic Trade, 1620–1740*, Copenhagen: Danish Science P; The Hague: Nijhoff, 1958.

Hall, Kenneth, *Maritime Trade and State Development in Early Southeast Asia*, Sydney and Wellington: Allen and Unwin, 1985.

Mabbett, Ian, and David Chandler, *The Khmers*, Oxford: Blackwell, 1996.

Marr, David G., and A. C. Milner, eds, *Southeast Asia in the 9th to 14th Centuries*, Singapore: ISEAS; Canberra: ANU, 1986.

Meilink-Roelofsz, M. A. P., *Asian Trade and European Influence in the Indonesian Archipelago between 1500 and about 1650*, The Hague: Nijhoff, 1962.

Reid, Anthony, *Southeast Asia in the Age of Commerce*, New Haven: Yale UP, 1988, 1993.

—— and Lance Castles, eds, *Pre-colonial State Systems in Southeast Asia*, Kuala Lumpur: MBRAS, 1975.

Subrahmanyam, Sanjay, *The Portuguese Empire in Asia, 1500–1700*, London and New York: Longman, 1993.

Wolters, O. W., *Early Indonesian Commerce: A Study of the Origins of Srivijaya*, Cornell UP, 1967.

—— *History, Culture and Religion in Southeast Asian Perspectives*, Singapore: ISEAS, 1982.

Indonesia

Andaya, Barbara Watson, *To Live as Brothers: Southeast Sumatra in the Seventeenth and Eighteenth Centuries*, U Hawaii P, 1993.

Andaya, Leonard Y., *The World of Maluku: Eastern Indonesia in the Early Modern Period*, U Hawaii P, 1993.

Anderson, Benedict R., and R. McVey, *A Preliminary Analysis of the October 1, 1965, Coup in Indonesia*, Cornell UP, 1971.

Anwar, Dewi Fortuna, *Indonesia in ASEAN*, New York: St Martin's P; Singapore: ISEAS, 1994.

Bastin, John, *The Native Policies of Sir Stamford Raffles in Java and Sumatra*, Oxford: Clarendon P, 1957.

Benda, Harry J., *The Crescent and the Rising Sun: Indonesian Islam under the Japanese Occupation, 1942–1945*, The Hague and Bandung: Van Hoeve, 1958.

Booth, Anne, *Agricultural Development in Indonesia*, Sydney: Allen and Unwin, 1988.

—— *The Indonesian Economy in the Nineteenth and Twentieth Centuries: A History of Missed Opportunities*, Basingstoke: Macmillan, 1998.

Breman, Jan, *Taming the Coolie Beast: Plantation Society and the Colonial Order in Southeast Asia*, Delhi: OUP, 1989.

Cribb, R., ed., *The Indonesian Killings, 1965–1966*, Clayton: Monash U, 1990.

Dahm, B., *Sukarno and the Struggle for Indonesian Independence*, trans. M. F. S. Heidhues, Cornell UP, 1969.

—— *History of Indonesia in the Twentieth Century*, trans. P. S. Falla, London: Pall Mall, 1971.

Dijk, C. van, *Rebellion under the Banner of Islam: The Darul Islam in Indonesia*, The Hague: Nijhoff, 1981.

Elson, R. E., *Javanese Peasants and the Colonial Sugar Industry: Impact and Change in an East Java Residency, 1830–1940*, Singapore: OUP, 1984.

—— *Village Java under the Cultivation System, 1830–1870*, St Leonards: Allen and Unwin, 1994.

Fasseur, Cornelis, *The Politics of Colonial Exploitation: Java, the Dutch and the Cultivation System*, trans. R. E. Elson and Ary Kraal, Cornell UP, 1992.

Feith, Herbert, *The Decline of Constitutional Democracy in Indonesia*, Cornell UP, 1962.

Henley, David E. F., *Nationalism and Regionalism in a Colonial Context: Minahasa in the Dutch East Indies*, Leiden: KITLV P, 1996.

Hindley, Donald, *The Communist Party of Indonesia*, UCP, 1964.

Ichlasul Amal, *Regional and Central Government in Indonesian Politics: West Sumatra and South Sulawesi, 1949–1979*, Yogyakarta: Gadjah Mada UP, 1992.

Ingleson, John, *Road to Exile: The Indonesian Nationalist Movement, 1927–1934*, Singapore: OUP, 1986.

—— *In Search of Justice: Workers and Unions in Colonial Java, 1908–1926*, Singapore: OUP, 1986.

Kahin, George McT., *Nationalism and Revolution in Indonesia*, Cornell UP, 1952.

Sartono Kartodirdjo, *Protest Movements in Rural Java*, Singapore: OUP; Jakarta: P. T. Indira, 1973.

Kell, Tim, *The Roots of Acehnese Rebellion, 1989–1992*, Cornell UP, 1995.

Kurasawa Aiko, 'Mobilization and Control: A Study of Social Change in Rural Java, 1942–1945', PhD thesis, Cornell U, 1988.

Legge, J. D., *Sukarno: A Political Biography*, Sydney: Allen and Unwin, 1972.

Leur, J. C. van, *Indonesian Trade and Society*, The Hague, Bandung: van Hoeve, 1955.

Lewis, Dianne, *Jan Compagnie in the Straits of Malacca, 1641–1795*, Athens: Ohio U, 1995.

Lindblad, J. Thomas, *Between Dayak and Dutch: The Economic History of Southeast Kalimantan, 1880–1942*, Dordrecht: Foris, 1988.

—— ed., *Historical Foundations of a National Economy in Indonesia, 1890s–1990s*, Amsterdam: North Holland, 1996.

Mackie, J. A. C., *Konfrontasi: The Indonesian-Malaysia Dispute, 1963–1966*, Kuala Lumpur: OUP, 1974.

McVey, Ruth, *The Rise of Indonesian Communism*, Cornell UP, 1965.

Nagazumi Akira, *The Dawn of Indonesian Nationalism: The Early Years of the Budi Utomo, 1908–1918*, Tokyo, 1972.

Niel, Robert van, *The Emergence of the Modern Indonesian Elite*, The Hague and Bandung: van Hoeve, 1960.

Nordholt, Henk Schulte, *The Spell of Power: A History of Balinese Politics, 1650–1940*, Leiden: KITLV P, 1996.

Osborne, Robin, *Indonesia's Secret War: The Guerrilla Struggle in Irian Jaya*, Sydney: Allen and Unwin, 1985.

Palmier, Leslie, *Indonesia and the Dutch*, London: OUP, 1962.

Pelzer, Karl J., *Planter and Peasant*, The Hague: Nijhoff, 1978.

Penders, C. L. M., and Uld Sundhaussen, *Abdul Haris Nasutio: A Political Biography*, St Lucia: UQP, 1985.

Ramage, Douglas E., *Politics in Indonesian Democracy: Islam and the Ideology of Tolerance*, London and New York: Routledge, 1995.

Reid, Anthony, *The Contest for North Sumatra: Atjeh, the Netherlands and Britain, 1858–1898*, Kuala Lumpur: OUP, 1969.

—— *The Indonesian National Revolution, 1945–1950*, Melbourne: Longman, 1974.

—— *The Blood of the People: Revolution and the End of Traditional Rule in Northern Sumatra*, Kuala Lumpur: OUP, 1979.

Remmelink, Willem, *The Chinese War and the Collapse of the Javanese State, 1725–1743*, Leiden: KITLV P, 1994.

Resink, G. J., *Indonesia's History between the Myths*, The Hague: van Hoeve, 1968.

Ricklefs, M. C., *A History of Modern Indonesia*, London: Macmillan, 1981.

—— *War, Culture and Economy in Java, 1677–1726*, Sydney: Allen and Unwin, 1993.

—— *The Seen and Unseen Worlds in Java, 1726–1749*, St Leonards: Allen and Unwin, 1998.

Sato Shigeru, *War, Nationalism and Peasants: Java under the Japanese Occupation, 1942–1945*, St Leonards: Allen and Unwin, 1994.

Schiller, Jim, *Developing Jepara in New Order Indonesia*, Clayton: Monash U, 1996.

Schmutzer, Eduard J. M., *Dutch Colonial Policy and the Search for Identity in Indonesia, 1920–1931*, Leiden: Brill, 1977.

Schwarz, Adam, *A Nation in Waiting: Indonesia in the 1990s*, St Leonards: Allen and Unwin, 1994.

Shiraishi Takashi, *An Age in Motion: Popular Radicalism in Java, 1912–1926*, Cornell UP, 1990.

Sundhaussen, Ulf, *The Road to Power: Indonesian Military Politics, 1945–1967*, Kuala Lumpur: OUP, 1982.

Sutherland, Heather, *The Making of a Bureaucratic Elite: The Colonial Transformation of the Javanese Priyayi*, Singapore: Heinemann, 1979.

Vos, Reinout, *Gentle Janus, Merchant Prince: The VOC and the Tightrope of Diplomacy in the Malay World, 1740–1800*, Leiden: KITLV P, 1993.

Williams, Michael Charles, *Communism, Religion and Revolt in Banten*, Athens: Ohio U, 1990.

East Timor

Hiorth, F., *Timor Past and Present*, Townsville: James Cook U, 1985.

Krieger, Heike, ed., *East Timor and the International Community: Basic Documents*, CUP, 1997.

Malaysia

Andaya, Barbara Watson, *Perak, the Abode of Grace: A Study of an Eighteenth-Century Malay State*, Kuala Lumpur: OUP, 1979.

Andaya, Leonard Y., *The Kingdom of Johore, 1641–1728*, Kuala Lumpur: OUP, 1975.

Black, Ian, *A Gambling Style of Government: The Establishment of the Chartered Company's Rule in Sabah, 1878–1915*, Kuala Lumpur: OUP, 1983.

Blythe, Wilfred, *The Impact of Chinese Secret Societies in Malaya: A Historical Study*, OUP, 1969.

Bonney, R., *Kedah, 1771–1821*, Kuala Lumpur: OUP, 1971.

Butcher, John G., *The British in Malaya, 1880–1941*, Kuala Lumpur: OUP, 1979.

Case, William, *Elites and Regimes in Malaysia: Revisiting a Consociational Democracy*, Clayton: Monash U, 1996.

Cheah Boon Kheng, *The Peasant Robbers of Kedah, 1900–1929: Historical and Folk Perceptions*, Singapore: OUP, 1988.

Chew, Daniel, *Chinese Pioneers on the Sarawak Frontier, 1841–1941*, Singapore: OUP, 1990.

Cowan, C. D., *Nineteenth-century Malaya: The Origins of British Political Control*, London: OUP, 1961.

Crouch, Harold, *Government and Society in Malaysia*, St Leonards: Allen and Unwin, 1996.

Drabble, J. H., *Rubber in Malaya, 1876–1922: The Genesis of the Industry*, Kuala Lumpur: OUP, 1973.

Ghosh, K. K., *Twentieth-century Malaysia: Politics of Decentralization of Power, 1920–1929*, Calcutta: Progressive, 1977.

Gullick, J. M., *Indigenous Political Systems of Western Malaya*, London: Athlone, 1958.

—— *Rulers and Residents: Influence and Power in the Malay States, 1870–1920*, Singapore: OUP, 1992.

Heng Pek Koon, *Chinese Politics in Malaysia: A History of the Malaysian Chinese Association*, Singapore: OUP, 1988.

Kaur, Amarjit, *Bridge and Barrier: Transport and Communications in Colonial Malaya, 1870–1957*, Singapore: OUP, 1985.

—— *Economic Change in East Malaysia: Sabah and Sarawak since 1850*, Basingstoke: Macmillan, 1998.

Kratoska, Paul, *The Japanese Occupation of Malaya*, St Leonards: Allen and Unwin, 1998.

Lau, Albert, *The Malayan Union Controversy, 1942–1948*, Singapore: OUP, 1991.

Leigh, Michael B., *The Rising Moon: Political Change in Sarawak*, Sydney UP, 1974.

Milner, Anthony, *The Invention of Politics in Colonial Malaya*, CUP, 1995.

Pringle, Robert, *Rajahs and Rebels: The Ibans of Sarawak under Brooke Rule, 1841–1941*, London: Macmillan, 1970.

Reece, R. H. W., *The Name of Brooke: The End of White Rajah Rule in Sarawak*, Kuala Lumpur: OUP, 1982.

Roff, Margaret Clark, *The Politics of Belonging: Political Change in Sabah and Sarawak*, Kuala Lumpur: OUP, 1974.

Roff, William R., *The Origins of Malay Nationalism*, Yale UP, 1967.

Stockwell, A. J., *British Policy and Malay Politics during the Malayan Union Experiment, 1942–1948*, Kuala Lumpur: MBRAS, 1979.

Turnbull, C. M., *The Straits Settlements, 1826–67*, London: Athlone, 1972.

Wong Lin Ken, *The Malayan Tin Industry to 1914*, Tucson: U Arizona P, 1965.

Yeo Kim Wah, *The Politics of Decentralization: Colonial Controversy in Malaya, 1920–1929*, Kuala Lumpur: OUP, 1982.

Yong, C. F., and R. B. McKenna, *The Kuomintang Movement in British Malaya, 1912–1949*, Singapore UP, 1990.

Singapore

Chew, Ernest C. F., and Edwin Lee, *A History of Singapore*, Singapore: OUP, 1991.

Tremewan, C., *The Political Economy of Social Control in Singapore*, Basingstoke: Macmillan, 1994.

Yong, G. F., *Chinese Leadership and Power in Colonial Singapore*, Singapore: Times Academic P, 1991.

Brunei

Brown, D. E., *Brunei: The Structure and History of a Bornean Malay Sultanate*, Brunei: Brunei Museum, 1970.

Hussainmiya, B. A., *Sultan Omar Ali Saifuddin III and Britain: The Making of Brunei Darussalam*, Kuala Lumpur: OUP, 1995.

McArthur, M. S. H., *Report on Brunei in 1904*, ed. A. V. M. Horton, Ohio U, 1987.

Saunders, Graham, *A History of Brunei*, Kuala Lumpur: OUP, 1994.

Singh, D. S. Ranjit, *Brunei, 1839–1983: The Problems of Political Survival*, Singapore: OUP, 1984.

Tarling, Nicholas, *Britain, the Brookes and Brunei*, Kuala Lumpur: OUP, 1971.

Philippines

Bankoff, G., *Crime, Society, and the State in the Nineteenth-Century Philippines*, Quezon City: Ateneo de Manila UP, 1996.

Doronila, Amando, *The State, Economic Transformation, and Political Change in the Philippines, 1946–1972*, Singapore: OUP, 1992.

Friend, Theodore, *Between Two Empires: The Ordeal of the Philippines, 1929–1946*, Yale UP, 1965.

Gopinath, Aruna, *Manuel L. Quezon: The Tutelary Democrat*, Quezon City: New Day, 1987.

Gowing, P. G., *Muslim Filipinos: Heritage and Horizon*, Quezon City: New Day, 1979.

Grunder, G. A., and William E. Livezey, *The Philippines and the United States*, Norman: U Oklahoma P, 1951.

Guerrero, L. M., *The First Filipino*, Manila: Historical Conservation Society, 1963.

Ileto, Reynaldo C., *Pasyon and Revolution: Popular Movements in the Philippines, 1840–1910*, Quezon City: Ateneo de Manila UP, 1979.

de Jesus, Edilberto C., *The Tobacco Monopoly in the Philippines*, Quezon City: Ateneo de Manila UP, 1980.

Kerkvliet, Benedict J., *The Huk Rebellion*, UCP, 1977.

Larkin, John A., *The Pampangans: Colonial Society in a Philippine Province*, UCP, 1972.

Majul, C. A., *The Political and Constitutional Ideas of the Philippine Revolution*, Quezon City: UPP, 1967.

——— *Muslims in the Philippines*, Quezon City: UPP, 1973.

May, R. J., and F. Nemenzo, eds, *The Philippines after Marcos*, New York: St Martin's, 1985.

Owen, Norman G., *Prosperity without Progress: Manila Hemp and Material Life in the Colonial Philippines*, UCP, 1984.

Paredes, Ruby R., ed., *Philippine Colonial Democracy*, Yale UP, 1988.

Reid, Robert H., and Eileen Guerrero, *Corazon Aquino and the Brushfire Revolution*, Baton Rouge: Louisiana State UP, 1995.

Rosenberg, David A., ed., *Marcos and Martial Law in the Philippines*, Cornell UP, 1979.

Starner, Frances L., *Magsaysay and the Philippine Peasantry*, UCP, 1961.

Sturtevant, David R., *Popular Uprisings in the Philippines, 1840–1940*, Cornell UP, 1976.

Warren, James F., *The Sulu Zone, 1768–1898*, Singapore UP, 1981.

Wickberg, Edgar, *The Chinese in Philippine Life, 1850–1898*, Yale UP, 1965.

Burma

Aung-Thwin, Michael, *Pagan: The Origins of Modern Burma*, U Hawaii P, 1985.

Cady, John F., *A History of Modern Burma*, Cornell UP, 1958.

Cheng Siok-Hwa, *The Rice Industry of Burma, 1852–1940*, Kuala Lumpur: OUP, 1968.

Johnstone, W. C., *Burma's Foreign Policy: A Study in Neutralism*, Harvard UP, 1963.

Koenig, William J., *The Burmese Policy, 1752–1819*, Ann Arbor: U Mich, 1990.

Lieberman, Victor B., *Burmese Administrative Cycles*, Princeton UP, 1984.

Pollak, Oliver B., *Empires in Collision: Anglo-Burmese Relations in the Mid-nineteenth Century*, Westport: Greenwood, 1979.

Ramachandra, G. P., 'Anglo-Burmese Relations, 1795–1826', PhD thesis, U Hull, 1977.

Silverstein, Josef, ed., *Independent Burma at Forty Years: Six Assessments*, Cornell UP, 1989.

Singhal, D. P., *The Annexation of Upper Burma*, Singapore: Eastern Universities P, 1960.

Smith, Donald E., *Religion and Politics in Burma*, Princeton UP, 1965.

Tarling, Nicholas, 'The Fourth Anglo-Burmese War': Britain and the Independence of Burma, Gaya: Centre of South East Asian Studies, 1987.

Taylor, Robert H., *The State in Burma*, U Hawaii P, 1987.

Tinker, Hugh, *The Union of Burma: A Study of the First Years of Independence*, OUP, 1957.

Thailand

Akin, Rabibhadana, *The Organization of Thai Society in the Early Bangkok Period*, Cornell UP, 1969.

Anderson, Benedict R. O'G., and Richard Mendiones, *In the Mirror: Literature and Politics in Siam in the American Era*, Bangkok: Duang Kamol, 1985.

Batson, Benjamin J., *The End of the Absolute Monarchy in Siam*, Singapore: OUP, 1984.

Brown, I. *The Elite and the Economy in Siam, c. 1890–1920*, Singapore: OUP, 1988.

Chaiyan Rajchagool, *The Rise and Fall of the Thai Absolute Monarchy*, Bangkok, Cheney: White Lotus, 1994.

Darling, Frank C., *Thailand and the United States*, Washington: Public Affairs P, 1965.

Fineman, Daniel, *A Special Relationship: The United States and Military Government in Thailand, 1947–1958*, U Hawaii P, 1997.

Hewison, Kevin, *Bankers and Bureaucrats: Capital and the Role of the State in Thailand*, Yale UP, 1989.

Hong Lysa, *Thailand in the Nineteenth Century*, Singapore: ISEAS, 1984.

Hunsaker, B., et al., *Loggers, Monks, Students and Entrepreneurs: Four Essays on Thailand*, DeKalb: Northern Illinois U, 1996.

Ingram, J. C., *Economic Change in Thailand since 1850*, Stanford UP, 1955.

Kobkua Suwannathat-Pian, *Thailand's Durable Premier Phibun through Three Decades, 1932–1957*, Kuala Lumpur: OUP, 1995.

Riggs, Fred W., *Thailand: The Modernization of a Bureaucratic Policy*, Honolulu: East-West Center P, 1966.

Stowe, Judith A., *Siam becomes Thailand*, London: Hurst, 1991.

Surin Pitsuwan, *Islam and Malay Nationalism: A Case Study of the Malay-Muslims of Southern Thailand*, Bangkok: Thammasat U, 1985.

Tej Bunnag, *The Provincial Administration of Siam*, Kuala Lumpur: OUP, 1977.

Vella, W. F., *Chaiyo!*, U Hawaii P, 1978.

Wyatt, David, *Thailand: A Short History*, Yale UP; Chiang Mai: Transvin, 1984.

Vietnam

Duiker, William J., *The Rise of Nationalism in Vietnam, 1900–1941*, Cornell UP, 1976.

——— *U.S. Containment Policy and the Conflict in Indochina*, Stanford UP, 1994.

Engelbert, Thomas, and C. E. Goscha, *Falling out of Touch: A Study on Vietnamese Communist Policy towards an Emerging Cambodian Communist Movement, 1930–1975*, Clayton: Monash Asia Institute, 1995.

Hue-Tam Ho Tai, *Radicalism and the Origins of the Vietnamese Revolution*, Harvard UP, 1992.

Le Thanh-Khoi, *Le Viet-Nam: Histoire et Civilisation*, Paris: Editions de Minuit, 1965.

Li Tana, *Nguyen Cochinchina*, Cornell UP, 1998.

Marr, David G., *Vietnamese Anticolonialism, 1885–1925*, UCP, 1971.

——— *Vietnam, 1945: The Quest for Power*, UCP, 1995.

Murray, Martin J., *The Development of Capitalism in Colonial Indochina (1870–1940)*, UCP, 1980.

Osborne, Milton E., *The French Presence in Cochinchina and Cambodia: Rule and Response (1859–1905)*, Cornell UP, 1969.

Taylor, Keith W., *The Birth of Vietnam*, UCP, 1983.

Thai Quang Trung, *Collective Leadership and Factionalism: An Essay on Ho Chi Minh's Legacy*, Singapore: ISEAS, 1985.

Tonnesson, Stein, *The Vietnamese Revolution of 1945*, Oslo: IPRI; London: Sage, 1991.

Tuck, Patrick J. N., *French Catholic Missionaries and the Politics of Imperialism in Vietnam, 1857–1914: A Documentary Survey*, Liverpool UP, 1987.

Woodside, Alexander B., *Vietnam, and the Chinese Model: A Comparative Study of Nguyen and Ch'ing Civil Government in the First Half of the Nineteenth Century*, Harvard UP, 1971.

—— *Community and Revolution in Modern Vietnam*, Boston: Houghton Mifflin, 1976.

Cambodia

Chandler, David P., *Brother Number One: A Political Biography of Pol Pot*, Boulder: Westview, 1992.

Corfield, Justin, *Khmers Stand Up! A History of the Cambodian Government, 1970–1975*, Clayton: Monash U, 1994.

Jackson, Karl D., ed., *Cambodia, 1975–1978: Rendezvous with Death*, Princeton UP, 1989.

Kiernan, Ben, and Chantou Boua, eds, *Peasants and Politics in Kampuchea, 1942–1981*, London: Zed; New York: Sharpe, 1982.

Leifer, Michael, *Cambodia: The Search for Security*, London: Pall Mall, 1967.

Smith, Roger M., *Cambodia's Foreign Policy*, Cornell UP, 1965.

Tully, John, *Cambodia under the Tricolour Flag*, Clayton: Monash Asia Institute, 1996.

Laos

Dommen, Arthur J., *Conflict in Laos*, London: Pall Mall, 1964.

Gunn, Geoffrey C., *Political Struggles in Laos (1930–1954)*, Bangkok: Duang Kamol, 1988.

—— *Rebellion in Laos*, Boulder: Westview, 1990.

Stuart-Fox, Martin, *Buddhist Kingdom, Marxist State: The Making of Modern Laos*, Bangkok, Cheney: White Lotus, 1996.

Cities and Buildings

Abeyasekere, Susan, *Jakarta: A History*, Singapore: OUP, 1987.

Edwards, Norman, *The Singapore House and Residential Life, 1819–1939*, Singapore: OUP, 1990.

Gullick, J. M., 'The Bangunan Sultan Abdul Samad', JMBRAS, 65, 1 (1992), pp. 27–38.

Kernial Singh Sandhu and Paul Wheatley, eds, *Melaka: The Transformation of a Malay Capital, c. 1400–1980*, 2 vols, Kuala Lumpur: OUP, 1983.

Lee, Edwin, *Historic Buildings of Singapore*, Singapore: Preservation of Monuments Board, 1990.

Lockard, Craig A., *From Kampung to City: A Social History of Kuching Malaysia, 1820–1970*, Athens: Ohio U, 1987.

McGee, T. G., *The Southeast Asian City*, London: Bell, 1967.

Pearn, B. R., *History of Rangoon*, Rangoon, 1929, reprint 1971.

Turnbull, C. M., *A History of Singapore, 1819–1975*, Kuala Lumpur: OUP, 1977.

Index

This is mainly an index of places and personalities. It is intended also to list the activities of Southeast Asian states more fully than of those outside the region, European or Asian. To aid readers who wish to pursue the history of particular Southeast Asian states, the main entries are set in bold.